AF594558

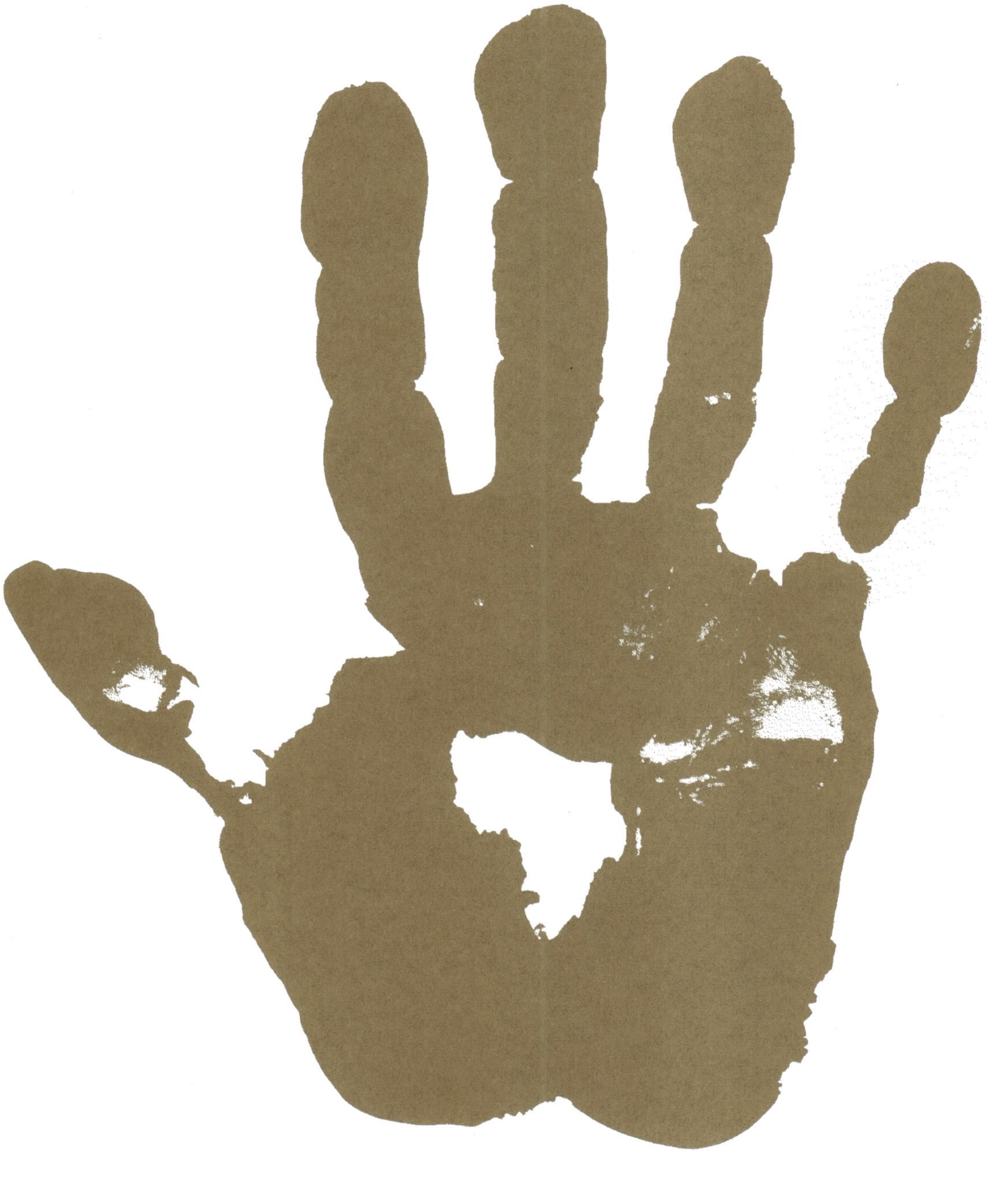

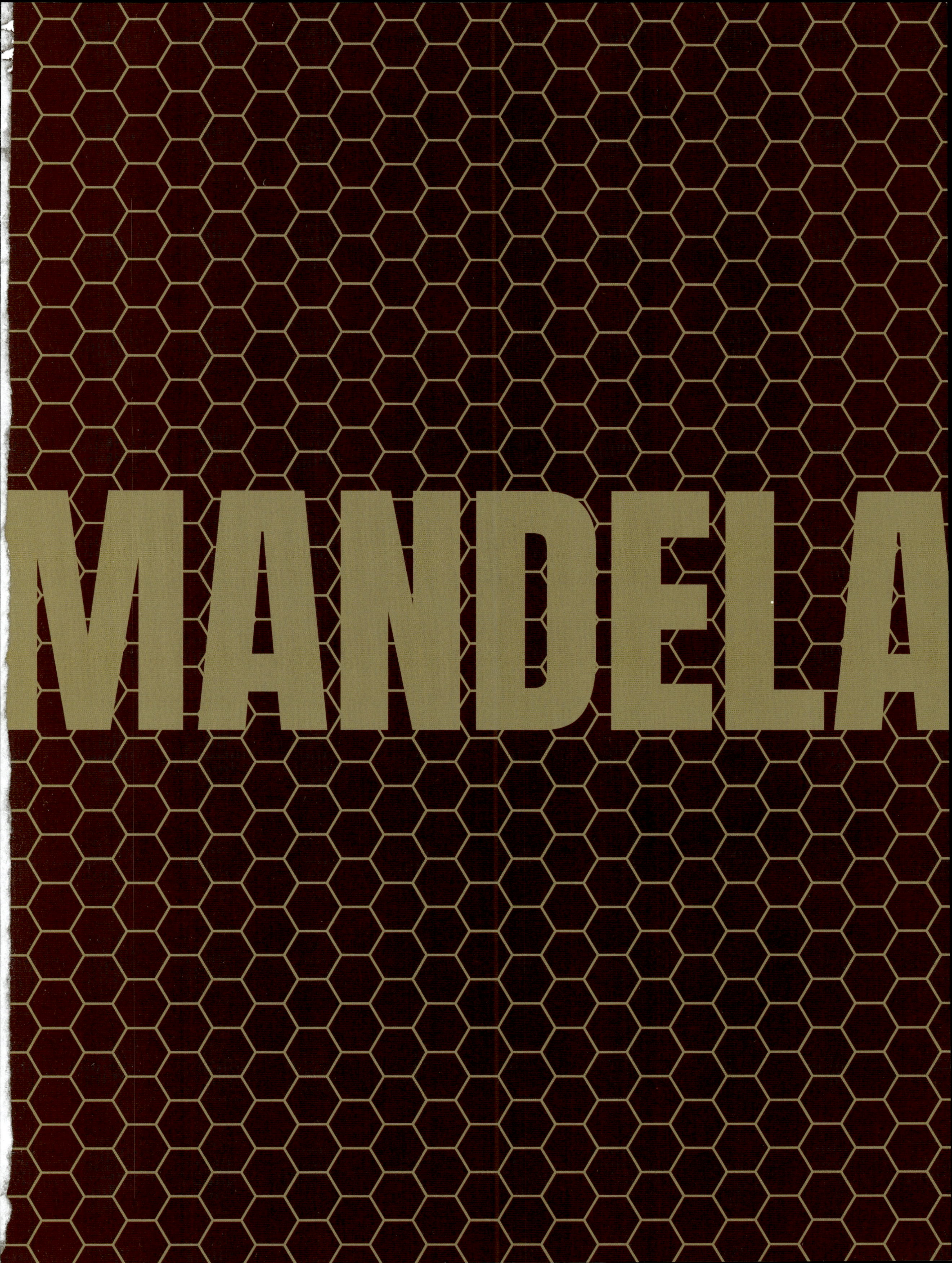
MANDELA

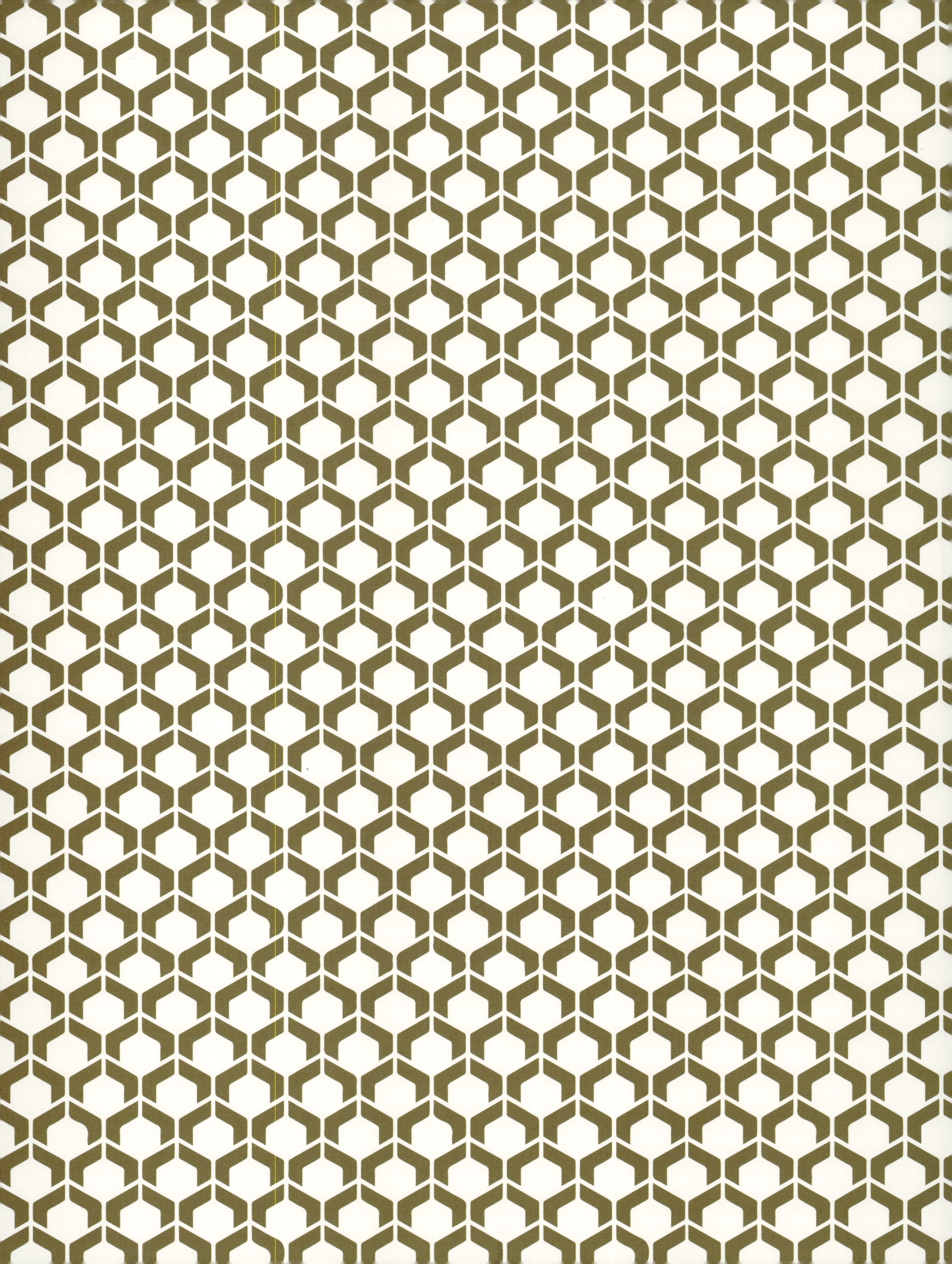

IN HONOR OF AN EXTRAORDINARY LIFE

MANDELA

DR. PHUMLA MAKAZIWE MANDELA

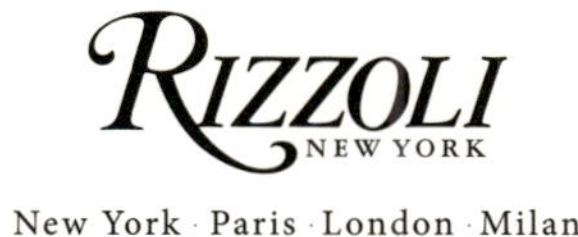

New York · Paris · London · Milan

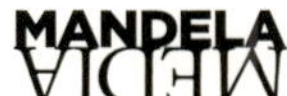

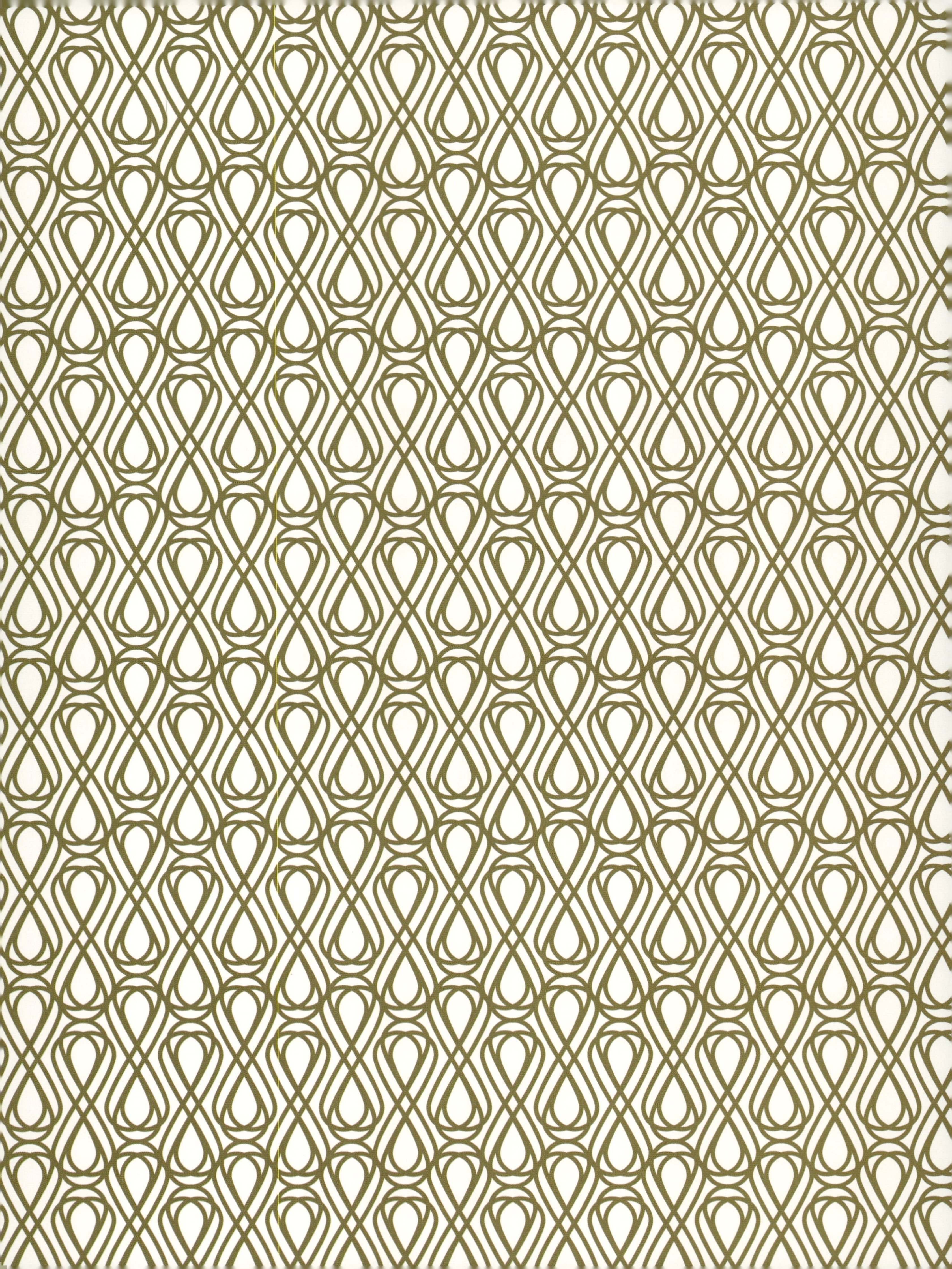

Table of Contents

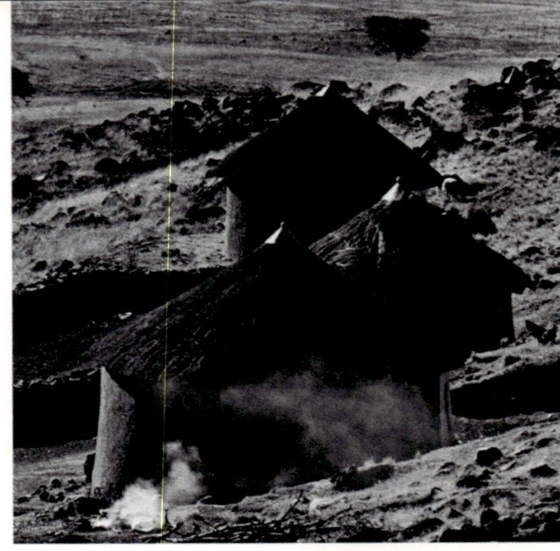

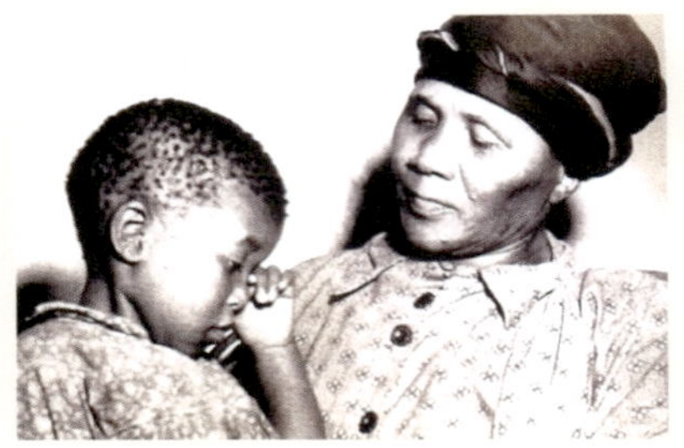

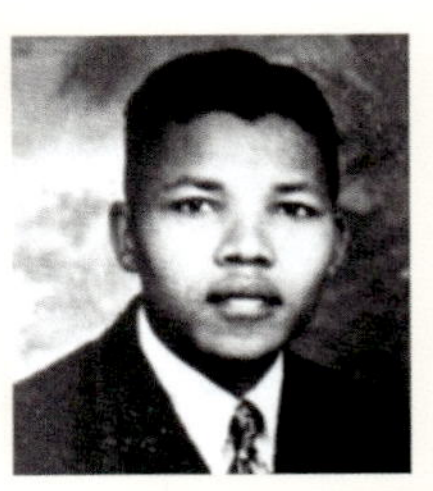

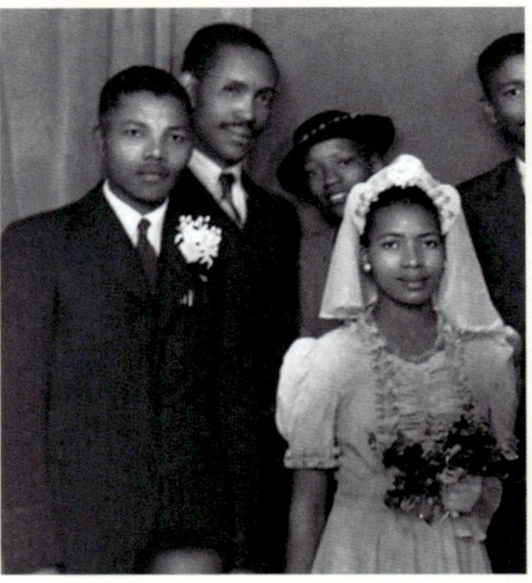

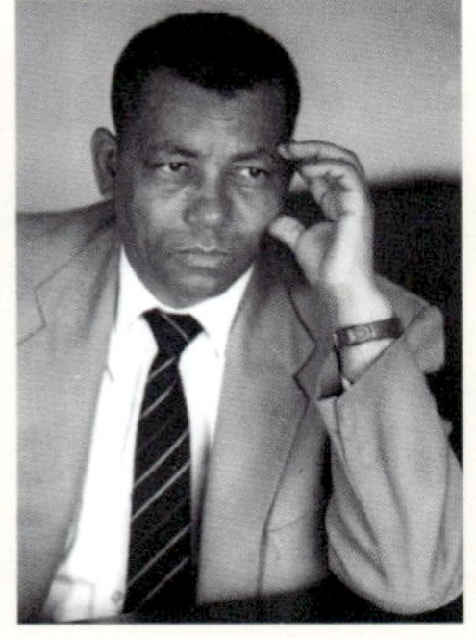

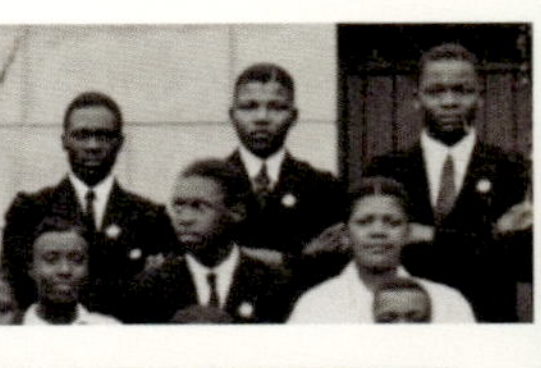

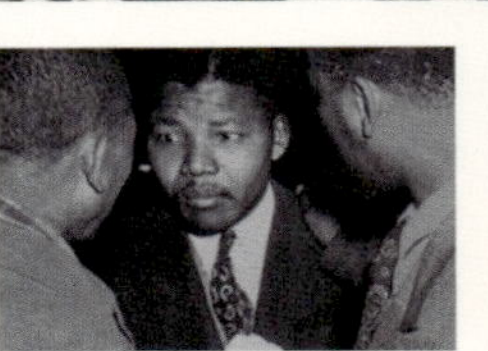

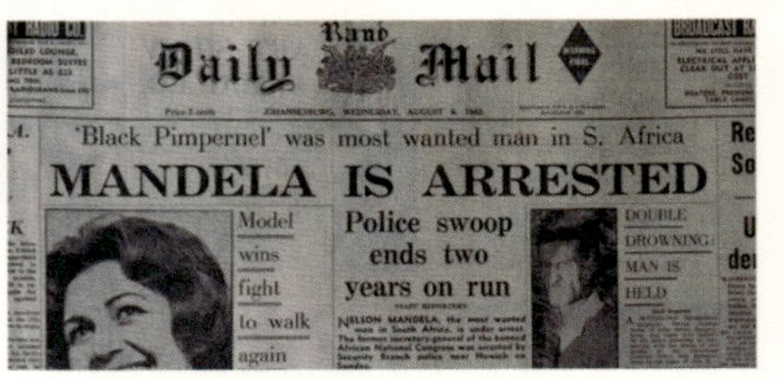

Rand Daily Mail

'Black Pimpernel' was most wanted man in S. Africa

MANDELA IS ARRESTED

Model wins fight to walk again

Police swoop ends two years on run

DOUBLE DROWNING: MAN IS HELD

Nelson Rolihlahla Mandela

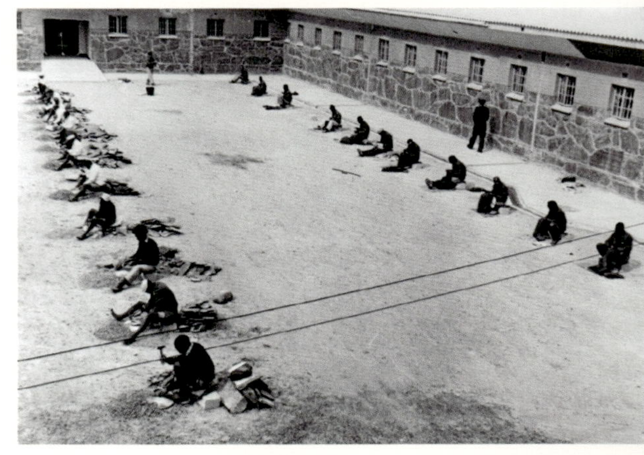

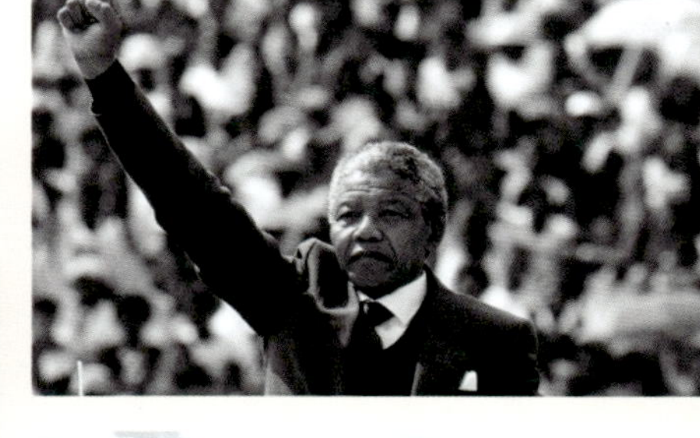

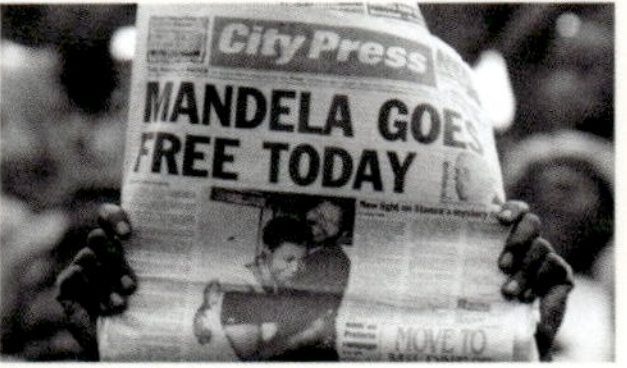

City Press

MANDELA GOES FREE TODAY

MOVE TO

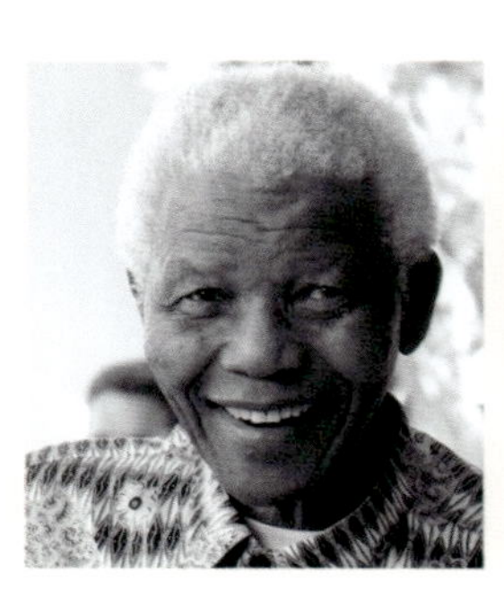

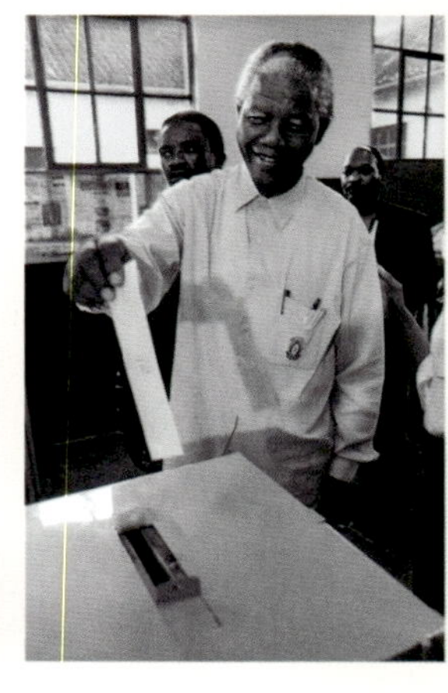

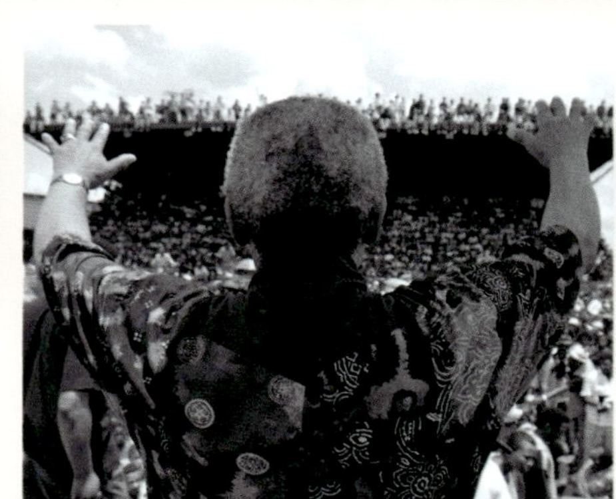

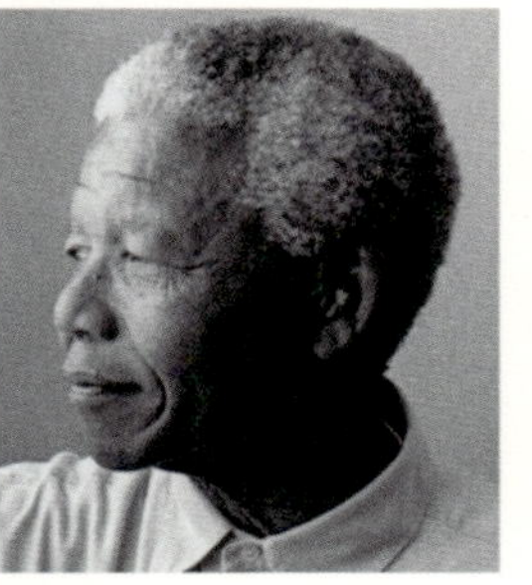

1918

1918 Born in Mvezo

1925 First member of family to attend school

1927 Entrusted to the Regent of the Thembus in Mqhekezweni

1934 Undergoes initiation rites
1934–1940 Attends Clarkebury, Healdtown, and Fort Hare schools

1941

1941 Flees to Johannesburg to escape an arranged marriage
1943 Studies for a law degree at University of the Witwatersrand; meets Walter Sisulu
1948 Elected president of the African National Congress (ANC) Youth League

1950

1952 Sets up first Black law practice in South Africa; ANC volunteers are arrested, charges dismissed
1956 Mandela and 158 others arrested, charged with treason, case dismissed four years later
1960 Sharpeville Massacre, ANC banned
1961 Mandela goes underground
1962 Though under house arrest Mandela travels Africa to raise support; arrested upon return
1963 Raid at Liliesleaf uncovers plans for guerrilla warfare, Mandela and others charged, Rivonia Trial begins

1964

1964 Sentenced to life in prison on Robben Island for sabotage and conspiracy

1982 Moved to Pollsmoor Prison in Capetown, release offered if he denounces violence; Mandela rejects offer

1985 South African President Botha offers Mandela's release again if he denounces armed struggle; Mandela rejects offer

1990

1990 Released from prison

1991 End of apartheid

1994

1994 Elected president of South Africa

1999

1999 Retirement

2013

2013 Passing

1944–1958 **Married to Evelyn Mase**

CHILDREN
Makaziwe Mandela-Amuah
Makgatho Mandela
Madiba Thembekile Mandela
Makaziwe Mandela

1958–1996 **Married to Winnie Mandela**

CHILDREN
Zindziswa Mandela
Zenani Mandela

1998–2013 **Married to Graça Machel**

At Time of Passing
GRANDCHILDREN 18
GREAT-GRANDCHILDREN 14

Reverend Al Sharpton

My work for social justice and civil rights follows the example, courage, and commitment of many throughout history and around the globe. I have been continually inspired by the advocates of nonviolent change who have preceded me, notably Nelson Mandela.

Mandela changed the direction of world history with his work to democratize South Africa. He faced unspeakable cruelty—every brutality that can be done to a man, other than murder, was done to him—yet he maintained his dignity and dedication to his cause. He spent twenty-seven years in jail and came out willing to forgive those who imprisoned him. He is an eternal example, not only that revolution is possible, but that reconciliation is possible. He said to me once that "Revolution without reconciliation is not a revolution at all. You just changed who is in power, without changing how you are in power." I have always remembered his guidance. His very presence contained greatness, and every person who was as lucky as I was to meet him knew this.

He had an unmatched, unquantifiable gravity, yet simultaneously carried himself with great humility. Mandela lost years with his family due to his imprisonment, and even when he was free, his dedication to his work limited his personal time. He shared so much of himself with the world, and the world is the better for it. It is fitting that his daughter has written this book, as his family continues their generosity in sharing him with the world. I will never forget his role in my life as a mentor and a leader, and I know many others feel the same.

This book will teach current and future generations about Mandela's story and his impact. The start of the book describes his childhood in Mvezo, and his experiences as a lawyer and young activist—young people will benefit from imagining him as a young man, before he grew into the influential figure he became. He is not an untouchable figure but a real man whose youth shaped him, and perhaps the humanity of his beginnings will inspire other young people to imagine their own potential impact. The book's coverage of his years of imprisonment and his lifelong fight for justice will further inspire readers. The concluding sections on his release, presidency, and legacy fully cement the depiction of the icon we know today. His actions and determination prove an individual can change their community and the world without lowering themselves to violence and incivility. Mandela not only successfully challenged institutions of bigotry, bias, and hate, but he did it without internalizing the very things he was fighting. He changed the course of global politics and the lives of millions, and he also set an example for generations of activists such as myself. Mandela inspires me and many others to be better in every way, to transcend the pettiness that so often infiltrates politics, and aspire to true equality.

Mandela's goals of equality and equity remain universal needs for society today. His life's struggle brought the world forward, but there is much work left to be done when it comes to equality regardless of gender, race, sexual orientation, and socioeconomic status. In his honor, we learn about his life, take lessons from his wisdom, and take up his call to continue fighting for justice. As he often said, "It always seems impossible until it's done."

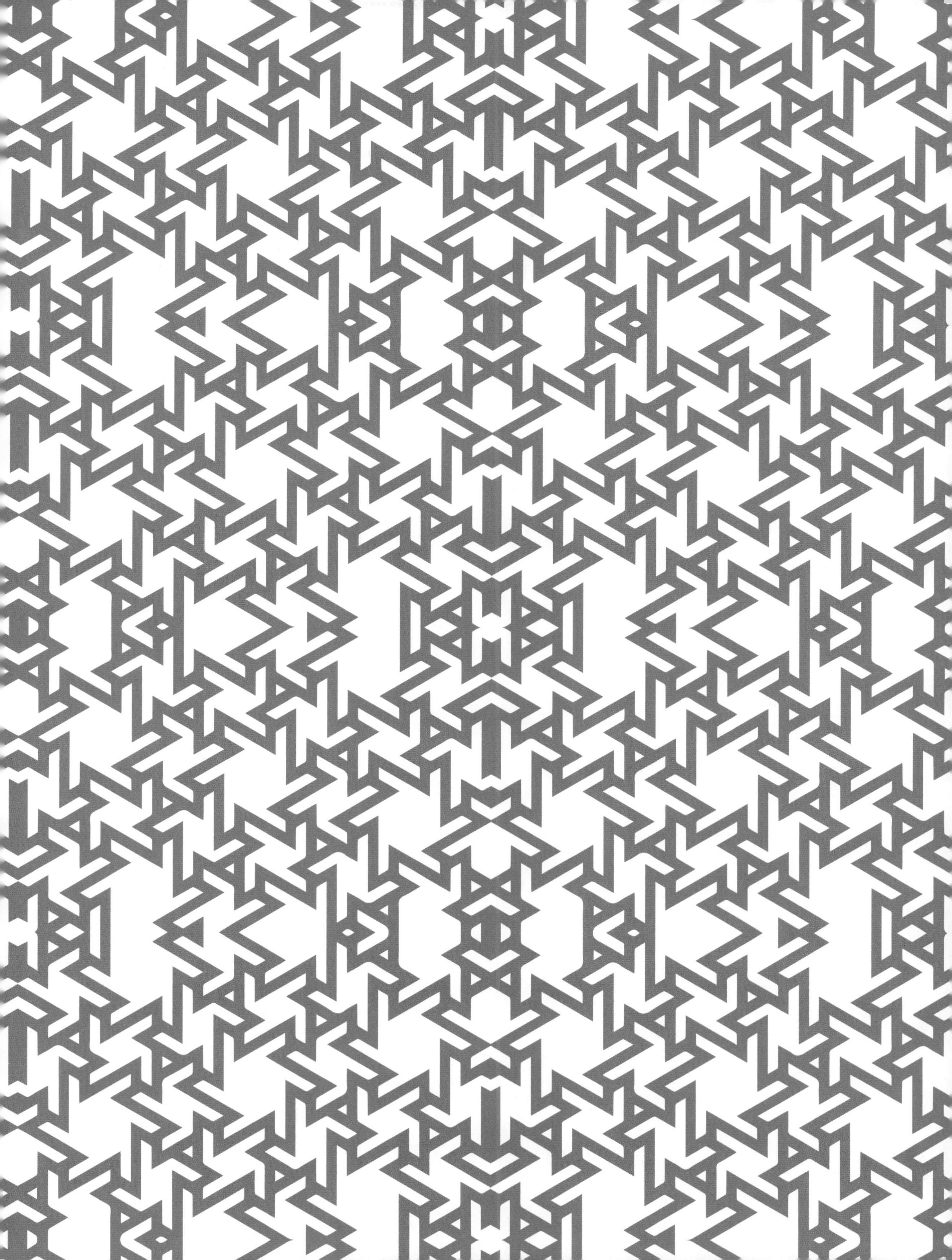

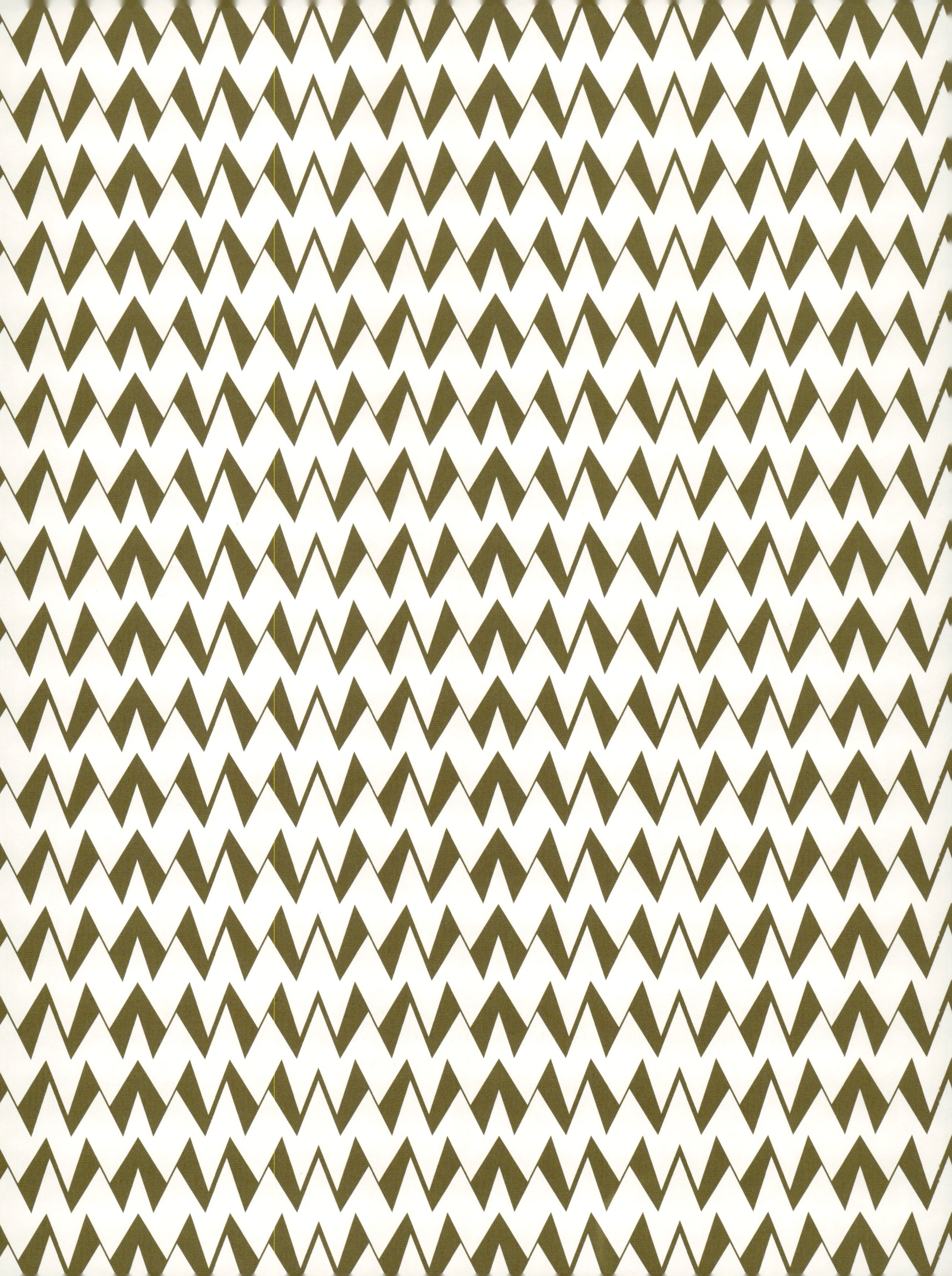

Joff Van Reenen

I met Dr. Phumla Makaziwe Mandela, Nelson Mandela's daughter, when she interviewed me for the auction she wanted conducted for her father's centenary gala celebrations. I was extremely keen to conduct the sale, not least because I had met Tata Mandela by chance about two decades earlier while he was state president.

What struck me about Dr. Maki was the deep knowledge, understanding, and passion she exuded for people and cultures. What struck me about Tata Mandela was how tall he was. I'm 6'3" and he towered over me. Whenever I tell the story of how I literally bumped into him, I get goose bumps and the hair on the back of my neck stands up.

I am part of the generation of South Africa's youth that was given democracy and I remember my first voting experience, at the age of eighteen, being the referendum. I was in the last SADF (South African Defence Force) conscription intake before it became the SANDF (South African National Defence Force), which was difficult because I was raised with no preconceived ideas of different cultures. My parents were liberal, and they taught me good values and to think for myself—things for which I will be forever grateful.

Meeting Dr. Maki was probably one of the scariest moments of my life. She asked me to meet her at her late father's home in the Houghton suburb of Johannesburg. We sat in the lounge, where she served me tea, which was a little overwhelming both because of the location and because Dr. Maki carries much of her father in her. She has a wonderfully powerful presence—one of deep understanding of the world and warm compassion for the people and things in it. When she asked me if I would auction off a collection of her dad's drawings, I nearly fainted. It is without a doubt the highlight of my career.

Growing up and living through two very different South African worlds, I saw both the best and the worst of our incredible country and its history. Getting to know Dr. Maki and the rest of her family has been, and continues to be, a privilege that I do not take lightly.

Paging through this book you will experience some very personal images of Tata Madiba, thanks to his very private family. I continue to be awed by how colossal his imprint and legacy were on our fledgling democracy. How did one man change the course of history of an entire country and for millions around the world? The photos in this book will help you to understand the man, father, farmer, herder, teacher, president, statesman, and philosopher.

My life was forever changed for the better by getting to know Dr. Maki and her incredible family's legacy. I have a much deeper understanding of South Africa's past, our cultures, and our heritage, and I will forever be indebted to the Mandelas for this enlightenment. I hope this book helps enlighten you, too.

Noëlla Coursaris Musunka

Some people have a legacy that is so far-reaching it's hard to put into words. Nelson Mandela, a significant hero of mine, is one of those people. Through his determination, self-sacrifice, and fight for freedom, he changed the lives of millions for the better.

It was the greatest honor for me to receive an award from the House of Mandela at the Nelson Mandela centenary celebrations in 2018. Madiba was a courageous, compassionate, and dynamic leader who inspired positive changes in my beloved home continent of Africa and across the world. An elder who cared deeply about the young, he was a champion in the fight against inequality throughout his long life, including the inequality faced by many in accessing quality education. His example inspired my own dreams to bring transformative education to girls and their communities in the Democratic Republic of the Congo (DRC).

I was born in Lubumbashi, in the DRC, but my father died suddenly when I was five, and my mother was forced to send me to live with relatives in Europe. This opened up opportunities that never would have been afforded me in my home country. When I returned at age eighteen, I knew I had to pay it forward, and Malaika, the nonprofit organization I ultimately started in 2007, was born in my heart. Changemakers like Mandela, who do extraordinary things, start out as ordinary people. Ordinary people who make a choice to give what they have for the benefit of others who are disadvantaged, who choose to fight for what they believe in, no matter the personal cost. Empowerment was a priority for Madiba.

It is also a core priority for me and the leaders at Malaika as we work toward my dream of uplifting people through education and health. Malaika strives to empower youth, and I believe African youth are the key to unlocking Africa's economic potential. Africa has the youngest population in the world—70 percent of sub-Saharan Africa is under the age of thirty; our young people must drive Mandela's legacy into the future.

I am immensely proud to be among the next generation of leaders who are lifting African people up and helping them to unleash their potential. With dynamic and creative illustrations, this book will connect with new audiences and bring Mandela's powerful story to life in a new way, creating a domino effect that will keep his spirit alive and motivate future generations who need to go further than we have. I sincerely hope it will inspire and educate, as well as trigger dreams and actions that will help Africa rise to greater heights over the decades to come.

I hope that Mandela is watching his beloved home become the beautiful Africa he envisioned.

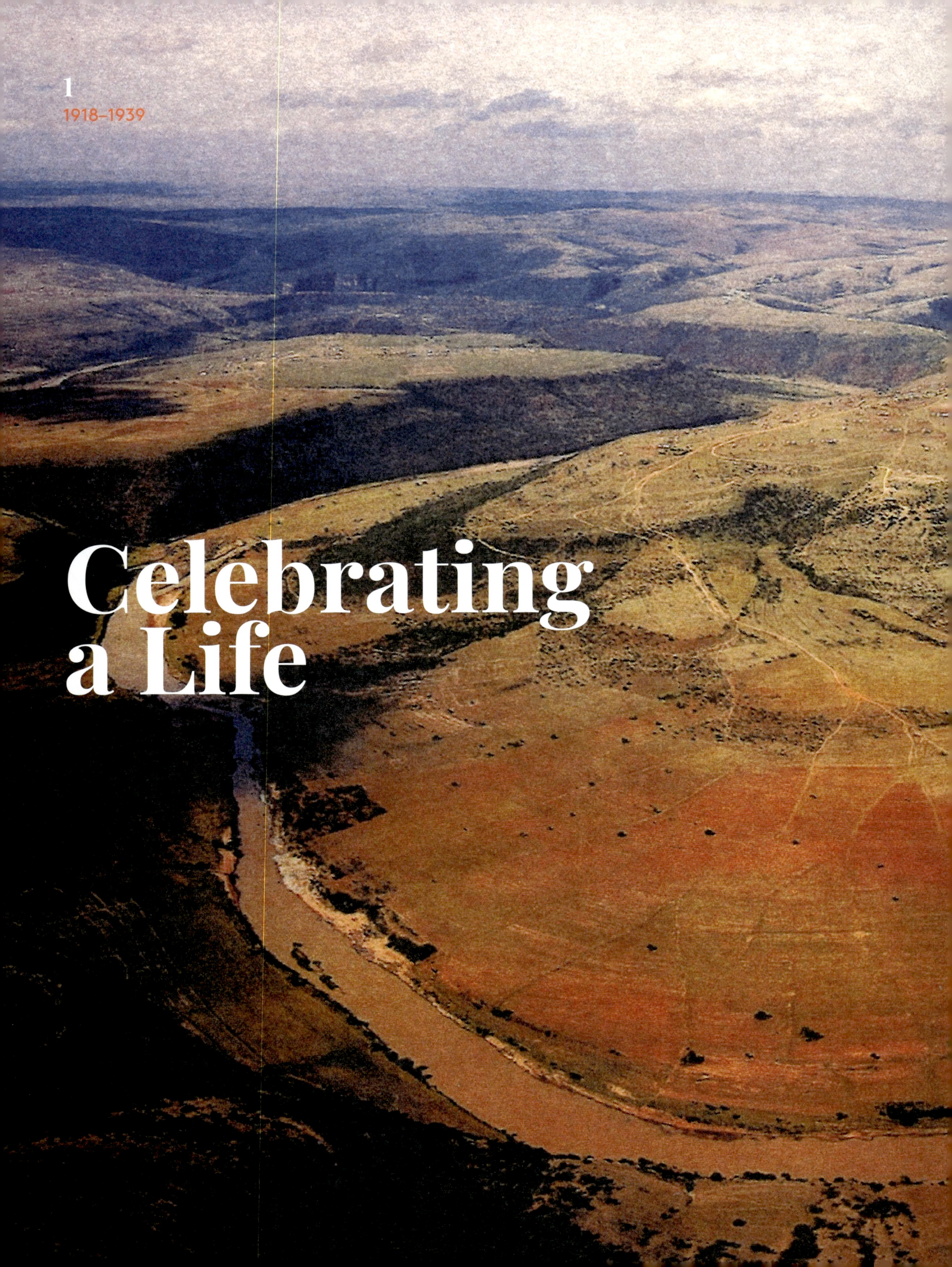

1

1918–1939

Celebrating a Life

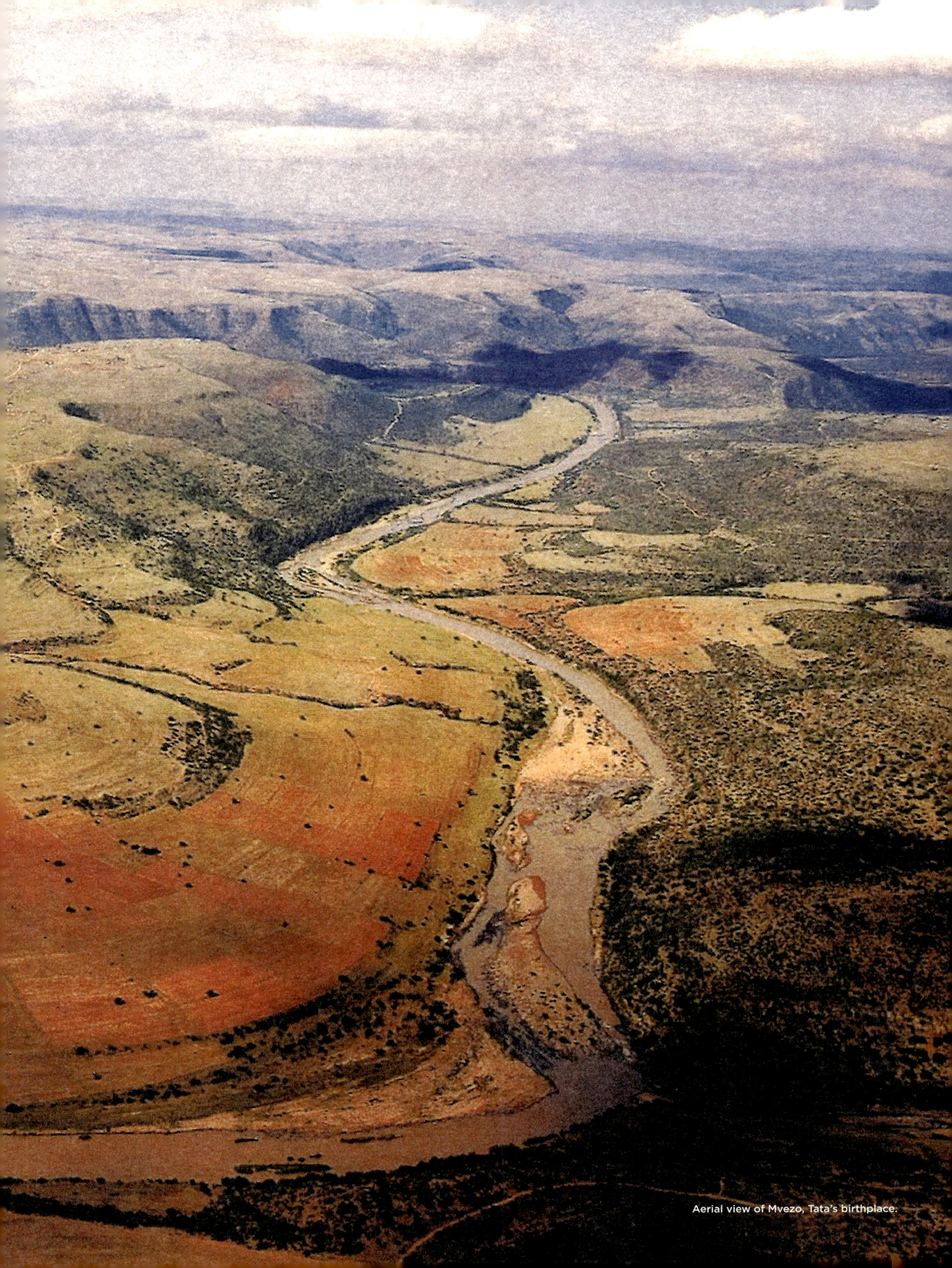

Aerial view of Mvezo, Tata's birthplace.

Our Source of Inspiration

The past is a prologue for the House of Mandela. An important lesson in life is to always learn from those who have traveled the road before us. We learn lessons from the past that we use now and in the future. We consciously capture these lessons, use them as guides in our lives, and communicate the lessons through art, words, and actions.

As a father and grandfather, Nelson Rolihlahla Mandela consistently emphasized that he was shaped by the cultural traditions and values of his ancestral roots.

Our ancestors were committed to compassion and a spirit of human solidarity, and above all embraced the view that individuals derive meaning from being part of a group. As the progeny of the House of Mandela, we believe that the time has come for us to recall everything that is good, honorable, and inspiring in our past and embrace it.

Our history and lineage is like a welcoming circle of friendship. It shelters us from the loneliness and isolation of life. It gives us a mooring, a center in our life as we crisscross the world. Our ancestors showed us the way and inspire us to live up to our highest ideals, and for that we are grateful.

Maki Mandela

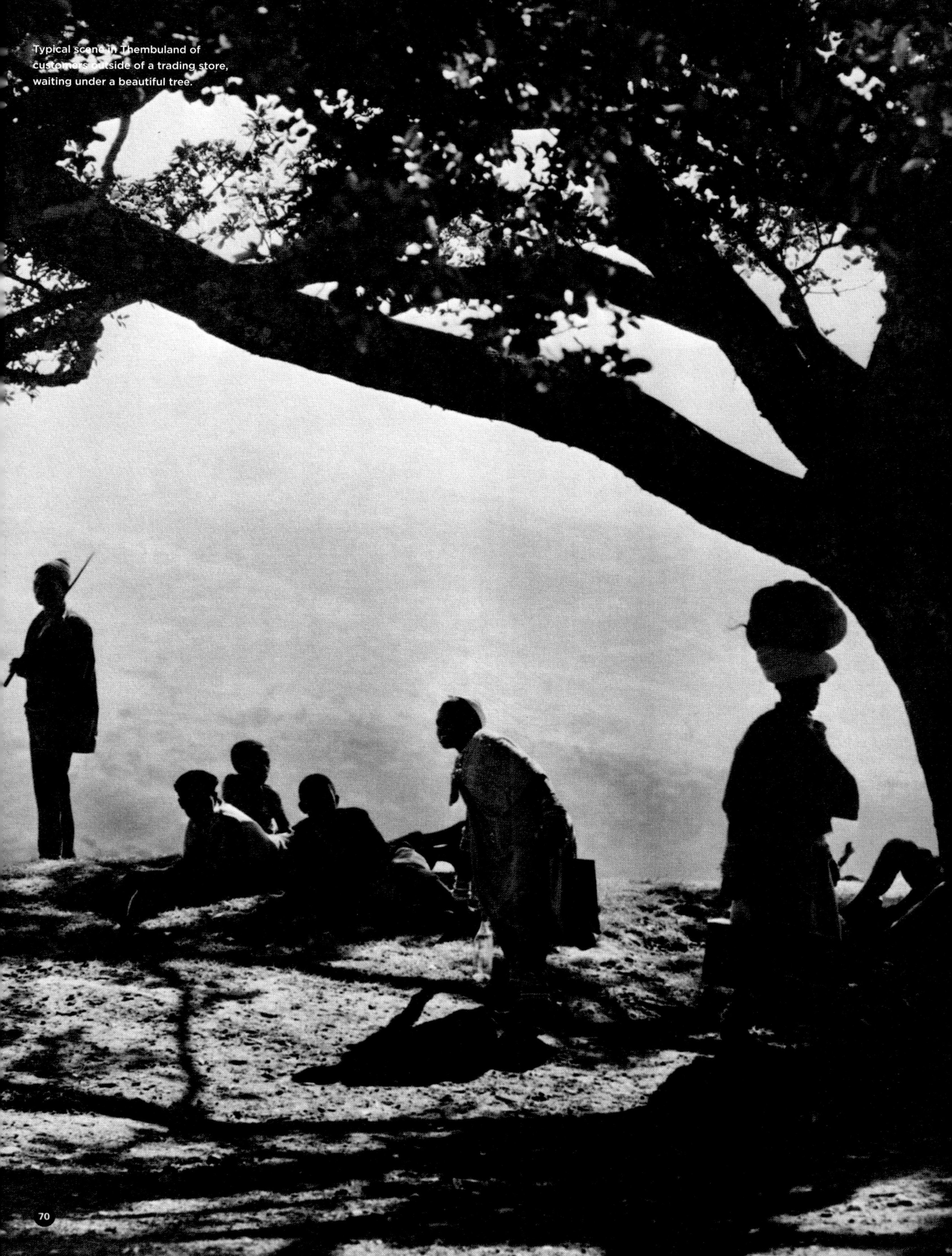

Typical scene in Thembuland of customers outside of a trading store, waiting under a beautiful tree.

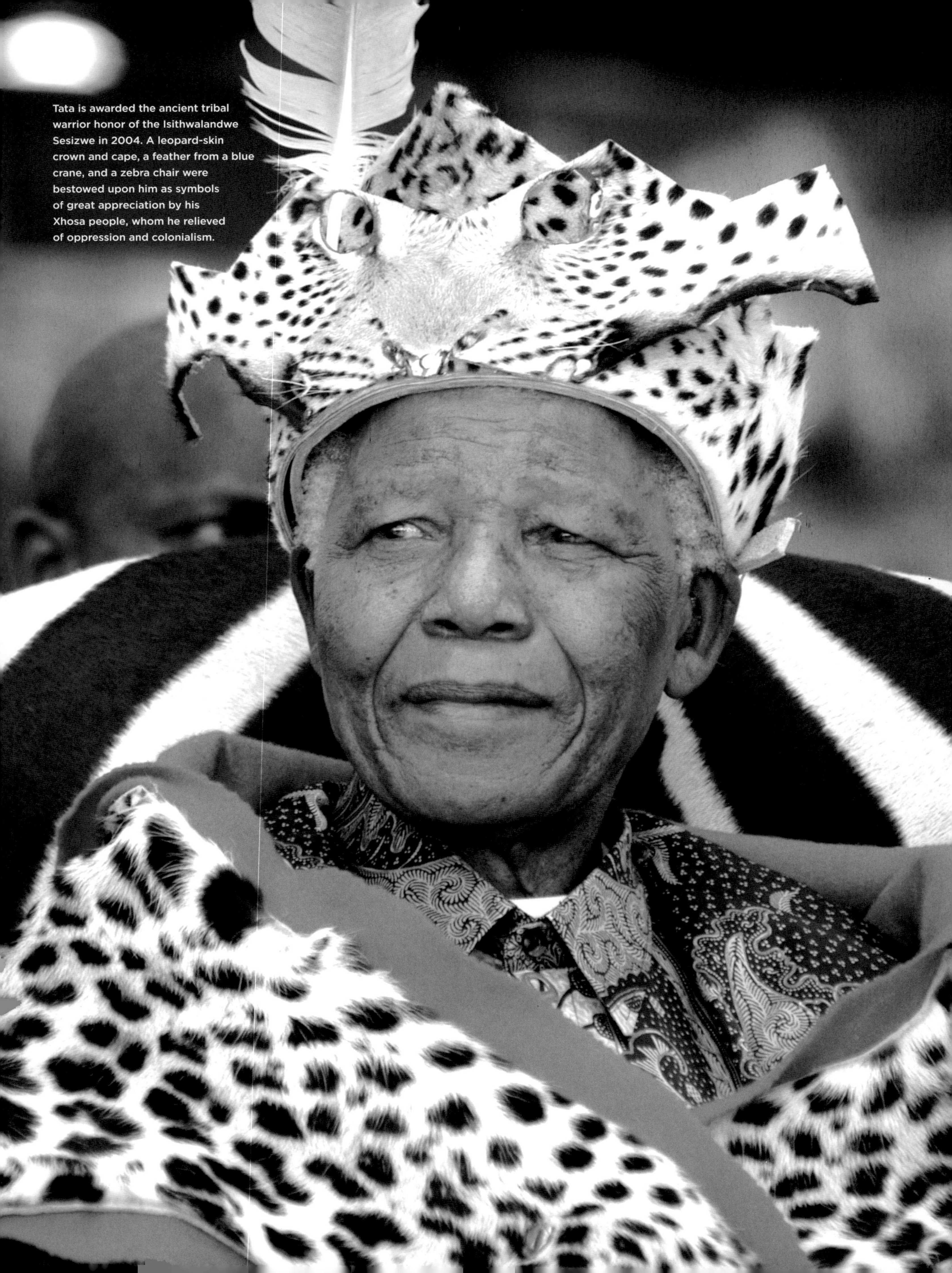

Tata is awarded the ancient tribal warrior honor of the Isithwalandwe Sesizwe in 2004. A leopard-skin crown and cape, a feather from a blue crane, and a zebra chair were bestowed upon him as symbols of great appreciation by his Xhosa people, whom he relieved of oppression and colonialism.

In Praise of the Ancestors

Even now the forefathers still live
They are not overcome by the power of the whirlwind.
The day that sealed their eyes that did not conquer them.
Even the tall boulder that stands over them
Casts only a humble shadow over their resting place
They are the great voice that carries the epics.

The Ancestors have come to listen to our songs,
Overjoyed they shake their hands in ecstasy.
With us they celebrate their eternal life.
They climb the mountain with their children
To put the symbol of the ancient stone on its forehead.

We honor those who gave birth to us
With them we watch the spectacle of the moving mists.
They have opened their sacred book to sing with us
They are the mystery that envelops our dream.
They are the power that shall unite us.
They are the strange truth of the earth.
They came from the womb of the universe
Restless they are, like a path of dreams,
Like a forest sheltering the neighboring race of animals.

Yes, the deep eye of the universe is in our chest
With it we stare at the centers of the sky.
We sing the anthems that celebrate their great eras.
For indeed life does not begin with us.

Mazisi Kunene
Exiled poet, supporter, and organizer of the anti-apartheid movement in Europe and Africa

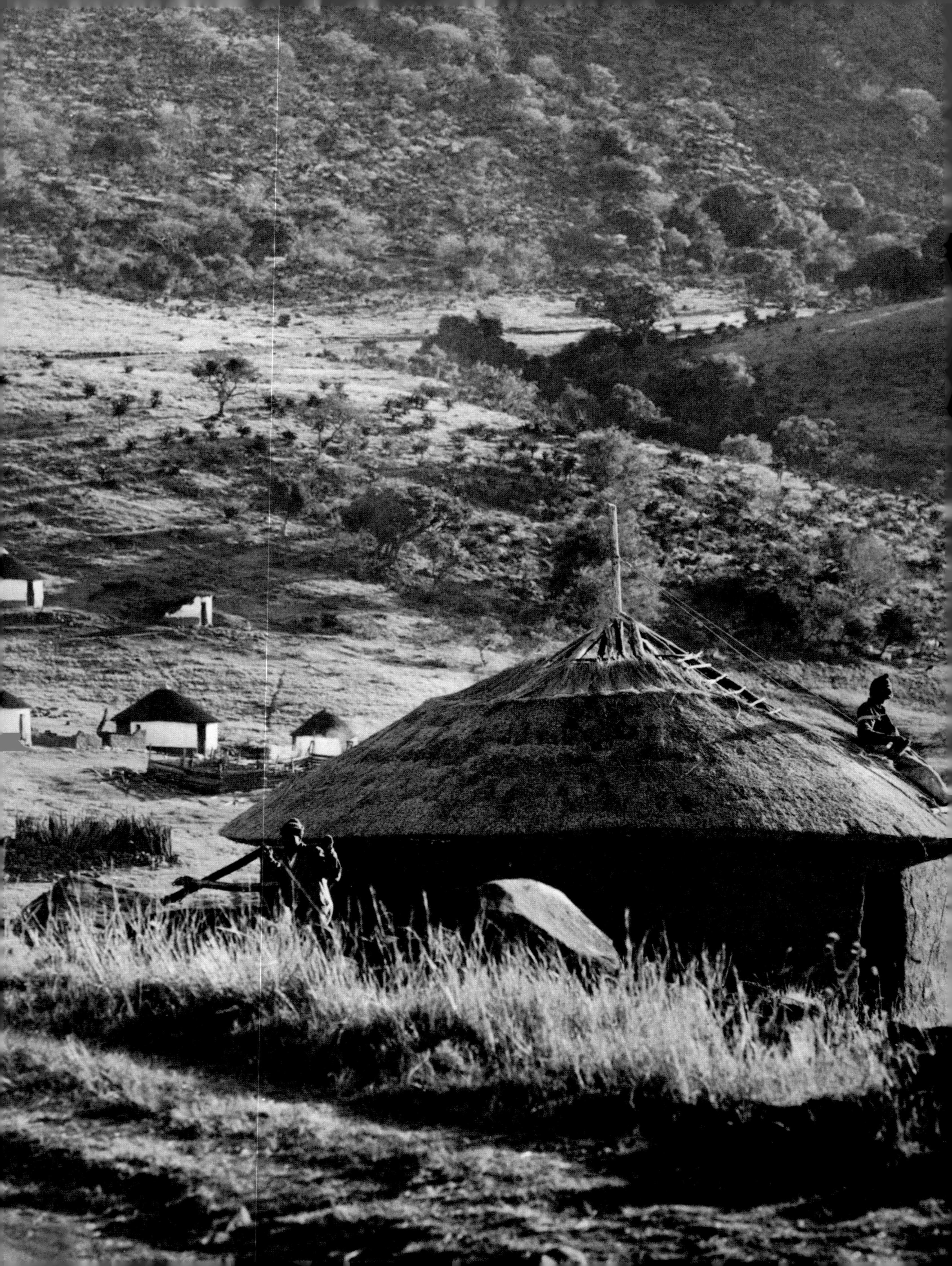

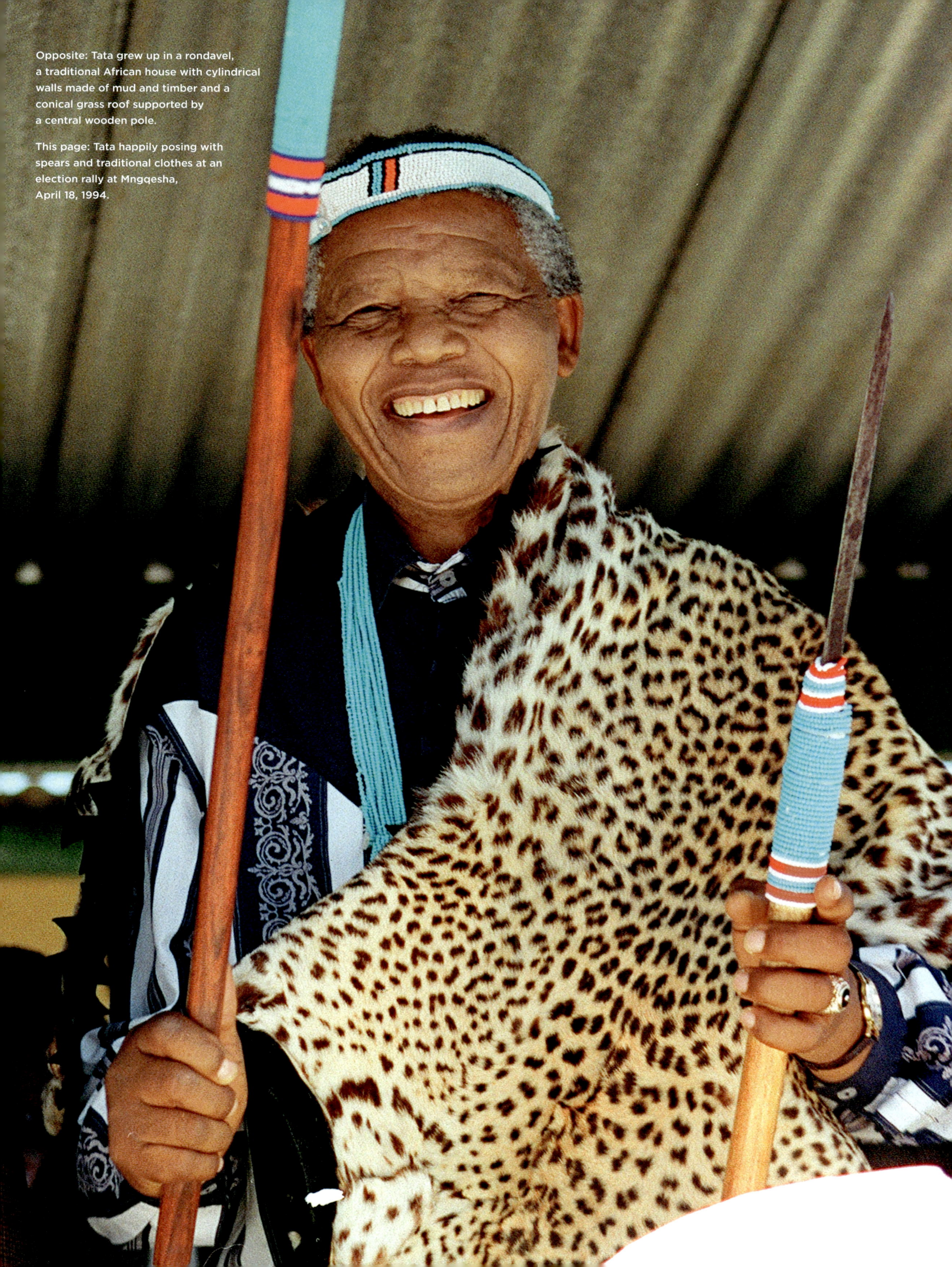

Opposite: Tata grew up in a rondavel, a traditional African house with cylindrical walls made of mud and timber and a conical grass roof supported by a central wooden pole.

This page: Tata happily posing with spears and traditional clothes at an election rally at Mngqesha, April 18, 1994.

Nelson Rolihlahla Mandela

This is a story about my father ("Tata," in the Xhosa language). It is a story that clearly defines who he was, where he came from, and how the lessons he learned from his ancestors, parents, and cultural traditions helped to shape him.

On July 18, 1918, Tata was born in the small village of Mvezo on the banks of the Mbashe River near Umtata (Transkei's largest town), about 560 miles (900 km) south of Johannesburg.

Mvezo is home to various Xhosa-speaking peoples. Transkei is bordered toward the west by the high Drakensberg mountains and toward the east by the Indian Ocean. The scenic beauty of this fertile land of rolling hills and many rivers is unparalleled.

Tata was a proud son of the Mandela family. He belonged to the abaThembu ethnic group and a branch of the Left Hand House of the royal abaThembu lineage. Tata is often referred to as "Madiba," but this is his clan name. Each Xhosa belongs to a clan that traces its descent back to a specific forefather. The Madiba clan is our ultimate reference. It is the source of our identity and pride. When one is called by one's clan name, which is far more important than a surname, it is a sign of deep respect. It refers to the ancestor from whom a person is descended and immediately provides an identity in terms of ethnicity and geographic status.

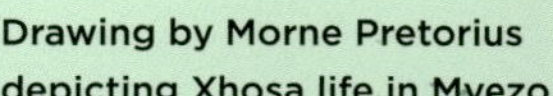

Drawing by Morne Pretorius depicting Xhosa life in Mvezo.

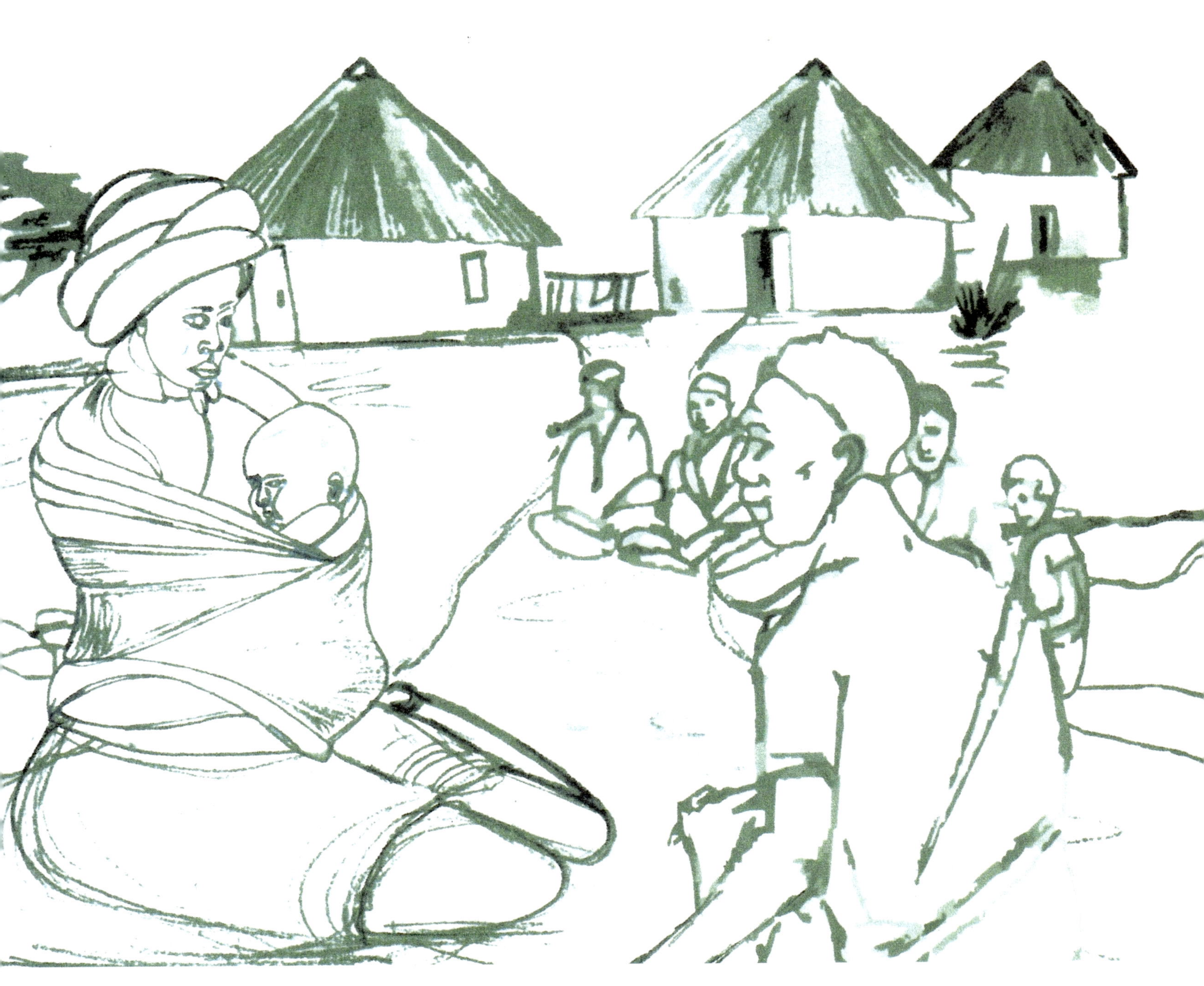

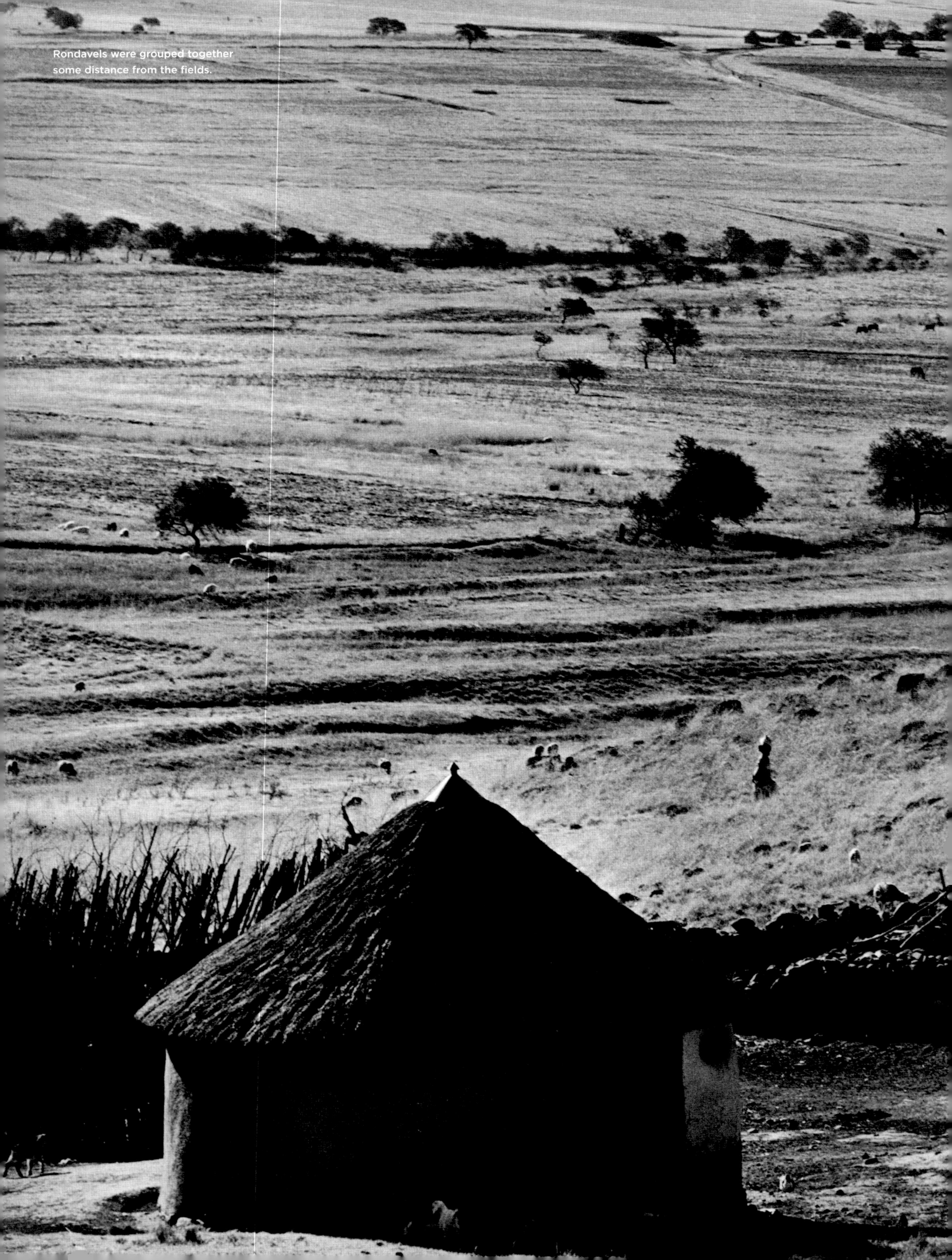

Rondavels were grouped together some distance from the fields.

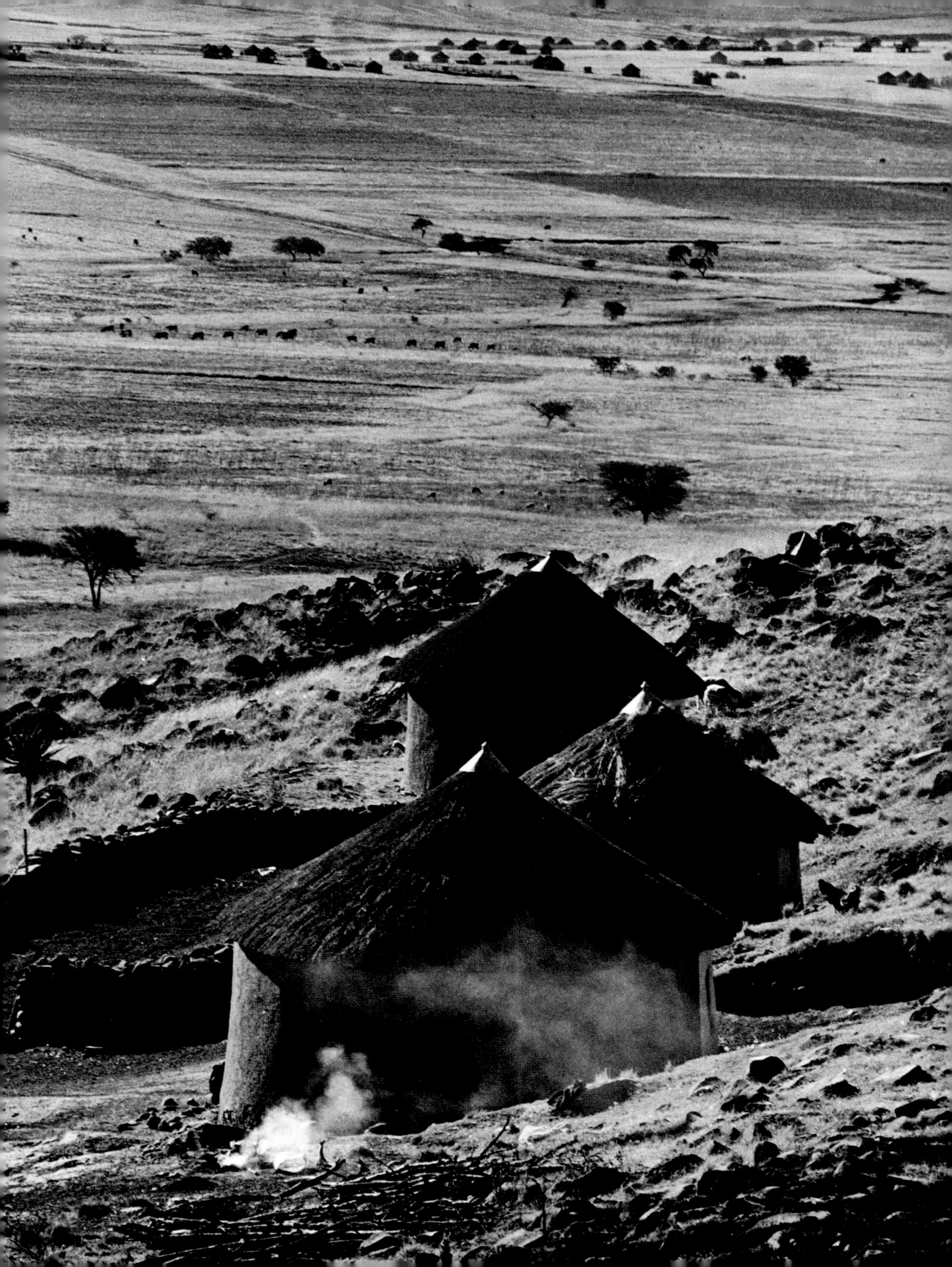

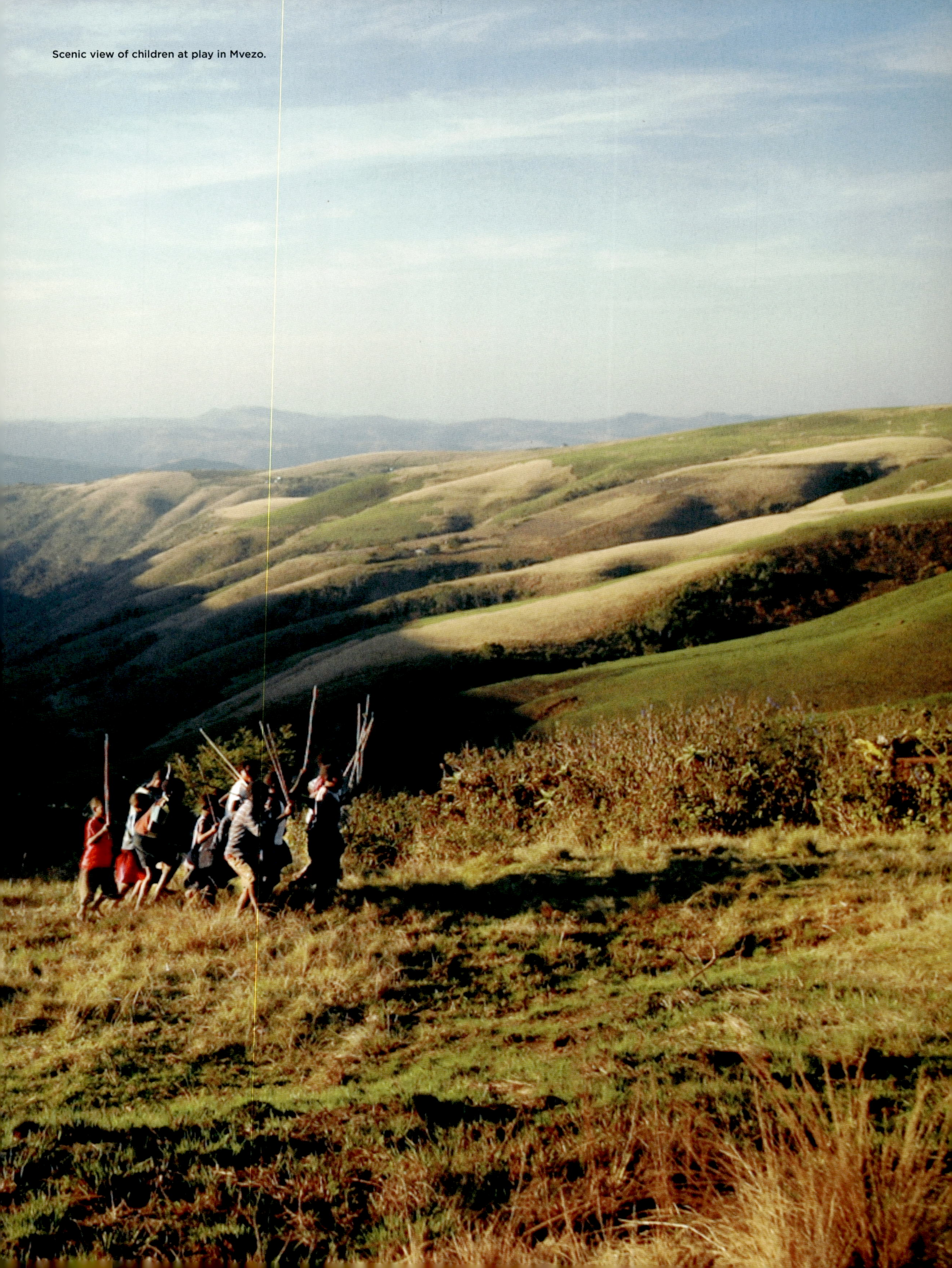

Scenic view of children at play in Mvezo.

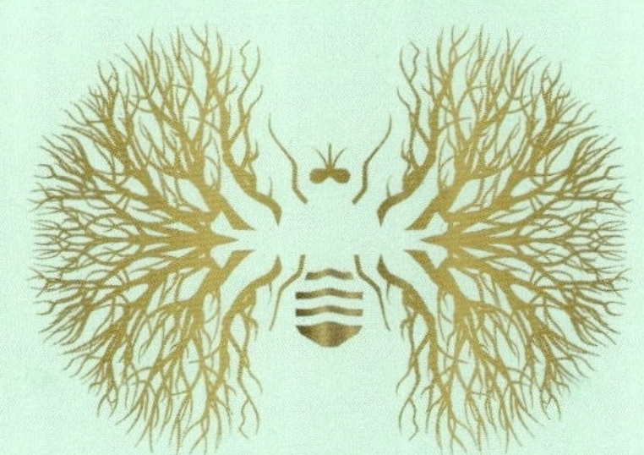

“The family tree is like a vine that grows; it’s who we are and where we come from.” Tukwini Mandela

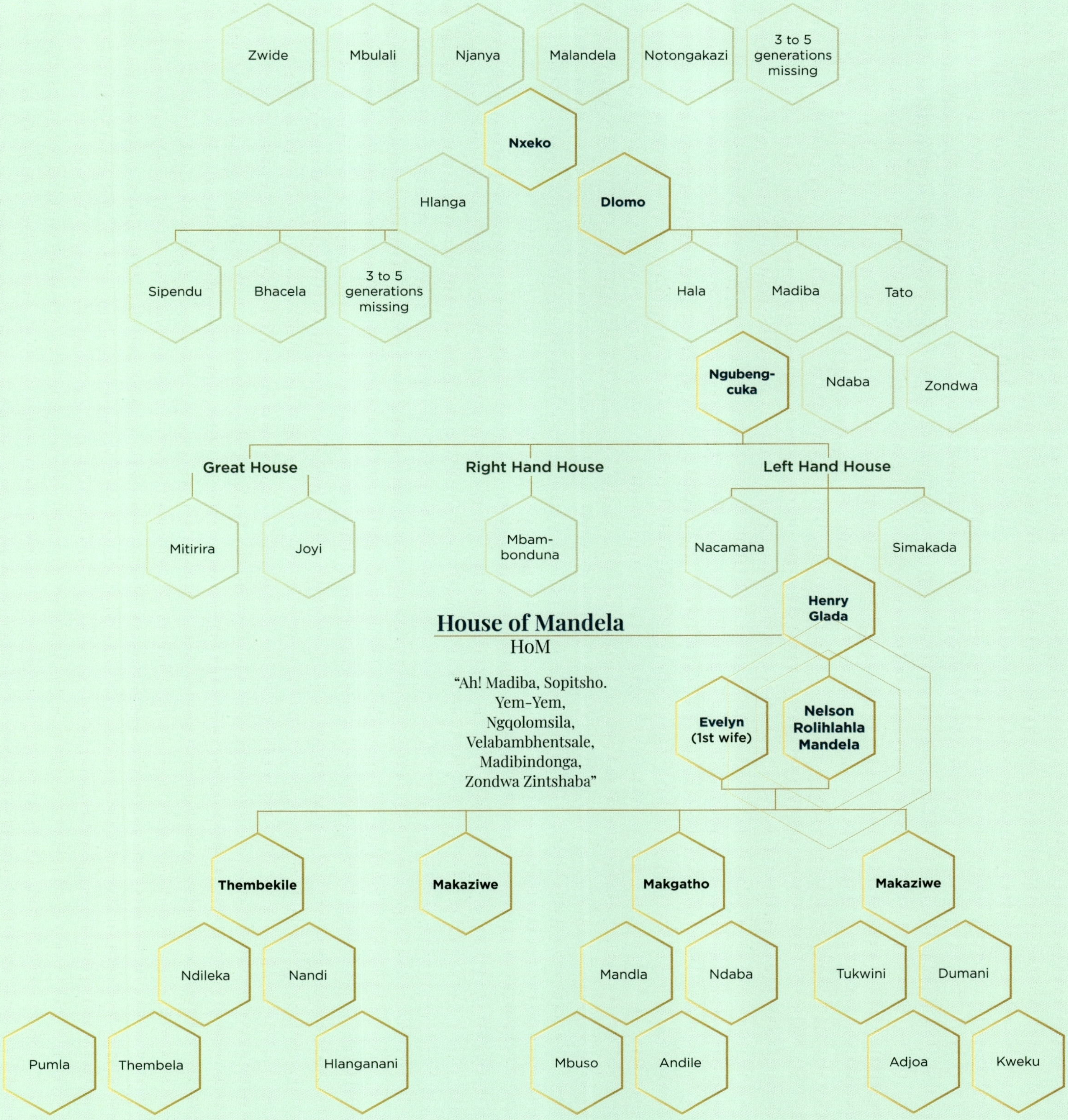

Zwide
Mbulali
Njanya
Malandela
Notongakazi
3 to 5 generations missing

Nxeko

Hlanga
Dlomo

Sipendu
Bhacela
3 to 5 generations missing

Hala
Madiba
Tato

Ngubeng-cuka
Ndaba
Zondwa

Great House
Right Hand House
Left Hand House

Mitirira
Joyi
Mbam-bonduna
Nacamana
Simakada

Henry Glada

House of Mandela

HoM

“Ah! Madiba, Sopitsho.
Yem-Yem,
Ngqolomsila,
Velabambhentsale,
Madibindonga,
Zondwa Zintshaba”

Evelyn (1st wife)
Nelson Rolihlahla Mandela

Thembekile
Makaziwe
Makgatho
Makaziwe

Ndileka
Nandi
Mandla
Ndaba
Tukwini
Dumani

Pumla
Thembela
Hlanganani
Mbuso
Andile
Adjoa
Kweku

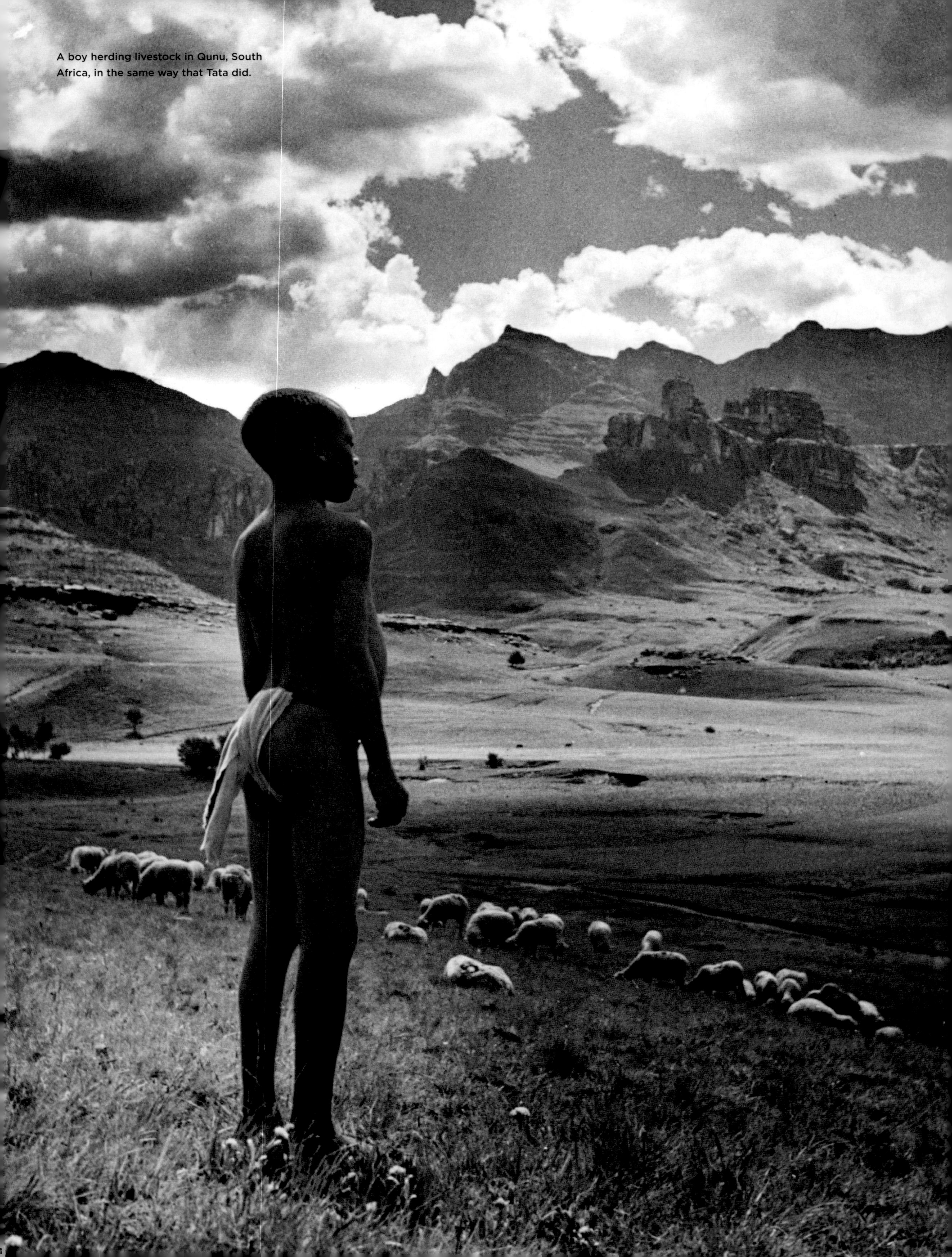

A boy herding livestock in Qunu, South Africa, in the same way that Tata did.

In South Africa, kinship and lineage are the articulating principles of social organization and the basis of social integration. Lineage is the most important unit among the Thembu people. For centuries, lineage relationships have been the foundation of our social life, customs, and laws. They are fundamental to our upbringing.

The abaThembu ruling lineage can be traced back more than twenty generations to King Zwide in the 1080s. The Mandela family is part of this lineage by both blood and custom. By the beginning of the eighteenth century, Thembuland was a well-established kingdom in the Eastern Cape. King Ngubengcuka, the fourth monarch, ruled from 1800 to 1830. He established a unified Thembuland that stretched from Umthatha to present-day Queenstown. As was the custom, he had three wives who constituted the three principal royal houses: the Great House, the Right Hand House, and the Left Hand House. From the Left Hand House, King Ngubengcuka had two sons, Simakade and Mandela, my great-grandfather, who was born in 1820 and whose name was used as a surname for all his children. Mandela had four children, one of whom was Chief Mphakanyiswa Gadla Mandela, my grandfather. Chief Mphakanyiswa had nine children; Nelson Rolihlahla Mandela is the only son from his first wife.

Tata, in *Long Walk to Freedom,* described my grandfather

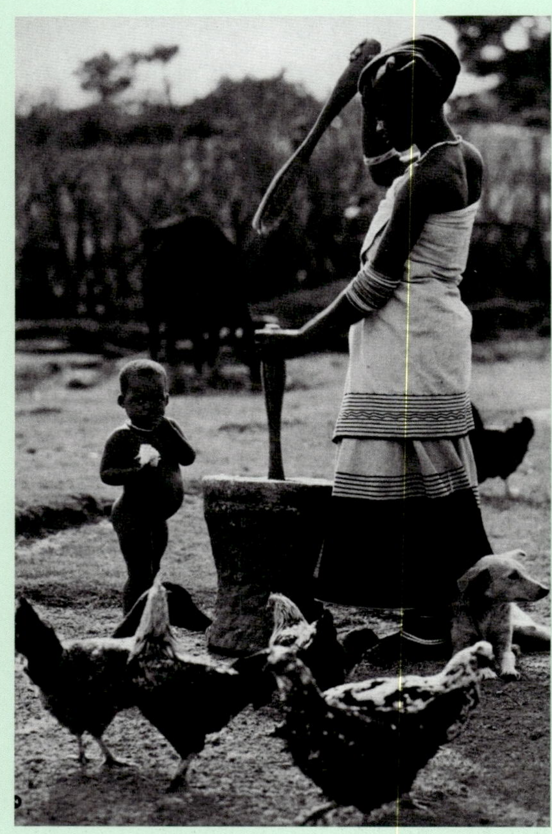

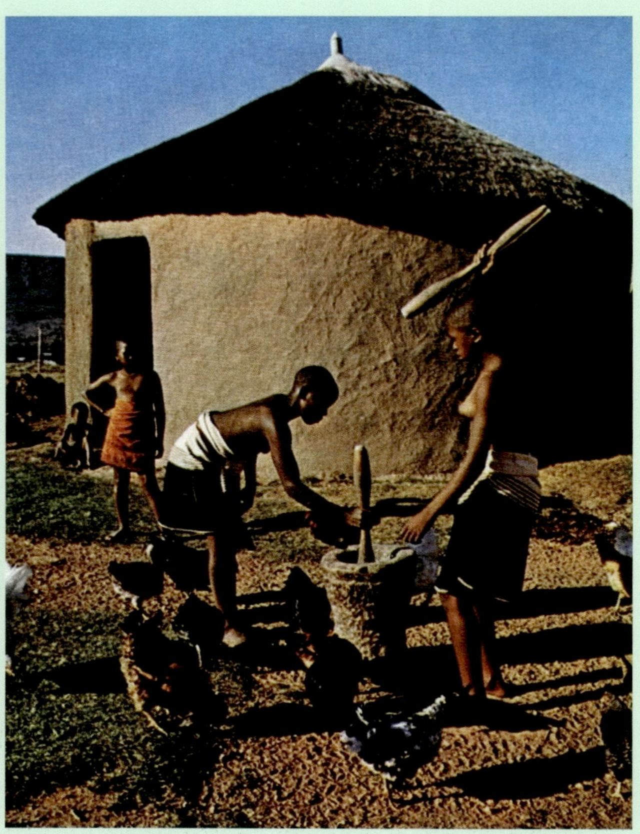

These photographs portray traditional daily life, much as it was like for Tata.

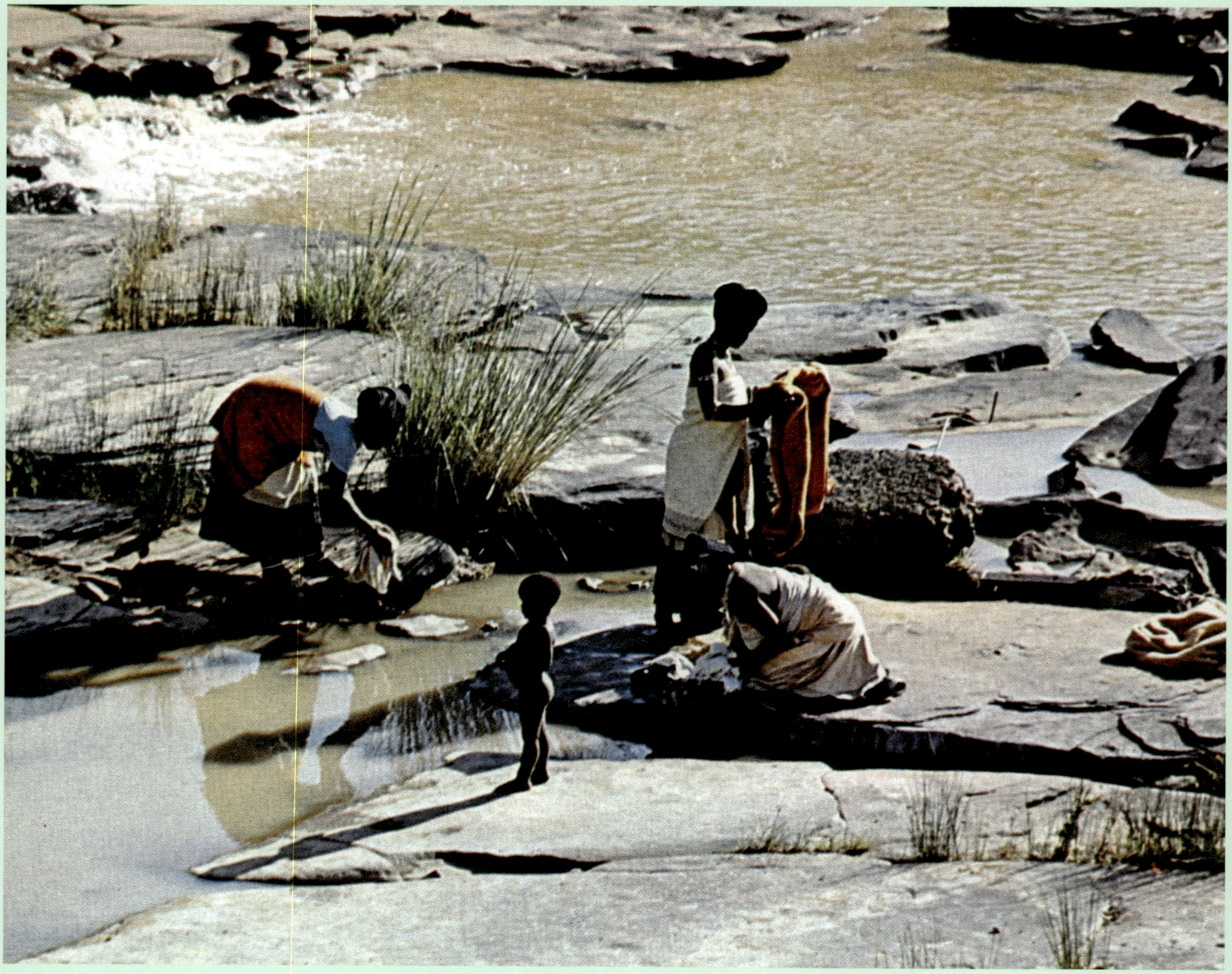

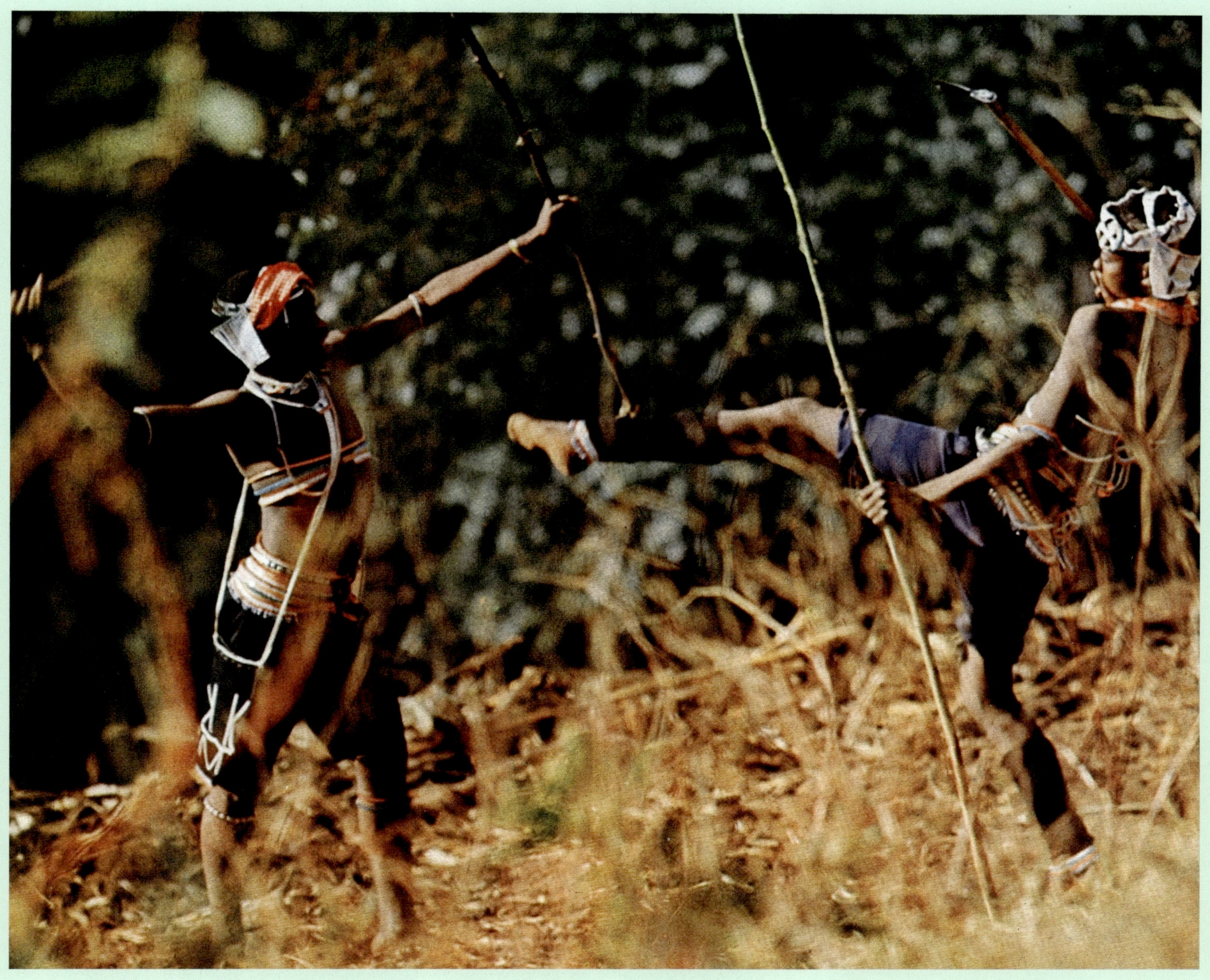

Tata used to play stick games with cousins and other young boys in the village.

as dignified in manner and appearance. He was tall and dark, and Tata would often try to emulate him by rubbing ash in his own hair. My grandfather was very strong-willed, a trait that I believe was passed down to my father.

My grandfather has often been referred to as the prime minister of Thembuland in the early 1900s; however, no such title existed. Rather, he was a trusted custodian of Xhosa history, and a respected and valued counselor to King Dalindyebo and King Jongintaba during their reigns; he often accompanied them on their travels and when meeting government officials. Tata's own interest in history was greatly inspired and encouraged by his father. Despite not being able to read or write, my grandfather was widely known to be an excellent orator, able to engage, entertain, and teach his audiences.

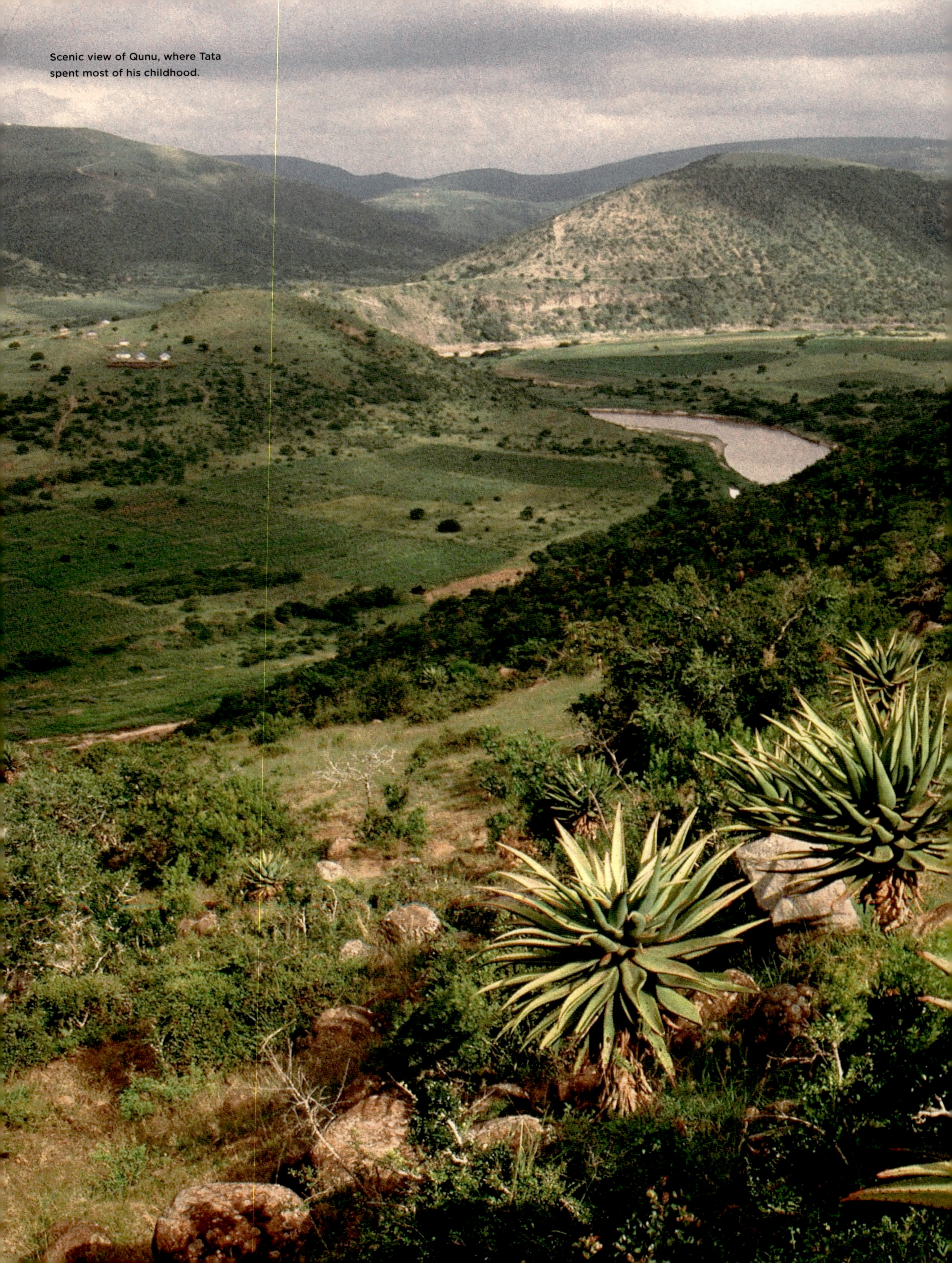

Scenic view of Qunu, where Tata spent most of his childhood.

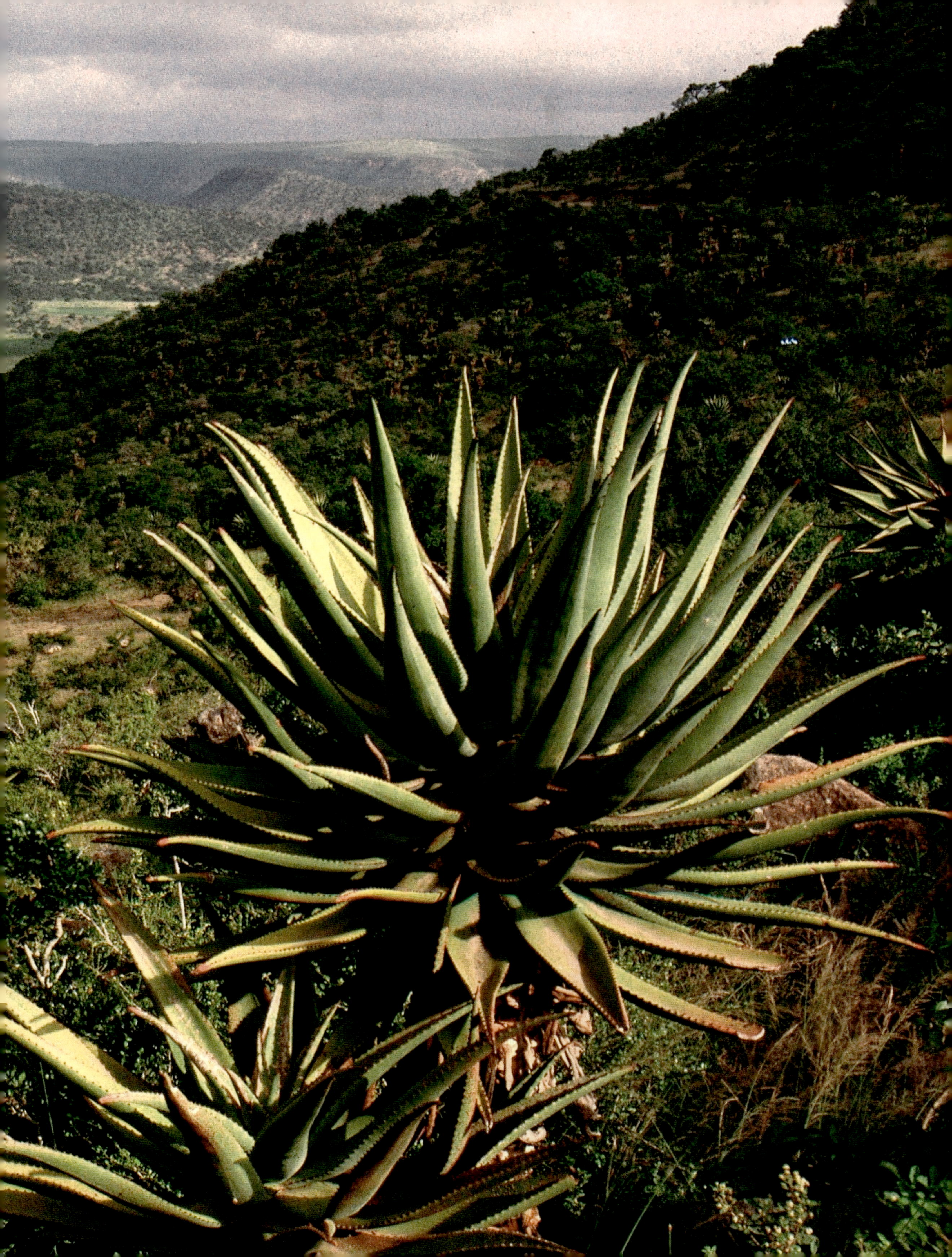

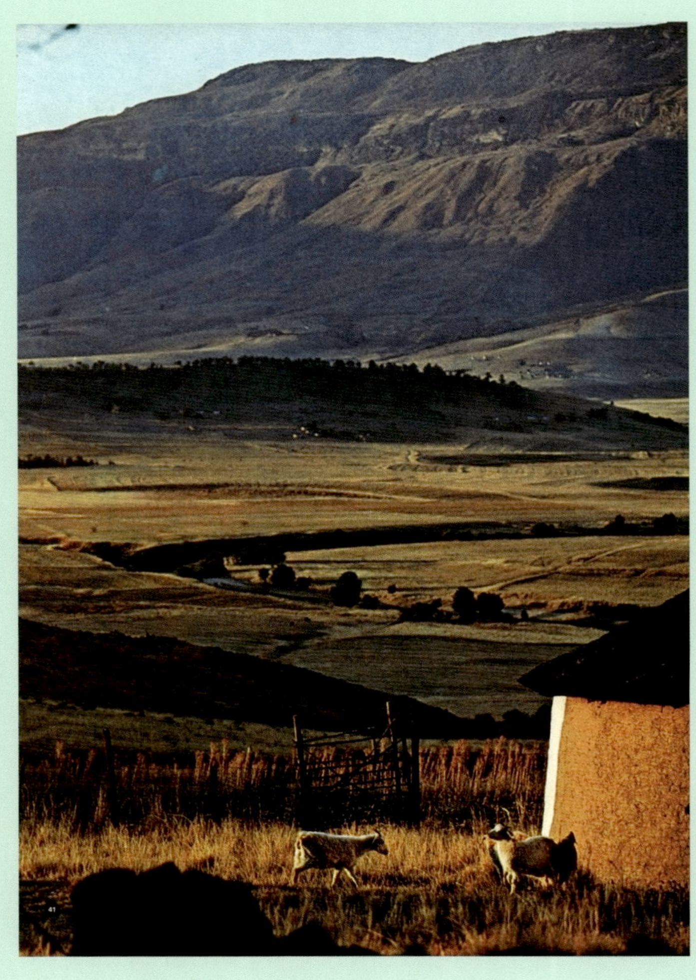

In 1919, my grandfather was deposed from his chieftainship because of insubordination to a local magistrate. He lost most of his income and moved to the village of Qunu.

The village of Qunu was small with a population of only a few hundred people. Like other families, Tata lived in a beehive-shaped hut called a rondavel made with mud walls; a wooden central pole supported a peaked grass roof that allowed smoke to escape. The doorway was low, and the adults had to stoop to enter. The floors in the huts were made of crushed anthills, the grainy soil having the right consistency to pack down for hard floors. It was kept smooth by regularly wiping it with fresh cow dung. Groups of huts were built together to form a residential area in proximity to the fields.

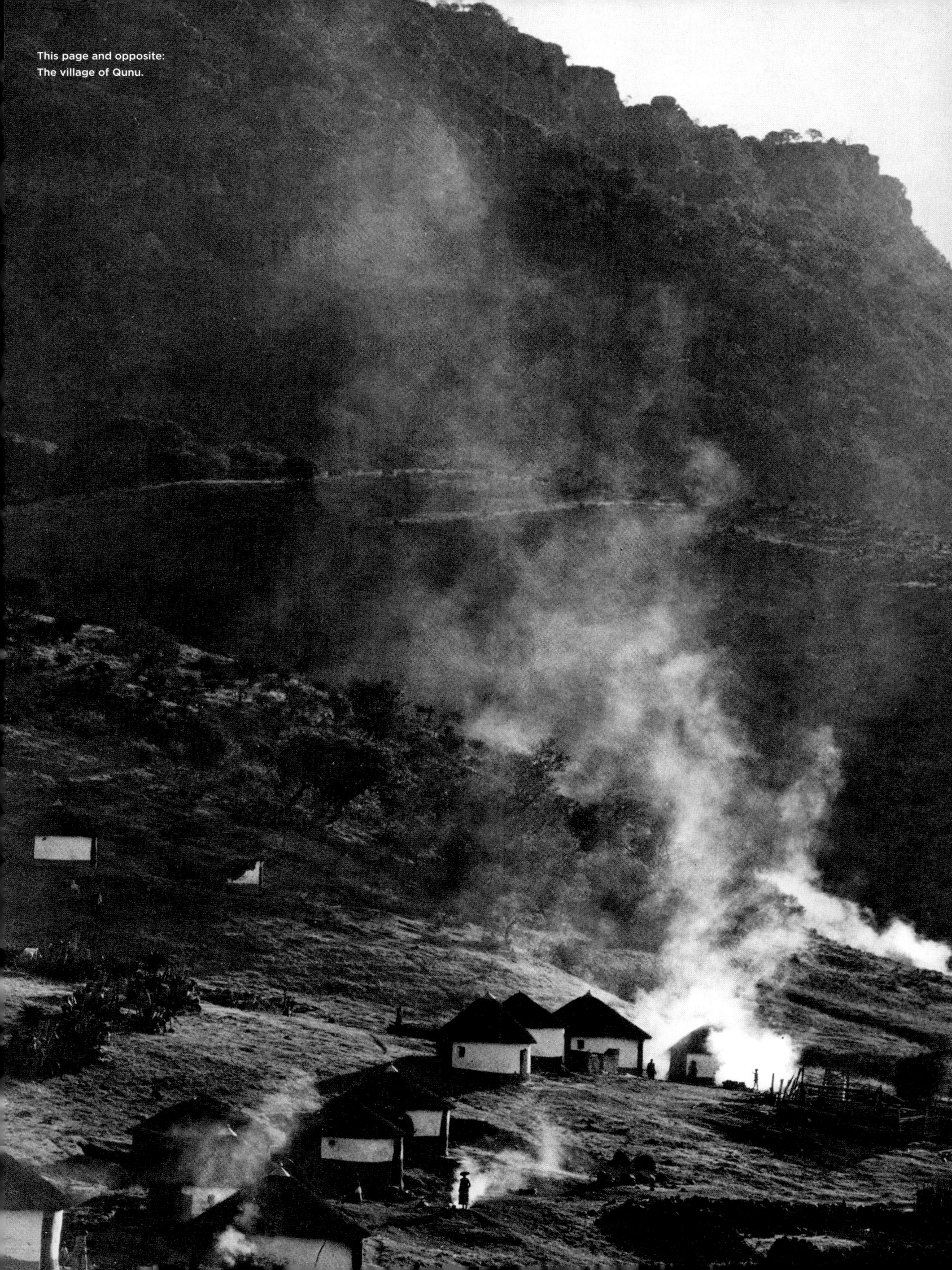

This page and opposite:
The village of Qunu.

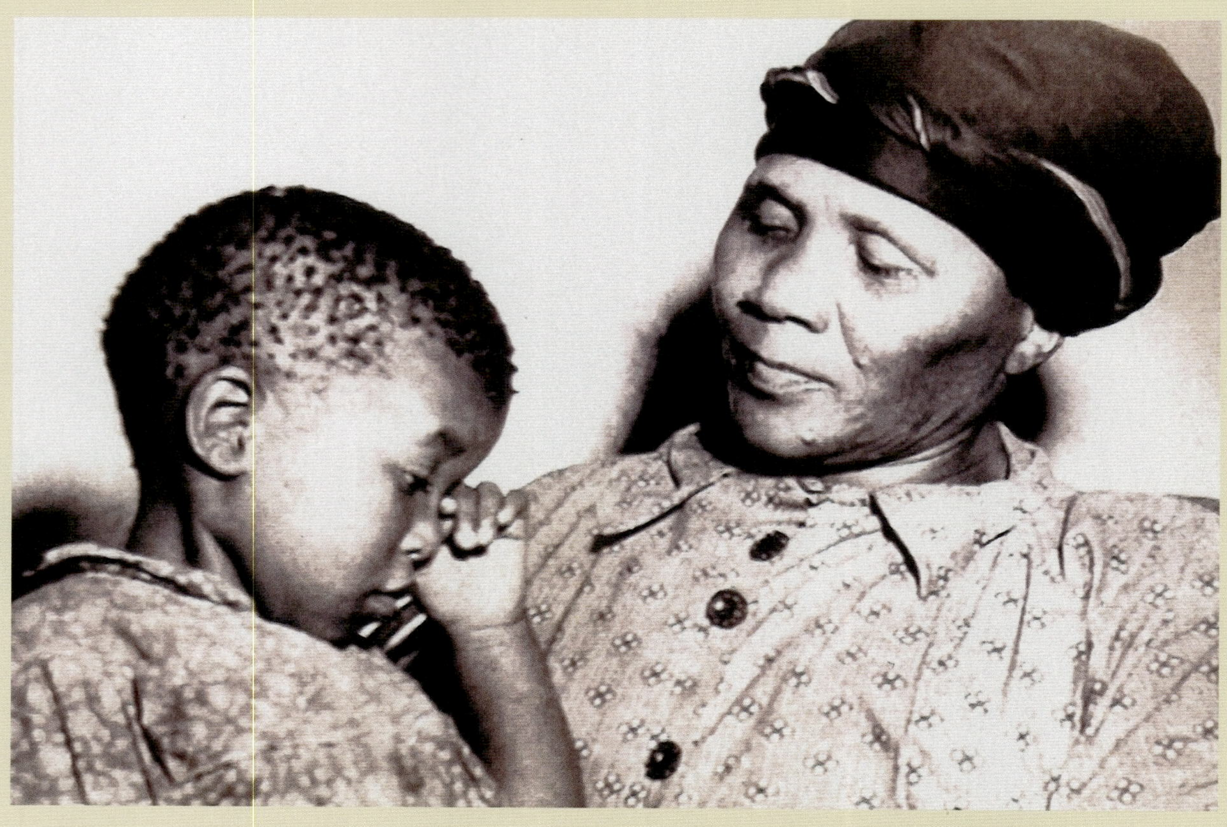

My grandmother, Nonqaphi Nosekeni Fanny Mandela, with one of her granddaughters, Nomfundo Mandela.

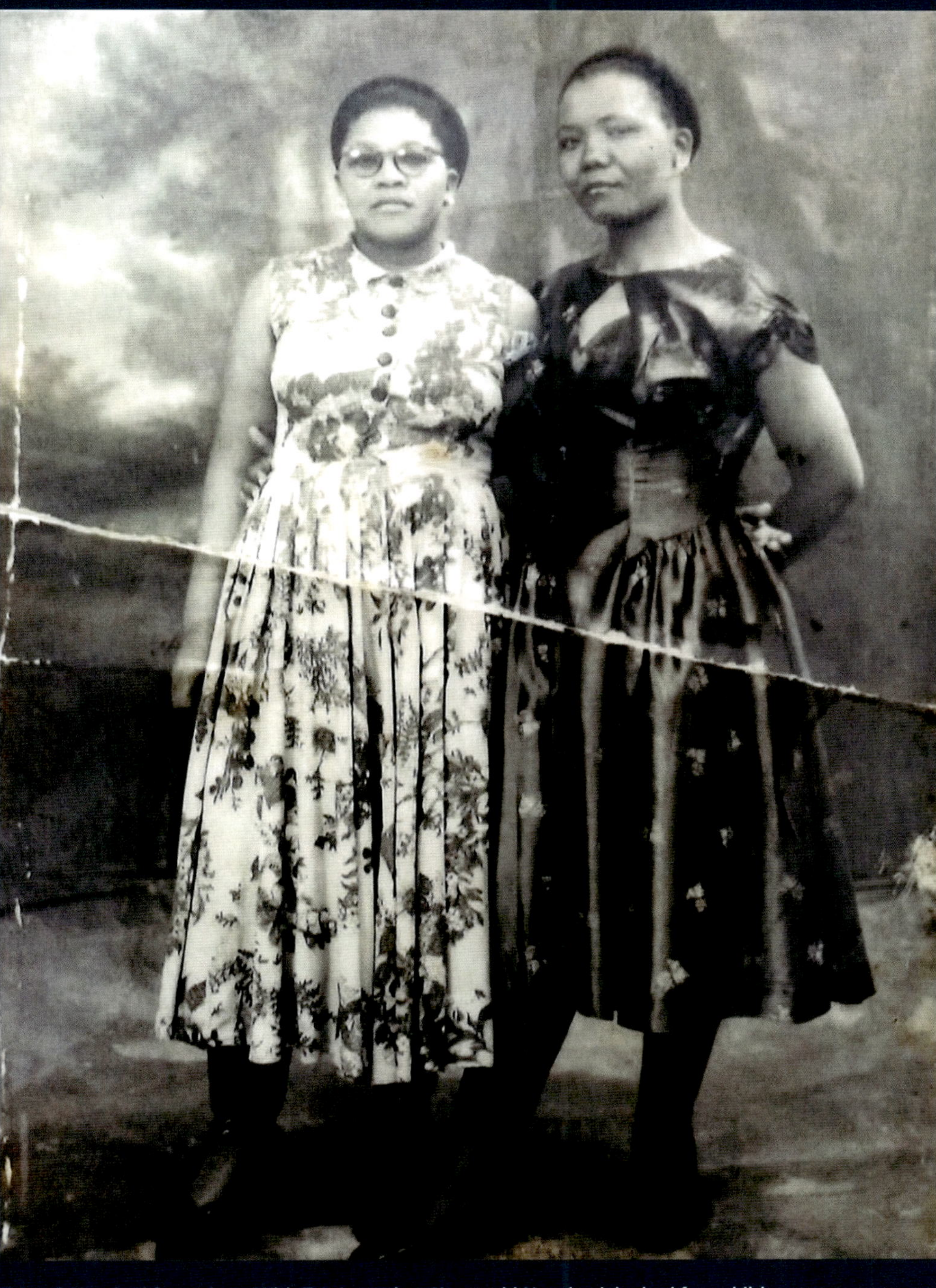

Tata's father had four wives. With Tata's mother, Nonqaphi Nosekeni, he had four children: Tata and three daughters. Shown here are Tata's oldest sister, Baliwe (*left*), and Makhutswana (Leabie), the youngest.

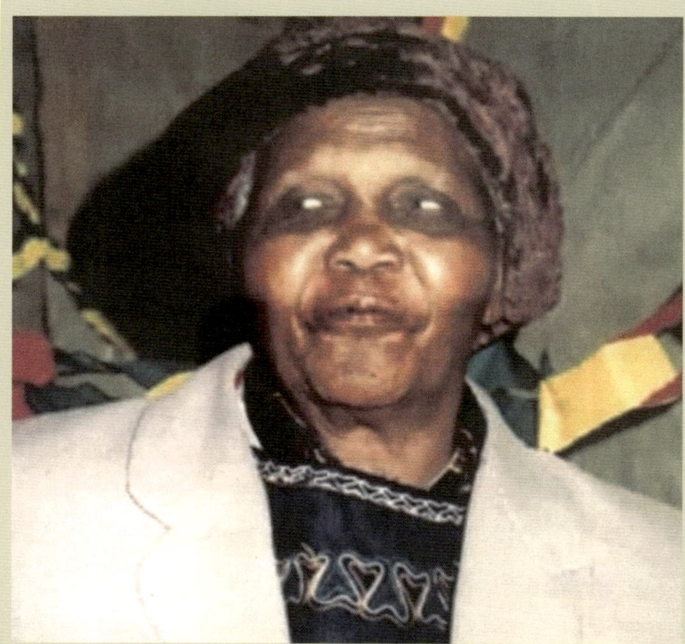

Tata's sister Natancu remained in the Transkei. Later, when Tata was imprisoned on Robben Island, he would look forward to her visits. She would bring news and gossip about the village and relatives to share with him.

The land belonged to the state. Africans at that time could not own a private title in South Africa.

Instead in the 1800s and early 1900s, chiefs were in custody of the land and would allocate property to villagers. By virtue of custom and colonial policies, women in Thembuland were allocated indirect usufruct rights, allowing them all the advantages derived from the use of the land belonging to their husbands. My grandmother Nosekeni and my aunts were the chief producers of agricultural foodstuffs and cash crops in our area while also doing all the housework.

They collected wood and cow dung to make fire for cooking and fetched water from the nearby river. Most men were working in the mines or on remote white-owned farms. Women and children wore garments made of blankets dyed in ochre. The only Western-style clothing was worn by a few Christians living in the village. With no roads, they walked well-worn paths to the fields for water and then back home.

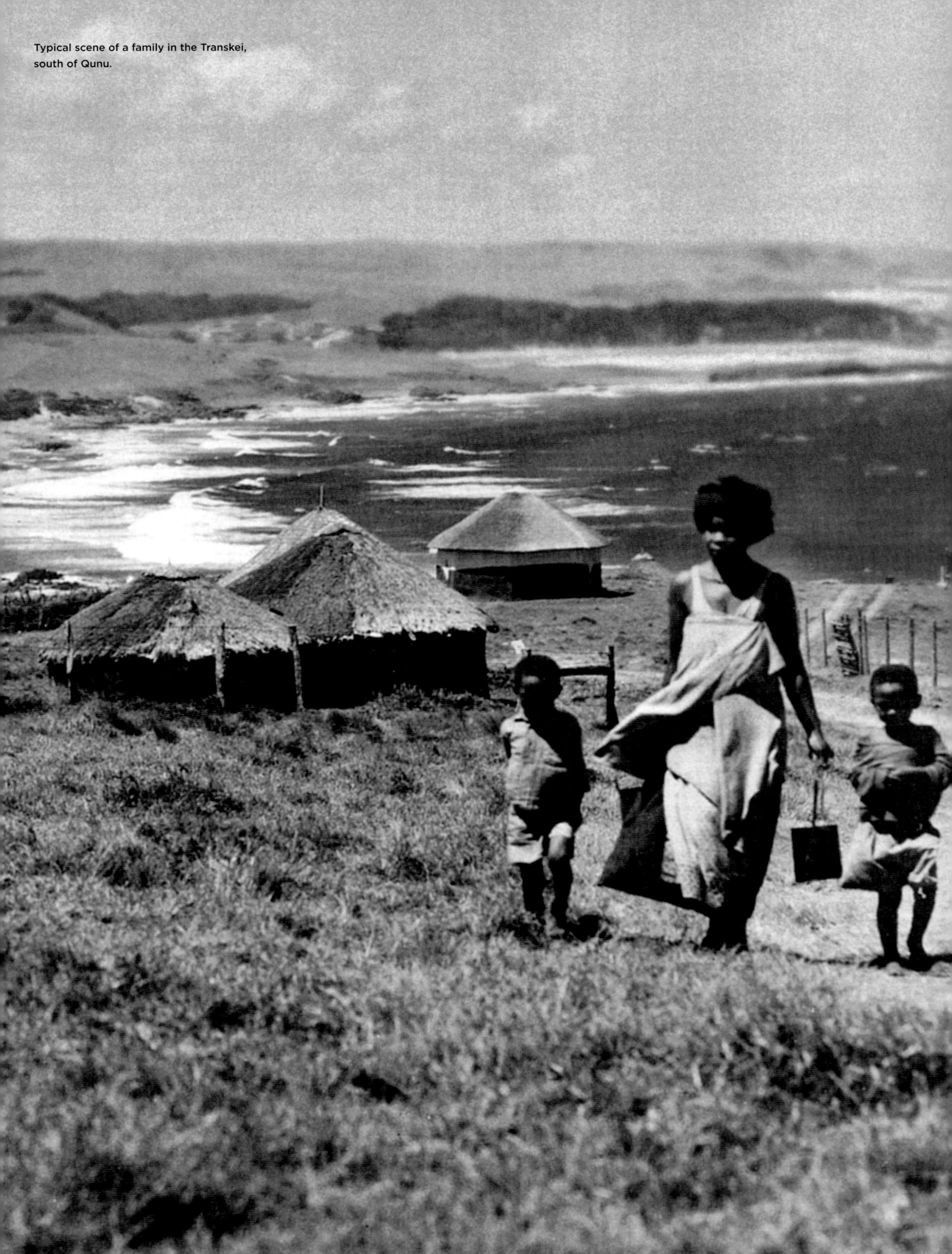

Typical scene of a family in the Transkei, south of Qunu.

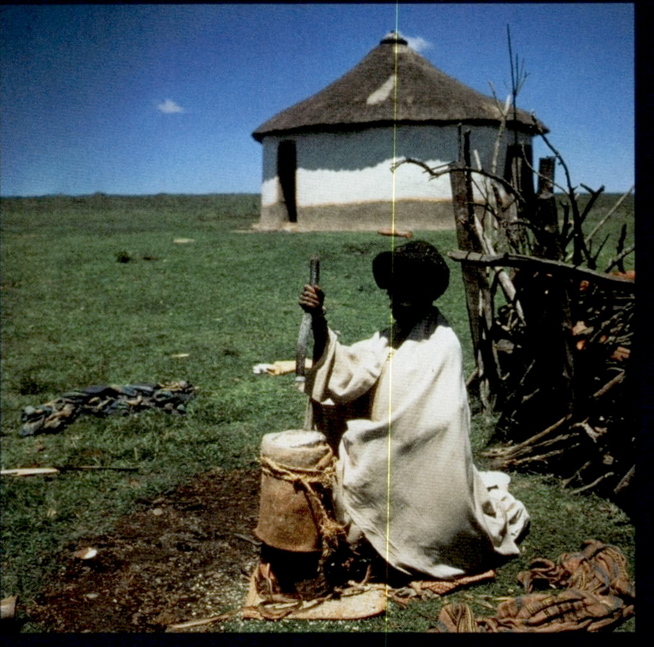

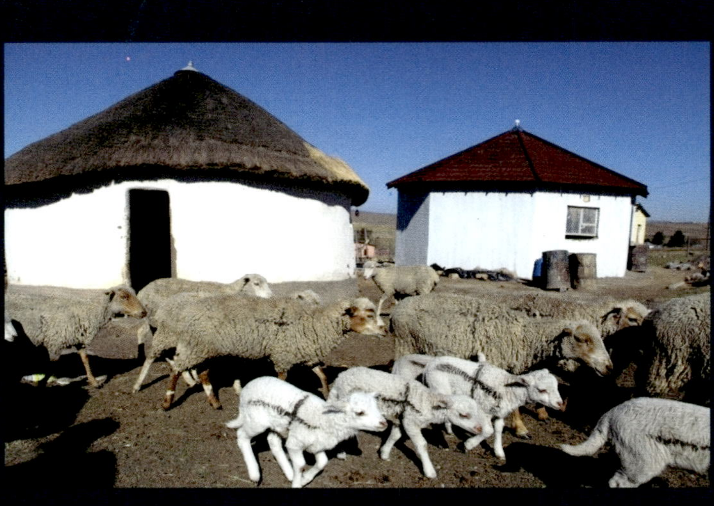

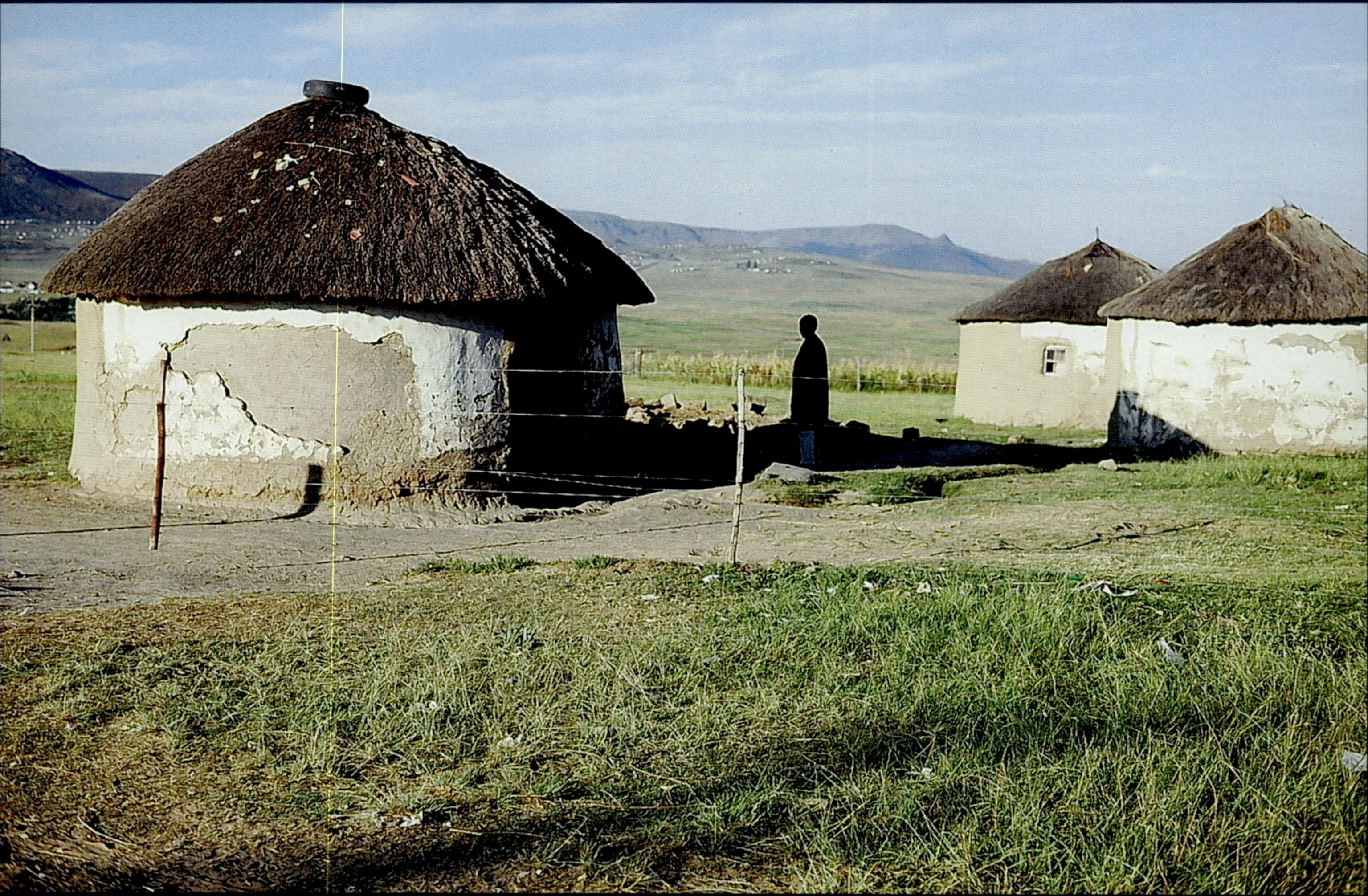

This page and opposite: Young men took care of cattle, sheep, and goats. They were also responsible for tilling and planting, and transporting goods by

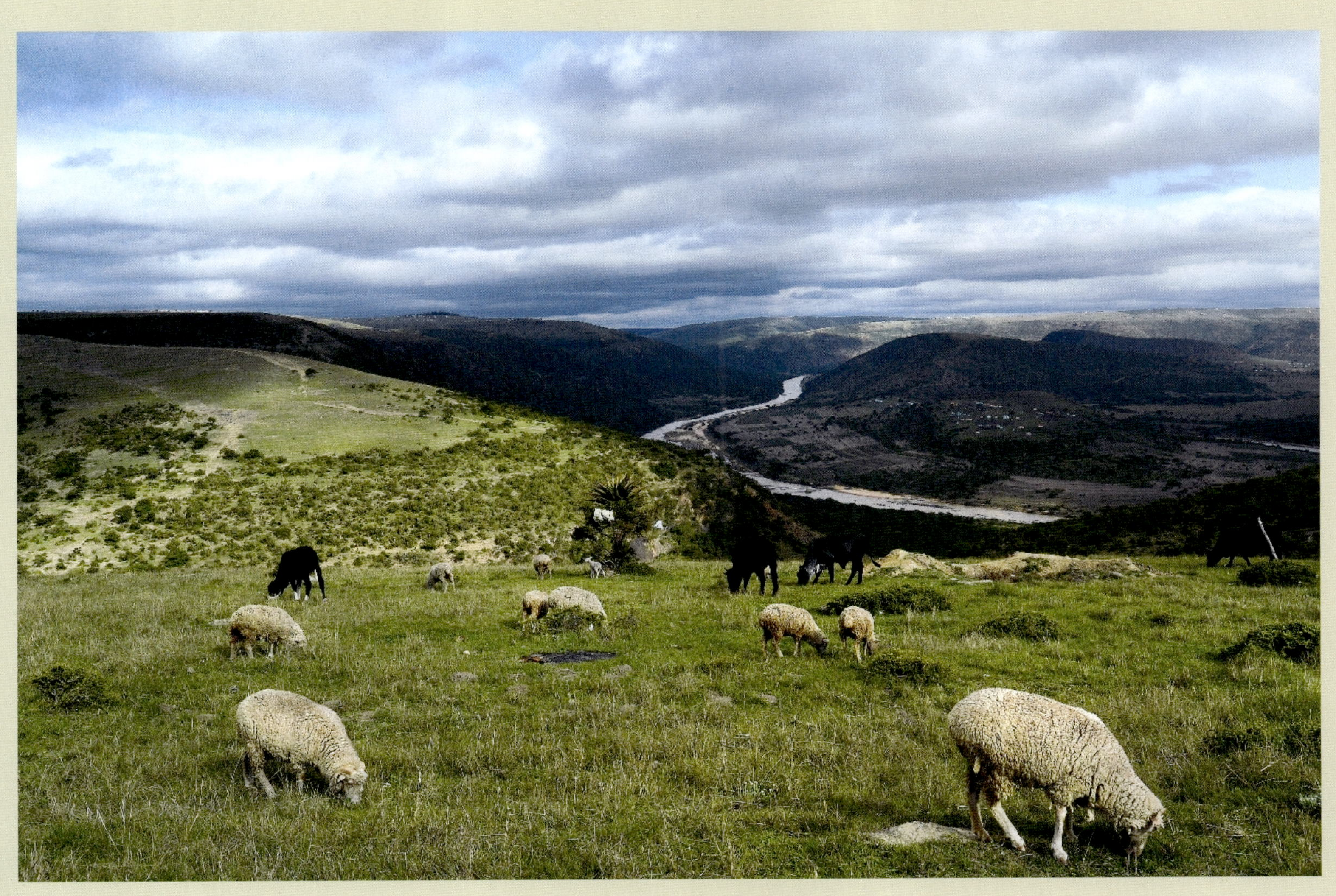

My grandmother owned three huts: one was used as a kitchen, the second as a bedroom, and the third as a storage facility.

The major food staple was corn, which was prepared in various ways. It could be pounded or ground using two stones. It would either be made into bread or the corn kernels would be mixed with beans to make umngqusho or umphokoqotho (a mixture with sour milk that was Tata's favorite). While corn was at times in limited supply, milk from cows and goats was always plentiful. My grandmother's household was often filled with relatives, cousins, and other local children. Tata's childhood was never lonely, and he often expressed that his fondest memories of his boyhood were in Qunu. He felt that this was where his roots were and where he wanted to spend his retirement years and be buried. Both of his parents were buried there, and it is also where he built his own home when he was released from prison in February 1990.

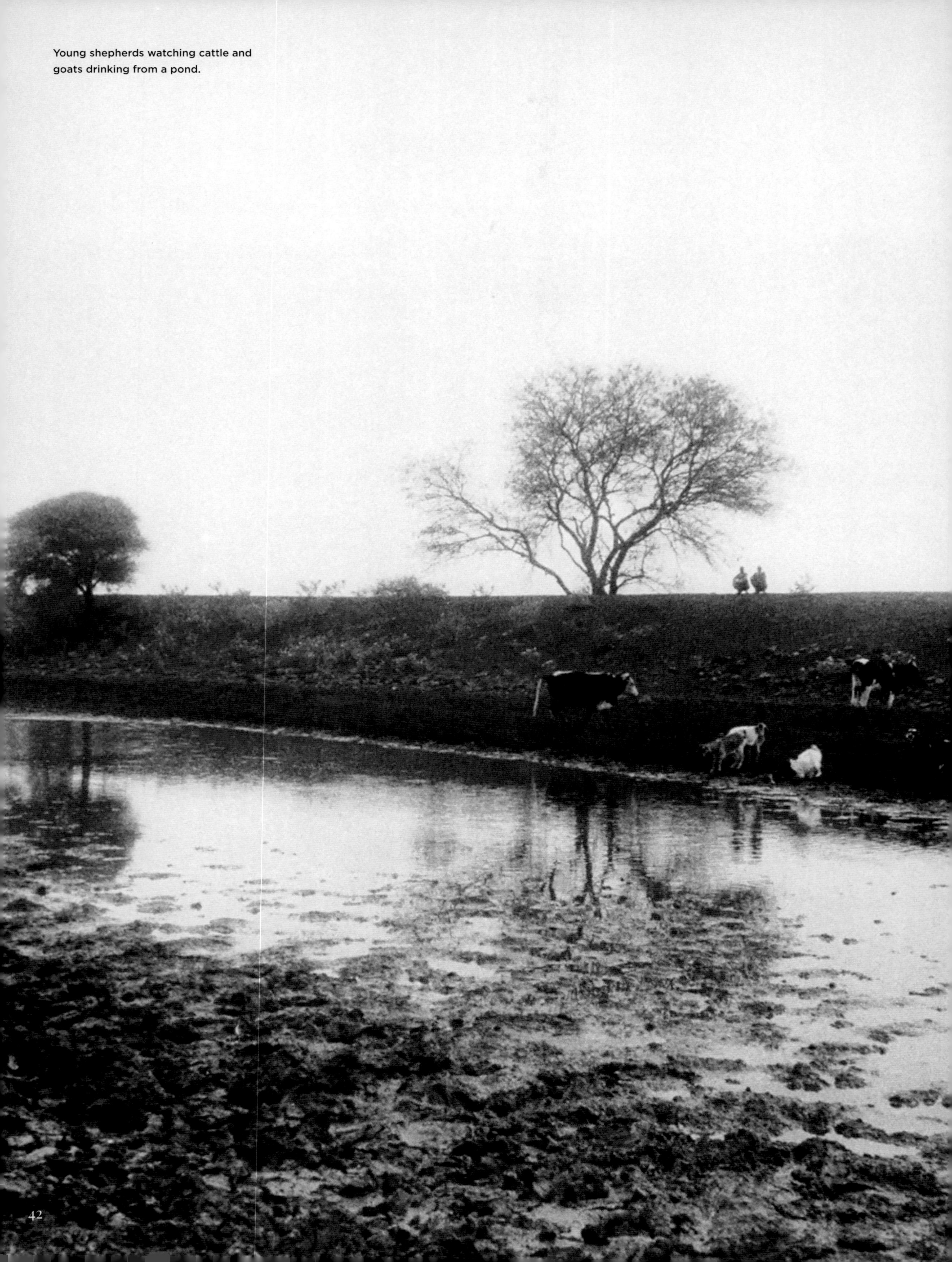

Young shepherds watching cattle and goats drinking from a pond.

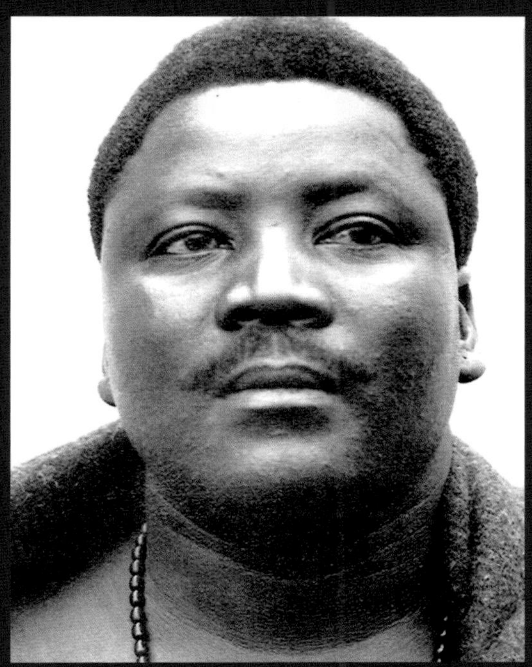

Jongintaba

Chief regent of the Thembu people, who was appointed to be Tata's guardian by his dying father.

When he was dying from lung disease in 1930, Tata's father entrusted him to his close relative Chief Jongintaba Dalindyebo, the supreme chief of the Thembus. Wearing an old khaki shirt and trousers made from his father's clothes, Tata arrived later that year with his trunk at the Great Place palace in Mqhekezweni. Jongintaba was a handsome and well-dressed man who inspired in Tata a lasting interest in clothes. He also set an example of benign authority and leadership by consensus that Tata followed in later years. Tata shared a simply furnished rondavel with the regent's son, Justice, who became like a brother to him. He went to a local school there (later he went to school in Qokolweni, near Umtata). While living in Mqhekezweni, he listened to the stories told by the chiefs who visited. He was inspired by their kinship and took pride in learning from his people. In particular, he gained an understanding of the past from uTata uJoyi, a relative whose grandfather was one of the sons of king Ngubengcuka, the king of the Thembus in the 1800s.

According to Tata, joy and ubuntu (the spirit of community, caring for one another, compassion, and kindness, especially within African societies) ended when the tyranny of white people was established and African ancestral lands were stolen. Tata was inspired to regain it for all South Africans. In 1934, sixteen-year-old Tata underwent the traditional Xhosa initiation ceremony into manhood. His circumcision was held on the banks of the Mbashe River, where many of his ancestors experienced the same rituals. The custom of circumcision is used to mark the entrance into manhood and is regarded as the most solemn occasion in the life of a man. For two months or more afterward, initiates, known as abakhwetha, live in isolation in a specially constructed grass hut or lodge. It is usually built in a secluded area where they enjoy complete privacy, as women may not look upon their faces during this period. An instructor, who looks after the initiates, and a young errand boy also live at the lodge.

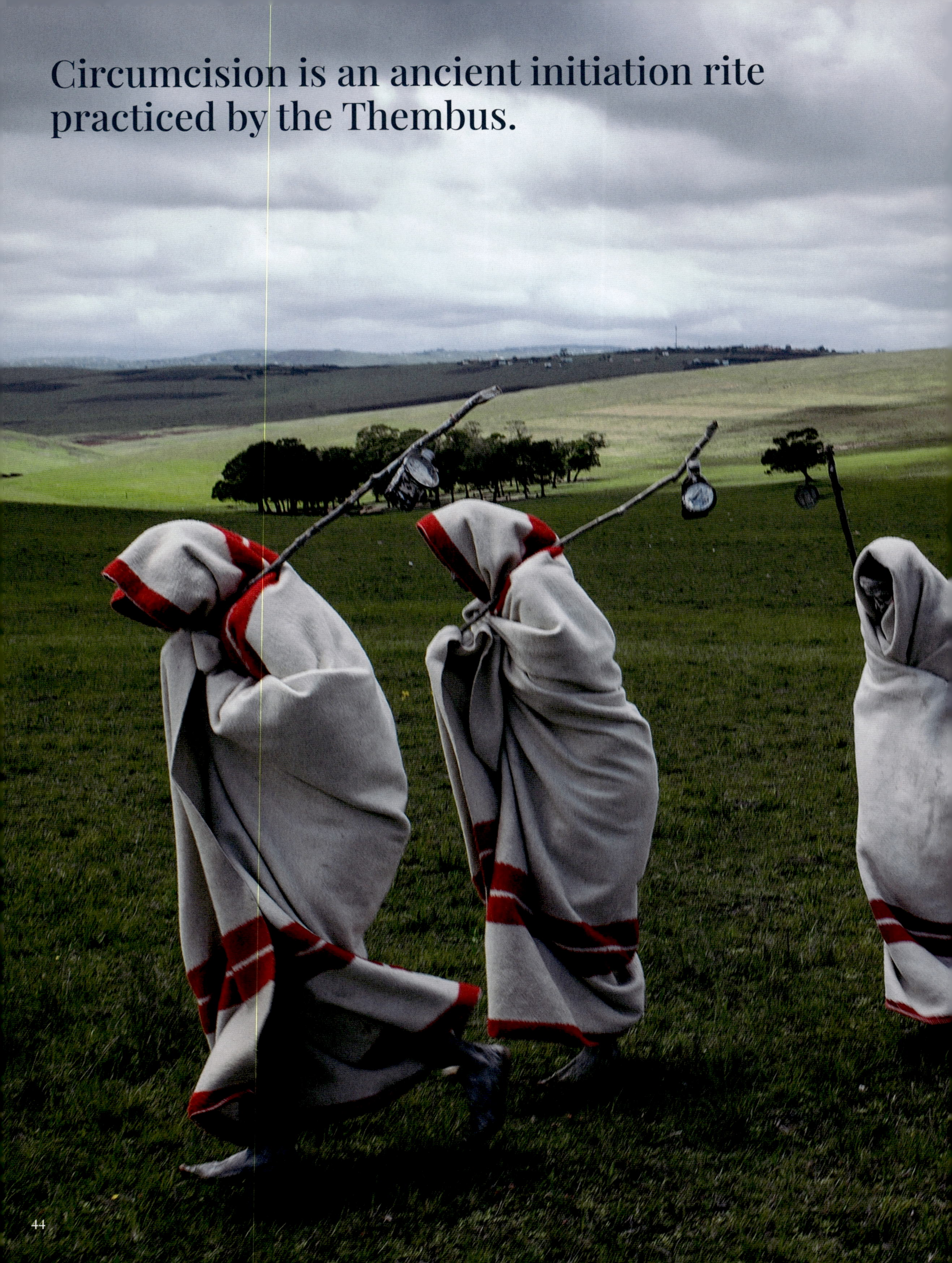

Circumcision is an ancient initiation rite practiced by the Thembus.

The circumcision ritual serves as a rite of passage from boyhood to manhood. In the Thembu culture, a boy would not be allowed to get married or establish his own household if not circumcised. He would not be regarded as a grown man. Although this ritual is still widely practiced, its prevalence has been affected by changes in value systems, the emergence of new diseases, and the fact that several boys have died following traditional circumcisions. Some boys opt for hospital circumcisions, and other families are now circumcising their sons at birth. However, many Thembu men opt for the traditional initiation rite because it is still regarded as an educational process in which boys are taught about their social responsibilities and their conduct as men. Because circumcision is considered a formal incorporation into cultural life and the Thembu religion, paying homage to ancestors, after the age of eighteen or twenty there is a stigma attached to those who have not gone through the ritual.

Girls also go through a rite of passage to womanhood called intonjane. This ritual takes place after a girl begins menstruating. It is symbolic of the girl's sexual maturity and ability to conceive. It is still practiced in some rural areas.

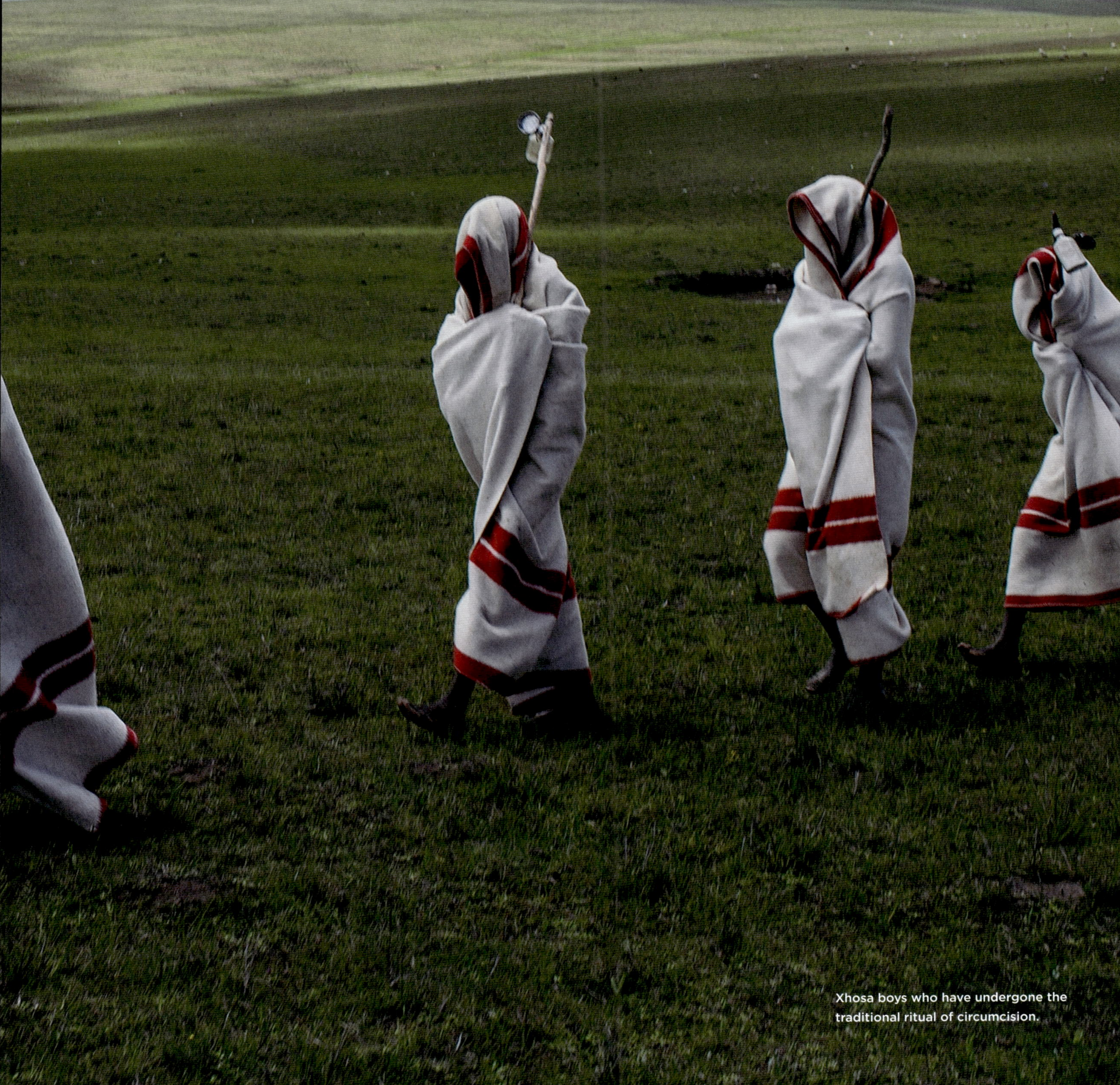

Xhosa boys who have undergone the traditional ritual of circumcision.

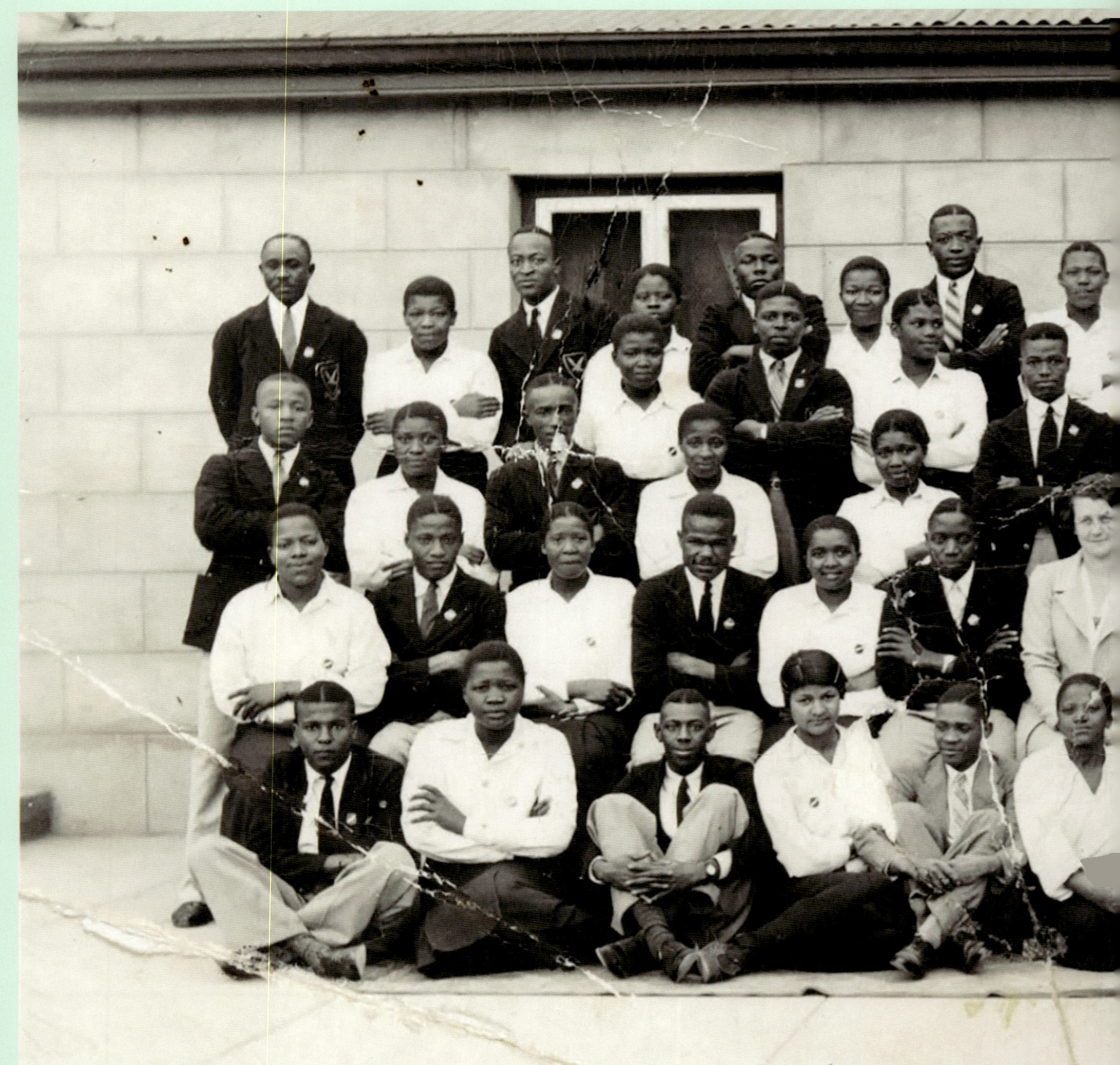

Tata had a strong sense of destiny tied to his roots. From a young age, he was being groomed by his guardian to one day be counselor to the Thembu king. In his teenage years, at the reputable missionary schools of that era, he emulated the boys from more "sophisticated" African families who studied there. However, he never envied them. He secretly relished the fact that "the country boy" could even rival them in their worldliness.

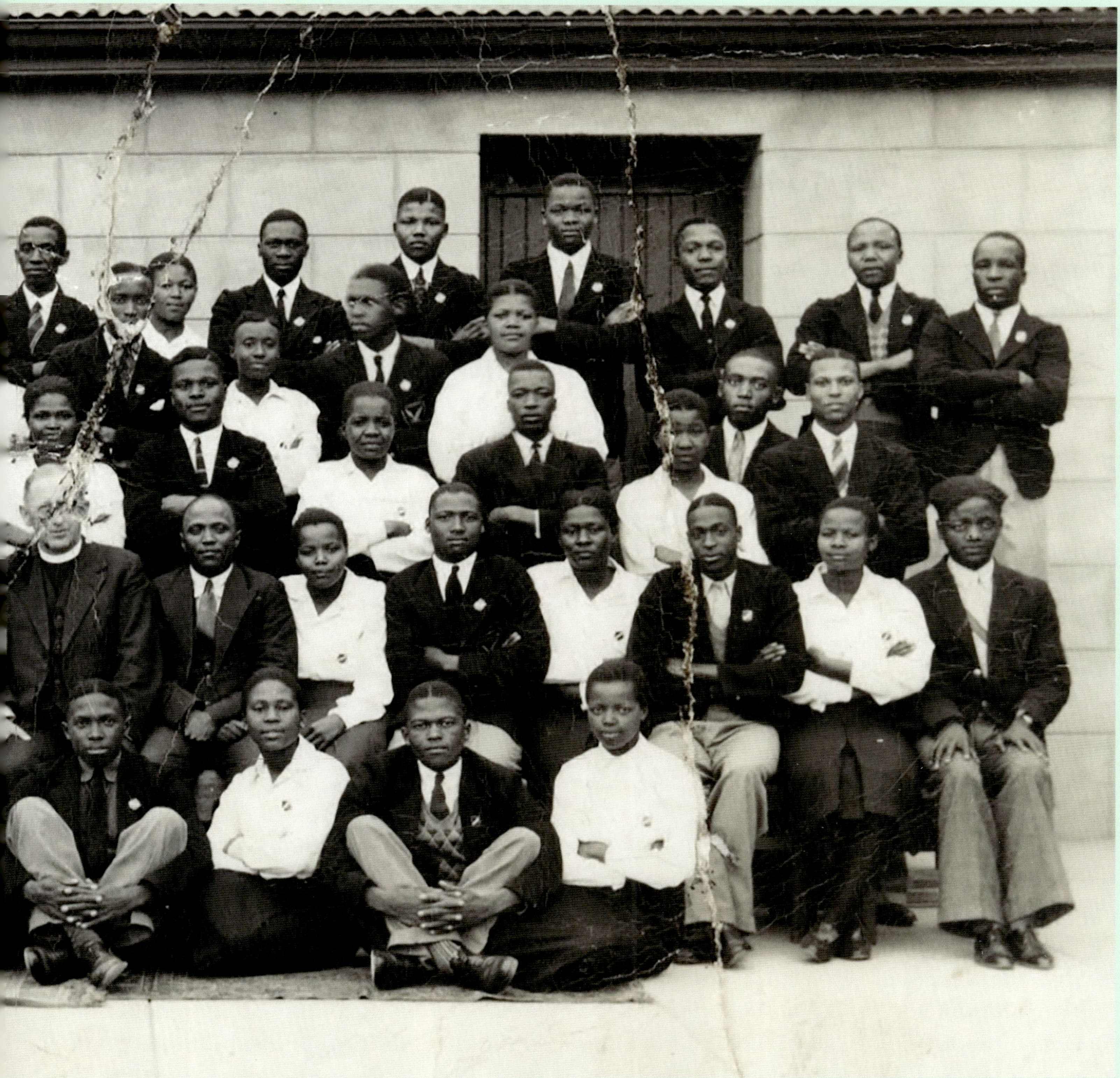

While living in Mqhekezweni, Tata was sent to good missionary schools by his guardian, Chief Jongintaba. Later, he completed his secondary education in Clarkebury, where he received his junior certificate. His schooling in Clarkebury broadened his horizons, and he met students from all over South Africa, many from sophisticated families. After two years there, Tata continued his education at Healdtown, a Wesleyan Methodist mission school in Fort Beaufort in the Eastern Cape. He displayed strong leadership qualities and was appointed as a prefect in his first year there.

Healdtown School, 1938. Tata is in the back row (*fifth from the right*) with his hair parted on the side. Below: Tata attended Clarkebury Mission School from 1934 to 1935.

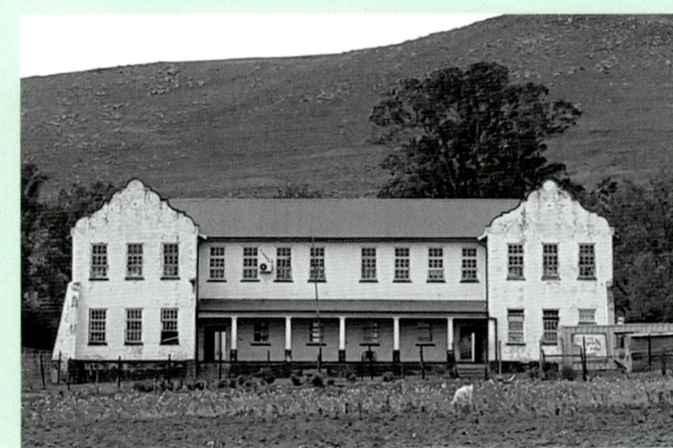

As the boy in a family who had lost a father, Tata had a deep longing to provide for his mother and sisters. He was well aware of all the wealth and prestige they had lost after his father's death. He wanted them to be able to afford things they'd been denied before. He truly believed that a BA graduate from Fort Hare would fulfill his dream of building his mom a home in Qunu, with nice furniture and a garden.

Although the teaching staff was dedicated to providing their students with a good education, at times their Christian values were contradicted by their tolerance of and bias toward the racist colonial system. Missionaries rejected all African traditional rituals and customs, believing them to be based on superstition, and felt that their role was to save the souls of African people. Tata graduated from Healdtown in 1938 and enrolled at the University College of Fort Hare in Alice the following year. From its founding in 1916 until its incorporation in 1959 into the apartheid system, Fort Hare was the most important and influential institution of higher education for Black Africans. The university drew scholars from all over Africa and counts such political activists as Oliver Tambo, Robert Mugabe, and Desmond Tutu among its alumni. Fort Hare was about twenty miles from Healdtown, in the municipality of Alice. It was the only residential center of higher education for non-white people in South Africa at that time. Although the country was not yet under Afrikaner Nationalist rule, the society was highly segregated. Fort Hare attracted Indian and Colored students, and Black students from all over southern, central, and eastern Africa. Tata said that for young Black students it was "Oxford, Cambridge and Harvard all rolled into one." Tata began his studies for a bachelor of arts degree at Fort Hare but was expelled for joining a student protest. In 1942, he completed his degree through the University of South Africa (UNISA) while also apprenticing for one of the biggest law firms in Johannesburg. He began studying for an LLB (undergraduate bachelor of law) degree at the University of the Witwatersrand in 1943, but left the university in 1949 without graduating. To enter the legal profession in the 1940s, an attorney's diploma with five years of apprenticeship was required, which Tata qualified for on March 27, 1952, through his apprenticeship and passing his qualification exam. Later that year, he and his friend Oliver Tambo opened the first Black-owned legal practice in Johannesburg. They offered affordable, and often free, legal advice to Africans who could not afford the standard fees. The Mandela and Tambo law firm later closed because of their involvement in the struggle against apartheid. With their increasing interest and work in politics, the principals no longer had the time to devote to the law firm.

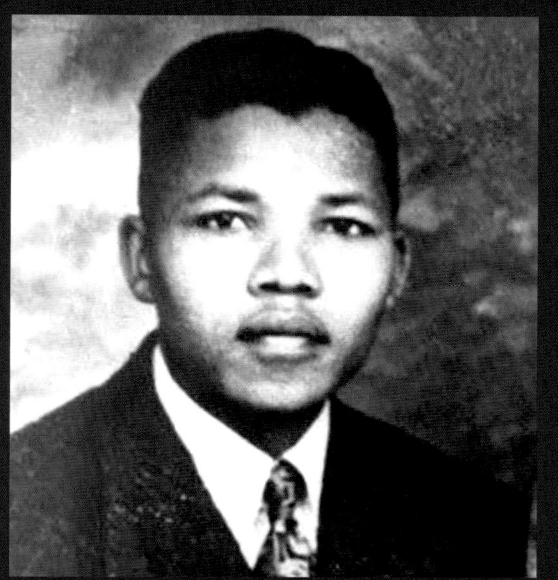

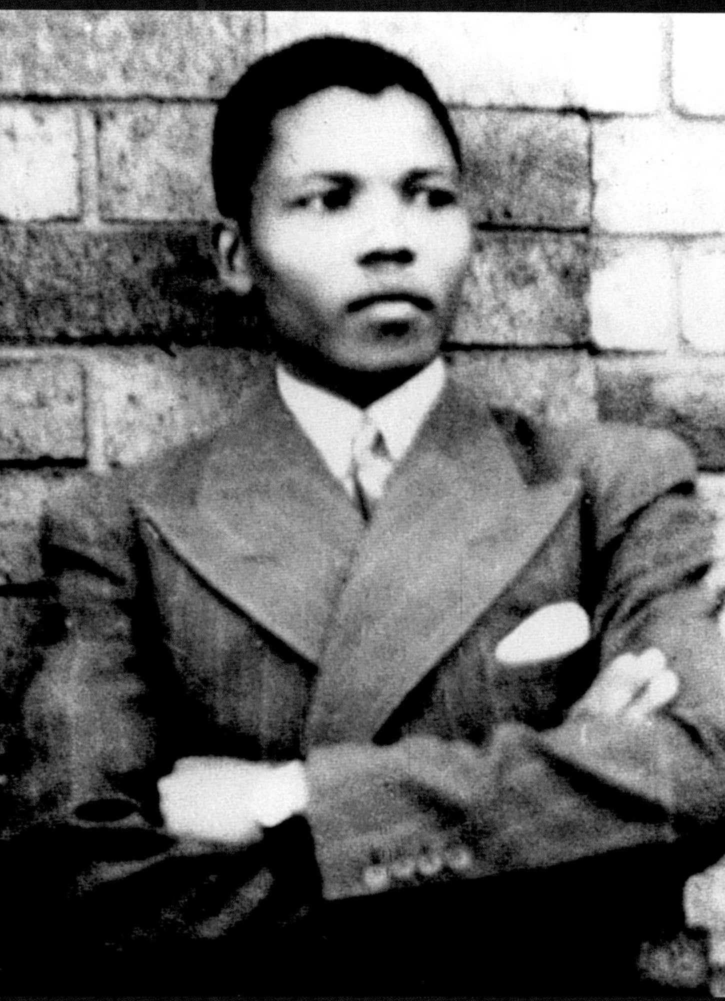

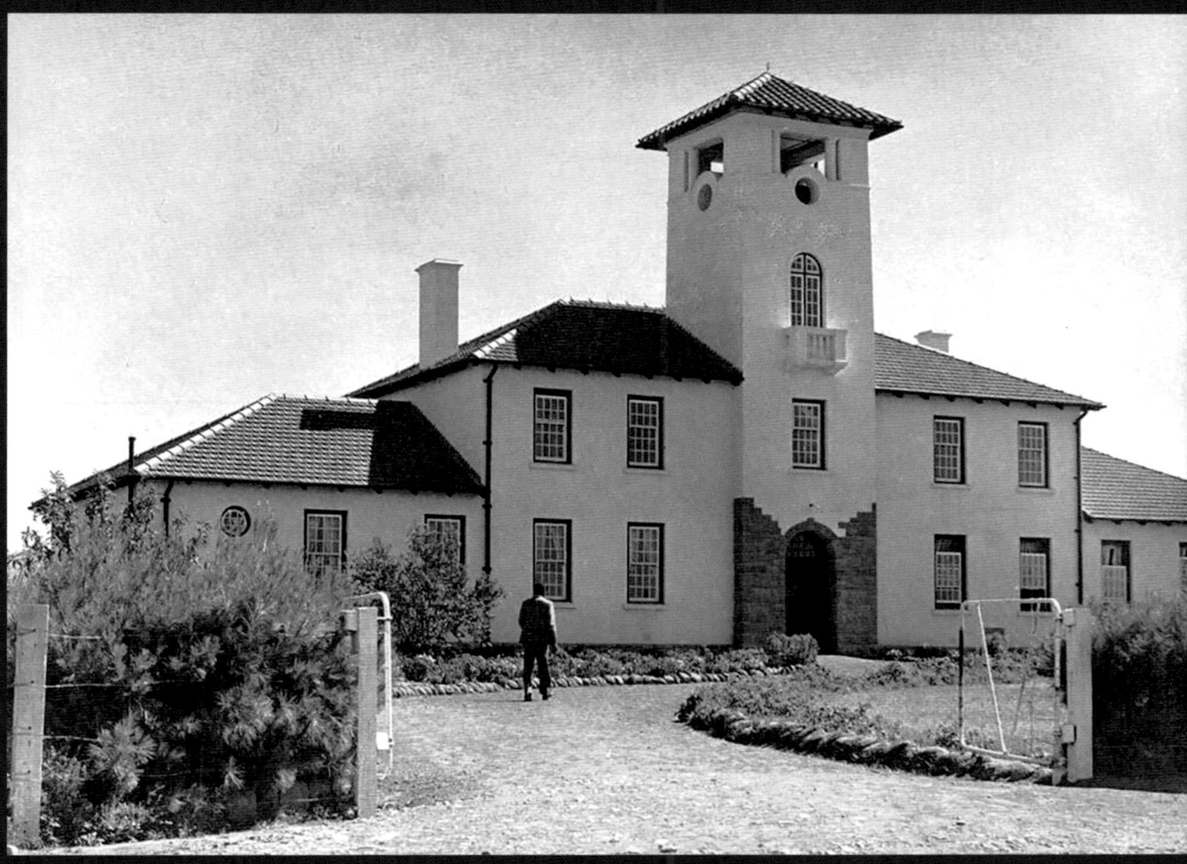

Top: Tata during his school years.

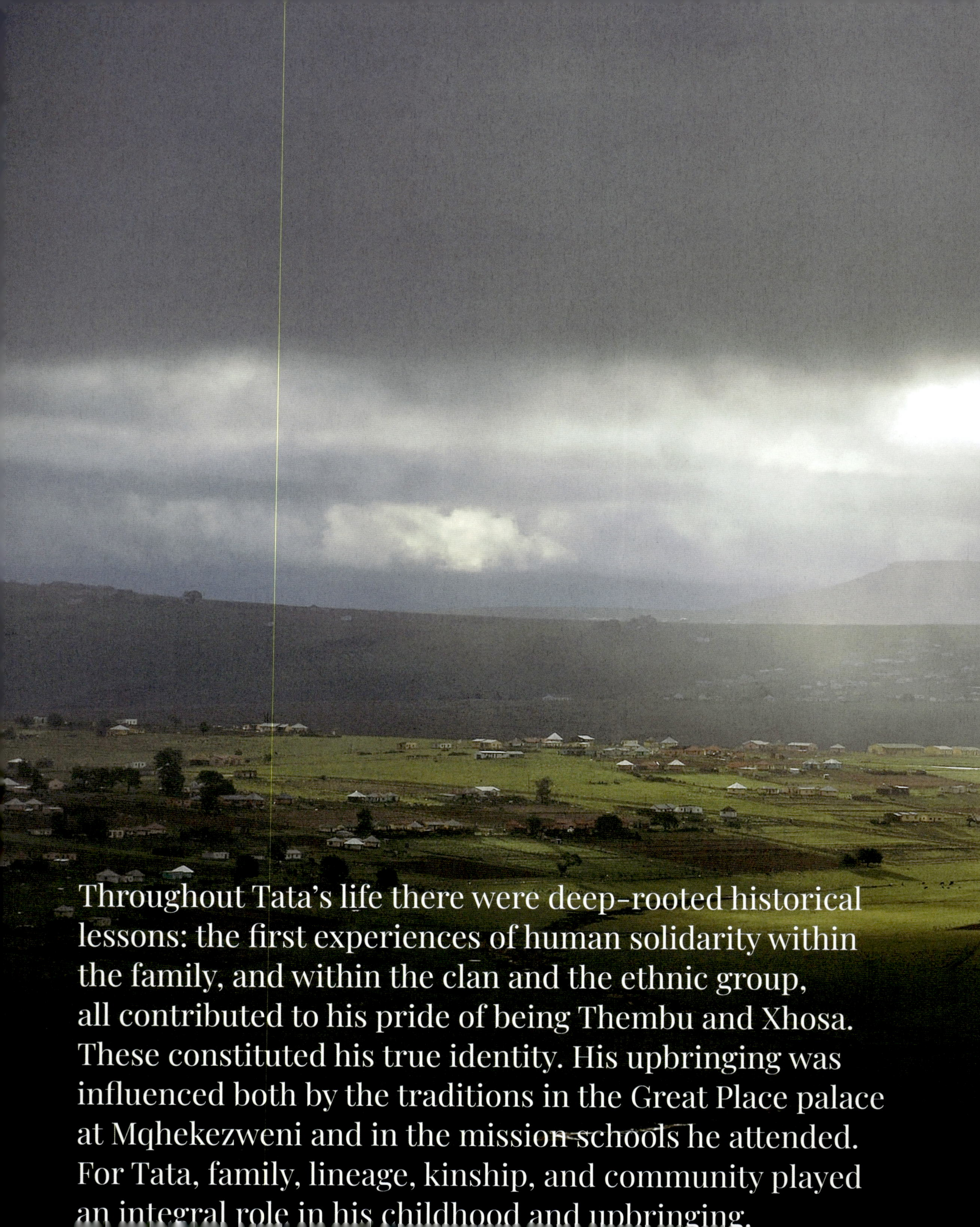

Throughout Tata's life there were deep-rooted historical lessons: the first experiences of human solidarity within the family, and within the clan and the ethnic group, all contributed to his pride of being Thembu and Xhosa. These constituted his true identity. His upbringing was influenced both by the traditions in the Great Place palace at Mqhekezweni and in the mission schools he attended. For Tata, family, lineage, kinship, and community played an integral role in his childhood and upbringing.

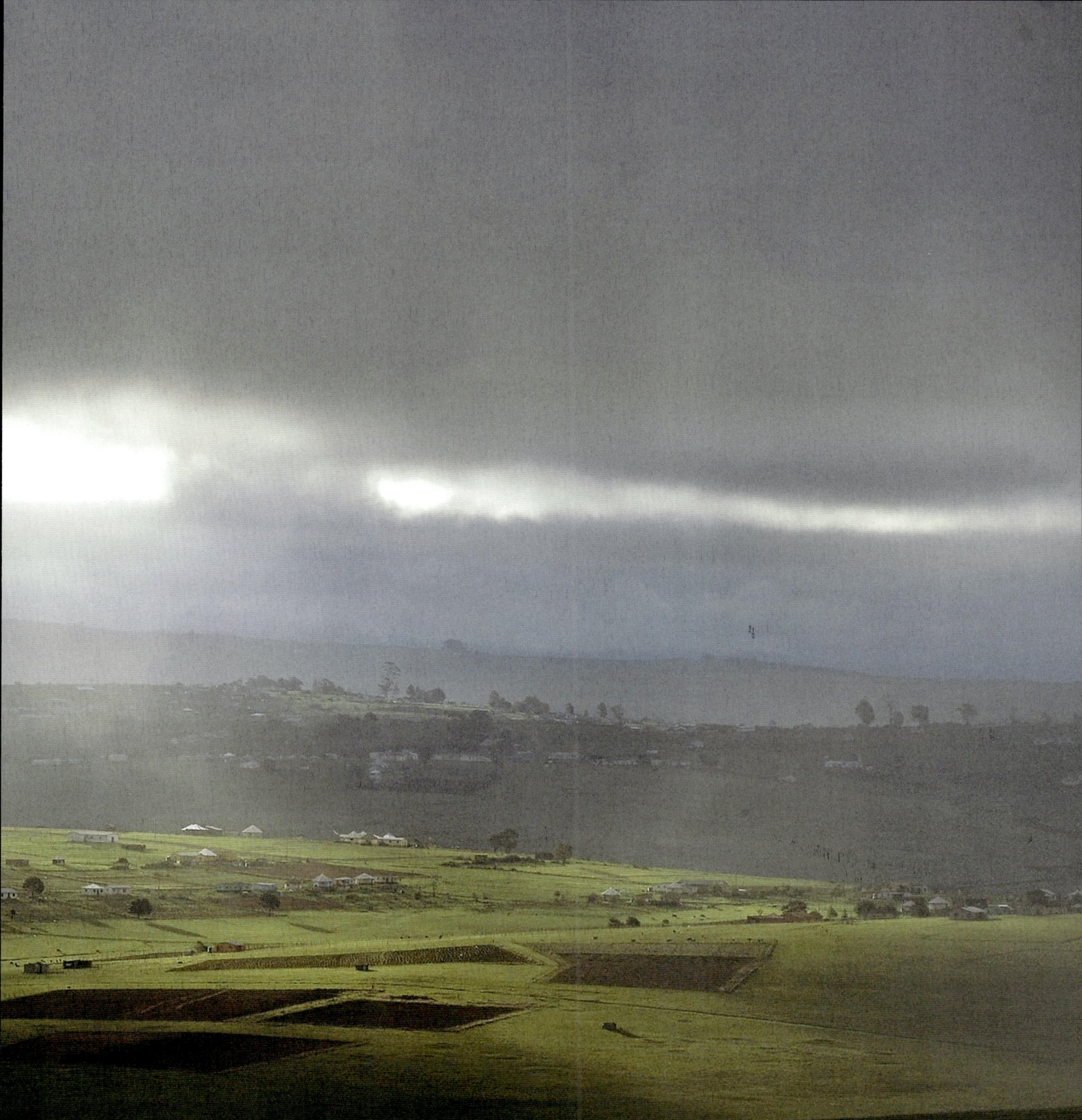

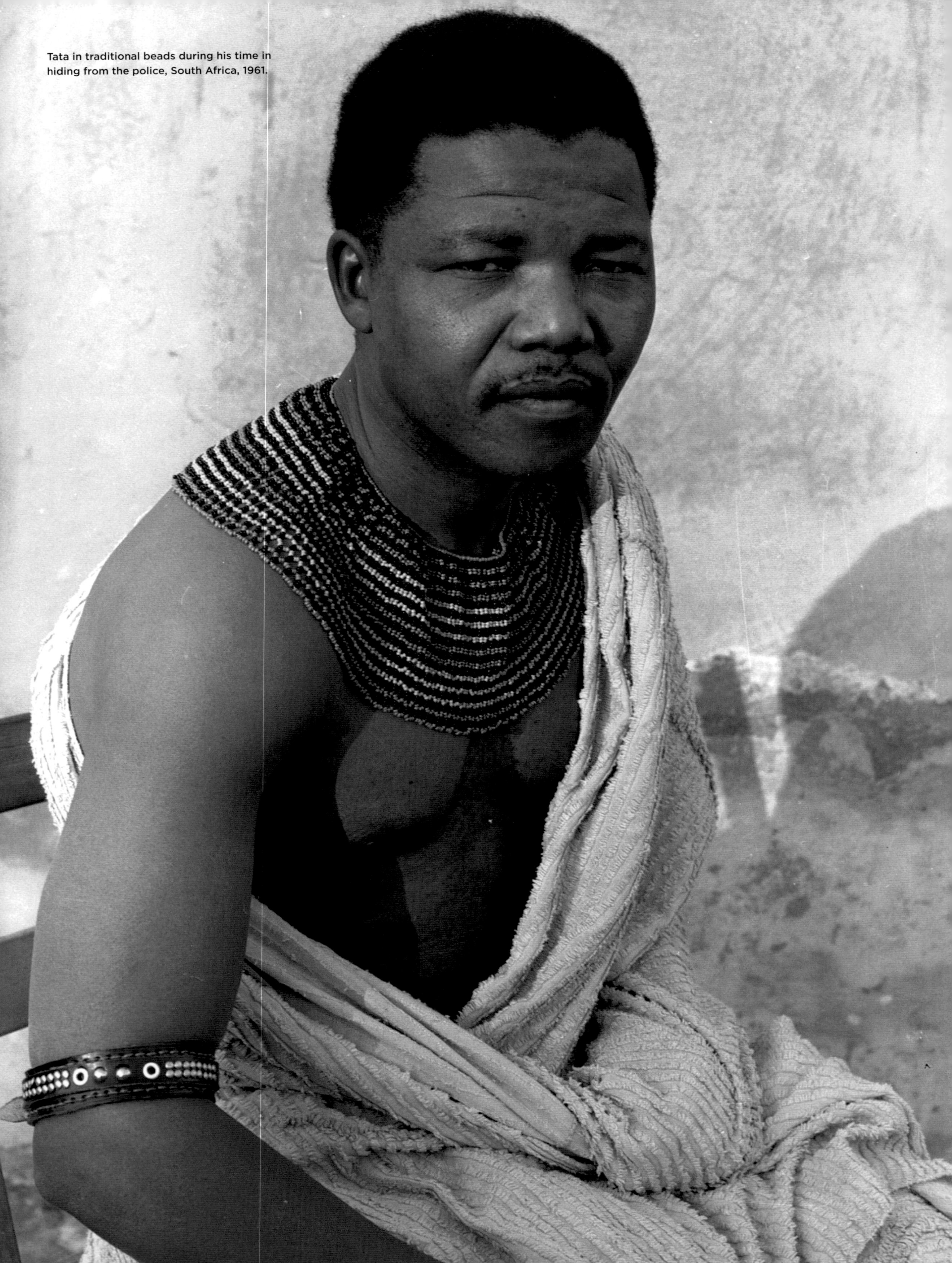

Tata in traditional beads during his time in hiding from the police, South Africa, 1961.

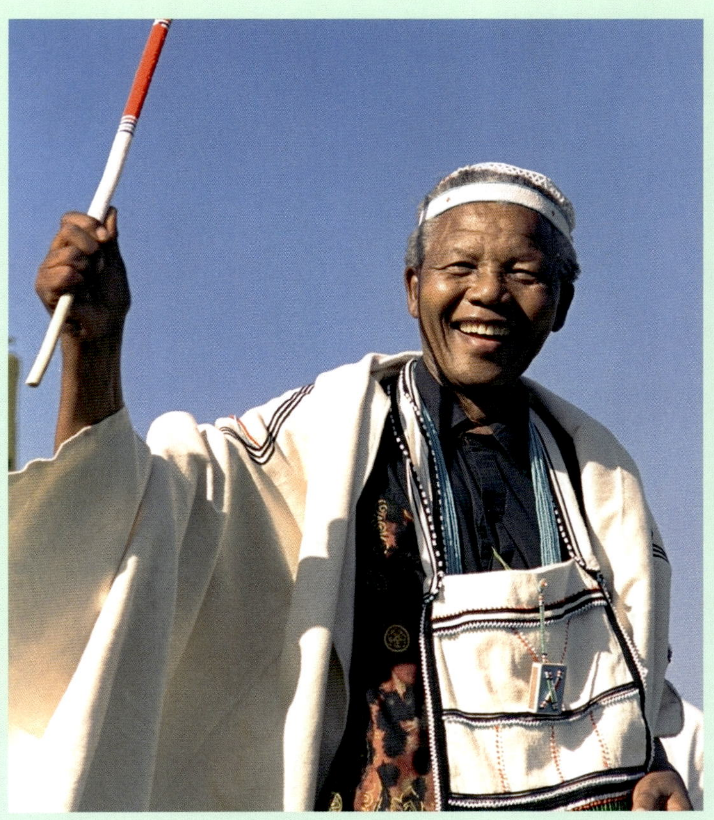

Campaigning in the Eastern Cape in 1994.

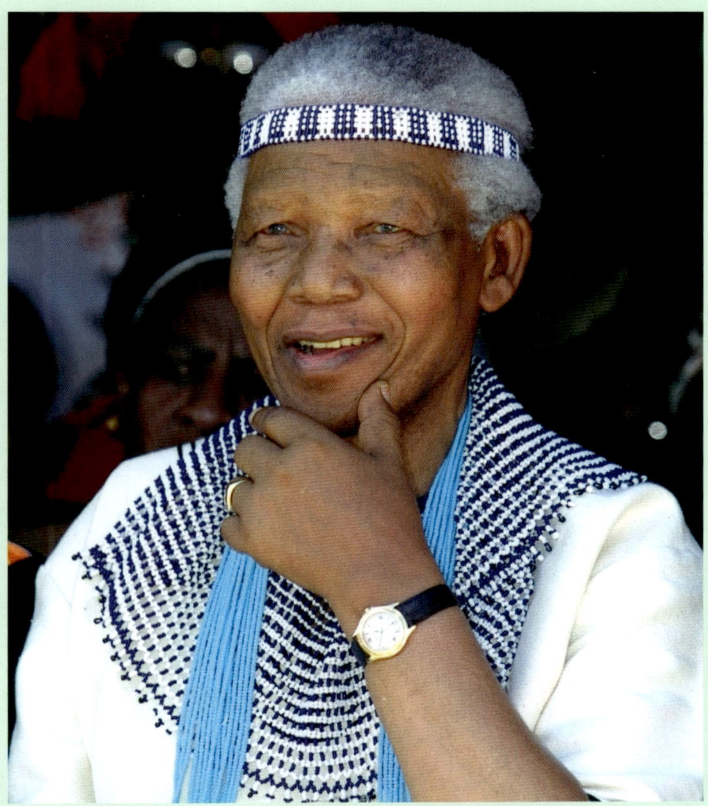

In traditional Xhosa dress as a member of the Thembu royal family at the wedding of his great grandnephew Prince Mfundo-Mhrara in Mthatha, December 2002.

Tata was proud of his Xhosa roots and enjoyed wearing traditional attire.

When Tata became president, he chose to not wear suits and instead wore what would later be known as "Madiba shirts," a type of shirt said to date back to Egypt's first dynasty. He felt that a suit was too confining, and that these colorful, loose-fitting shirts were closer to traditional attire and would bring him closer to his people. Tata was given a batik shirt by Indonesia's president Suharto and others were made by a local shirtmaker, but most of Tata's shirts came from Stefano Ricci, the renowned Italian designer. Tata was drawn to long-sleeved shirts with a pocket, and especially loved bold and colorful prints.

The Thembu tribe, like all Xhosa-speaking people, are very proud and their cultural heritage, and clothing, food, and dance are close to their hearts. Traditional Xhosa dress is made of woven cotton, dyed beautiful ochres, turquoises, and other colors, and is distinguished by unique styles and patterns. Traditionally, the women's clothing and ornaments show the stages of their lives. The women usually wear a traditional skirt, an umbhaco, which is decorated with bias binding, buttons, and beads; a beaded top called a vulwakabini; and a colorful braided turban. The Thembu are known for their beautiful beadwork and it forms an important part of their traditional dress. They usually wear long necklaces of multicolored beads as well as beaded bracelets on the arms and ankles. Thembu women would often be seen smoking long decorative pipes made of wood, frequently decorated with colorful beads. Xhosa men would often wear animal skins around their loins or a wraparound ankle-length skirt made of woven cotton. They would throw an animal skin blanket over their shoulders, and would also wear a decorative head scarf, a long necklace, and beaded arm bands.

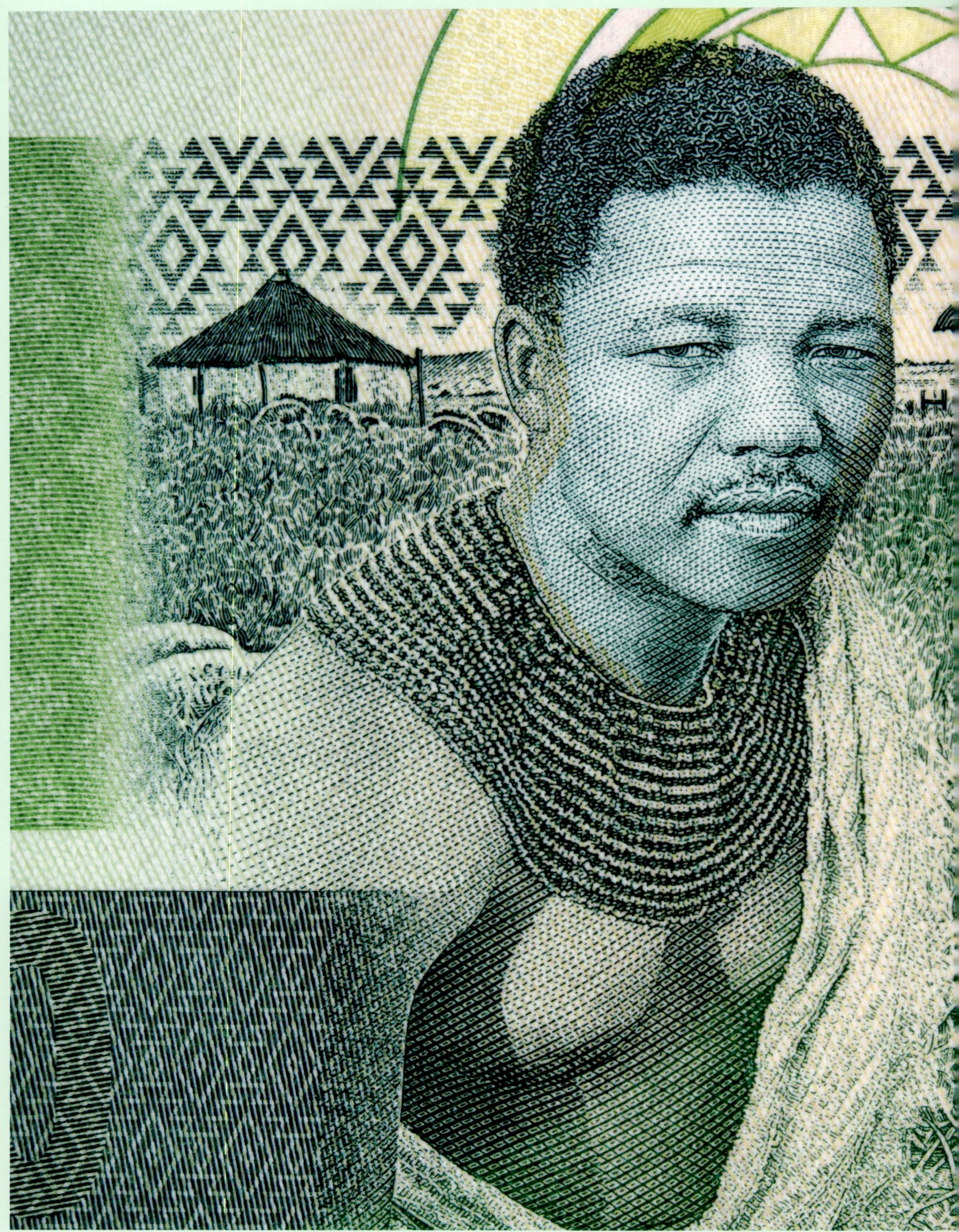

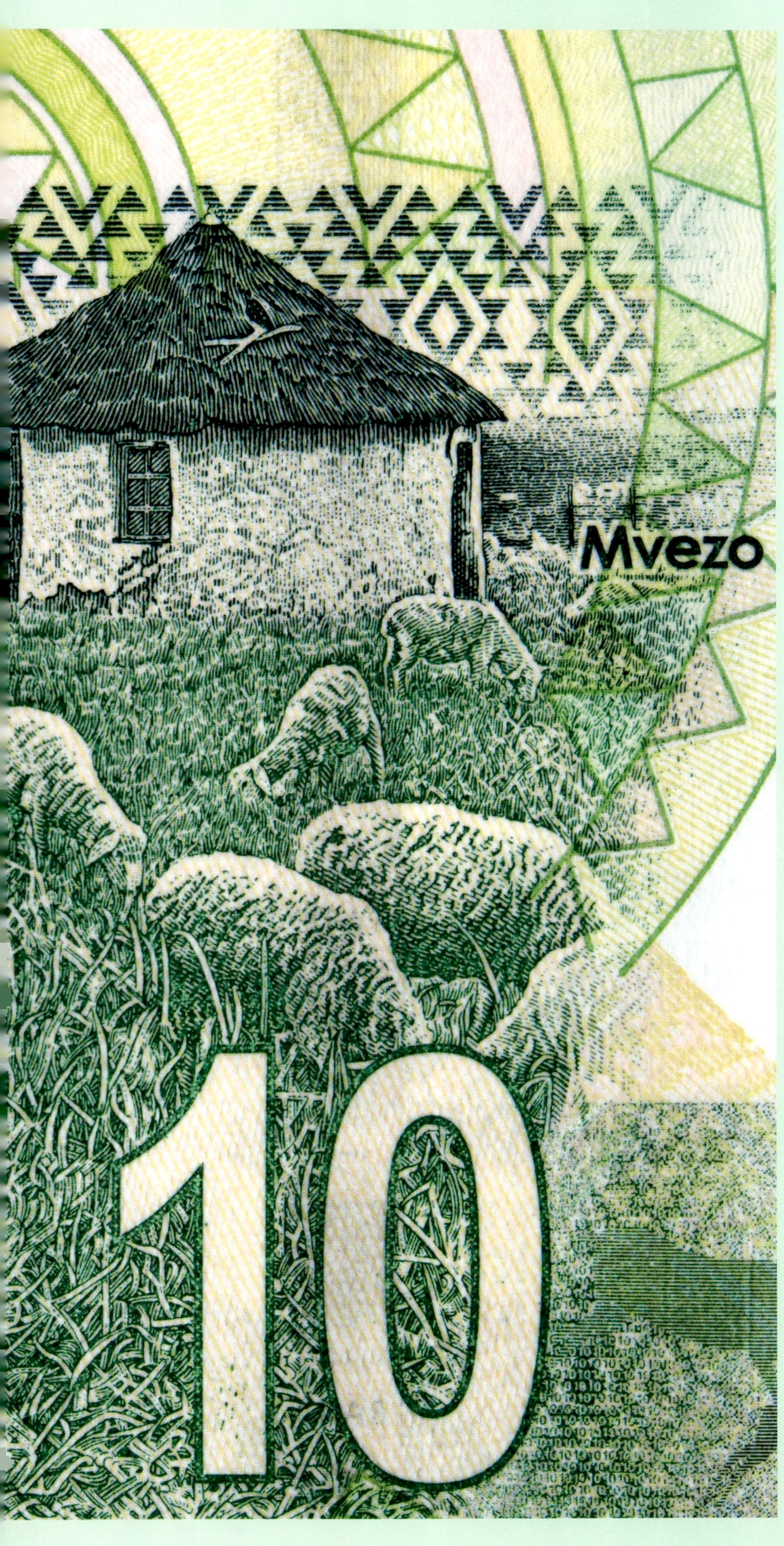

South African banknote featuring
Tata in traditional Xhosa dress.

2

1941–1949

Escaping to the City of Gold: Johannesburg

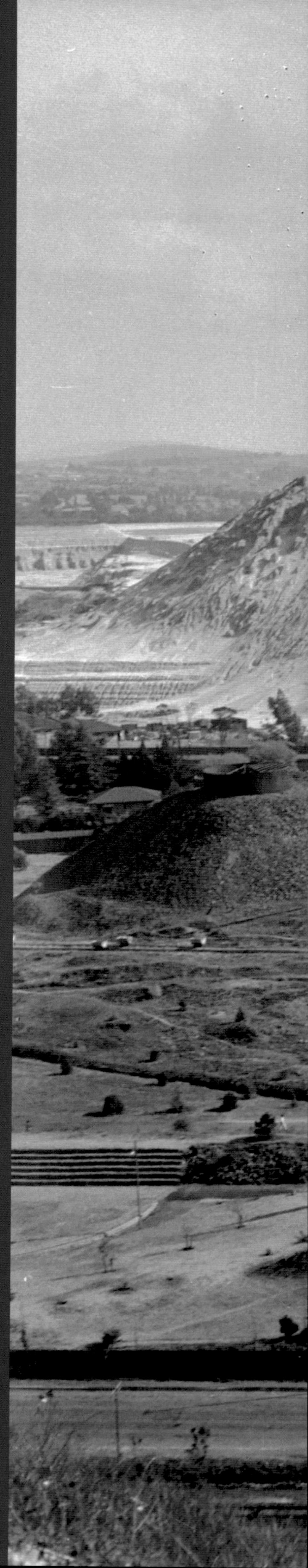

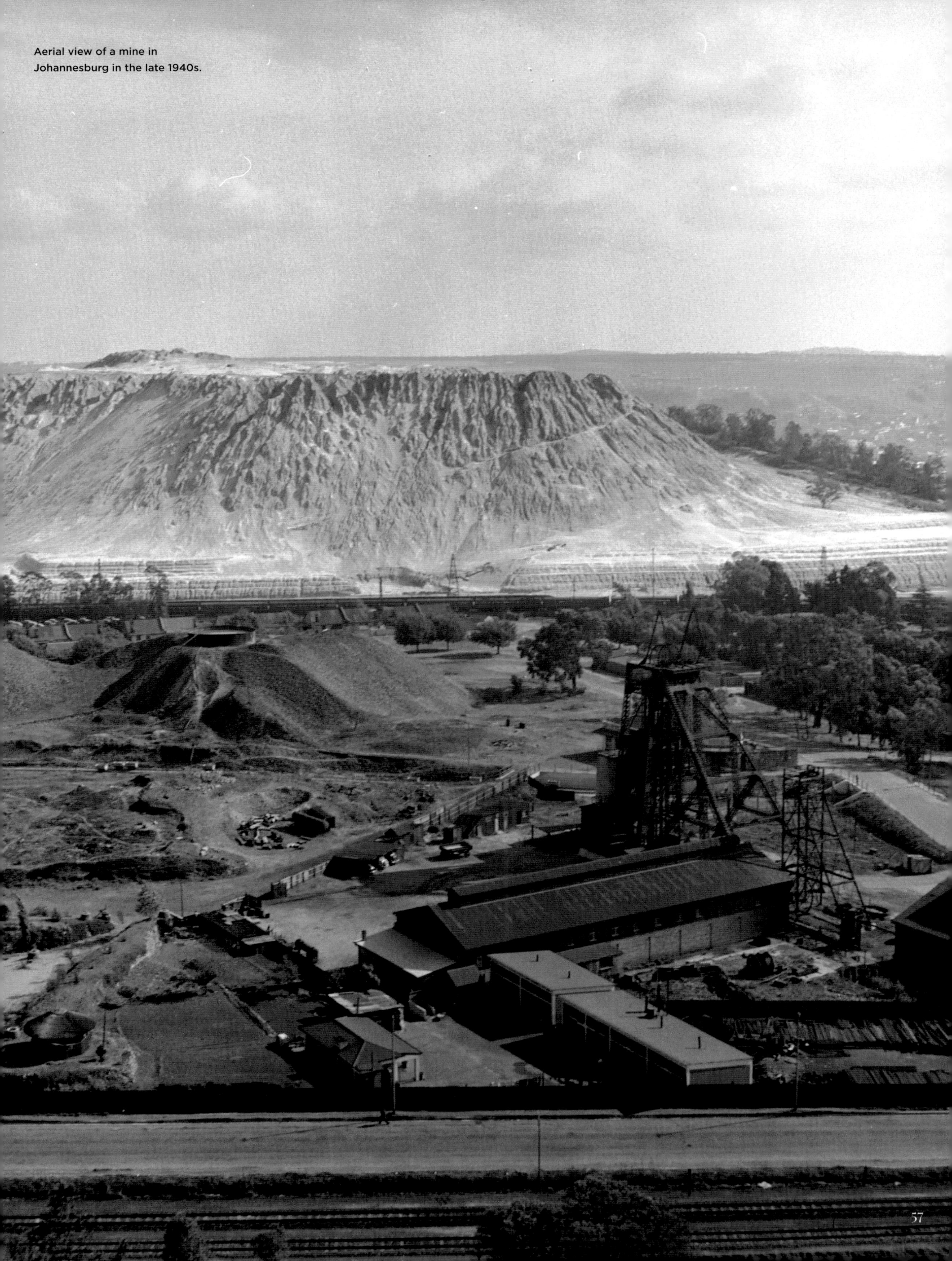

Aerial view of a mine in Johannesburg in the late 1940s.

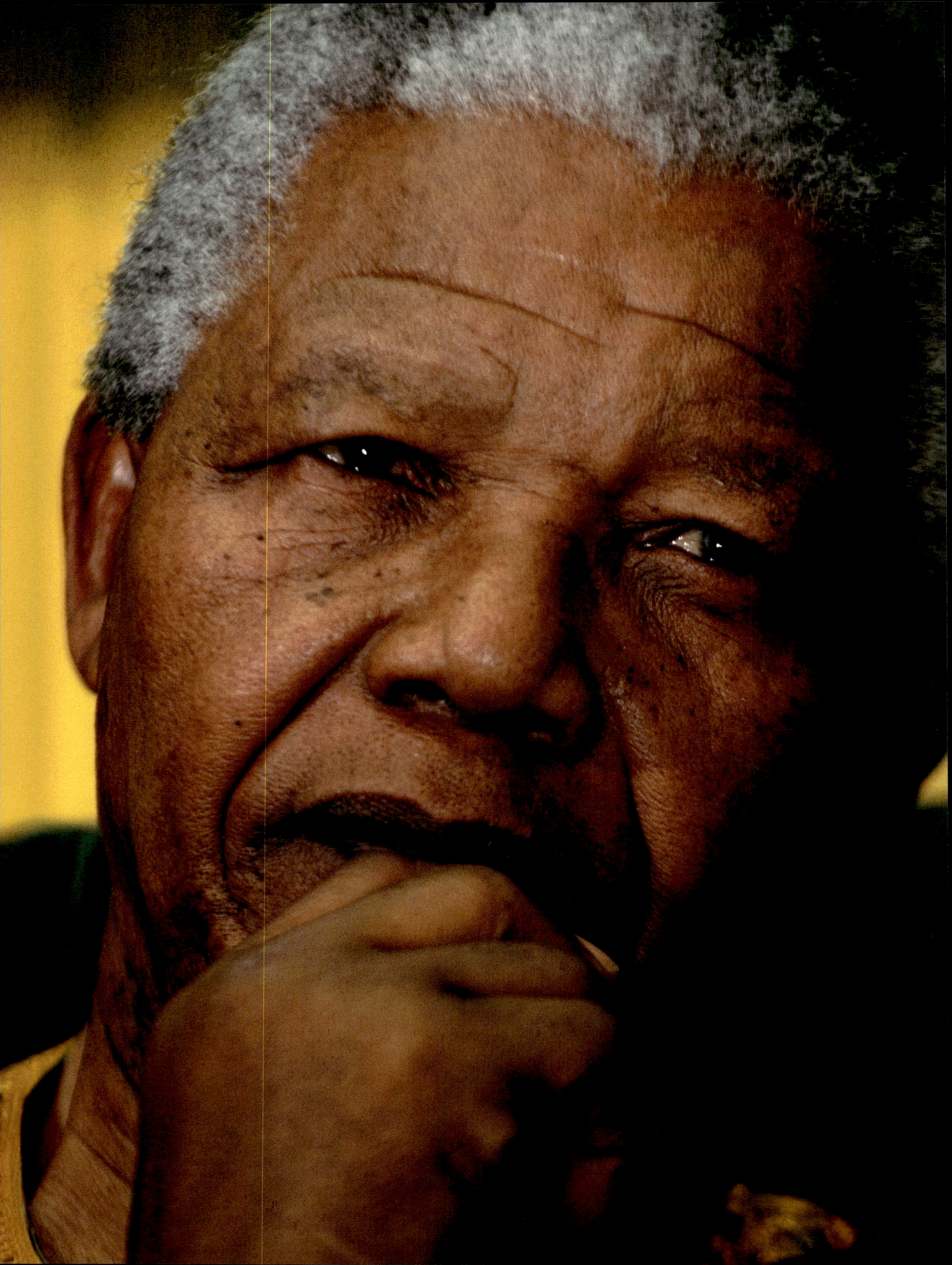

“What counts in life
is not the mere fact
that we have lived:
it is what difference
we have made to the lives
of others that will determine
the significance of the
life we lead.”

Tata being interviewed for a documentary on his life in 1994

After Tata left Fort Hare, he was in a state of limbo. By the time he went back home, Justice was also returning from college. After a few days, the regent called them and announced that before he could journey to the land of the ancestors, it was his duty to see that his two sons were properly married. Tata and Justice decided that night that they would escape and go to Johannesburg.

They stole two cows, which they sold to a local trader who assumed that they were selling the cows at the behest of the regent. With that money, they were able to travel from Umtata to Johannesburg. On the way they stopped in Queenstown, where they encountered challenges. In the early 1940s, the movement of Africans from one magisterial district to another was governed by a number of restrictions and laws. One had to be over sixteen and be in possession of a dompas, a passbook that one was required to present on demand to any white policeman or civil servant. Failure to do so could mean arrest, a jail sentence, or a fine. The pass stated where the bearer lived, who his chief was, and whether he had paid the annual poll tax, a tax levied only on Africans. (Later, the passbook was changed to a reference booklet, containing detailed information that had to be signed by one's employer every month.) With the help of a friend, Tata and Justice were able to get the necessary documents and catch a ride to Johannesburg from a white woman.

Once there, they discovered a town unlike anything they had encountered before. Gold and diamond mines were at the center of Johannesburg's economy in the 1940s, and were strictly segregated, with enclosed compounds and hostels for Black workers, who made up the majority of the mining labor force.

The so-called Mineral Revolution of the later nineteenth century had profoundly changed the nature of the South African social and political landscape and marked the beginning of the country's transition from an agricultural to an industrial economy. Diamonds were discovered first in Kimberly in 1867, and gold in Witwatersrand just twenty years later. These discoveries prompted a rush in the development and production of large-scale mining machinery, as well as tremendous shifts in the nation's demographics and the onset of urbanization, as each

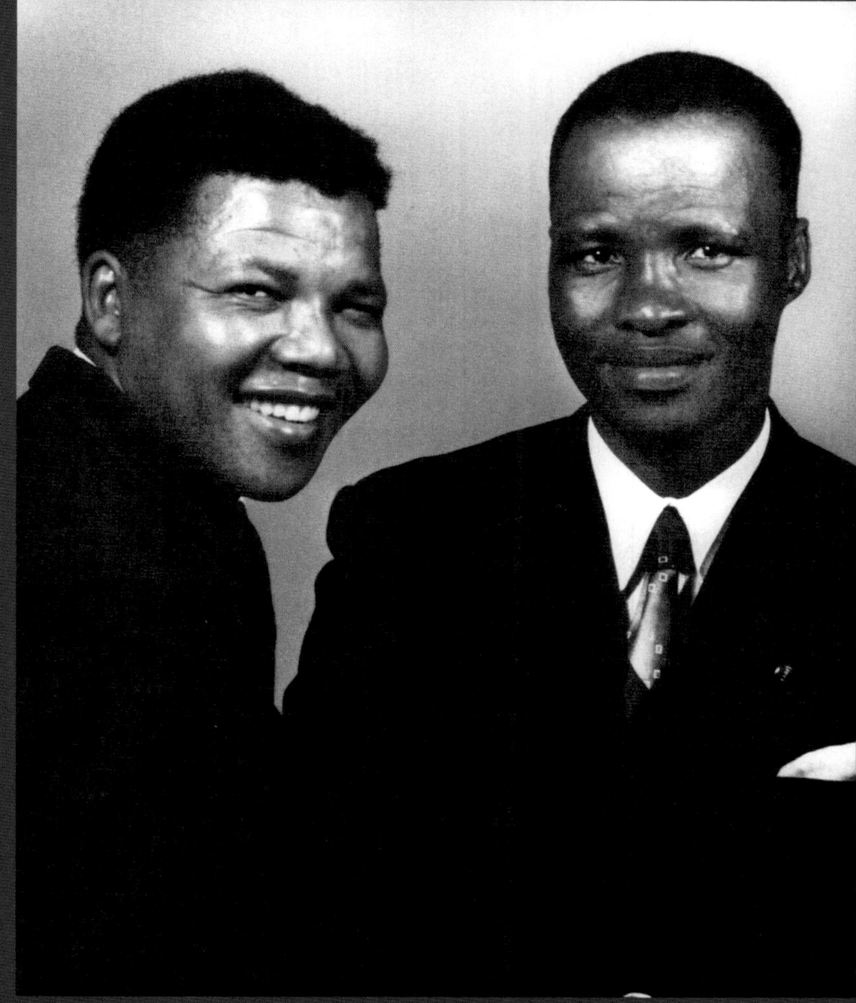

Tata and K. D. (Justice) Matanzima.

new mine drew more and more prospective workers to its region from across the continent. In turn, as the scale of the gold- and diamond-mining industries escalated, institutionalized forms of labor control over Africans were implemented throughout the country to create labor for the cities and towns where these minerals were mined. Africans were dispossessed of their land through forced resettlements and had to migrate for work. Migrants ensured that cheap labor was available from rural areas; these workers were not wage laborers who could freely sell their services to other employers. The single-sex hostels were further segregated into ethnic groups as part of the divide and rule tactic of the mine owners. Factional fighting between groups was rife but it was not discouraged—it served to prevent any unification of Blacks in protests against the mining houses, and it reinforced the power of the chiefs in the rural areas. Johannesburg was known colloquially among Blacks as "Egoli," meaning "City of Gold," but these streets were not paved with the shiny metal. There was the incessant noise of mine shaft lifts, drilling, dynamite blasting rock, and men shouting orders. Miners walked around cloaked in dust or drenched in sweat. At night white workers went to their own residences and Black workers to their hostels where they ate, slept, and socialized in a room full of narrow, concrete bunks laid out side by side. Tata and Justice found temporary accommodations in Crown Mines, one of the larger gold mines, with an induna, a Black supervisor, in the mining compound. Tata was lucky enough to be employed as a night watchman (with a new uniform that included a helmet and boots, a whistle, a flashlight, and a knobkerrie or club). Within three months he would become a clerk at the mine. "There is nothing magical about a gold mine," Tata would later recall in *Long Walk to Freedom*. "Barren and pockmarked, all dirt and no trees, fenced in on all sides, a gold mine resembles a war-torn battlefield."

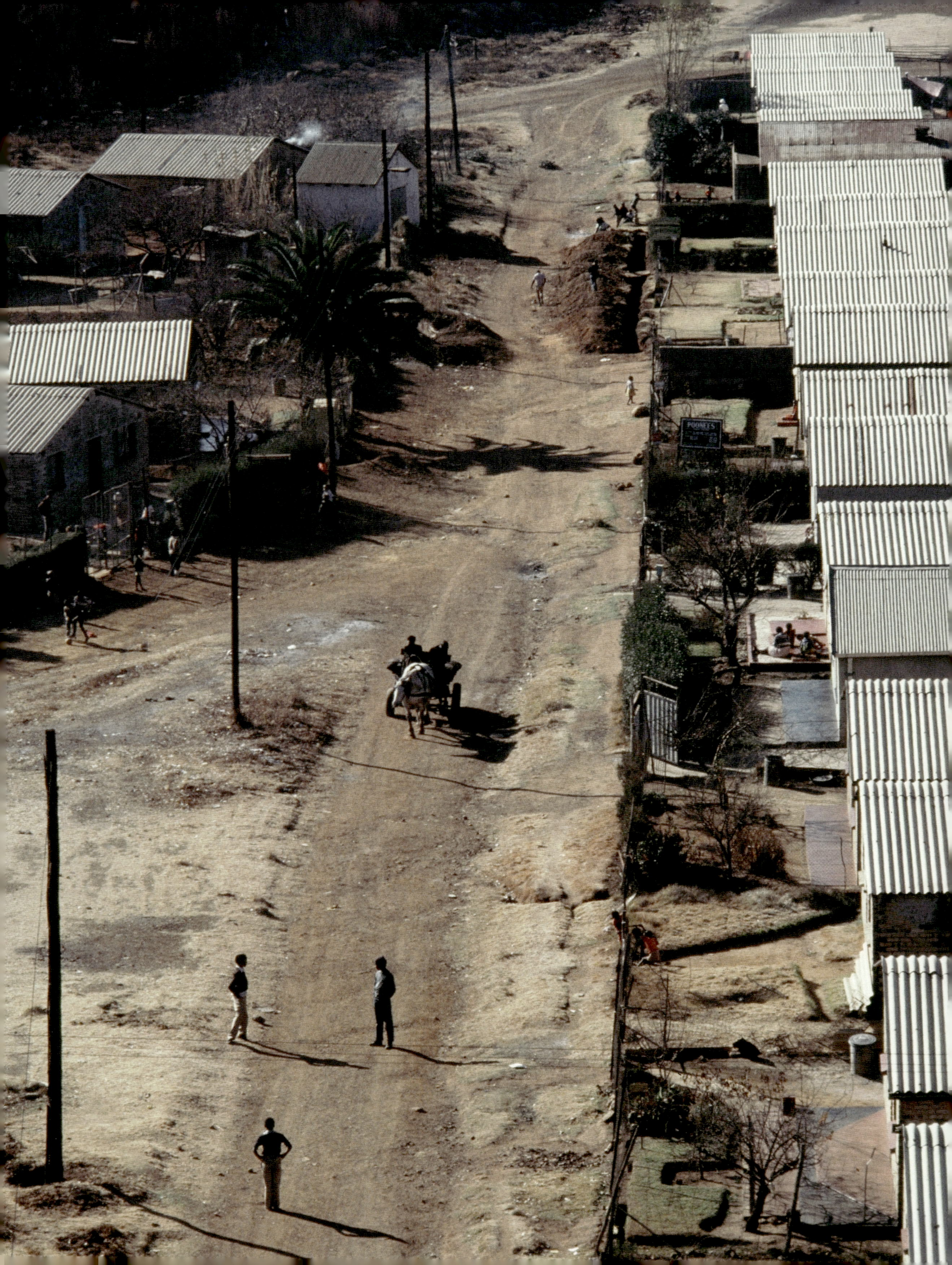

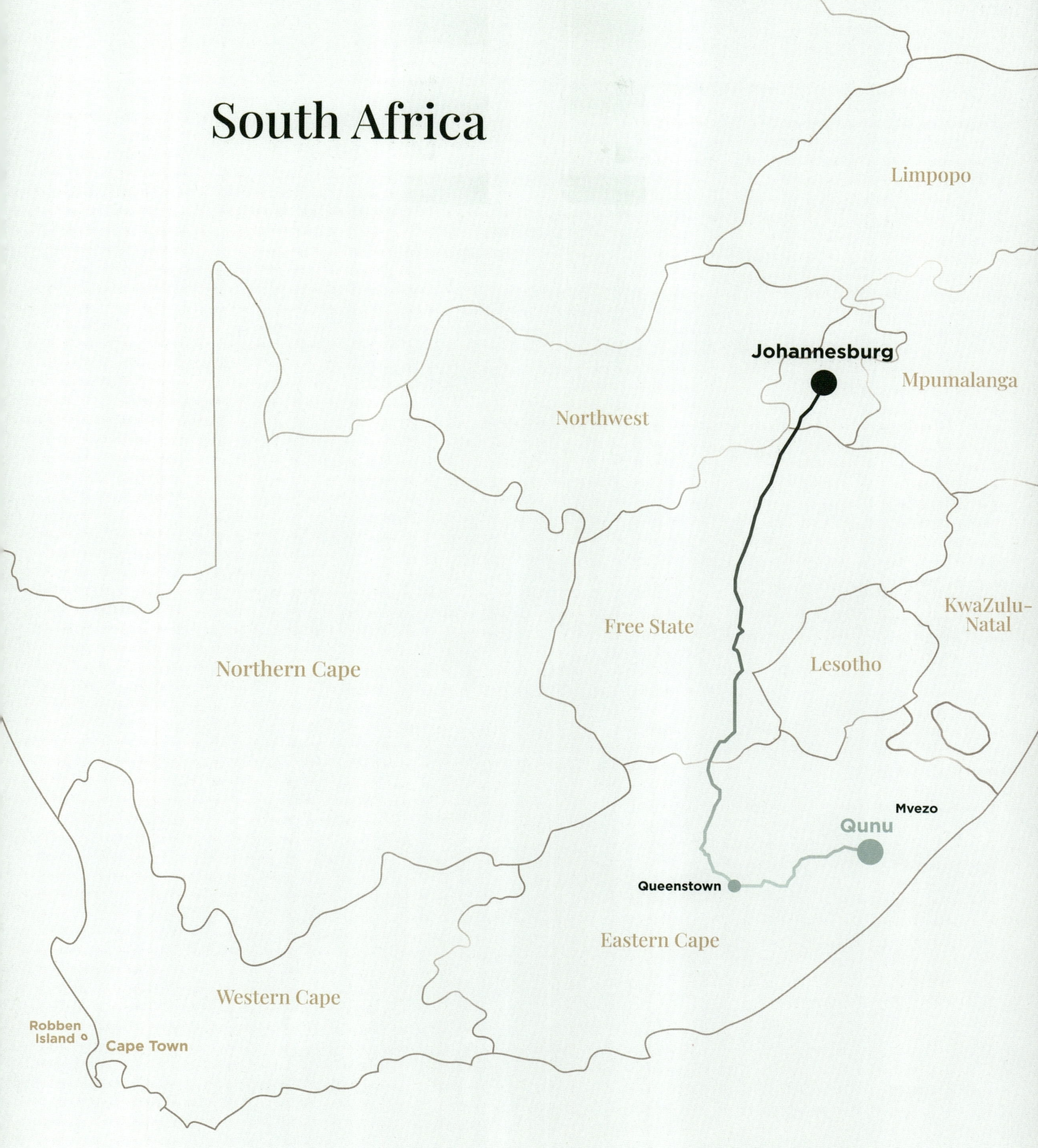

Opposite: Township road leading to Johannesburg.

Tata and Justice escaped Qunu and made their way to Johannesburg through an area of South Africa they had never traveled. They faced many challenges on this journey, from finding transportation to acquiring the necessary documents to leave their homeland.

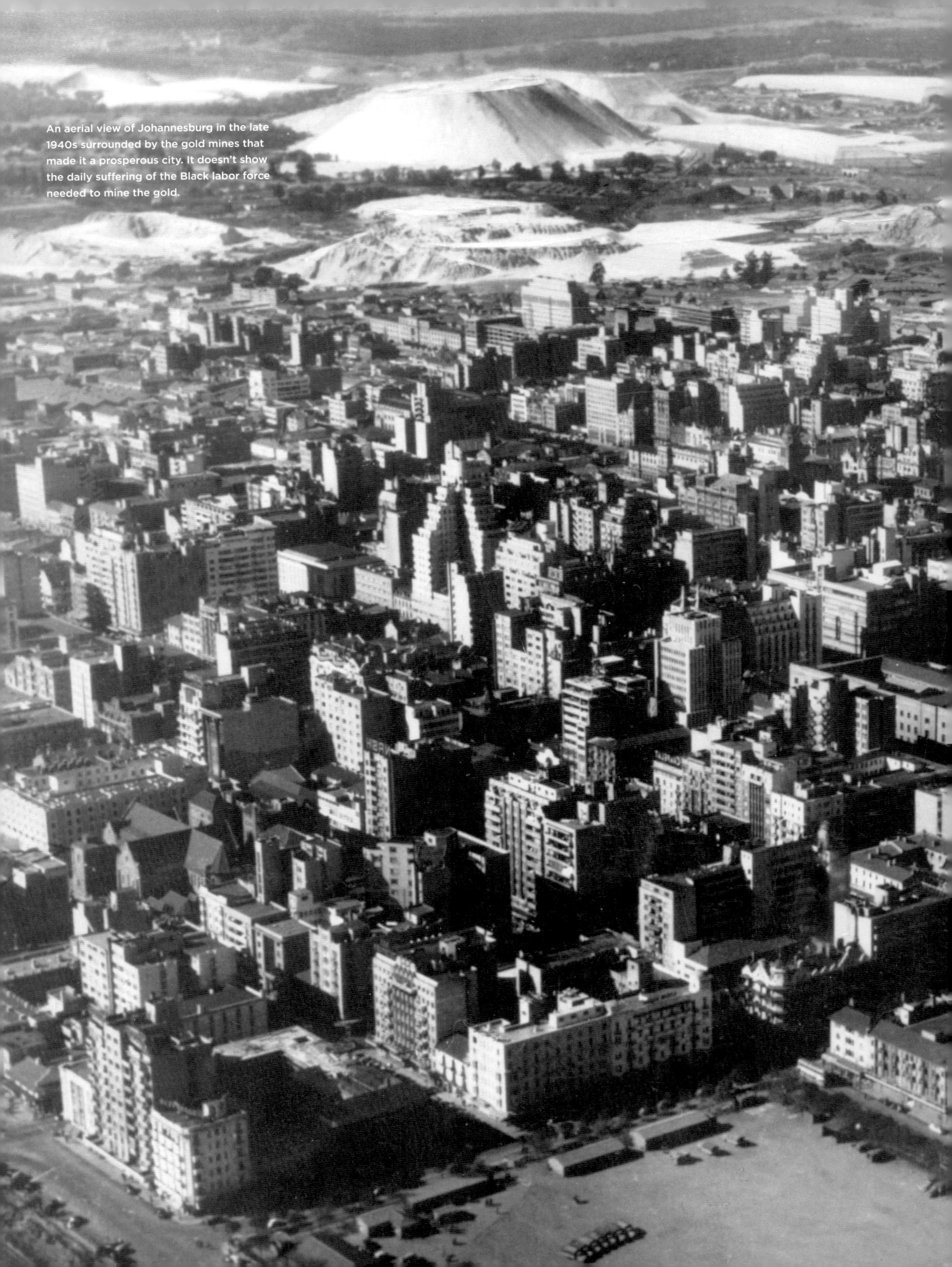

An aerial view of Johannesburg in the late 1940s surrounded by the gold mines that made it a prosperous city. It doesn't show the daily suffering of the Black labor force needed to mine the gold.

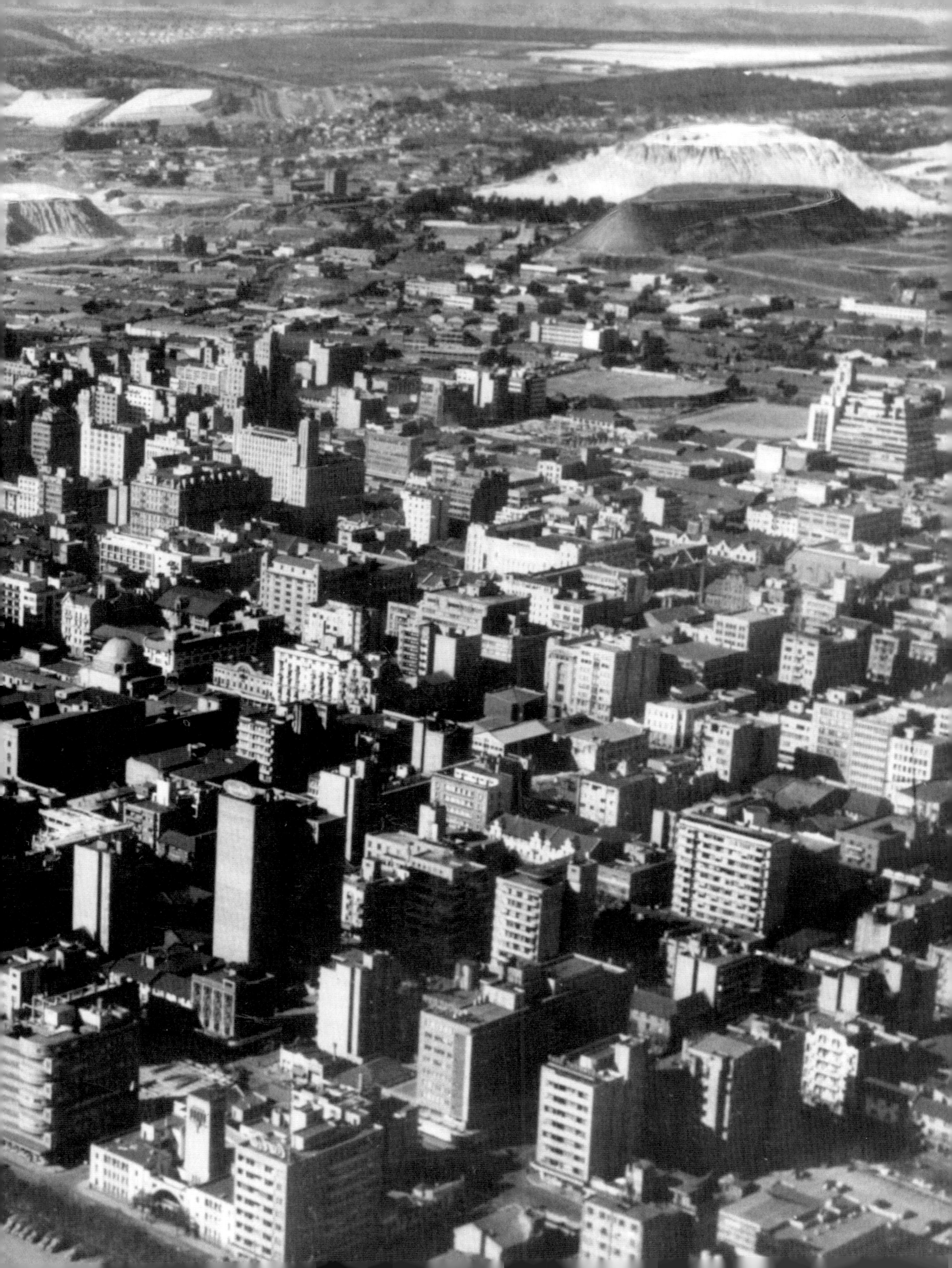

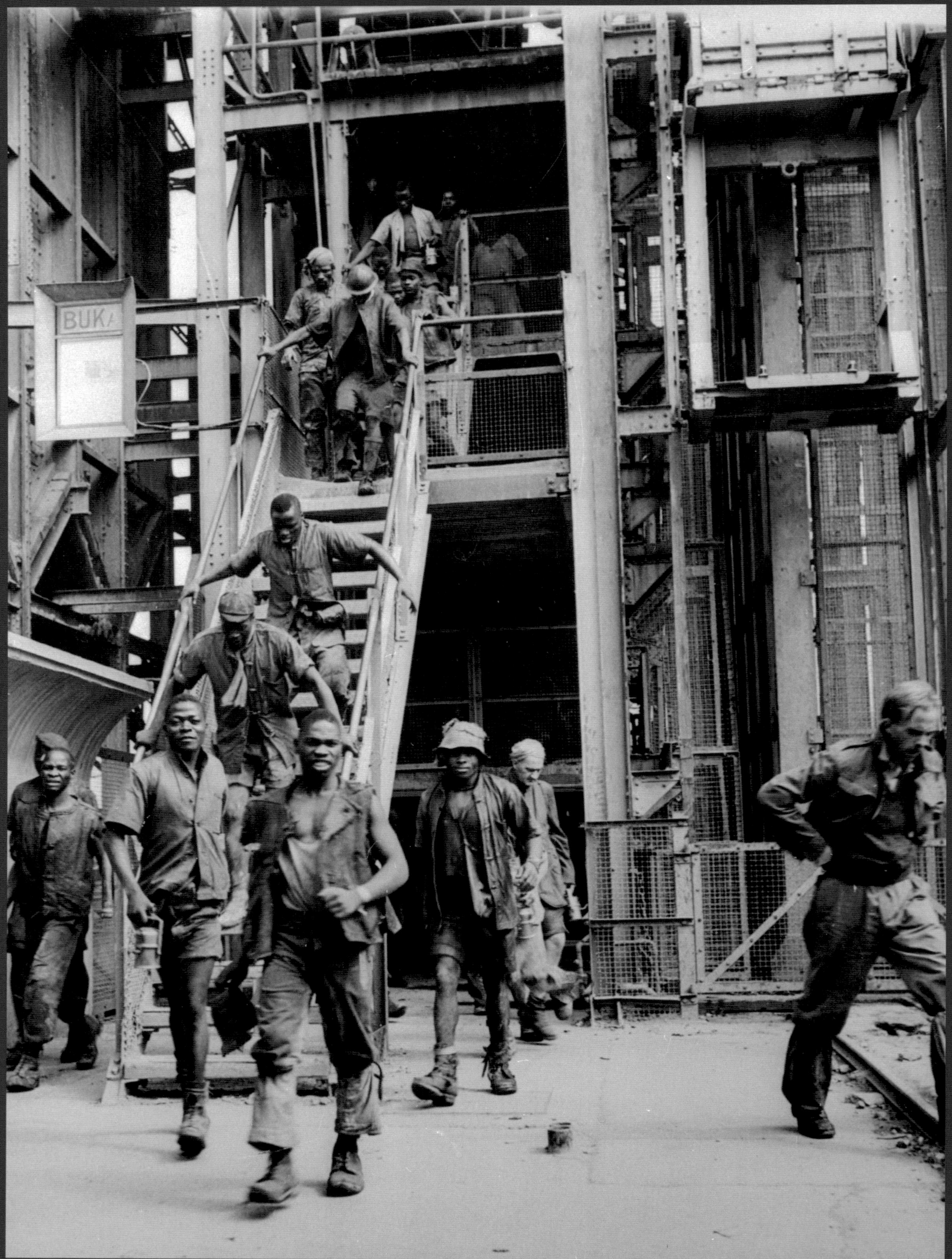
BUK

The mines were difficult and dangerous places to work. Life was hard and harsh in the mining compounds.

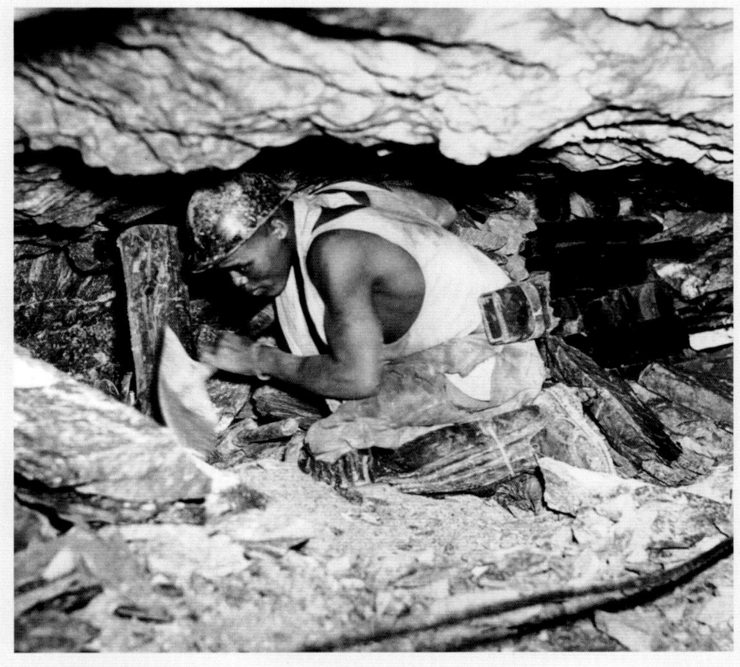

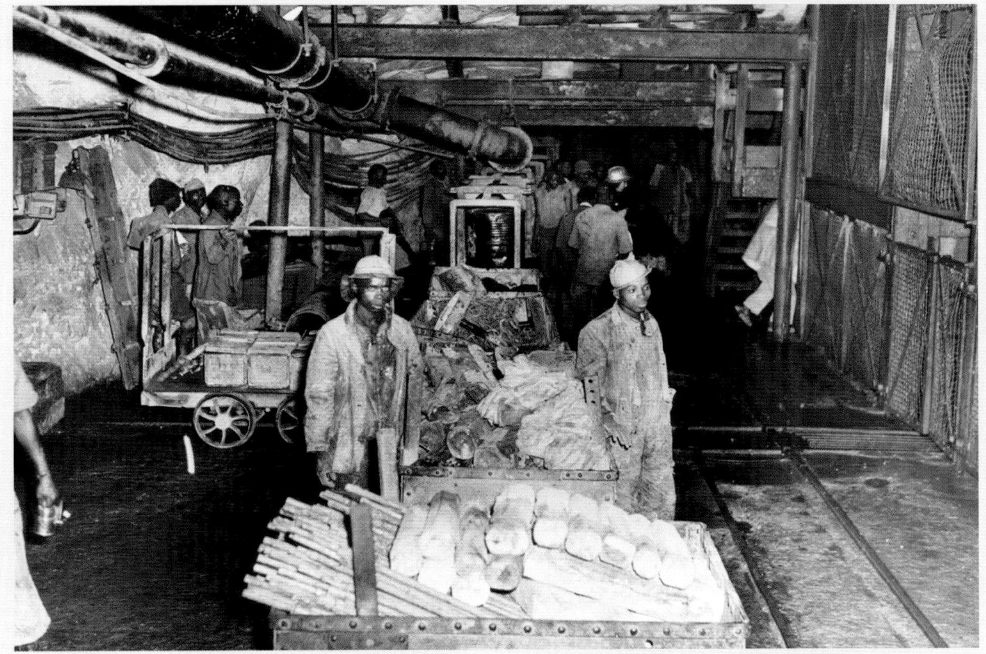

It was here that Tata was first exposed to the exploitation of Black workers and the cruelty inflicted on them. Previously, he had just heard stories that were told within the Great Place palace.

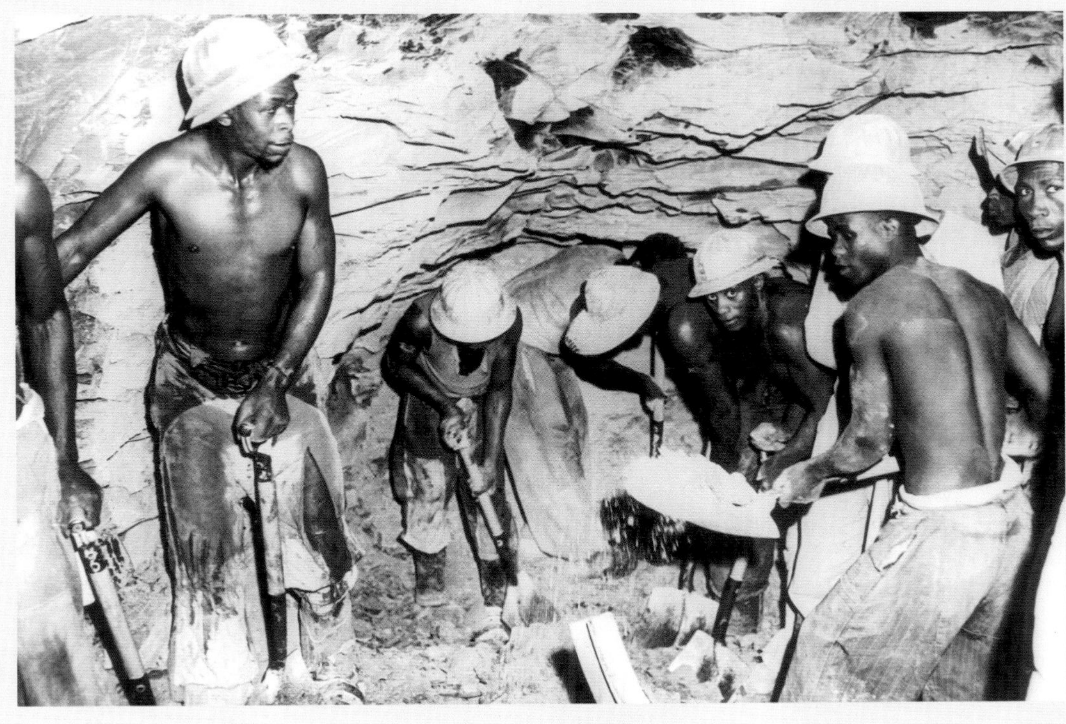

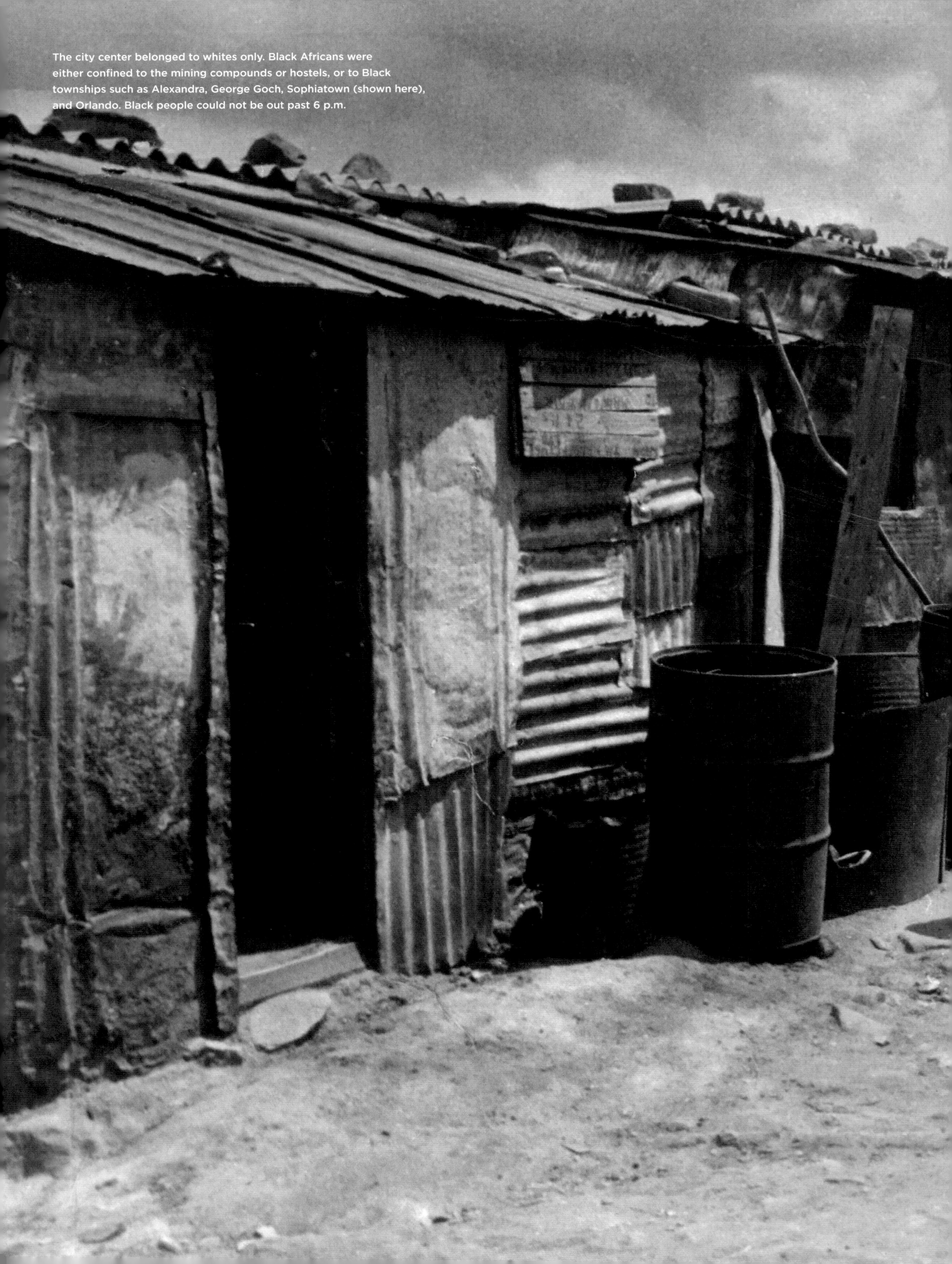

The city center belonged to whites only. Black Africans were either confined to the mining compounds or hostels, or to Black townships such as Alexandra, George Goch, Sophiatown (shown here), and Orlando. Black people could not be out past 6 p.m.

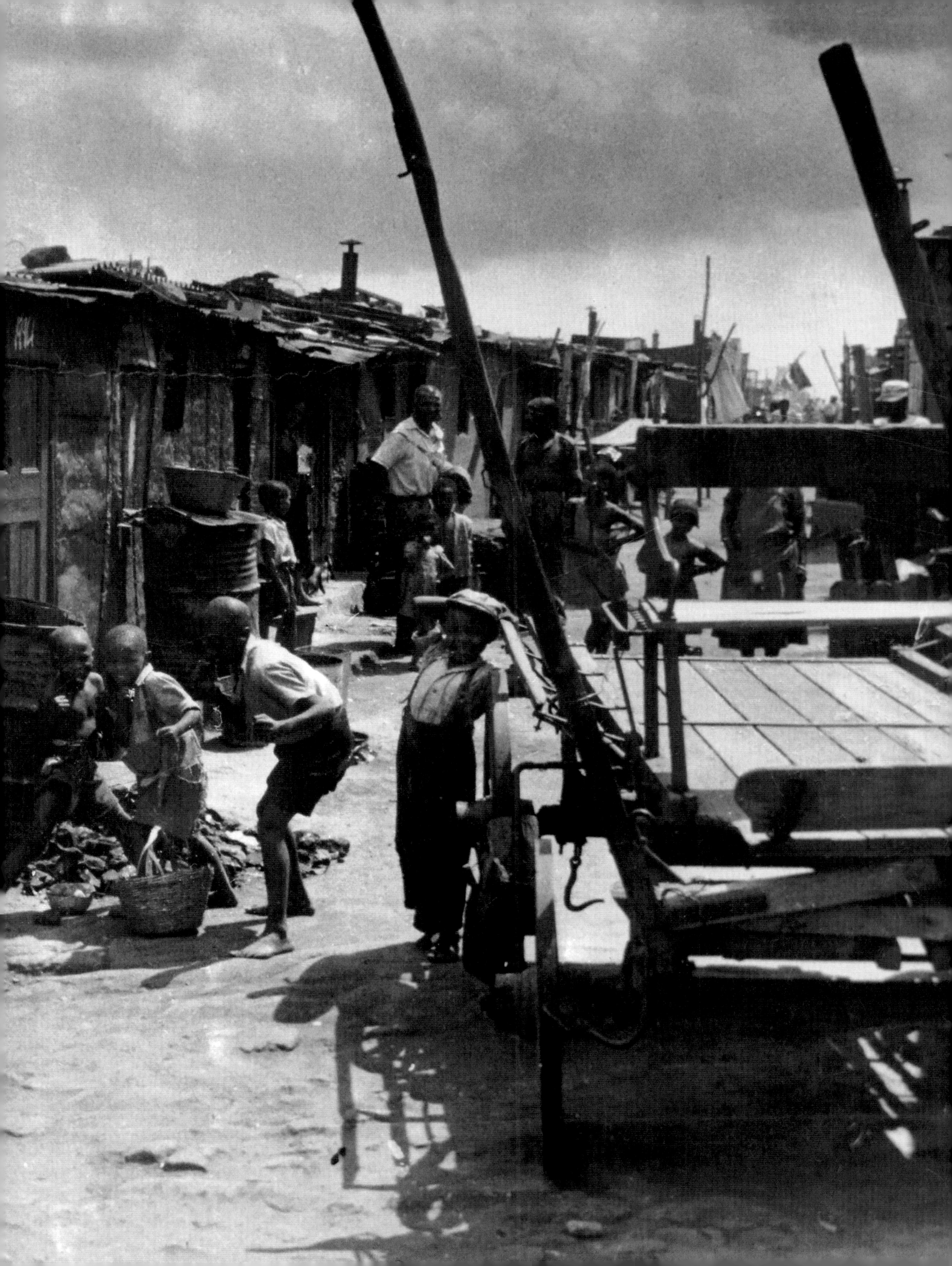

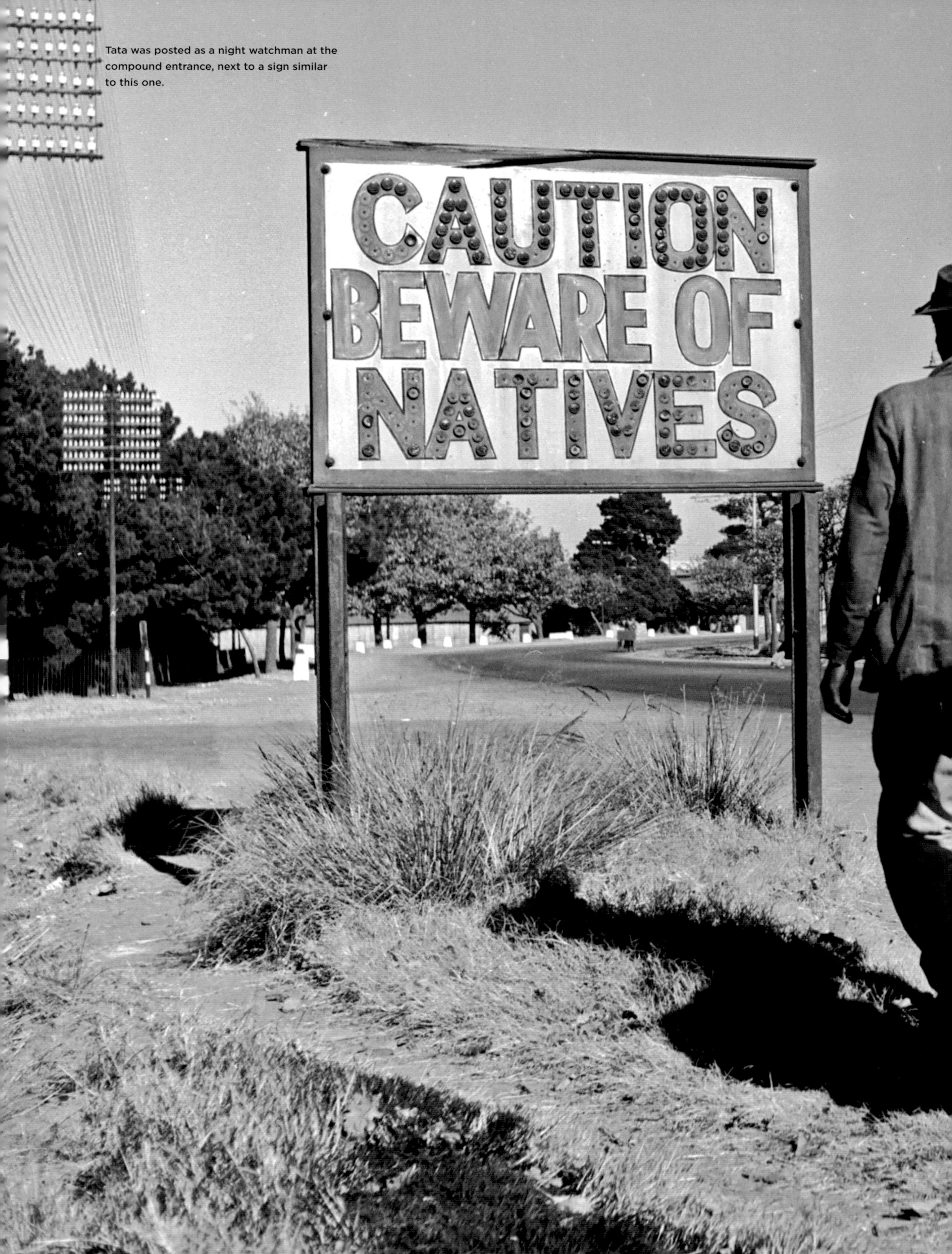

Tata was posted as a night watchman at the compound entrance, next to a sign similar to this one.

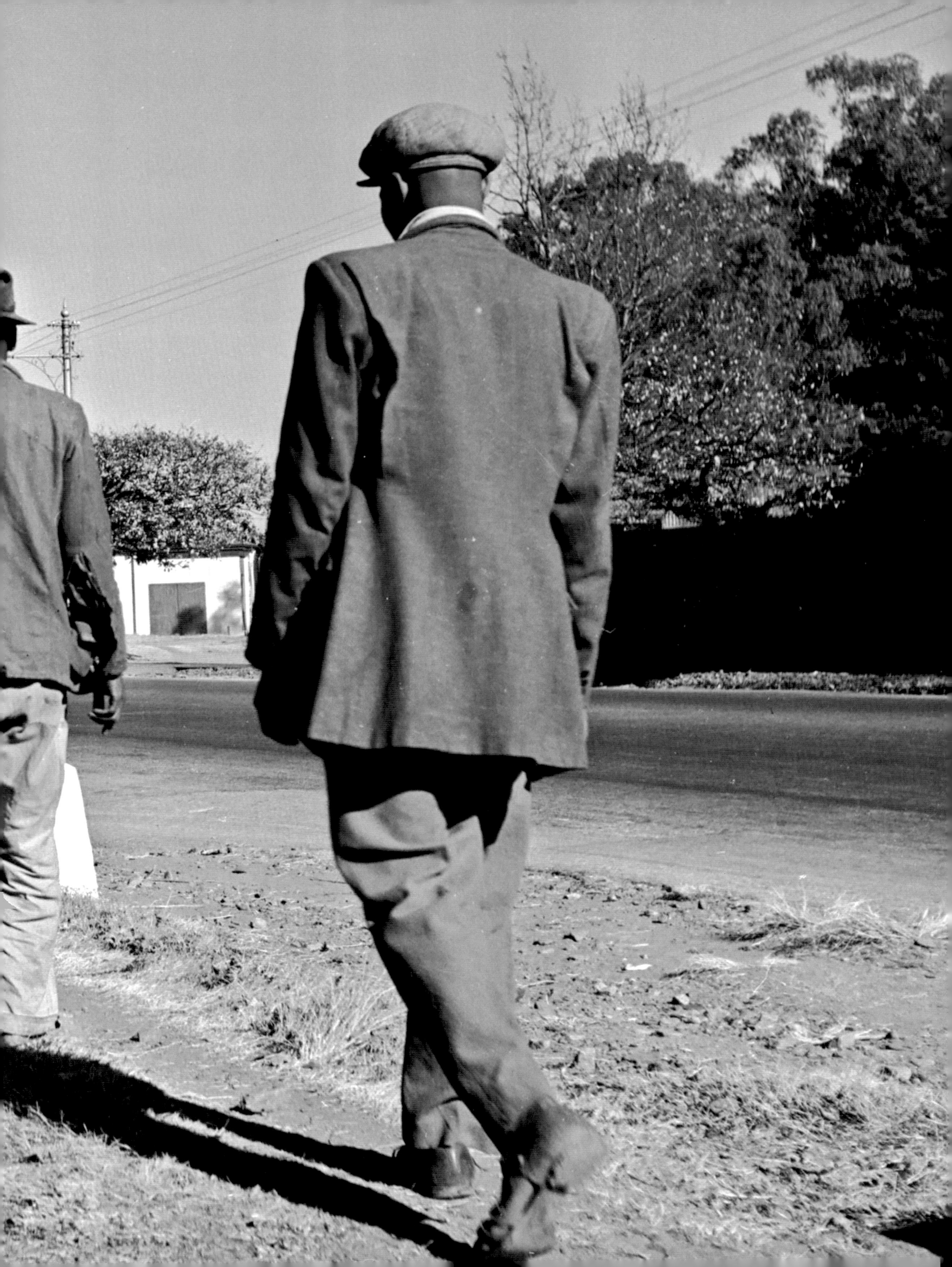

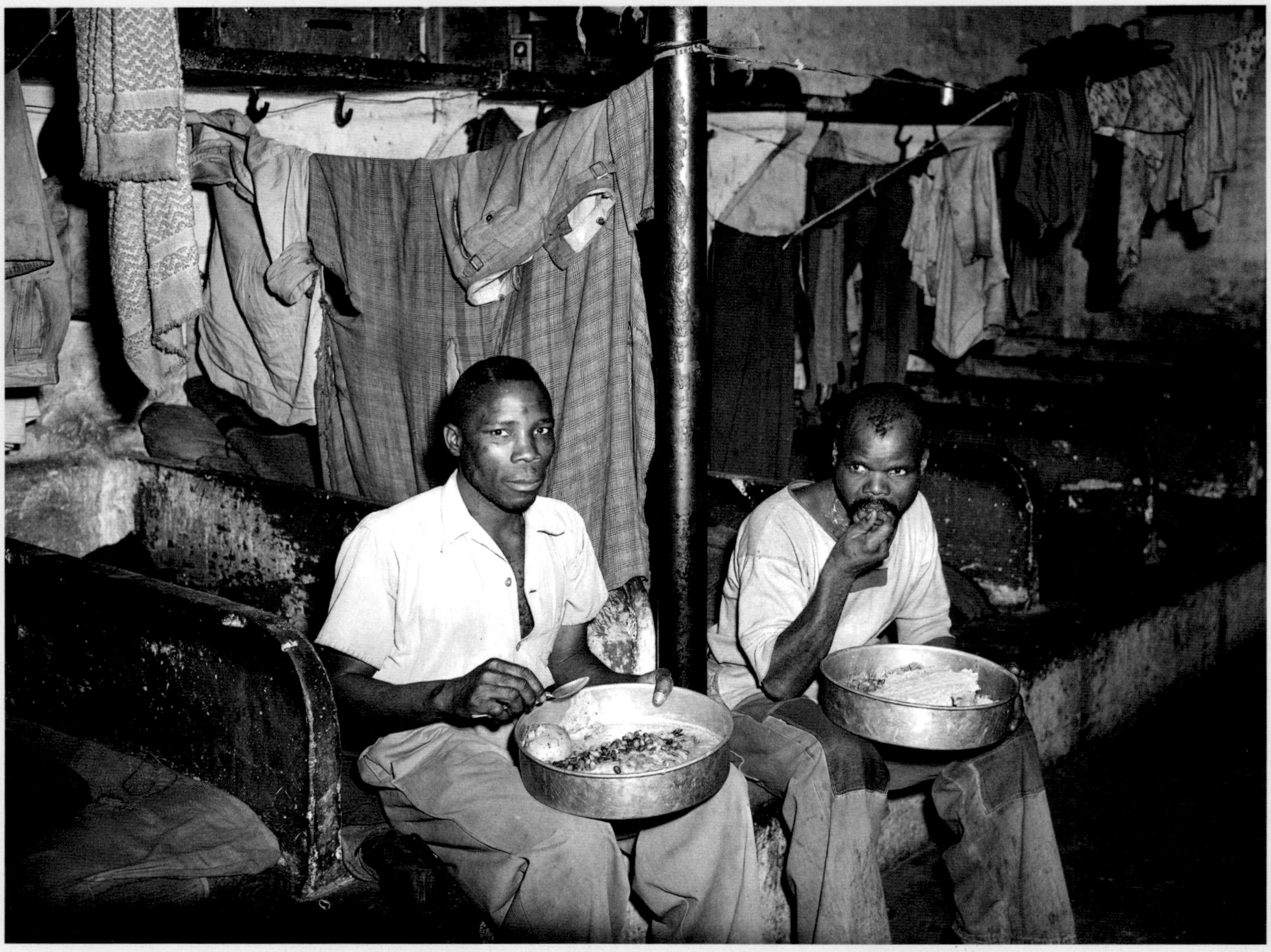

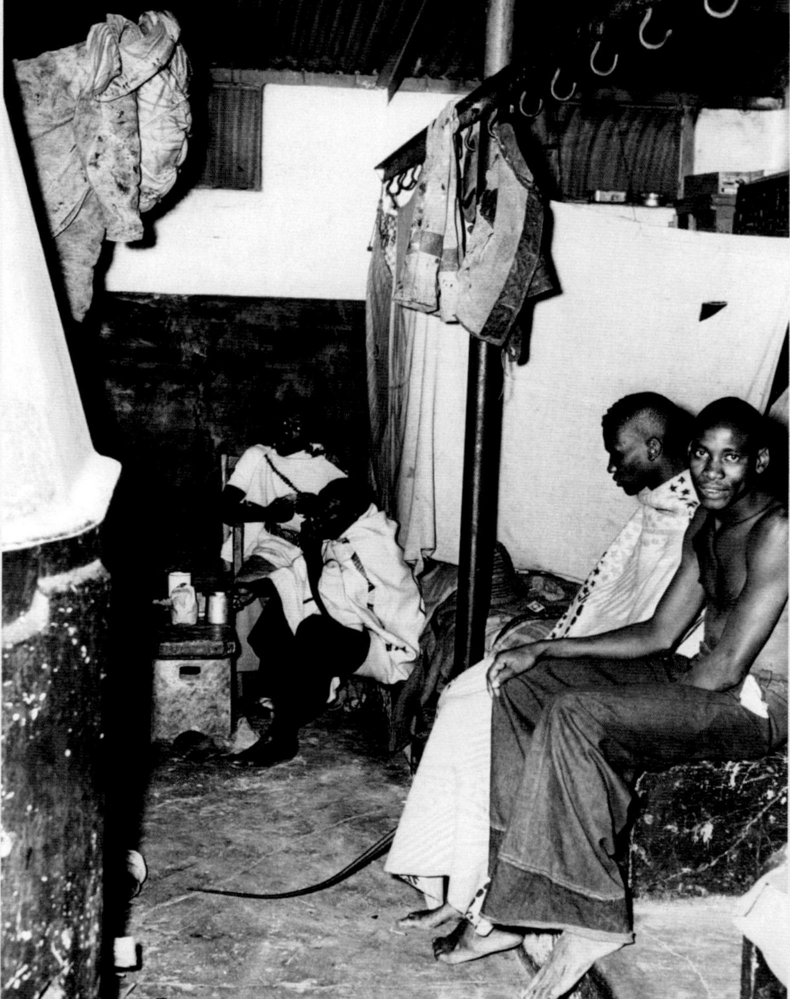

Black miners in the mining compound. They slept and ate in very crowded conditions.

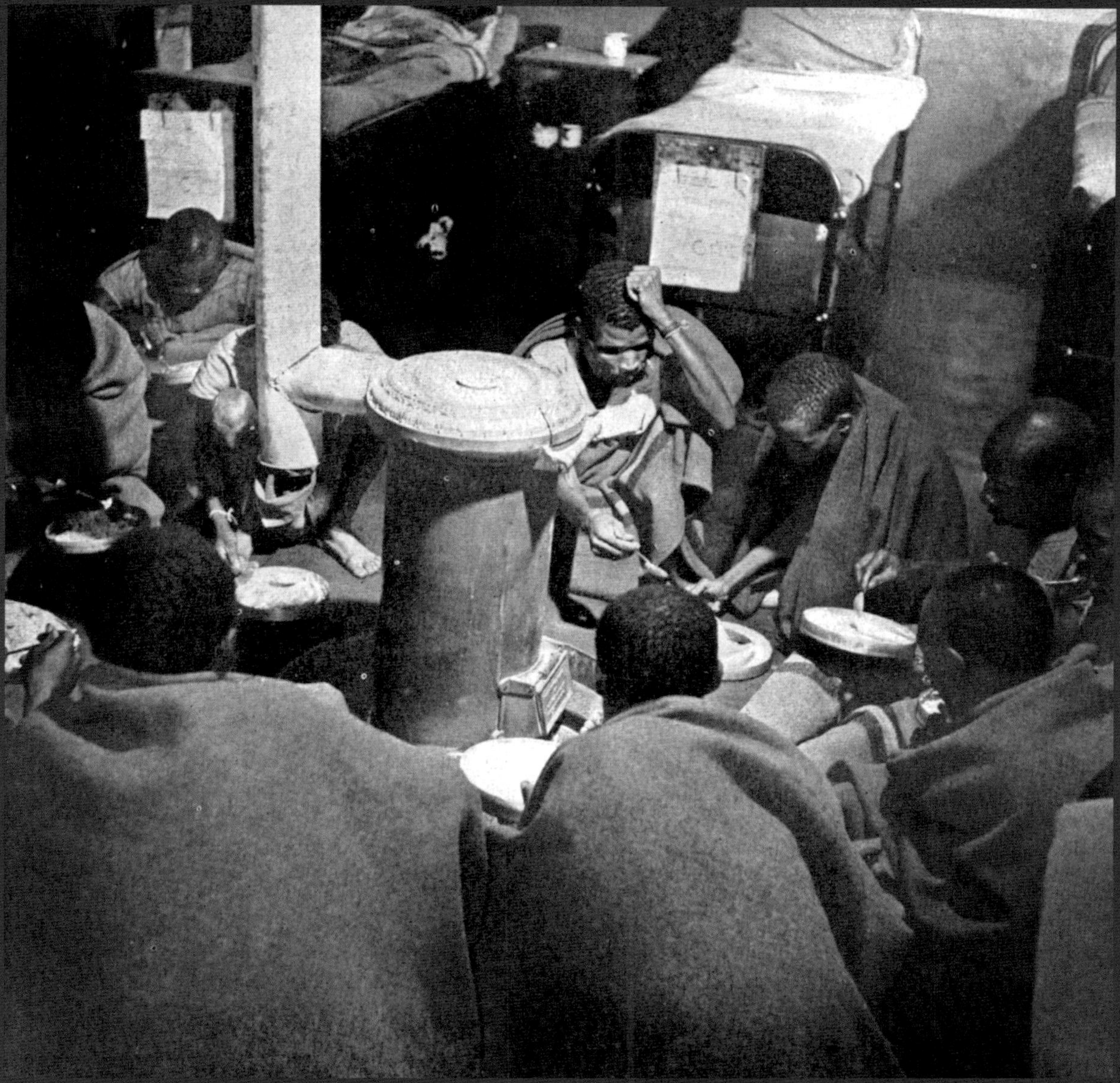

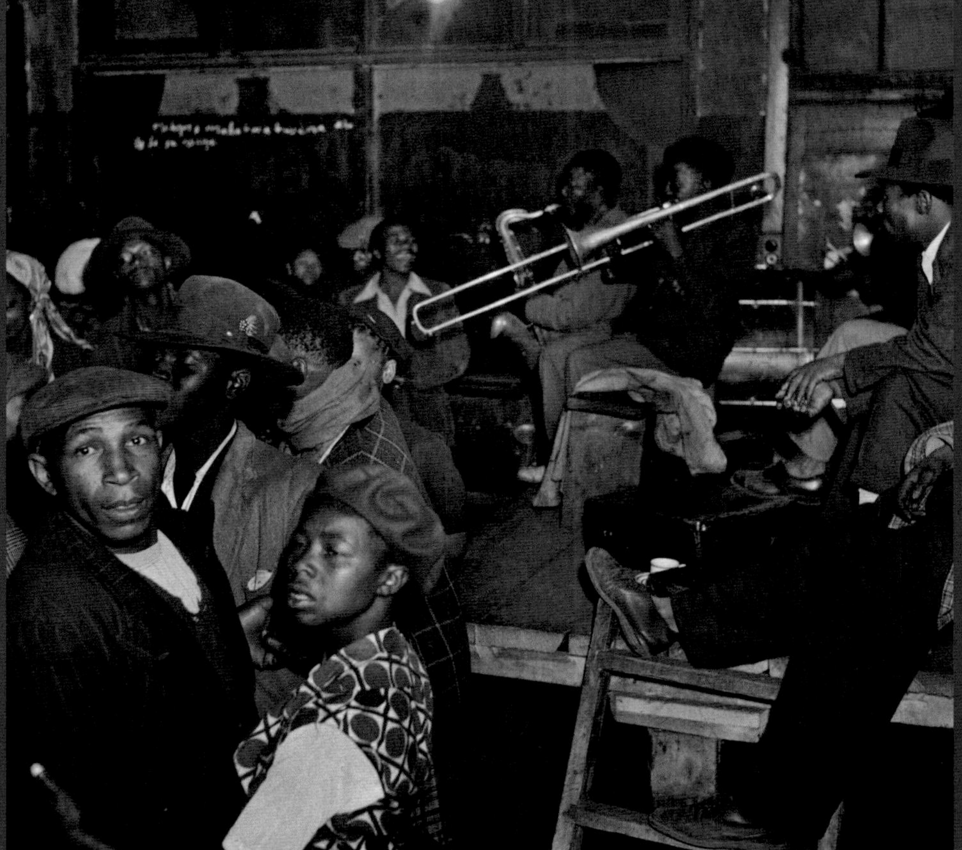

Life on the weekend in the Black townships.

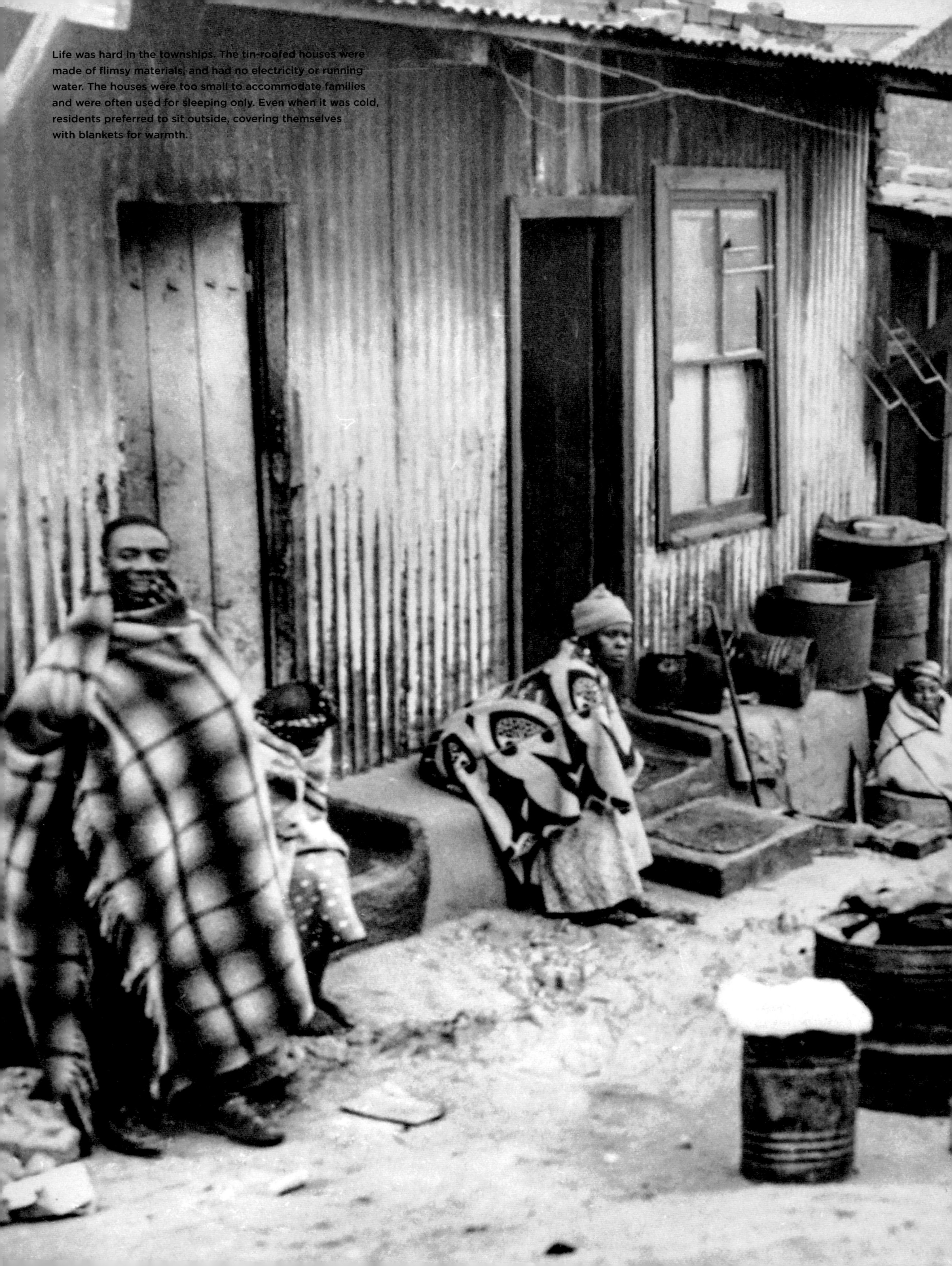

Life was hard in the townships. The tin-roofed houses were made of flimsy materials, and had no electricity or running water. The houses were too small to accommodate families and were often used for sleeping only. Even when it was cold, residents preferred to sit outside, covering themselves with blankets for warmth.

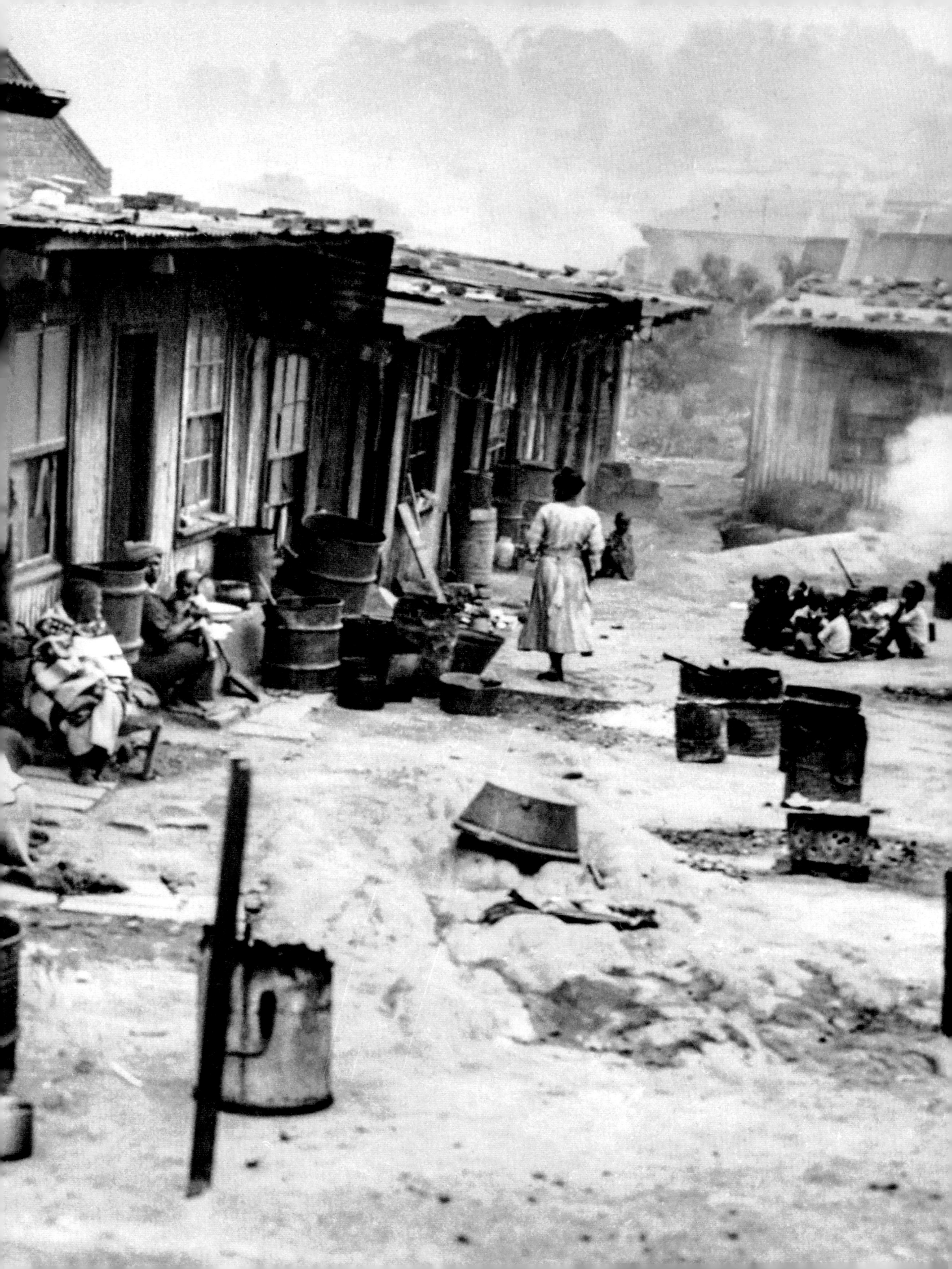

Walter Sisulu

After boasting that he and Justice had run away from home and deceived the regent, the two were dismissed from the mine and ordered to return home to Mqhekezweni.

Tata did not wish to return home and went to stay with a cousin, Garlick Mbekeni, in George Goch. Garlick was a warm, friendly person who was instrumental in helping Tata find a job with a legal firm in Johannesburg.

Garlick took him to the city center and introduced him to Walter Sisulu. This was a meeting that would change the course of Tata's life on a personal and professional level in ways he could never have anticipated, and this would lead to us kids all knowing him only as Uncle Walter.

At their first meeting, Uncle Walter was very impressed with the young Nelson Mandela—his royal connections, his dignified bearing, and the evident ambition all indicated a potential for success. He saw a young man with high ideals and great qualities who was destined to play an important part in the community.

Uncle Walter was also a homeboy, from Thembuland and a member of the Gcina clan. Born out of wedlock in Ngcobo in 1912, he was the son of Alice Sisulu and Victor Dickinson, a white government official who acknowledged his paternity and contributed to the child's early upbringing, but he never lived with them. After a few years, he moved away and lost touch with his African family. Uncle Walter only ever identified as Black and Xhosa.

Uncle Walter spent his childhood with his aunt in Cofimvaba, dropping out of school in standard five (grade 7) and leaving home to work at the mines in Johannesburg in 1928. Just sixteen, he was deemed too young for underground work and released from his contract. For the next few years, he found employment in a variety of unskilled jobs before his dismissal after leading a strike at a biscuit factory. He then began a career as a small businessman, selling advertising for *Bantu World*, the main African newspaper, and identifying potential African account holders for the Union Bank.

In 1939, he opened Sitha Investments, the only Black-owned real estate agency in South Africa, which bought and sold property in Alexandra and Sophiatown.

Tata was, of course, equally impressed with Uncle Walter. By that time he was a well-known person around Orlando township, which later became one of the townships of Soweto. He led a successful choir and a Xhosa cultural organization, the Orlando Brotherly Association, that held meetings where members would read aloud and discuss Xhosa epic poetry. He was already active with the African National Congress (ANC). Throughout the 1960s he chaired a local chapter of the ANC, then a body with only a few thousand members concentrated mainly in

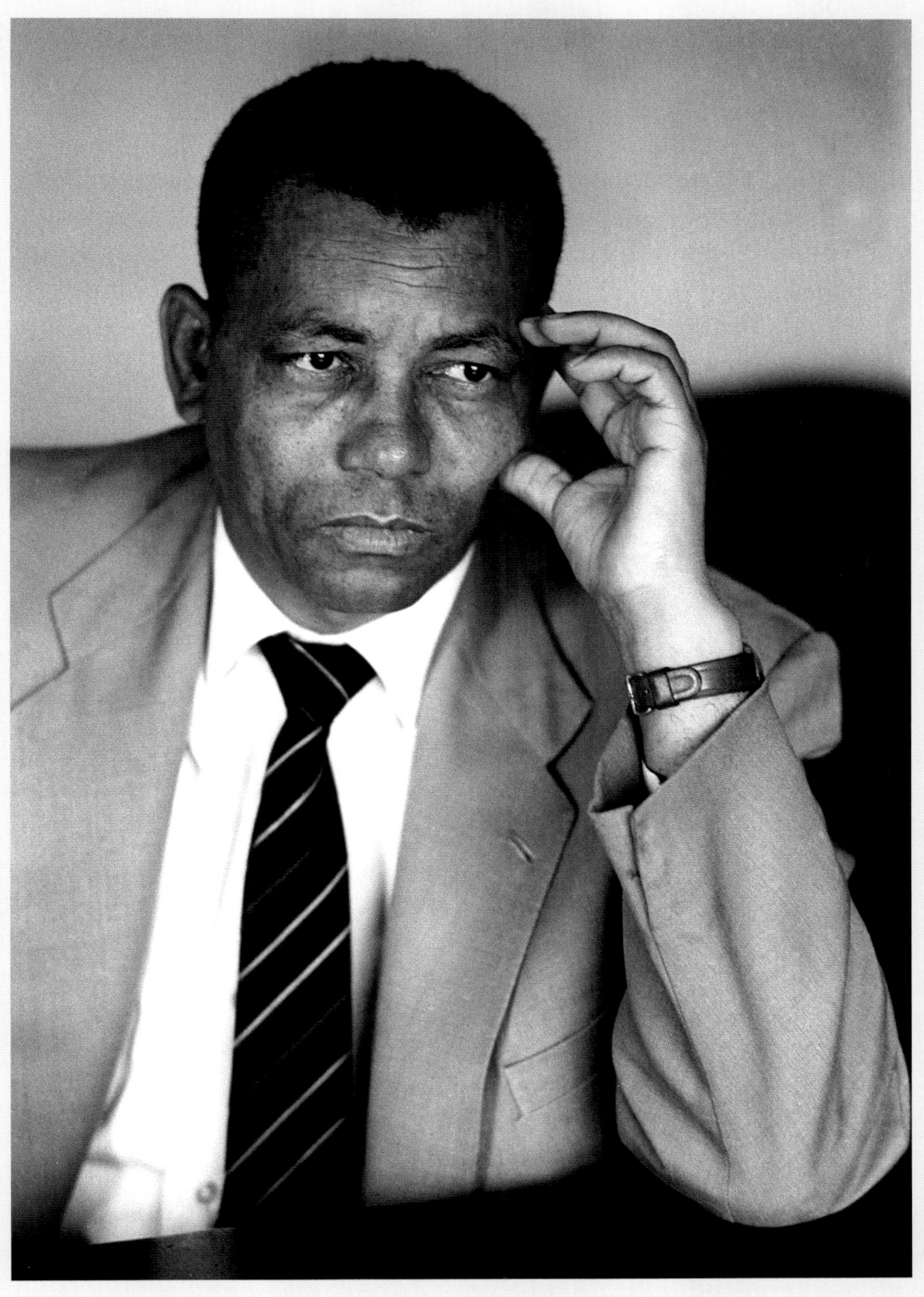

Tata's first encounter with Walter Sisulu marked the beginning of his most enduring friendship.

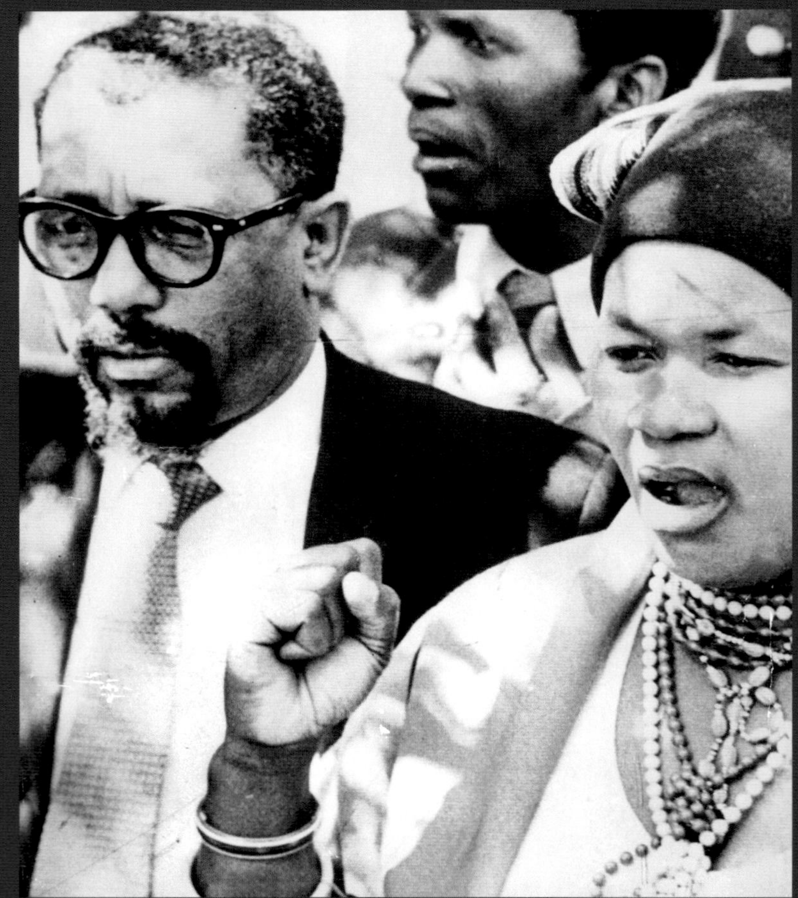

Johannesburg, Durban, and Port Elizabeth. Tata explained why he was in Johannesburg. On learning that he was an ex-law student from Fort Hare, Uncle Walter immediately introduced him to Witkin, Sidelsky, and Eidelman—the largest law firm in Johannesburg. They were a group of white, liberal Jewish lawyers who handled business from both white and Black clients. In addition to trying conventional law cases, they oversaw property transactions for African customers. Uncle Walter brought the firm clients who needed a mortgage. The firm would handle their loan applications and then take a commission, which it would split with the estate agent, Sitha Investments. Lazar Sidelsky agreed to hire Tata as an article clerk while he also completed his BA degree.

This was an amazing opportunity for Tata: in South Africa, to be a practicing lawyer, one must complete not just a relevant degree and other qualifying exams but also serve an apprenticeship for a number of years—called "serving articles." Tata worked in his job at the firm during the day while studying at night through the University of South Africa (UNISA). This was another respected educational institution that, at the time, offered credits and degrees via correspondence courses to students of all races. Through Uncle Walter, Tata was introduced to many people in the city. He was to learn an interesting lesson. Tata had been taught that to be a leader you had to have a university degree. He therefore believed that proficiency in English and success in business were definitely due to high academic achievement. It was with great surprise that he learned from his cousin Garlick that Uncle Walter had no formal education beyond grade 7 or 8. Tata had to rethink his beliefs. He found that even with all the courses in English that he had completed, his English was not as fluent or as eloquent as many of the men he met in Johannesburg—men who had not even completed a school certificate.

I think that Tata was very fortunate to meet Walter Sisulu when he did. The gesture of kindness that Walter extended to him was to change the course of my father's life in a way that he himself had not anticipated.

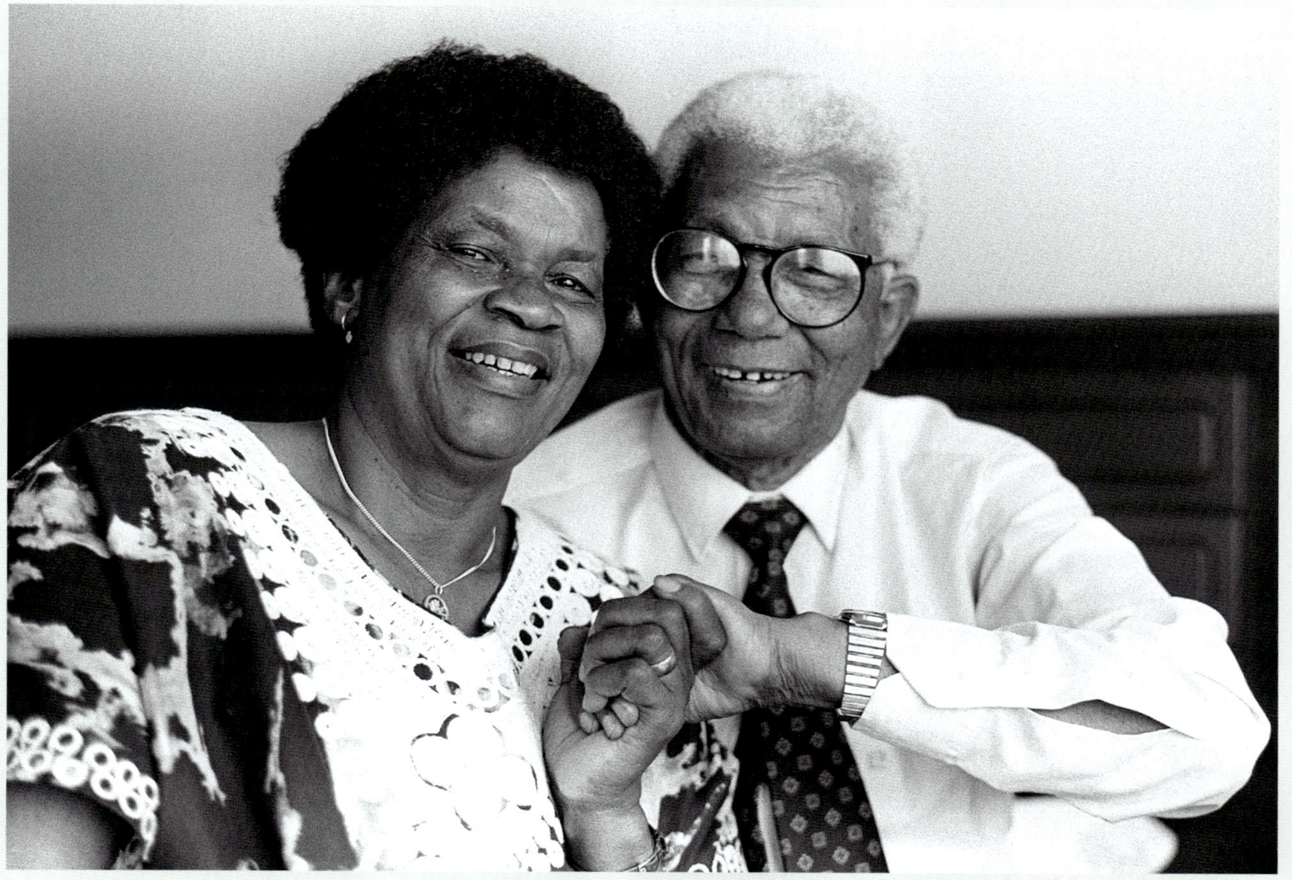

Opposite: Anti-apartheid ANC leaders Albertina and Walter Sisulu in Johannesburg.
Above: Albertina and Walter Sisulu in their Soweto home, October 1989.
Right: Tata, Albertina, and Walter Sisulu at a rally in Soweto, February 1990.
Below: Tata and Walter Sisulu raise their fists in the garden of Desmond Tutu's residence in Cape Town, one day after Tata's release, February 1990.

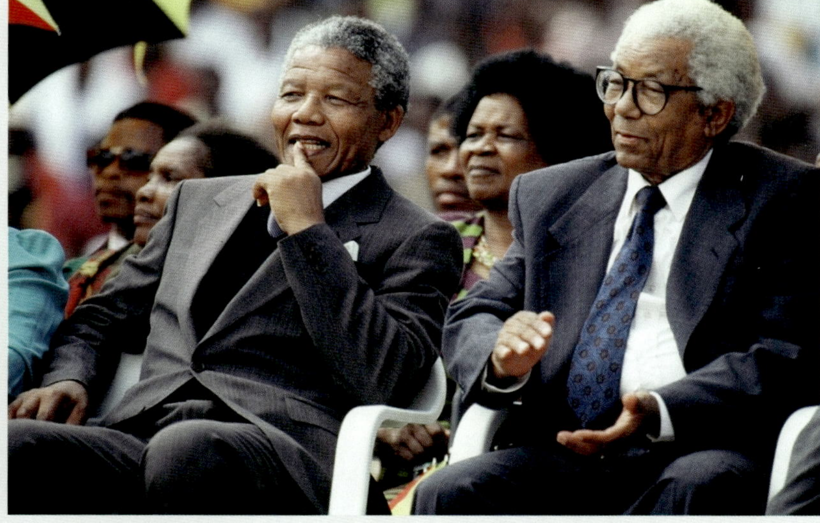

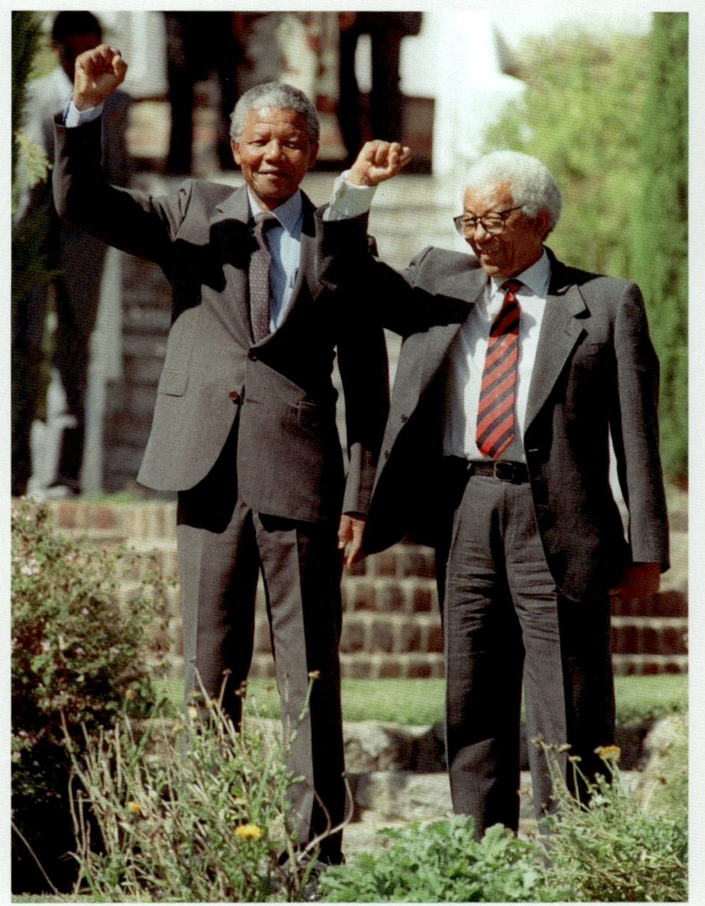

I was six years old when Tata met Walter Sisulu, and we considered Uncle Walter (as we came to call him) and Albertina as a part of our family. Tata and Uncle Walter were rarely around, and even when they were, Uncle Walter's house was the center of political meetings and activity. On the very rare occasions when we saw them, Uncle Walter was warm, affectionate, and loving. We wanted to visit him during his incarceration in Pretoria prison and on Robben Island, but we were not permitted to; only his immediate family was allowed—the same conditions that applied to Tata.

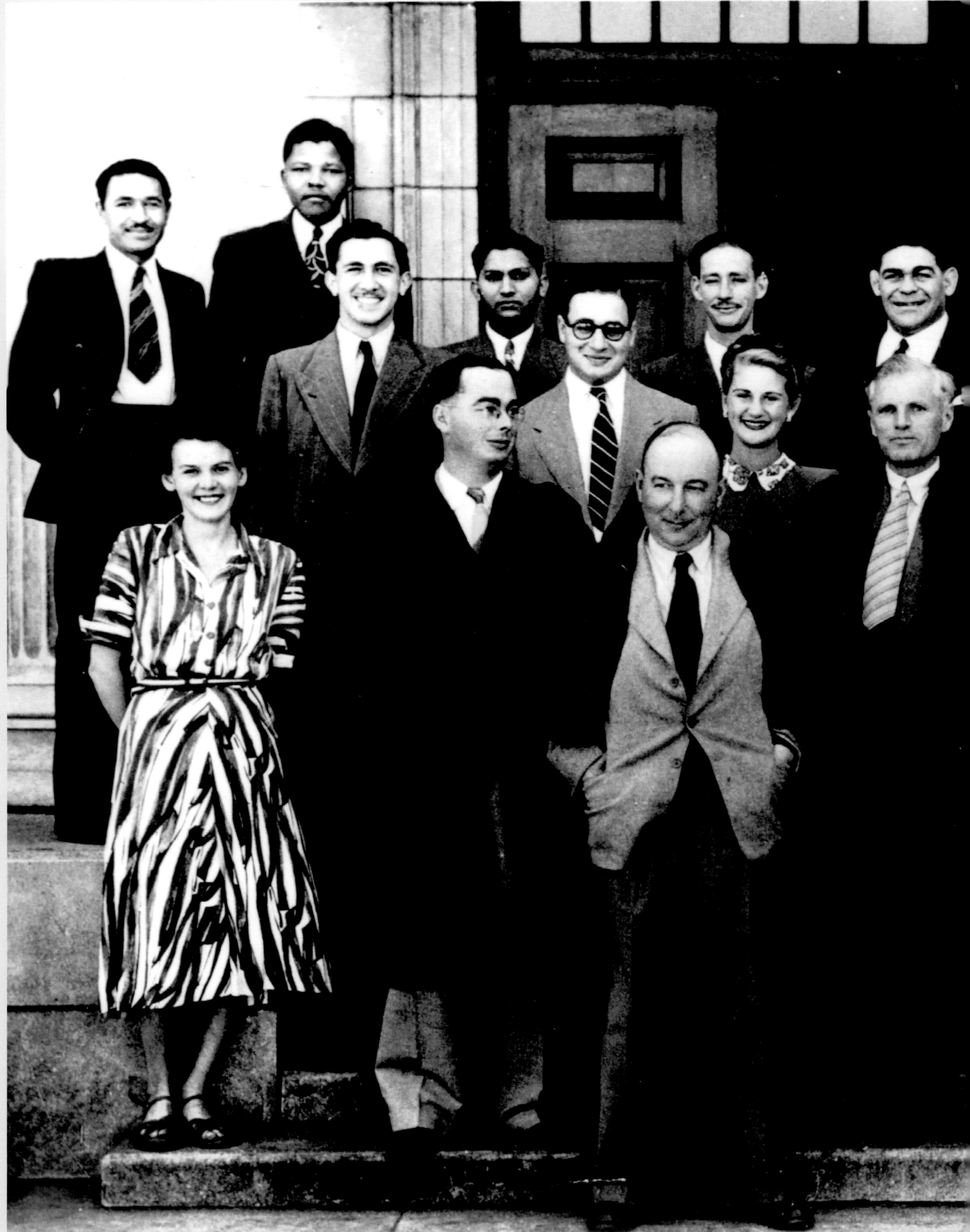

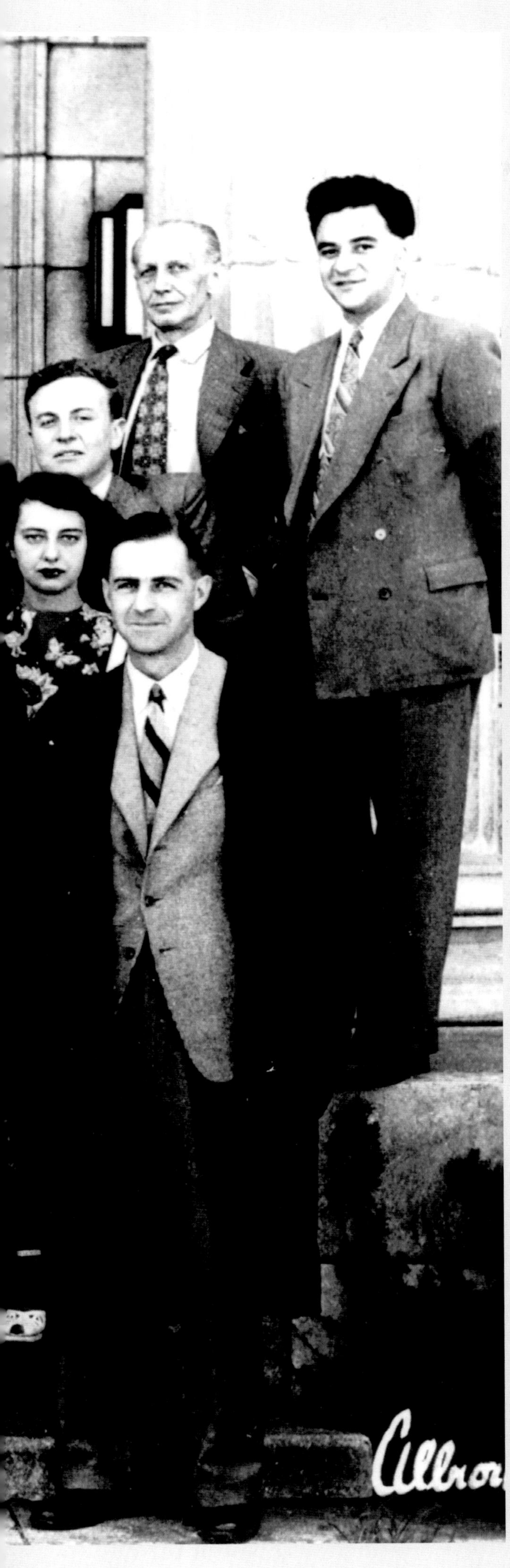

Tata studied law at the University of the Witwatersrand (Wits University) from 1943 to 1949. As the only Black African student there he faced racism, yet he befriended liberal, communist, Jewish, and Indian students. A meaningful friendship arose between Tata and Joe Slovo, an opponent of the apartheid system. Slovo had a leadership role in the ANC and was later a commander of the ANC's military wing, uMkhonto we Sizwe.

Wits University, Faculty of Law, 1949. Back row (*left to right*): S. Essak, Tata, N. Mazenzarb, M. Liebengerg; middle row: Henry Nathanson, R. Bhoolia, Julian Phillips, J. Moller; front row: Daphne Clarke, Prof. Ellison Kahn, Prof. H. R. Hanlo, Joe Slovo, Helen Goldfoot (dean's secretary), Prof. Scholtens, Unity Fictor, Prof. Exton Burchell.

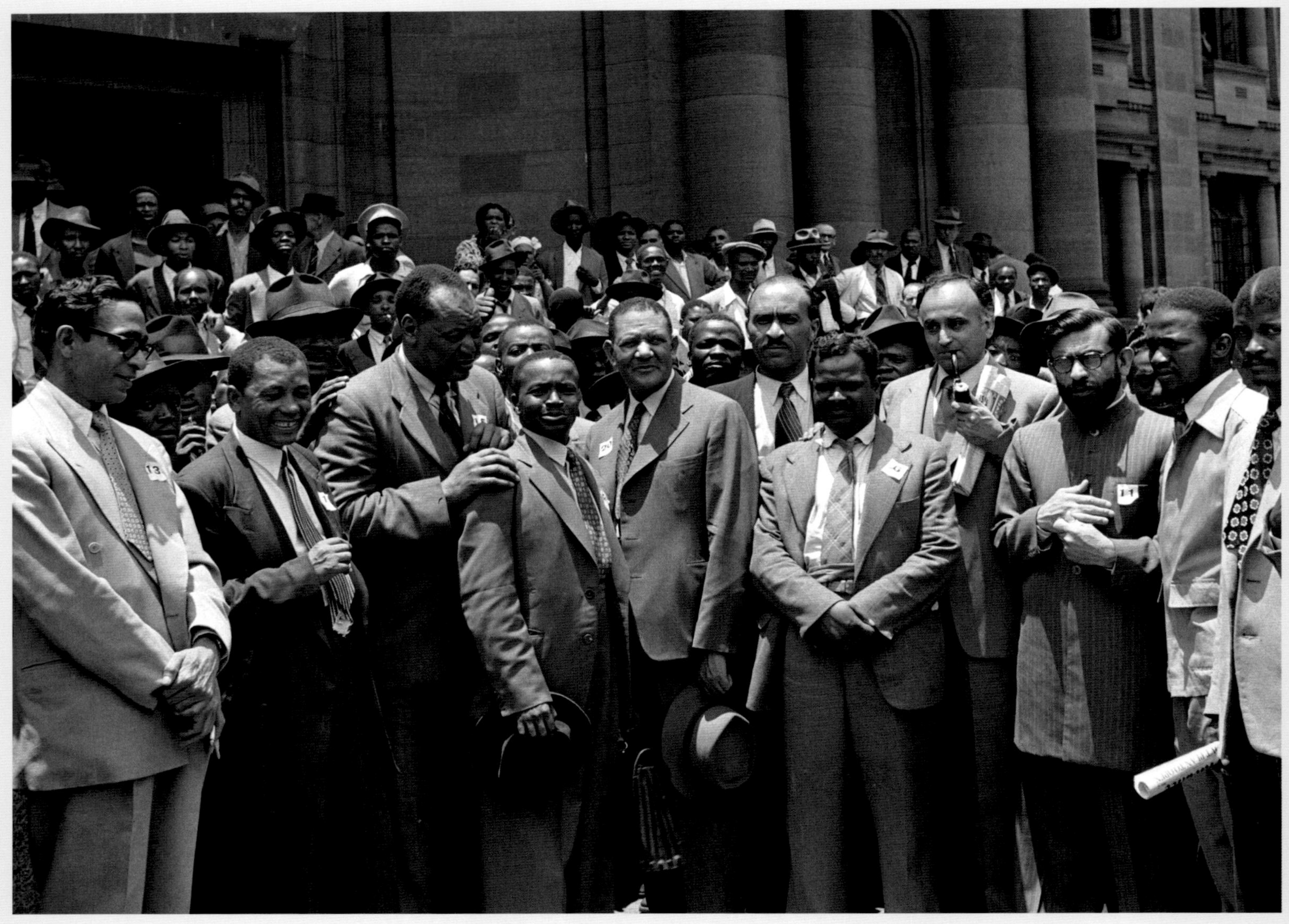

Uncle Walter encouraged Tata and many young African men to join the ANC. Above: Some of the twenty anti-apartheid campaigners charged with contravening the Suppression of Communism Act during the Defiance Campaign of Civil Disobedience pose outside Johannesburg Magistrates Court after their trial, September 1952.

Uncle Walter and Tata's friendship would stand the test of time—through the struggle of twenty-seven years in prison and beyond. Tata was honored by his older mentor's warmth, affection, and trust. Uncle Walter had the authority of a cultural brother in the city. He was a friend, a family member, and a key influence in Tata's life. When Tata got a job as an article clerk and could afford to rent a room, he moved to "Dark City," the poorest section of Alexandra township. For Tata, a country boy, life in Alexandra was exciting but also perilous. The township had some nice homes, but it was mostly an impoverished neighborhood. Most homes were either in complete disrepair or tin-roofed shacks without electricity or running water. Gangsters known as tsotsis were very much a part of life, and shebeens, illegal saloons, were on every street. It was a far cry from Tata's comforting birthplace and exposed him for the first time to extreme poverty and racial discrimination that he had not yet experienced firsthand. It was, however, one of the few areas of the country where Black Africans could acquire freehold property and run their own affairs—to Tata, it was an urban promised land.

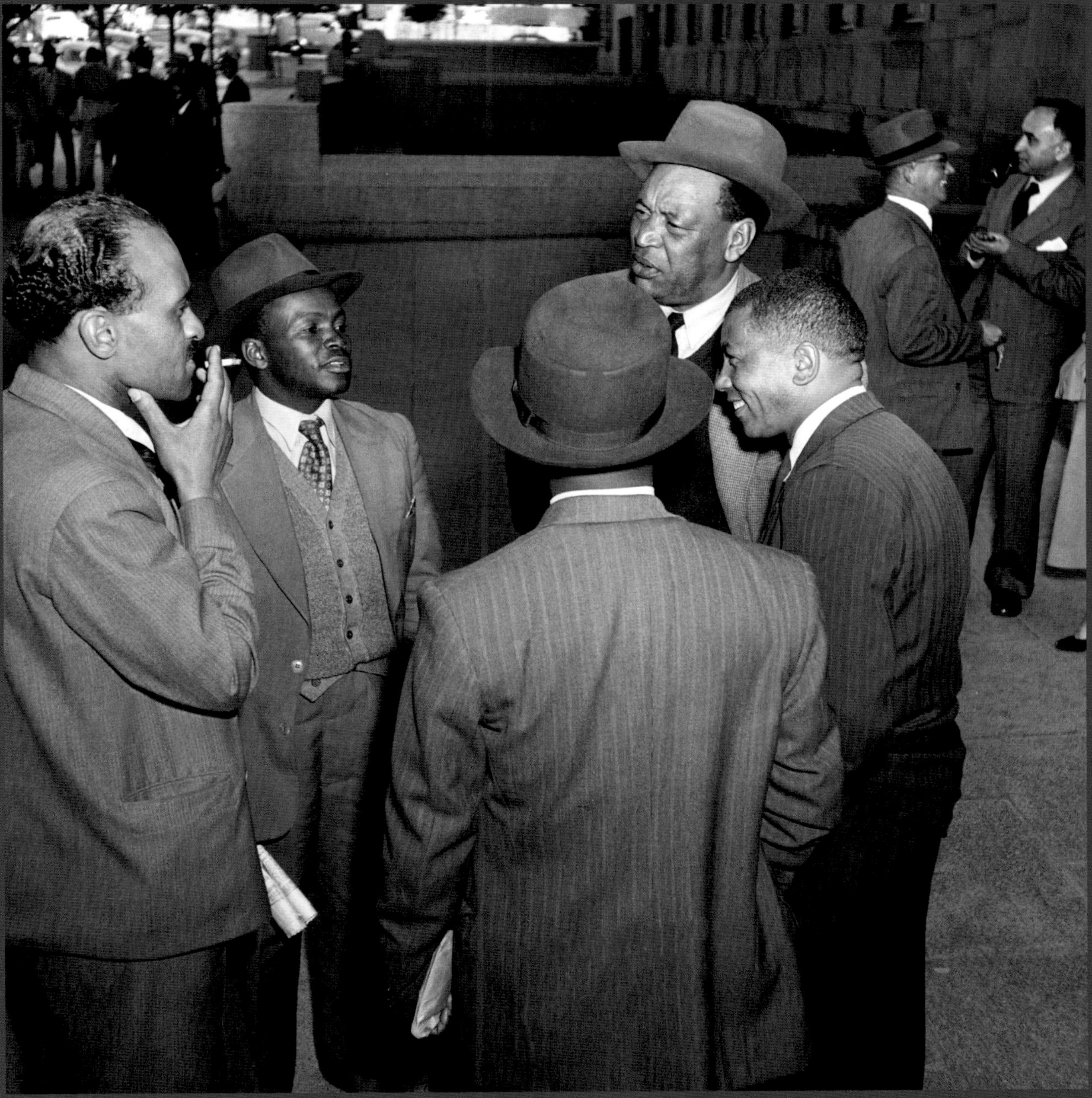

Above: Uncle Walter, on far right, and other defendants, in the trial of twenty anti-apartheid campaigners, discuss the case with their lawyers outside Johannesburg Magistrates Court, during the Defiance Campaign of Civil Disobedience.

Right (*from left*): Defendants Yusuf Dadoo, Baboo Dadoo, and Uncle Walter. Yusuf Dadoo was the president of the South African Indian Congress.

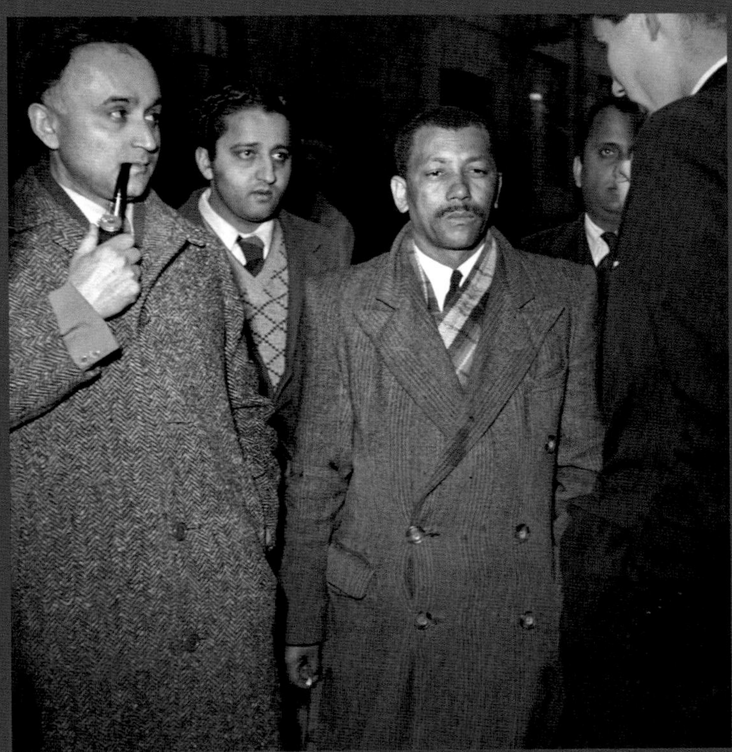

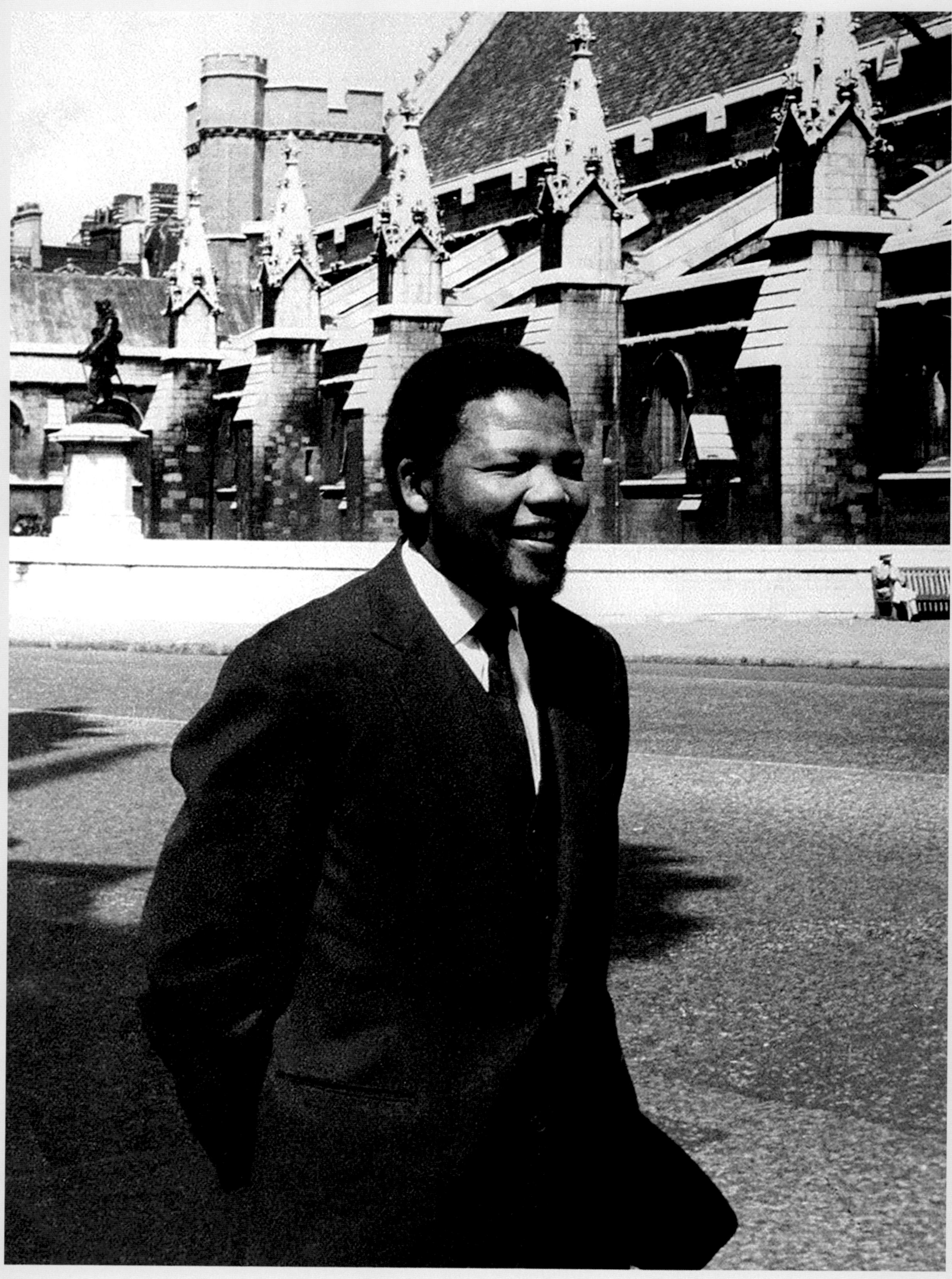

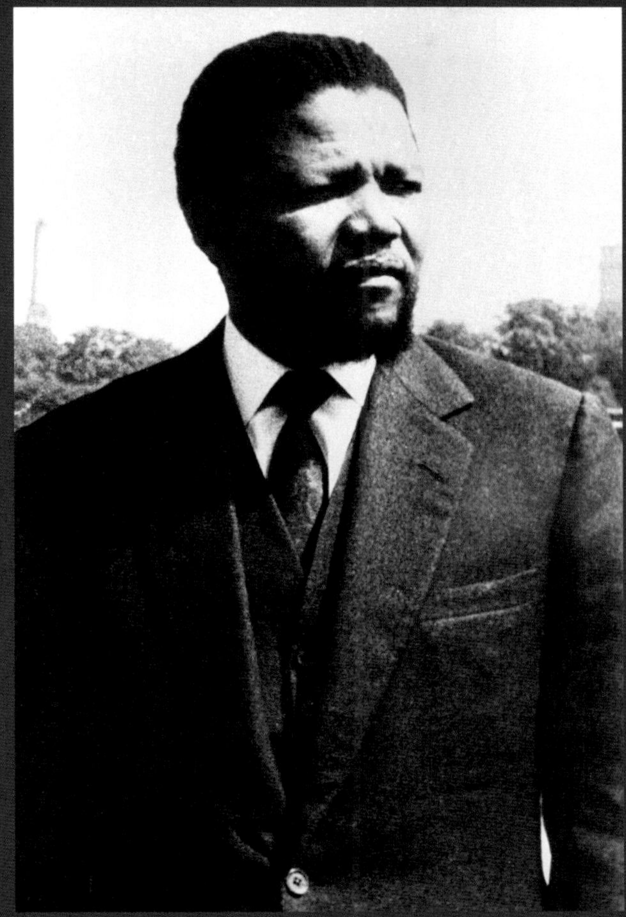

Opposite: Tata on a visit to London, 1962.

Above: Tata in the early 1960s.

Throughout his years in the city, Tata remained proud of his royal Thembu roots and always returned to them. The social connections provided by kinship networks remained important even after he moved to Johannesburg. Ever since he and Justice left home without the regent's permission, Tata had felt guilty that his actions had shown disrespect to his guardian, so he was happy to be able to reconcile when the regent visited Johannesburg. And later, when he was unable to attend the regent's burial in 1942, Tata found great solace in the fact that they had made peace before his death. The regent's wisdom and ability to keep people united by listening to and respecting other opinions was a lesson that Tata would carry with him in both his private life and political career.

"I cannot pinpoint a moment when I became politicized, when I knew that I would spend my life in the liberation struggle. I had no epiphany, no singular revelation, no moment of truth, but a steady accumulation of a thousand slights, a thousand indignities, and a thousand unremembered moments, produced in me an anger, a rebelliousness, a desire to fight the system that imprisoned my people."

Tata in *Long Walk to Freedom*, referring to the period in his life when he became an activist

Below: A woman sitting in the wagon reserved for white people, protesting the systematized racial segregation in South Africa.

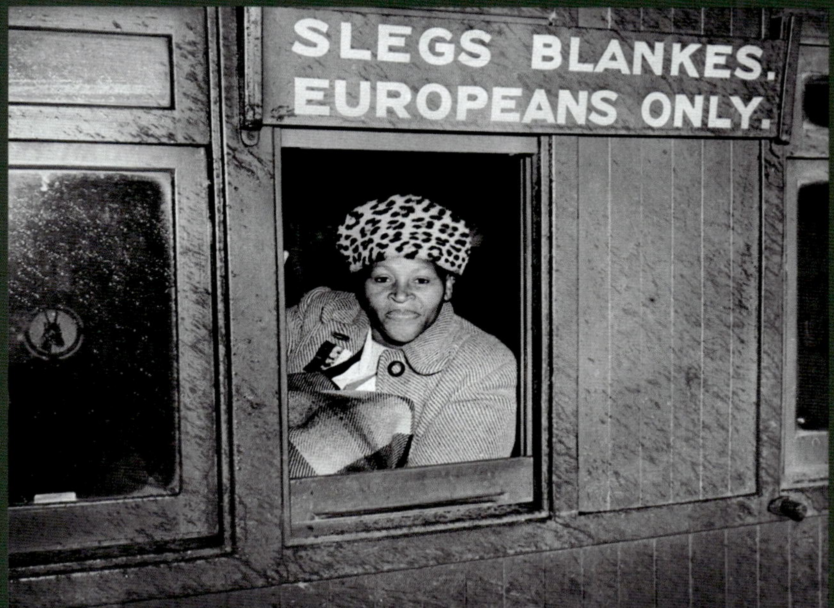

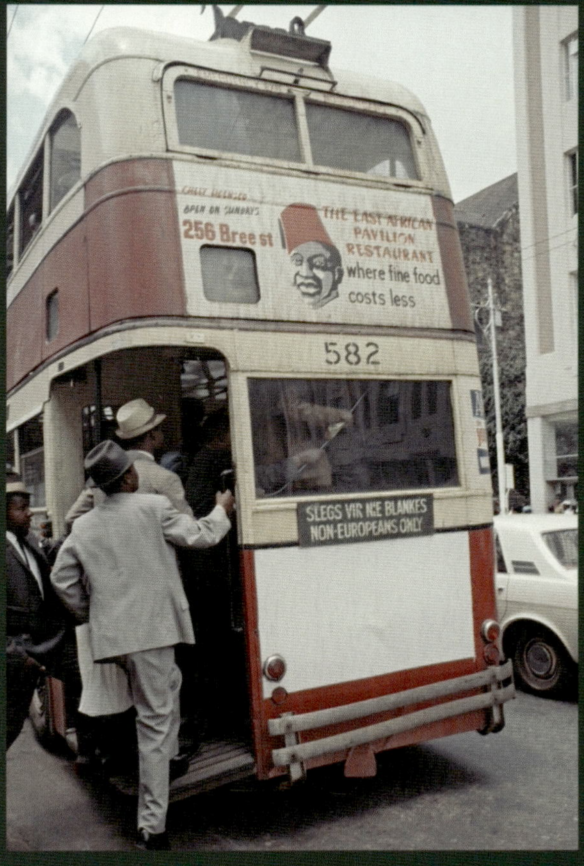

Non-Europeans were not allowed to use elevators and were only allowed on segregated trolleys.

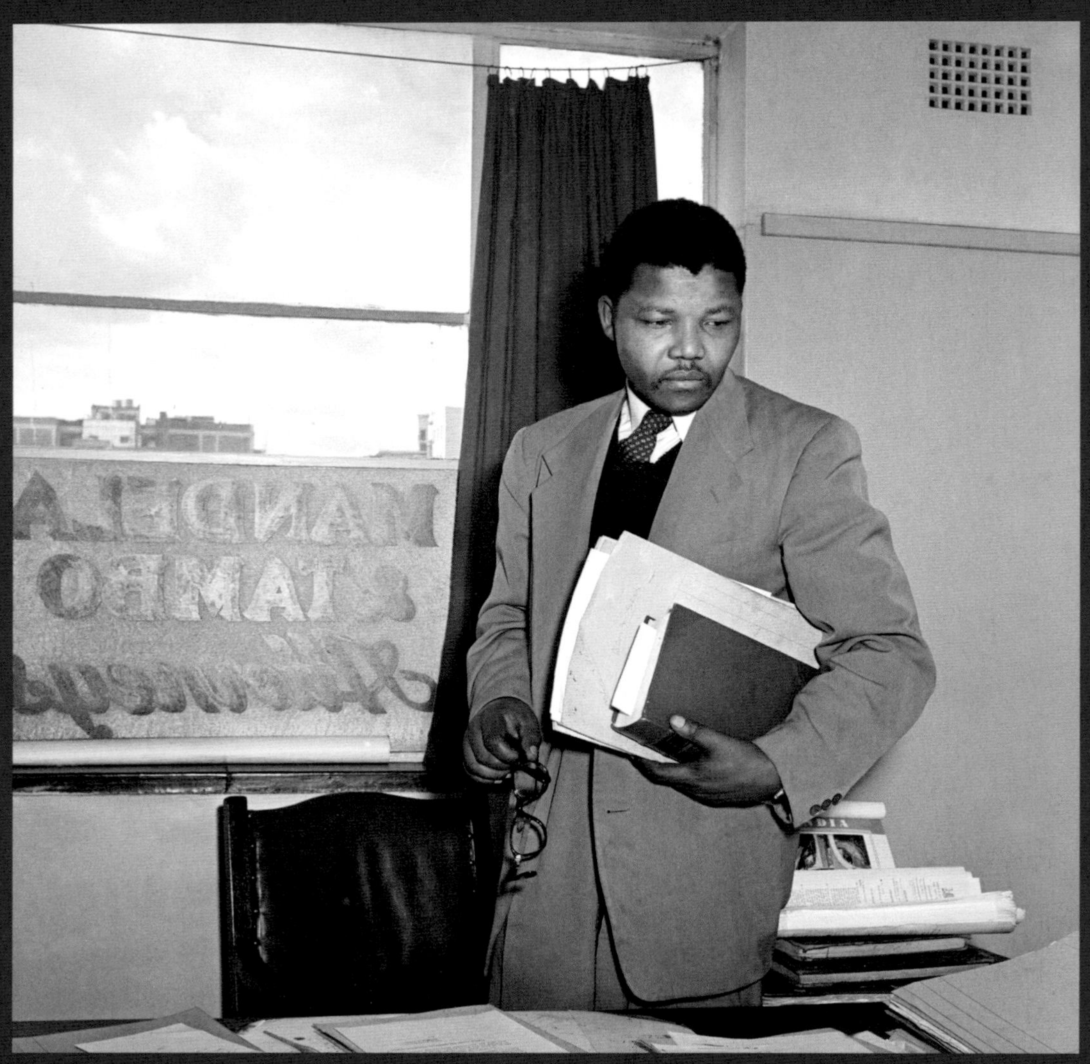

Tata and Oliver Tambo opened Johannesburg's first Black-owned law partnership in 1952. They both joined in the struggle to liberate South Africa and went on to lead the ANC. The demands of their political work ultimately made it impossible to continue the practice, and they closed it in 1960.

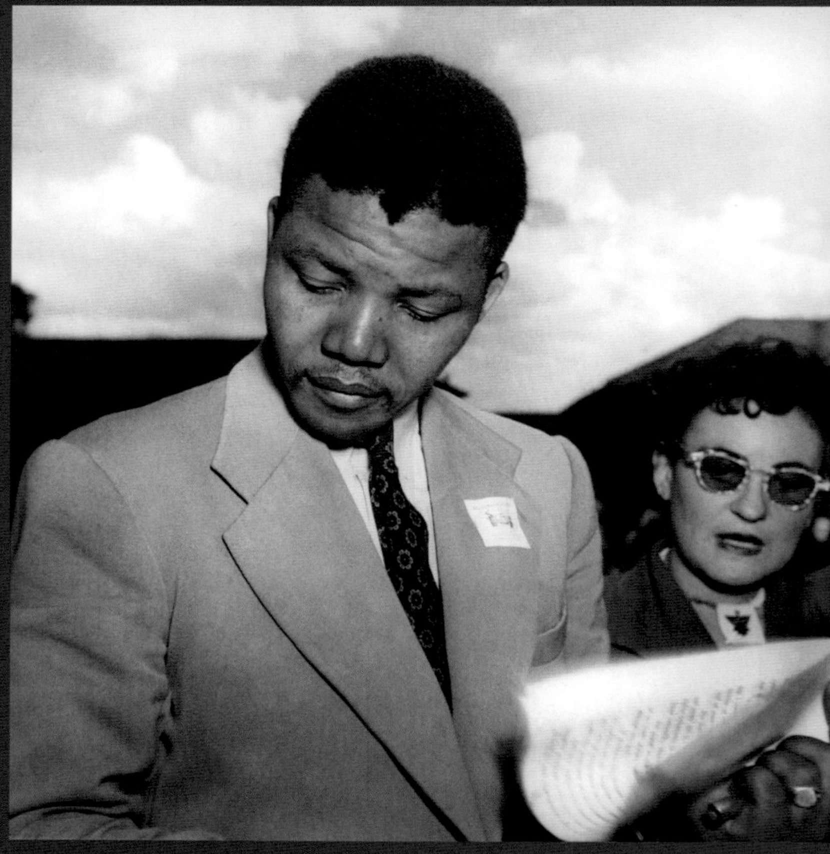

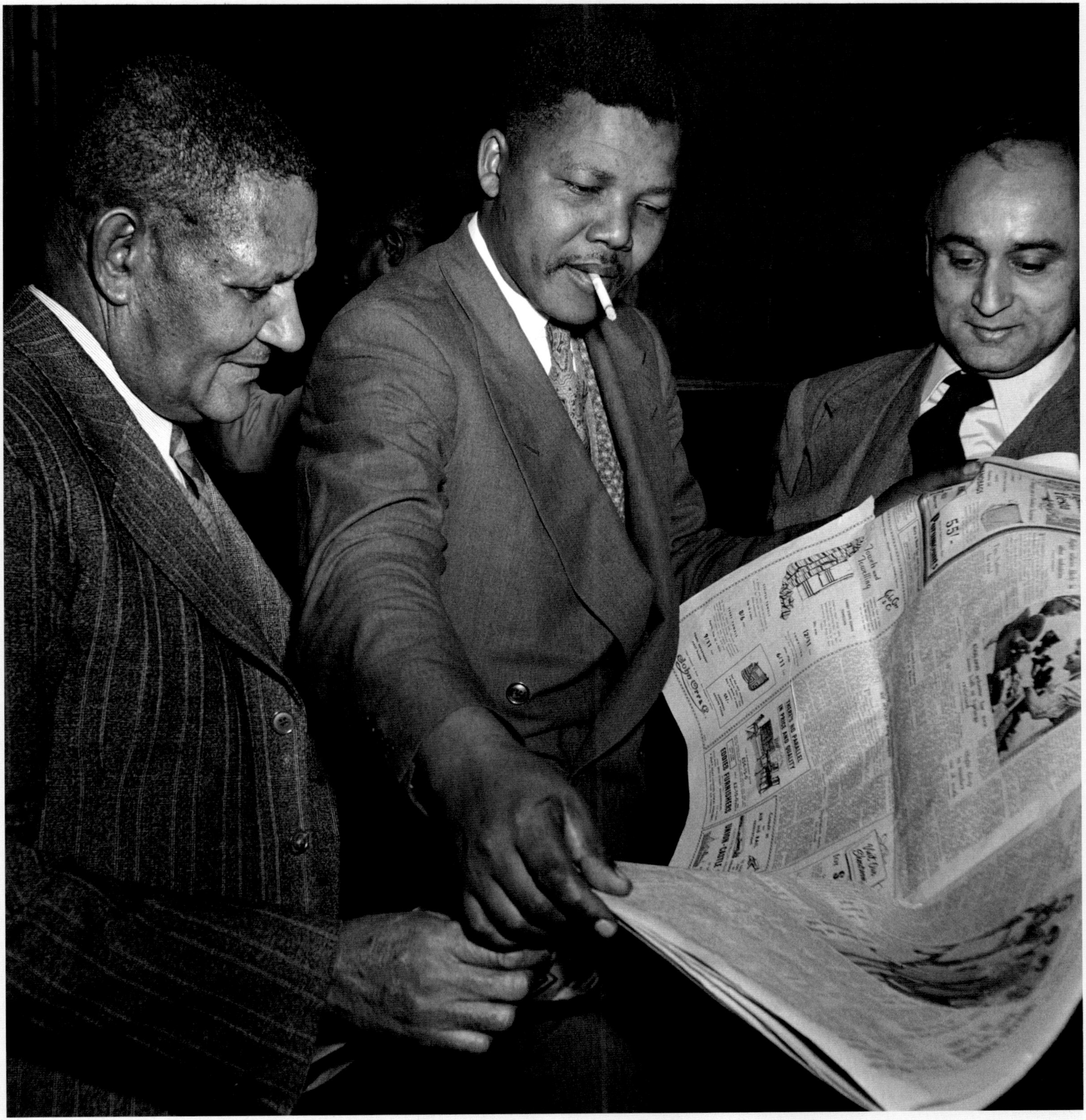

Opposite (*above*): Tata in the office of Mandela and Tambo in Johannesburg, which provided free or affordable legal representation to Blacks.

Opposite (*below*): Tata with fellow activist Ruth First at an ANC conference in Bloemfontein, South Africa.

Above (*left to right*): African National Congress leader J.S. Moroka, Tata (leader of the ANC Youth League), and president of the South African Indian Congress Yusuf Dadoo outside a Johannesburg courtroom during a trial connected with the Defiance Campaign.

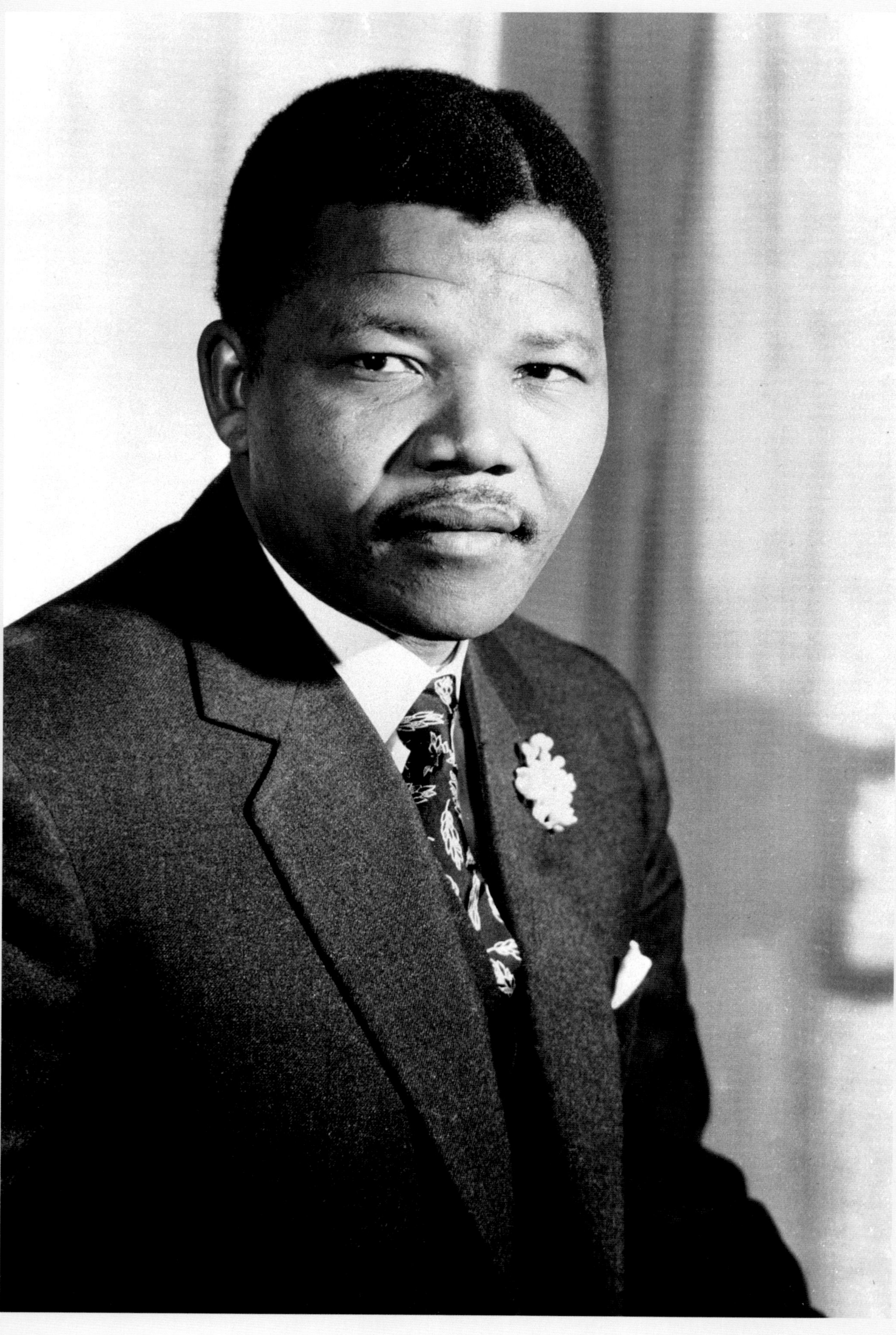

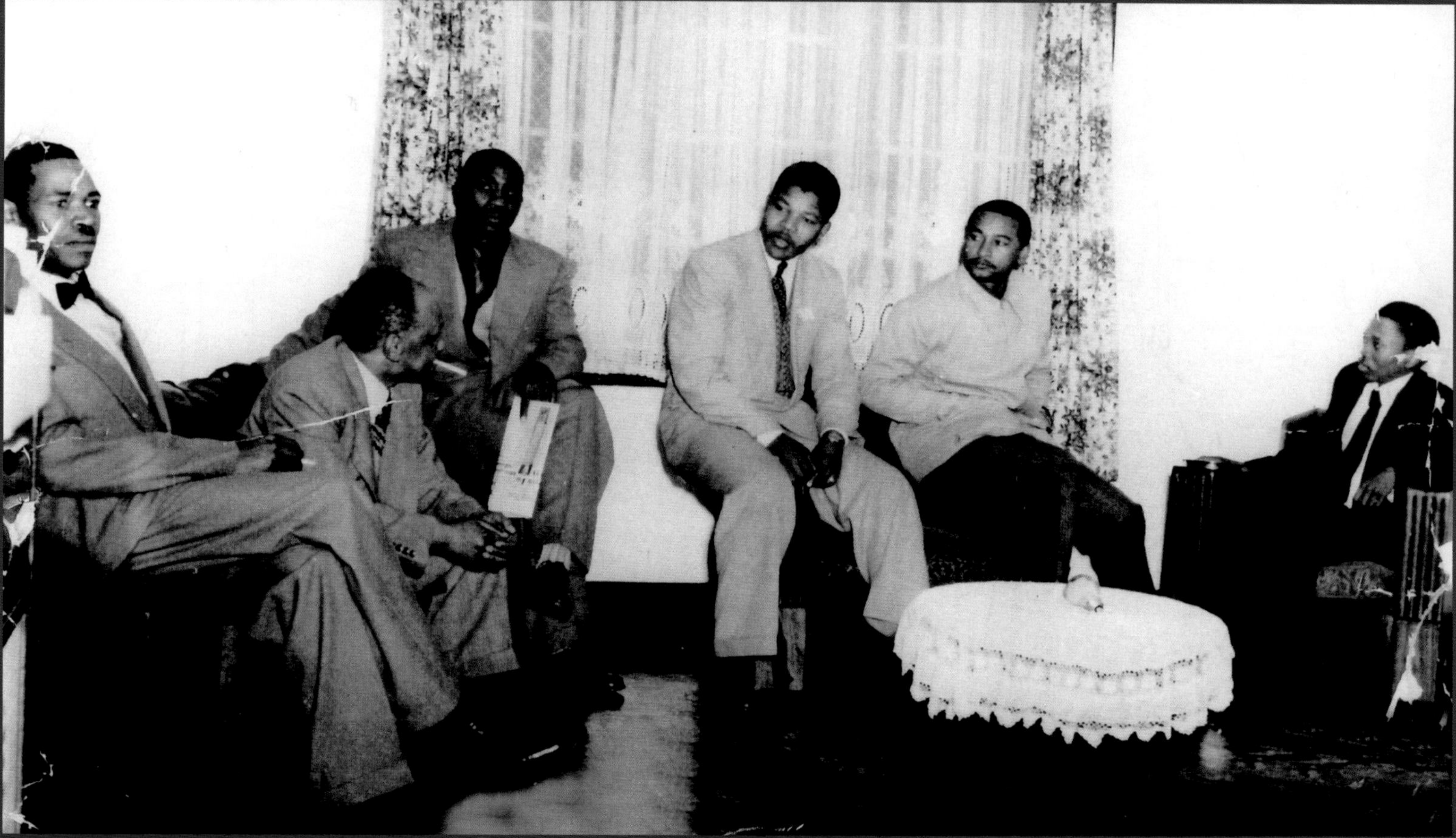

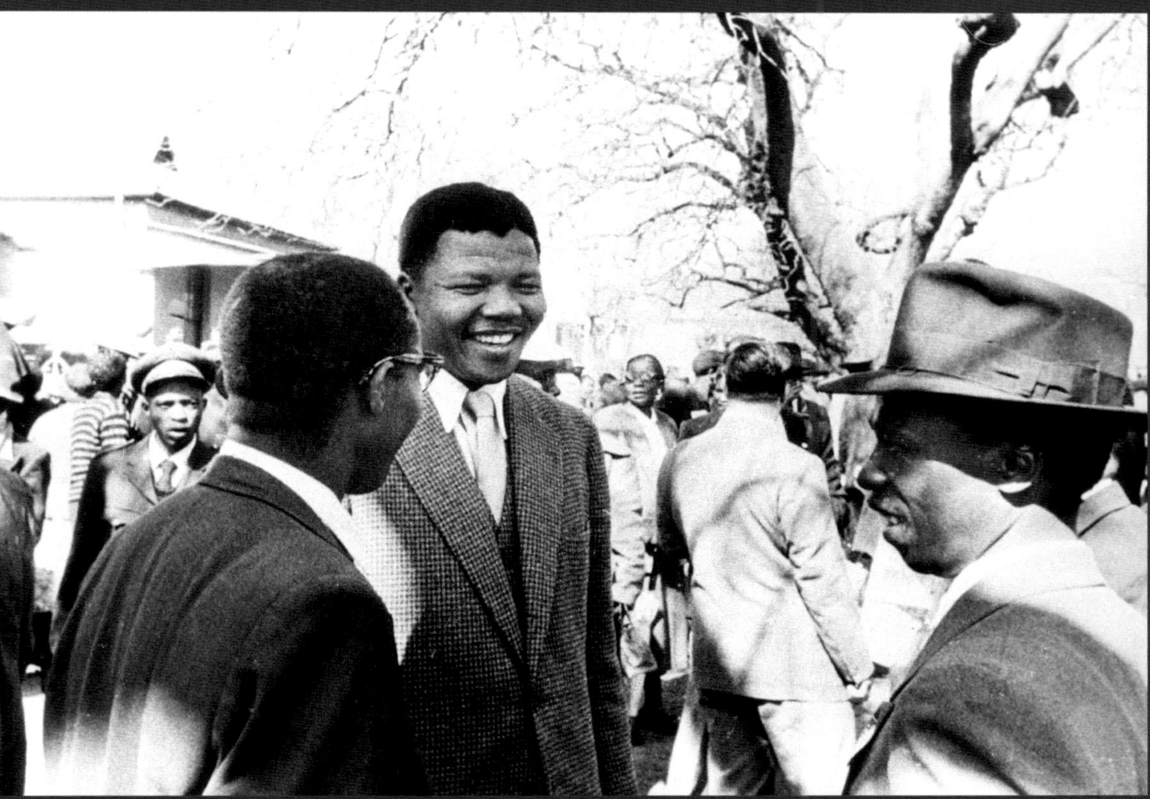

Opposite: Mandela becomes national
president of the ANC Youth League, 1951.

Tata and Joe Slovo, the head of the Communist Party in South Africa. They met as students at Wits University.

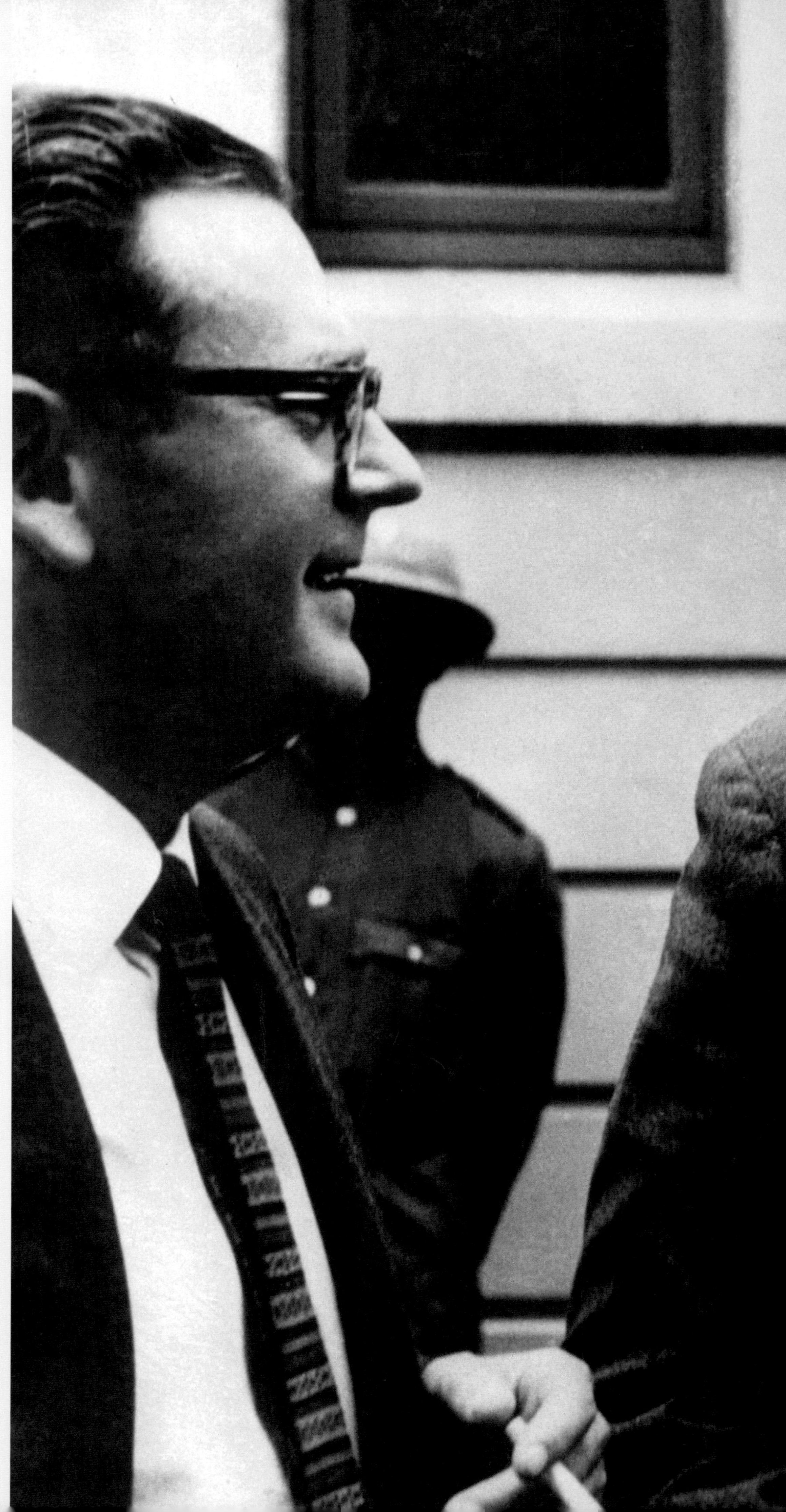

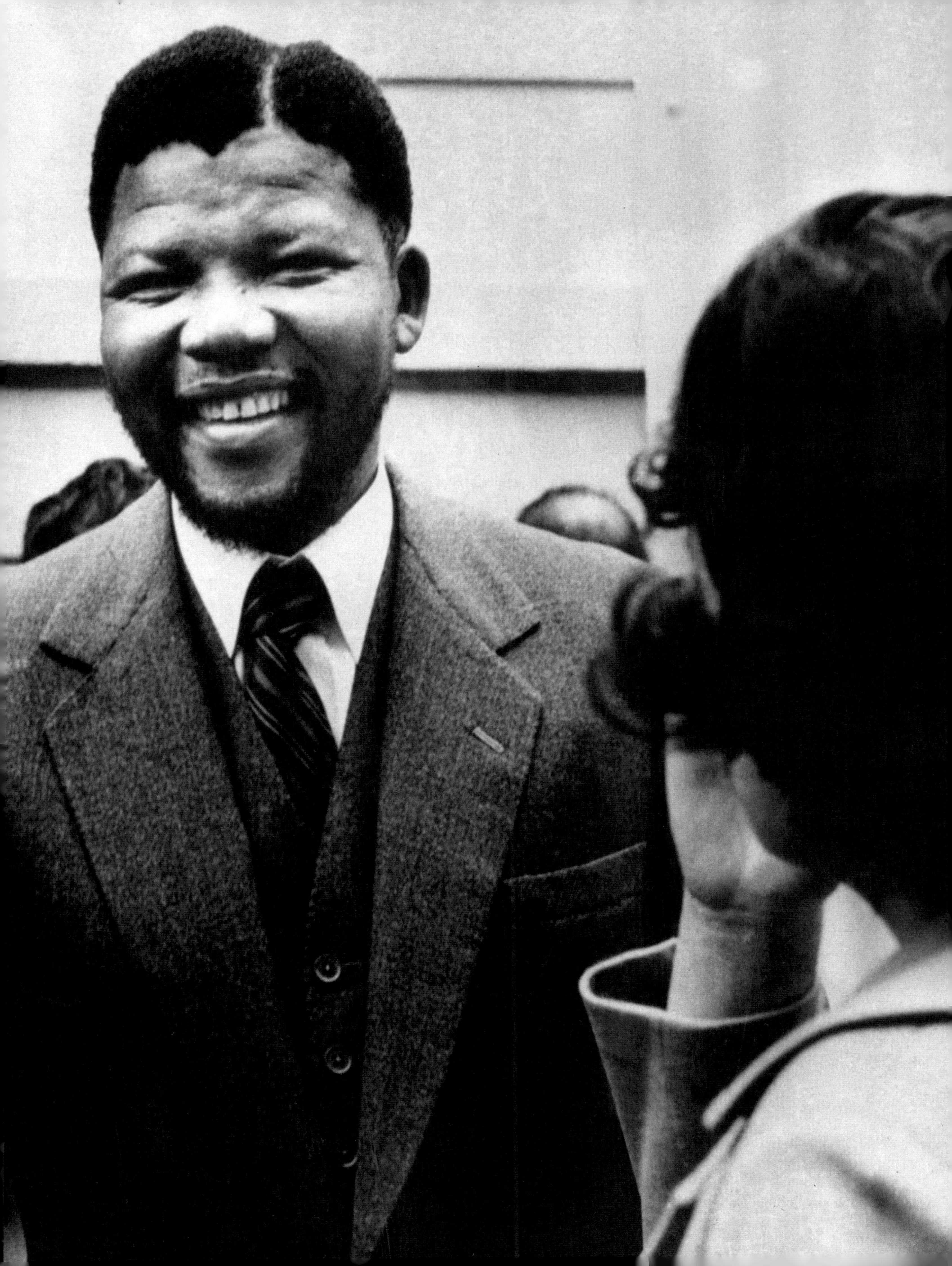

3

1950–1962

The Troublemaker

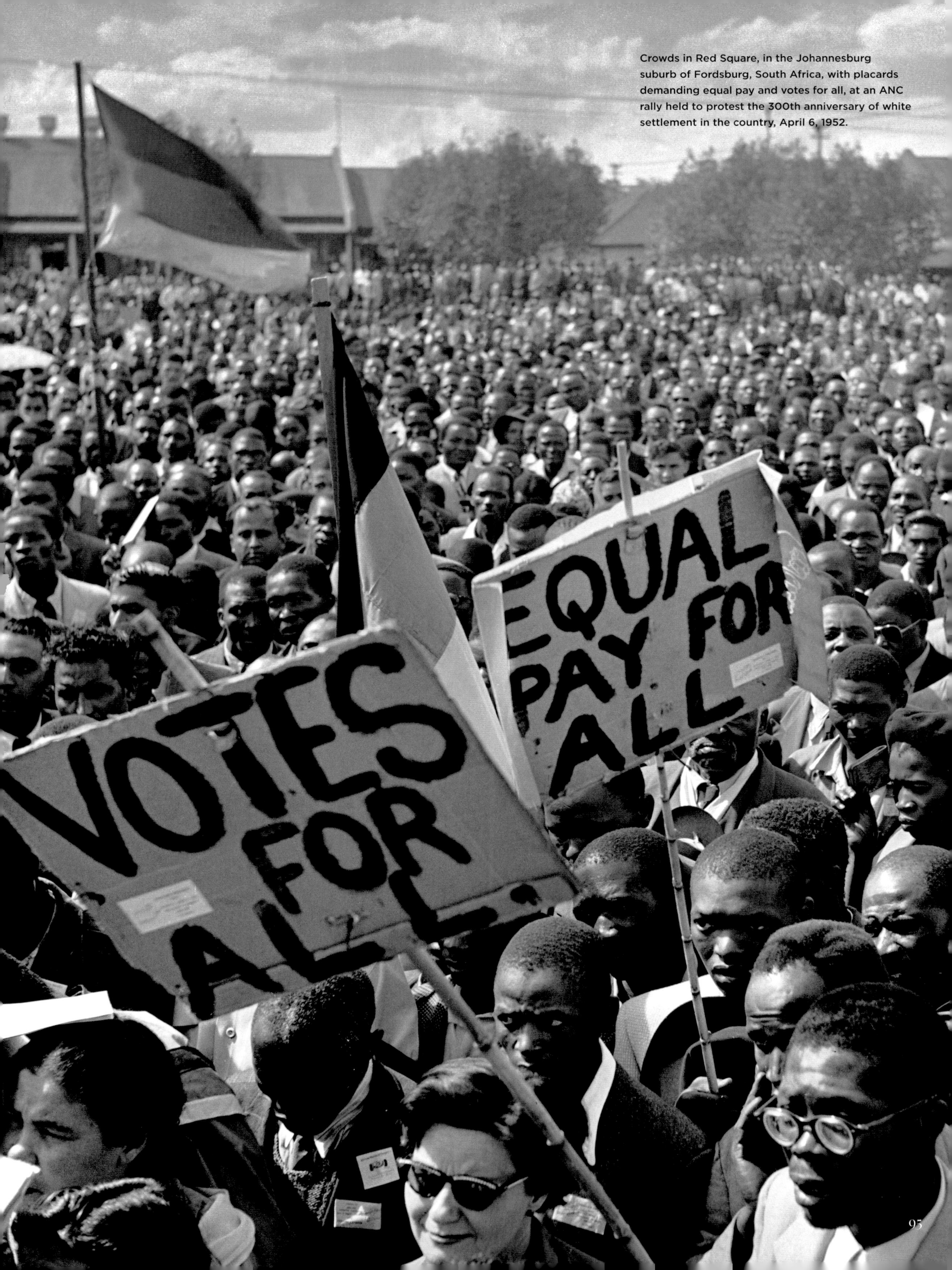

Crowds in Red Square, in the Johannesburg suburb of Fordsburg, South Africa, with placards demanding equal pay and votes for all, at an ANC rally held to protest the 300th anniversary of white settlement in the country, April 6, 1952.

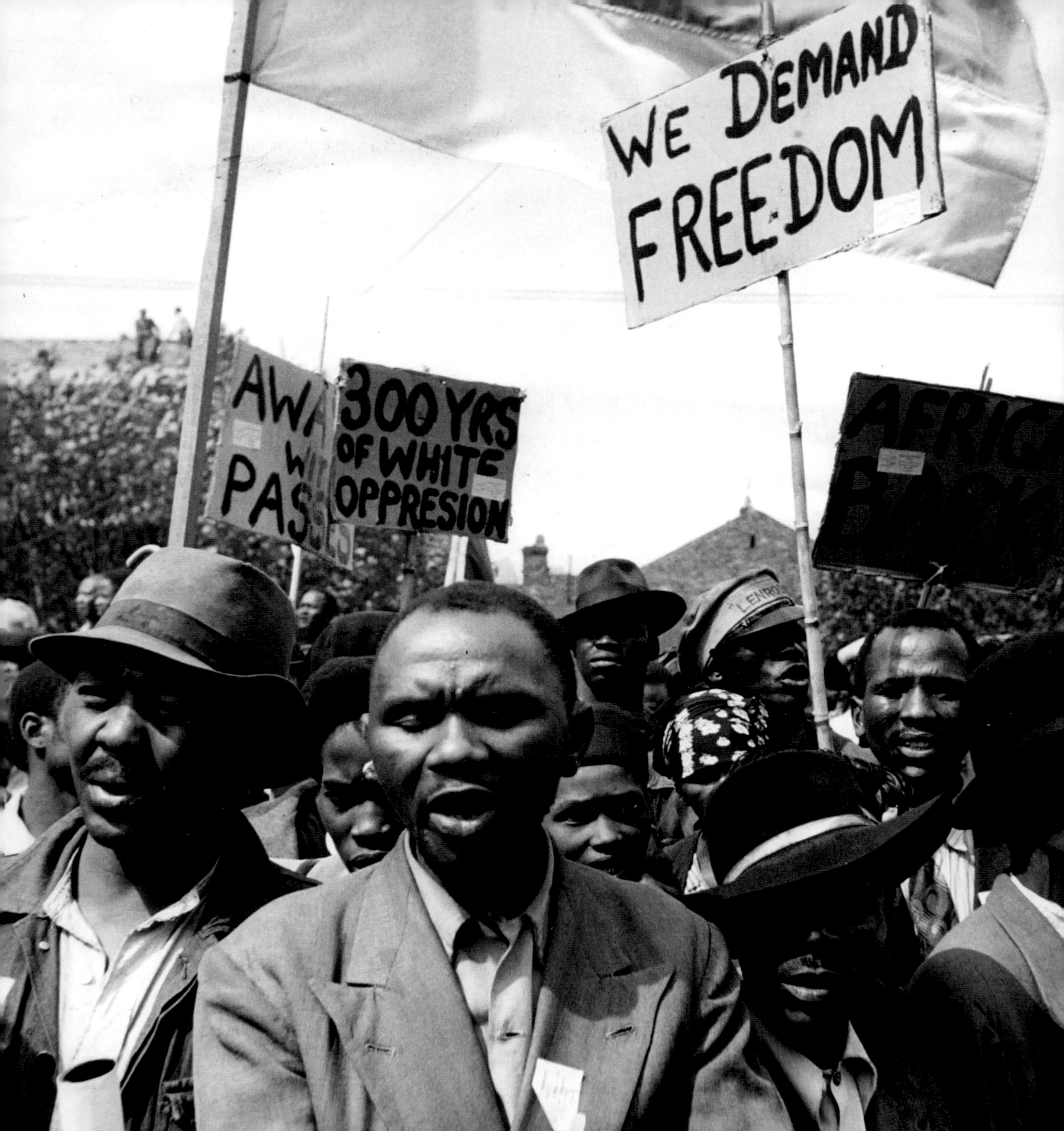

Black Africans at a Johannesburg protest defying a ban on such gatherings, 1952.

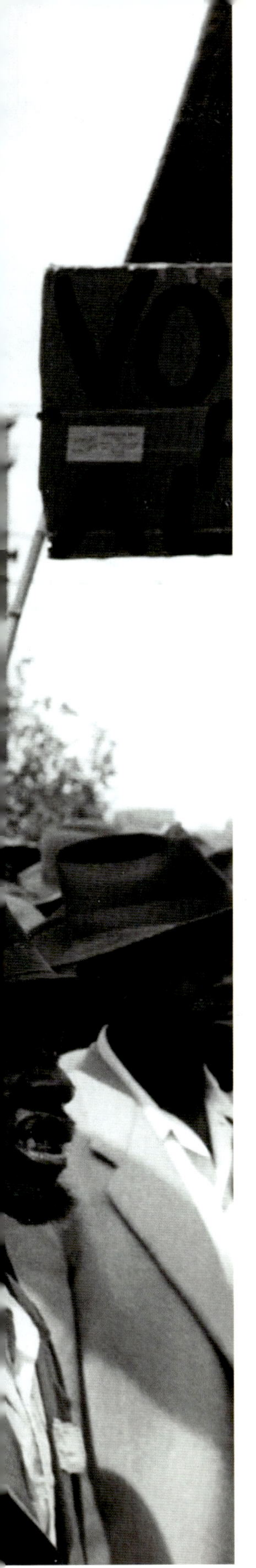

"For my own part
I have made a choice,
I will not leave South Africa,
nor will I surrender.
Only through hardship,
sacrifice, and militant action,
can freedom be won.
The struggle is my life,
I will continue fighting
for freedom until the
end of my days."

Tata's press statement, June 20, 1961

Tata's *Struggle* drawing.

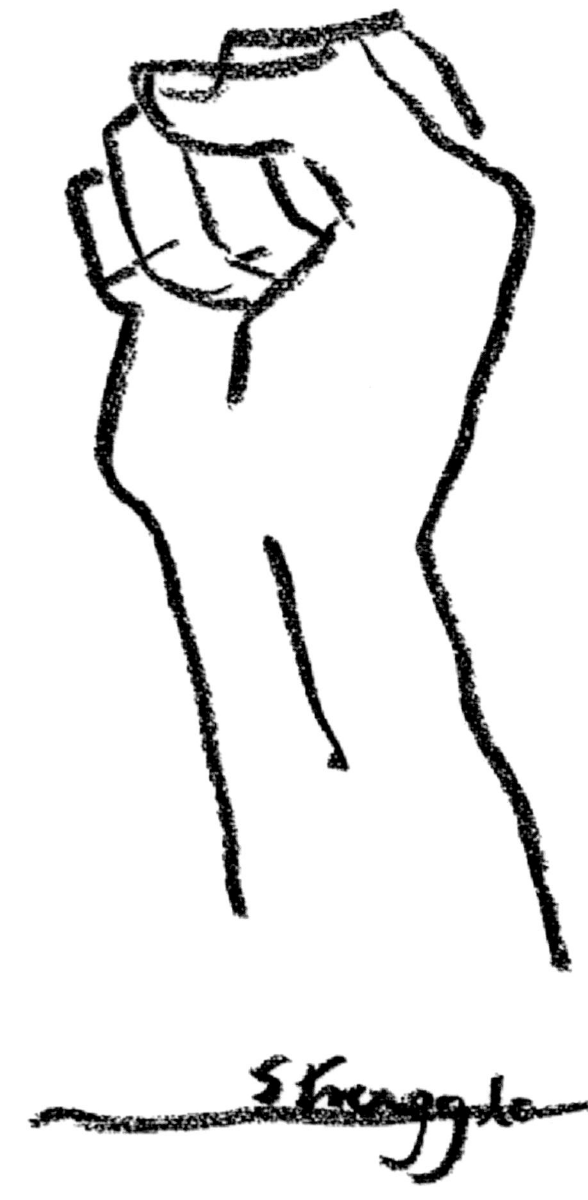

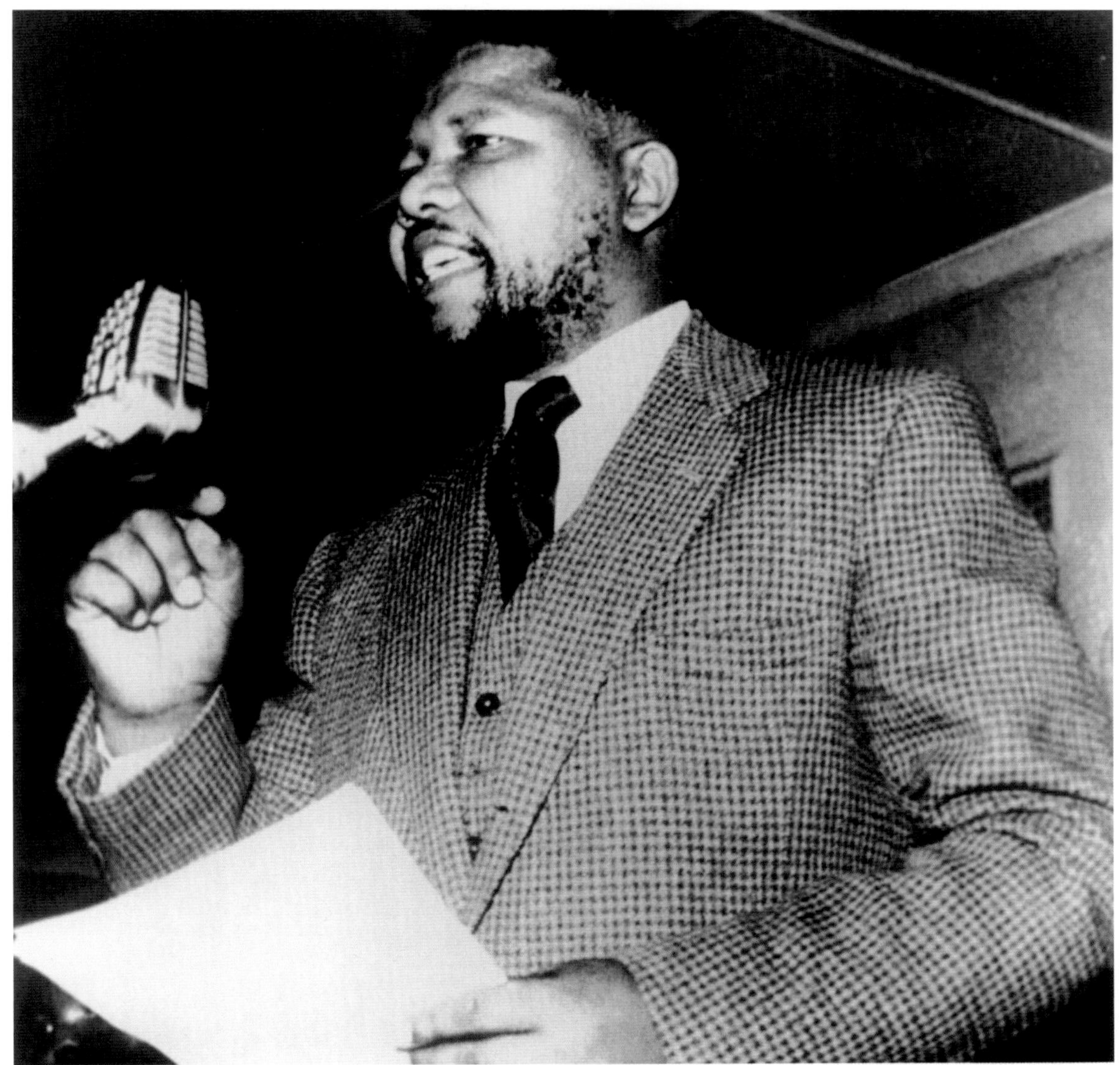

Tata during a speech to the ANC, 1961.

In 1944, Tata joined the ANC. He, Anton Lembede, A. P. Mda, Oliver Tambo, and Walter Sisulu formed the ANC Youth League in Johannesburg. Lembede was elected as the organization's first president and they adopted an Africanist and militant orientation, which rejected participation in such governmental boards as the Native Representative Council, which they perceived to be unrepresentative of Black concerns. Tata had met several communists when he was attending the University of the Witwatersrand as a part-time student, and their beliefs had an impact on his political development. The major contribution to his political formation, however, was from people who were closer to him, relatives and friends he met during his visits to Sisulu's home, where there were heated discussions about the brutal effects of apartheid on Black people. Initially the manifesto of the ANC Youth League emphasized the national liberation of Africans, which would be achieved by Africans themselves. There were opposing views about following a purely African nationalist agenda. Some Youth Leaguers felt that a nationalism that could include sympathetic whites was desirable. Ultimately, they opted for a multiracial form of struggle. In 1946, the African Mine Workers' Union strike was organized by labor activists in the ANC, such as Gaur Radebe, whom Tata had met at the Sidelsky law firm. Miners throughout South Africa, especially in the Transvaal, where most of the country's gold was mined, were paid two shillings a day. The Chamber of Mines had repeatedly ignored the union's demand to improve wages and the living conditions of the mine workers. Seventy thousand mine workers participated in the strike and, as usual, the strike was met with brutal force by the police and twelve miners died.

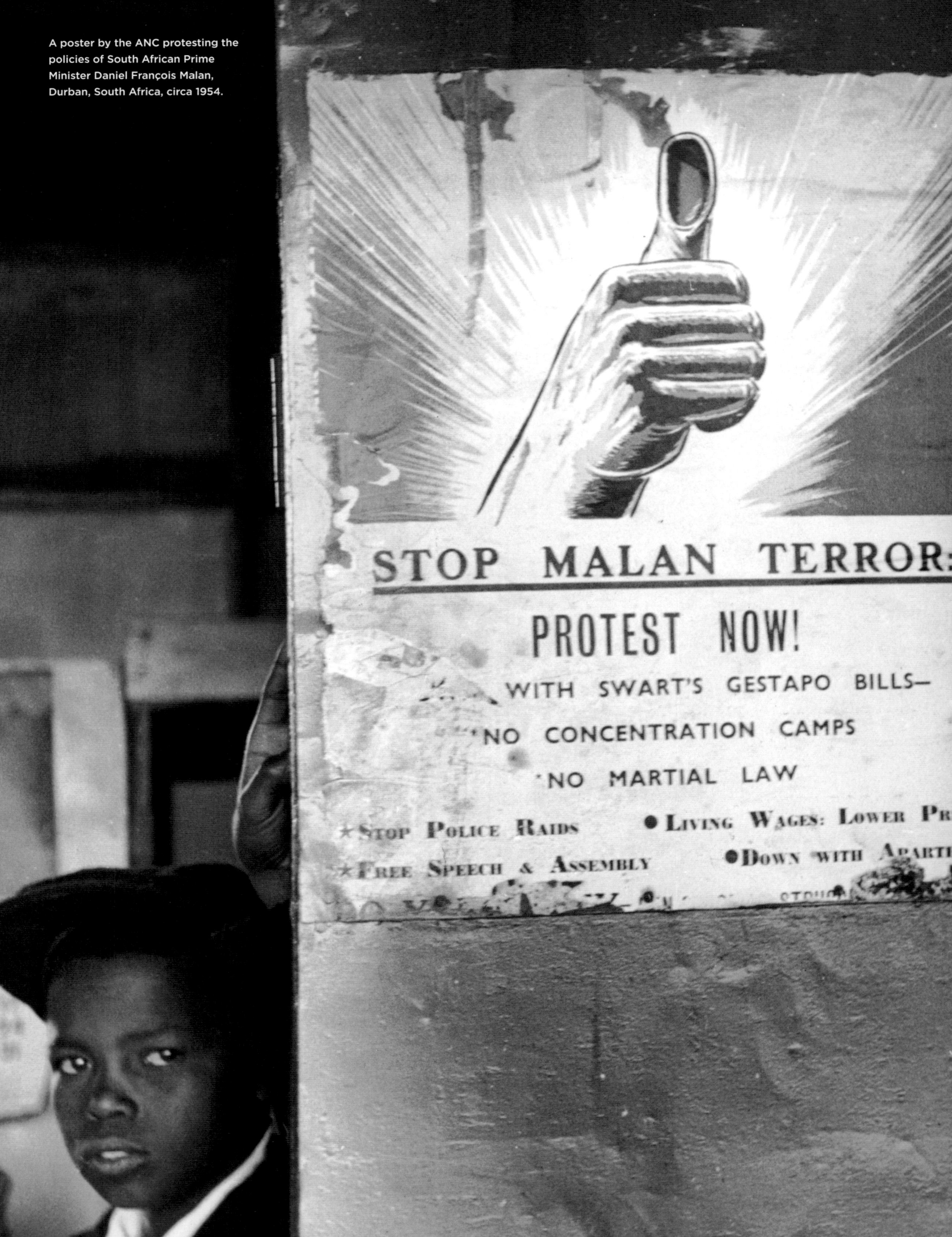

A poster by the ANC protesting the policies of South African Prime Minister Daniel François Malan, Durban, South Africa, circa 1954.

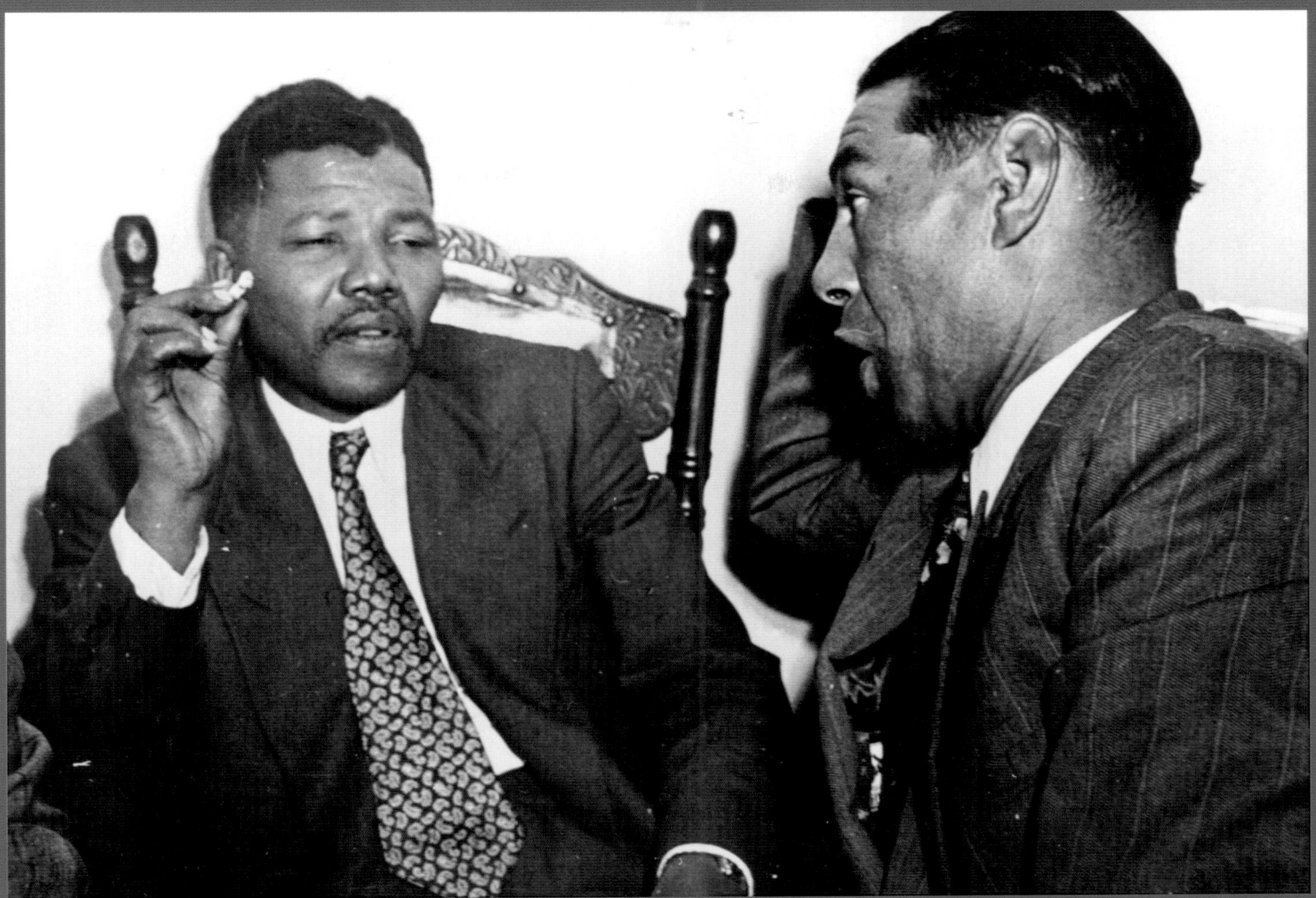

Tata in discussion with C. Andrews, a Cape Town teacher, circa 1950.

In 1947, Tata was elected to the executive committee of the ANC in the Transvaal. From that time on he became fully committed—as he said, he was bound heart and soul to the struggle against apartheid and freeing his people from racial oppression. In 1948, after the Afrikaner Nationalists won power from the British, they consolidated and solidified the racist laws in South Africa: Indians could not move freely in and out of KwaZulu-Natal; Africans were not allowed to vote or move freely, among other oppressive laws. Within weeks, the apartheid government curbed trade unions, scrapped the limited franchises of the Indian, Colored, and African people, and prohibited mixed marriages. The Immorality Act quickly followed, making sexual relations between whites and non-whites illegal. The Population Registration Act labeled all South Africans by race, making physical appearance the single most defining factor of an individual.

When the Group Areas Act was passed in 1950, it imposed control over interracial property transactions and property occupation throughout South Africa. It created a framework for varying levels of government to establish particular neighborhoods where only Blacks or whites could reside. The Group Areas Act was used to demolish all the houses in certain areas and displace everyone who was not of the designated group; hundreds of thousands of people were ultimately affected. This happened in both urban and rural areas where the land was either fertile or had valuable mineral resources.

The act, designed to support apartheid, perpetuated the status quo of white supremacy and resulted in the continued control of the African labor market to support rapid economic development.

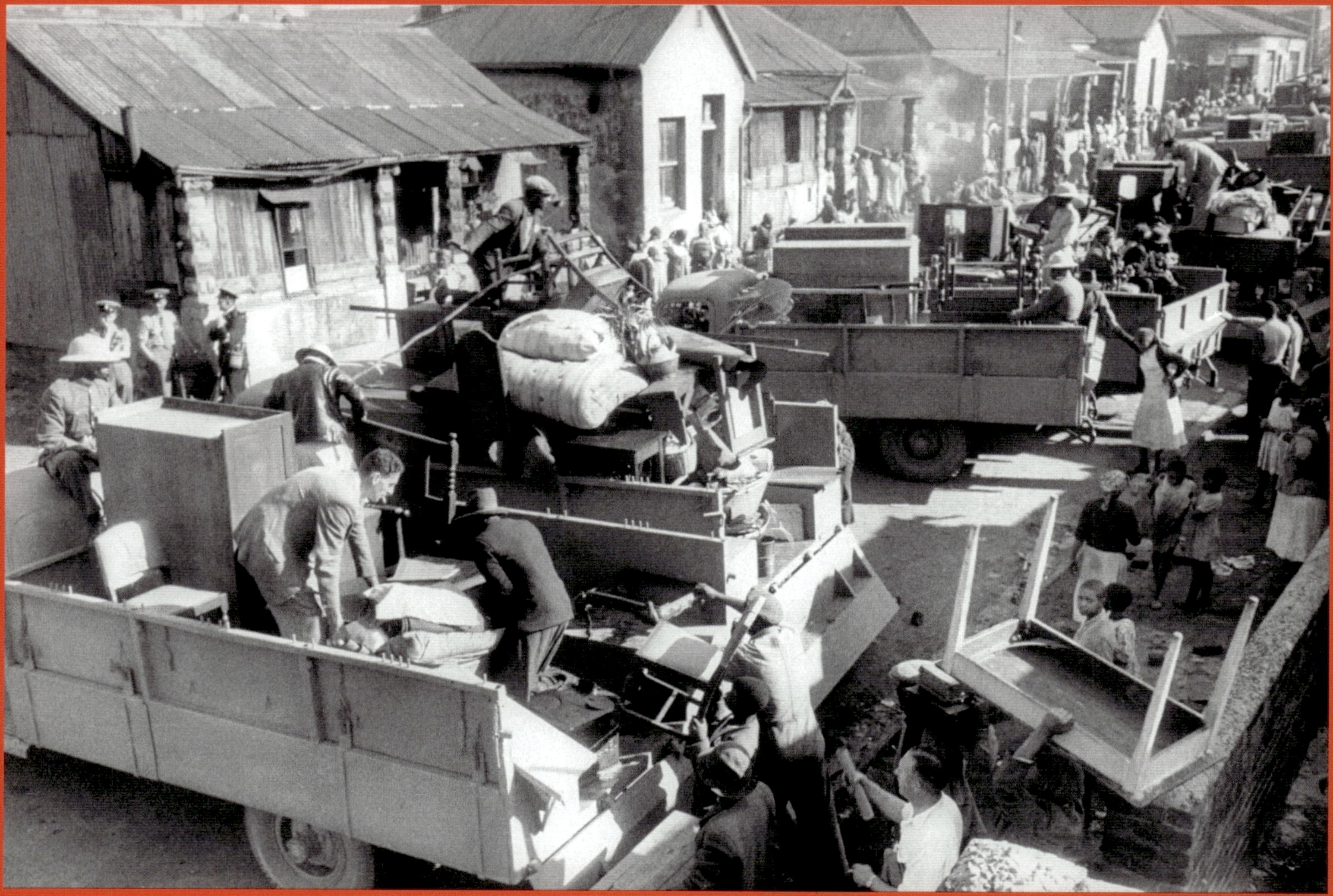

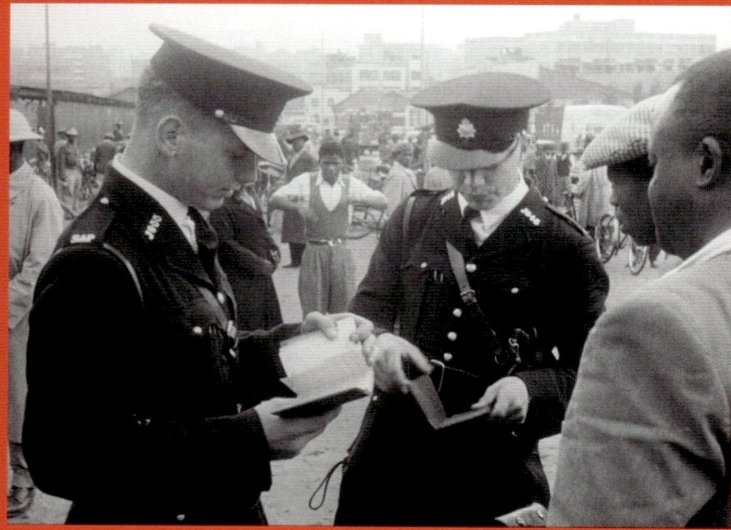

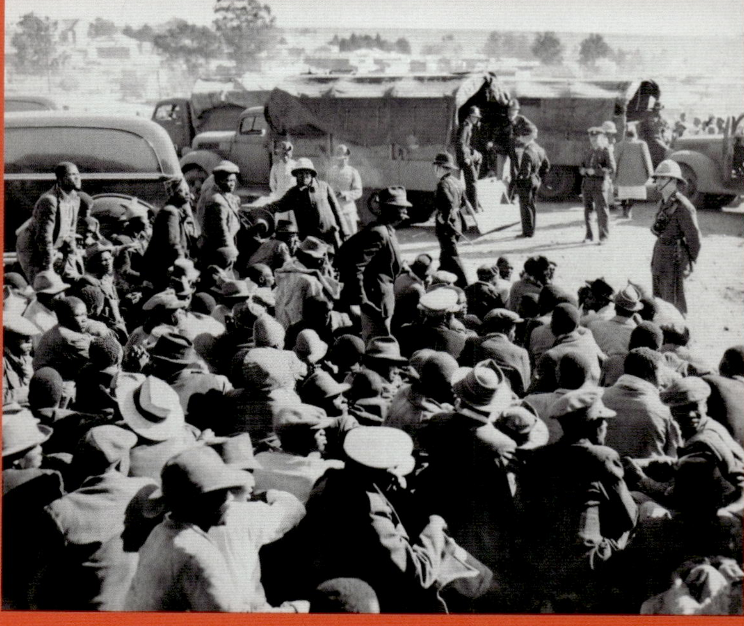

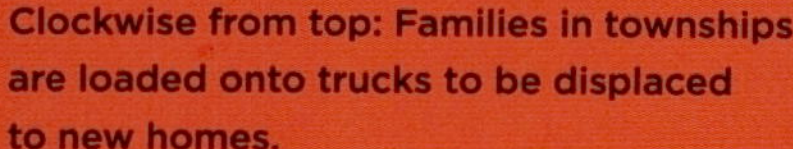

Clockwise from top: Families in townships are loaded onto trucks to be displaced to new homes.

Non-whites being detained by police in a township of Johannesburg, 1947.

Non-whites are required to carry passbooks. Here a policeman and an interpreter check the papers of a man bound for Johannesburg to spend six months working in the mines.

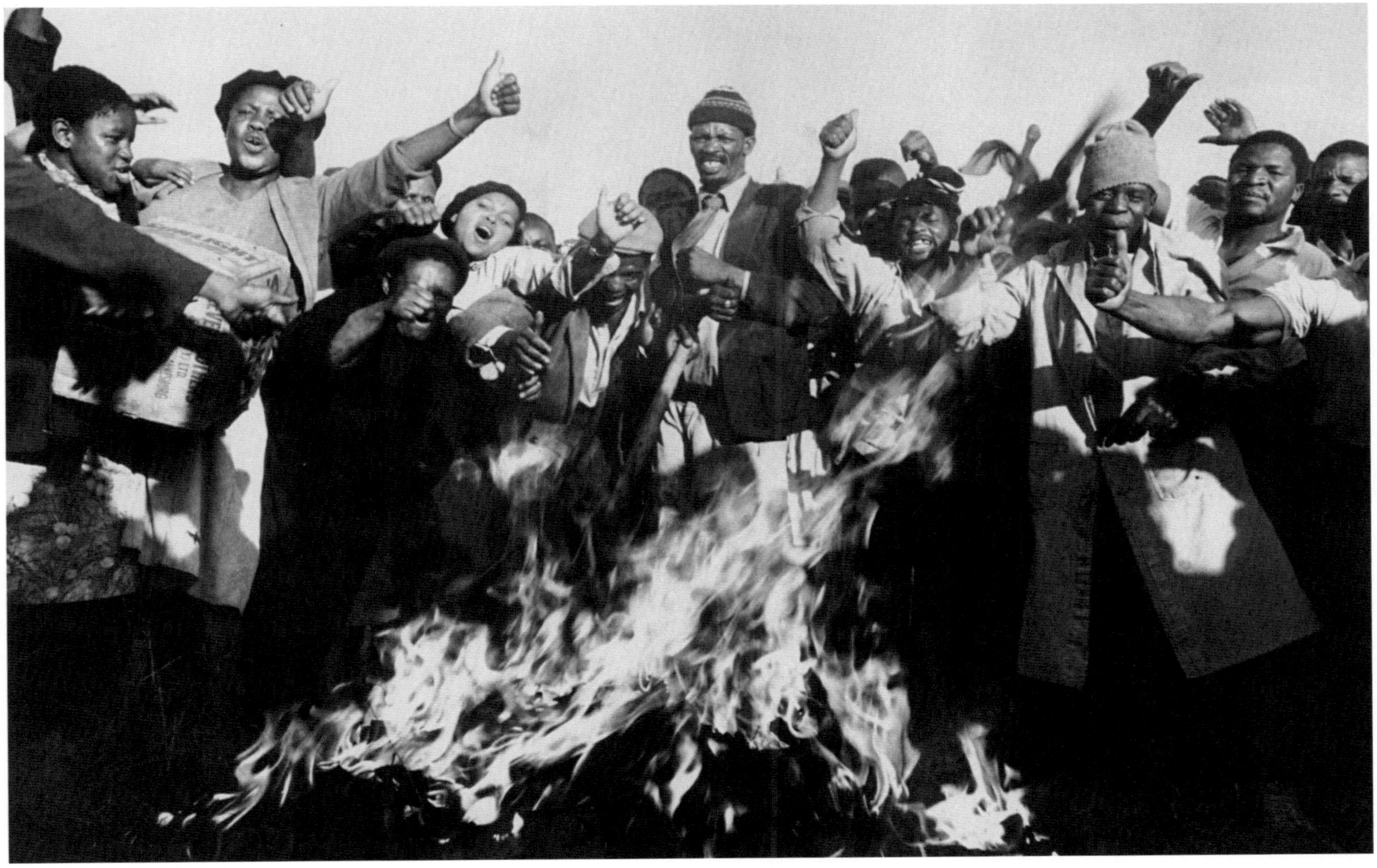

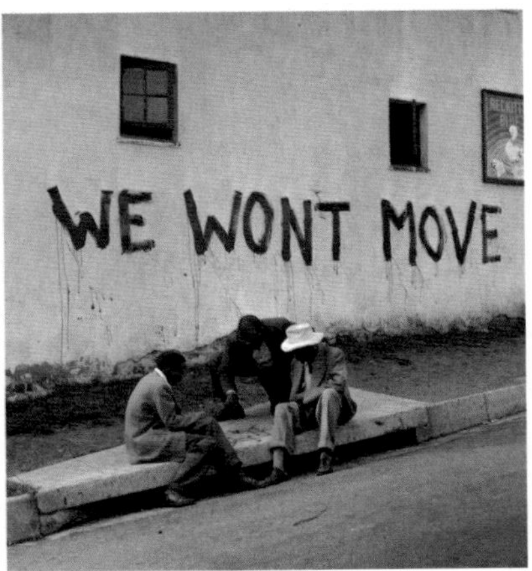

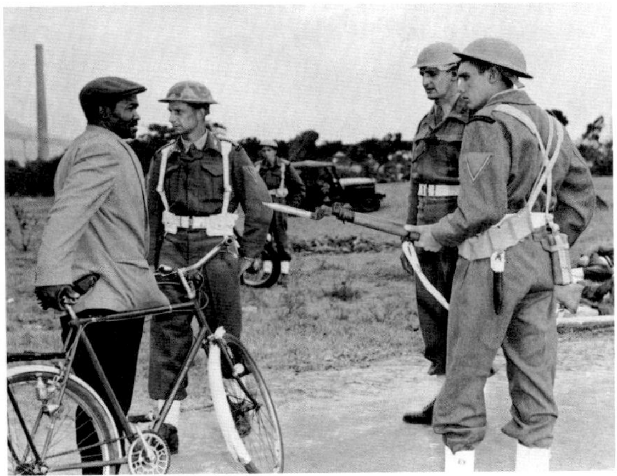

Clockwise from above: Protesters burning African passbooks during a race riot.

Despite the official state of emergency, Black protesters tried to march to Cape Town to demand the release of Black leaders arrested after the Sharpeville Massacre, March 21, 1960.

The slogan "We Won't Move" appears on a wall in Sophiatown, a suburb of Johannesburg, 1955. The Group Areas Act of 1950 allowed the government to relocate the Black inhabitants of Sophiatown to the surrounding countryside, having allocated specific living areas to people of specific races.

Forced removals took place in many cities and towns of South Africa. The oppressive segregation laws led to the creation of the Defiance Campaign, which became the largest nonviolent resistance in South Africa of that era, and marked the first time all racial groups joined forces under the leadership of the ANC and the South African Indian Congress. The Defiance Campaign was launched on June 26, 1952—people were asked not to go to work as an act of rebellion, and it was dubbed the National Day of Protest and Mourning. People burned their passbooks or entered places that were designated "whites only," which was against the law. By December, 8,067 protesters across the country had been arrested. Although the offenses were minor and relatively small penalties were imposed, the government became concerned and reacted by arresting national leaders. All were charged under the Suppression of Communism Act, but were released on bail.

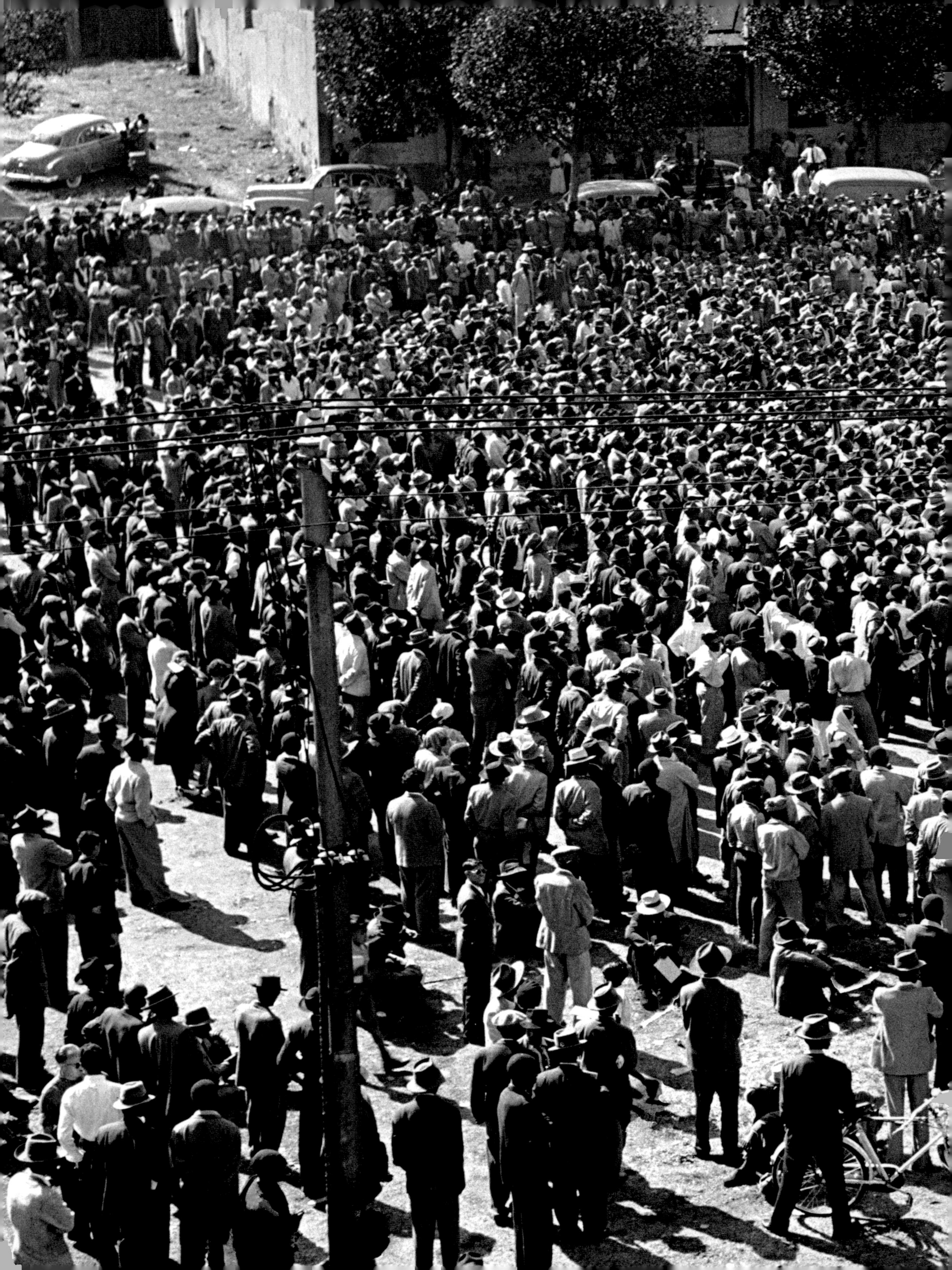

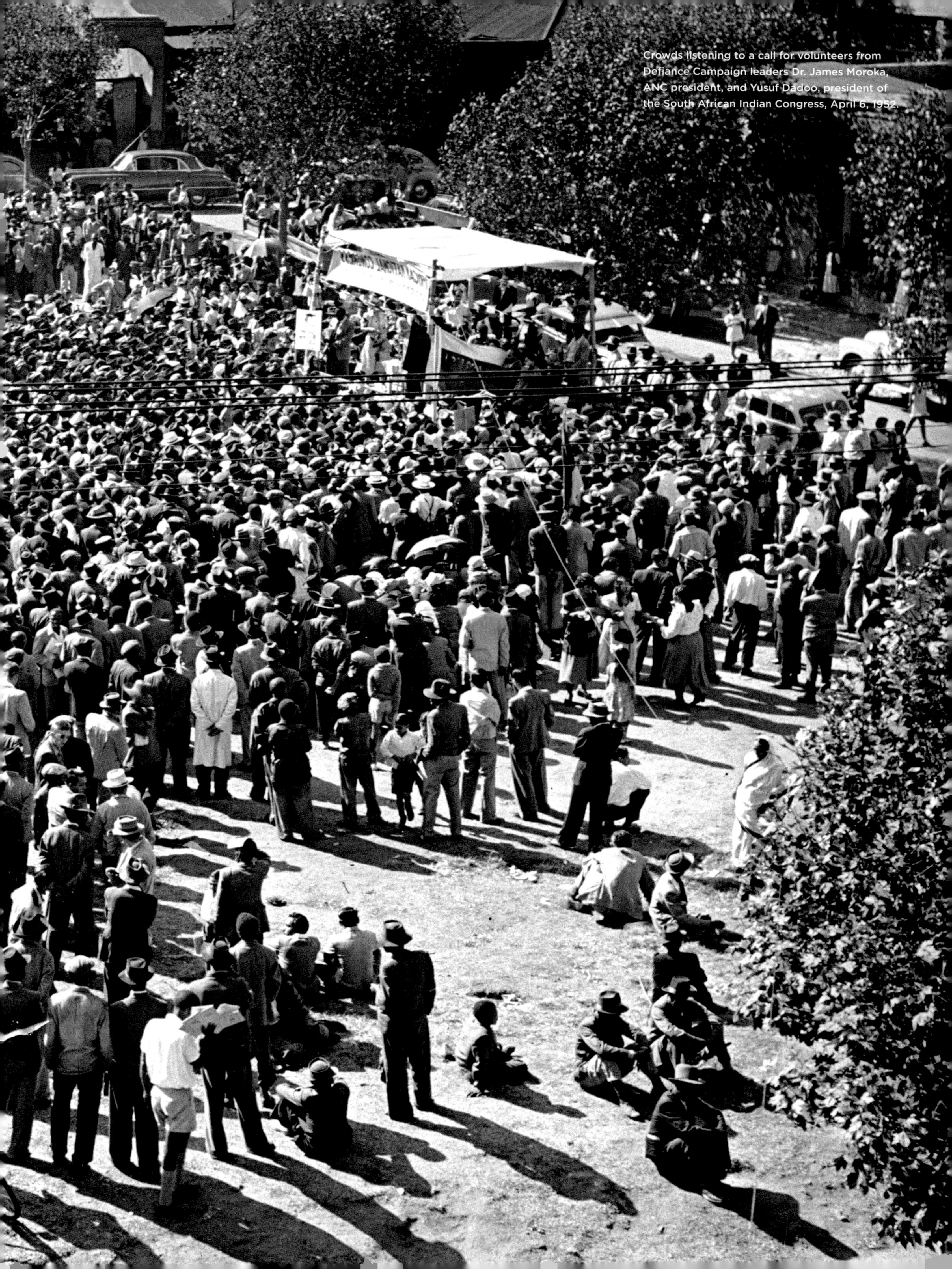

Crowds listening to a call for volunteers from Defiance Campaign leaders Dr. James Moroka, ANC president, and Yusuf Dadoo, president of the South African Indian Congress, April 6, 1952.

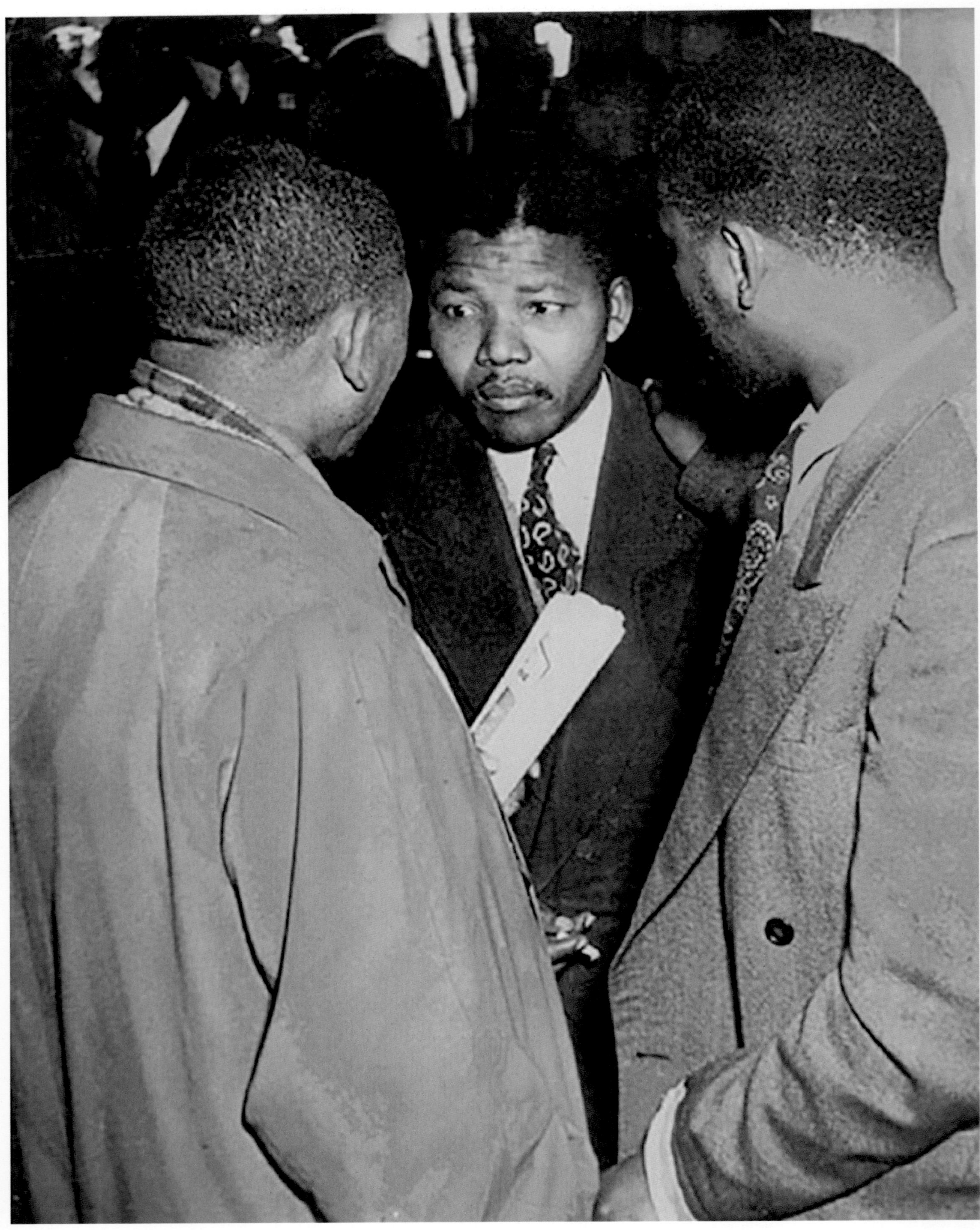

Dr. Moroka, Tata, and Dadoo
during the 1952 Defiance Campaign.

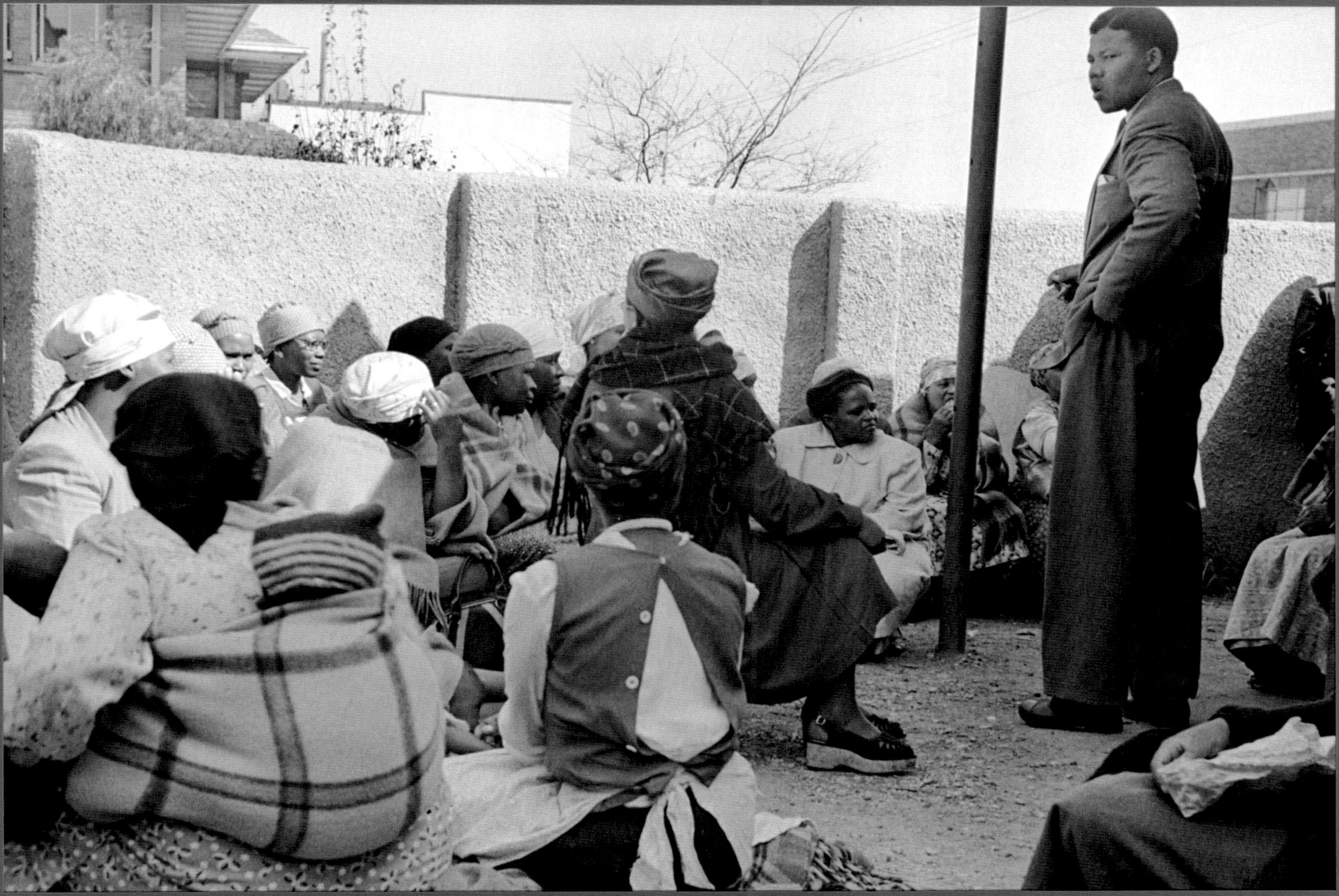

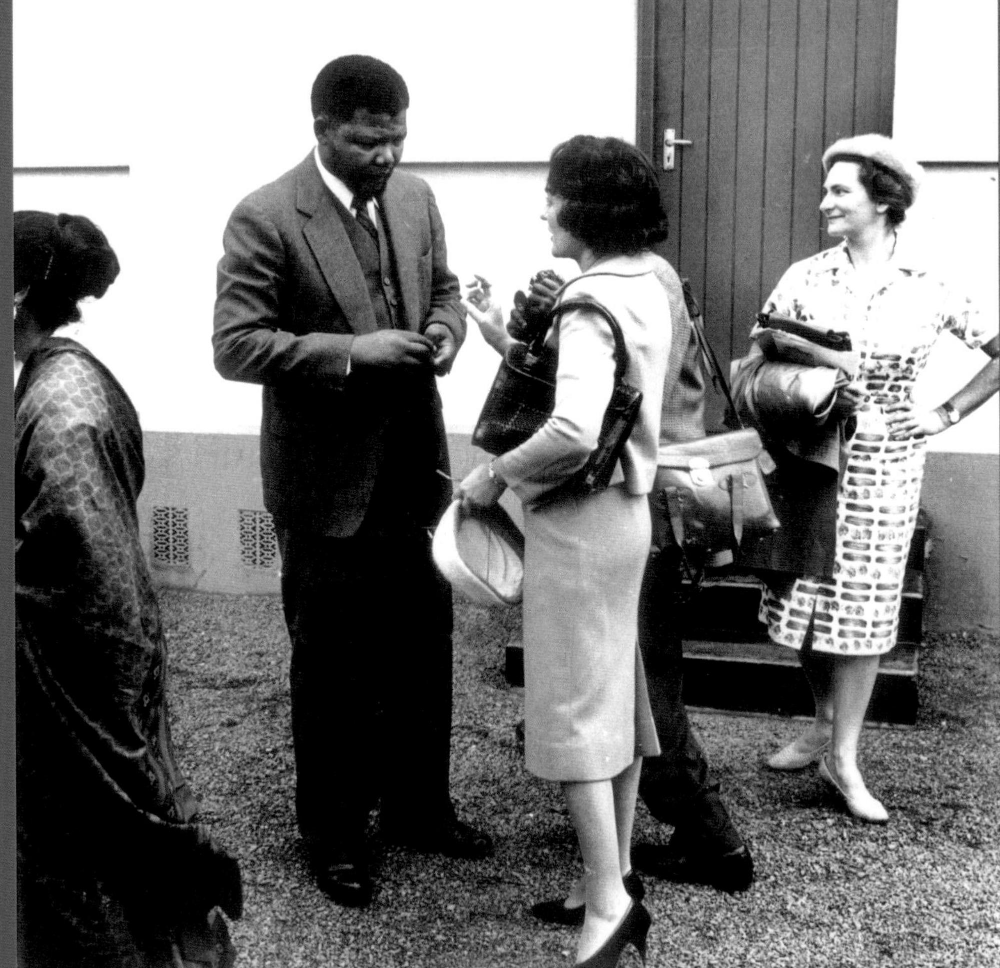

Above: Tata addressing a group of twenty-one women he represented before their court appearance on charges of public disturbance. It was alleged that the women roared, shouted, made noises, and quarreled, thereby attracting a crowd, or engaged in other riotous behavior. The women pleaded not guilty, May 1955.

Left: Tata speaking with journalist and political activist Ruth First.

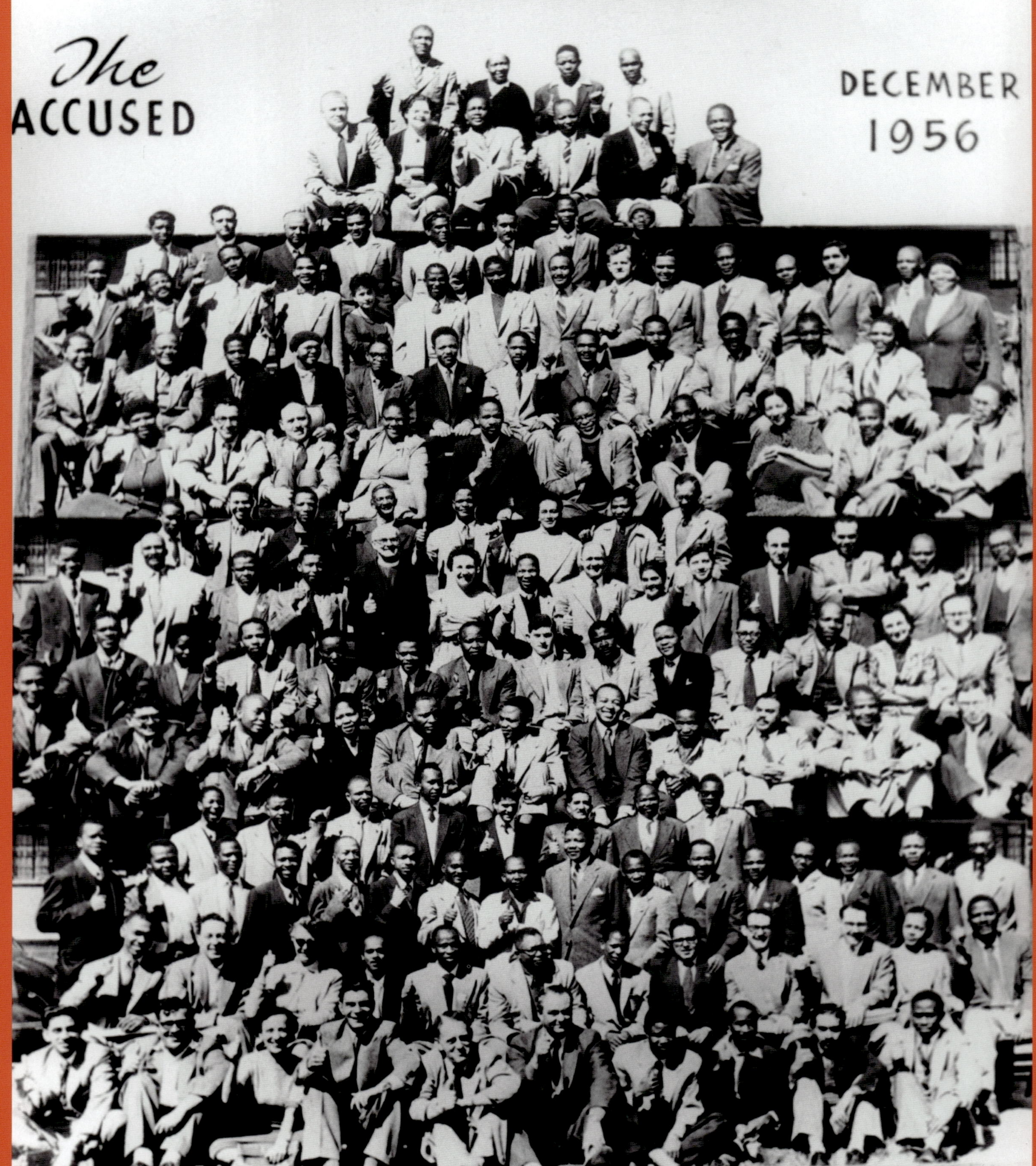

More than 150 Congress leaders were arrested in 1956. Tata is in the center of the third row from the bottom.

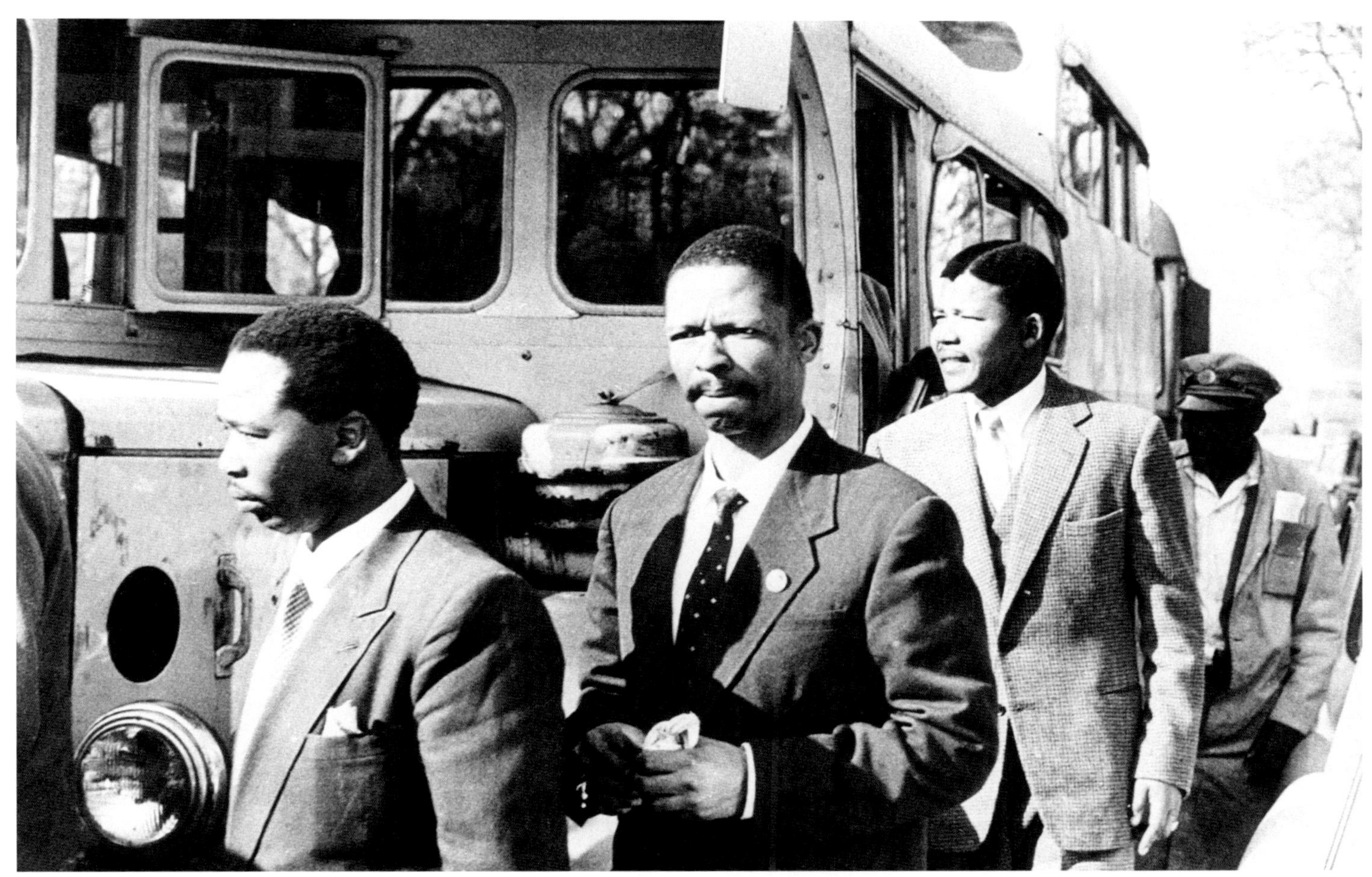

Tata arrives with ANC colleagues at the Pretoria High Court for the 1956 Treason Trial.

"Apartheid is the embodiment of racialism, oppression, and inhumanity of all previous white supremacist regimes. To see the real face of apartheid, we must look beneath the veil of constitutional formulas, deceptive phrases, and playing with words."

Tata's statement published by the ANC in 1976, while he was on Robben Island

In 1956, in an escalation by the government, leading figures from the ANC, along with other organizers, were arrested on charges of high treason and tried under an indictment covering a period that began on October 1, 1952. Arrests occurred all over the country during the peaceful protests of the Defiance Campaign, and its existence marked a new chapter in the struggle for freedom. The ANC grew to 100,000 members and it emerged as a grassroots-based organization. Tata felt a great sense of accomplishment and satisfaction. The campaign freed him from any lingering sense of doubt or inferiority. It liberated him from being overwhelmed by the power and seeming invincibility of the white man and his institutions. Tata felt that he now was a true freedom fighter.

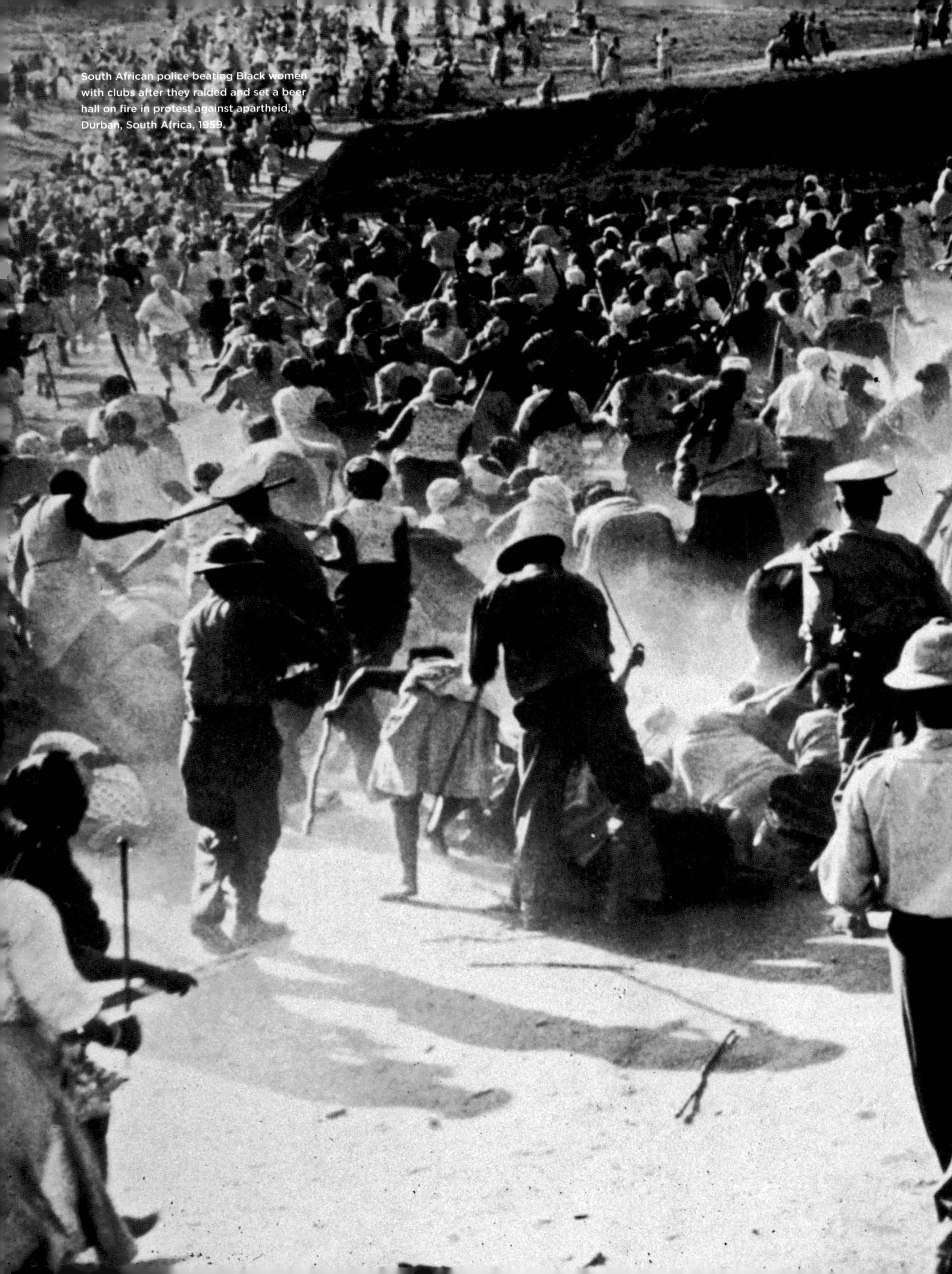

South African police beating Black women with clubs after they raided and set a beer hall on fire in protest against apartheid, Durban, South Africa, 1959.

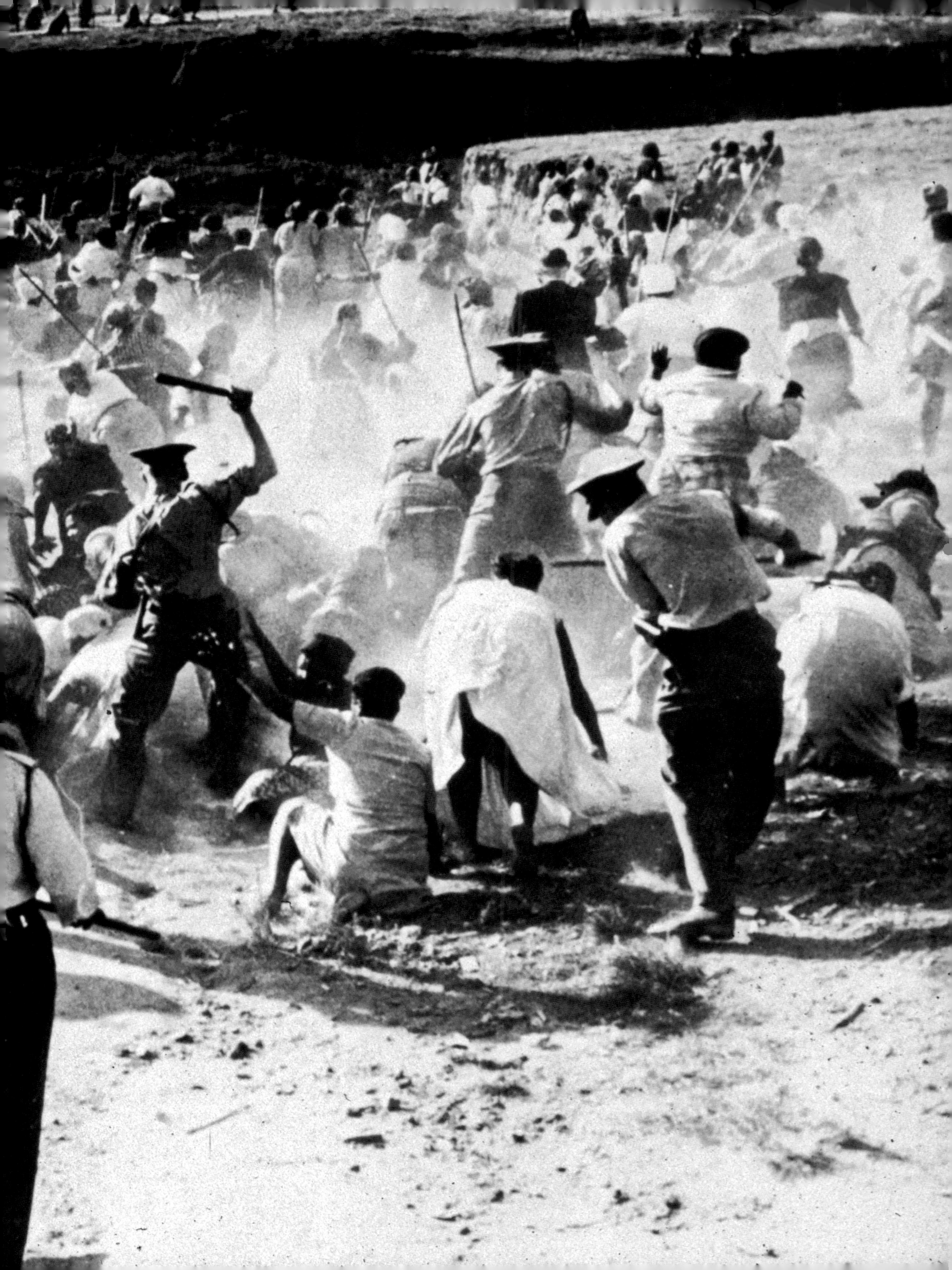

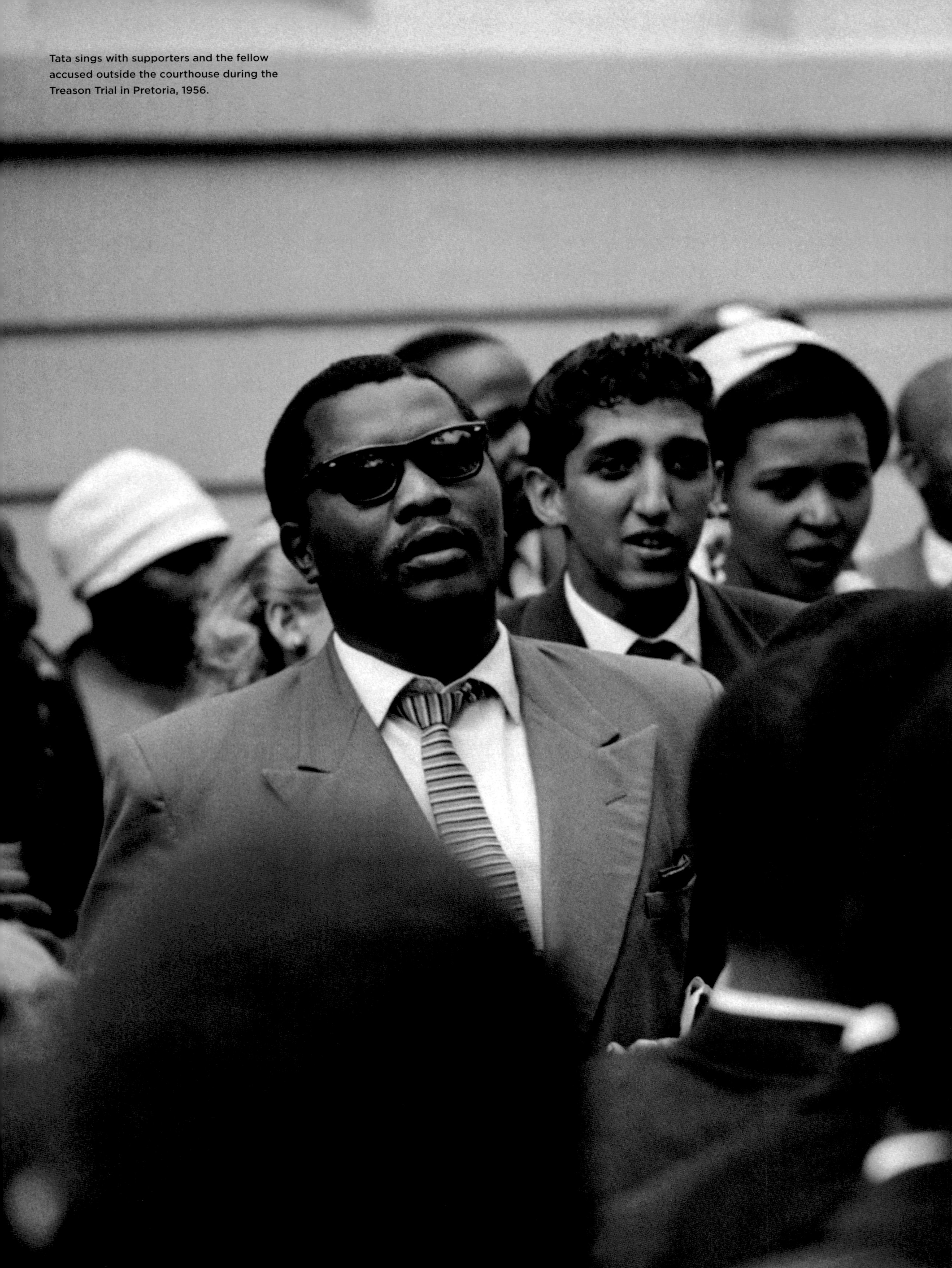

Tata sings with supporters and the fellow accused outside the courthouse during the Treason Trial in Pretoria, 1956.

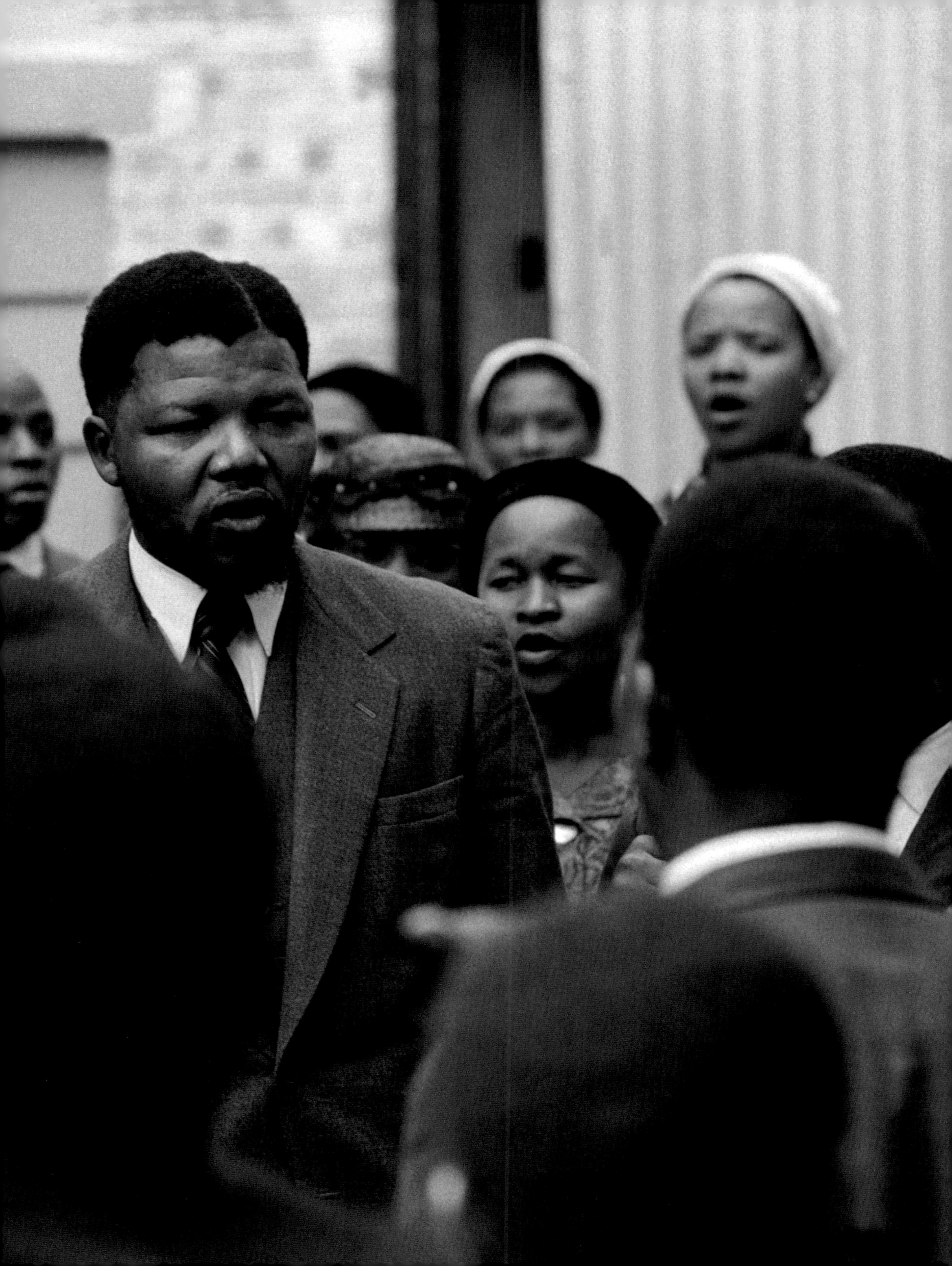

These photographs were taken on the rooftop of a newspaper building in September 1957 in the Johannesburg central business district. Tata, a fan of boxing, was persuaded to take time off for relaxation during the Treason Trial, and photographer Bob Gosani managed to persuade him, after a day of sitting in the dock, to shadowbox with professional featherweight champion Jerry Moloi. These widely seen images were originally published in *Tauza: Bob Gosani's People*, the iconic photography book of 1950s South Africa.

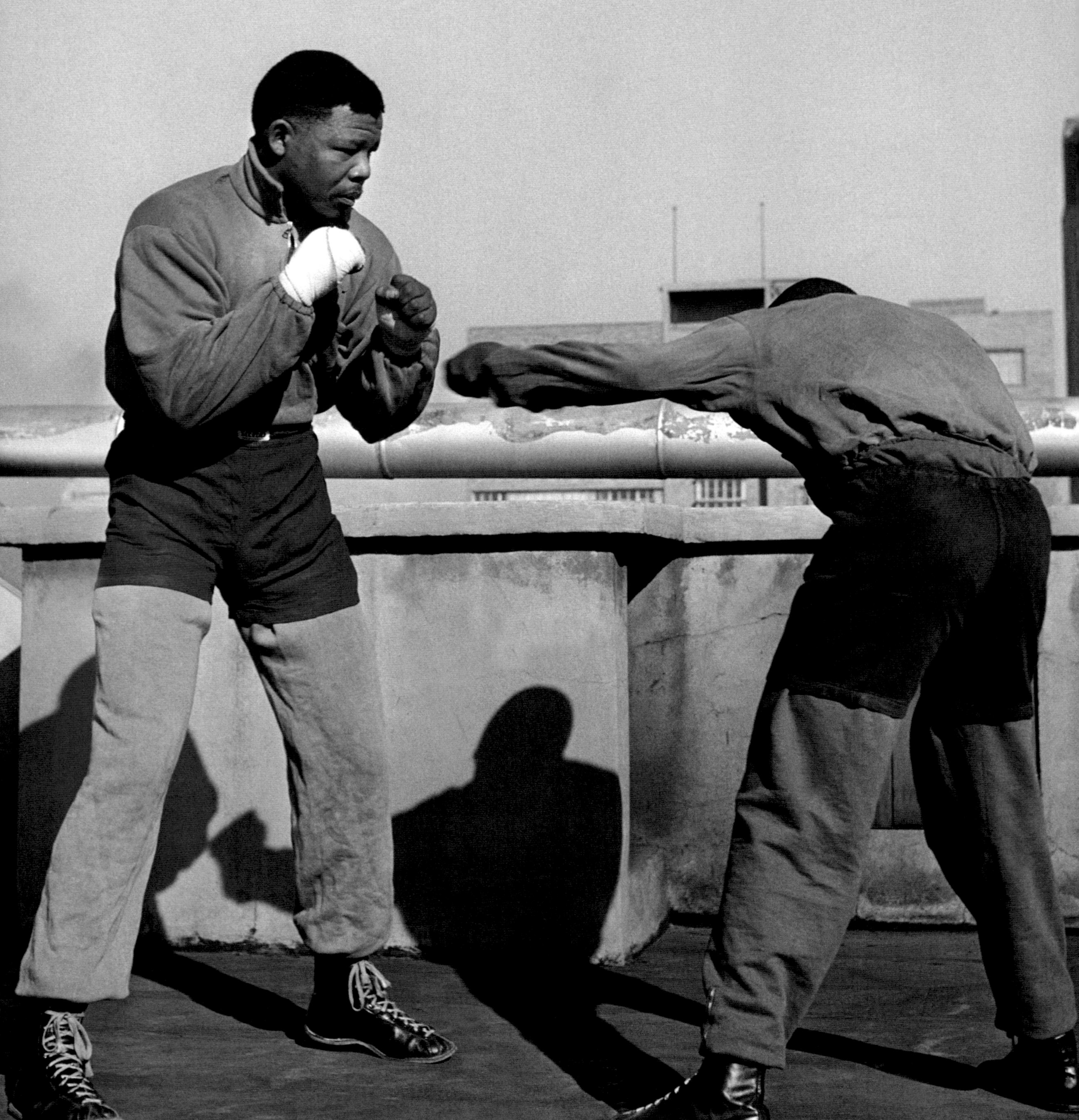

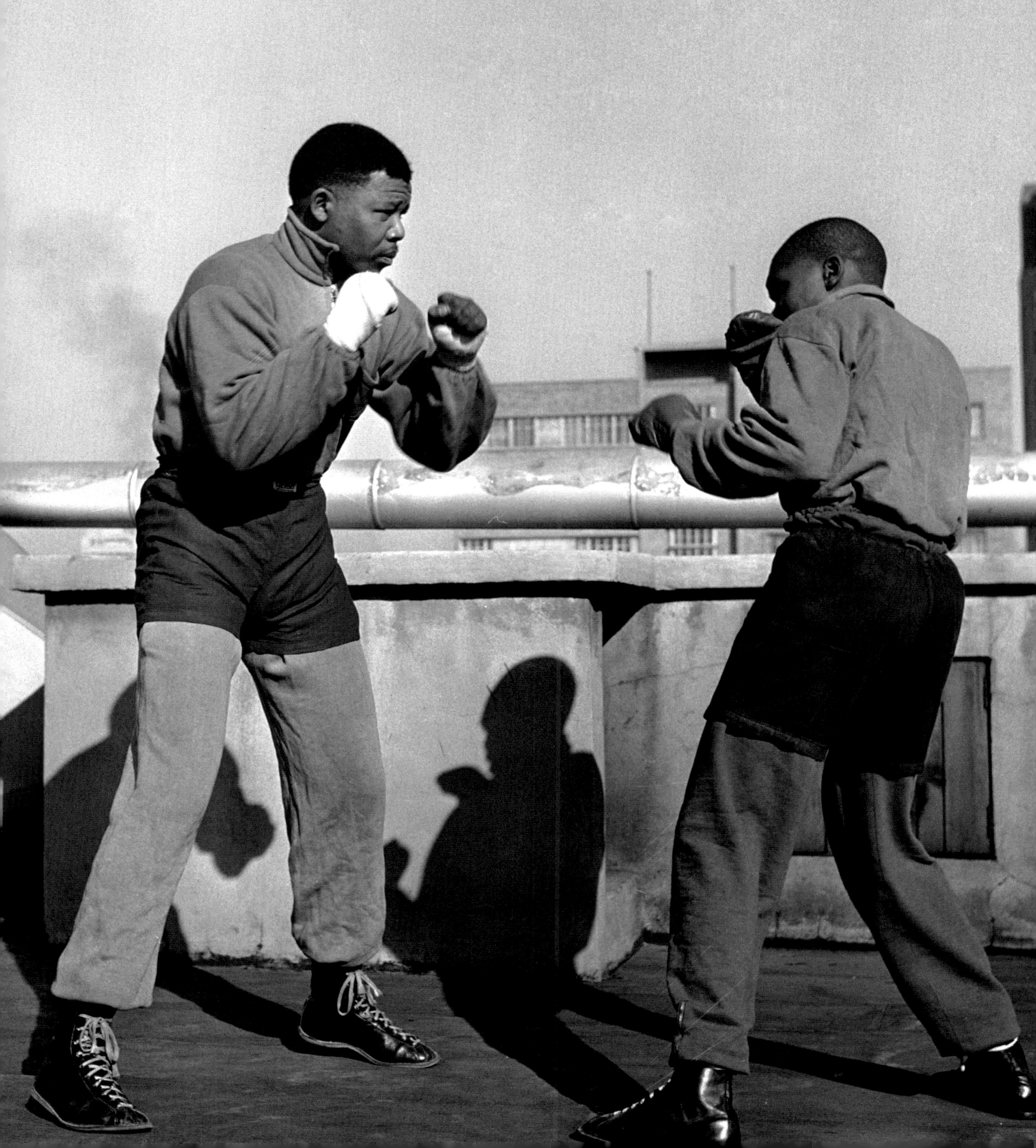

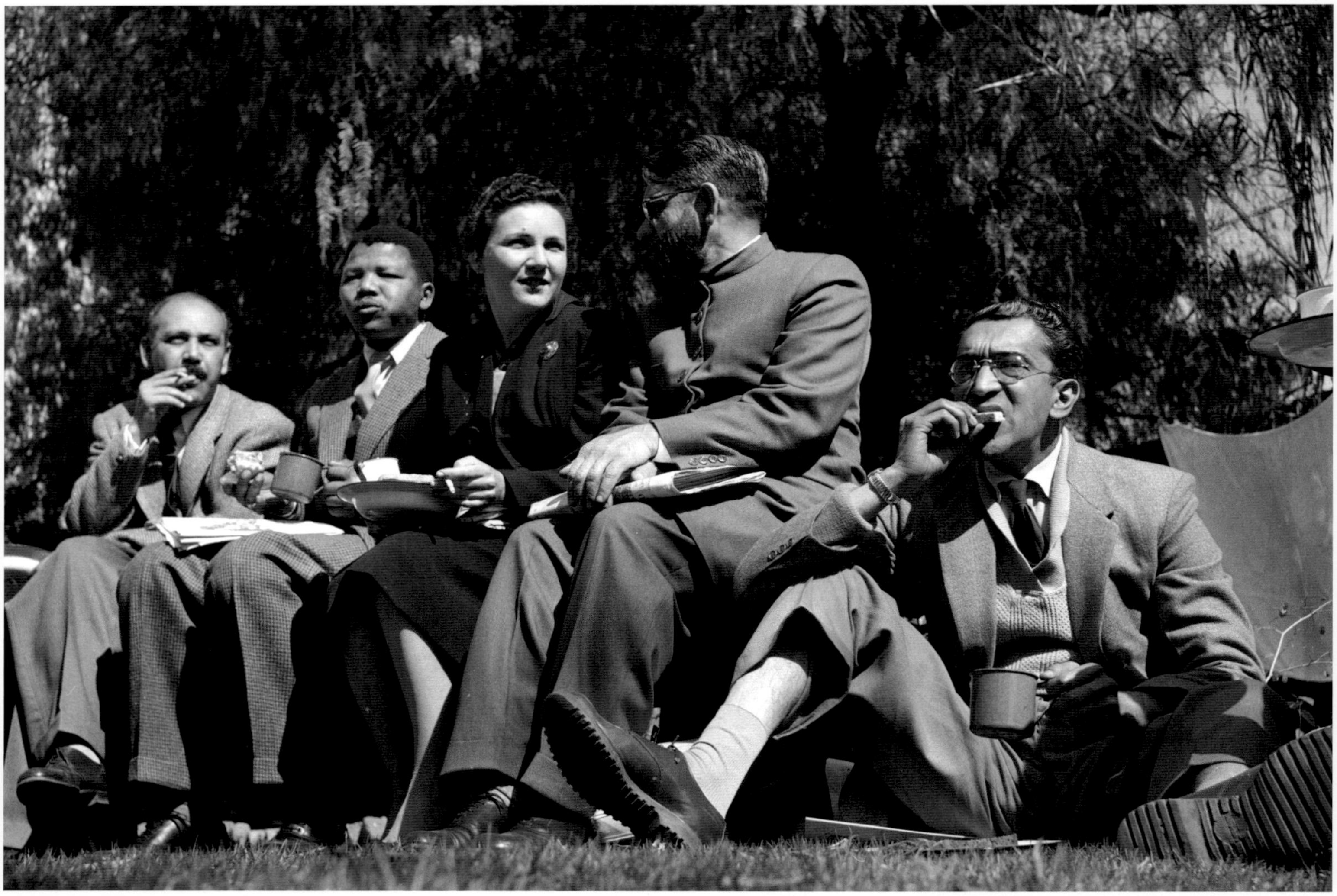

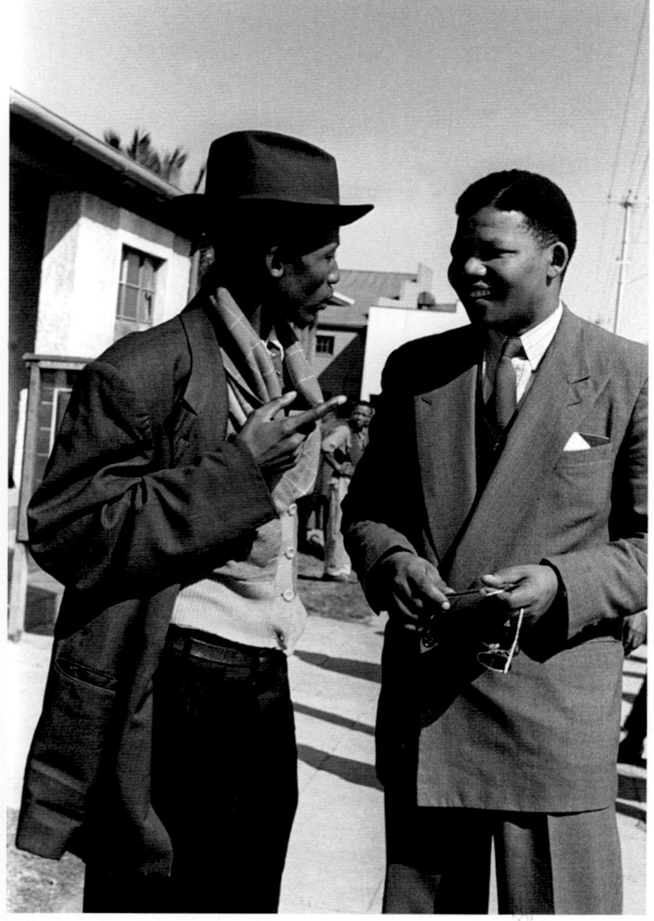

Above: Tata taking a tea or lunch break during the Treason Trial at the old synagogue, which was converted into a court, September 1958. The trial, of 156 people, lasted from 1956 to 1961.

Left: Tata with Peter Nthite, another Youth League leader in the ANC, during a lunch break at the Treason Trial, circa 1958.

Opposite: Defendants Moses Kotane and Tata leave a courtroom during the Treason Trial, 1958.

"We plan to make government impossible. There would be other forms of mass pressure to force the race maniacs who govern our beloved country to make way for a democratic government of the people, by the people, and for the people. To seek for cheap martyrdom by handing myself to the police is naive and criminal. I have chosen this latter course, which is more difficult and which entails more risk and hardship than jail. I have had to separate myself from my dear wife and children, from my mother, and sisters, to live as an outlaw in my own land. I have had to close my business (the Mandela Tambo Law Firm) to abandon my profession, and live in poverty and misery."

Press statement issued by Tata while in hiding, June 26, 1960

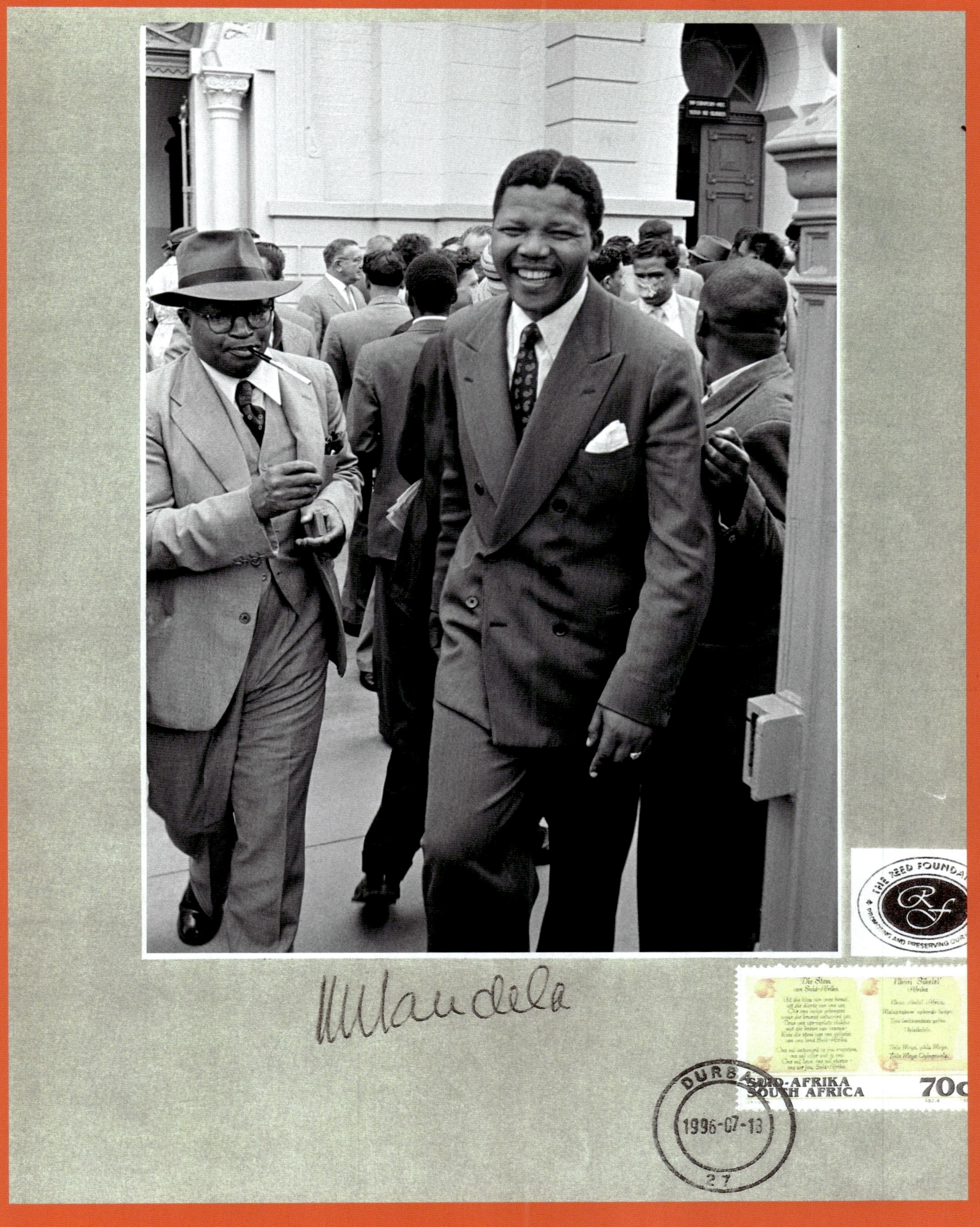

The arrest of all 156 leaders of the ANC, Indian Congress, Cape Coloured Congress, and the unions in 1956 was intended to break the power of the Congress Alliance once and for all, since previous measures by the government had not worked. The accused faced charges claiming that they had participated actively in the campaign to create the Freedom Charter. According to the prosecution, the charter called for the abolition of all racial discrimination and the granting of equal rights to all. Combined with the slogan "Freedom

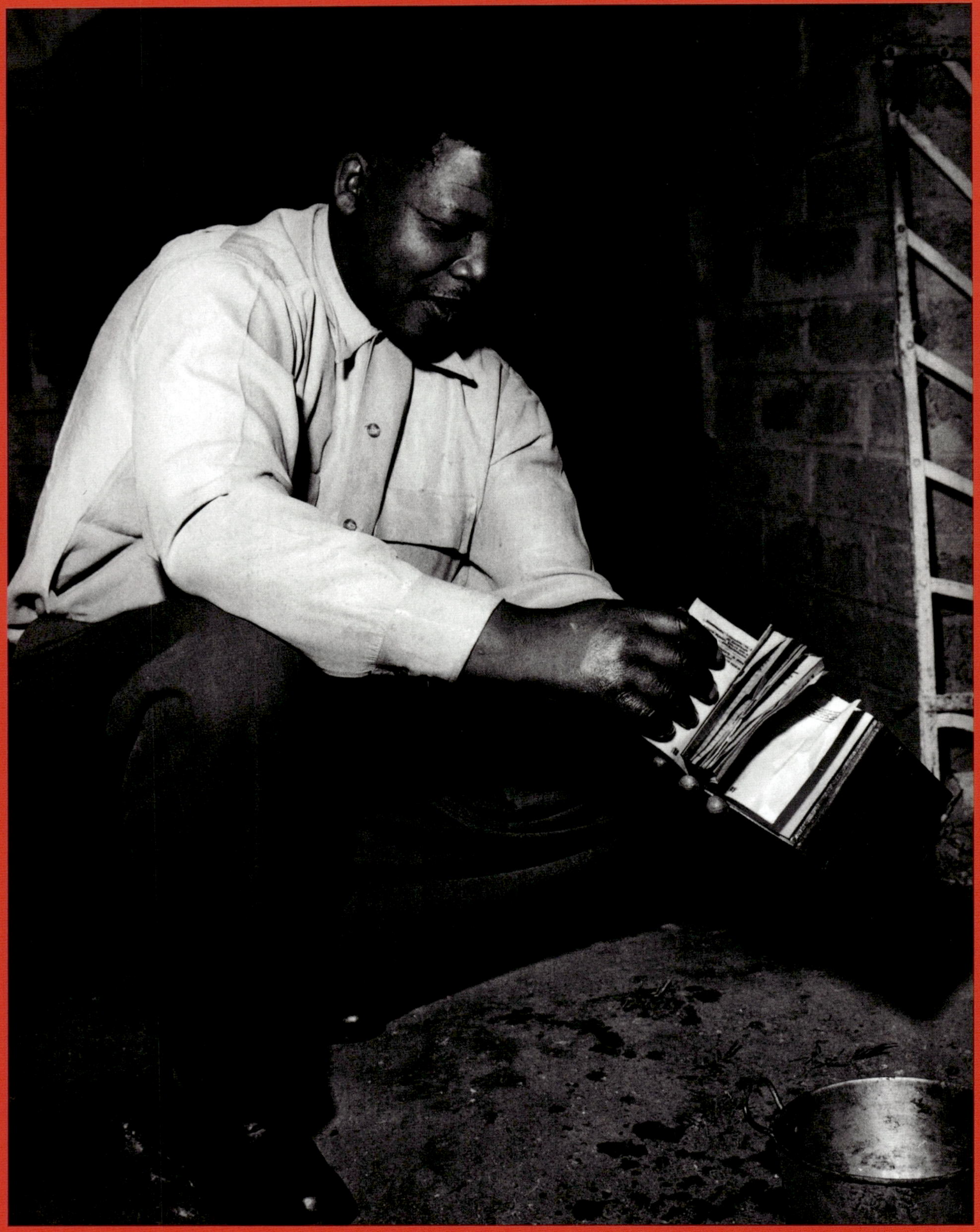

Tata burning his passbook in protest of the Sharpeville Massacre. He was at home under house orders prohibiting him from attending political gatherings or moving out of Johannesburg.

Tata learned through experience that fighting the brutal system of apartheid was a lonely, painful journey. He was banned from participating in any political activity and his movements were restricted. Banning was meant to break one's spirit—emotionally and psychologically. During this period Tata longed for freedom of movement.

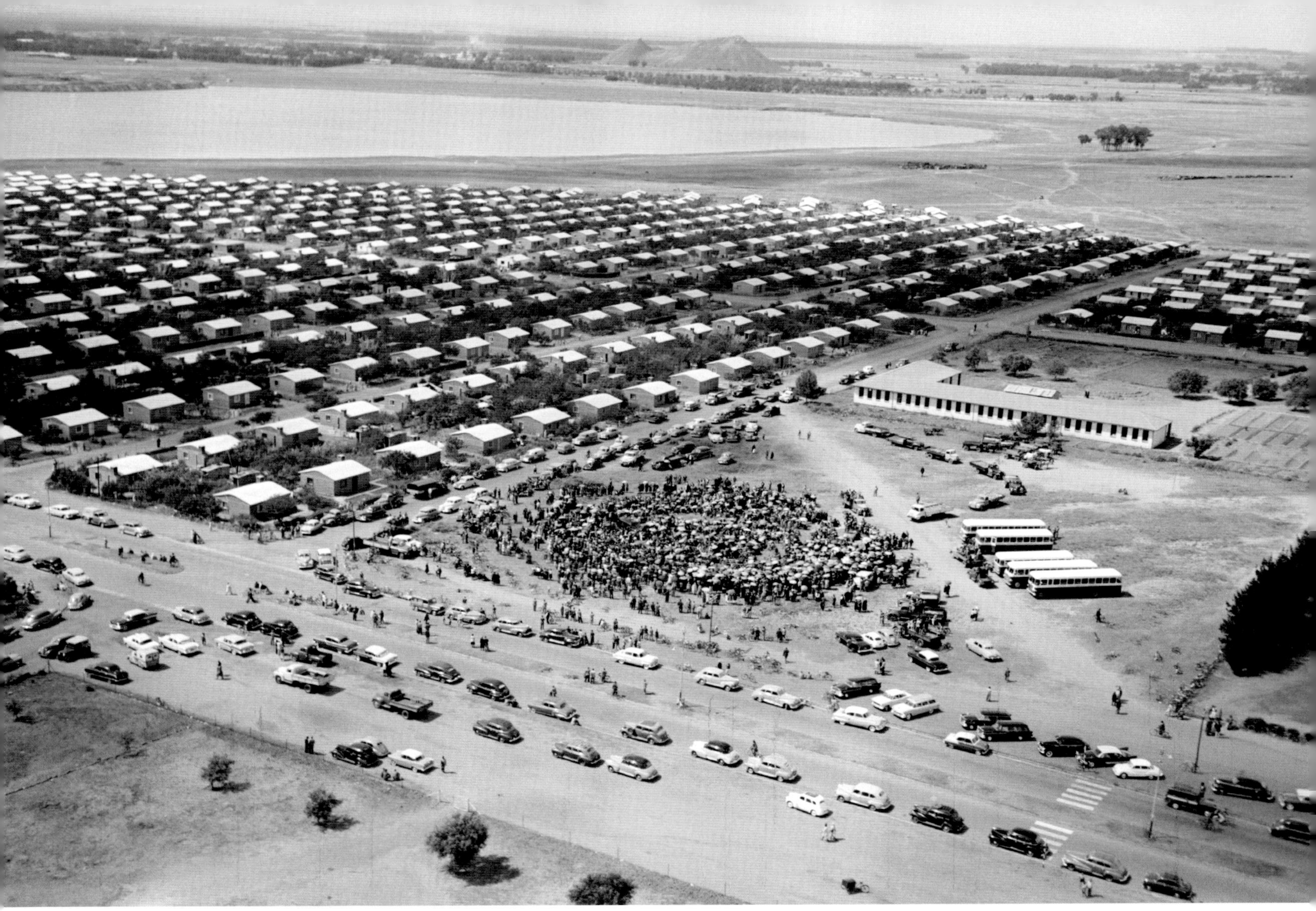

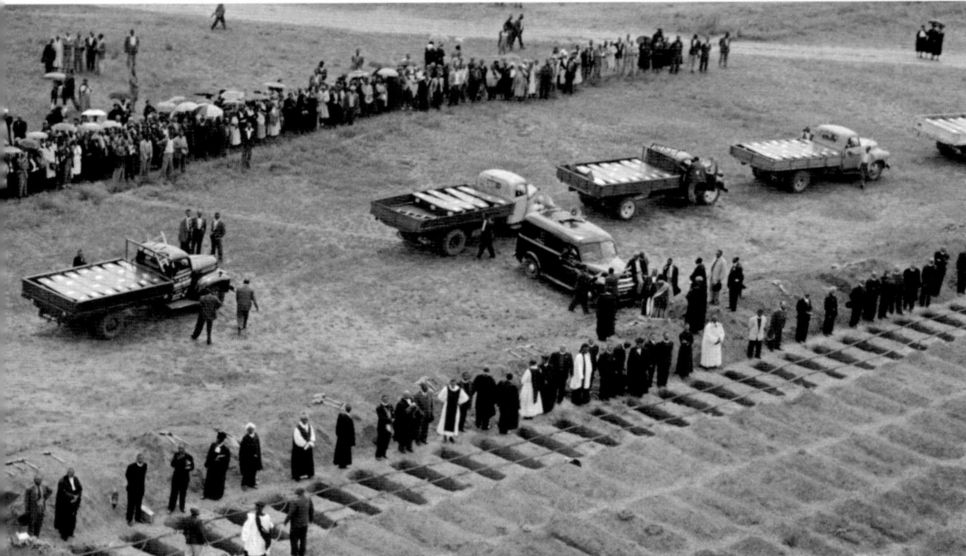

Above: Aerial view of Sharpeville, 1960.

Left: Bodies arrive on flatbed trucks to be buried in a graveyard near the township of Sharpeville following the Sharpeville Massacre, March 24, 1960.

Tata's *Freedom* drawing.

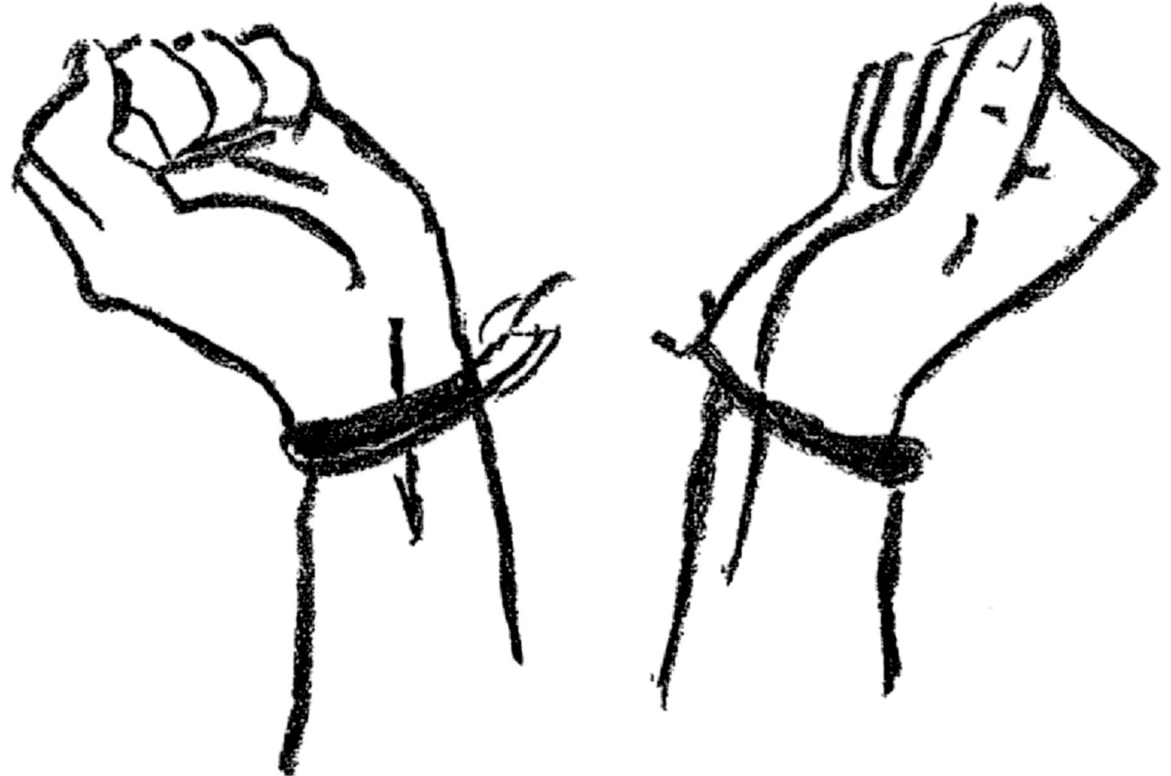

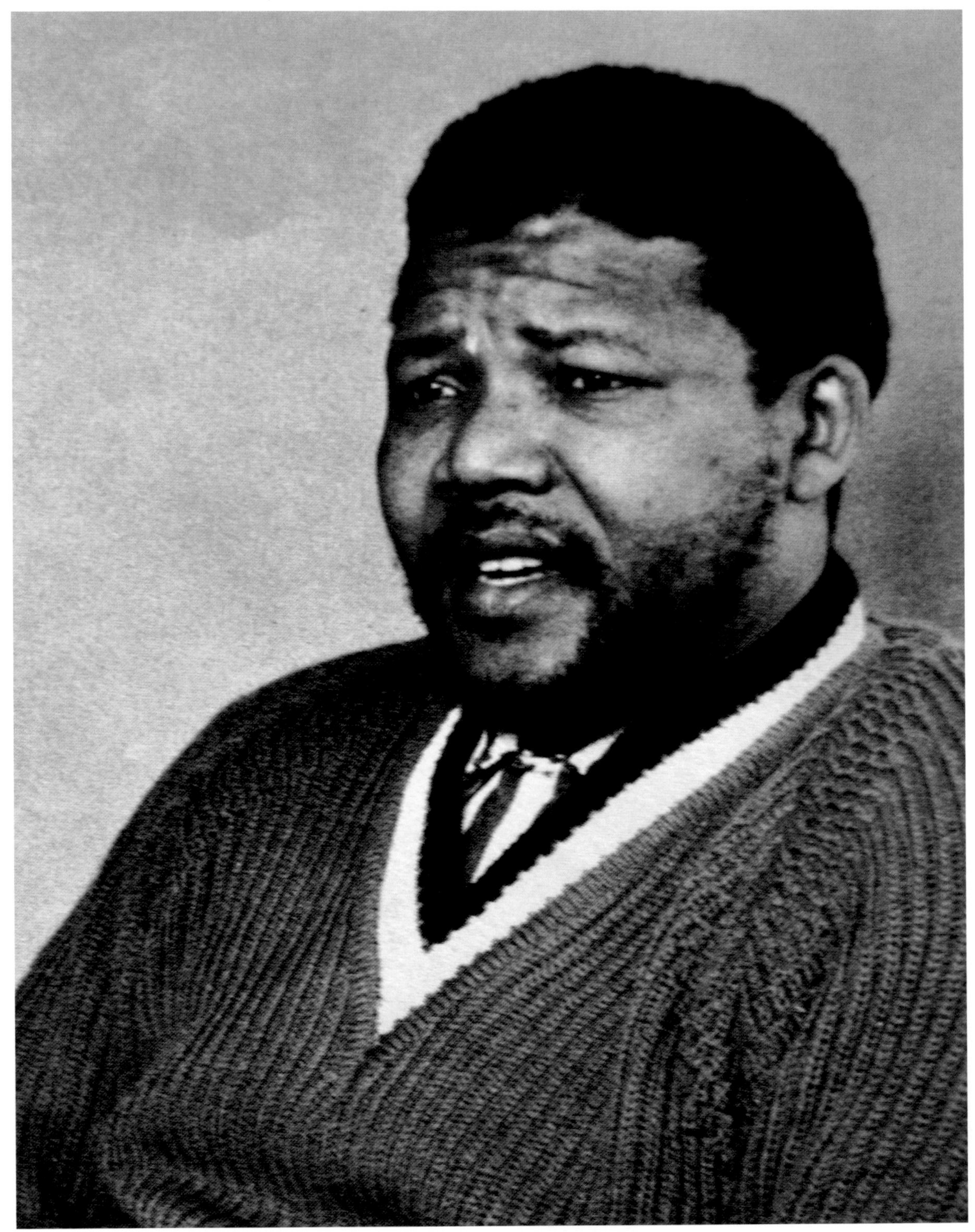

Tata circa 1962.

"Living underground requires a seismic psychological shift. I became a creature of the night. I would keep my hideout during the day, and would emerge to do my work when it became dark. I was terribly lonesome for my wife and family." Tata in *Long Walk to Freedom*

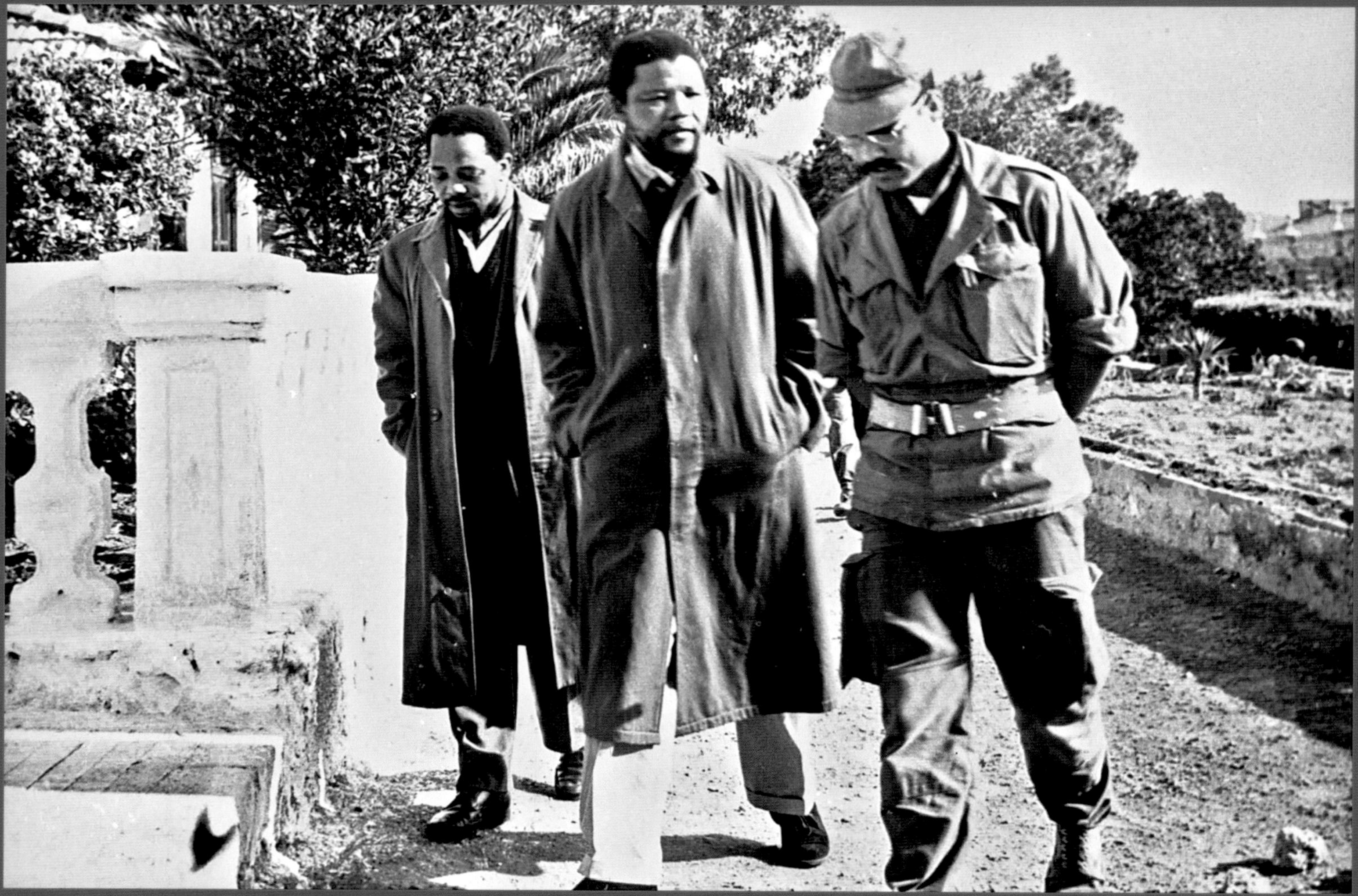

Above: Tata in Algeria, 1962.

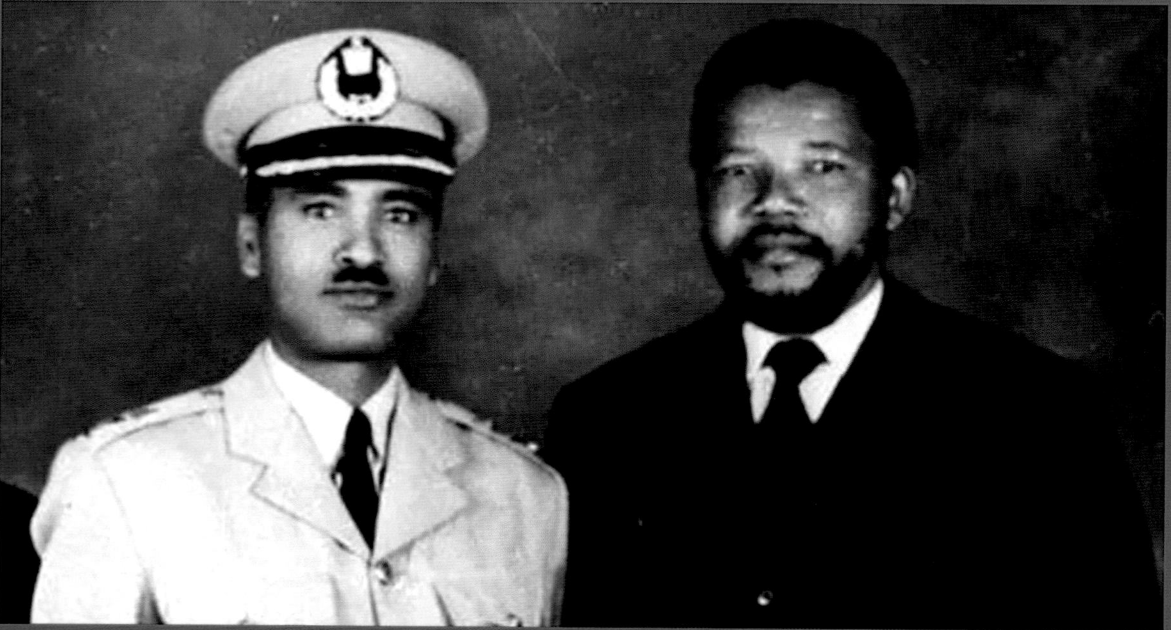

Left: Ethiopian general Tadesse Birru with Tata, while Tata was studying military affairs in Ethiopia, 1962.

Emperor Haile Selassie of Ethiopia was fully committed to the freedom, independence, unity, and development of Africa. He strongly supported our liberation struggle. He permitted Tata to get an Ethiopian passport, allowing him to travel to other African countries and the UK.

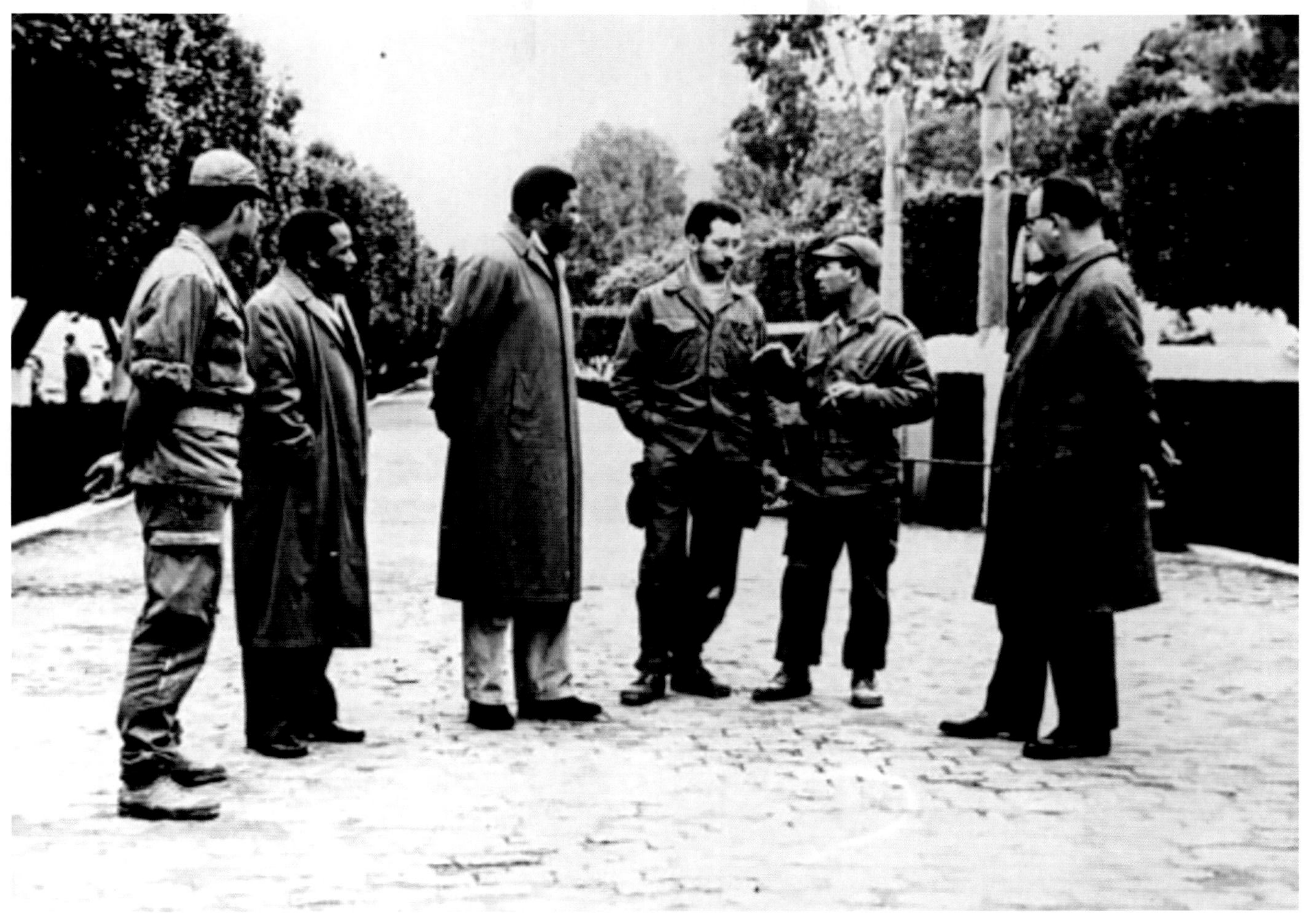

Tata received military training
in Morocco and Algeria, 1962.

Tata was the first South African liberation fighter to receive military training in Algeria. He was very grateful for the support. He claimed that Algeria made him a man.

"There comes a time in the life of a nation when there remain only two choices, submit or fight."

Tata in *Long Walk to Freedom*

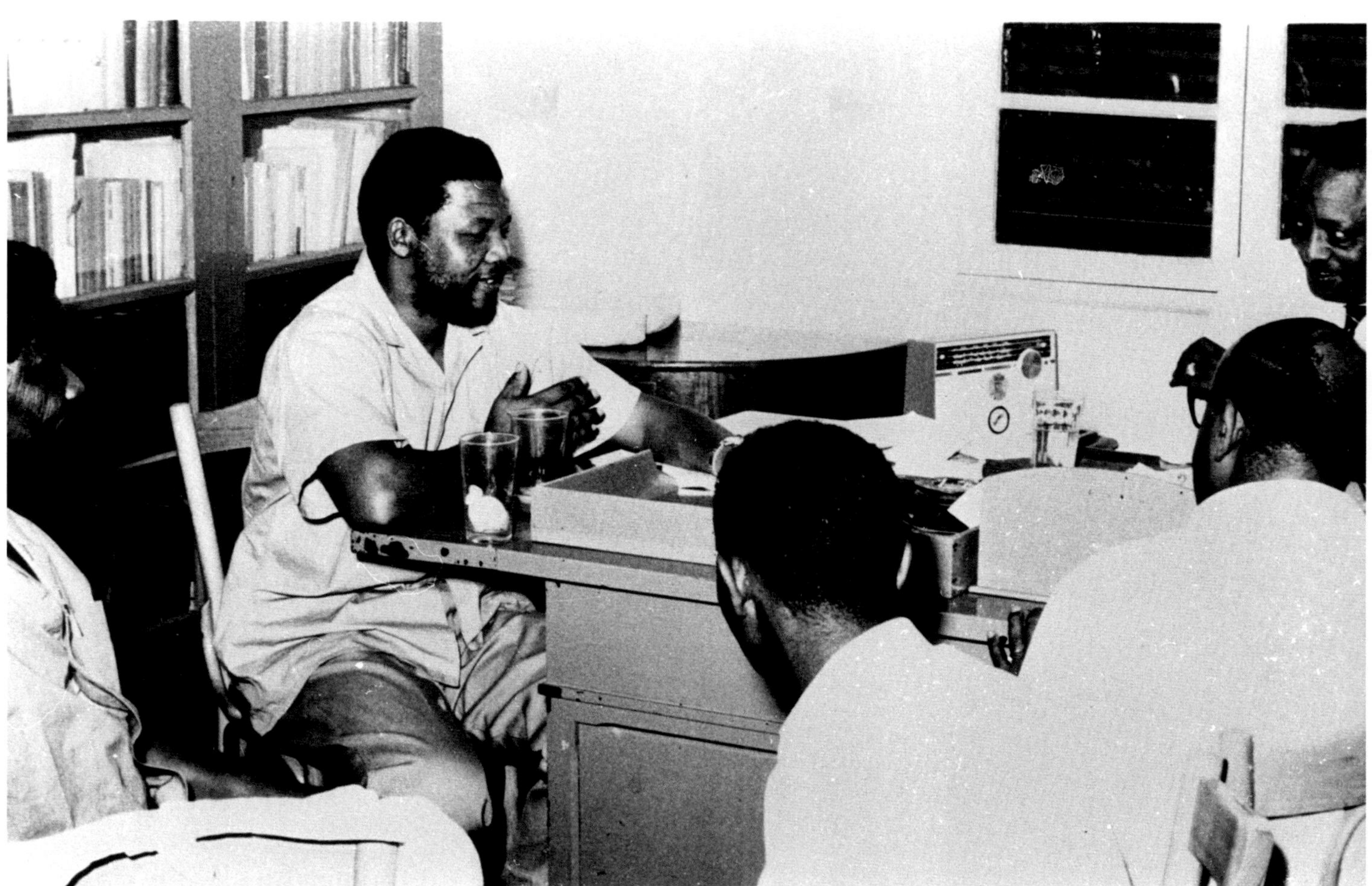

Tata being interviewed by a radio station in Addis Ababa, Ethiopia, while there for the Pan-African Freedom Conference.

Tata's fight for freedom was a lifelong endeavor. In that journey, the support, the cooperation, and the unity he found with other African nations and their people, was a remarkable bright spot. The emancipation of the South African people was a joint effort with a great deal of assistance from other African states. South Africa was inspired by its neighbors to pursue freedom at all costs. African leaders gave refuge to exiled activists, and helped train soldiers of uMkhonto we Sizewe, the military wing of the ANC. Africa empowered South Africa. In October 1961, Tata was driven to Liliesleaf Farm in Rivonia, which was the headquarters of the ANC and a safe house for those in hiding. He lived there under the alias David Motsamayi and was able to leave the house frequently in disguise. In January 1962, Tata was smuggled out of the country without official travel documents. He made his way via Lobatse, Botswana, to attend the Pan-African Freedom Conference in Ethiopia, met several leaders from the Organization of African Unity in Addis Ababa, Ethiopia, and canvassed for both military and financial support. Tata felt that by traveling the continent, he would be visiting his own genesis, unearthing the roots of what made him an African.

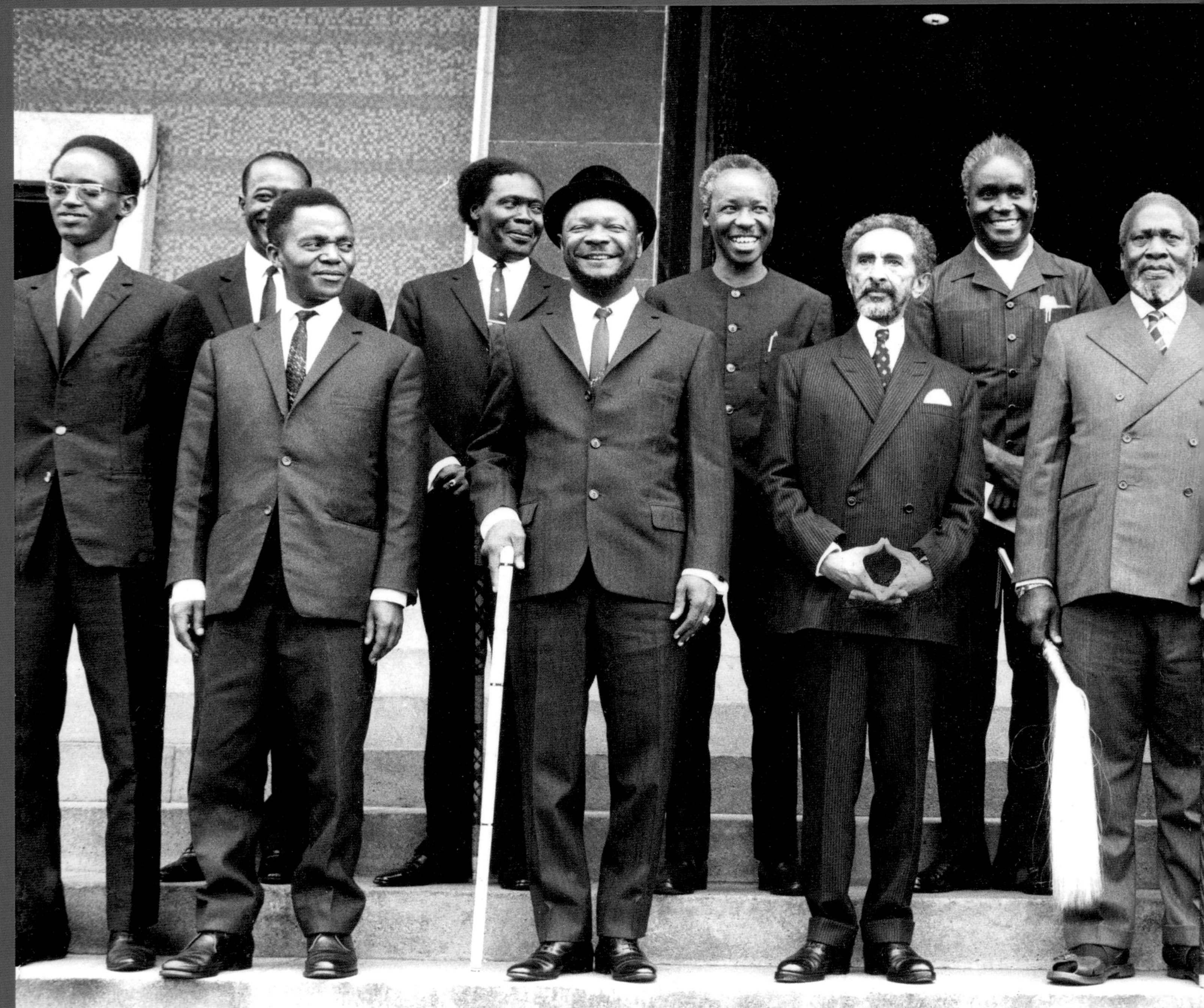

The founders of the Organisation of African Unity (OAU), who were also the leaders of some of the African states Tata addressed.

Léopold Sédar Senghor
Senegal

Modibo Keita
Mali

King Hassan II
Morocco

Habib Bourguiba
Tunisia

Muammar Gaddafi
Libya

Gamal Abdel Nasser Hussein
Egypt

Ibrahim Abboud
Sudan

Emperor Haile Selassie
Ethiopia

Milton Obote
Uganda

Julius Kambarage Nyerere
Tanzania

Sir Seretse Khama
Botswana

Sir Alhaji Abubakar Tafawa Balewa
Nigeria

Kwame Nkrumah
Ghana

William Tubman
Liberia

Sir Milton Augustus Strieb Margai
Sierra Leone

Ahmed Sékou Touré
Guinea

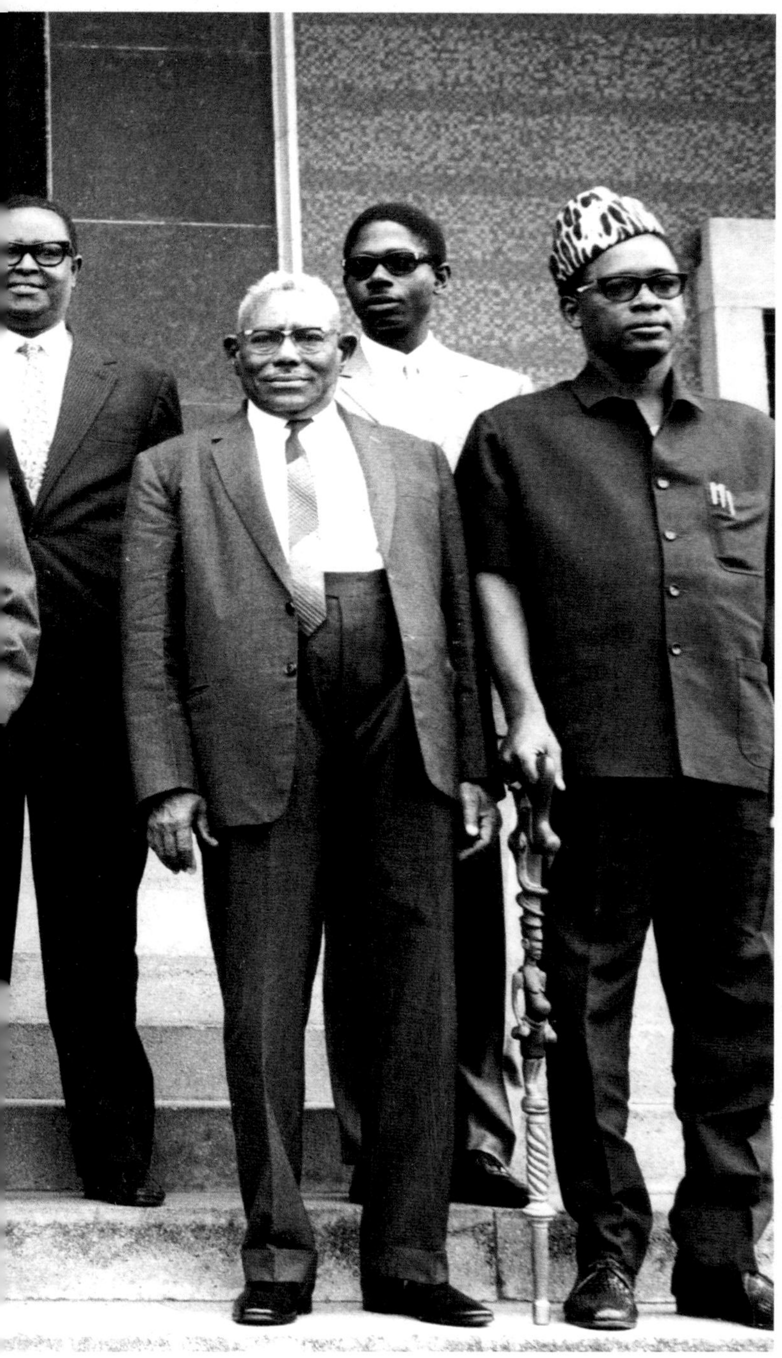

An excerpt from Nelson Mandela's speech at the Pan-African Freedom Conference

"The delegation of the African National Congress, and I particularly, feel specially honored by the invitation addressed to our organization by the Pan-African Freedom Movement of East and Central Africa (PAFMECA) to attend the historic conference and to participate in its deliberations and decisions. The extension of the PAFMECA area to South Africa, the heart and core of imperialist reaction, should mark the beginning of a new phase in the drive for the total liberation of Africa—a phase that derives special significance from the entry into PAFMECA of independent states of Ethiopia, Somalia, and Sudan.

"It was not without reason, we believe, that the secretariat of PAFMECA chose as the seat of this conference the great country of Ethiopia, which, with hundreds of years of colorful history behind it, can rightly claim to have paid the full price of freedom and independence. His Imperial Majesty, himself a rich and unfailing fountain of wisdom, has been foremost in promoting the cause of unity, independence, and progress in Africa, as was so amply demonstrated in the address he graciously delivered in opening this assembly. The deliberations of our conference will thus proceed in a setting most conducive to a scrupulous examination of the issues that are before us.

"At the outset, our delegation wishes to place on record our sincere appreciation of the relentless efforts made by the independent African states and national movements in Africa and other parts of the world, to help the African people in South Africa in their just struggle for freedom and independence. The movement for the boycott of South African goods and for the imposition of economic and diplomatic sanctions against South Africa has served to highlight most effectively the despotic structure of the power that rules South Africa, and has given tremendous inspiration to the liberation movement in our country. It is particularly gratifying to note that the four independent African states that are part of this conference, namely, Ethiopia, Somalia, Sudan, and Tanzania (formerly Tanganyika), are enforcing diplomatic and economic sanctions against South Africa. We also thank all those states that have given asylum and assistance to South African refugees of all shades of political beliefs and opinions. The warm affection with which South African freedom fighters are received by democratic countries all over the world, and the hospitality so frequently showered upon us by governments and political organizations, has made it possible for some of our people to escape persecution by the South African government, to travel freely from country to country and from continent to continent, to canvass our point of view and to rally support for our cause. We are indeed extremely grateful for this spontaneous demonstration of solidarity and support, and sincerely hope that each and every one of us will prove worthy of the trust and confidence the world has in us."

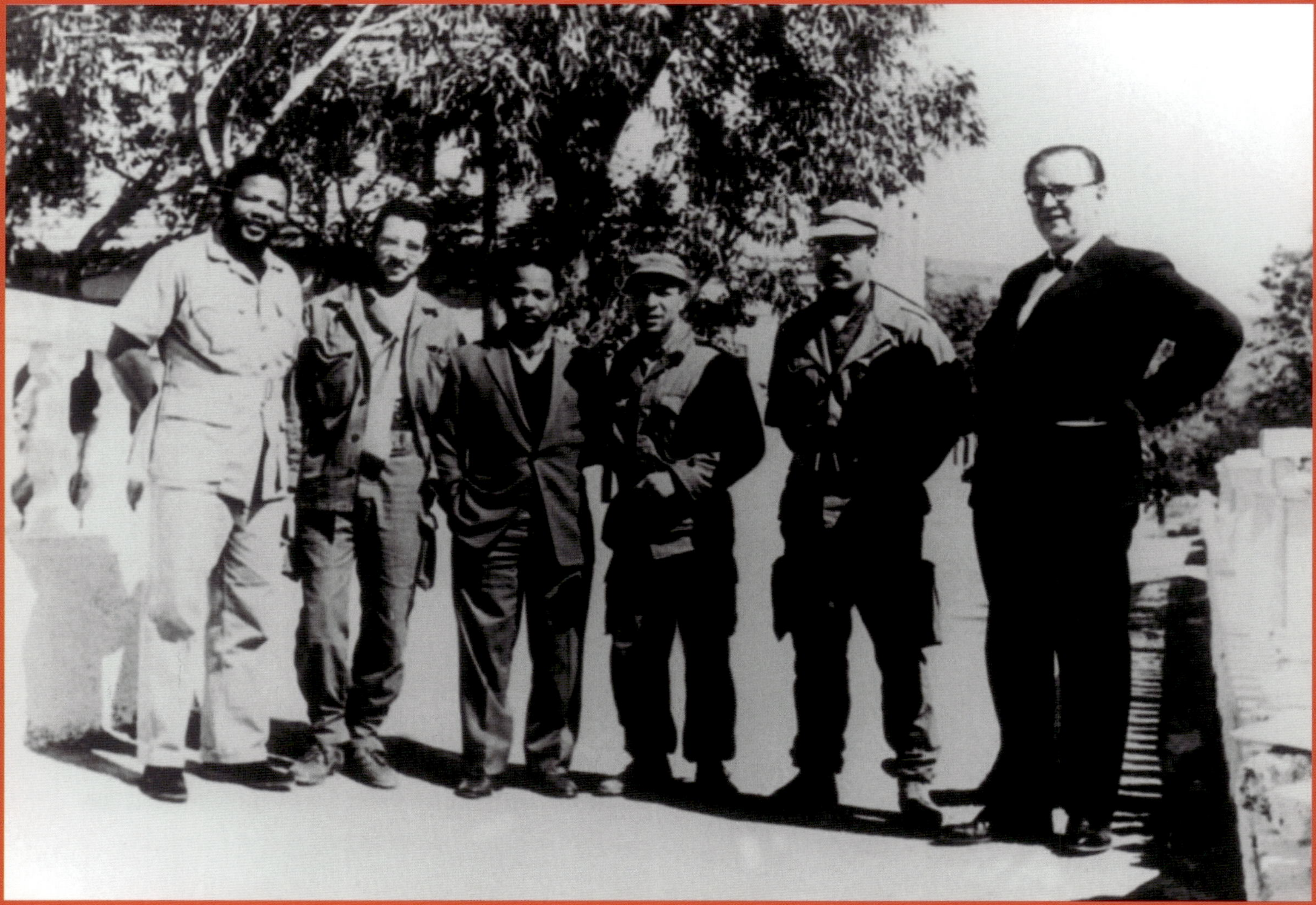

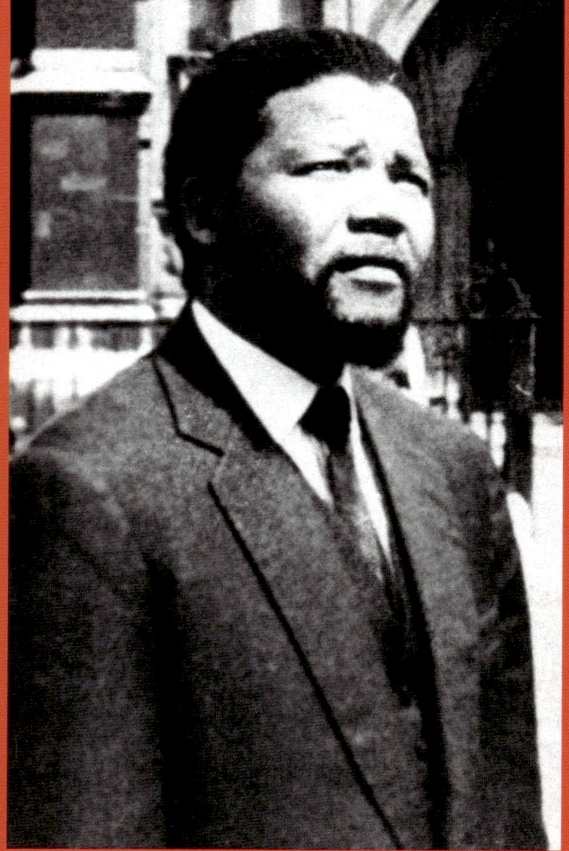

Above: Tata (*left*), with commanders of the Algerian army, 1962.

Left: Tata, circa 1962.

"Do not look the other way; Do not hesitate. Recognize that the world is hungry for action, not words. Act with courage and vision."

From a speech Tata delivered for the Campaign To End Poverty at Trafalgar Square in London in 2005

1962

While under house arrest, Tata set off on a clandestine trip in Africa to raise support for the armed struggle.

January 3
Nelson Mandela attends the Pan-African Freedom Conference in Addis Ababa, Ethiopia, as the ANC representative

January 11
Mandela leaves South Africa and arrives in Lobatse, Botswana

January 17
Mandela warned by Bechuanaland Immigration that he might be kidnapped by the South African police

January 19
Mandela and Joe Matthews (a leader in the ANC Youth League with Mandela and a friend from Fort Hare) fly to Mbeya, Tanzania (formerly Tanganyika)

January 20
Mandela and Matthews meet with John Mwakangale MP, a member of the Tanganyika African National Union

January 21
Mandela arrives in Dar es Salaam, Tanzania

January 25
Mandela arrives in Lagos, Nigeria

January 29
Mandela visits the Ethiopian Embassy in Nigeria for a visa to Ethiopia

January 30
Mandela arrives in Addis Ababa, Ethiopia, to address the Pan-African Freedom Movement of East and Central Africa (PAFMECA) Conference

February 5
Mandela attends an evening function at the Ghanian Embassy in Addis Ababa

February 6
Mandela finishes his address on behalf of the ANC to the PAFMECA Conference in Addis Ababa

February 8
Mandela and his delegation are received by Emperor Haile Selassie in Ababa

February 12
Mandela arrives in Cairo, Egypt, and checks in to the Continental Hotel

February 17
Mandela and Oliver Tambo take an hour-long boat trip on the Nile River in Cairo

February 19
Mandela speaks with the Czechoslovakian ambassador to Egypt in Cairo

February 25
Mandela arrives in Tripoli, Libya

February 27
Mandela arrives in Tunis, Tunisia

March 3
Mandela meets Ahmed Bennour of the General Union of Students in Tunisia

March 5
Mandela meets President Habib Bourguiba of Tunisia, who advises him on "methods and tactics"

March 6
Mandela flies from Tunis to Casablanca, Morocco

March 9
Mandela meets Dr. Mostefai, head of the Algerian diplomatic mission in Morocco

March 20
Mandela and Robert Resha visit the Zegangan base of the Algerian Liberation Front in Morocco

March 25
Mandela witnesses Algerian liberation leader Ahmed Ben Bella inspecting fighters in Morocco

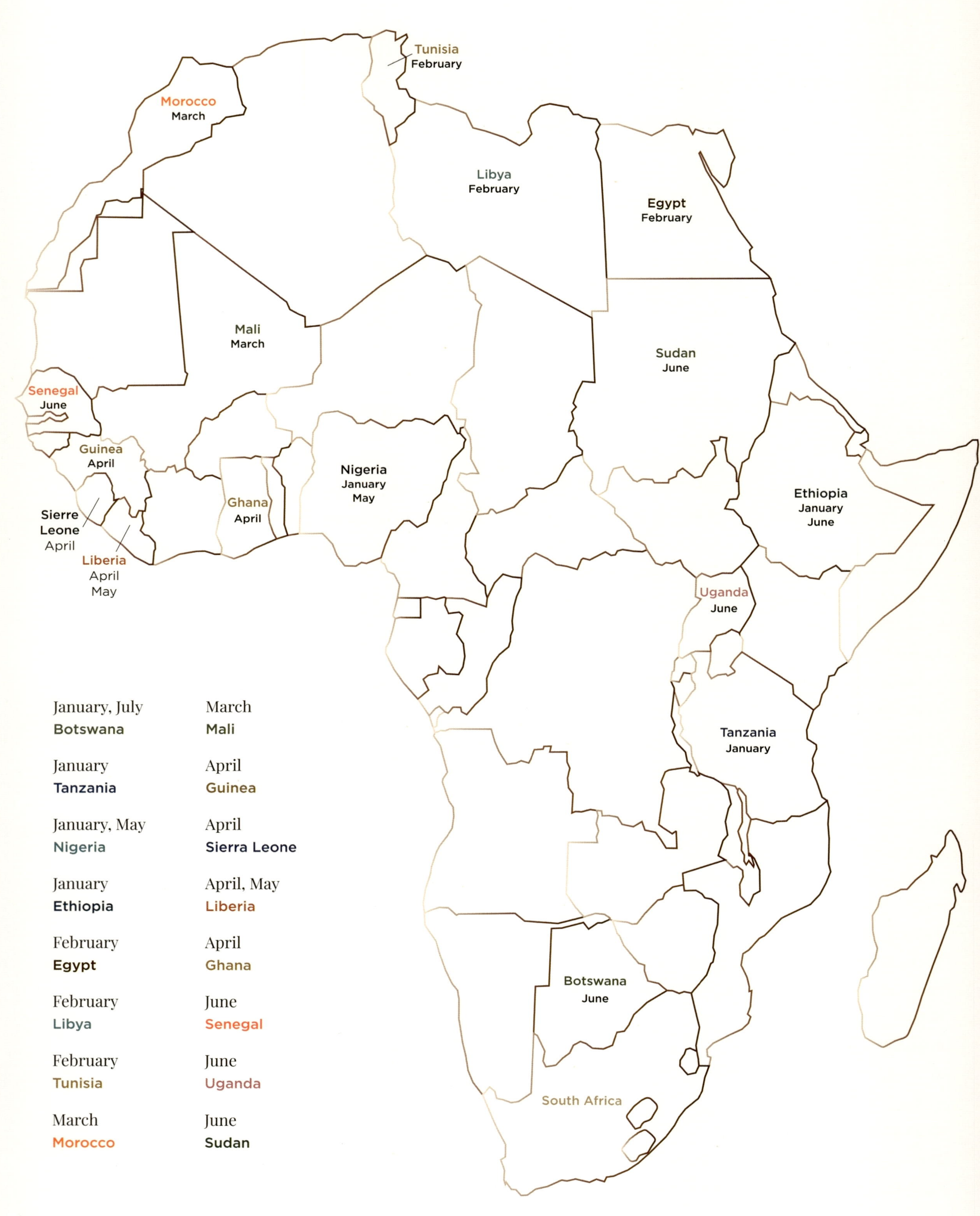

Tunisia
February
Morocco
March
Libya
February
Egypt
February
Mali
March
Sudan
June
Senegal
June
Guinea
April
Nigeria
January
May
Ethiopia
January
June
Ghana
April
Sierre
Leone
April
Liberia
April
May
Uganda
June
Tanzania
January
Botswana
June
South Africa
January, July
Botswana
January
Tanzania
January, May
Nigeria
January
Ethiopia
February
Egypt
February
Libya
February
Tunisia
March
Morocco
March
Mali
April
Guinea
April
Sierra Leone
April, May
Liberia
April
Ghana
June
Senegal
June
Uganda
June
Sudan

March 28

Mandela leaves Morocco for Mali

March 28

Mandela arrives in Bamako, Mali

April 2

Mandela visits the Ministry of Foreign Affairs in Mali

April 6

Mandela meets Doudou Gueye, the secretary general of the Union of Pan-African Journalists

April 11

Mandela has a two-hour discussion in Mali with Ghana's ambassador, Salifu Yakubu

April 12

Mandela arrives in Conakry, Guinea

April 16

Mandela arrives in Freetown, Sierra Leone

April 17

Mandela attends the National Assembly of Sierra Leone and meets members of parliament

April 19

Mandela arrives in Monrovia, Liberia

April 27

Mandela arrives in Accra, Ghana

May 3

Mandela visits Tema Harbour in Accra

May 17

Mandela arrives in Lagos, Nigeria

May 22

Mandela visits the Amechi region in Nigeria

May 27

Mandela has a forty-five-minute stopover in Accra, en route to Monrovia, Liberia

May 30

Mandela meets Guinea's president Ahmed Sékou Touré, who pledges his full support

June 1

Mandela arrives in Dakar, Senegal

June 2

Mandela meets Senegal's minister of justice, Gabriel d'Arboussier, and stays at the Hotel de la Paix in Dakar

June 5

Mandela meets President Léopold Sédar Senghor of Senegal, who promises assistance in the struggle against apartheid

June 10

Mandela meets Ugandan prime minister Milton Obote

June 19

Mandela arrives in Khartoum, Sudan

June 29

Mandela receives a lesson in demolitions during military training in Ethiopia

July 24

Mandela returns to South Africa through Botswana

August 5

Mandela is arrested at Howick in KwaZulu-Natal

August 5

Mandela makes a brief appearance in the Johannesburg Magistrates Court on charges of leaving the country without a passport and inciting workers to strike

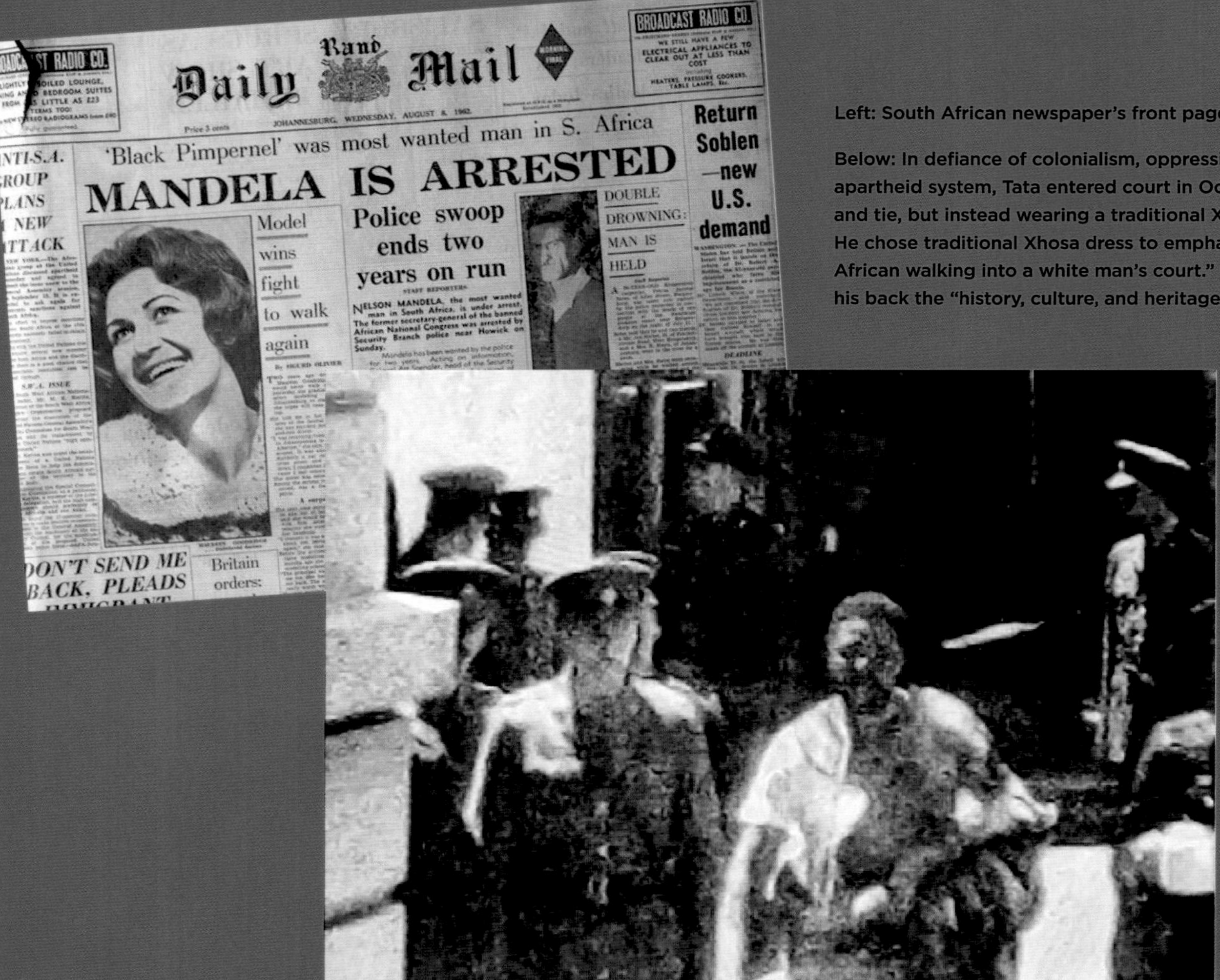

BROADCAST RADIO CO.

Rand Daily Mail

JOHANNESBURG, WEDNESDAY, AUGUST 8, 1962.

'Black Pimpernel' was most wanted man in S. Africa

MANDELA IS ARRESTED

Police swoop ends two years on run

NELSON MANDELA, the most wanted man in South Africa, is under arrest. The former secretary-general of the banned African National Congress was arrested by Security Branch police near Howick on Sunday.

Model wins fight to walk again

DOUBLE DROWNING: MAN IS HELD

Return Soblen —new U.S. demand

DON'T SEND ME BACK, PLEADS

Britain orders:

Left: South African newspaper's front page about Tata's arrest.

Below: In defiance of colonialism, oppression, and the brutal apartheid system, Tata entered court in October 1962, not in a suit and tie, but instead wearing a traditional Xhosa leopard-skin kaross. He chose traditional Xhosa dress to emphasize that he was a "Black African walking into a white man's court." He was literally wearing on his back the "history, culture, and heritage" of his people.

Tata realized that the fear of being imprisoned could not stop him from continuing to fight for justice and freedom.

In July 1962, Tata returned from the Pan-African Freedom Conference having galvanized support for the newly formed uMkhonto we Sizwe. On August 5, seventeen months after going underground, on his way from KwaZulu-Natal to give a report to Chief Albert Luthuli about his trip, Tata was arrested after a tip-off to the police. In November, he was sentenced to five years in prison for incitement to strike and leaving the country without a passport. He was held for six months in a Pretoria prison and then transferred to the Robben Island prison. In July 1963, while Tata was serving his five-year prison sentence, the police raided Liliesleaf Farm, where they confiscated several papers and evidence, including a significant document titled "Operation Mayibuye," a written strategic proposal for guerrilla combat in South Africa. Due to the evidence found, Tata and ten other co-defendants are charged with sabotage and conspiracy in the subsequent trial, known as the Rivonia Trial. During Tata's time underground, he became a symbol of rebellion and struggle, and throughout the Rivonia Trial, he personified a hallmark of justice in the court of the oppressor and the representative of the great ideals of freedom and democracy in a society that dishonored those ideals.

A Black Man in a White Man's Court

"Why is it that in this courtroom I am facing a white magistrate, confronted by a white prosecutor, escorted by white orderlies? Can anybody honestly and seriously suggest in this type of atmosphere the scales of justice are very balanced? Why is it that no African in the history of this country has ever had the honor of being tried by his own kith and kin, by his own flesh and blood? I will tell your worship why: the real purpose of this rigid color bar is to ensure that the justice dispensed by the courts should conform to the policy of the country, however much that policy might be in conflict with the norms of justice accepted in judiciaries throughout the civilized world. Your worship, I hate racial discrimination and most intensely, and in all its manifestations. I have fought it all my life. I fight it now, and I will do so until the end of my days. I detest most intensely the setup that surrounds me here. It makes me feel that I am a black man in a white man's court. This should not be."

Extract from Tata's first court statement at the trial in 1962, where he conducted his own defense

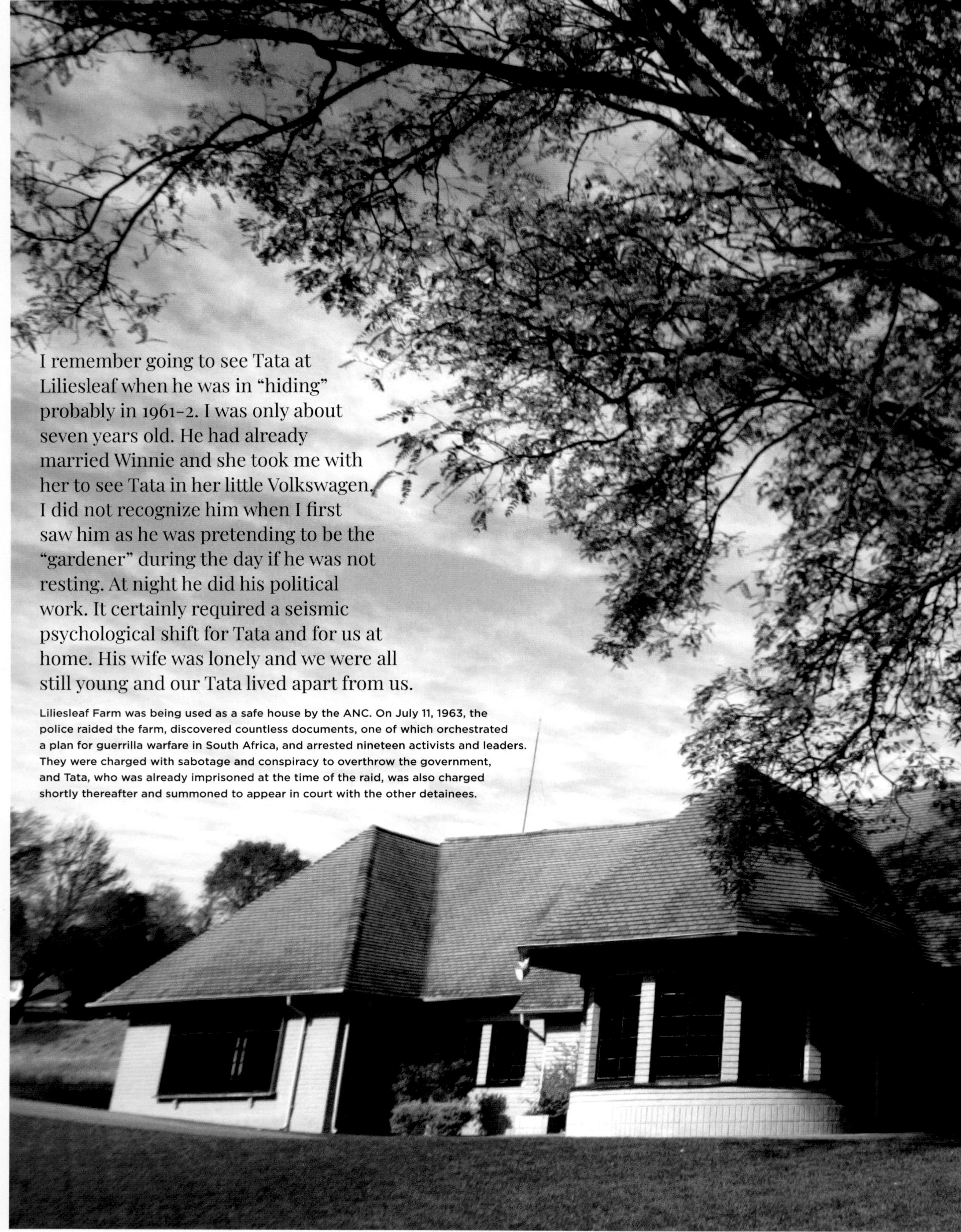

I remember going to see Tata at Liliesleaf when he was in "hiding" probably in 1961–2. I was only about seven years old. He had already married Winnie and she took me with her to see Tata in her little Volkswagen. I did not recognize him when I first saw him as he was pretending to be the "gardener" during the day if he was not resting. At night he did his political work. It certainly required a seismic psychological shift for Tata and for us at home. His wife was lonely and we were all still young and our Tata lived apart from us.

Liliesleaf Farm was being used as a safe house by the ANC. On July 11, 1963, the police raided the farm, discovered countless documents, one of which orchestrated a plan for guerrilla warfare in South Africa, and arrested nineteen activists and leaders. They were charged with sabotage and conspiracy to overthrow the government, and Tata, who was already imprisoned at the time of the raid, was also charged shortly thereafter and summoned to appear in court with the other detainees.

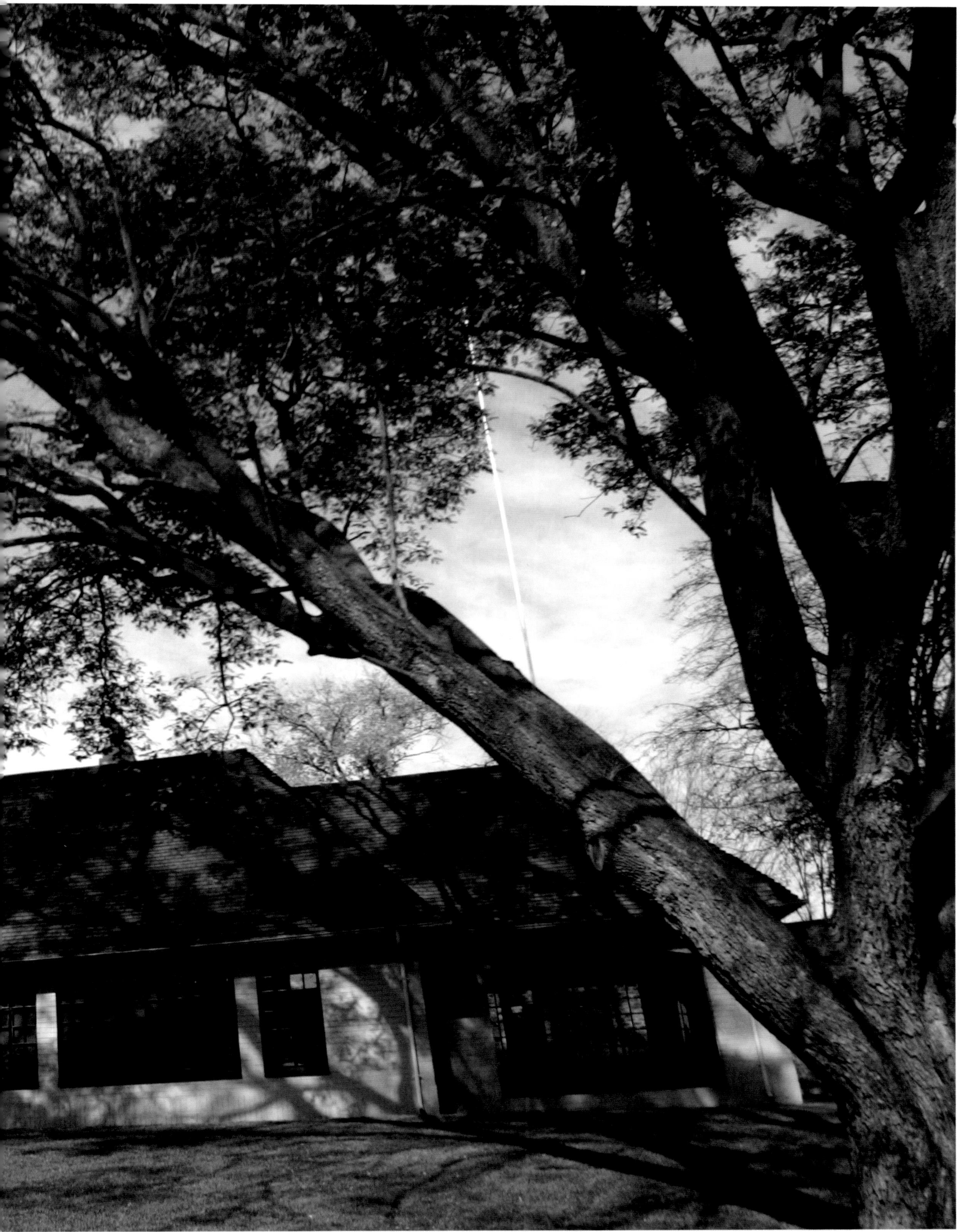

MANDELA TRIAL

LIFE OR DEATH

POST Reporters — Johannesburg

IT is believed that Nelson Mandela, Ruth Slovo (former Johannesburg Editor of "New Age"), James Kantor (the prominent Johannesburg lawyer), and 15 men — including Walter Sisulu — who were arrested in the raid on Arthur Goldreich's house in Rivonia, are among 30 people who will be charged in the Pretoria Supreme Court this Tuesday.

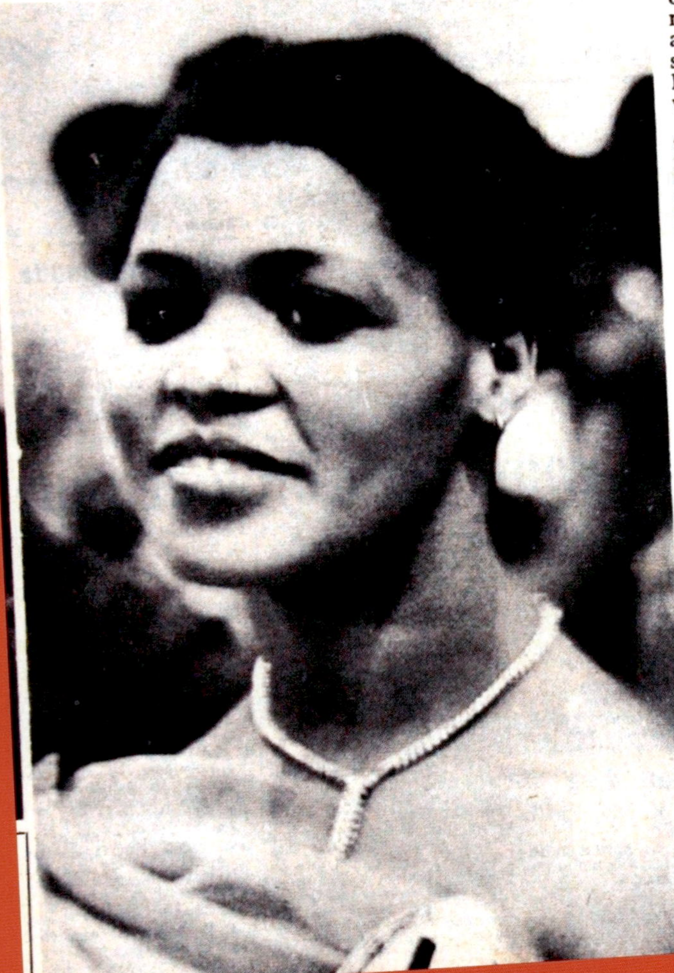

Nelson Mandela is the only one among the 30 who is not a 90-day detainee. He is at present serving a five-year sentence for incitement and leaving the country without a valid document.

These 30 are among 110 detainees who are expected to appear in Pretoria this week — in the biggest series of mass trials since the Treason Trial. A further six detainees are scheduled to appear on October 14.

A Johannesburg attorney who is appearing for some of the detainees told POST that he was originally told that they would be charged with high treason.

Later he learned that they would be charged with sabotage — which can carry the death penalty.

It is thought that their trial may take three or four months.

The names

Among the 30, it is reported, are: Govan Mbeki, Raymond Mhlaba, Dennis Goldberg, Dr. Hillar Festenstein, Joseph Mashifane, Frank Mogothlana, Thwadi Makena, Erasmus Makoe, Phillip Mokoto, Thomas Mashifane, Solomon Sepeng and B. A. Hepple, an advocate.

Dr. Percy Yutar, deputy attorney-general of the Transvaal, confirmed to POST yesterday that a number of 90-day detainees will appear in the Pretoria Supreme Court on Tuesday morning.

He said he did not know who the people were and what the charge or charges against them would be.

"We are working on the charges over the weekend and they should be ready on Tuesday morning," he said.

There is some speculation in legal and other circles as to whether Mrs. Hazel Goldreich will be among those charged.

South African newspaper announcing the Rivonia Trial.

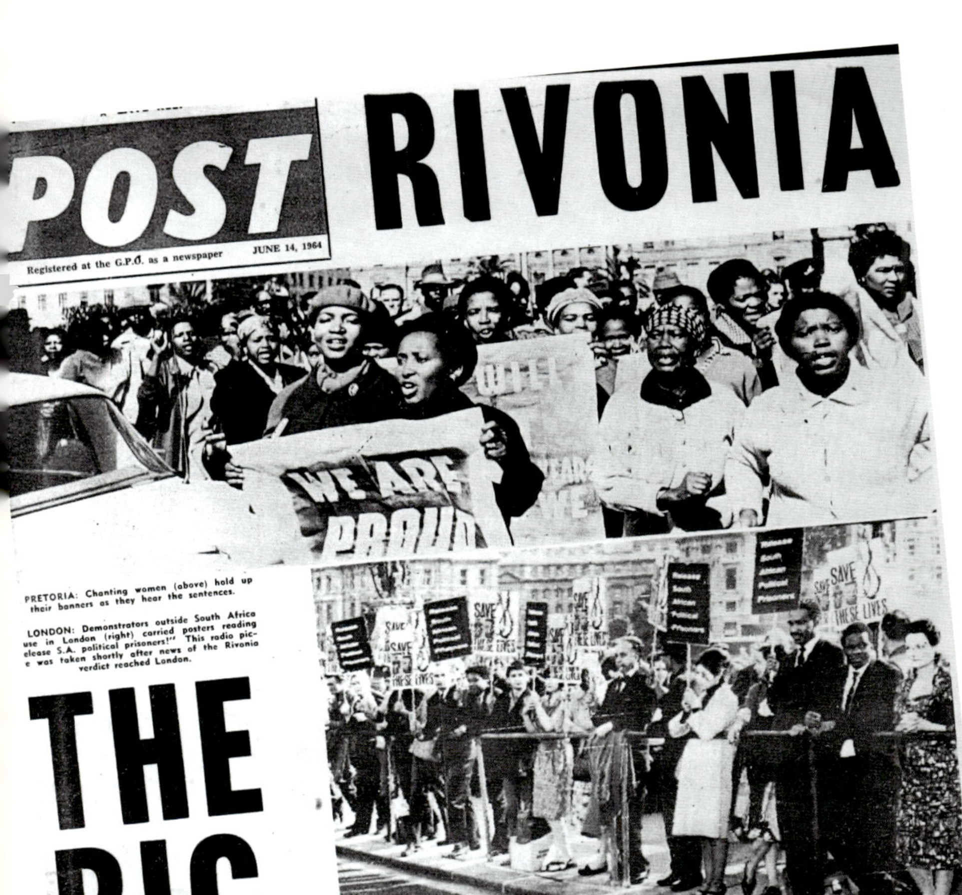

POST RIVONIA

Registered at the G.P.O. as a newspaper JUNE 14, 1964

PRETORIA: Chanting women (above) hold up their banners as they hear the sentences.

LONDON: Demonstrators outside South Africa ...use in London (right) carried posters reading ...elease S.A. political prisoners!" This radio pic... e was taken shortly after news of the Rivonia verdict reached London.

THE BIG PROTESTS

R400 £200 CASH PAYMENT PLAN FOR YOU

YOU CAN RECEIVE A CASH PAYMENT OF

...HE RIVONIA TRIAL is ... over. But the post-...ortem on Rivonia continues ...roughout the world this ...eekend.

Demonstrations in Britain pro-...ting against the life sentences ...posed on Mandela and the ...ier seven men are expected to ...ich a climax today (Sunday) at ...mass rally in Trafalgar Square. ...here have been protests at the ...ited Nations, in Paris, Algiers, ...saka and elsewhere.

...ress comment in Britain general-... praises the Judge-President, Mr. ...tice De Wet, for a fair trial but ...hes out at the Verwoerd regime.

Reaction in the townships of ...he Rand and elsewhere in South ...frica ranges from relief that ...he death sentence was not passed ...o shock at the fact that the Rivo-...ia men have been locked up for ...ife.

...arge police squads turned out in ...toria and on the road to Pre-...ia on Verdict Day and Sentence ...y. The police remained on the

SIX PAGES

TODAY POST brings yo... SIX pages of news an... pictures telling you a... about the Rivonia tria... Read the latest news o... this page and then turn ... pages 2, 3, 14, 15 and 2...

alert this weekend.

There were no reports of dist...ances.

Brigadier C. J. Joubert, of ... Security Branch, told POST ye... day: "Things are very quiet but... are prepared. There may be tro... — but we don't expect anythin...

British trade unions and o... nisations opposed to S... Africa's racial policies yeste... called for a massive turnout to... at the London rally to cond... the Rivonia sentences.

The mass rally, which is expe... to be attended by thousands,

Police at HOME

Front pages of South African newspapers reporting the sentence of life imprisonment for Tata and others following the Rivonia Trial, June 14, 1964.

SUNDAY EXPRESS

Registered at the G.P.O. as a newspaper.

...RICE 5c

JOHANNESBURG, JUNE 14, 1964.

"Already there"

RIVONIA MEN FLOWN IN SECRET TO ROBBEN ISLAND

EXPRESS REPORTER

THE seven non-White accused who were sentenced to life imprisonment in the Rivonia sabotage trial were secretly flown to Cape Town yes-...erday.

From there they were taken ...mmediately to Robben Island ... start serving their sentences.

A senior prisons officer told ... in Pretoria yesterday after-...oon: "All I can say is that they ...re there already."

Dennis Goldberg, the only White man sentenced, was not sent to Robben Island, since there is no accommodation there for White prisoners.

I understand from other sources that plans were originally made to fly the Rivonia men by military aircraft from Pretoria on Friday afternoon, within hours of the end of the trial.

However, the plans were changed for security reasons at the last moment, and they were flown to Cape Town some time before lunch yesterday.

The eight men found guilty are:

Nelson Mandela, Walter Sisulu, Dennis Goldberg, Ahmed Kathrada, Govan Mbeki, Raymond Mhlaba, Andrew Mlangeni and Elias Motsoaledi.

DEFENCE (CONSIDERING APPEAL) IS SHOCKED

By ANN CAVILL

THE sudden decision to send the Rivonia men to Robben Island came as a sur-...ise to the five-man defence ...eam.

The defence is spending the ... considering whether or not to appeal against the life sentences imposed by Mr. Justice Quartus de Wet in the Pretoria Supreme Court on Friday.

"This has come as a complete shock," a spokesman for the defence team said. "We knew nothing about the men being moved.

"On Friday we spoke to police officials and told them we would need to have further consultations with the prisoners before deciding about an appeal.

"We understood that the men would remain in Pretoria until the matter of appeal was settled."

The defence has 14 days in which to lodge an appeal. A final decision was to have been ... after discussions

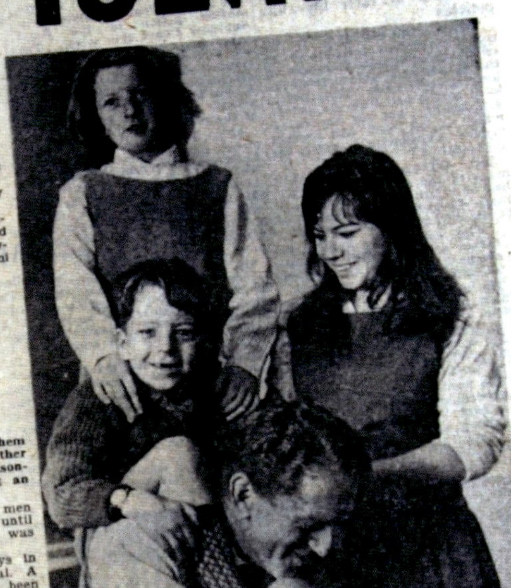

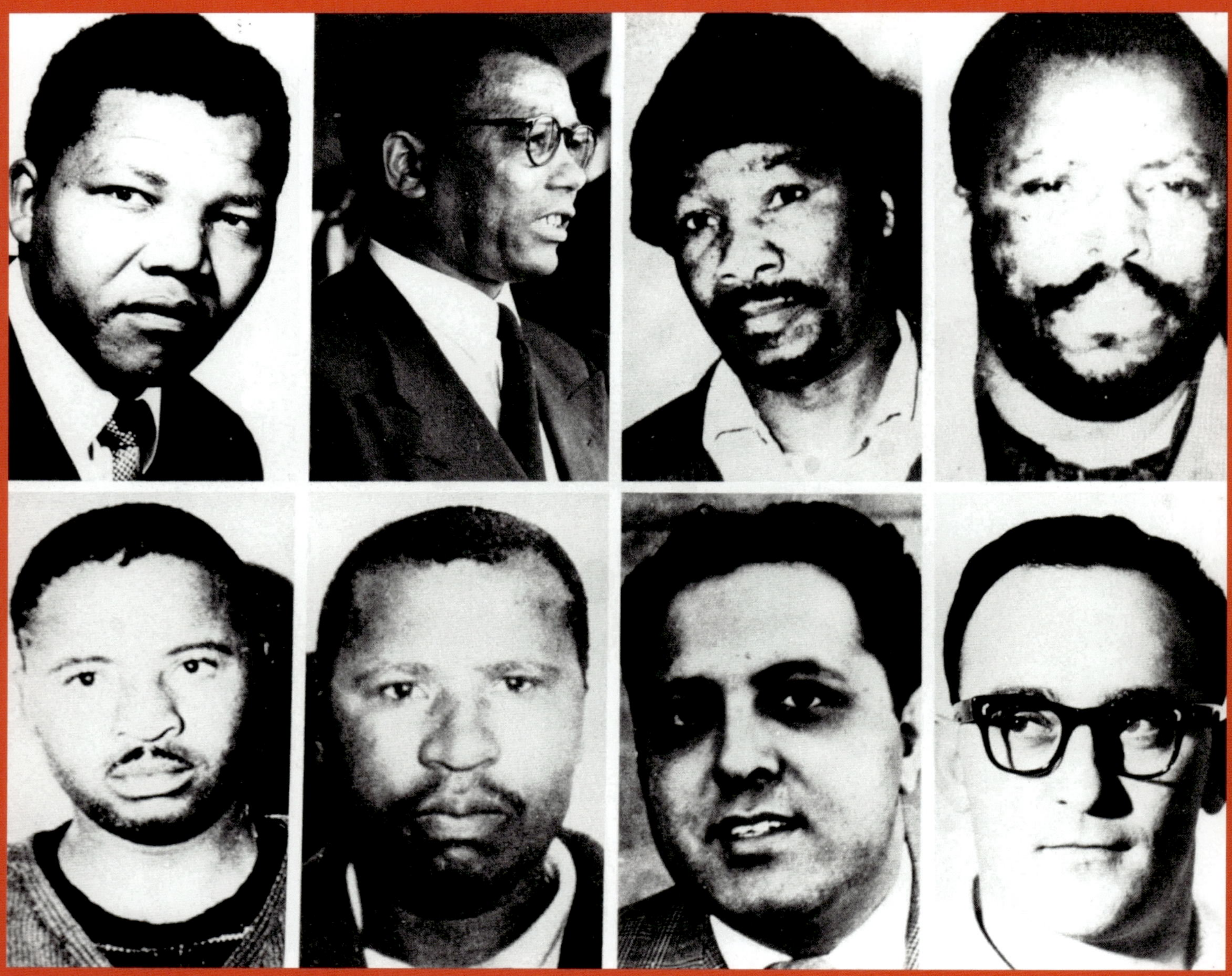

Clockwide from top left: Tata, Uncle Walter, Govan Mbeki, Raymond Mhlaba, Dennis Goldberg, Ahmed "Kathy" Kathrada, Andrew Mlangeni, and Elias Motsoaledi.

On June 12, 1964, at the Pretoria Supreme Court, the Rivonia Trial concluded with eight of the ten men accused being found guilty on all charges, and sentenced to life imprisonment.

Nelson Mandela (accused no. 1, guilty)
Walter Sisulu (accused no. 2, guilty)
Dennis Goldberg (accused no. 3, guilty)
Govan Mbeki (accused no. 4, guilty)
Ahmed Kathrada (accused no. 5, guilty on one charge)
Lionel Bernstein (accused no. 6, not guilty)
Raymond Mhlaba (accused no. 7, guilty)
James Kantor (accused no. 8, guilty)
Elias Motsoaledi (accused no. 9, guilty)
Andrew Mlangeni (accused no. 10, guilty)

Plea in Mitigation as Political Statement

"I would say that the whole life of any thinking African in this country drives him continuously to a conflict between his conscience on one hand, and the law on the other. This is not a conflict peculiar to this country. The conflict arises for men of conscience, for men who think and who feel deeply in every country. Recently in Britain, a peer of the realm, Earl (Bertrand) Russell, probably the most respected philosopher of the Western world, was sentenced and convicted for precisely the type of activities for which I stand before you today—for following his conscience in defiance of the law, as a protest against the nuclear weapons policy being followed by his own government. He could do no other than oppose the law and to suffer the consequences for it. Nor can I, nor many Africans in this country. The law as it is applied, the law as it has been developed over a long period of history, and especially the law as it is written and designed by the nationalist government is a law which, in our views, is immoral, unjust, and intolerable. Our consciences dictate that we must attempt to alter it. . . . Men, I think, are not capable of doing nothing, of saying nothing, of not reacting to injustice, of not protesting against oppression, of not striving for the good society and the good life in ways they see it."

Tata from his court statement

Charges

- Recruiting persons for training in the preparation and use of explosives and in guerrilla warfare for the purpose of violent revolution and committing acts of sabotage
- Conspiring to commit the aforementioned acts and to aid military units when they invaded the Republic
- Acting in these ways to further the objectives of communism
- Soliciting and receiving money for these purposes from sympathizers in Uganda, Algeria, Ethiopia, Liberia, Nigeria, Tunisia, and elsewhere

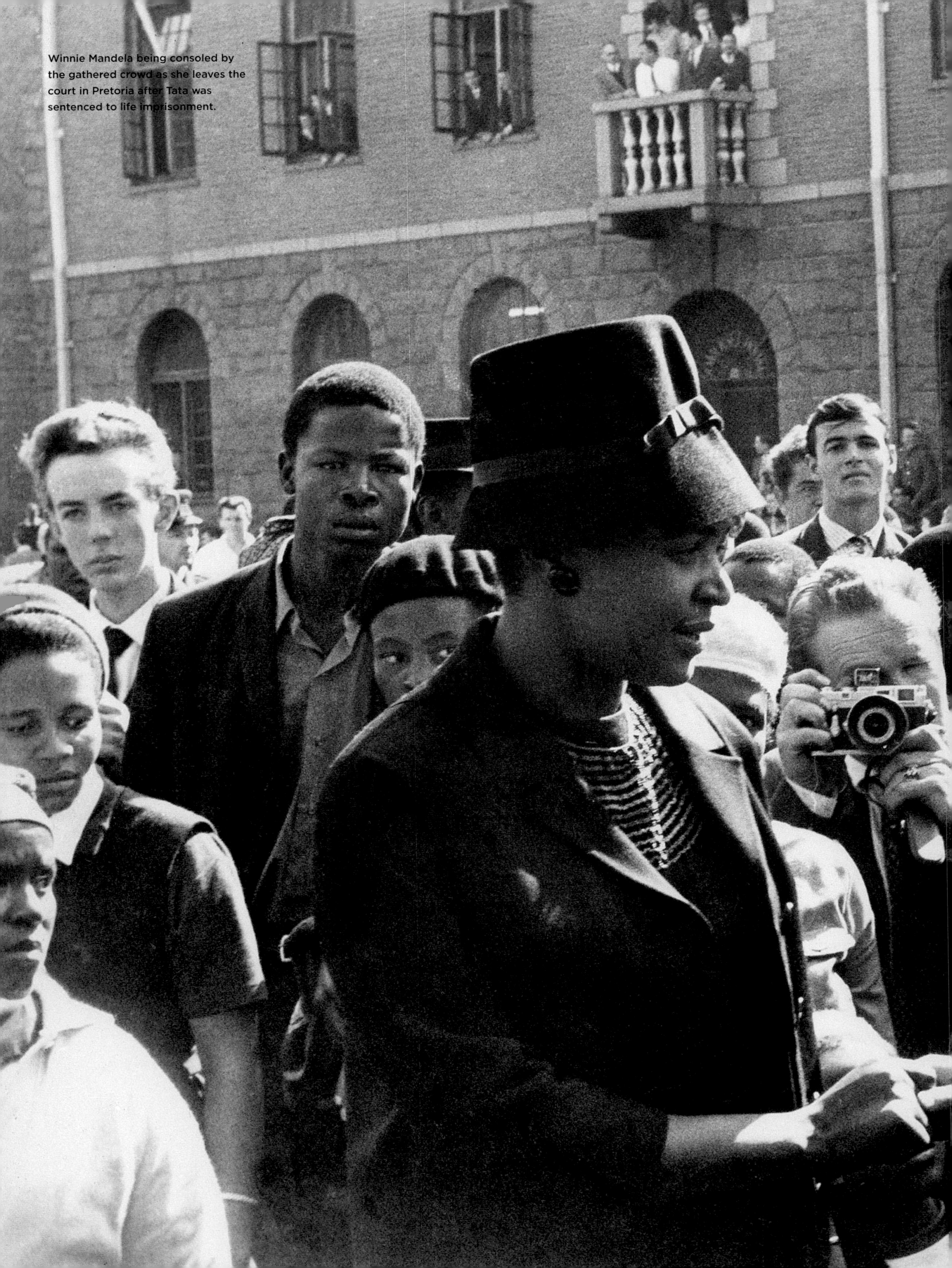

Winnie Mandela being consoled by the gathered crowd as she leaves the court in Pretoria after Tata was sentenced to life imprisonment.

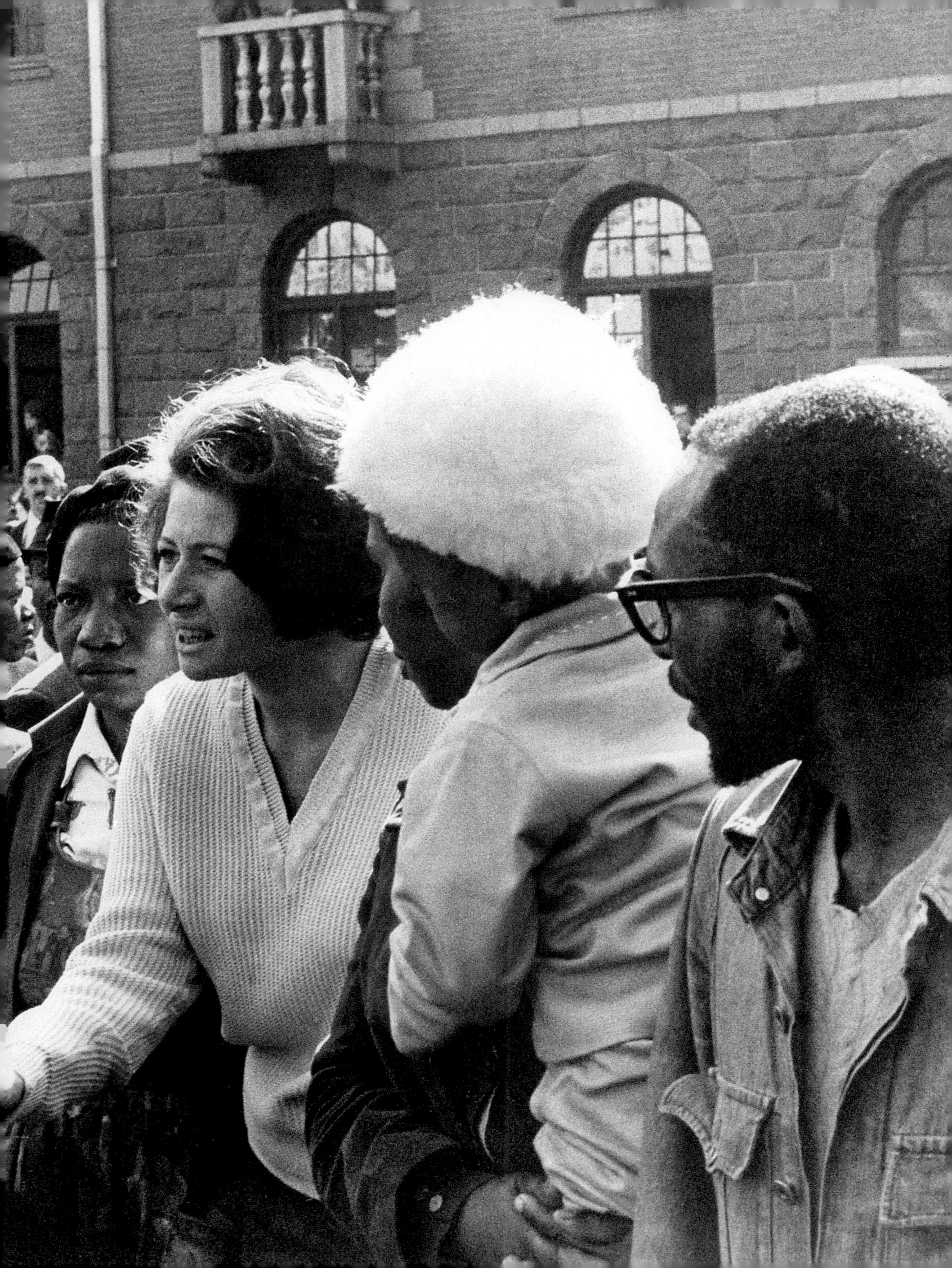

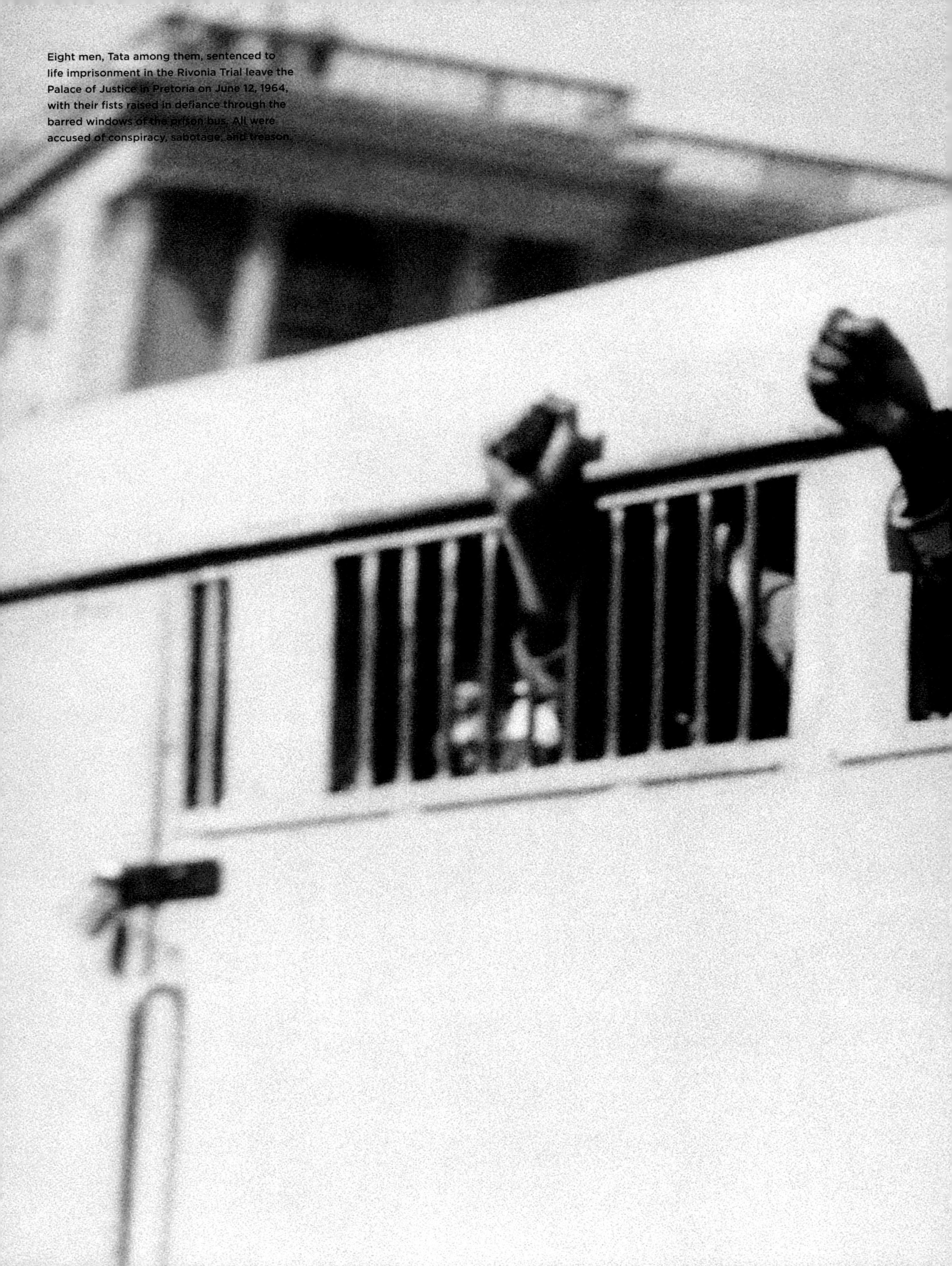

Eight men, Tata among them, sentenced to life imprisonment in the Rivonia Trial leave the Palace of Justice in Pretoria on June 12, 1964, with their fists raised in defiance through the barred windows of the prison bus. All were accused of conspiracy, sabotage, and treason.

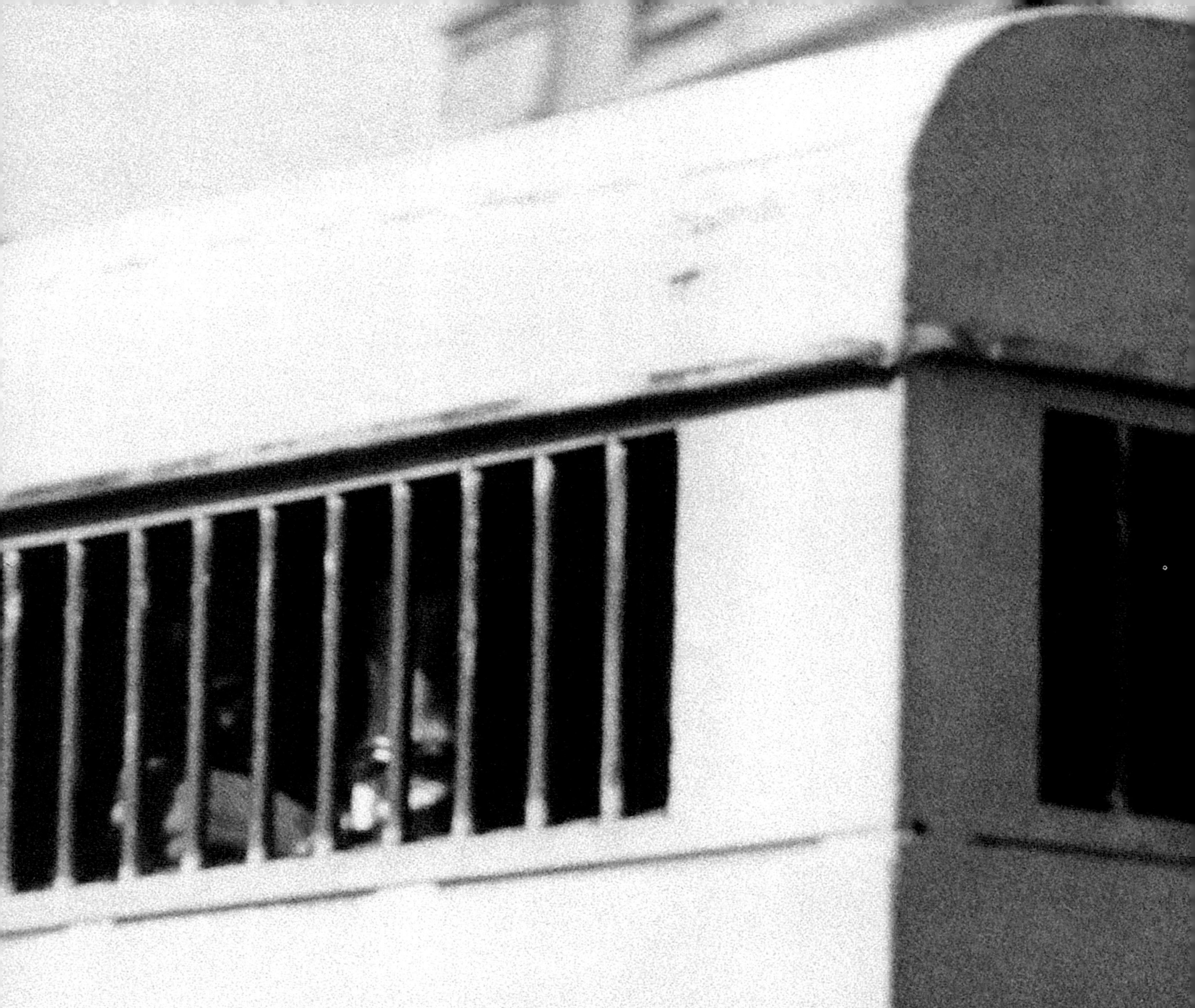

"During my lifetime I have dedicated my life to this struggle of the African people. I have fought against white domination, and I have fought against black domination. I have cherished the ideal of a democratic and free society in which all persons will live together in harmony and with equal opportunities. It is an ideal for which I hope to live for and to see realized. But, my Lord, if it needs to be, it is an ideal for which I am prepared to die."

During the trial, Tata speaking in the dock of the court on April 20, 1964

4

1964–1990

27 Years

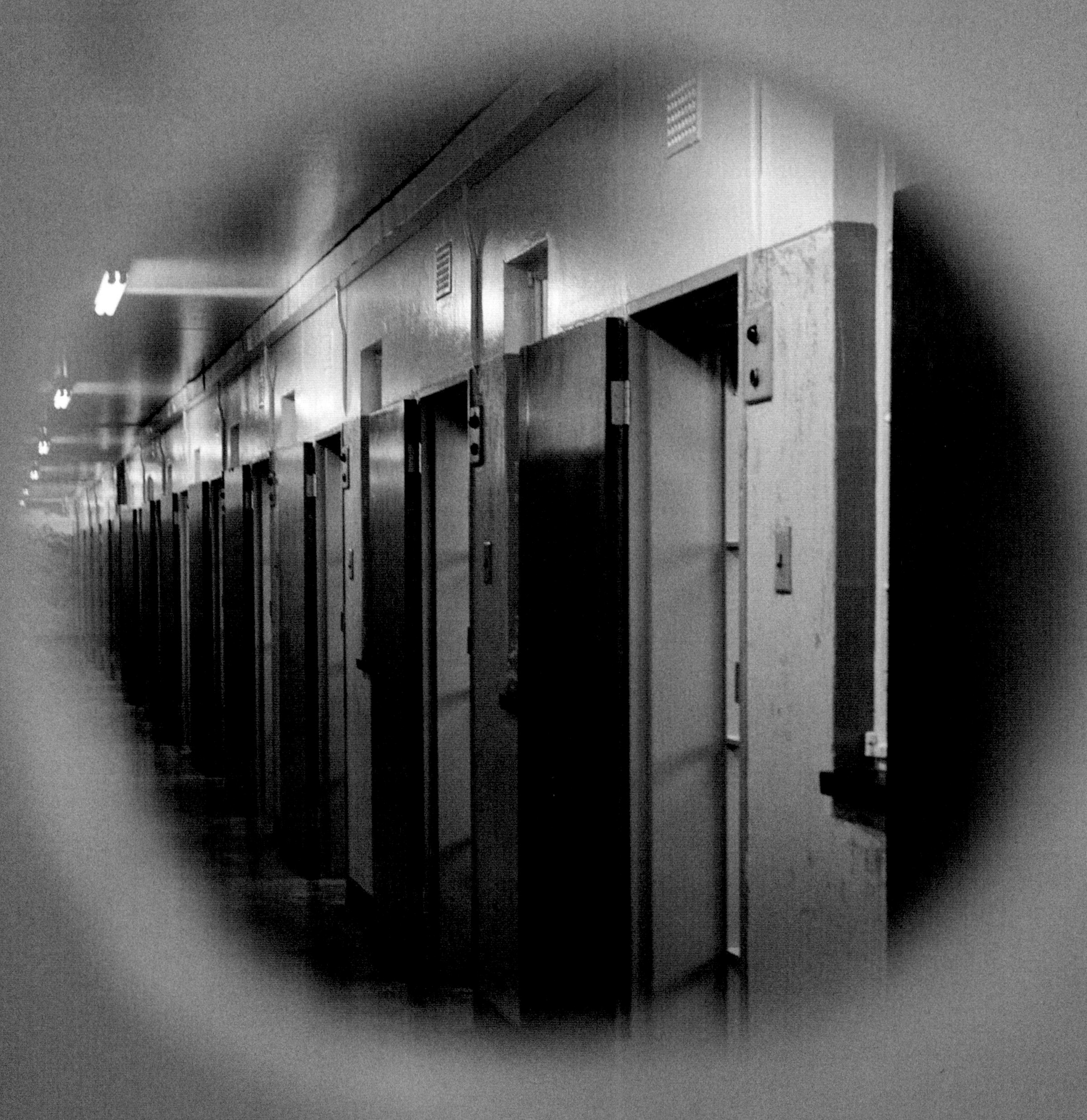

A hallway of the maximum-security prison on Robben Island.

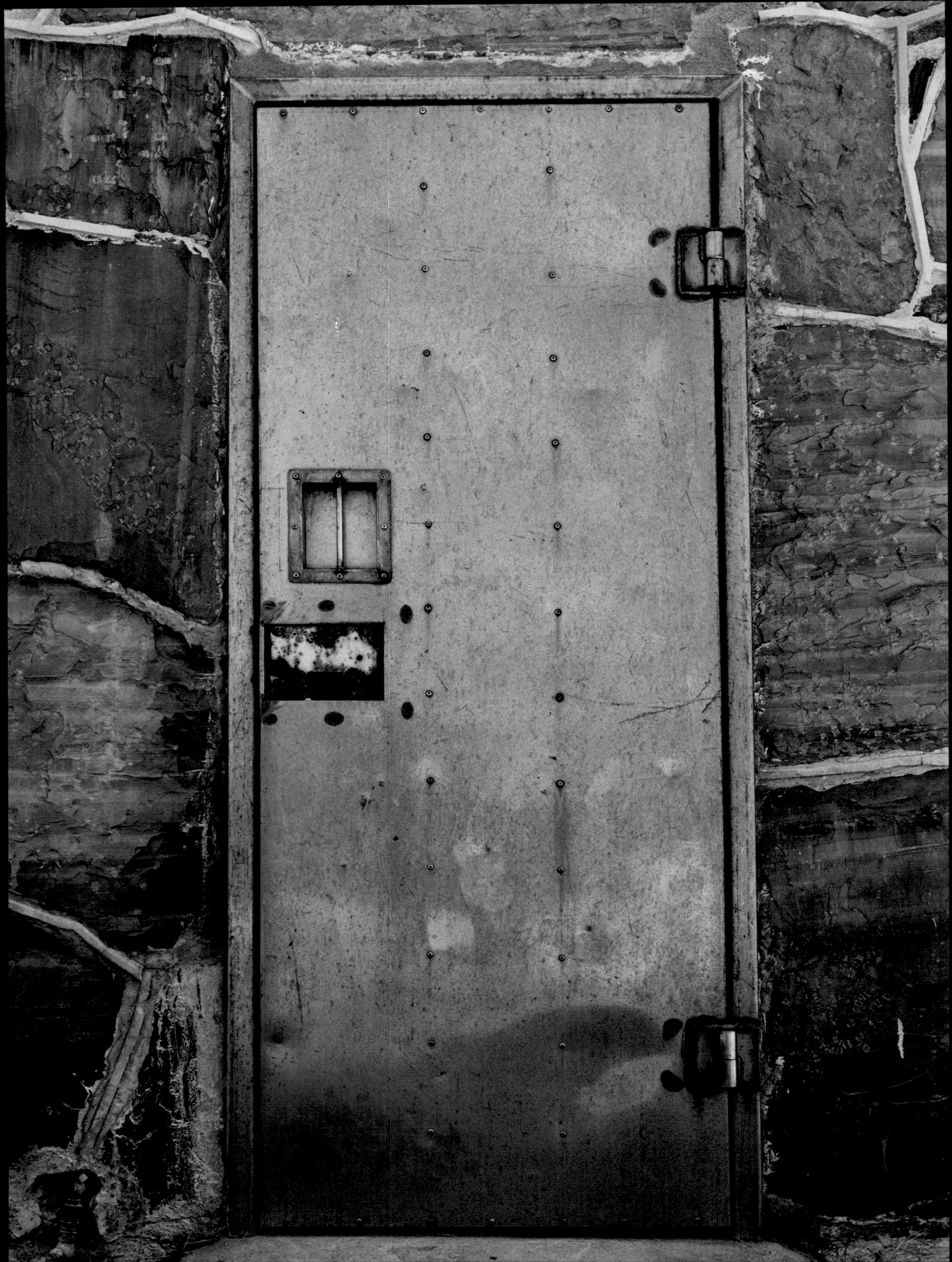

G.P.-S.13566—1961-62—10,000

Warrant of Committal: Supreme Court.
Lasbrief tot Gevangesetting: Hooggeregshof.

J. 278.

FOR GAOL USE.—VIR TRONKGEBRUIK.

Initials of Officer making entry and date.
Voorletters van beampte wat inskrywing maak en datum.

Date of discharge/Datum van ontslag

Appeal noted/Appèl aangeteken

Alterations in sentence/Veranderings in vonnis

~~466/64~~ Checked by/Nagegaan deur

R.C.A./R.A.A. No. 7/a-10-63. Case/Saak No. 386/63

Police Station/Polisiekantoor Marshall Square

D220/82.

In the Supreme Court of South Africa. ~~1165/63~~

In die Hooggeregshof van Suid-Afrika.

(Transvaal Provincial DIVISION.
-AFDELING.)

To the Sheriff of the Province of the Transvaal or his lawful Deputy.

GREETING.

WHEREAS at a Criminal Session of the Supreme Court of South Africa holden before me at Pretoria on the 12th day of June in the Year of our Lord One Thousand Nine Hundred and Sixty-four the undermentioned prisoner was duly convicted of the crime(s) undermentioned and was sentenced by the Judgment of the said Court to undergo the punishment(s) affixed to his (her) name in such place as may be prescribed by lawful authority:

THIS IS THEREFORE to command you in the name of the State to keep and detain the said prisoner in your Custody until he (she) shall have suffered the said punishment, or be discharged therefrom according to law.

Aan die Balju van die Provinsie ... of sy wettige Adjunk.

SALUUT.

NADEMAAL by 'n strafsitting van die Hooggeregshof van Suid-Afrika gehou voor my te ... op die ... dag van ... in die Jaar van ons Here Eenduisend Negehonderd ... ondervermelde gevangene skuldig bevind is aan ondervermelde misdaad/misdade en by vonnis van genoemde Hof veroordeel is om die straf (strawwe) by sy (haar) naam vermeld te ondergaan in sodanige plek as wat die wettige owerheid mag voorskryf:

SO DIEN DIT OM u te gelas om in die naam van die Staat genoemde gevangene in u bewaring te ontvang en te hou totdat hy (sy) genoemde straf ondergaan het of ooreenkomstig die wet daarvan onthef word.

Prisoner's Name. Naam van Gevangene.	Sentence. Straf.
Nelson Mandela Age/Ouderdom 45 years. Nationality/Nasionaliteit. S.A. Born. Race/Ras. Bantu Sex/Geslag. Male 1AAC Classification of fine must be stated. Klassifikasie van boete moet aangegee word. 1AAC 90.02.11 1AAC LDA	Imprisonment for life (all counts taken together for purposes of sentence) Of what Crime convicted. Aan watter misdaad skuldig bevind. (1) Sabotage in contravention of Sect. 21(1) of Act Nº 76 of 1962 (Two Counts) (2) Contravening section 11(a) read with sections 1 and 12 of Act Nº 44 of 1950, as amended; (3) Contravening section 3(1)(b), read with Section 2 of Act Nº 8 of 1953, as amended.

FOR WHICH THIS SHALL BE YOUR WARRANT.
WAARVOOR DIT U LASBRIEF IS.

90.02.11 RDA

Given under my hand, at / Gegee onder my hand te Pretoria this / op hede die 12th day of / dag van June 1964

Registrar.
Griffier.

Presiding Judge.
Voorsittende Regter.

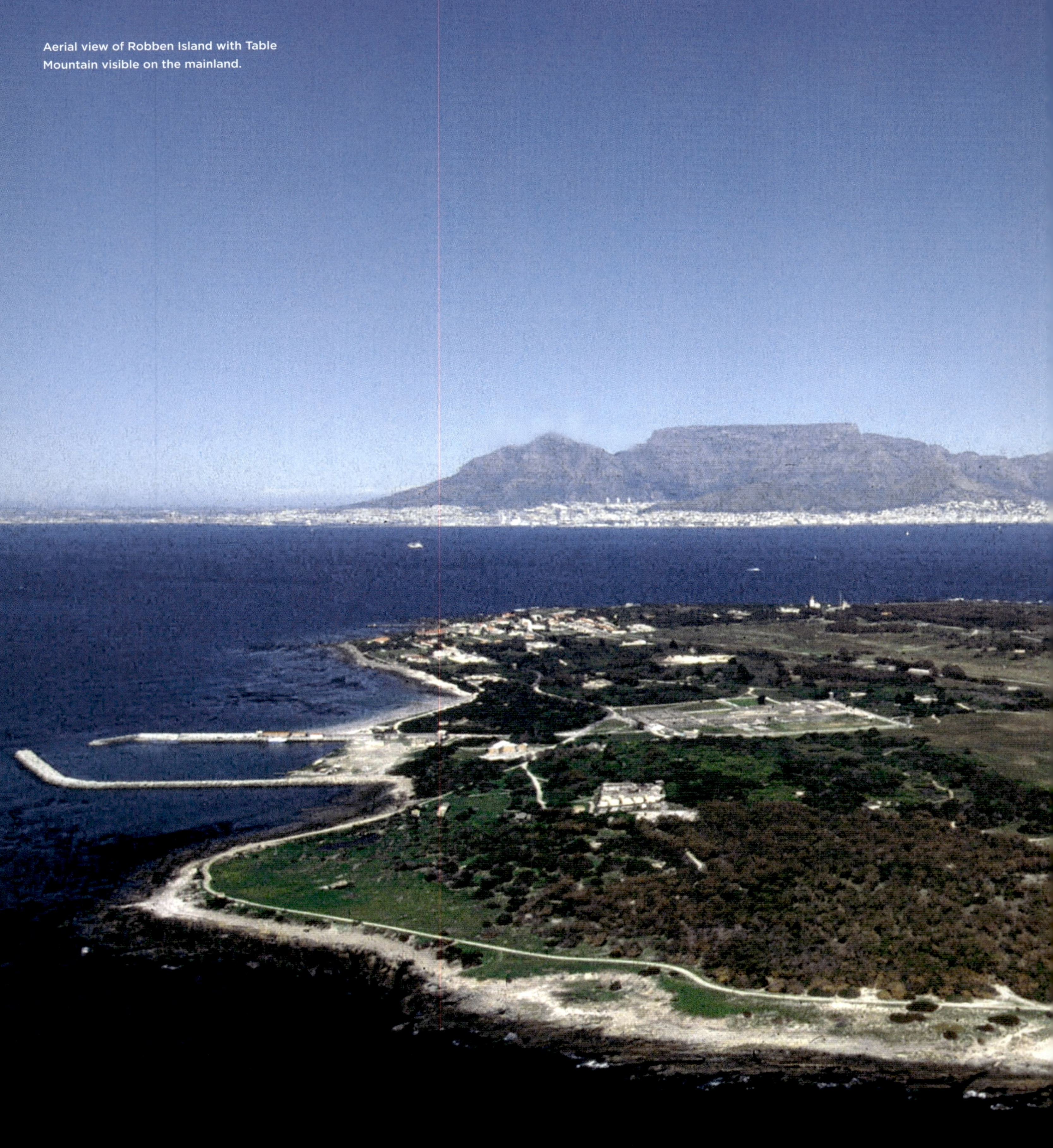

Aerial view of Robben Island with Table Mountain visible on the mainland.

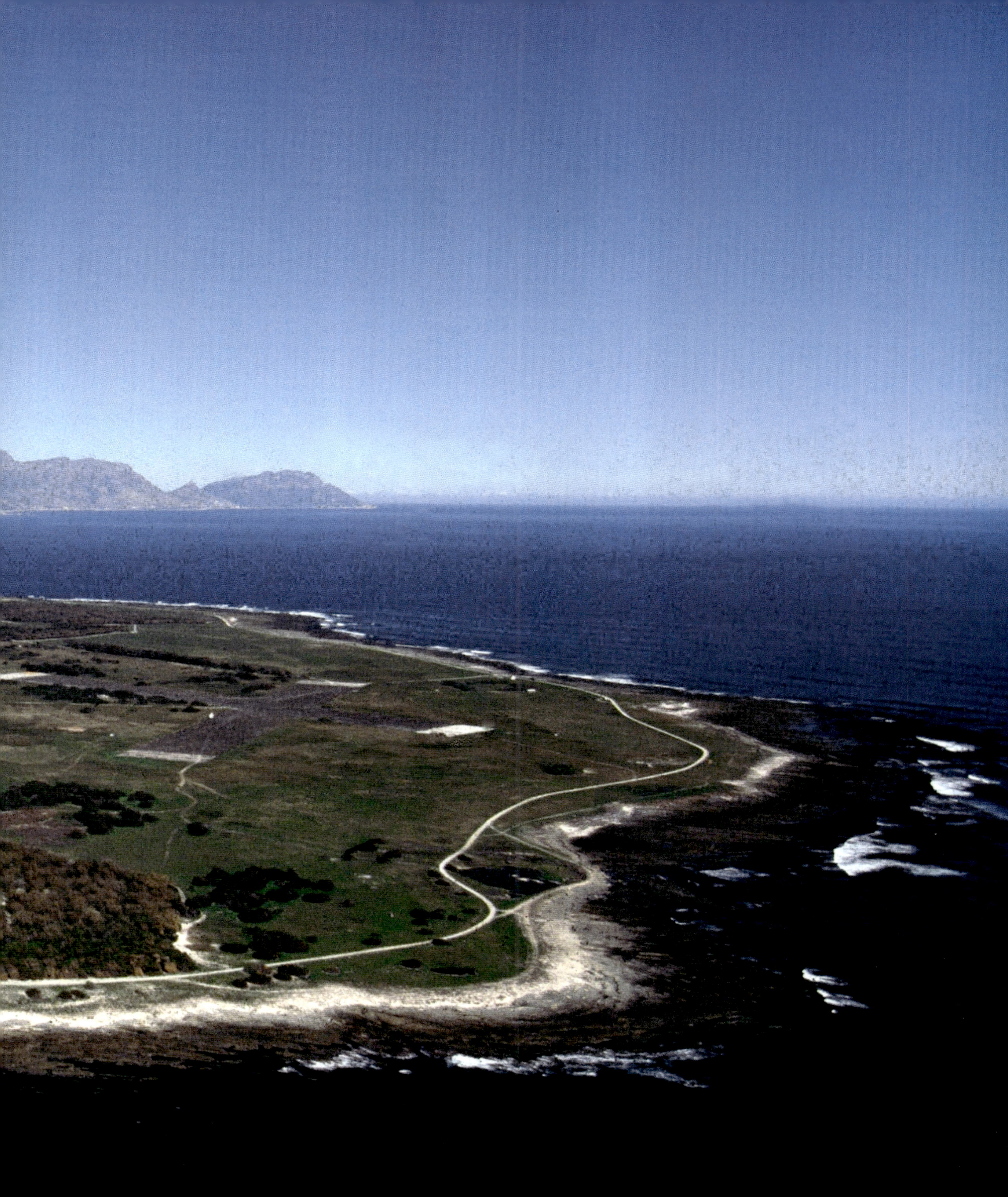

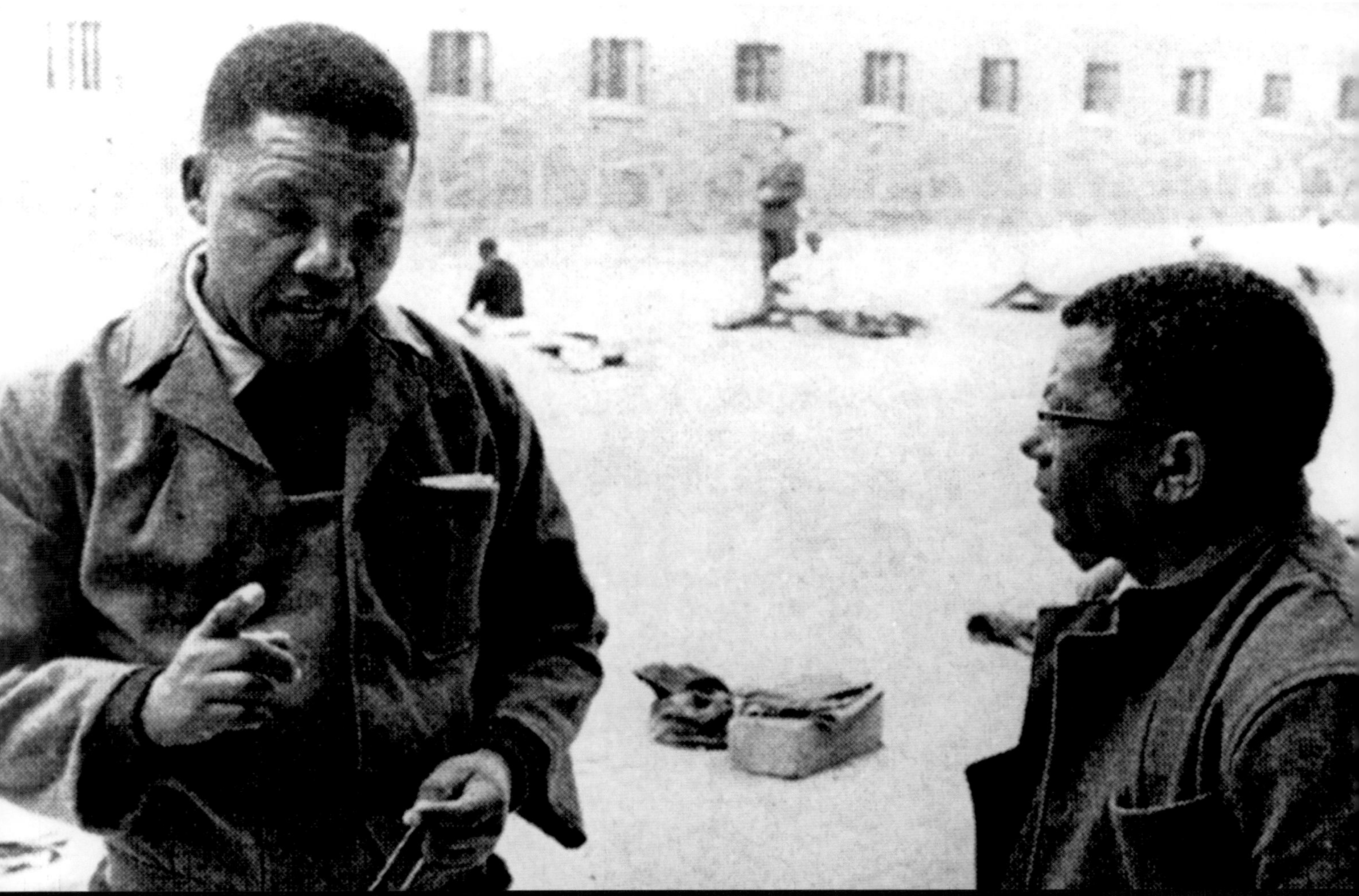

Robben Island has always been a place of sorrow.

In addition to being the location of a maximum-security prison mostly for political prisoners, Robben Island has been the site of a leper colony, a mental hospital, a jail during British colonial rule, and a military base. It is also the site of Tata's darkest years. Prison not only robbed him of his freedom, but the wardens attempted to take away his dignity. Inmates were forced to wear shorts—this was meant to infantilize the political prisoners and make them look like small boys. (In African culture at that time, only boys wore shorts.) They were required to eat the same food every day (stiff porridge in the mornings) and follow the same schedule. During his years on Robben Island, Tata was allowed visits only from immediate family members who had to apply to the prison commander for a visit, and he was allowed just a set number of visits and letters, both written and received. The letters he wrote often arrived with parts or pages missing.

Survival on Robben Island depended on inmate interdependency and support of one another. By understanding what the authorities were attempting to do and sharing that understanding with other inmates, their daily lives would be more tolerable. Furthermore, it was very hard, if not impossible, to resist alone. Tata did not know whether he would've been able to keep the spirit of resistance alive within him if it were not for the other inmates' courage, resolve, and determination to resist

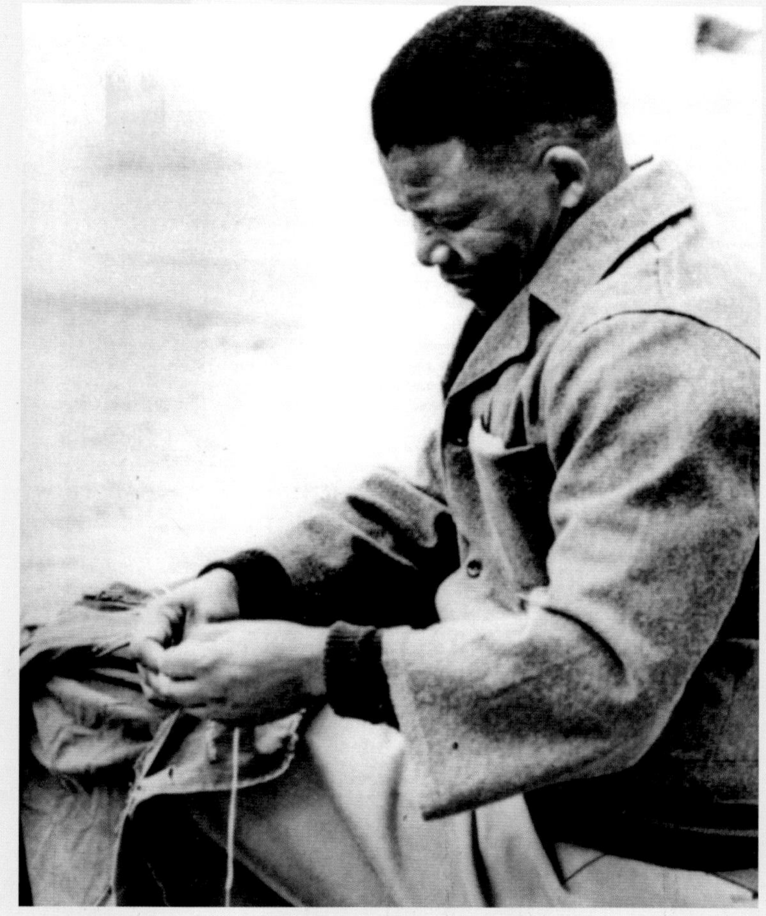

Opposite: Tata speaking with Uncle Walter in the prison's courtyard.

Right: Tata mending his prison clothes.

Below: Prisoners at work in the prison's courtyard.

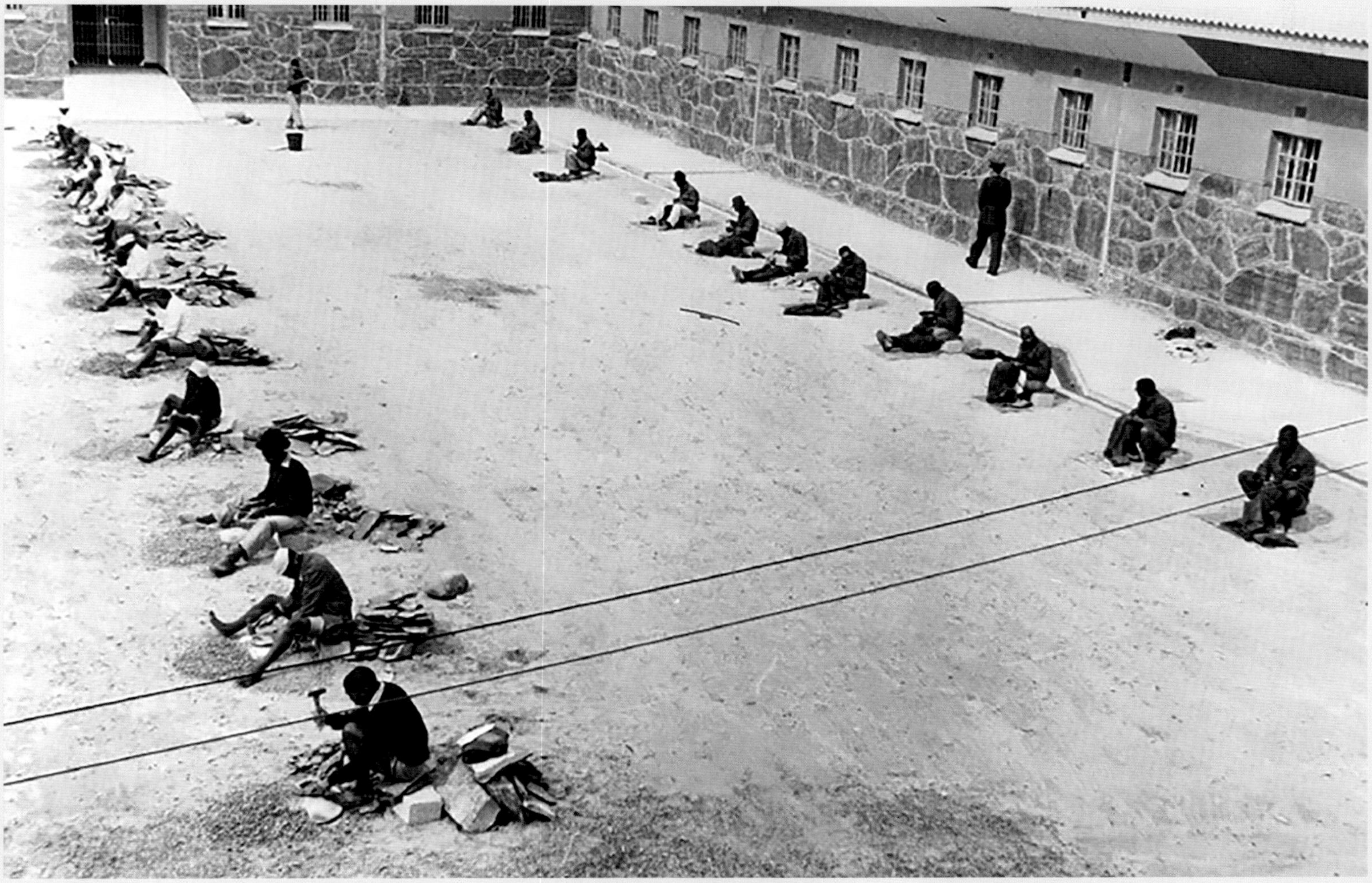

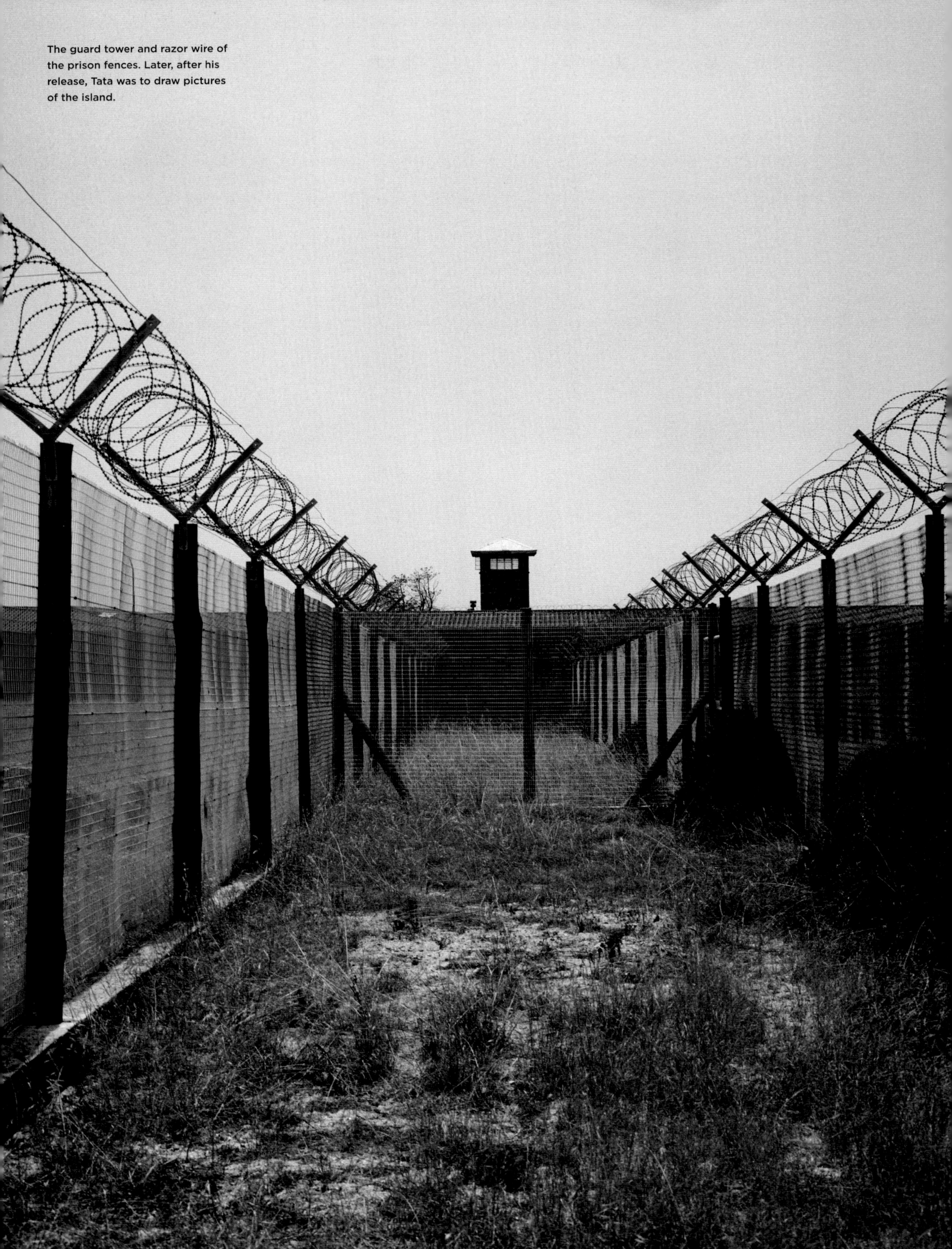

The guard tower and razor wire of the prison fences. Later, after his release, Tata was to draw pictures of the island.

Tata was not simply naive, he really seemed to have an inner knowledge that he would one day be free.

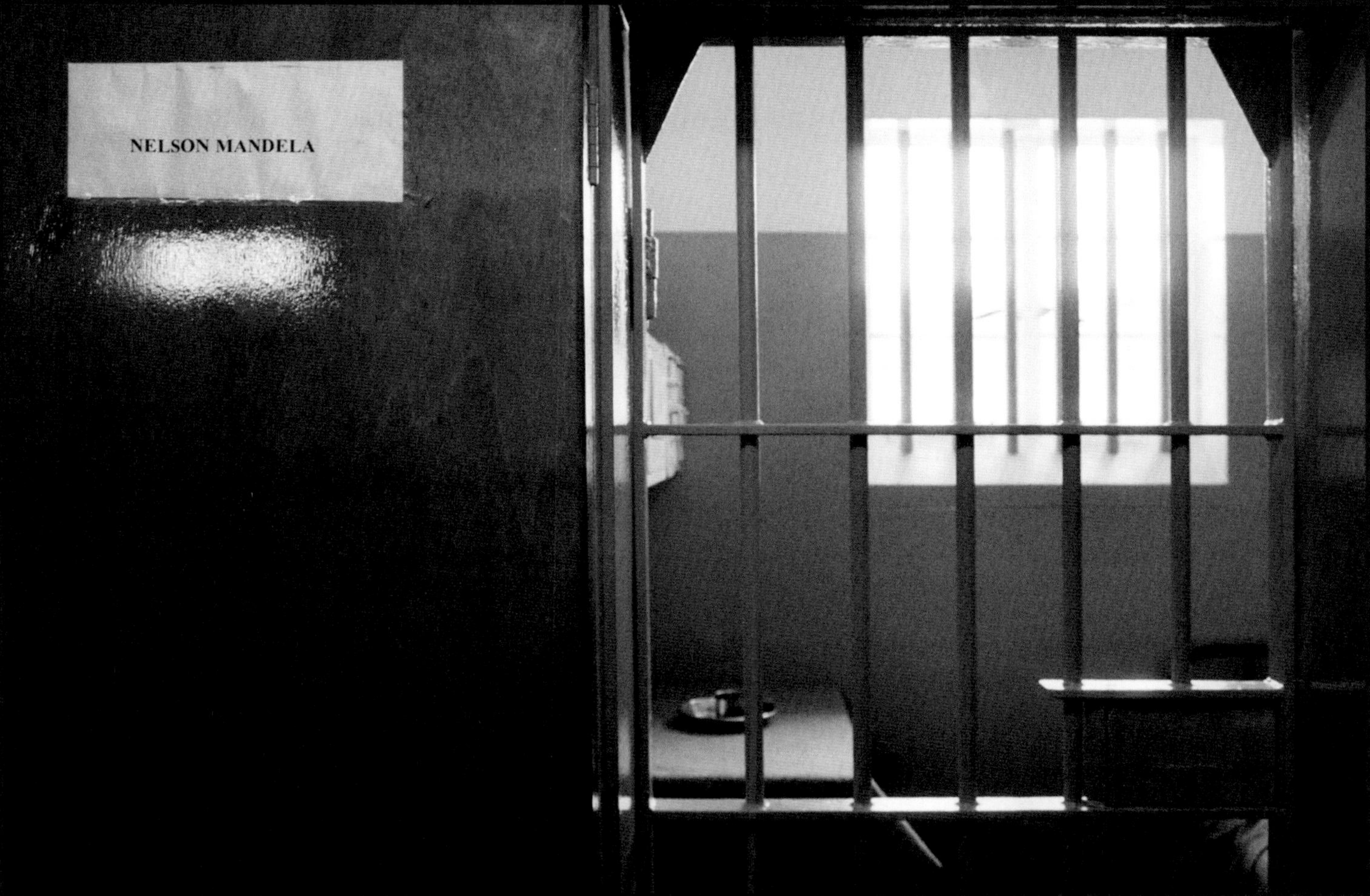

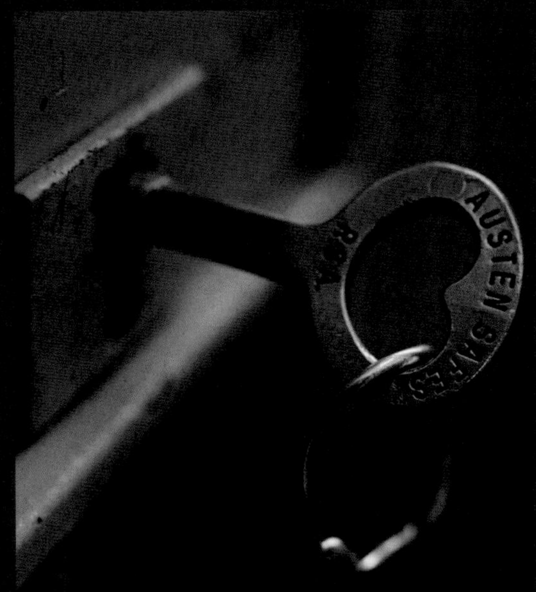

The deep sense of destiny related to his heritage as a young Thembu was translated into his political career and then sustained him during prison. He always said that "no one would rob him of his dignity." This was one of the objectives of prison wardens—to make a political prisoner know that he was worth nothing. It gave Tata something concrete to resist. He would face numerous opportunities to be miserable and even beaten down in prison during the next twenty-seven years, but he maintained his resolve not to despair but to hope that he would one day be free in a South Africa he believed was possible.

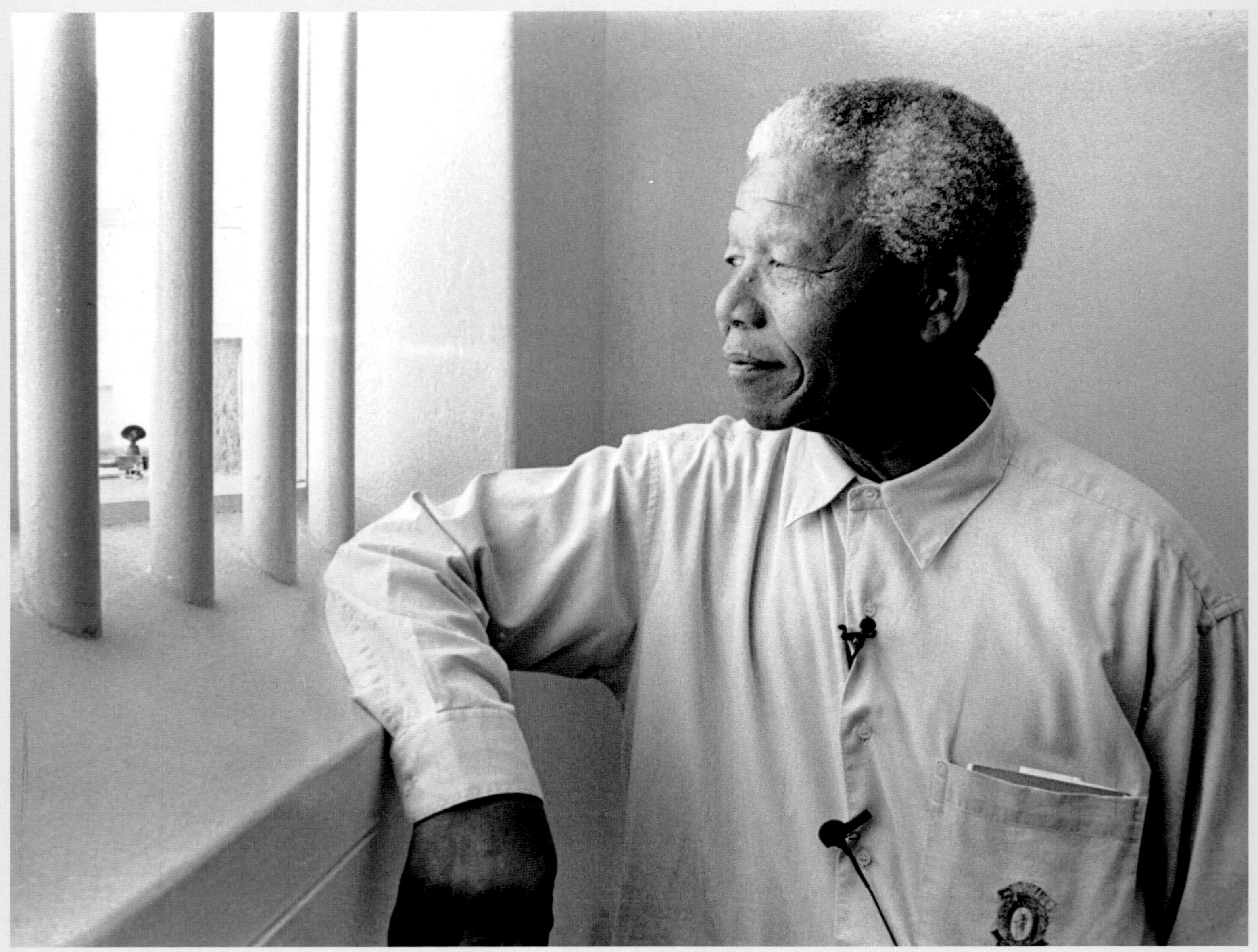

Two months after becoming president of South Africa, Tata visited the prison cell where he'd spent nearly three decades of his life, 1994.

Immediately following the Rivonia Trial, the eight men sentenced to life imprisonment were secretly transported at night in a Dakota military aircraft to Robben Island prison. Tata and other political prisoners occupied cells with no furniture; they slept on straw mats on the concrete floor and had only worn-out blankets to use during the cold nights. It was only after several protests and letters written to the prison officials in Pretoria that they were given beds. The doors to the cells did not close fully; there was a gap at the bottom of the door. With no running water in their cells, prisoners used metal buckets as toilets. Every day for thirteen years they worked in the island's quarry. The brutal work at the blindingly bright quarry damaged the eyes of most of the prisoners. A cave on the site was used to hide materials for study and as a shelter at lunchtime. In March 1982, after being held at Robben Island for eighteen years, Tata was transferred to Pollsmoor Prison in Tokai, Cape Town. He served the last fourteen months of his sentence in Victor Verster Prison in Paarl. On February 11, 1990, he was finally released. When Tata went to Robben Island in 1964, he was the 466th person to be incarcerated there and was given the now-infamous number 46664. This number has since been used as a symbol of perseverance against oppression.

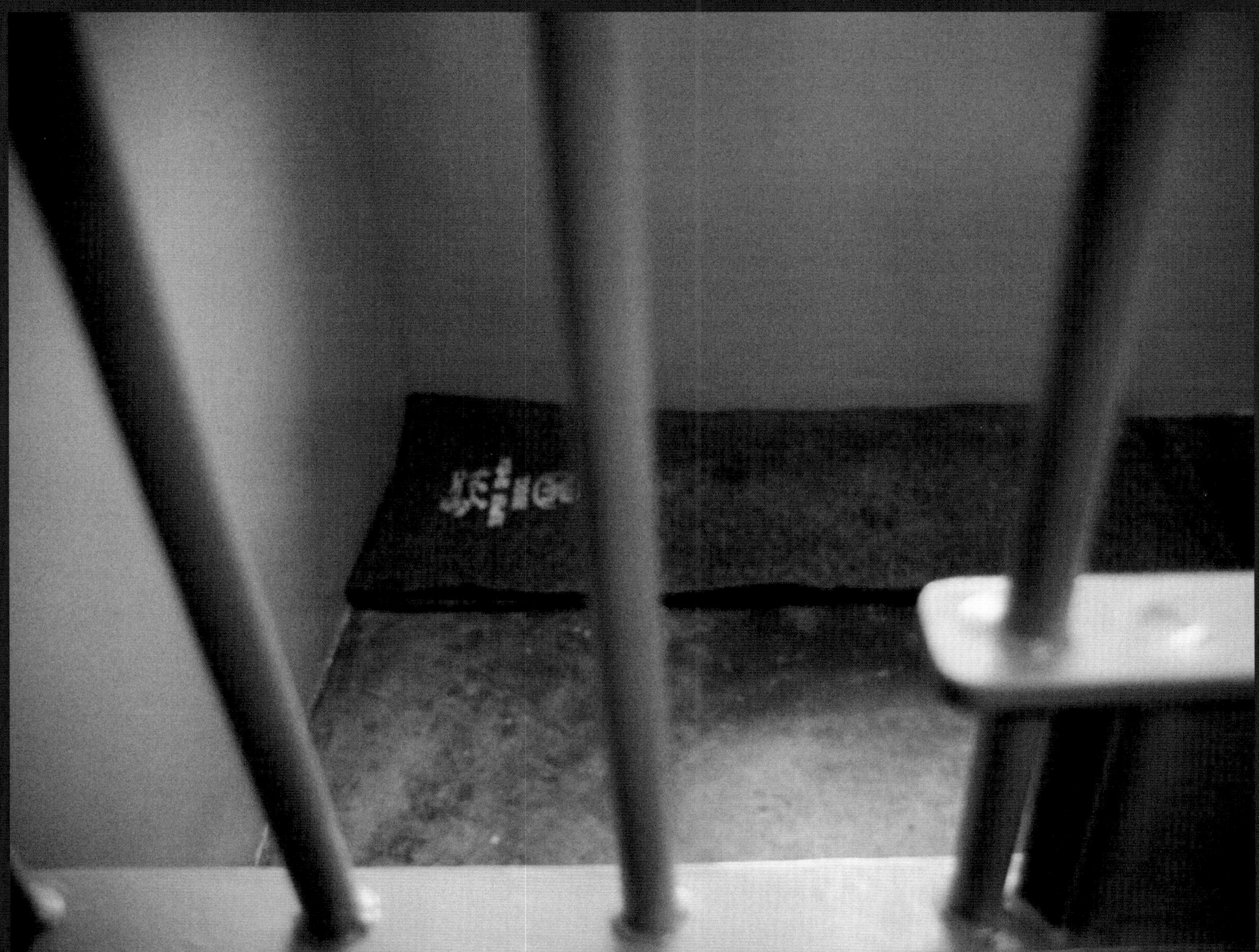
Tata's prison cell on Robben Island.

46664

* But for days I was lost in thought, wondering how I could show

I hope you have not forgotten the matter I raised in my letter of the 29th November 1969 relating to your own personal position. I hope at your next visit you will give me some progress report. I am anxious that you put yourself in a position whereby you will be able to guide the children in the choice of careers and in preparing them for such careers. The home atmosphere must exist which will encourage them to strive for the highest ideals in life, and this depends largely on you. Today your mother and mother-in-law are there to help you bring up Ndindi and Nandi, but sooner or later they will also pass to eternal rest, leaving you to fight all alone, and to face the difficult task of supervising the progress of the children. I shall say more on this matter when you come. In the meantime please read the letter again.

Nandi looks really fine in her maroon and white outfit. The green vegetation that forms the background to the photo is beautiful and reminds me of the happy and romantic days of my childhood. I can almost smell the sweet perfumes that must have filled the area where she posed. I have taken particular note of her mischievous smile. It is a charming picture and I am happy you sent it. I put it alongside that of Zeni and Zindzi.

Many thanks for the beautiful Xmas card you sent me. You must have combed the whole of Cape Town to get it. I like its bright red background and its artistic arrangement. I also received Ntombi's with the chocolate belle on the cover. The two of you must be little witches. You seem to know my tastes better than I do. They are really wonderful and was happy to receive them.

What is happening? Why have you not come? You wrote as far back as ~~December~~ November and told me that you had applied for a visiting permit. ~~Three~~ Four full months have passed and you have not turned up. Did you apply by registered letter? Do know I am looking forward to seeing you soon. Perhaps it may be advisable before you renew your application to phone Mum Winnie, Orlando 113, and find out if she has not already applied to come down.

My fondest regards to your mother and step-father and love to you, Ndindi, Ntombi and Lennard.

Yours affectionately,
Tata.

Mrs Lydia Thoko Mandela, "Hillbrow", ~~Retreat~~ 7th avenue, Retreat.

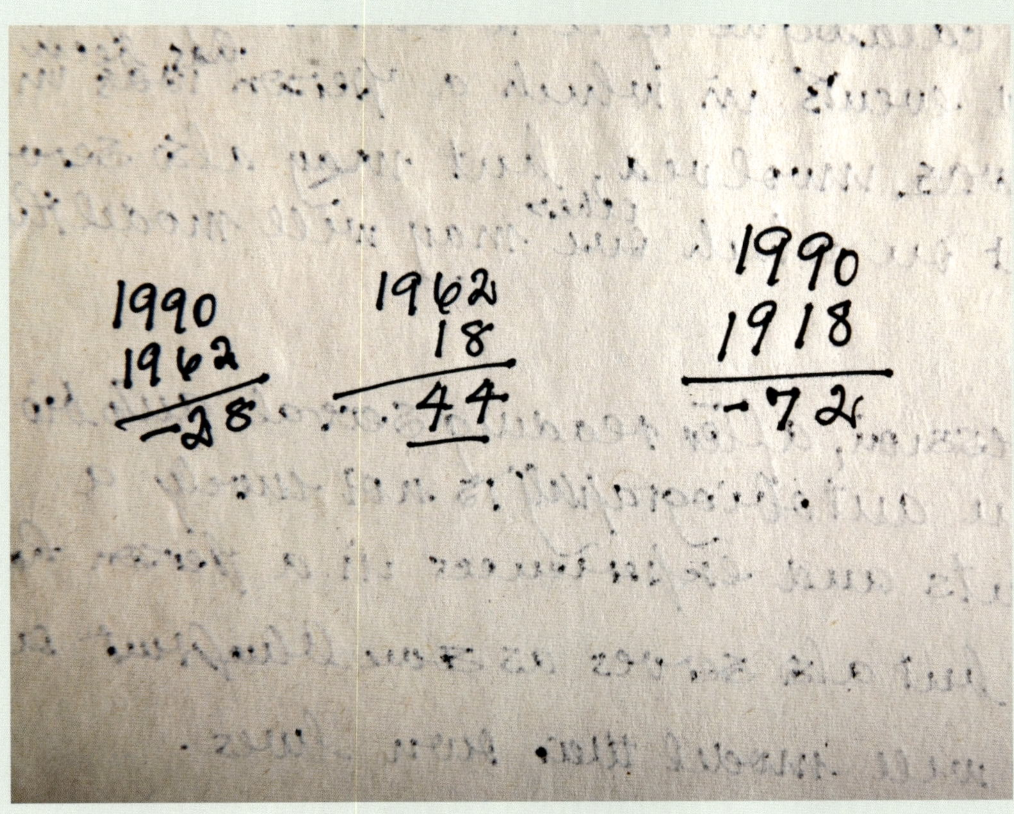

Opposite: Tata would keep his mind busy while alone in his cell by writing in his journal and writing letters to family and friends. Here he is writing to Thoko, my brother Thembi's fiancée.

Above: Tata calculating the number of years he spent in prison, including the years he was held while on trial. He was imprisoned when he was forty-four years old and released at the age of seventy-two.

Years later, Tata created a series of drawings of Robben Island along with handwritten notes to describe his sketches. While to many these years represented a period of hardship, an era to be forgotten, they were not to Tata. As was often the case, he looked at the world with eternal optimism.

"When it came to re-created visions of Robben Island, I needed to share this rich experience of culture which to me has a very special meaning. When I initially did the sketches in black chalk the images looked quite bleak.

I then thought that it should be a celebration and introduced bright and cheery colors, which I understand have become a new art form, and I hope that it will give you as much pleasure as I have had in creating these images."

Tata's thoughts on the Robben Island sketches, February 2003

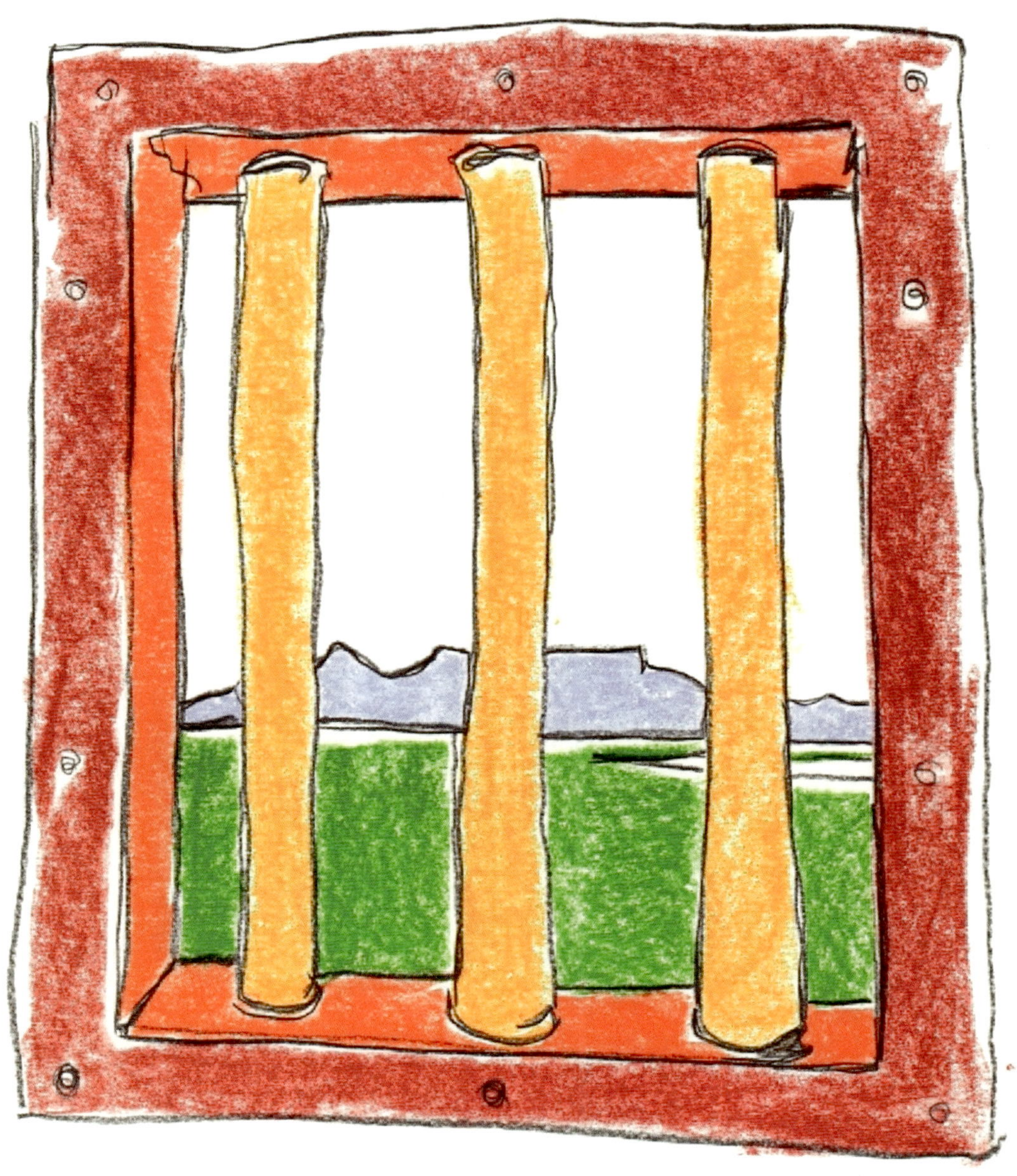

AP XXIV/L

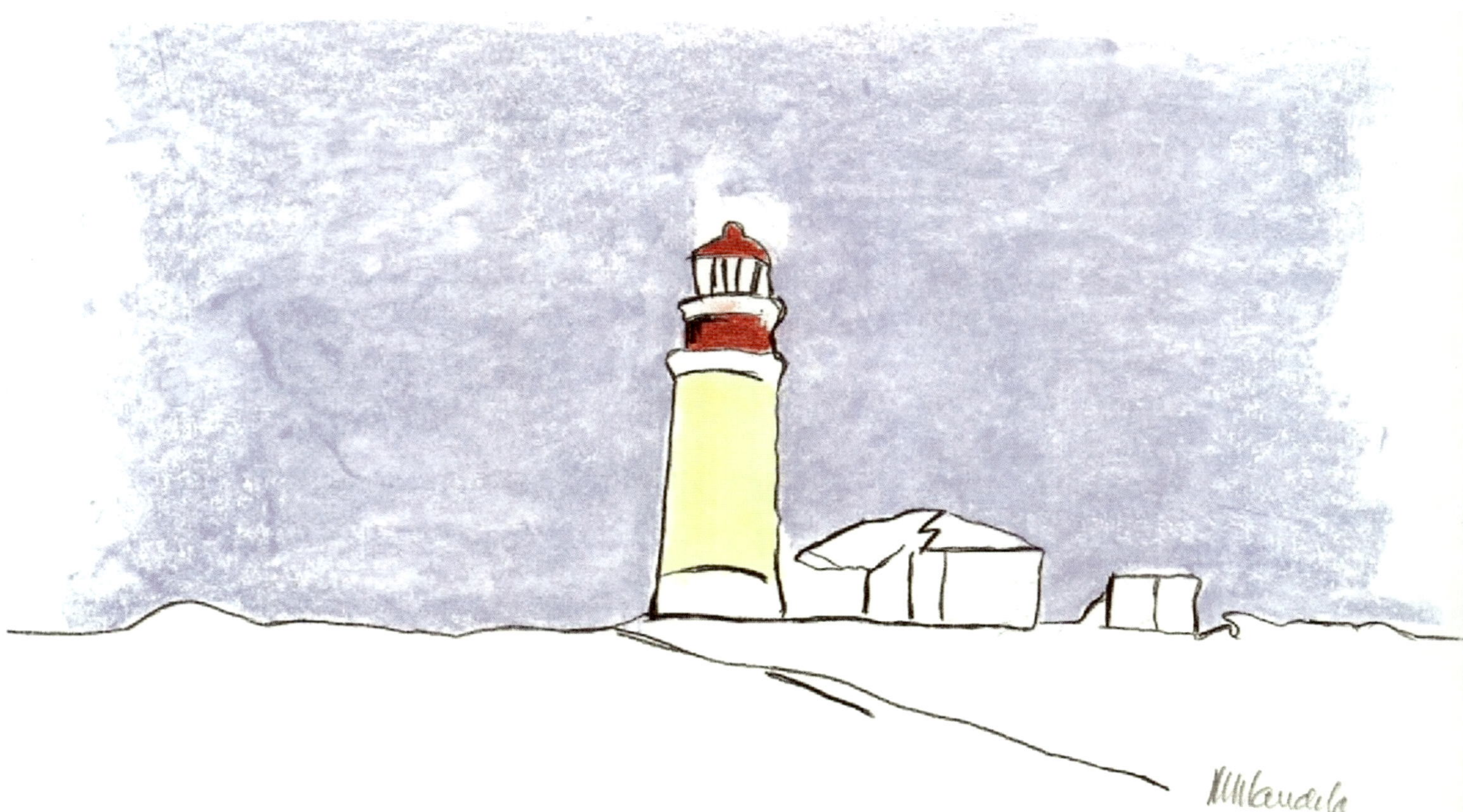

AP XXIV/L

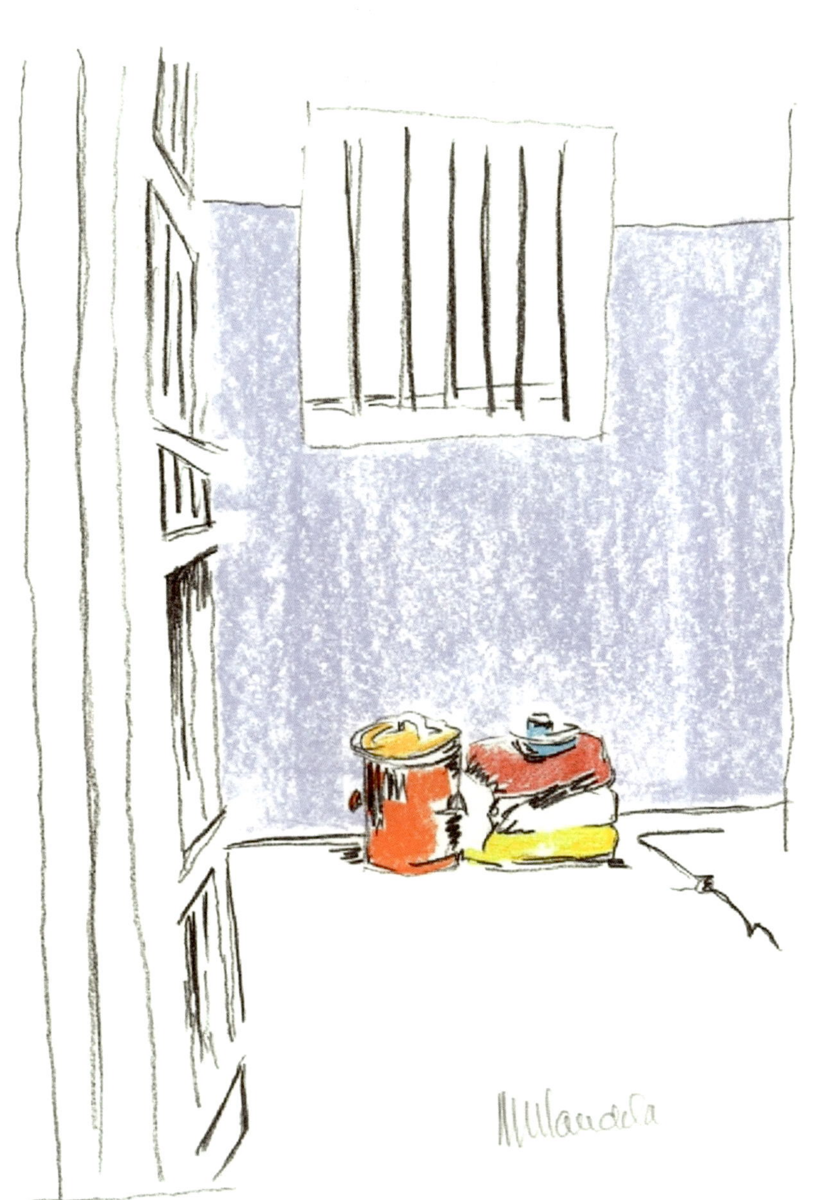

AP XXIV/L

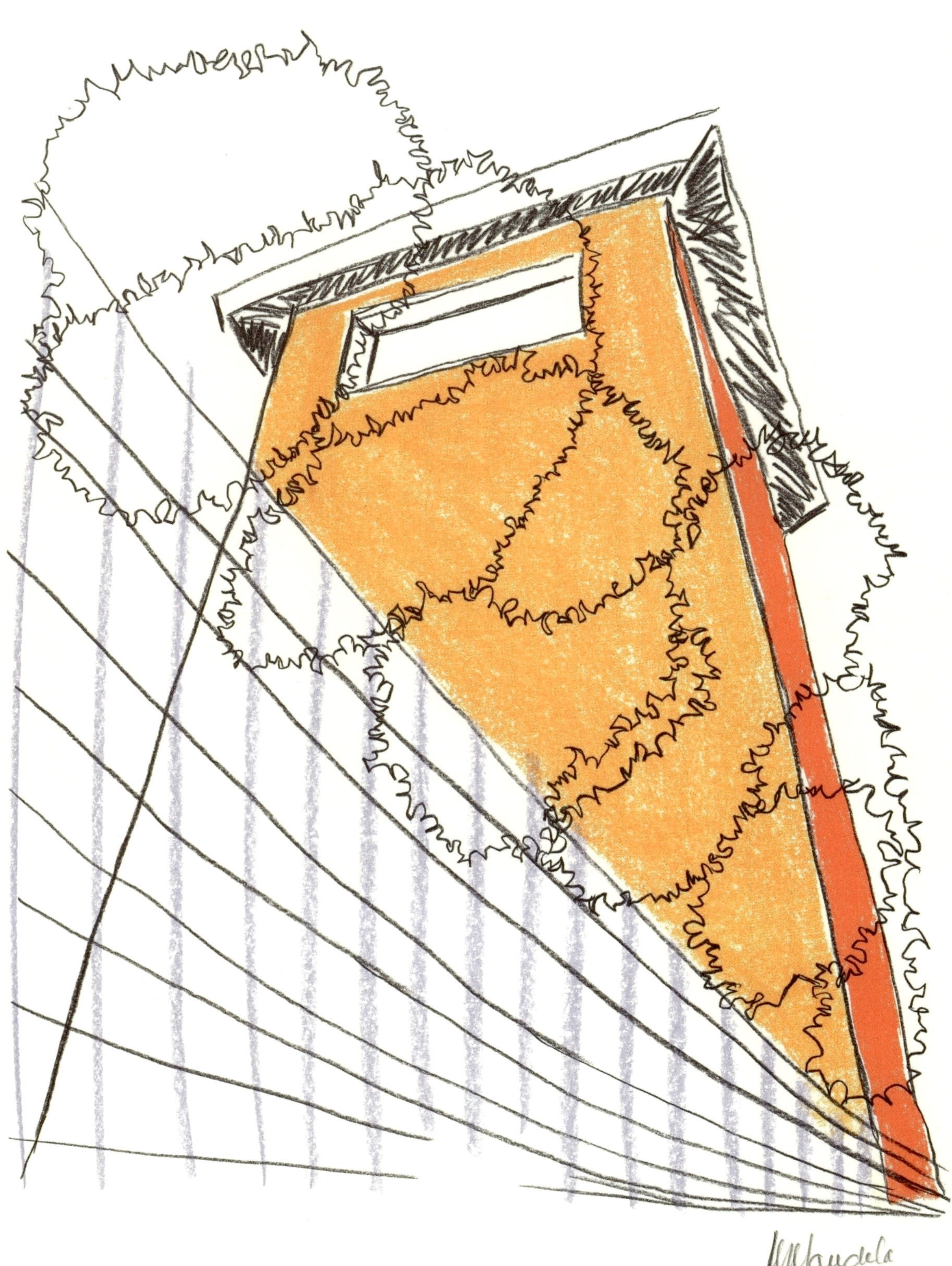

Tata describes the harsh reality of life on Robben Island, especially the watchful presence of the guard towers and the barbed wire.

Barbed wire fences and ominous towers became a tragic backdrop to life on Robben Island. At the time of my imprisonment, Robben Island was without question the harshest, most iron-fisted prison in the South African penal system. It was a remote and lonely island outpost for both prisoners and prison staff.

The racial divide on Robben Island was absolute. There were no black warders and there were no white warders demanded a master-servant relationship. There were no watches or clocks on Robben Island, we were dependent on bells and warders whistles and shouts as our time-pieces.

In the prison, the towers looked over us throughout the day. In this sketch I have attempted to pull together the two elements that overshadowed our lives for so many years: the towers and the ever-restraining barbed wire. The image shows the harsh reality that reminds me of our sacrifice and endurance, the use of more cheerful colours in the sketch is my way of presenting how we feel today.

NMandela

133/500

The courtyard in Robben Island prison was an unfriendly, empty and barren place. It was a sombre reminder of where I was. From the beginning of my imprisonment I asked to start a garden in the courtyard, to change this sad looking place. After years of refusing my request, we were finally given permission to plant a small garden on a narrow patch of earth against a wall. Being able to plant and nurture life in this prison courtyard offered me a sense of freedom and satisfaction that is hard to put into words even today. A garden is one of the few things in prison that one could control.

A powerful memory that I have is of a beautiful tomato plant that I coaxed from tiny seed to tender seedling to a strong plant that gave plump bright red juicy tomatoes. Despite my efforts the plant began to wither and die and nothing I did would heal it. When it died I took it carefully from the soil, washed its roots and buried it in a corner of the garden. I felt sad. It once again reminded me of where I was, and the hopelessness I felt at being unable to nourish other relationships in my life. My wife, my children, my family and my friends. It made me realise the beauty, simplicity and sacred value of family, of loved ones & friends. I swore to myself that I would never take another human being, their friendship or their love for granted ever again.

NMandela

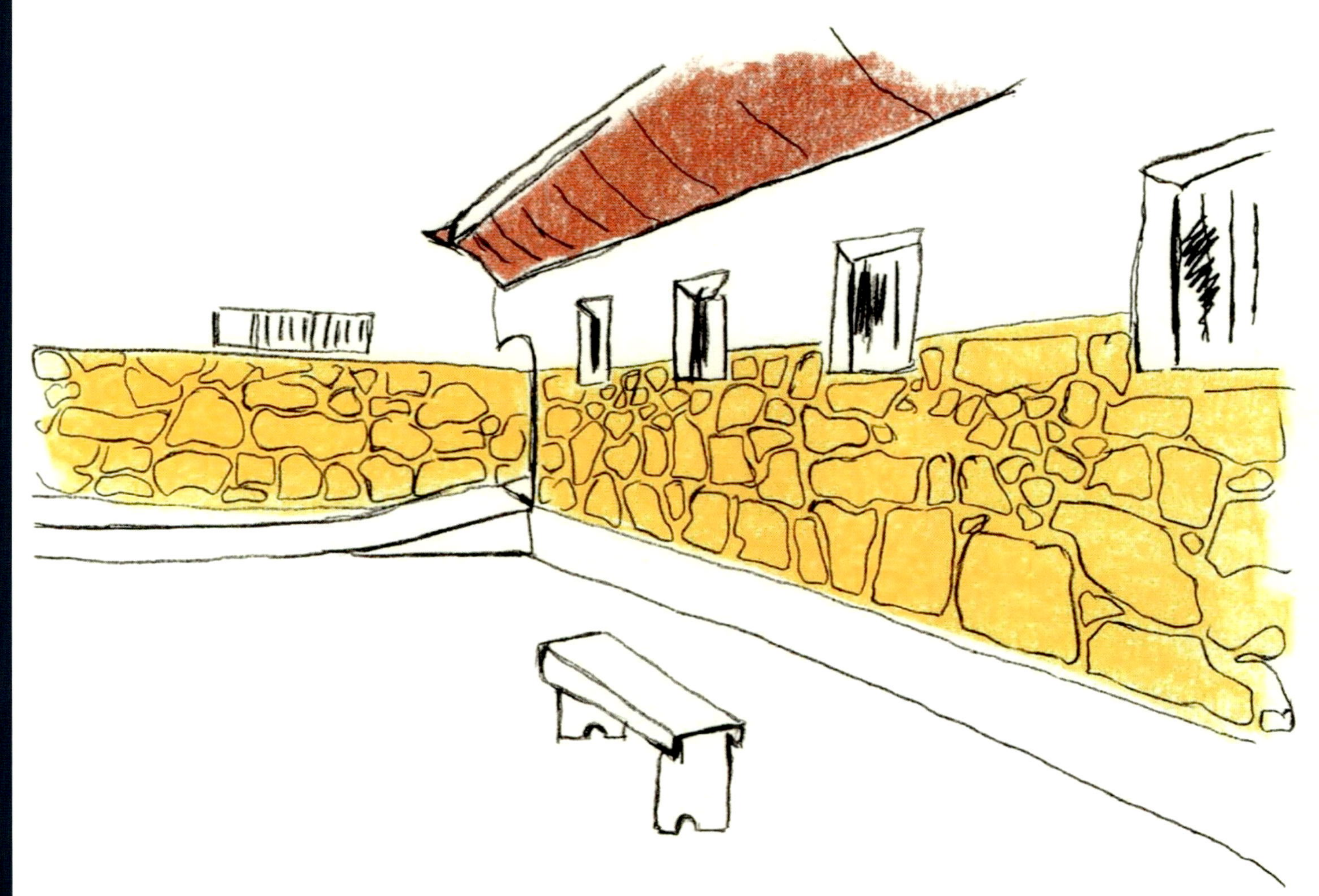

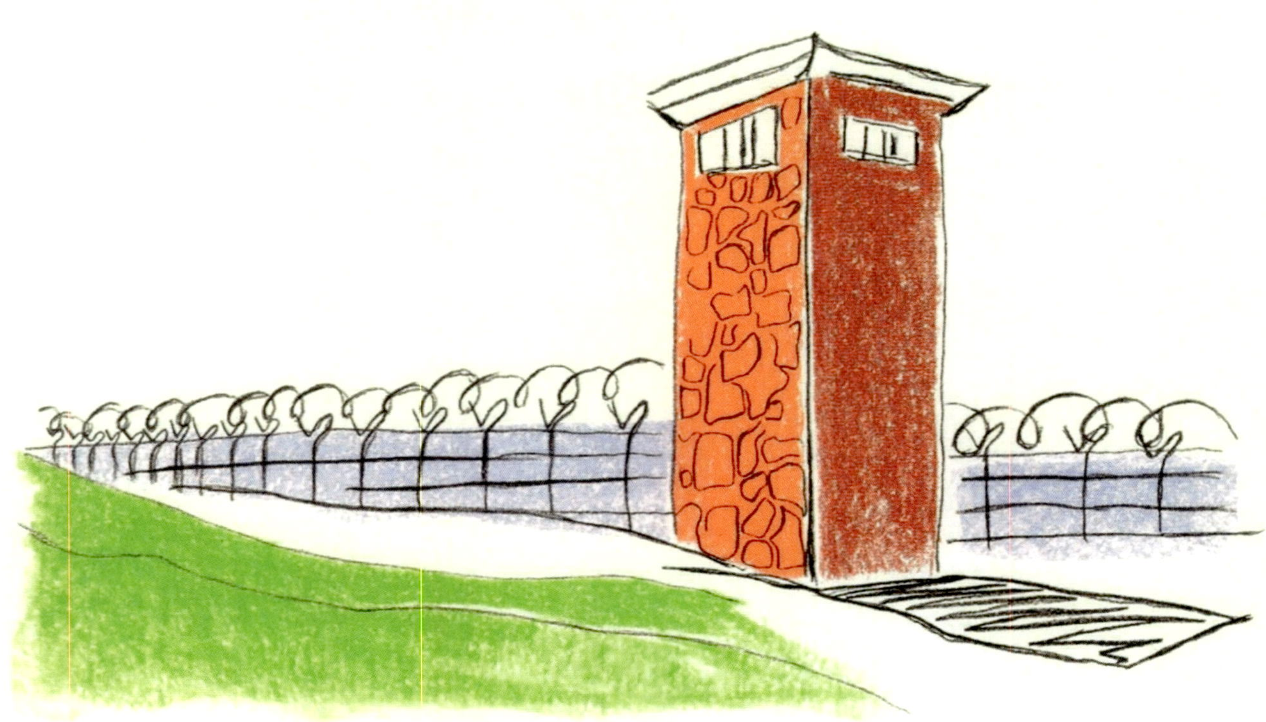

Prisoners on Robben Island, including Tata, departed from this area to work the quarries nearby, experiencing a sense of freedom at being able to walk in the open air, but upon their return each day, the tower reminded

The guard tower seen in this image marked the corner of the Robben Island prison compound. It was the point at which the dirt road from the stone quarry met the boundary patrol road. We worked the quarries for thirteen years as part of our "hard labour" sentence. It was hard work, but we did not mind, as it meant we could leave the prison compound and have the "freedom" to walk and talk together on the long road to the quarry. These were invigorating times.

We would feel the wind in our faces, see the birds flying in freedom and smell the eucalyptus blossoms. I remember seeing gemsbok and springboks grazing in the plains.

After a day of relative "freedom" the tower was a grim reminder as we returned to the prison each evening. Conversation between us would usually become less and less as we approached the tower.

The tower reminded us of exactly where we were and where we had expected to stay for the rest of our lives. How little we guessed at the great changes that would sweep our country in our lifetime... that in my lifetime I would exchange these prison walls for freedom, not just my freedom, but the freedom of all my country's peoples, a freedom which has become a symbol for all.

NMandela

In 1977 forced manual labour was ended after we maintained a two-year go-slow strike. We asked to do something more useful with our days instead of the monotony of mining lime and stone from the quarries. This action, however, robbed us of the opportunity to exercise, and after much effort we convinced the warders to allow us to convert the courtyard into a tennis court.

Prior to this, the prisoners were marched round and round the courtyard for half an hour every day. We used to walk around the courtyard quickly in single file under the watchful eye of the guards.

Our persistence paid off and we painted the cement courtyard surface to create a traditional tennis court layout. Strangely, Robben Island was the first opportunity for me to play tennis since university. I was by no means an expert, but the exercise was a welcome break from the walks to and from the quarry and round and round the yard.

Being able to exercise one's mind and body through play was an immensely freeing. Playing tennis and attending to my gardening became my two favourite hobbies on Robben Island. It was a strange sensation enjoying such civilised hobbies in such an uncivilised place. It caused me to reflect on the strange and perverse nature of apartheid, where they wrongly thought that one people's freedom could only be enjoyed at the expense and oppression of another.

NMandela

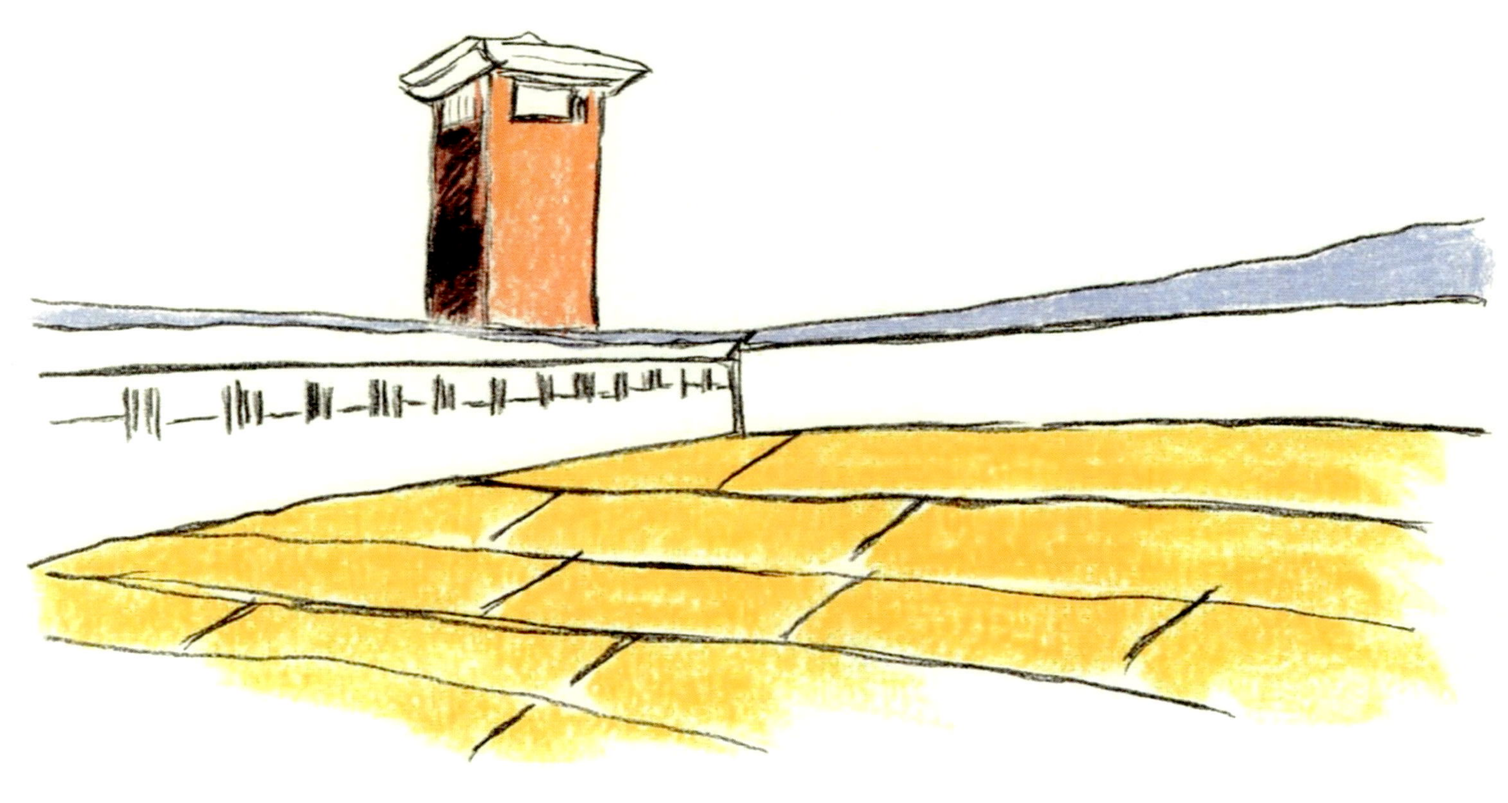

A sense of hope in a hopeless place: prisoners were allowed to paint the courtyard to resemble a tennis court.

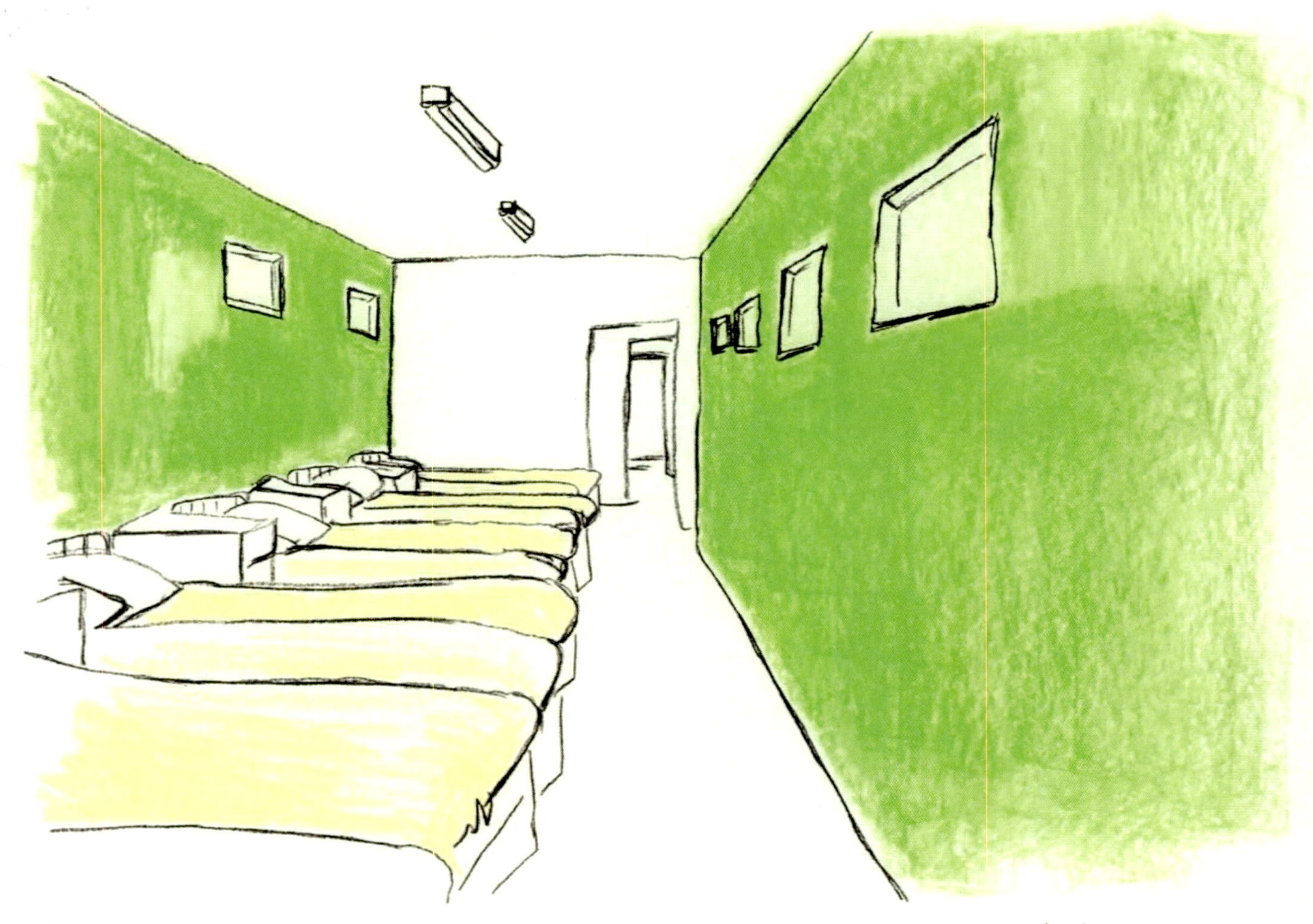

On Robben Island political and general prisoners were kept well apart. The only place where we could talk and share information with other inmates was in the prison hospital - and that thereby became more than just an infirmary. The hospital I have sketched here served as a secret and vital link between us and the rest of the world. Through the hospital, news about our families, our friends, the struggle and everyday events outside the prison would trickle through. It became one of our most important life lines to the outside world.

On arrival at the prison, all new prisoners were sent to the hospital for medical observation. On arrival one of the political detainees would feign illness and thereby gain access to the same space in the hospital where they would share their news with us.

As time passed the news became less depressing as we realised that the apartheid regime was weakening, that the voice of our struggle was being heard in the outside world and that a great wave of support was growing for all the people of South Africa.

Today I remember the stark hospital wards with fondness.. These memories, like this sketch are filled with joyous colours

NMandela

Today when I look at Robben Island I see it as a celebration of the struggle and a symbol of the finest qualities of the human spirit, rather than as a monument to the brutal tyranny and oppression of apartheid.

Robben Island is a place where courage endured in the face of endless hardship, a place where people kept on believing when it seemed their dreams were hopeless and a place where wisdom and determination overcame fear and human frailty.

It is true that Robben Island was once a place of darkness, but out of that darkness has come a wonderful brightness, a light so powerful that it could not be hidden behind prison walls, held back by a prison bars or hemmed in by the surrounding sea.

In these sketches entitled: My Robben Island, I have attempted to colour the Island sketches in ways that reflect the positive light in which I view it. This is what I would like to share with people around the world and, hopefully, also project the idea that even the most fantastic dreams can be achieved if we are prepared to endure life's challenges.

450/500

NMandela

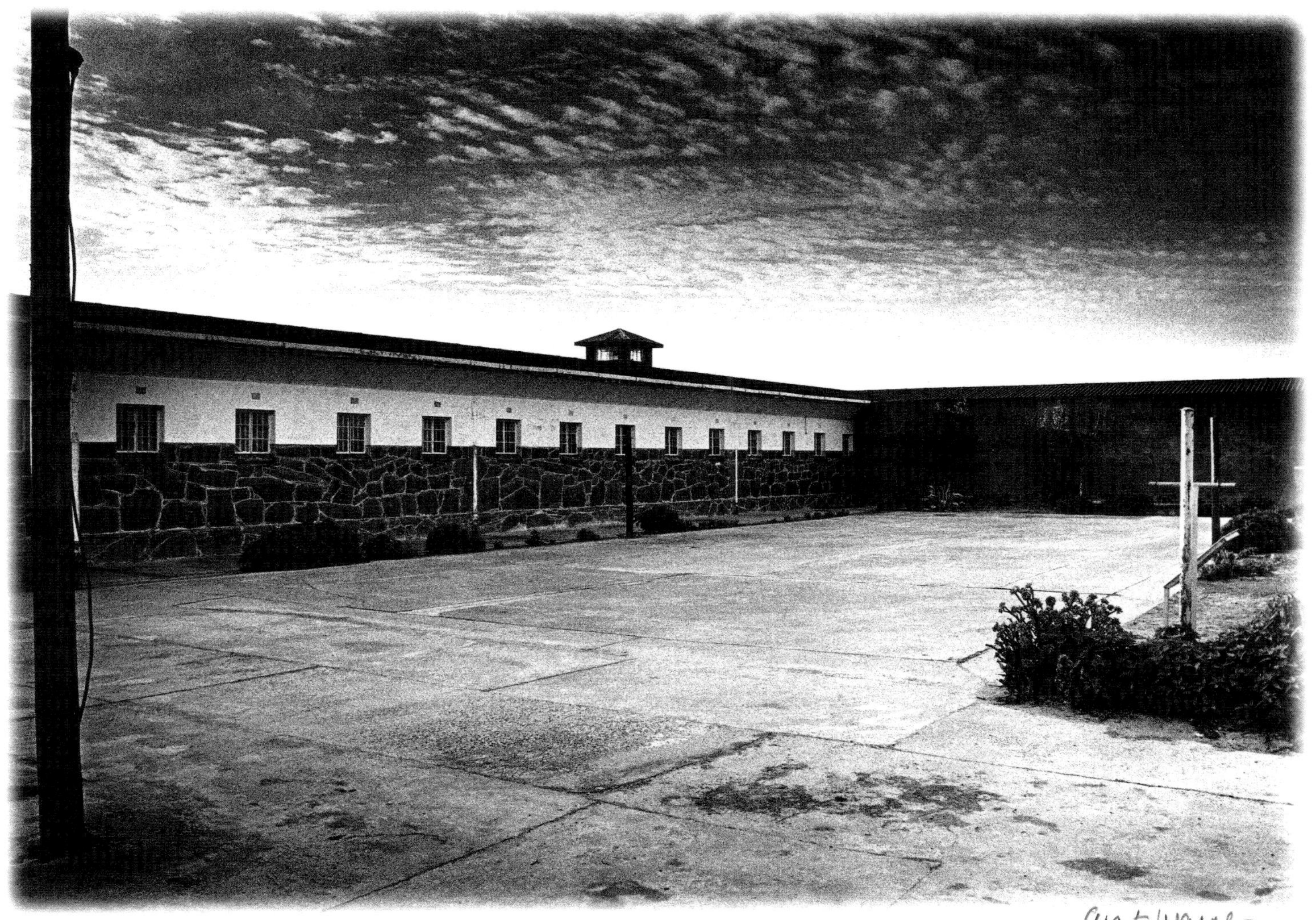

Example of a photo that inspired Tata's drawings of Robben Island.

5

The Family Man

"In truth, a family is what you make it. It is made strong, not by number of heads counted at the dinner table, but by the rituals you help family members create, by the memories you share, by commitment of time, caring, and love you show to one another, and by the hopes for the future you have as individuals and as a unit."

A quotation from author Marge Kennedy that I believe is a sentiment my father shared

Tata's sketch of a united family.

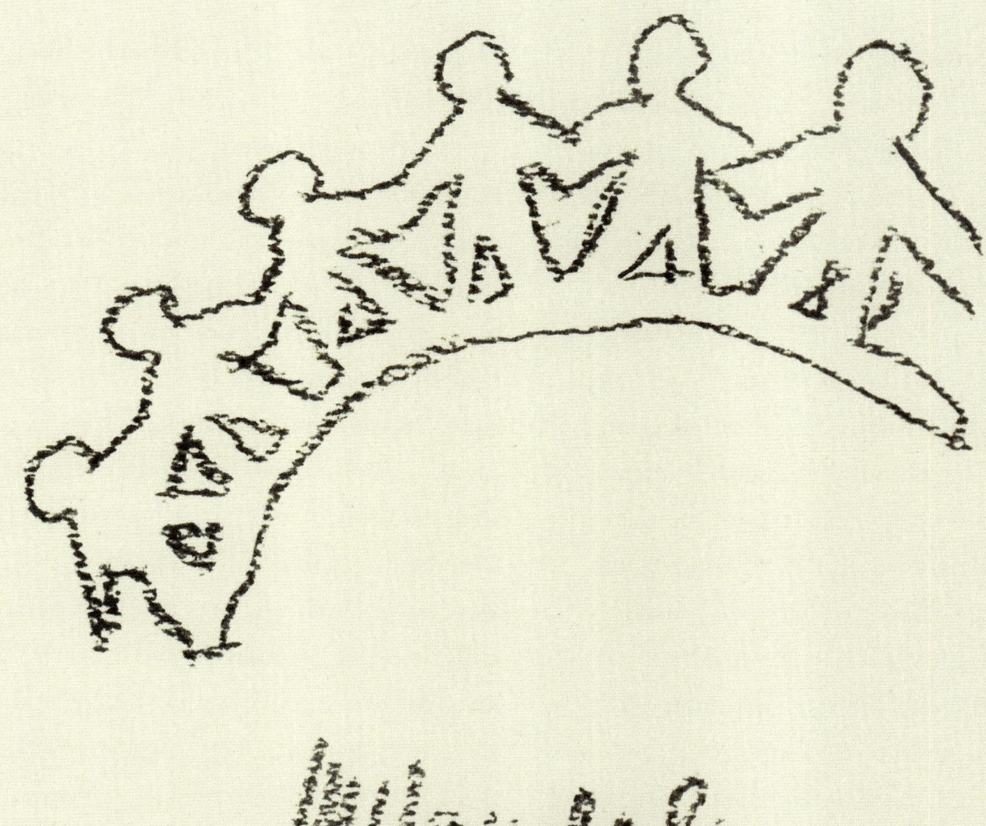

The choices that Tata made in life are not unique to him.

Many a man and woman made choices that sacrificed family for the good of society.

For Tata as a young Xhosa child, cultural life was about custom, ritual, and family connections that included those with our ancestors. He said "this was the alpha and omega of our existence, and it went unquestioned." The notion of "family" in African culture is not defined in the same way as the nuclear family of white Western culture. One's family is very broad. The sons and daughters of your siblings are considered your children, too. The children of your aunts and uncles are considered brothers and sisters. Your aunt is also your mother and your uncle is your father. There are no cousins, half-brothers, or half-sisters. We are all connected. The African concept of "Ubuntu" stems from this deep sense of family and community. Ubuntu means that people are human because of the other humans they are surrounded by—we are interconnected and interdependent and therefore all deserve kindness, care, respect, and dignity because of the mere fact that we are human. Tata often pointed out that it was his childhood nurturing, the experience of his childhood environment, his family values and culture, that shaped his identity, his view of family, and a great deal of his politics. His choices were also an outcome of his lineage. So, for a person like Tata in the sociopolitics of South Africa at that time, there was probably little choice between being an average husband and father and putting all one's energy behind the struggle for freedom for the greater African family.

Tata loved us but he also knew that there was a large, extended family that would not leave his wives or children hopeless. In the back of his mind, and as part of his culture, he believed they would be cared for by the greater family.

I think this is why many Black political figures could make the difficult choices to sacrifice conventional family life for the good of society. Our family was helped by people like K. D. Matanzima, who was considered a brother. Tata's younger brother—son of Tata's mother's sister—Sitsheketshe Mandela, helped us. And many more to whom we are forever grateful. The Sisulus were also considered family and not just through friendship. My mum's mum and Uncle Walter's mum were sisters. And when my brothers passed away, their children were my children and I was their mum. Tata loved his own family—we had no doubt about that—even though, in my youth, I only experienced his fatherhood from a distance. As children growing up in a modernizing society that was in huge transition, this affected each of us positively and negatively in different ways. It was not easy to resolve the fact that Tata was the "Father of the Nation" yet he could not be "there" for us! As an older man in retirement, he tried to make up for it. Instead of continuing for a second term as president of the nation, he made a choice for "family." He really wanted to spend more time with all of us as he had missed out on so much. He married three times. Had four children from his first wife, two with his second wife, eighteen grandchildren, and fourteen great grandchildren at the time of his passing, and more since.

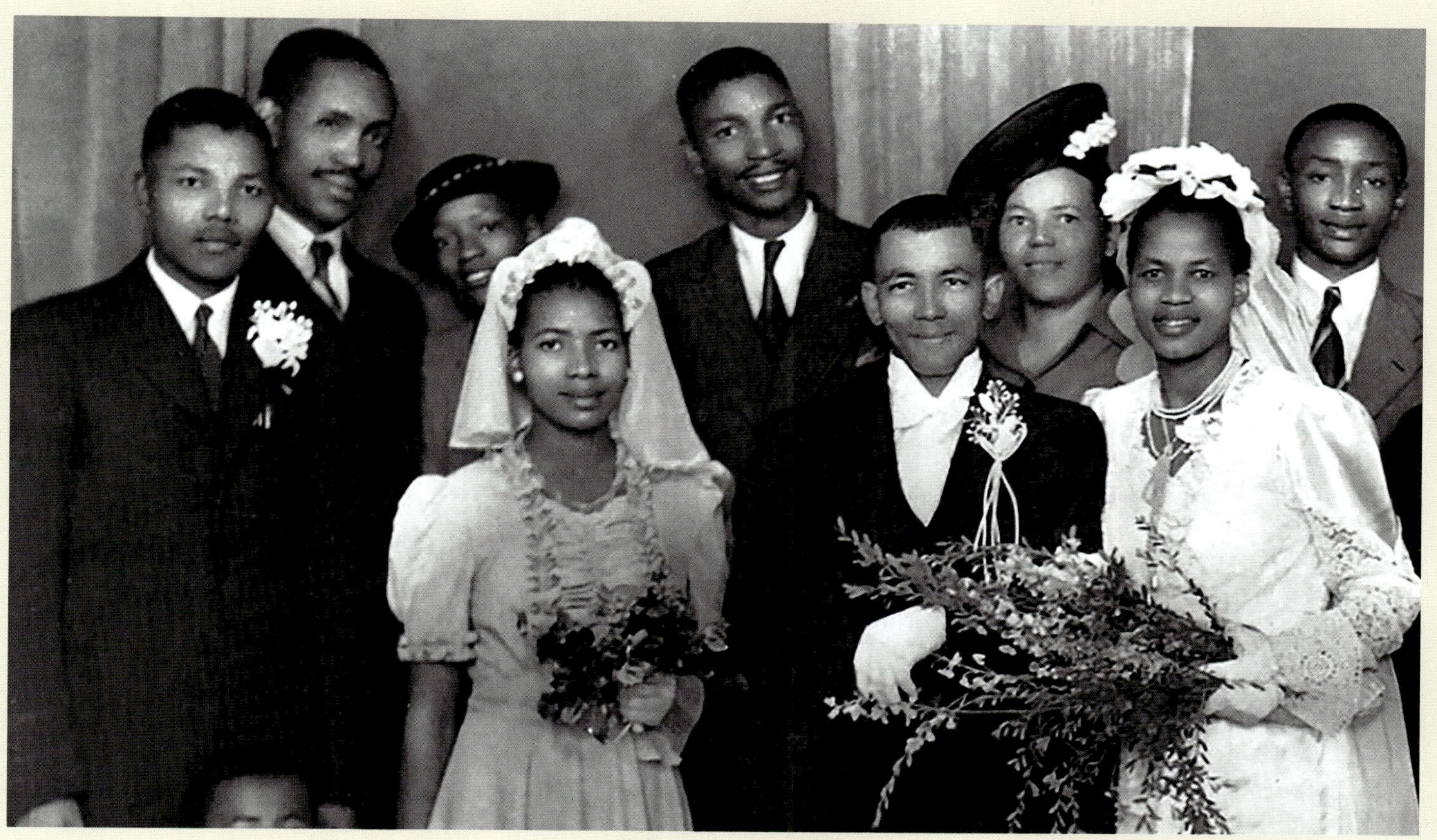

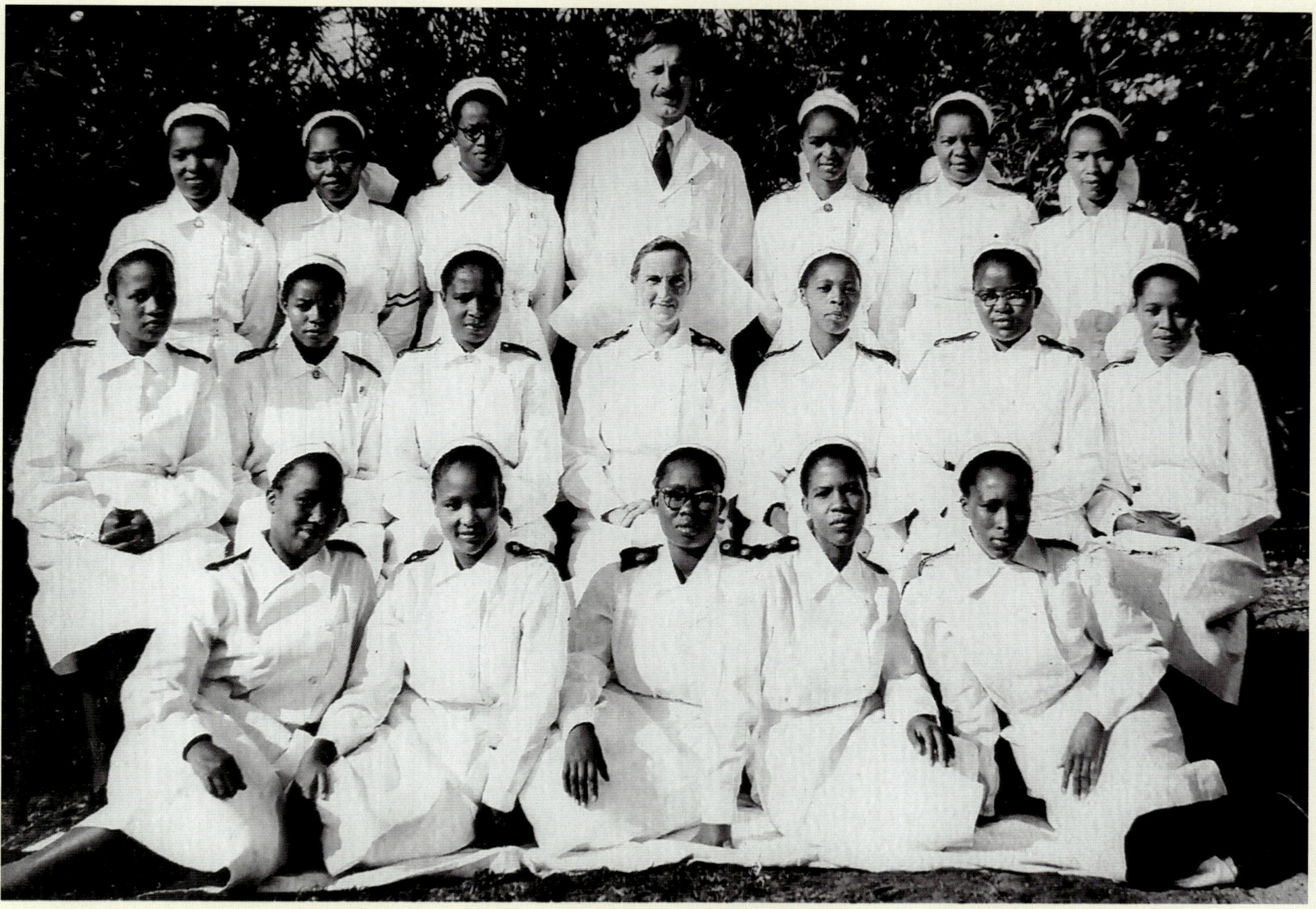

Top: Tata and my mum, Evelyn Ntoko Mase, at the wedding of their friends Walter and Albertina Sisulu.

Above: My mum (*third row, right*) at McCord Hospital training to be a midwife.

My Mother: Evelyn Ntoko

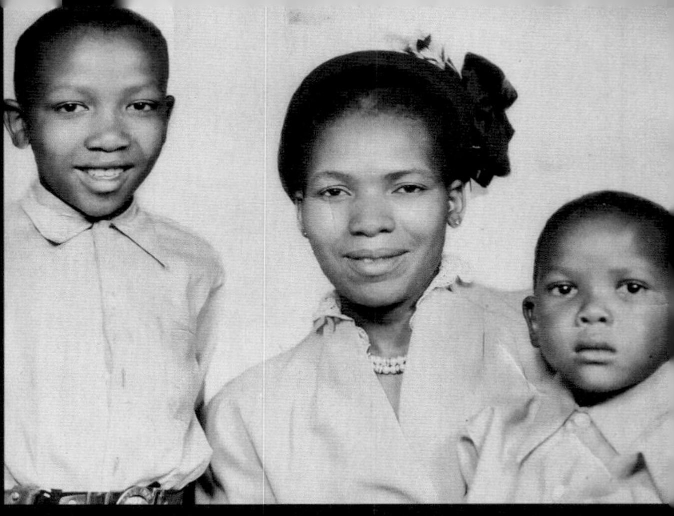

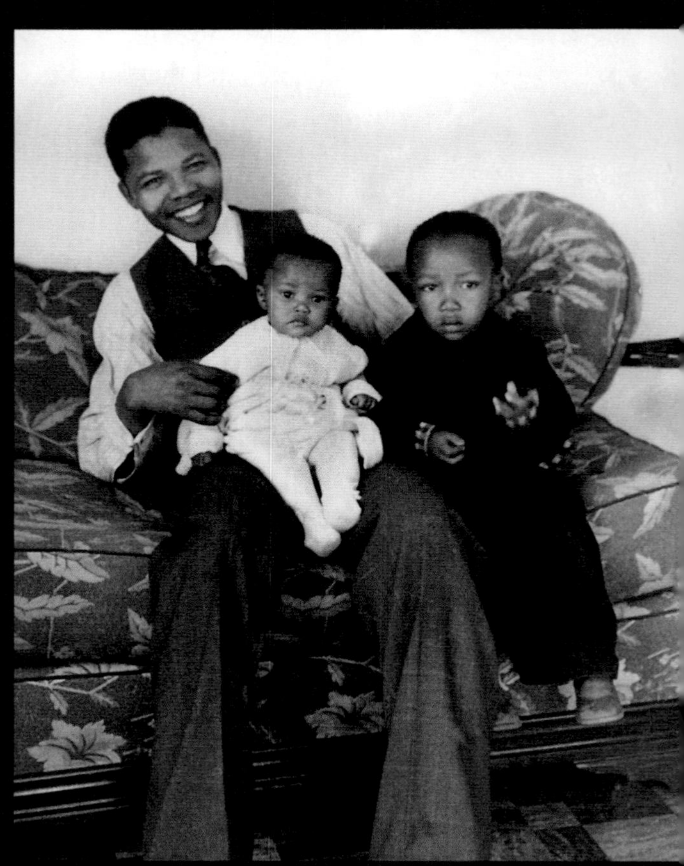

Top: My mum with my brothers, Thembekile (*left*) and Makgatho (*right*).

Above: Tata with late first daughter, Makaziwe, and Thembekile on the right.

Both my parents, Evelyn and Nelson Rolihlahla, were passionately committed to divergent passions. My mother was a committed member of the Jehovah's Witnesses and had no interest in politics. Tata, on the other hand, was a staunch member of the African National Congress.

Born Evelyn Ntoko Mase in Engcobo, Transkei, my mother lost her father, who was a miner, while still a baby. My grandmother passed away when my mother was twelve. She was sent to Soweto to join her brother, Samuel Mase. My uncle lived in Orlando East and owned a butcher shop. My mother's mum and Uncle Walter's mother were sisters, and the families were close. After high school, mum went to train as a nurse at Coronation Hospital in Johannesburg.

In the early 1940s mum caught the eye of Tata, who was a frequent visitor to the Sisulu home. He was attracted to her not only because she was pretty but she was quiet, centered (probably because of her faith as a Jehovah's Witness), and a little aloof. She was certainly unfazed by all the comings and goings of important people in the Sisulu household. My parents were married at the native commissioner's court in 1944, with Uncle Walter and Aunt Albertina as witnesses. The wedding was a simple affair. They lived with my uncle for some time, and they later secured their own home in Orlando West at No. 8115. They were married for fourteen years and had four children: Thembekile, Makaziwe 1, Makgatho, and myself, Makaziwe 2.

Families are like branches on a tree. We grow in different directions yet our roots remain as one.

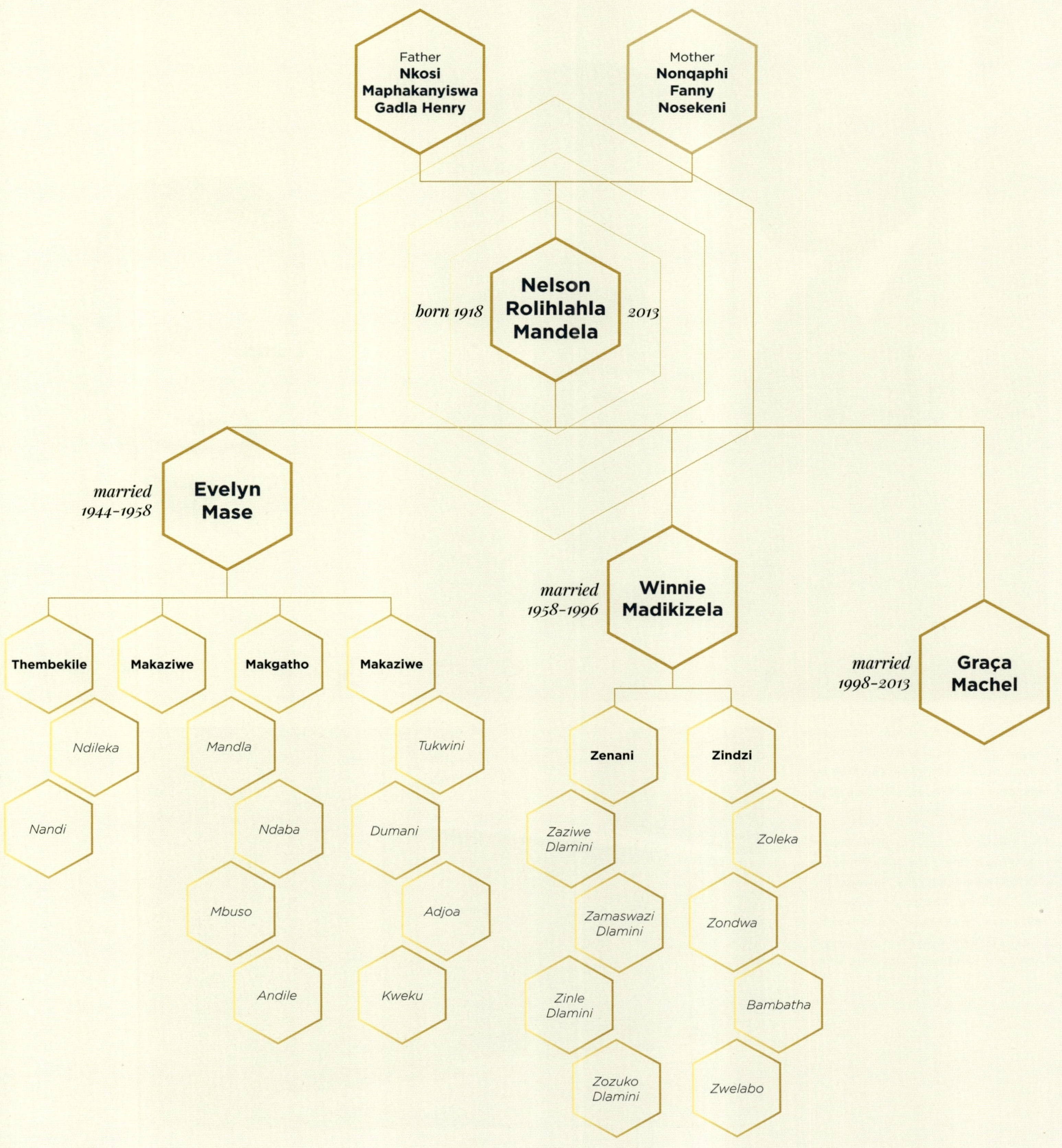

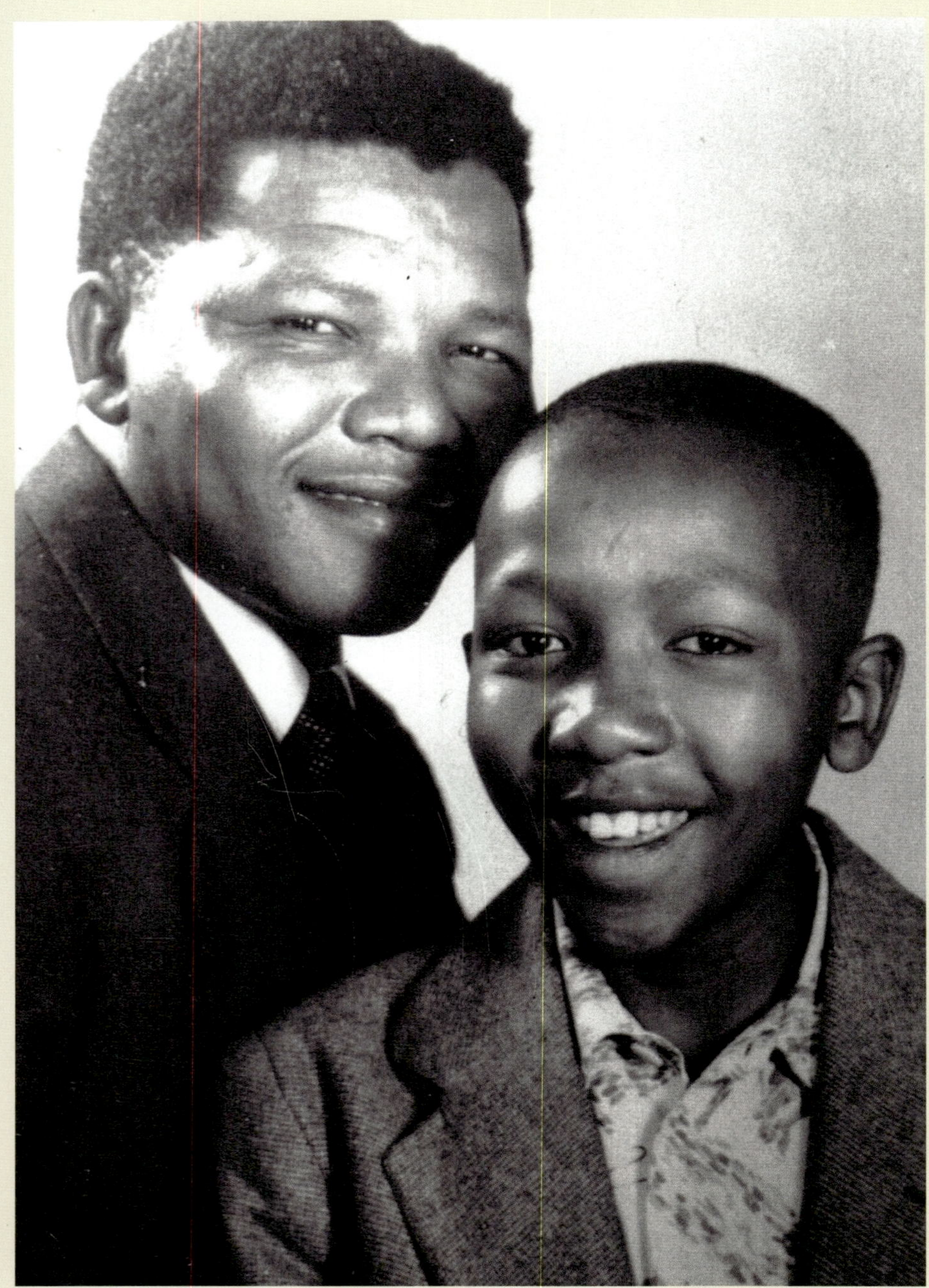

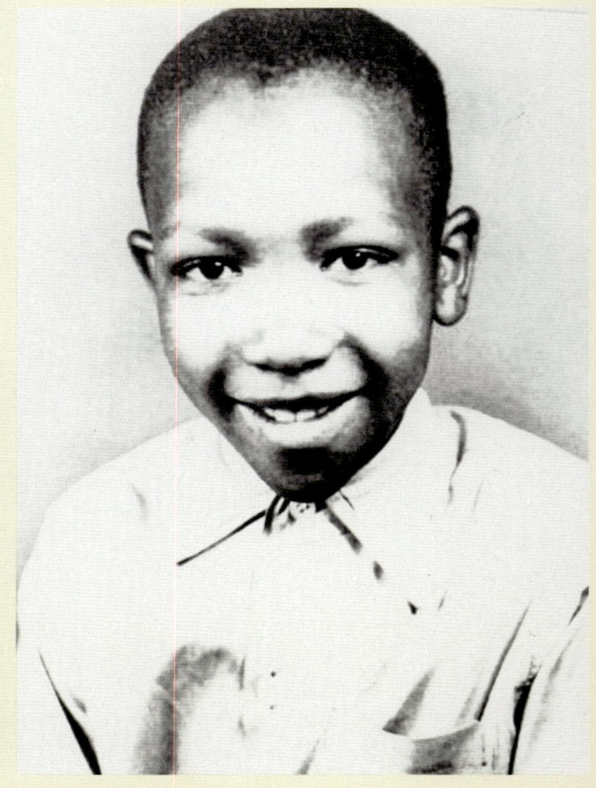

Above (*left*): Born in 1945, Thembekile "Styles" Mandela, shown with Tata. Above, right: My brother Thembekile's nickname was "Styles" because of his stylish fashion sense.

Right: Orlando West No. 8115. The house (now called the Mandela House) located in Orlando West, Soweto, in Johannesburg, was my home before Tata's twenty-seven-year imprisonment. Tata lived there with my mum, Evelyn. Later, Tata lived there with Miss Winnie.

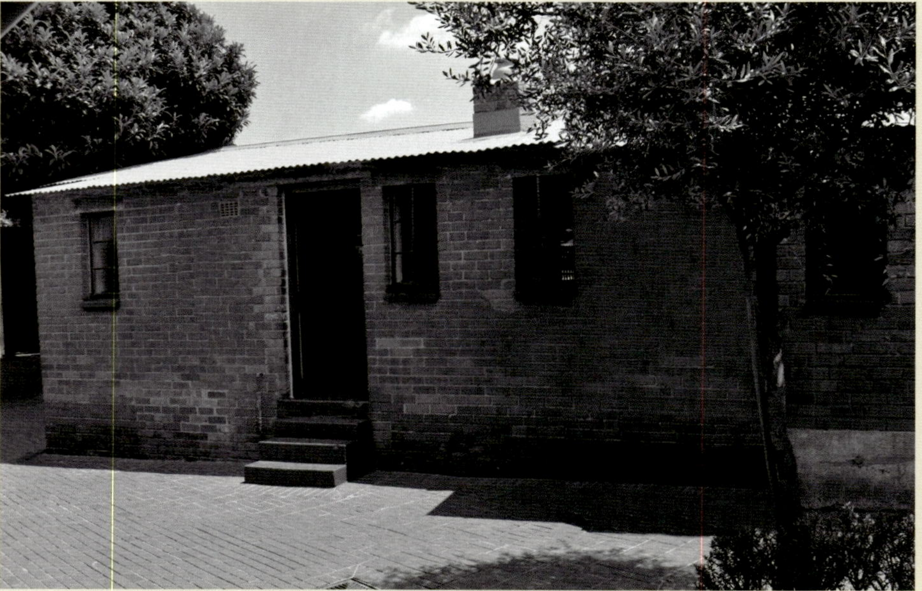

My mother, Evelyn, told me that Tata was a good father who was involved in family life. He would spend time with us, take the boys, Thembi and Makgatho, to sporting events, he would bathe us, feed us, and tell us bedtime stories. He enjoyed being a family man even after they divorced. Tata would pick us up every Friday and we would spend the weekends with him in Orlando West. When he was forced to go underground, he dearly missed the simple pleasures of being a husband and a father.

Orlando West was located in the heart of today's Soweto. By the time my parents were assigned a house, Orlando had more than twelve thousand houses arranged in densely packed plots on the east and west of the Klip River. Orlando West was eleven miles from the Johannesburg city center and was connected by railway and bus commutes. My parents would later make improvements to Orlando West No. 8115. They created an outbuilding with two more rooms as well as a garage. In the mid-1950s the house would have indoor plumbing but no electricity. In those days, the combined salary of my parents was about twenty-five pounds a month, so they lived comfortably. However, six months into their marriage, mum became the breadwinner after Tata completed his articles and committed to full-time study. Mum was earning a salary of seventeen pounds a month. Even after the reduction in their shared salaries, the Mandelas were considered part of the social elite, professionals (lawyer and nurse) with aristocratic connections. Both my parents remained part of the elite. My mother was one of only a few African nurses at that time (1950s). Tata was in a profession that was considered prestigious in African society. People often stopped my dad on the street and invited him into their homes, his position as a member of the royal Thembu nation and a lawyer afforded him high status. Both my parents maintained life-long friendships that they made during this time. An example is "Aunt" Adelaid, who became one of mother's closest friends. They met at a wedding they all attended. Tata and mum were both elegantly dressed, and together were the center of attention. Tata was already practicing law and his reputation as a prominent leader was taking hold. Aunt Adelaid was also a nurse, and began a lifelong friendship with my mum that evening. Over the years she often spoke about what a beautiful couple my parents were. My mum and Aunt Adelaid remained friends until Mum passed away.

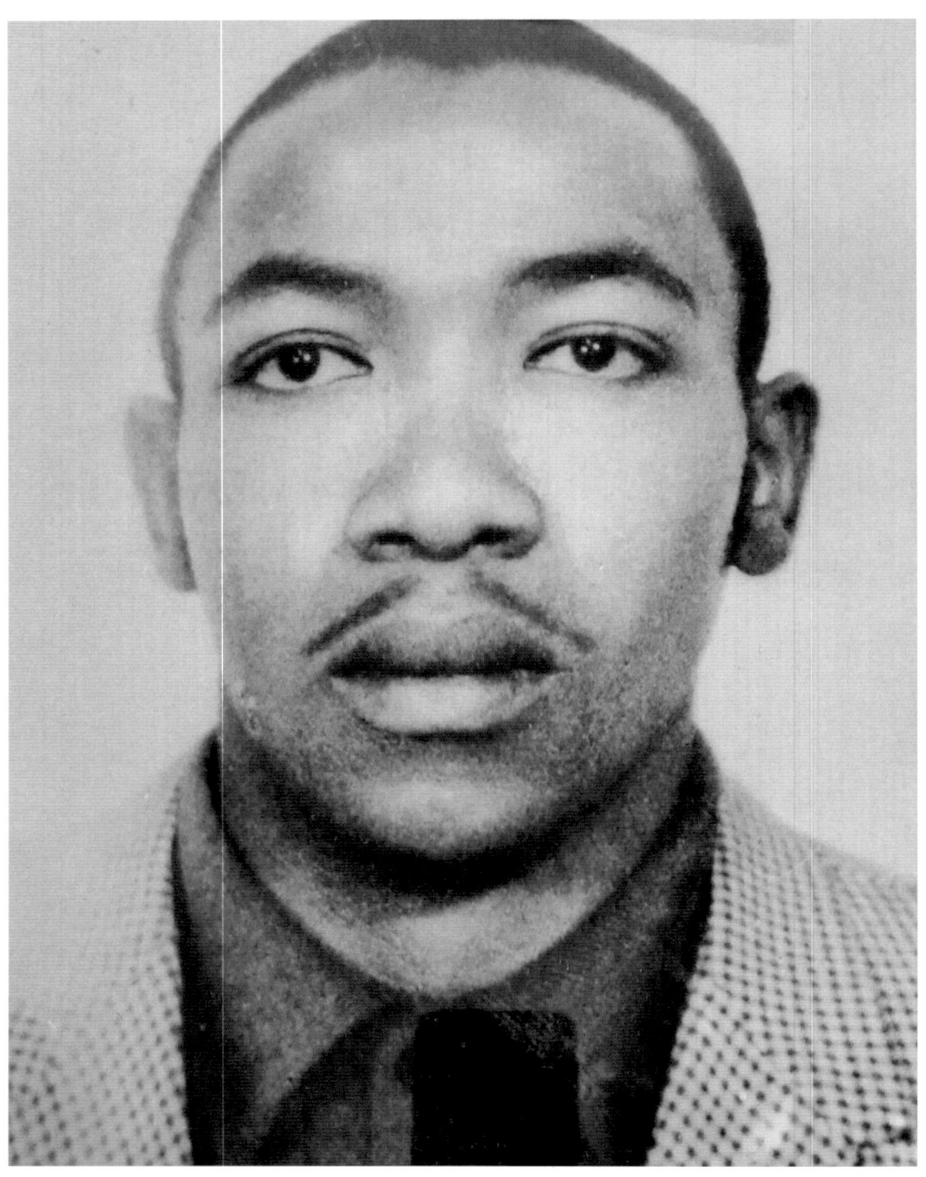

Thembekile at age twenty.

Madiba Thembekile "Thembi" Mandela

Tata remembered Thembekile as a solid, happy boy who resembled Mum more than him. Born on February 23, 1945, he was given the name Madiba, which is a clan name, but was better known by his nickname "Thembi." As a teenager he was given a new nickname, "Styles," as he was always well dressed. Tata was very proud that he had produced an heir and that the Mandela name and the Madiba clan would grow. It was the responsibility of every Xhosa male to ensure that the family name would be forever perpetuated. In patriarchal societies, the lineage is perpetuated through males, as it was believed or required that females would take on the surname of their husband's family.

Although politics prevented Tata from spending a lot of time at home, he enjoyed domestic life. He doted on Thembi, bathing, feeding, and playing with him. On some evenings when he was at home, he would look after Thembi at night and change his nappies. When Thembi was young, Tata would pick him up after work and they would drive to the Orlando Community Center, where they would do an hour of exercise; skipping rope, shadow boxing, and weight-lifting.

In 1958, I was only four and Thembi was twelve when our parents divorced. I remember being traumatized by their separation and Thembi was also deeply affected. He stopped being enthusiastic about school and became withdrawn and quiet.

Because Tata wanted a better education for all of us, Thembi was also sent to a boarding school in Swaziland for his high school years at St. Christopher's, an all-boys school located in Luyengo, then a British protectorate. During his high school years, Thembi met a girl, Thoko Mhlanga, from Alexandra township. Thoko got pregnant, and Thembi dropped out of school. Thoko adopted the surname "De Jager" from a relative so that she could be classified as "colored" and live in Retreat, Cape Town, close to her mother, which was a residential area for coloreds. As a colored person in the Cape you were offered more benefits and preferential treatment than Africans; in terms of employment, housing, health care, and amenities.

In Retreat, my brother and Thoko went into the liquor-bootlegging business, which was quite lucrative. He was able to assist my mother financially. They bought themselves a beautiful house in Clermont, Pinetown, in KwaZulu-Natal. My brother lived there until he died in a car accident on July 13, 1969. During his stay in Cape Town, Thembi did not make any attempt to see Tata on Robben Island. He was very bitter about how Tata had treated Mum and refused to reconcile with him.

T TO BUY at SOLLY RAMER'S
The Liquor Specialists'
's a reason!

STOP PRESS

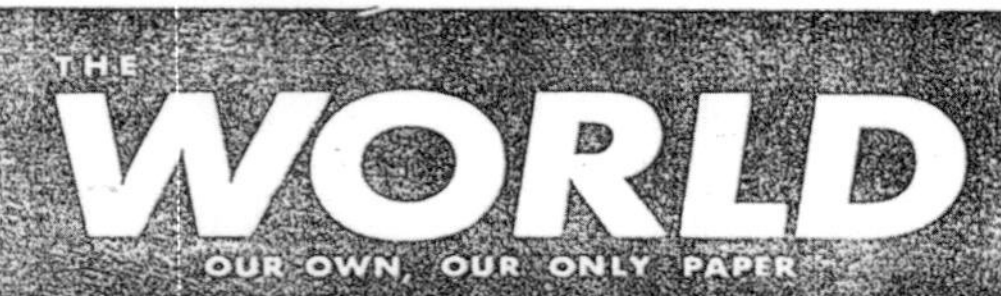

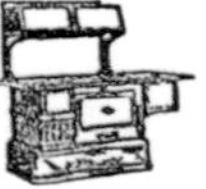

KEEP WARM THIS WINTER

Keep warm for as little as 75c per week. We are trade-in specialists and pay the best prices on your old stove.

UNION GRAMOPHONE SALOONS
51 HARRISON STR., JOHANNESBURG.

at the G.P.O. ewspaper.

WEDNESDAY, JULY 16, 1969

Price 2c

ANDELA'S SON DIES IN CRASH

By Thandi Maqubela

MR. THEMBEKILE MADIBA MANDELA, the 24-year-old son of Rivonia trialist, Nelson Mandela, who is serving life imprisonment on Robben Island, died this week following a car smash in Cape Town.

Thembekile, who was travelling with his fiancee Miss Lydia Mhlanga (24), was on his way to Cape Town after spending a long weekend at Nongoma in Zululand.

Mr. Mandela was due to be married to Lydia very soon. They had two children, Ndileka (4) and Nandi (1).

Another passenger who was with the couple, Mrs. Irene Simelane, is also reported to have died on the spot.

Lydia's condition is said to be "very critical". She is in hospital.

The news of Thembekile's death was broken to Mrs. Evelyn Mandela, a nurse at Pimville clinic who was Nelson Mandela's wife, before he got married to Winnie Mandela.

BROKE NEWS

Mrs. Mandela was just preparing to go to work yesterday morning when a group of relatives came to break the news to her.

This morning reporters found she had already left for Cape Town, with the intention of trying to bring back the corpse for

(Continued on back Page)

rl ns 00 ize

RED rand is h for a 12- win. Yet this ng Beatrice 919 Zone 1, ohannesburg,

the lucky reader who 00 first prize s World-Af- ty contest.

WEEK

second week at a student 00 in compe- by the

t pharmacist wanath Hos- homas Ranu- ek won our licap R400

who is a student at ko Higher Diepkloof, f the three o correctly inners of the rld-Afmark" competitors. nd prize of Julius Sha- 77 Jabulani, hird prize of Julia Koena North. whose intelli- her age, said going to put in the bank go to High wants to dressmaker

all has not ected her re- with her ers and bro- feels that et something 500. ne more than

n back Page)

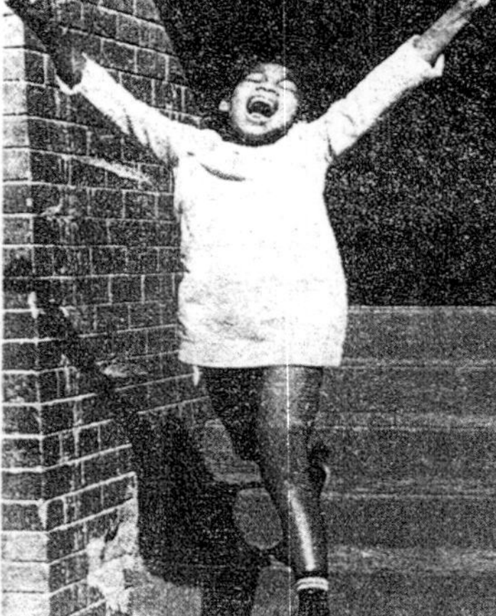

Twelve-year-old Beatrice Makaba whoops with joy after learning that she won the first prize of R500 in the WORLD-AFMARK "Choose the Winners" contest.

3 MEN HEAD FOR THE MOON TODAY

THIS AFTERNOON a huge rocket will blast three men into space from Cape Kennedy, U.S.A. Two of them will land on the moon in five day's time—if all goes well.

The spaceship — Apollo 11 — will start circling the moon on Sunday. Shortly after that, the moon landing ship will separate from the main ship with two of the spacemen aboard.

It will fly down to the moon's surface, and land in the middle, of the huge plain of dust known as the Sea of Tranquility.

On Monday millions of lucky people all over the world will watch the greatest adventure of the century on television as the two spacemen step down from their landing craft onto the moon's surface.

It will all be filmed on television, and sent "live"

(Continued on back Page)

Top T.P. club wins R250 — see page 2

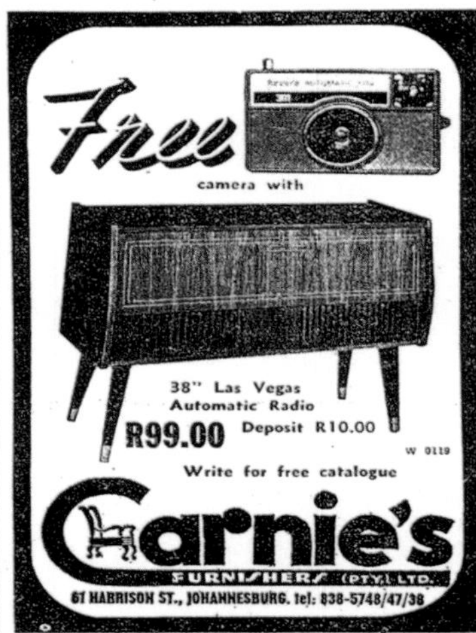

"I do not have words to express the sorrow, or the loss I felt. It left a hole in my heart that can never be filled."

Tata, on the loss of Thembekile, in *Long Walk to Freedom*

Tata was called to the Robben Island office and given a telegram from Makgatho, informing him that Thembi, his eldest son, had died in a car accident in Toursrivier, in the Western Cape. Thembi was twenty-five years old and was a father of two young children, Ndileka and Nandi.

Tata was heartbroken by this news and spent the day with Uncle Walter by his bedside. It was a loss too great for any exchange of words, so they sat together holding hands in silence. Tata requested permission to attend Thembi's funeral. He wanted to be there to rest his spirit in peace and to try to come to terms with the enormous loss. His request was denied. Unable to attend Thembi's funeral, Tata was left only with the memories of his son as a young boy, when he was underground in the years before he divorced my mum. There is the story of the day Thembi wore Tata's shirt that went all the way down to his knees. It reminded Tata of how, as a young boy himself, he had worn his father's clothes as a form of comfort and also as a symbol of his role as "son" in the family when his father died. In Thembi's case he was certainly showing his father that while he was in hiding, he was terribly missed. He said that he would "take care of the family" while Tata was gone. Thembi indeed looked after the family while he was alive. He even introduced Mum to the Institute of Race Relations (a liberal think tank promoting the ideas and policy solutions necessary to address economic investments to reduce poverty and unemployment). The institute gave me and Makgatho better financial aid for high school and paid for all my fees when I was at university in South Africa.

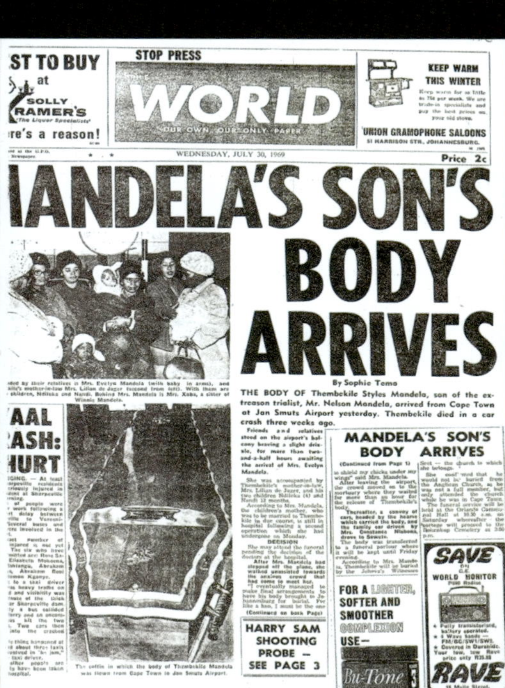

STOP PRESS

THE WORLD

OUR OWN, OUR ONLY PAPER

WEDNESDAY, JULY 30, 1969

Price 2c

MANDELA'S SON'S BODY ARRIVES

By Sophie Temo

THE BODY OF Thembekile Styles Mandela, son of the ex-treason trialist, Mr. Nelson Mandela, arrived from Cape Town at Jan Smuts Airport yesterday. Thembekile died in a car crash three weeks ago.

Friends and relatives stood on the airport's balcony braving a slight drizzle, for more than two-and-a-half hours awaiting the arrival of Mrs. Evelyn Mandela.

She was accompanied by Thembekile's mother-in-law, Mrs. Lilian de Jager, and his two children Ndileka (4) and Nandi 12 months.

According to Mrs. Mandela, the children's mother, who was to be married to Thembekile in due course, is still in hospital following a second operation which she had undergone on Monday.

DECISION

She may attend the funeral pending the decision of the doctors at the hospital.

After Mrs. Mandela had stepped off the plane, she walked unassisted towards the anxious crowd that had come to meet her.

"I eventually managed to make final arrangements to have his body brought to Johannesburg for burial. For like a hen, I must be the one

(Continued on back Page)

The coffin in which the body of Thembekile Mandela was flown from Cape Town to Jan Smuts Airport.

HARRY SAM SHOOTING PROBE — SEE PAGE 3

MANDELA'S SON'S BODY ARRIVES

(Continued from Page 1)

to shield my chicks under my wings" said Mrs. Mandela.

After leaving the airport, the crowd moved on to the mortuary where they waited for more than an hour for the release of Thembekile's body.

Thereafter, a convoy of cars, headed by the hearse which carried the body, and the family car driven by Mrs. Constance Mlahoma, drove to Soweto.

The body was transferred to a funeral parlour where it will be kept until Friday evening.

According to Mrs. Mandela, Thembekile will be buried by the Jehova's Witnesses Sect — the church to which she belongs.

She confirmed that he would not be buried from the Anglican Church, as he was not a full member, but only attended the church while he was in Cape Town.

The funeral service will be held at the Orlando Communal Hall at 10.30 a.m. on Saturday whereafter the cortege will proceed to the Doornkop Cemetery at 3.00 p.m.

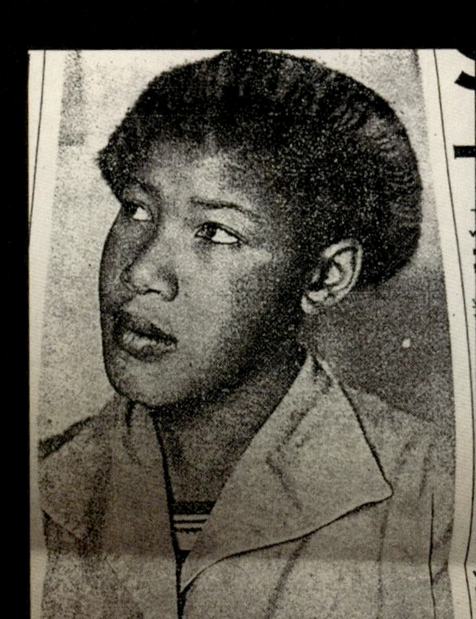

Newspapers of the day covered my brother's passing.
Right: A photo of me from an article about the surviving children.

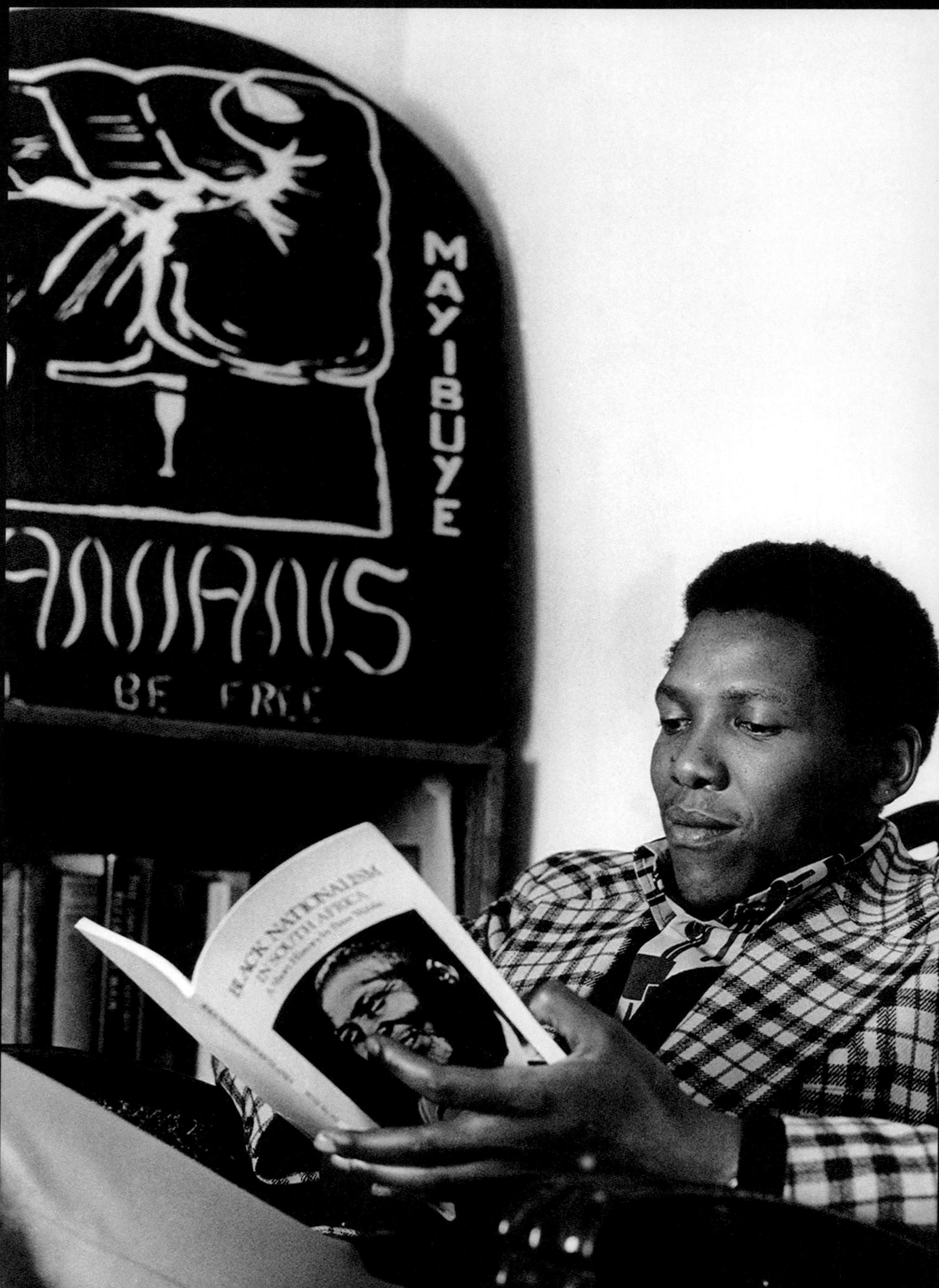

Makgatho Mandela at home at
No. 5118 in Orlando East.

"To be the father of a nation is a great honor, but to be the father of a family is a greater joy."

Tata in *Long Walk to Freedom*

Makgatho Lewanika Mandela

Makgatho was born on June 26, 1950, the day of protest organized by the African National Congress (ANC). He was the second son of my parents. Tata was with Mum for a few minutes and left to join the protest. Makgatho was named after the second president of the ANC, Sefako Mapogo Makgatho, and his second name, Lewanika, was from Sefako's father, a leading chief in Zambia.

Unlike Thembekile, Makgatho's experience with our dad was spent in fleeting moments, when he would arrive home late or early in the morning. Tata would sometimes take him around Orlando township in his car. Makgatho's recollections of Tata when he was young were that Tata was hardly at home, and he only spent real time with him when Tata was in hiding.

Makgatho attended primary school in Swaziland with Uncle Walter's son, Zwelakhe Sisulu. They lived with a family and went to a local school. They had an unhappy experience that first year because they were away from family and in new surroundings.

In their second year, they were transferred to St. Lucia, a boarding school in Manzini, Swaziland. Makgatho completed his matriculation in Orlando East in Soweto. After completing high school, Makgatho worked for a number of years with a local insurance company in the city of Johannesburg.

Makgatho visited Tata on Robben Island once or twice a year as permitted by the prison warden. Tata was not happy that Makgatho had not pursued higher studies after high school and insisted in every letter he wrote to him that he should go back to school. In his forties, Makgatho went back to school and studied law at the University of Natal in Durban.

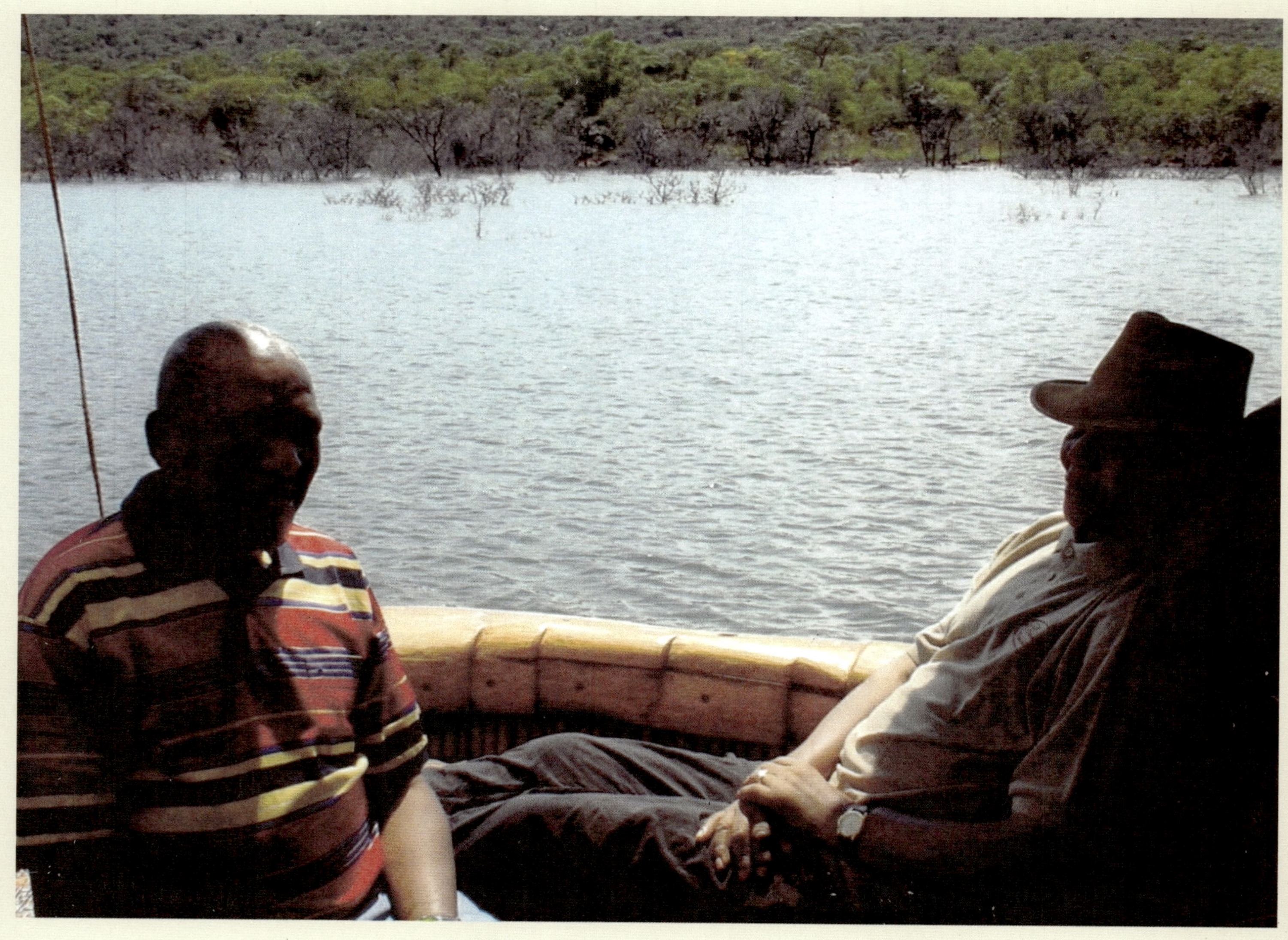

"Tata was a father who was there but not there physically. Even when I was born he was there for only a brief moment. We had expected that once he was free we could at last spend time with him, but his plate was always full. We have to accept that Tata is married to politics and enjoy the breakfasts, lunches, dinners, birthdays we have with him. These, for us, need to be our cherished moments."

Makgatho's thoughts on cherished moments he spent with Tata

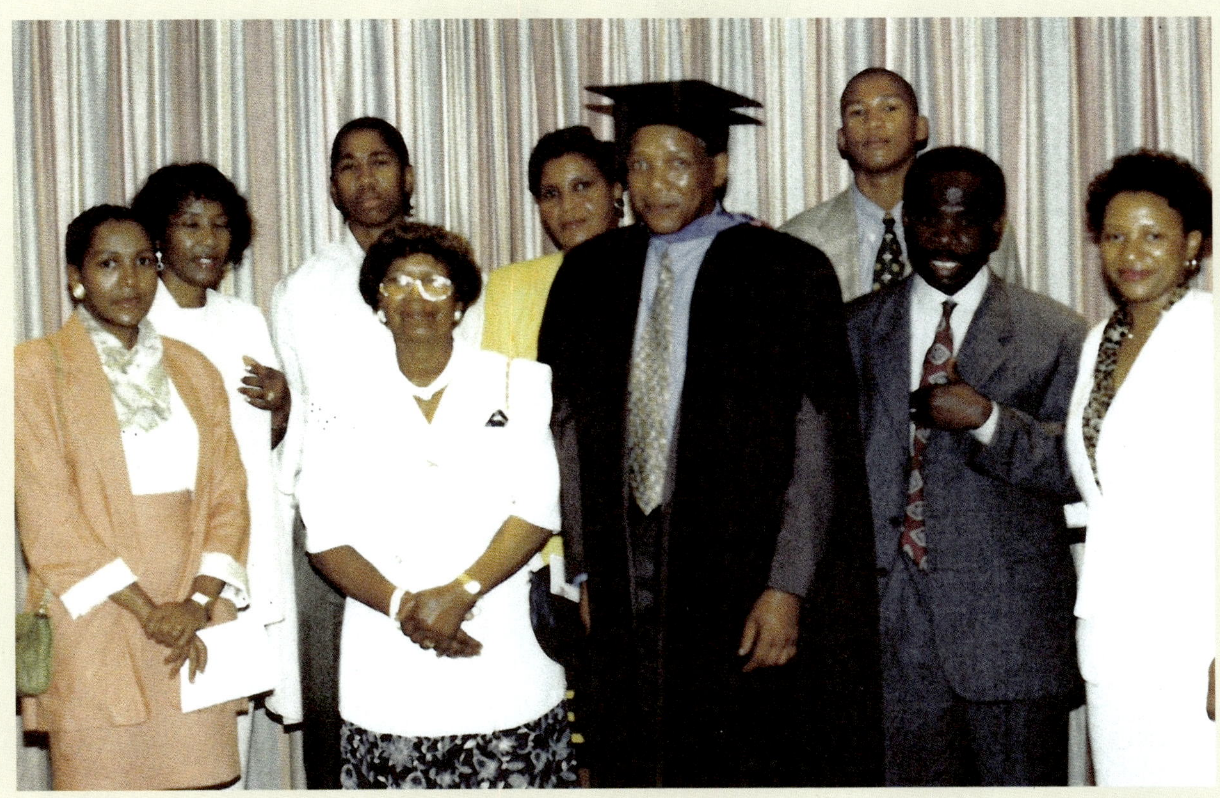

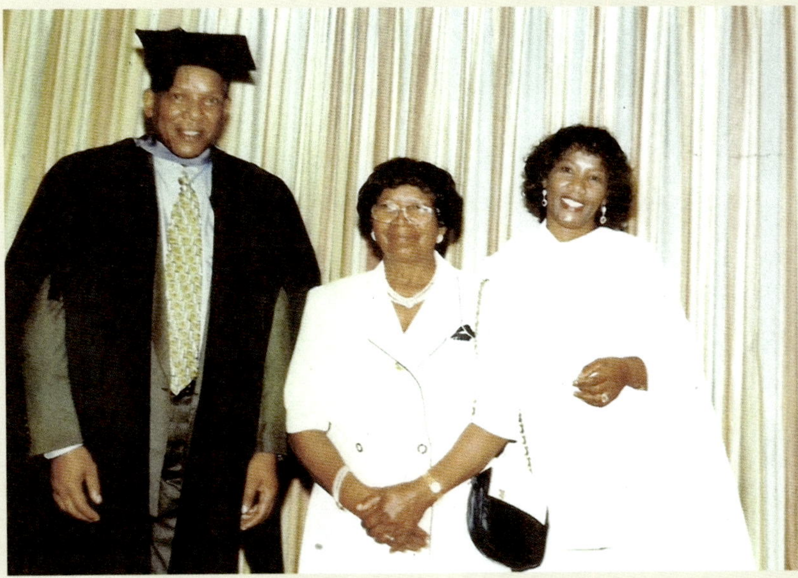

Above: Makgatho at his graduation surrounded by family. Front row (*left to right*): Thembi's older daughter, Ndileka; our Mum; Makgatho; my husband, Isaac Amuah; and Thembi's younger daughter, Nandi. Below: Tata and Makgatho after the bar ceremony.

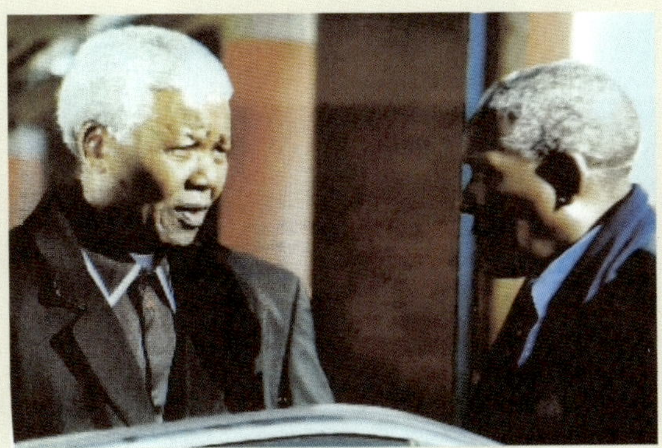

Opposite: Makgatho with Tata on a riverboat at Shambala Private Game Reserve.

Above: Makgatho, our mum, and me at Makgatho's graduation from the University of Natal, where he earned a law degree.

Right: Tata with Makgatho when he was admitted to the bar.

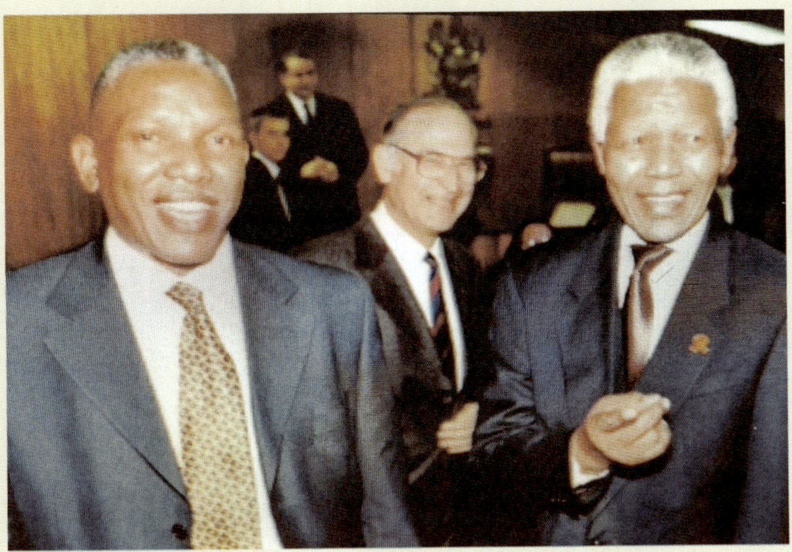

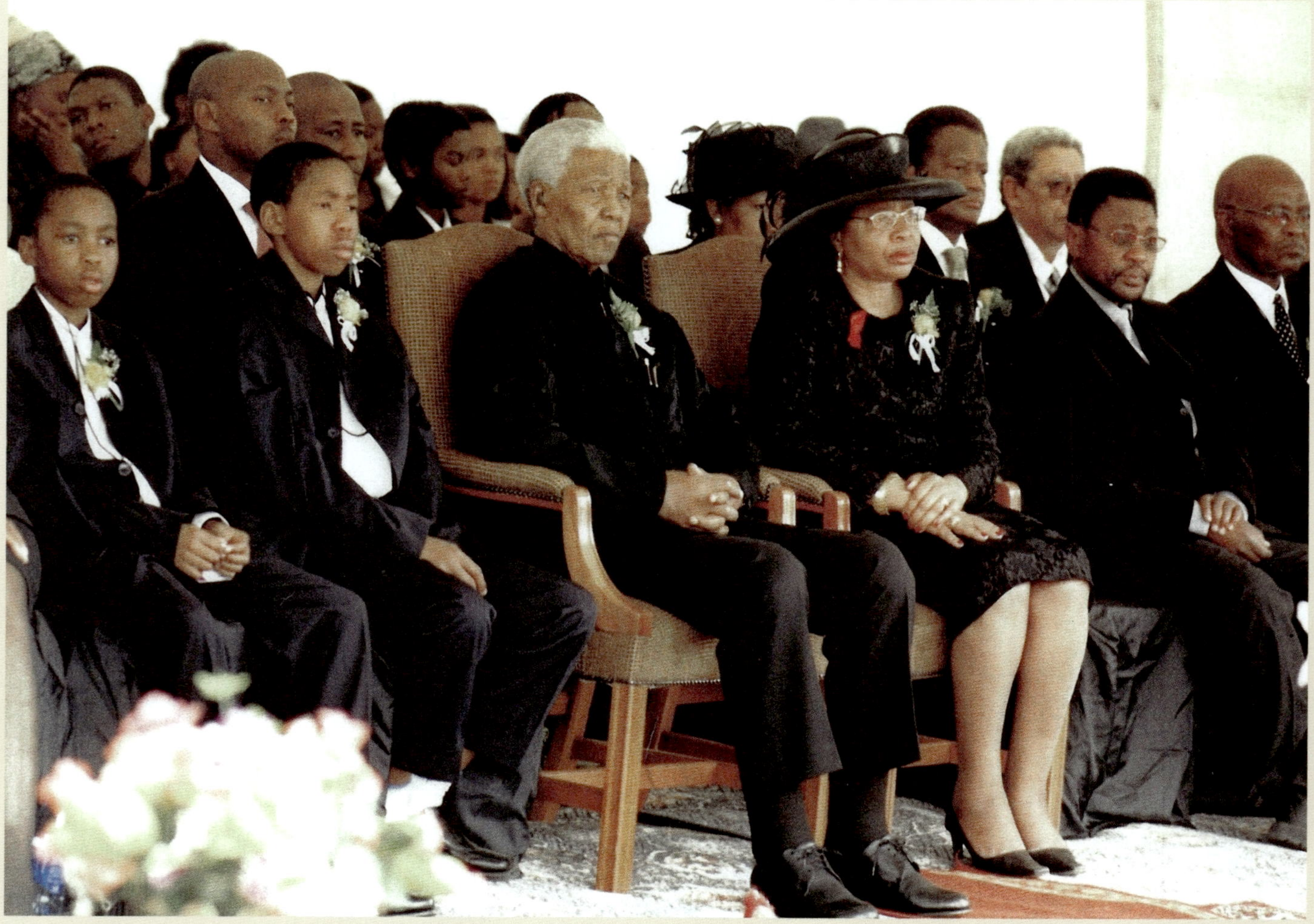

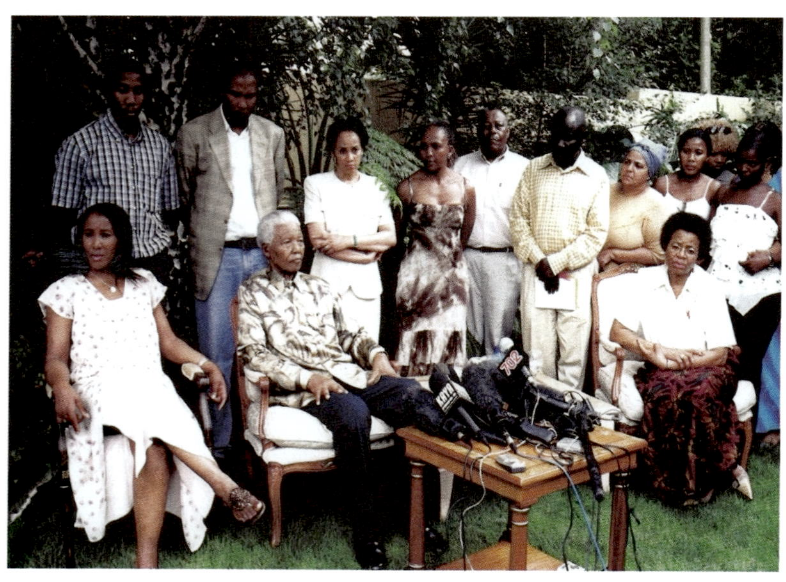

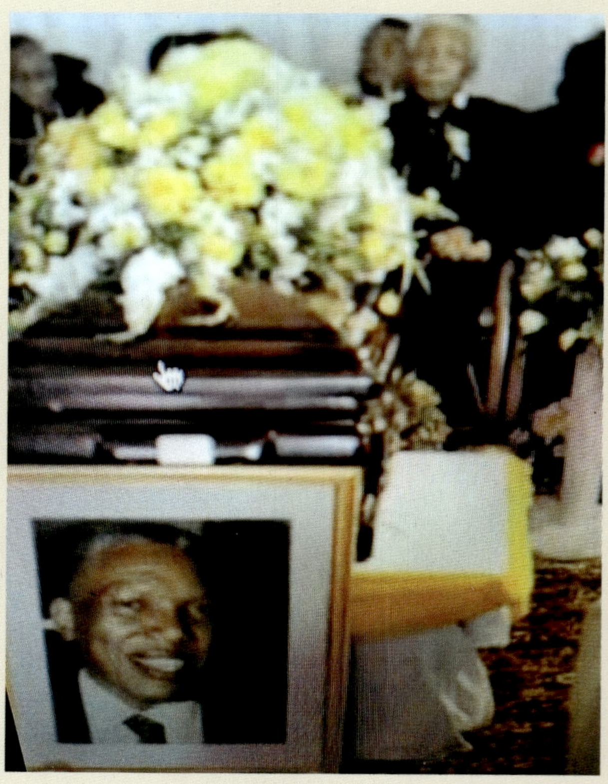

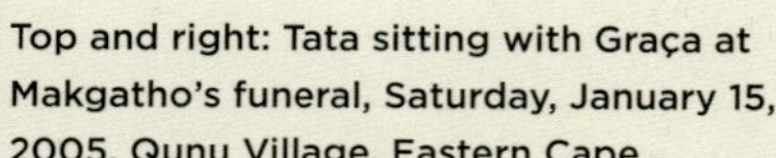

Top and right: Tata sitting with Graça at Makgatho's funeral, Saturday, January 15, 2005, Qunu Village, Eastern Cape.

Above: Tata speaking to the press about Makgatho's HIV status and death at his funeral in Qunu, surrounded by family.

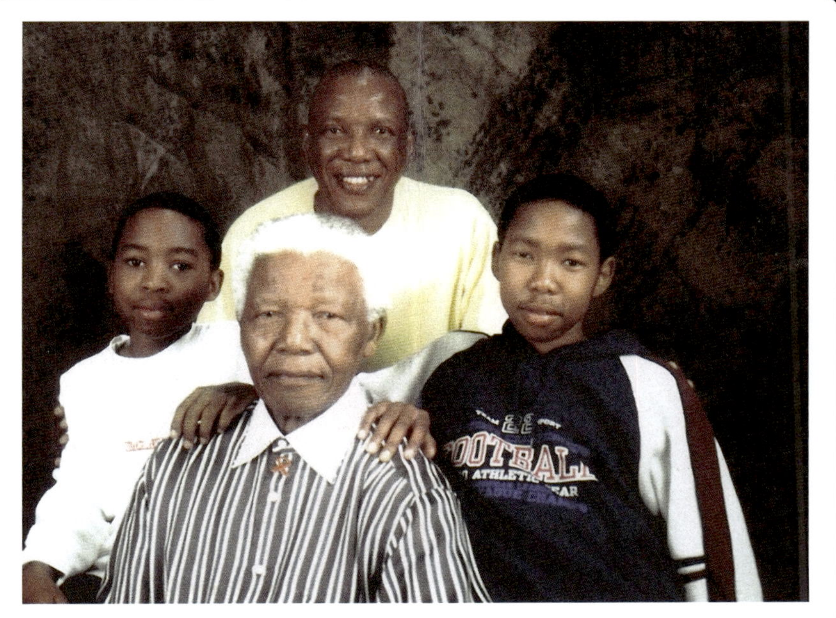

Tata and Makgatho, flanked by Makgatho's two young sons, Mbuso (*right*) and Andile (*left*).

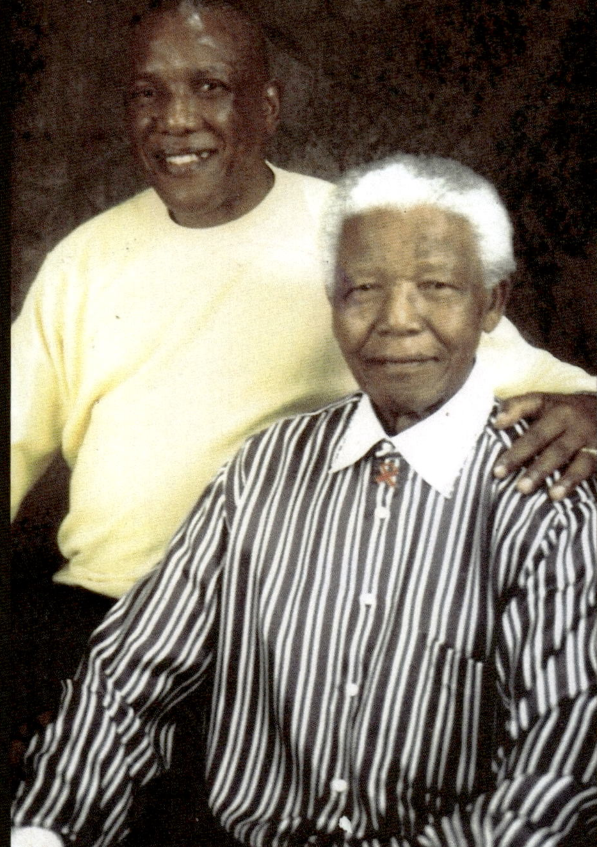

Makgatho did his articles at Webber Wentzel, a Johannesburg law firm, and later worked for a short time with lawyer Ismail Ayob, then at the Standard Bank legal department. Makgatho died of an AIDS-related illness. Tata knew long before Makgatho was hospitalized that he had HIV, as I had told him over lunch two years earlier. Those weeks that Makgatho was in the hospital, Tata visited every day, in the mornings and evenings. When Makgatho got out of a coma at one point, Tata was so excited that he promised to slaughter a cow for the medical staff. But a couple of days later, Makgatho went into a deep coma and silently slipped away on January 6, 2005, at Linksfield Hospital in Johannesburg. He left behind four sons: Mandla, Ndaba, Mbuso, and Andile. For years after, when we were gathered around the table and we would talk about Makgatho, Tata would stand up and leave.

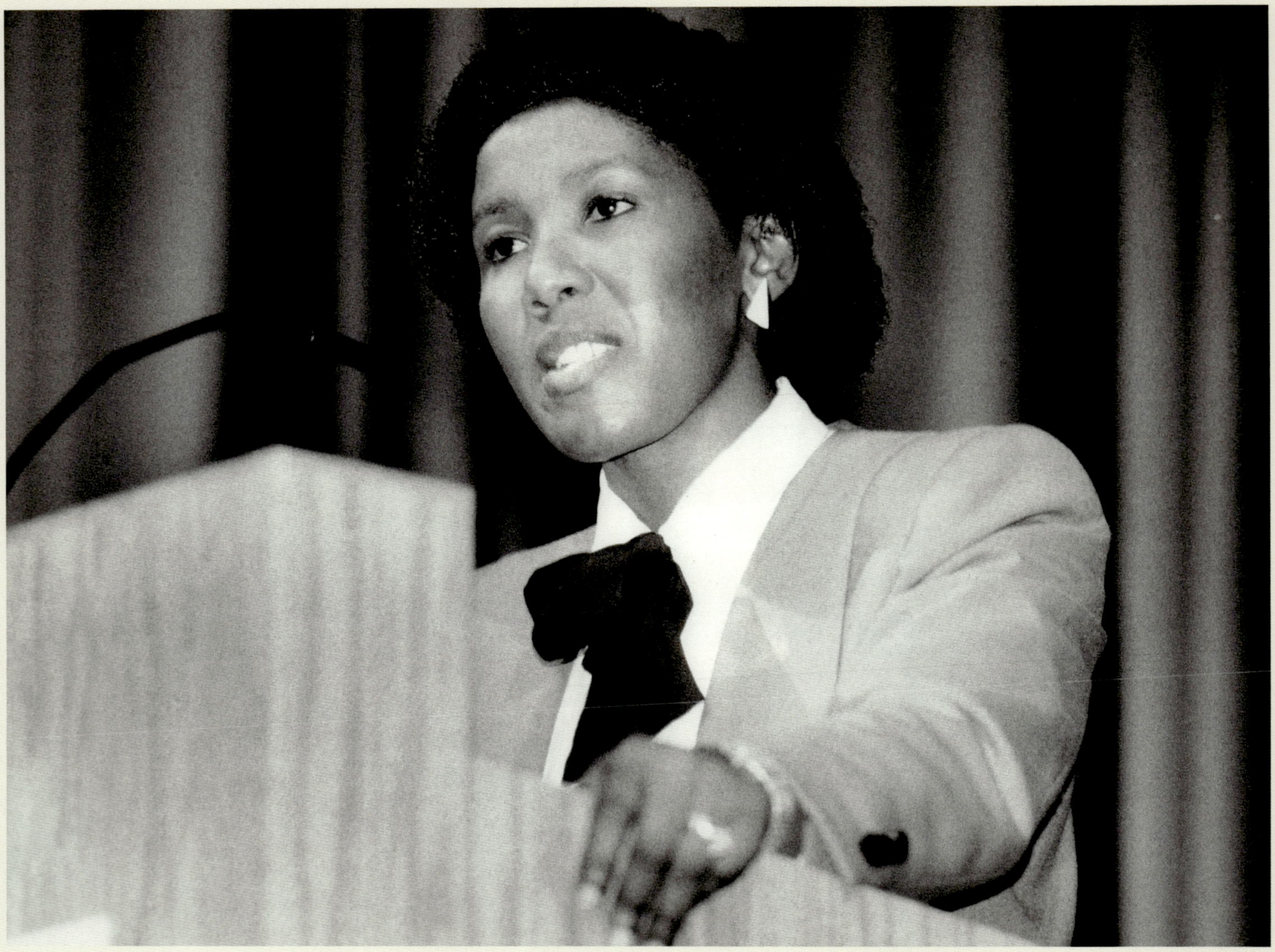

Delivering a speech while I was at university.

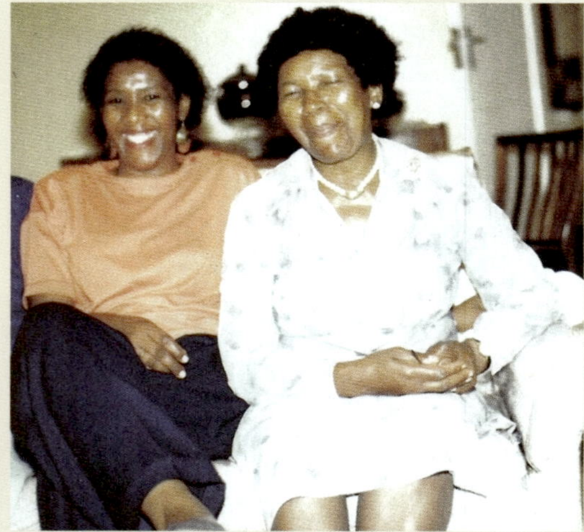

With my mother.

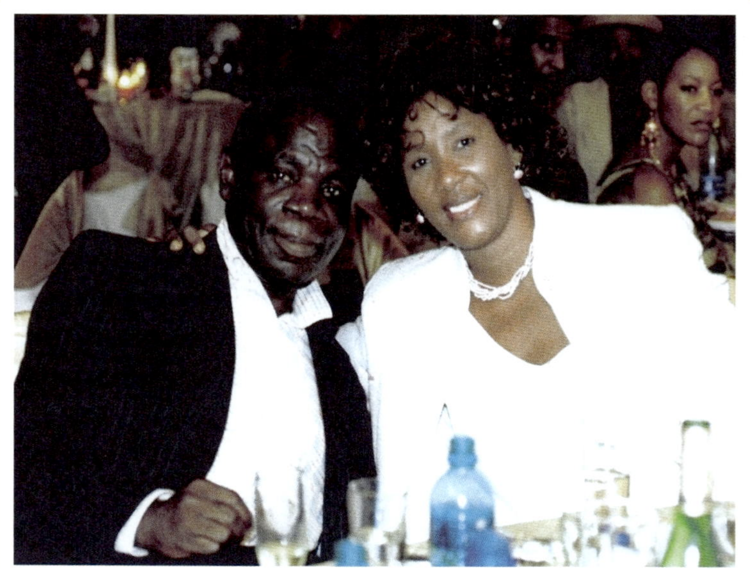

With my husband, Isaac Amuah.

"Makaziwe was still very small, and I remember one day, when I was not in prison or in court, I visited her at crèche (nursery school) unannounced. She had always been a very affectionate child, but that day when she saw me, she froze. She did not know whether to run to me or retreat, to smile or frown. She had some conflict in her small heart, which she did not know how to resolve. It was very painful."

Nelson Mandela, *Long Walk to Freedom*

Pumla Makaziwe Mandela

I was born Pumla Makaziwe (Maki/Maka) Mandela. I was named after my late sister Makaziwe, who died in infancy. I am the fourth and only surviving child of Nelson Mandela and Evelyn Mase. Just as my brothers were sent to school in Swaziland, I was seven years old when I was whisked away to a Roman Catholic school, St. Theresa Primary School, with my cousins Beryl and Lindiwe Sisulu. I completed my high school at Orlando High and then went on to qualify as a social worker at the University of Fort Hare, and then received an honors degree in sociology at the University of Natal in Durban. I hold a master's degree and a PhD in sociology and anthropology from the University of Massachusetts at Amherst.

I rarely saw Tata when I was growing up. He was remarried, absorbed in politics, and had become more distant from his family as a result of living underground. When I was young, he did not relish being away from his family or being deprived of the company of his children. One night when I was two years old, he was home with a number of friends. As he was leaving, I woke up and asked if I could come along with him. I think from an early age I had come to realize that I had a dad in name only. Tata could not give up his life in the struggle and that had a traumatic effect on all the children at a very tender age in our lives.

I was seven years old when I saw my father face-to-face, and it would be another nine years before I could see him again. I had to be sixteen and have an identity document before I could apply to visit him. After that I would visit him on Robben Island once or twice a year. The first time I visited Robben Island, I was so excited, although the journey to Cape Town by train and then by boat was not such a pleasant one. When we got to the island, I was pulled aside and told by the prison commander James Gregory that I had to communicate with Tata only in English and no politics were to be discussed. I would sit in the waiting room until I was

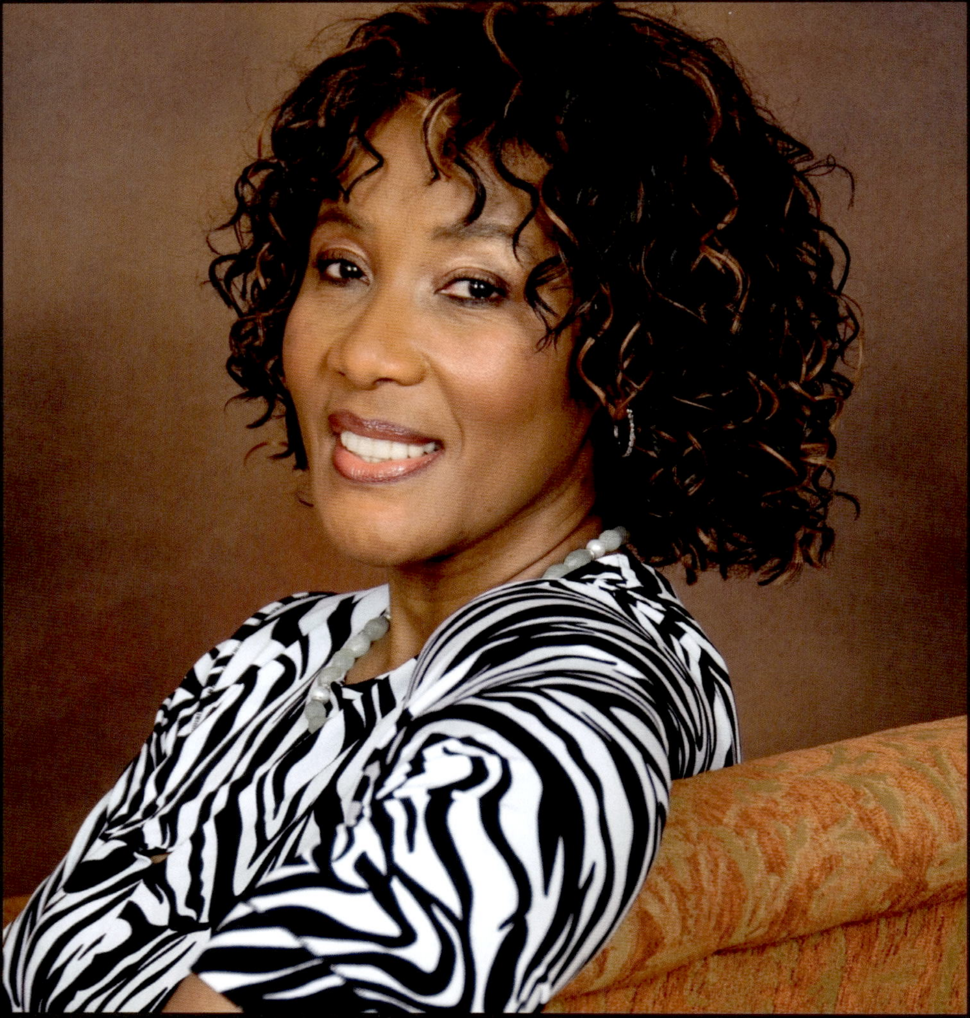

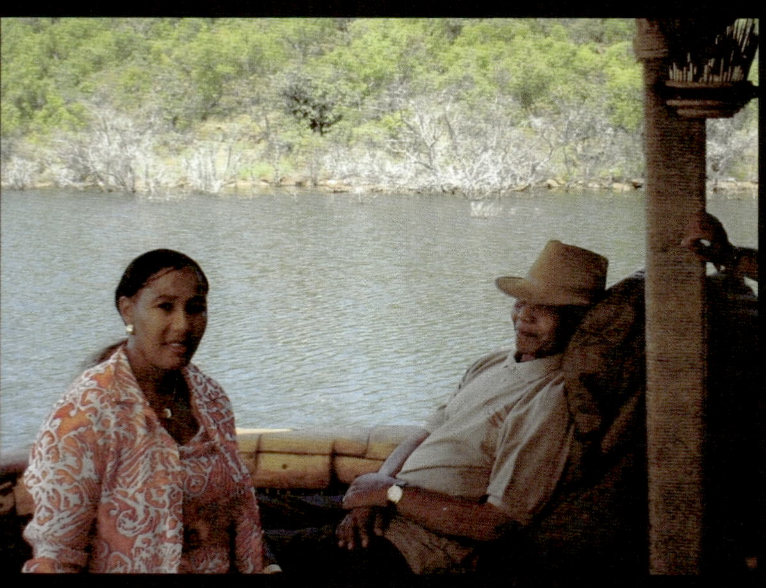

Tata and me on the river in the Shambala Private Game Reserve.

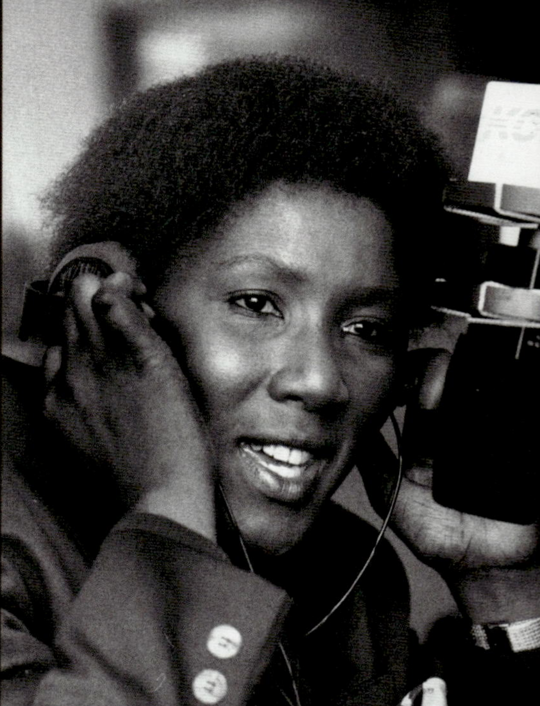

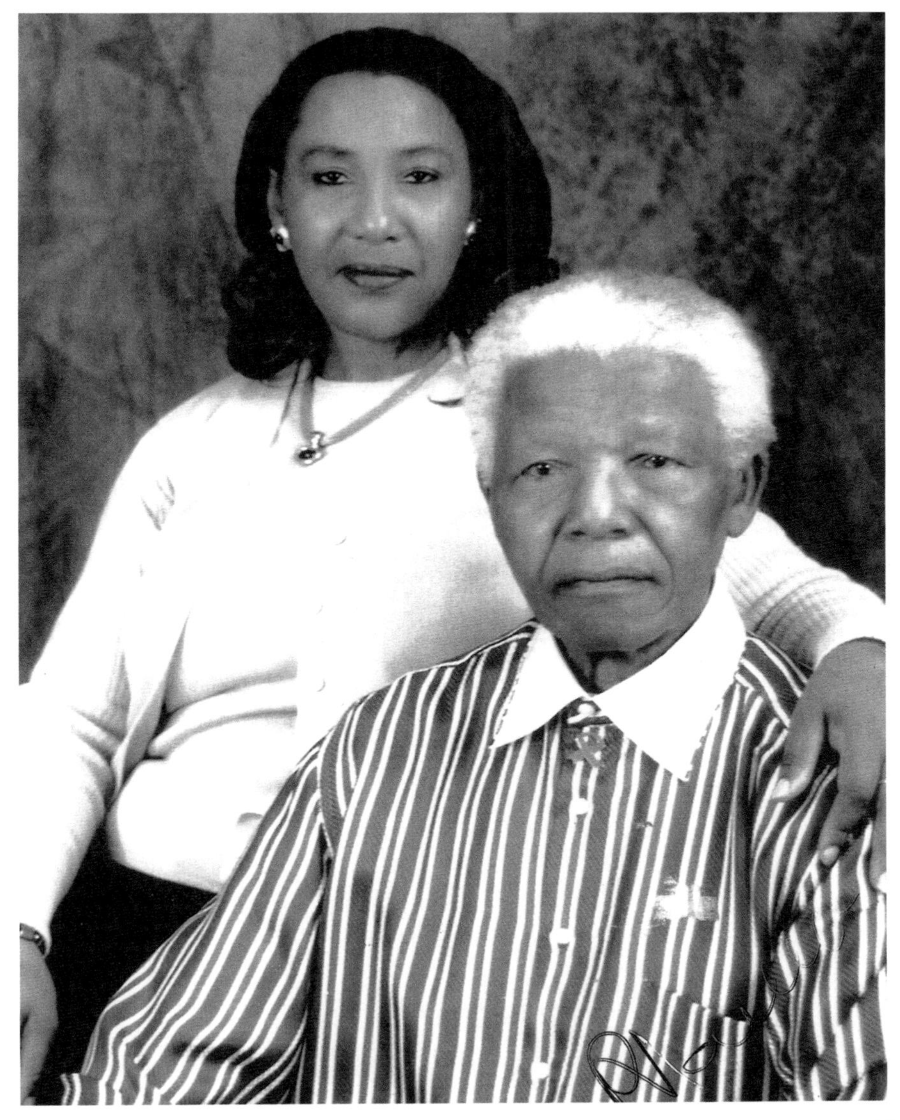

Me and Tata.

called. Finally, my turn came. I was expecting to hug Tata, but there was no such thing. I was brought to a visitor's booth where we were separated by a glass panel. We had to use the telephones provided on each side to speak to each other. We kissed the glass window. Tata was very happy to see me. He asked me to stand up, so he could see how tall I had grown. We spoke about family and school. We were only allowed thirty minutes and the visit was over. Later, Tata was transferred to Pollsmoor Prison, and then, just before he was released, to Victor Verster Prison. I would write to Tata, but he was only allowed a certain number of letters every year. At times one would get letters that were missing a paragraph or certain sentences. But Tata was a very good writer and never missed a birthday.

Tata valued education above everything else and encouraged me to go back to school after my first marriage collapsed. I applied to the University of Fort Hare in Alice, in the Eastern Cape, where I got my first degree in social work.

Tata and I did not see eye to eye on a few things, especially family issues—mainly how he treated my brother Makgatho. I believe Tata loved his grandchildren very much and actually spoiled them, but he was awkward with his own children. By the time he was released from jail, we were grown people who had grown up with little of his influence on us. We acknowledged that as the price of his commitment to the liberation of the people of South Africa.

Tata's grandchildren at his ninetieth birthday celebration.

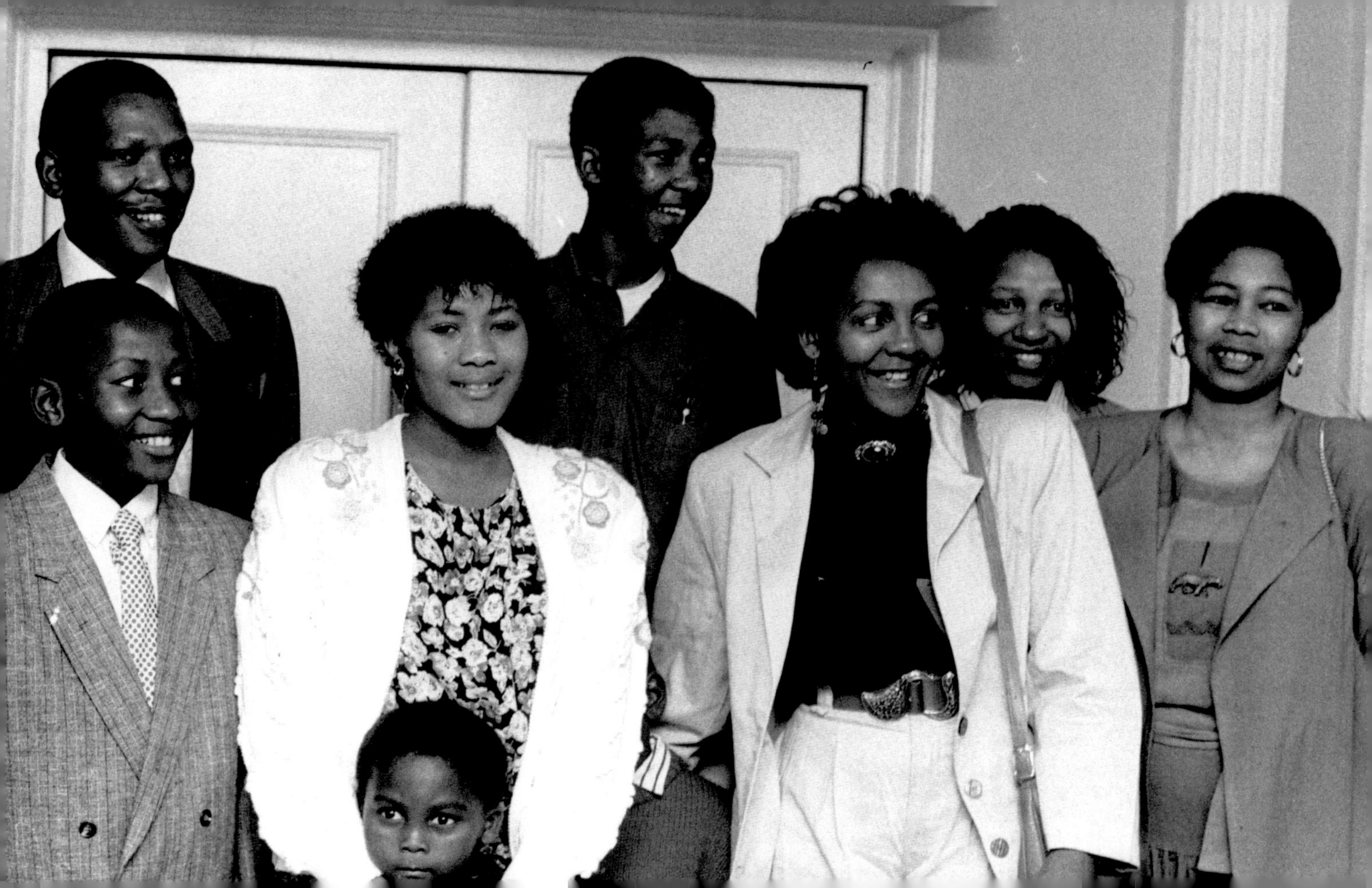

Nomzamo Winifred "Winnie" Zanyiwe Madikizela Mandela

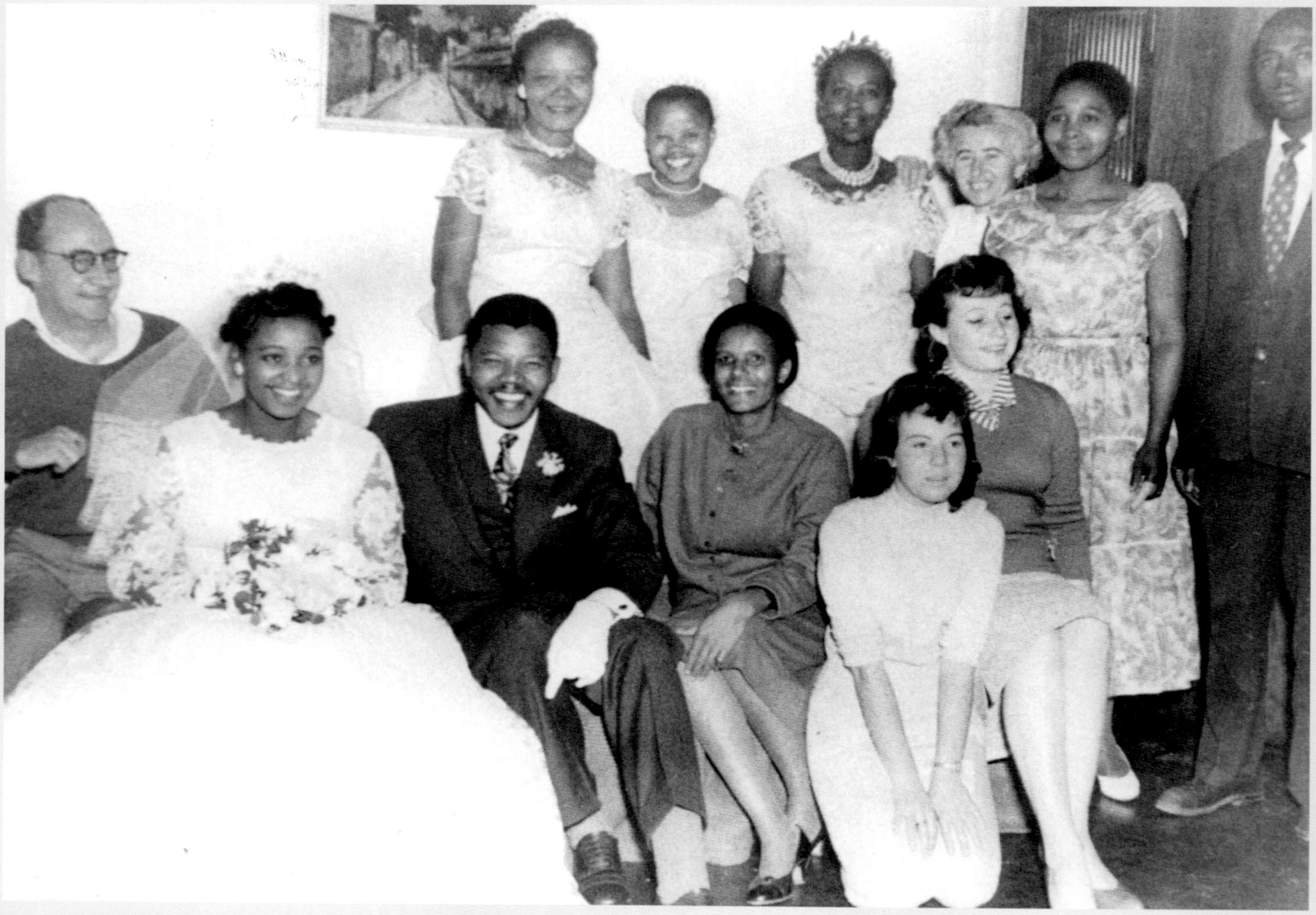

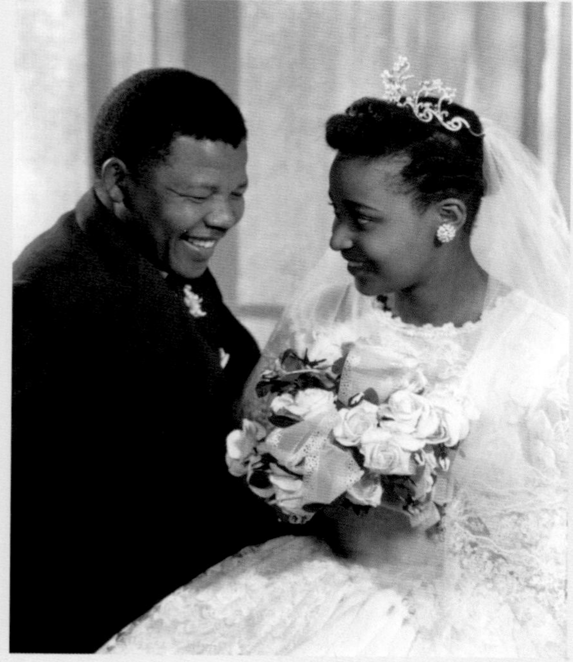

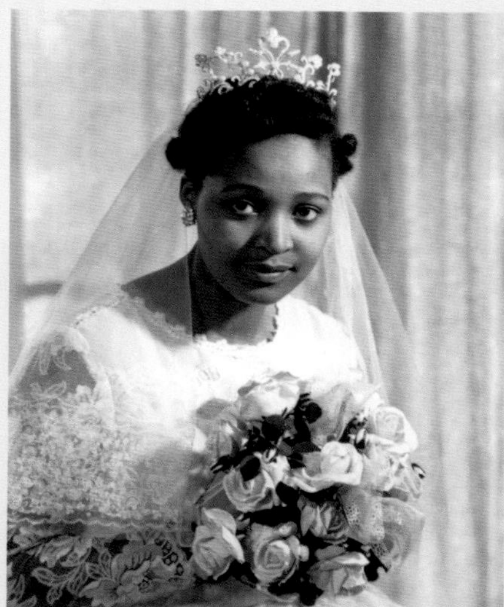

This page and opposite: Tata and Winnie Mandela with family and guests on their wedding day in 1958.

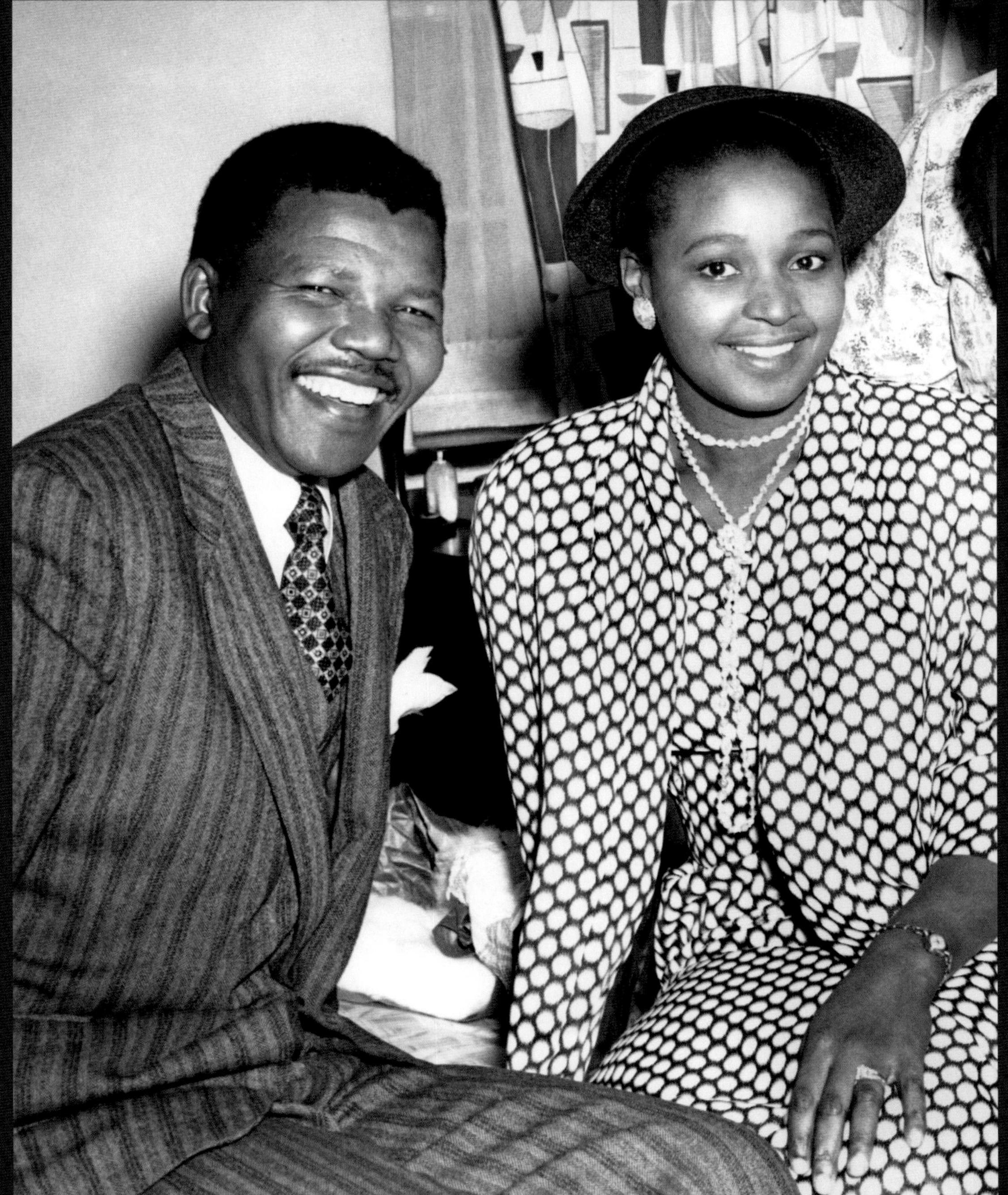

Winifred Madikizela, whom I would come to call "MaWinnie," was working as a social worker at Baragwanath Hospital in Soweto, Johannesburg. She was twenty-two years old when she met Tata in 1957; he was sixteen years her senior. After a short courtship, they got married in 1958. By then, Tata was already fully engaged in politics and banned in South Africa. To be able to attend his wedding he had to seek permission. Their marriage was robust, but it was also a lonely one for MaWinnie as Tata was always busy with ANC meetings, the Treason Trial, and legal work. Zenani, their first child, was born on February 5, 1959. The name Zenani means "What have you brought to the world?" It's a name, as my father has pointed out, whose meaning really symbolizes a challenge—a name that suggests certain expectations will be placed on the person to whom it was given.

On March 29, 1961, all Treason defendants were found not guilty. This happy news had come soon after the birth of their second child, Zindziswa, on December 23, 1960.

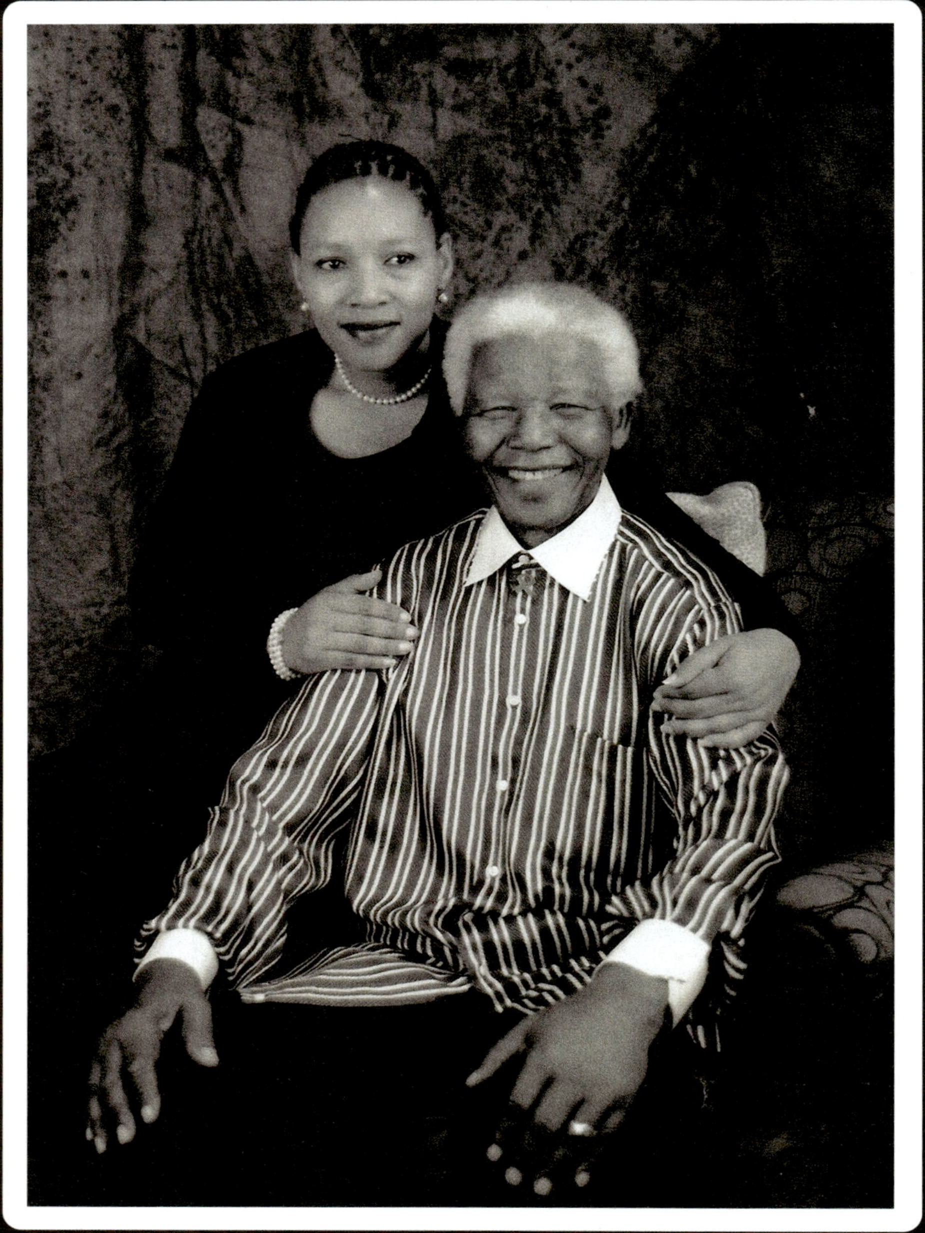

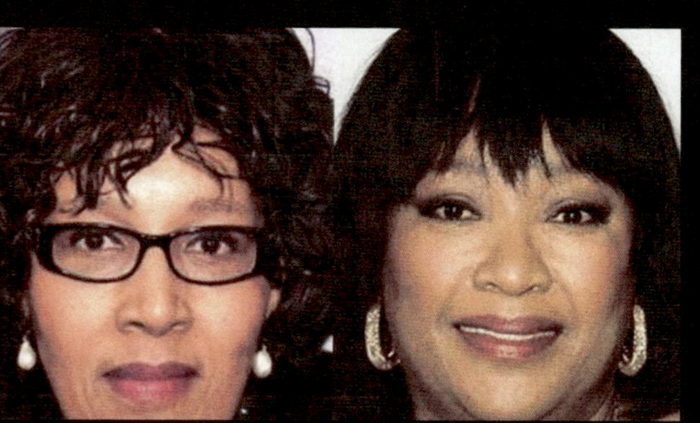

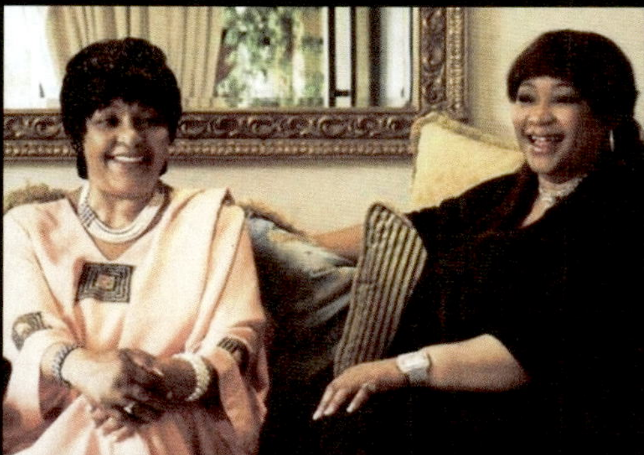

Zenani and Zindziswa

Thembekile, Makgatho, and I visited Orlando West No. 8115 from time to time, or we would all go together with MaWinnie to visit Tata in hiding. The period when Tata was in hiding was an unusual time for MaWinnie. It was a time when Tata was known as the "Black Pimpernel." He was arrested in Howick, Natal, and sentenced to five years imprisonment on August 5, 1962. MaWinnie visited Tata regularly in prison. In 1962, she was banned from speaking publicly, and her movements were restricted to the district of Johannesburg. Winnie was sent to prison on numerous occasions. She was a politician in her own right and was instrumental in keeping Tata's name and the struggle in the limelight for most of Tata's years in prison. Prison was tough for both Tata and MaWinnie. At one point he wrote to her:

> The cell is an ideal place to learn to know yourself, to search realistically and regularly the process of your own mind and feelings. In judging our progress as individuals, we tend to concentrate on external factors such as one's social position, influence and popularity, wealth and standard of education. . . . But internal factors may be even more crucial in assessing one's development as a human being. Honesty, sincerity, simplicity, humility, pure generosity, absence of vanity, readiness to serve others—qualities which are within easy reach of every soul—are the foundations of one's spiritual life. . . . At least, if for nothing else, the cell gives you the opportunity to look daily into your entire conduct, to overcome the bad and develop whatever is good in you.

When Tata was released from prison on February 11, 1990, life became a blur of activities, international travel, and negotiations for a new dispensation; and the couple grew apart and divorced in March 1996. Although divorced, MaWinnie continued to participate in family meetings—birthday parties, weddings, funerals, and Christmas gatherings, whether in Johannesburg or Qunu in the Transkei—until she passed away on April 2, 2018.
Both Zenani and Zindziswa went to school in Swaziland at Waterford Kamhlaba United World College of Southern Africa and while there Zenani met and married Prince Thumbumuzi Dlamini. Tata always emphasized education to all his children, and he was concerned that Zenani had not completed high school when she got married. He was nevertheless excited by her marriage into a royal Swazi family. He was also delighted when she left for America with her family to study at Boston University. Zenani was later appointed South Africa's ambassador to Argentina from 2012 until 2017, after which she was appointed South African high commissioner to Mauritius. In 2019, she was appointed as the South African ambassador to South Korea.
Zindziswa was a poet and a diplomat. She served as South Africa's ambassador to Denmark in 2014 until she passed away on July 13, 2020, from Covid-19 complications.

My Father's Third Wife, Graça Machel

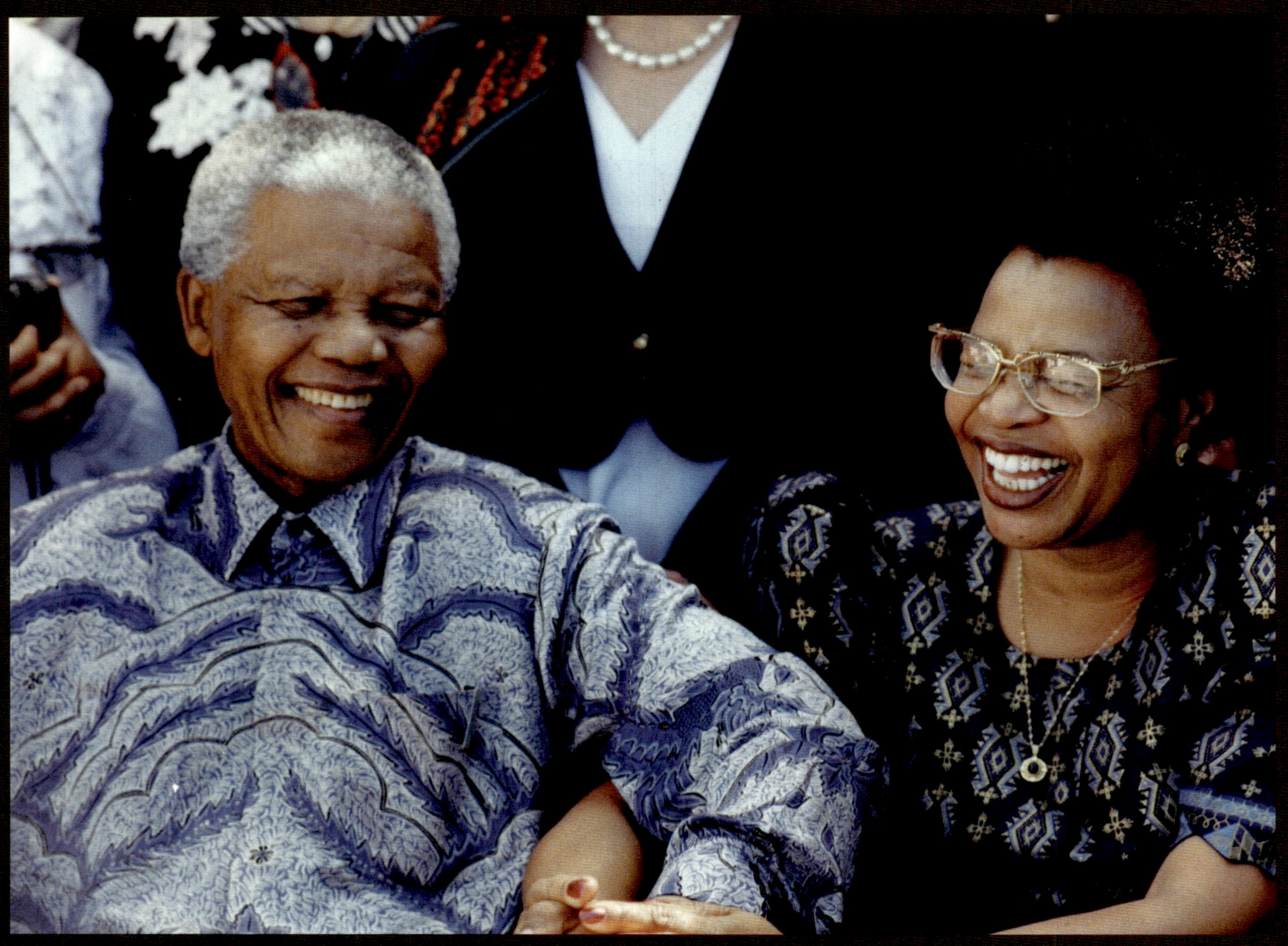

"I am in love with a remarkable lad."

Graça Machel

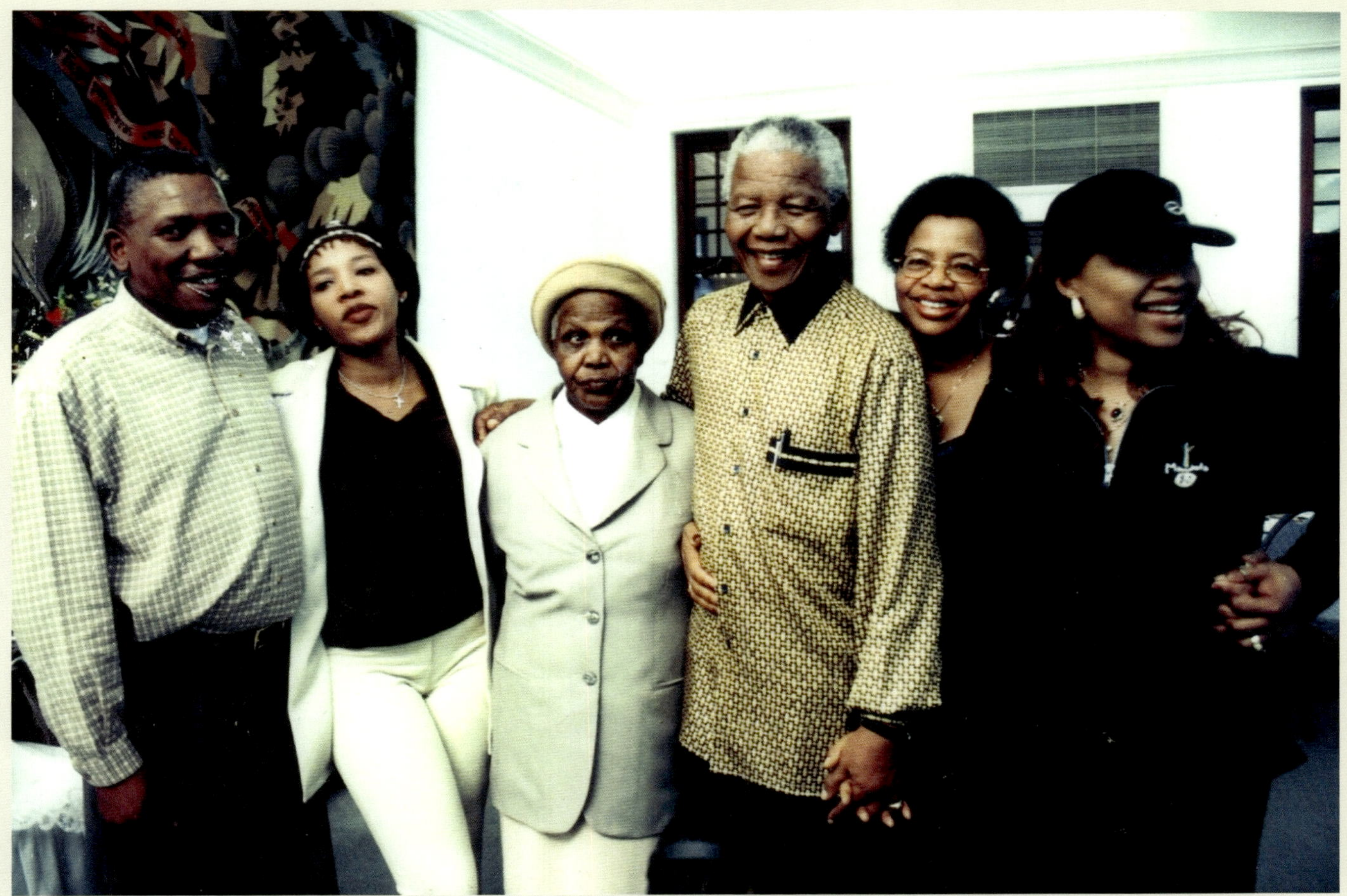

Left to right: Makgatho, Zeni, Aunt Notanal (my father's sister), Tata, Graça Machel, and Zindziswa at the president's residence in Pretoria the day Tata formally introduced Graça to his family and announced that they would get married.

In mid-1995, Tata began dating Graça Machel, the widow of the former president of Mozambique, Samora Machel, who had died in 1986. They dated for some time before getting serious about their relationship. She told a Portuguese newspaper, "Nelson and I were together some time before love came. It wasn't love at first sight. No, with me, things don't happen like that." By 1997, Graça had become Tata's consort and they would accompany each other on international visits. Graça would visit Tata in Johannesburg often. When Tata initially proposed to her, she did not readily accept as she was concerned about her obligations to her family and her country. "I belong to Mozambique," she told Tata's official biographer, Anthony Sampson, in an interview. "I will always be the wife of Samora Machel." Graça had six stepchildren from Samora Machel's first wife and two of her own with Samora: daughter Josina and son Malengane. At Tata and Graça's marriage, there were no more than sixteen specially invited guests present to witness the exchange of vows. Chief rabbi Cyril Harris blessed the couple and joined them in union. In a television interview, Tata spoke about his romance with Graça: "I'm in love with a lovely lady. I don't regret the reverses and setbacks because late in my life I'm blooming like a flower because of the love and support she's given me." In response, Graça told the press, "I am in love with a remarkable lad." Graça was married to Tata until he passed away on December 5, 2013. She lives in Maputo, Mozambique, and Johannesburg.

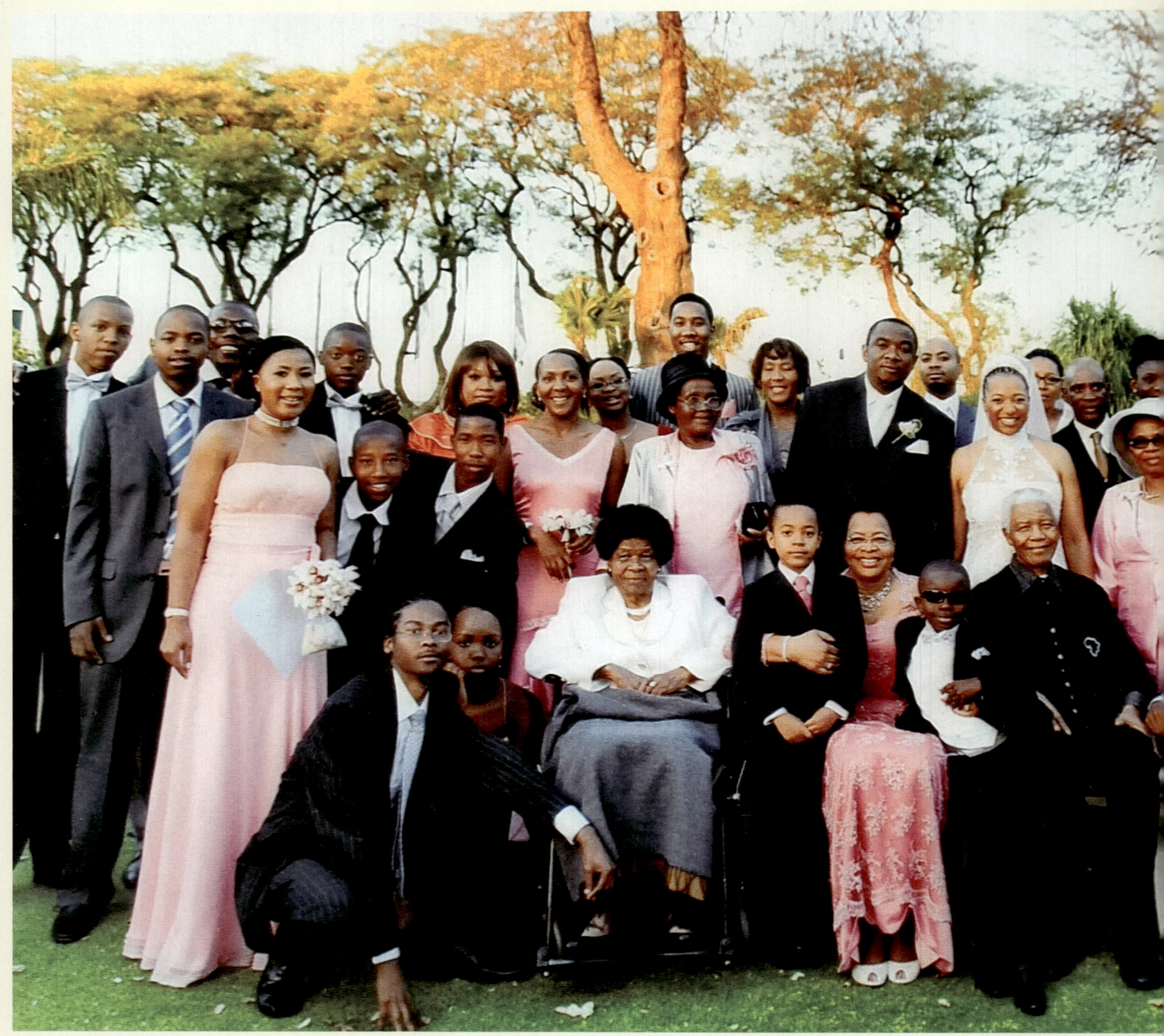

Tata surrounded by extended family at Nandi's wedding at the summer place.

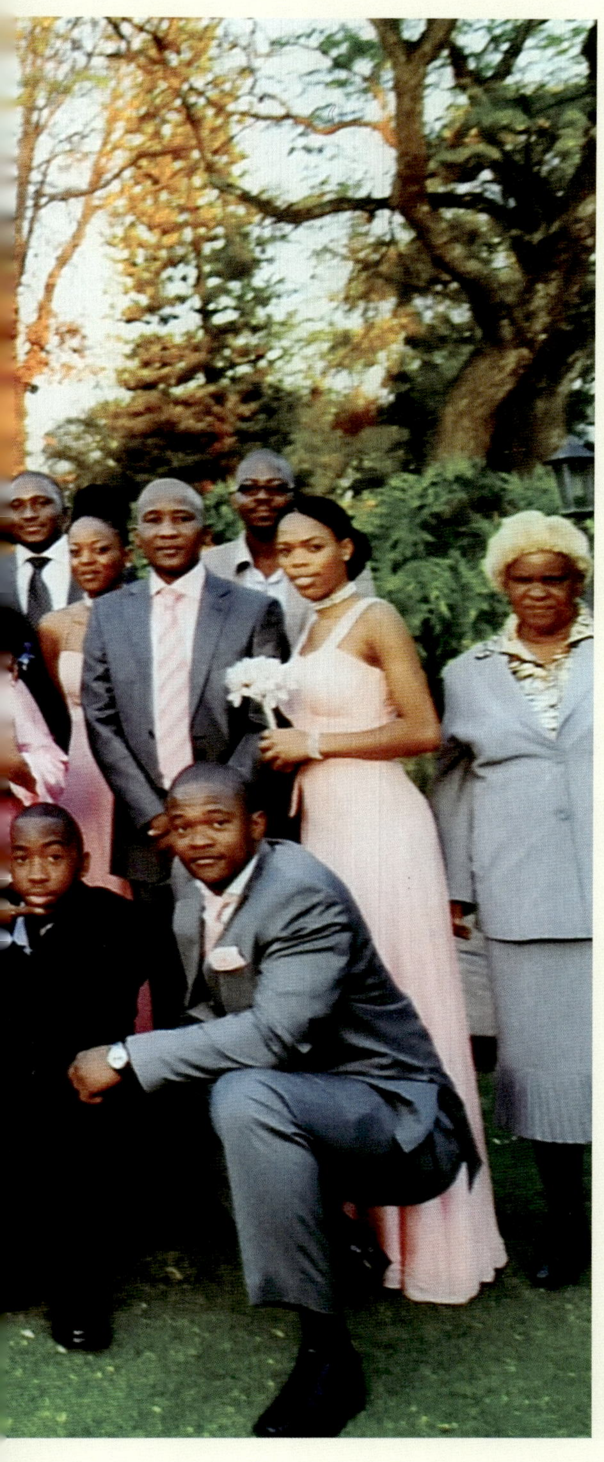

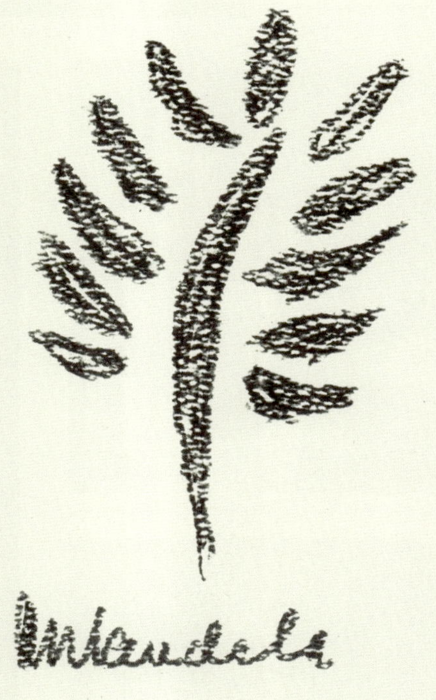

Tata never had any regrets about the sacrifices he made for the freedom of his people. However, he expressed regrets about the time he could have spent with his family. There is a consciousness of the price his children paid for a father who was often absent from his family, of a husband who left a young wife. This underlying consciousness of their pain when he was not there, when they needed him as an intimate, personal presence was expressed in his numerous letters. In one such letter, published in *Conversations with Myself*, Tata wrote that "I find it difficult to believe that I will never see Thembi again. . . . I had seen him towards the end of July 1962 . . . Then he was a lusty lad of 17 that I could never associate with death. He wore one of my trousers which was a shade too big and long for him. The incident was significant and set me thinking. . . . I was deeply touched, for the emotional factors underlying his actions were too obvious. For days thereafter my mind and feelings were agitated to realize the psychological strains and stresses my absence from home had imposed on the children."

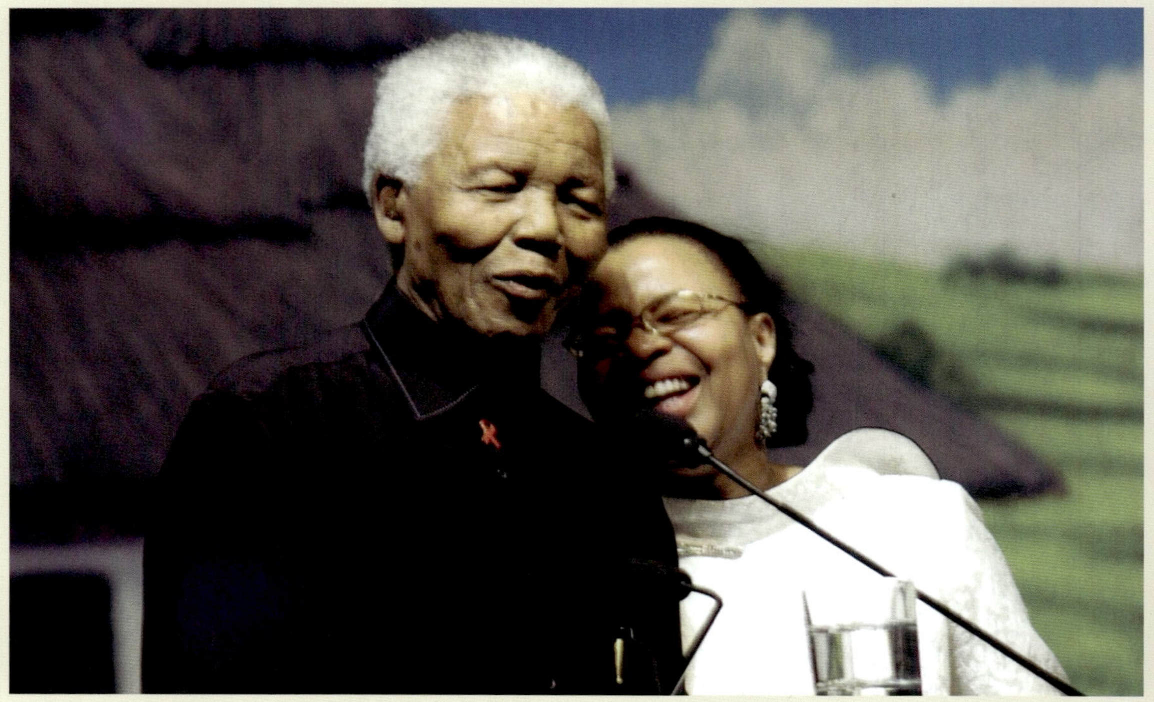

Tata and Graça at his eighty-fifth birthday party celebrating with family and friends.

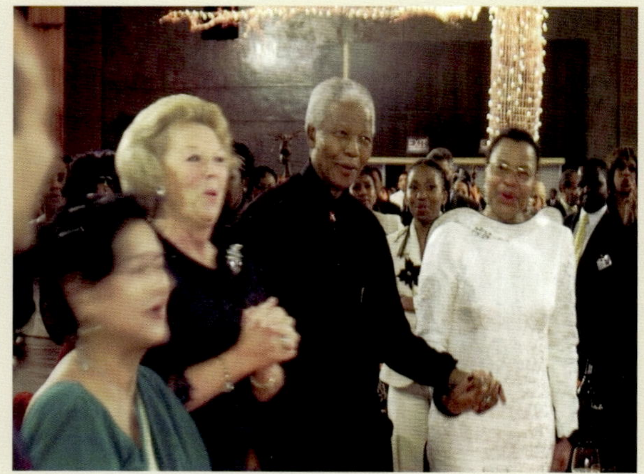

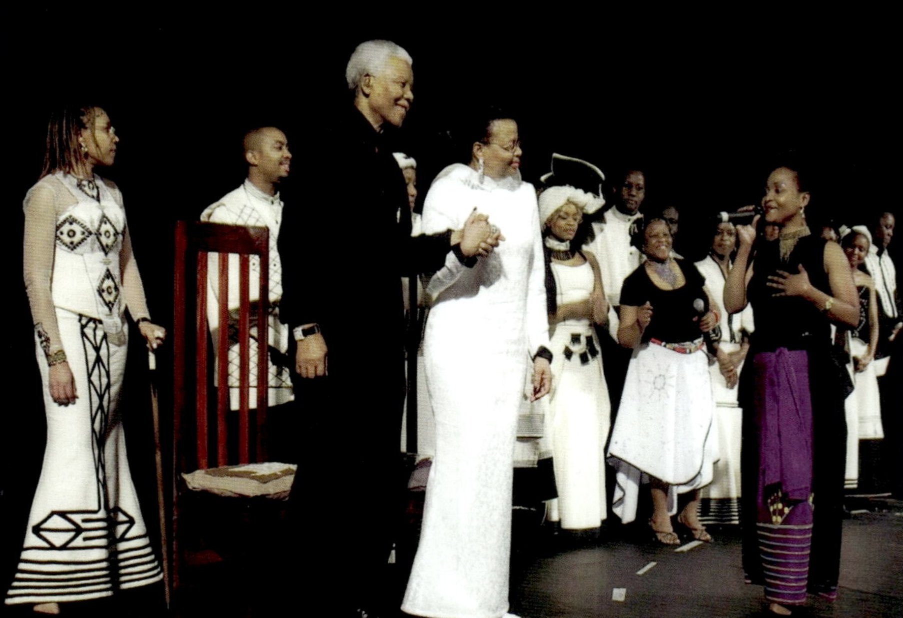

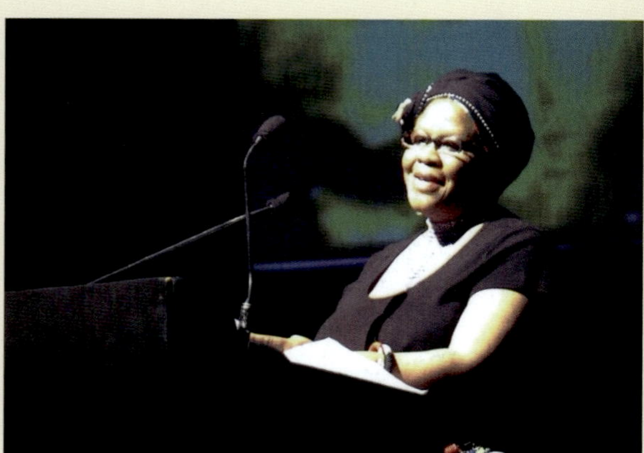

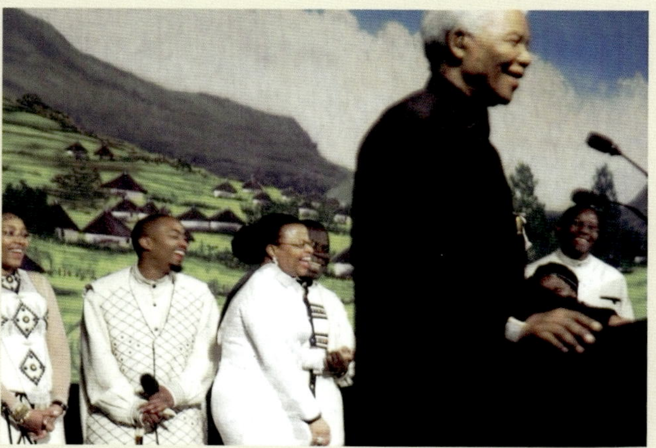

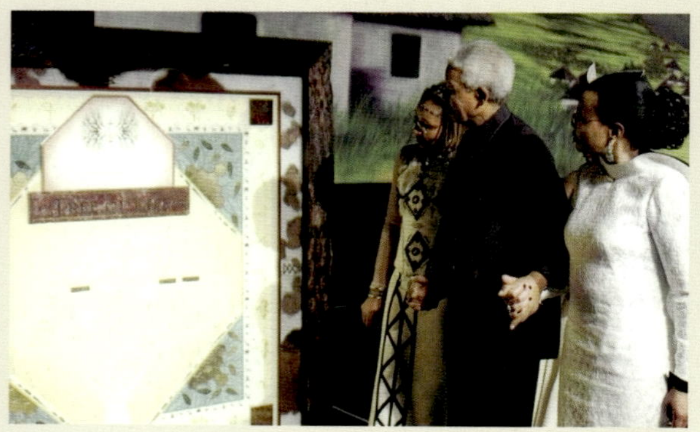

Left: A gift to Tata from the Mandela family—a frame made of railway ties with inlaid gold leaf messages from all over the world.

In 2003, the Mandela children and some of the older grandchildren planned a surprise birthday gala for Tata's eighty-fifth birthday and his fifth wedding anniversary to Graça. We raised money from an events management company in Johannesburg. The event was held at the Sandton Convention Centre with five hundred invited guests.

"Madiba, you have been always very warm. There was no time when you were indifferent. Happy birthday, Madiba."

Walter Sisulu

"Congratulations on your birthday, Madiba. Remember we are just the same age. You still are up and about as if you were a young boy. Happy birthday. May you have many more."

Albertina Sisulu

"Hi Madiba and Graça, We wish we could be there tonight to celebrate two incredible people, our most favorite people in the world. But we are stuck here in Chicago. I am finishing the seventeenth season of the *Oprah Winfrey Show*. Unfortunately, the show must go on. We wanted to send our love and heartfelt wishes to both of you. Madiba, we hope that you really enjoy your birthday and we hear that it will be quite a night to remember, comrade."

Oprah Winfrey and Stedman Graham

"Dear Tata, You occupy a special and significant place in our hearts because of your humility, your captivating smile, strength of your character, and most of all love for humanity. Your disciplined, courageous, fearless character is our legacy. May you have a happy birthday Madiba. God's blessings and long life to you, Tata."

Dr. Gigi Mberc

"Happy birthday, Madiba. I did not think you would make it to eighty-five. Your birthday must continue year after year. Happy fifth anniversary to a wonderful couple."

Amina Cachalia

"You are a special and precious gift to us in South Africa and the world. God be praised ukhole ukhukhobe."

Leah and Desmond Tutu

"Your inspiration and forgiveness will not only guide our family into the future but our entire nation. Thank you for the privilege of being a South African."

Richard and Karen Weilers

"Congratulations on your attainment of an eighty-fifth year of life. Wishing you many more years of happy and healthy living, spiritually, physically, and morally. May God Almighty continue to bless and sustain you and yours for all time."

Bishop Dabula Mpako

"You have taught us that every day we should reach out and touch someone, that we still have a lot to learn, that people will forget what we said or what we did, but they will never forget how you made them feel. For your eighty-fifth birthday, may God hold you in the palm of his hand and angels watch over you. All my love."

Wendy, a family friend

"You truly inspire us to be what we are. You are a true representation of what love is."

Graça

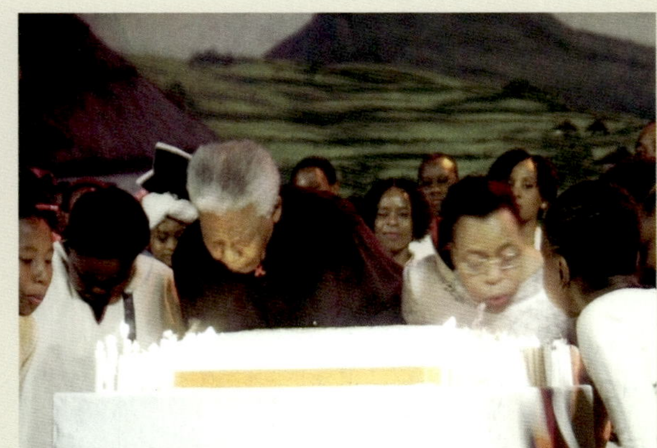

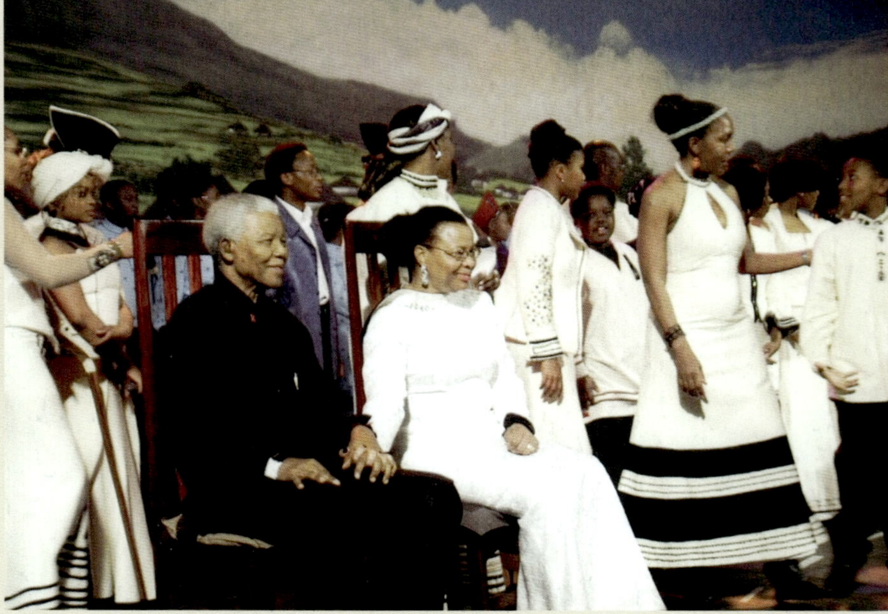

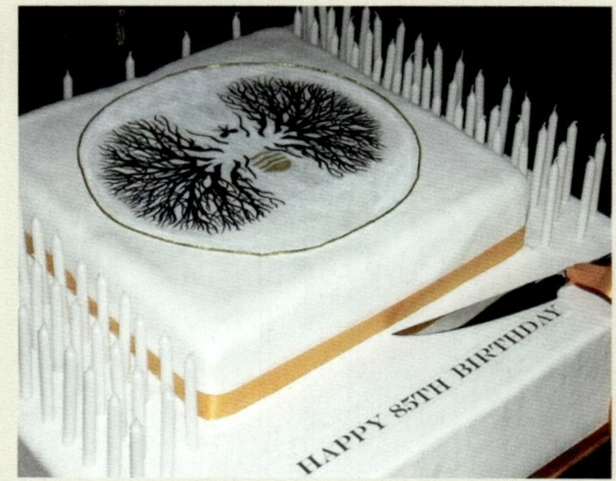

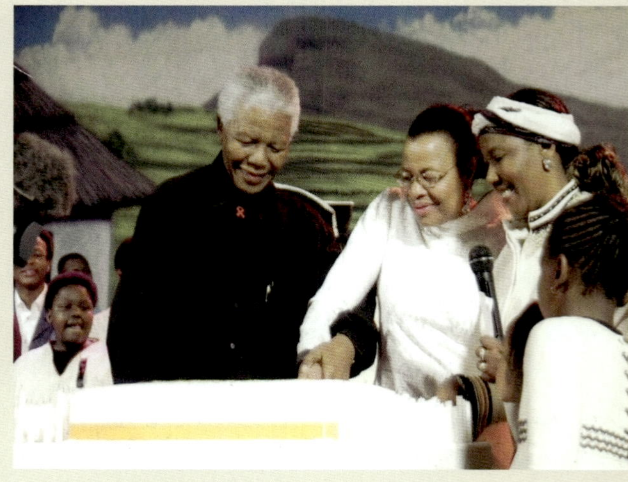

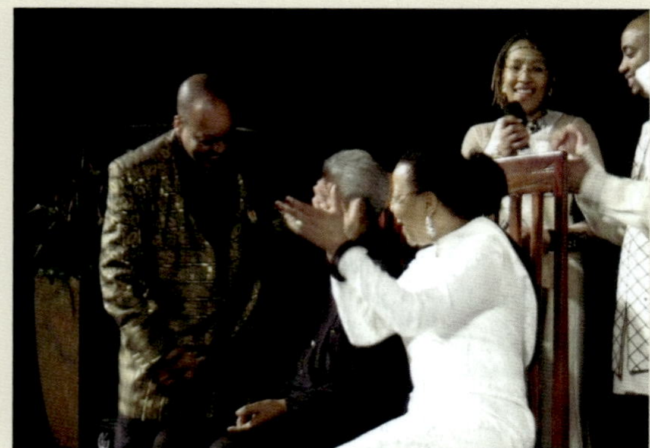

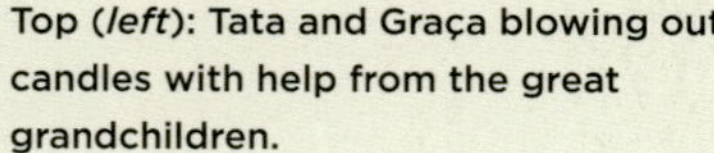

Top (*left*): Tata and Graça blowing out candles with help from the great grandchildren.

Above: South African president Jacob Zuma singing to Tata and Graça.

Right: Graça and me at the podium.

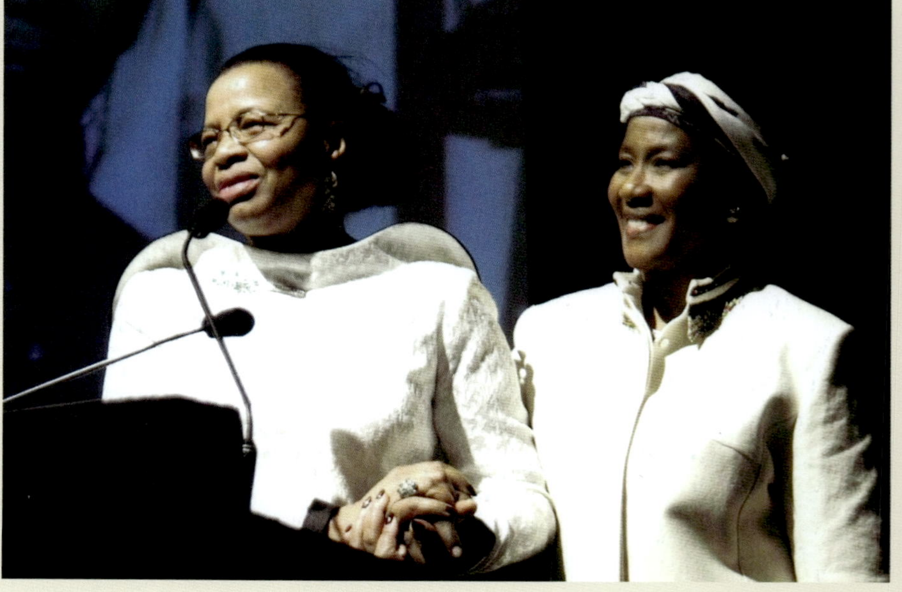

Clockwise from left: Ndileka, Stedman Graham, and my daughter, Tukwini. Oprah and Stedman made a surprise appearance at the birthday party.

Oprah and Tokyo Sexwale onstage. Tokyo was a political activitst who was also imprisoned on Robben Island for his anti-apartheid activities.

Left to right: My daughter Adjoa, Ndileka, Oprah, Tukwini, and me.

Tokyo singing with Oprah and Naomi Campbell.

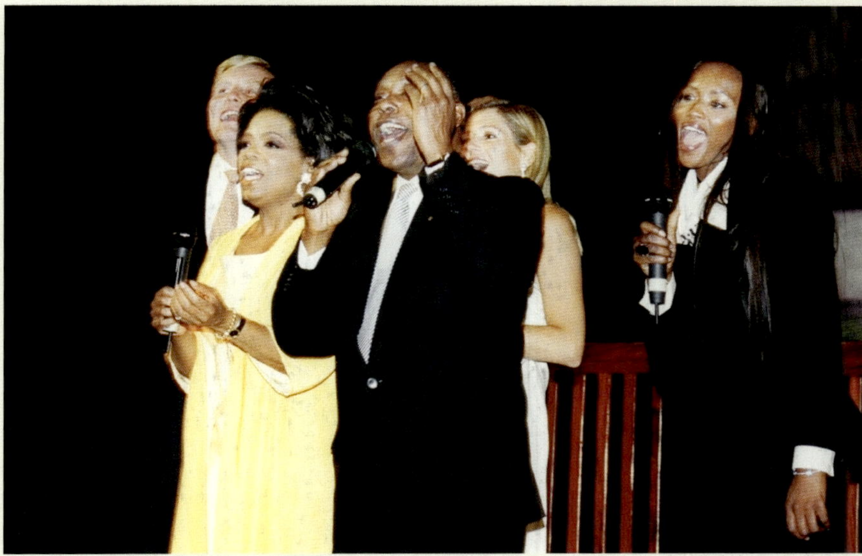

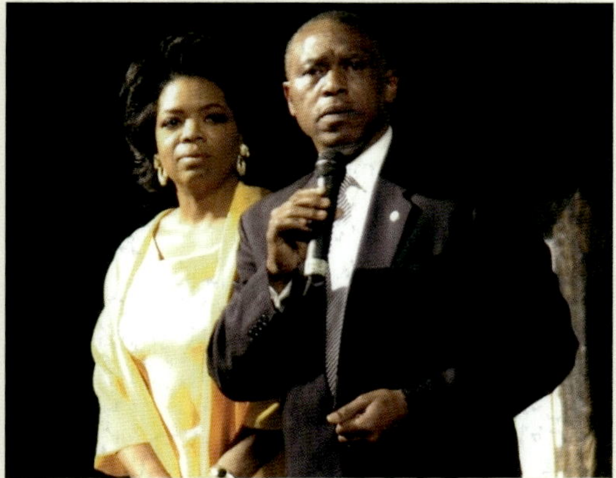

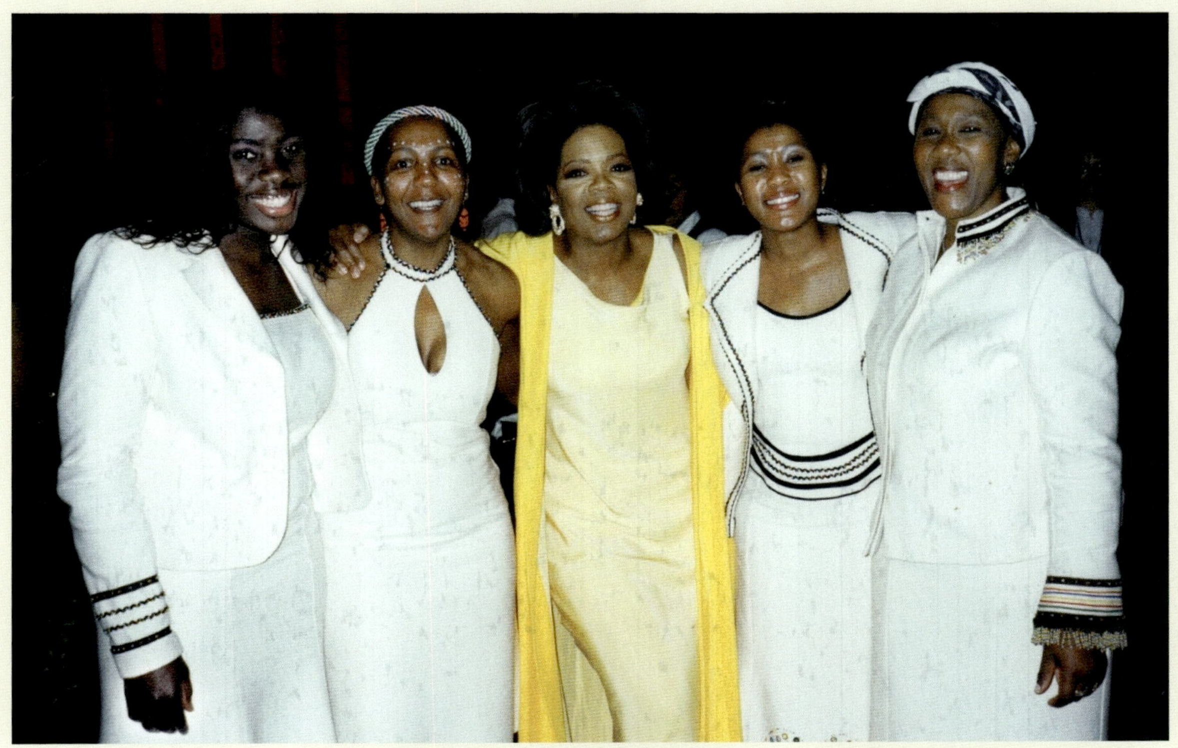

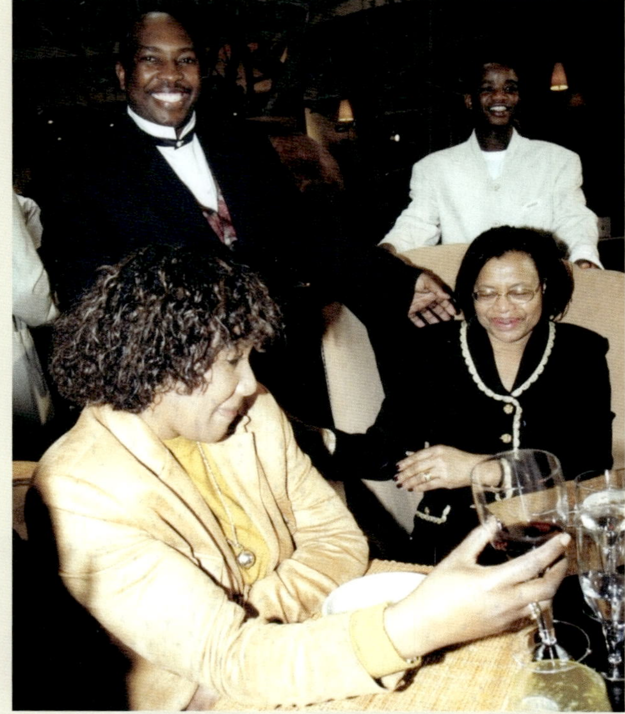

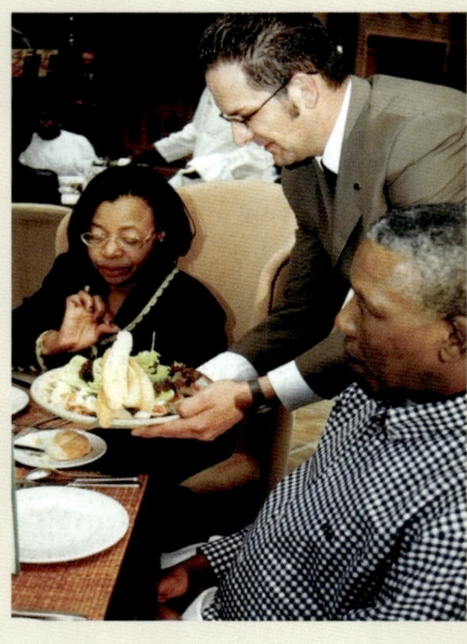

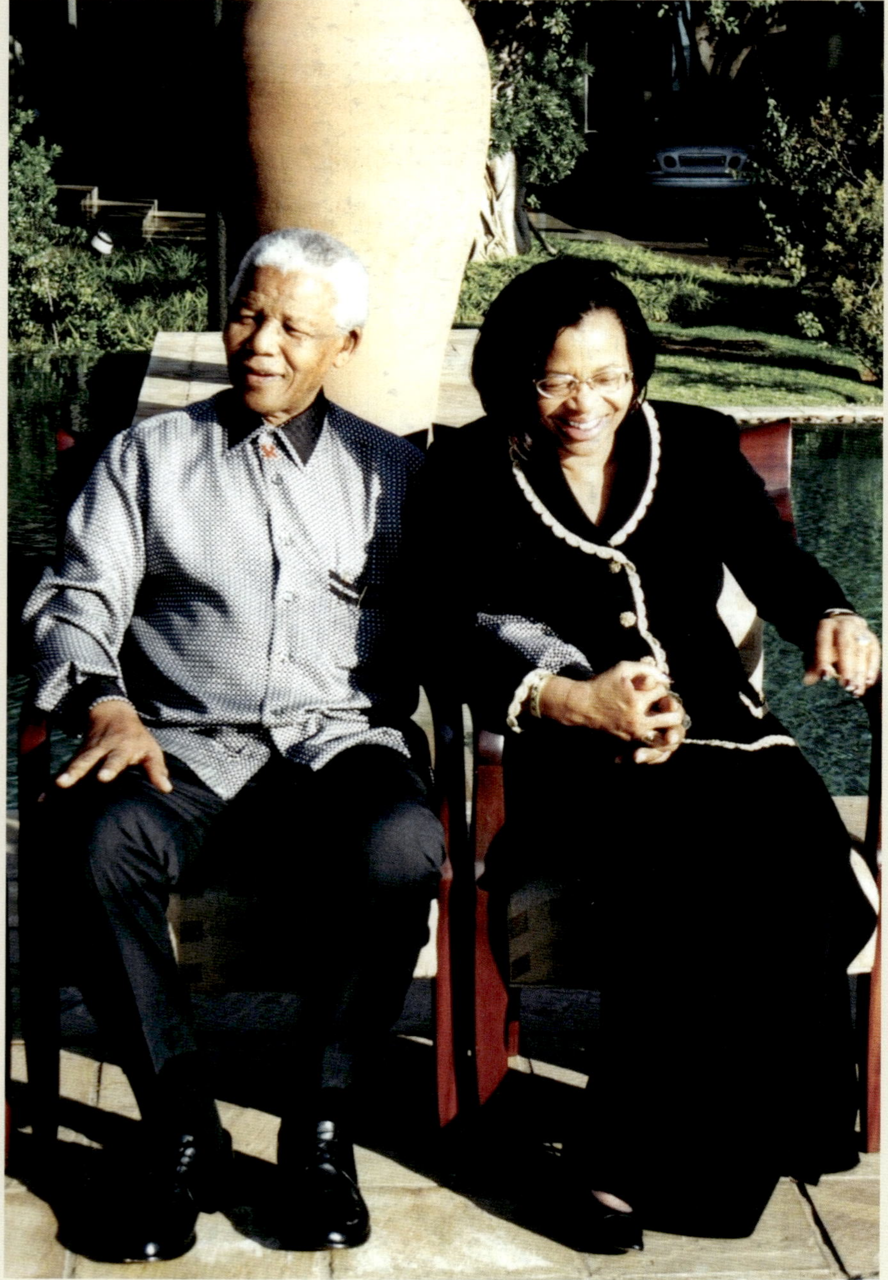

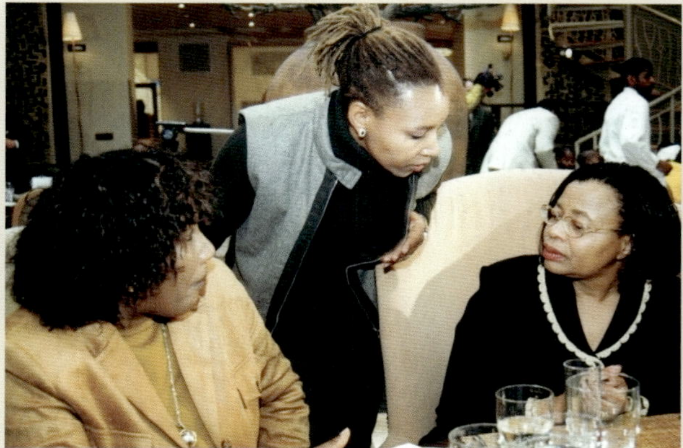

This page and opposite: Family Lunch at the Saxon Hotel in Sandhurst, Johannesburg.

Clockwise (*left to right*): Me and Graça; Graça and Makgatho; me, Zeni, and Graça; Tata and Graça.

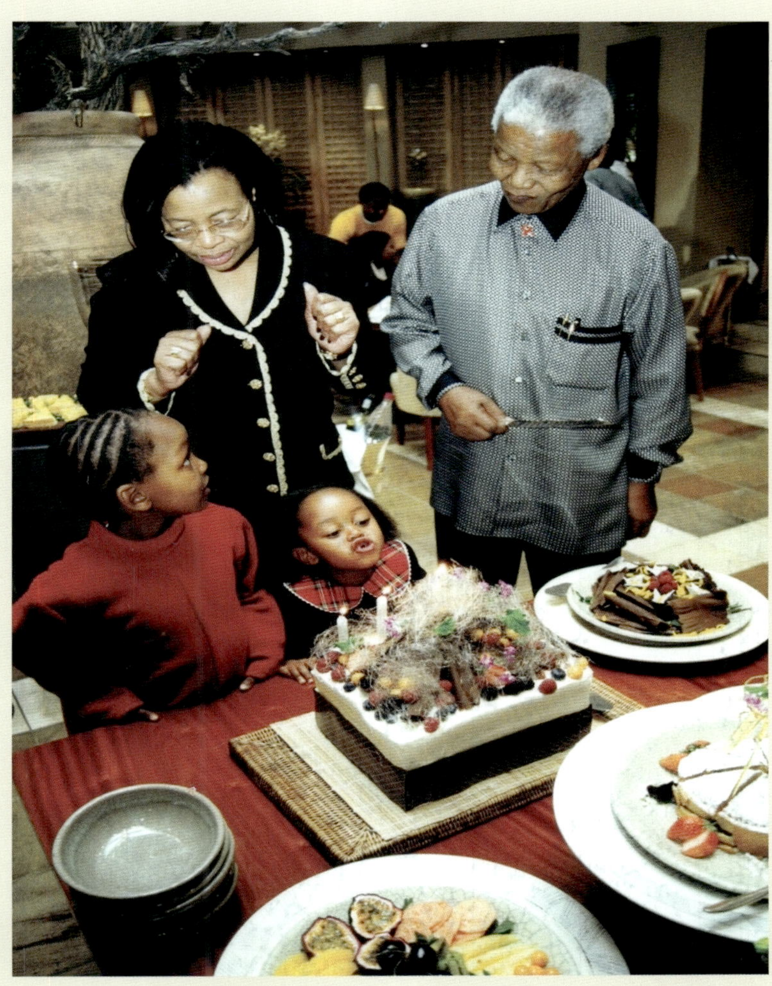

Below (*right*): Malenga Machel, Graça, and Tata.

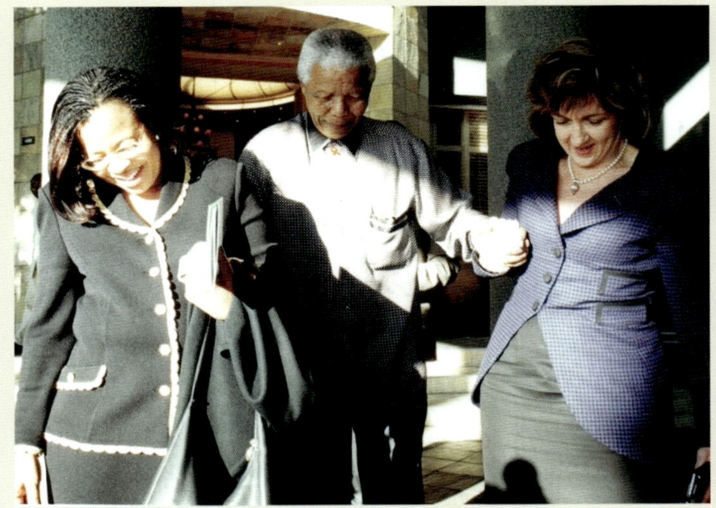

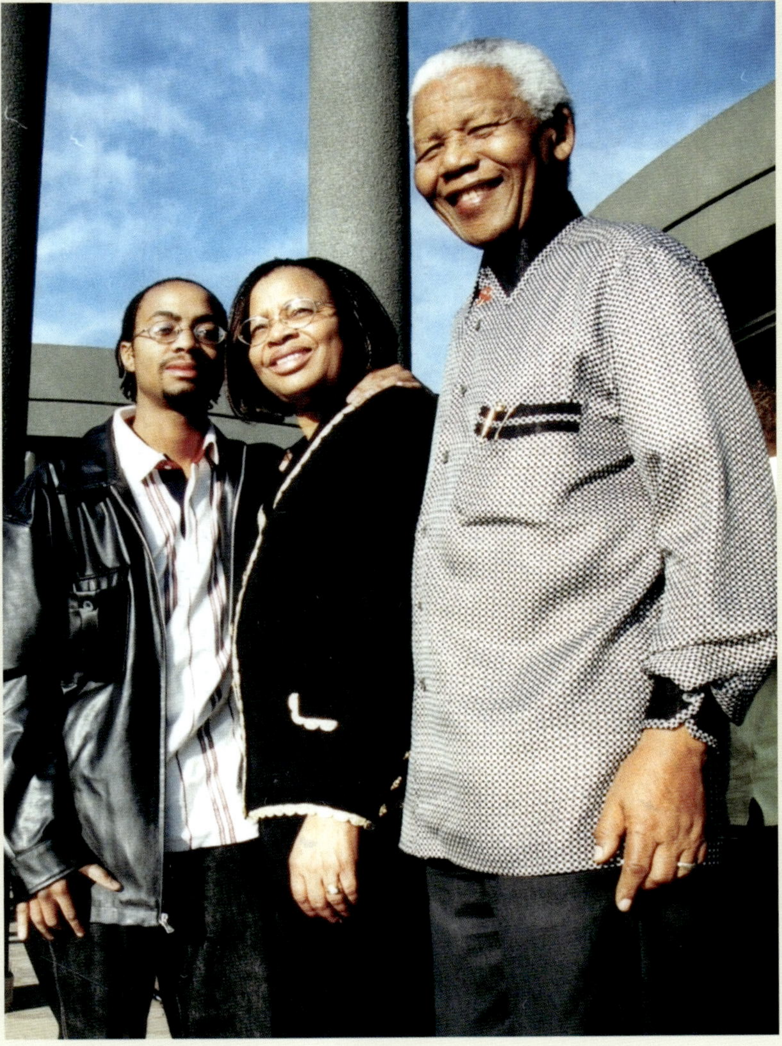

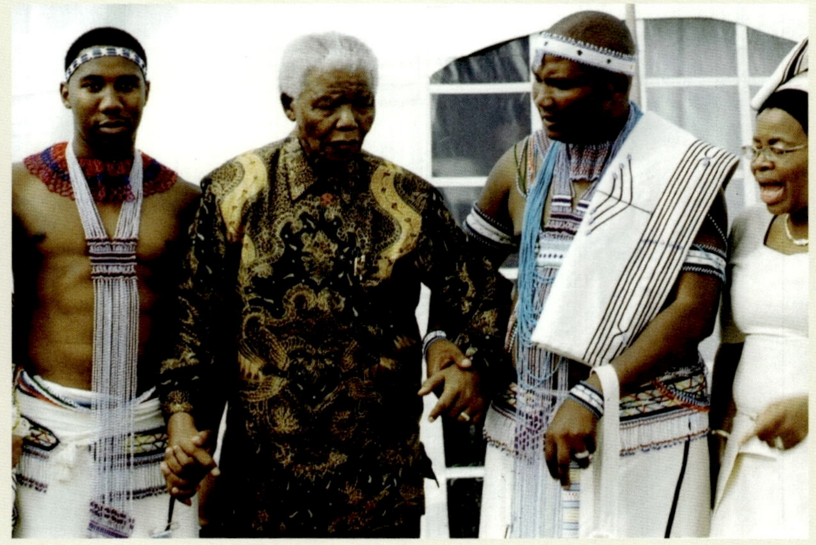

Left: Two of Makgatho's sons, Ndaba and Mandla, with Tata and Graça dressed for a traditional wedding in Qunu.

Below: Brothers Ndaba and Mandla.

Bottom (*left*): Tata, Graça, and Winnie at Tata's and Graça's wedding in Qunu.

Bottom (*right*): Mandla and his wife, and Tata with a Xhosa praise singer.

Opposite: Traditional dancers in Qunu.

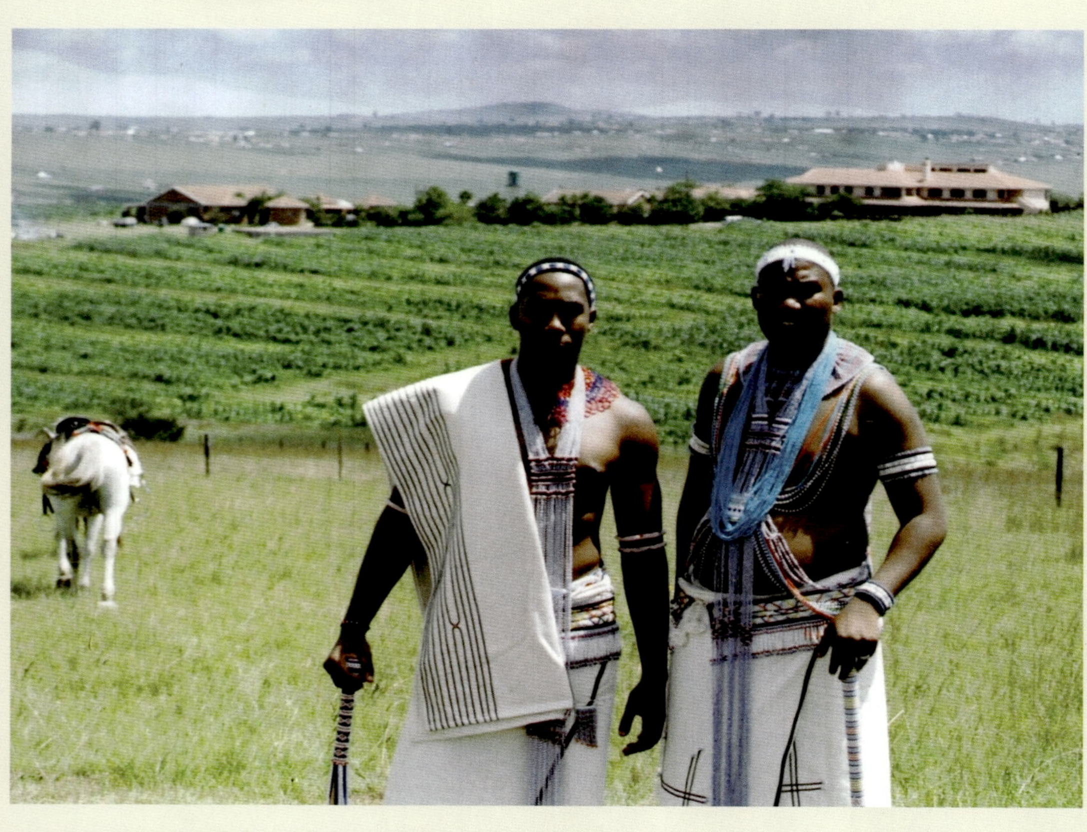

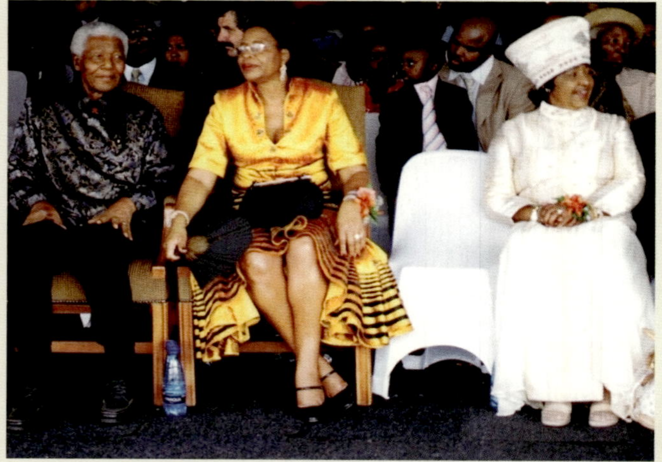

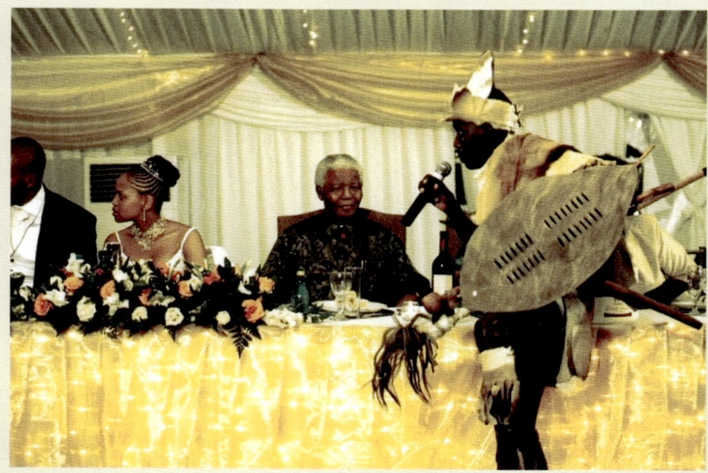

Events in Qunu—Tata's Beloved Home

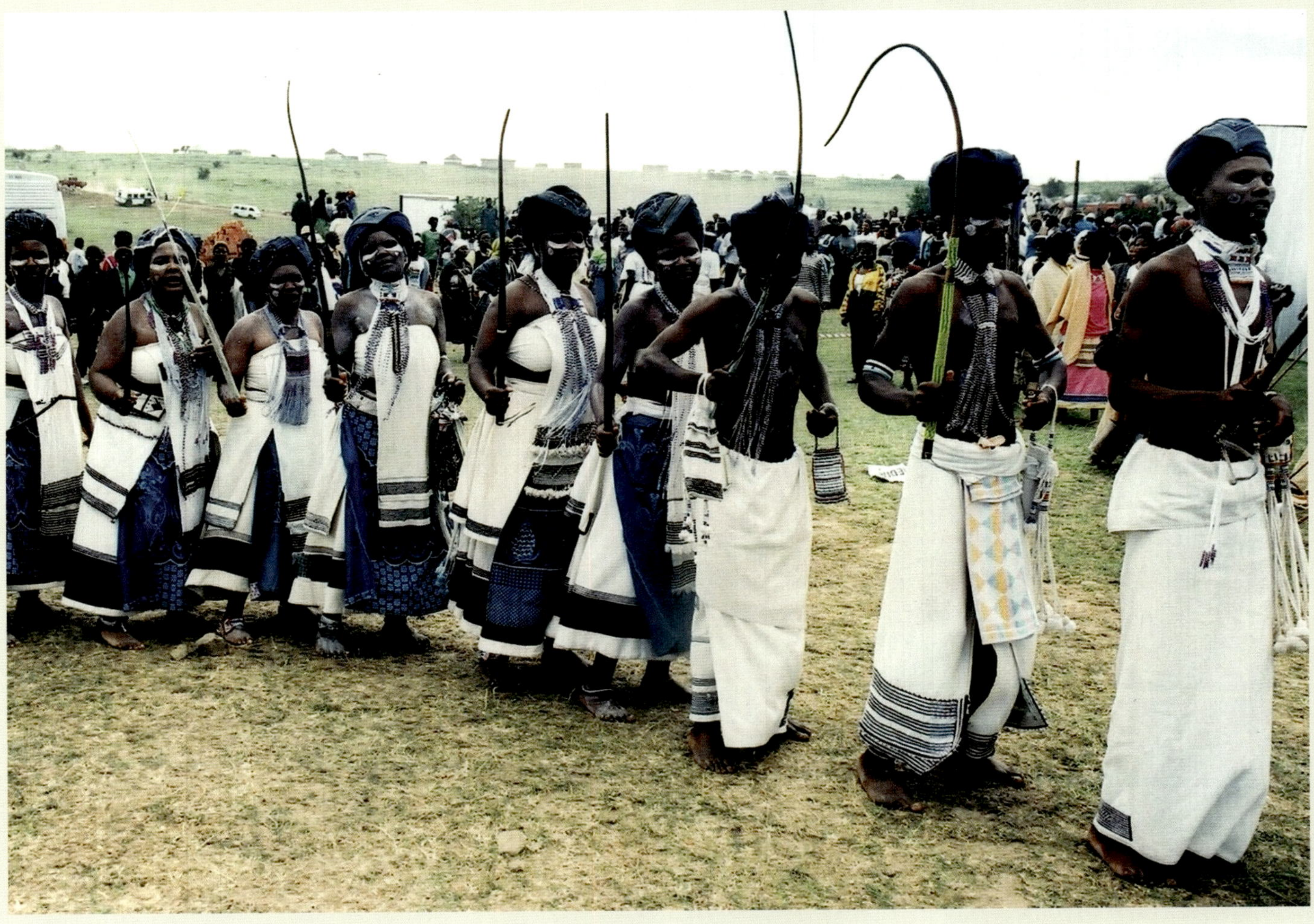

After Tata was released from prison in February 1990, he visited his birthplace to pay respect to his mother's grave. Qunu had always been very important to Tata. This is where he had fond memories of the warmth and simplicity of rural life, where the spirits of his ancestors roamed the hills. Tata always felt it important to be able to live close to one's place of birth. He built himself a country house and it was completed in 1993.

Part of his ancient, rural culture was that a man build his home close to his birthplace, and he told all of us children —even while he was in prison—that he wanted to be buried in Qunu, because his bones wouldn't rest anywhere else. In fact, he wished that his last breath would be in Qunu, but that was not to be.

Tata was really at home in Qunu, relaxed, talkative, and he encouraged the visit of chiefs and other family members. He would encourage us to visit Qunu often. "This is real home, where my roots and yours are," he would often say. "It becomes more important, the older you are, to go back to places where you have wonderful memories." Both his children who had passed away—Makaziwe 1 and Thembi—were exhumed from Johannesburg and interred in Qunu. When Makgatho passed away in Johannesburg, Tata made arrangements for his remains to be buried in Qunu. All important family events took place in Qunu.

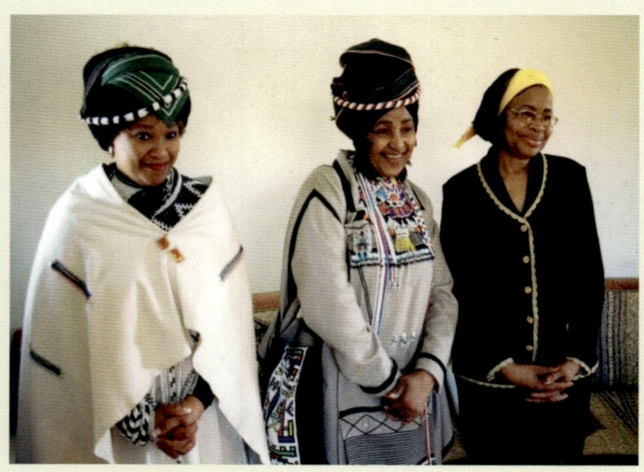

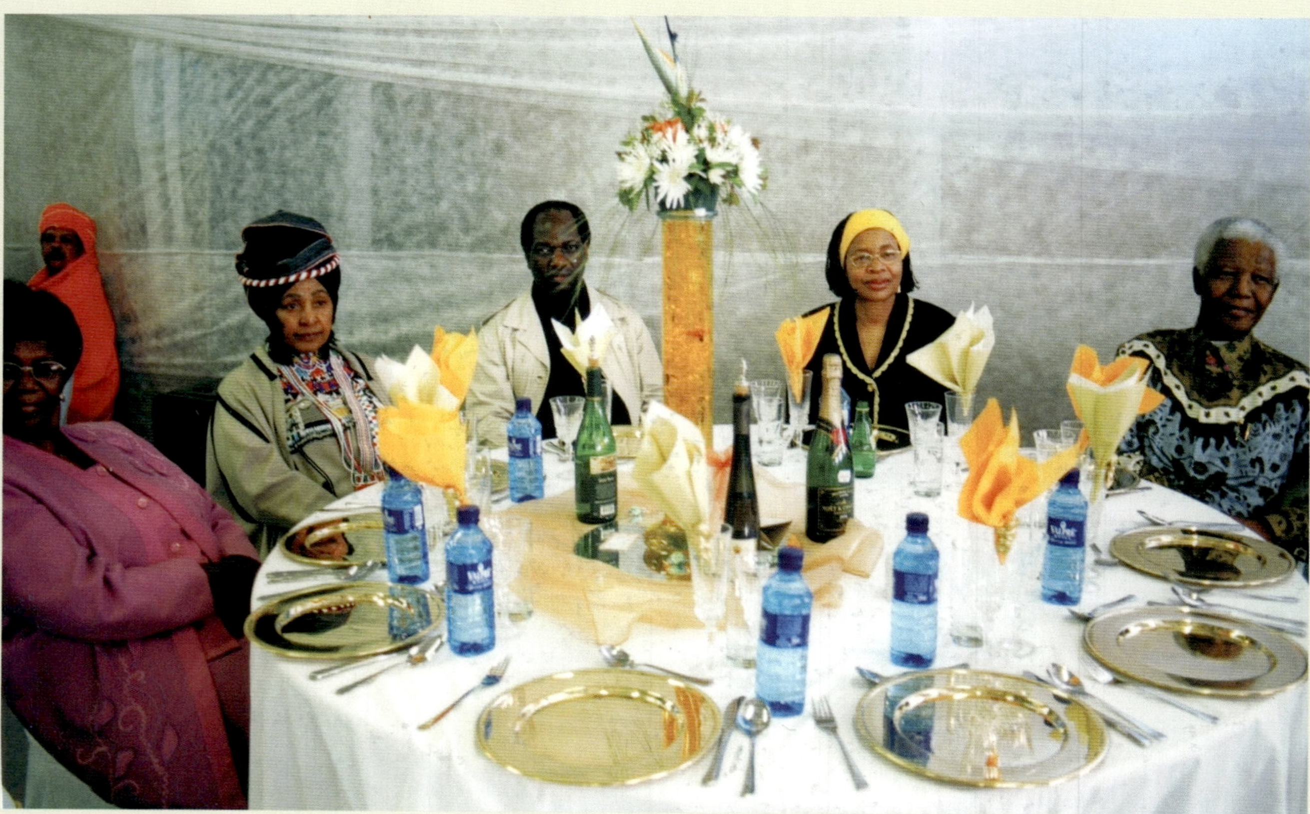

The eighty-eighth birthday lunch in Qunu.

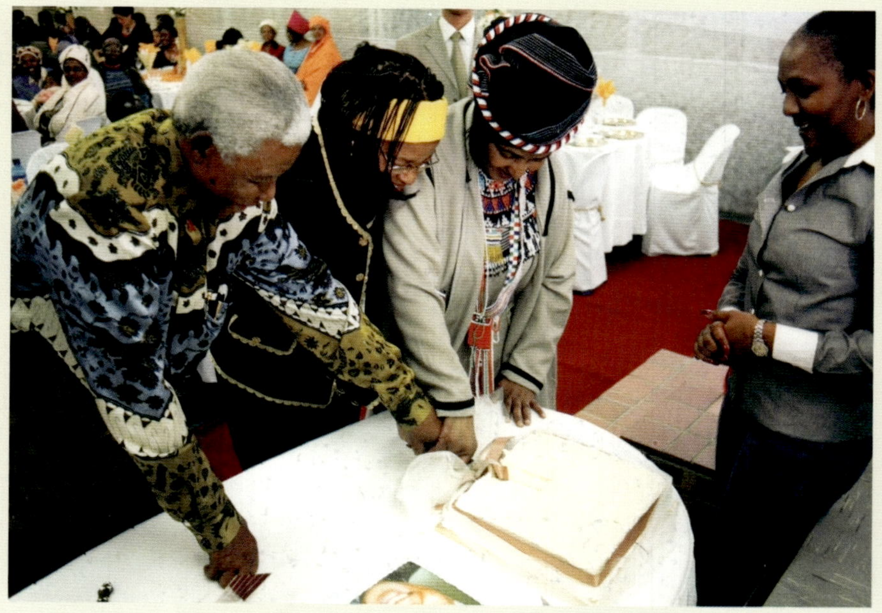

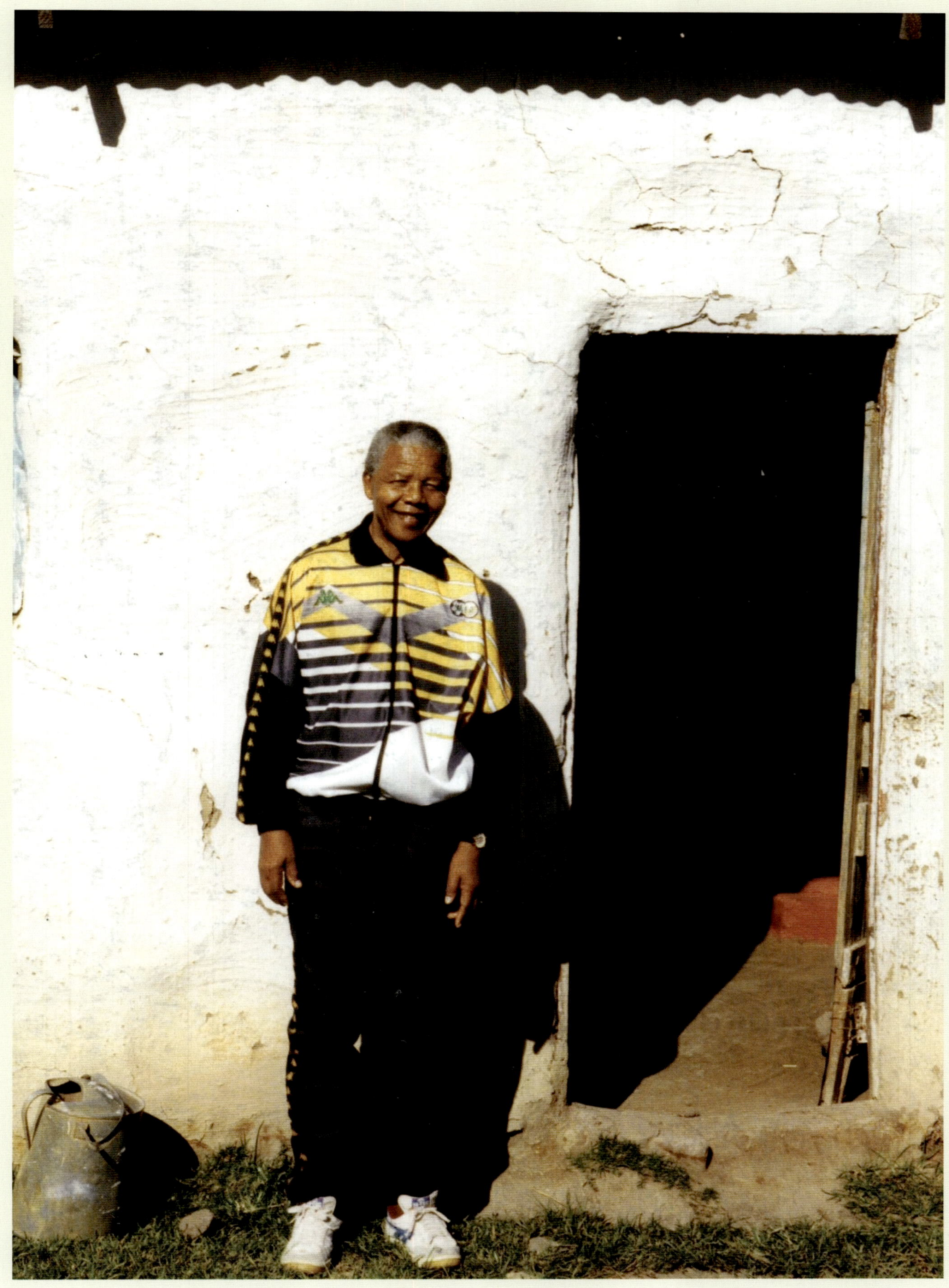

When Tata was in Qunu he would take long walks and visit some of the locals in the village.

Tata's Ninetieth Birthday Celebration and Tenth Wedding Anniversary

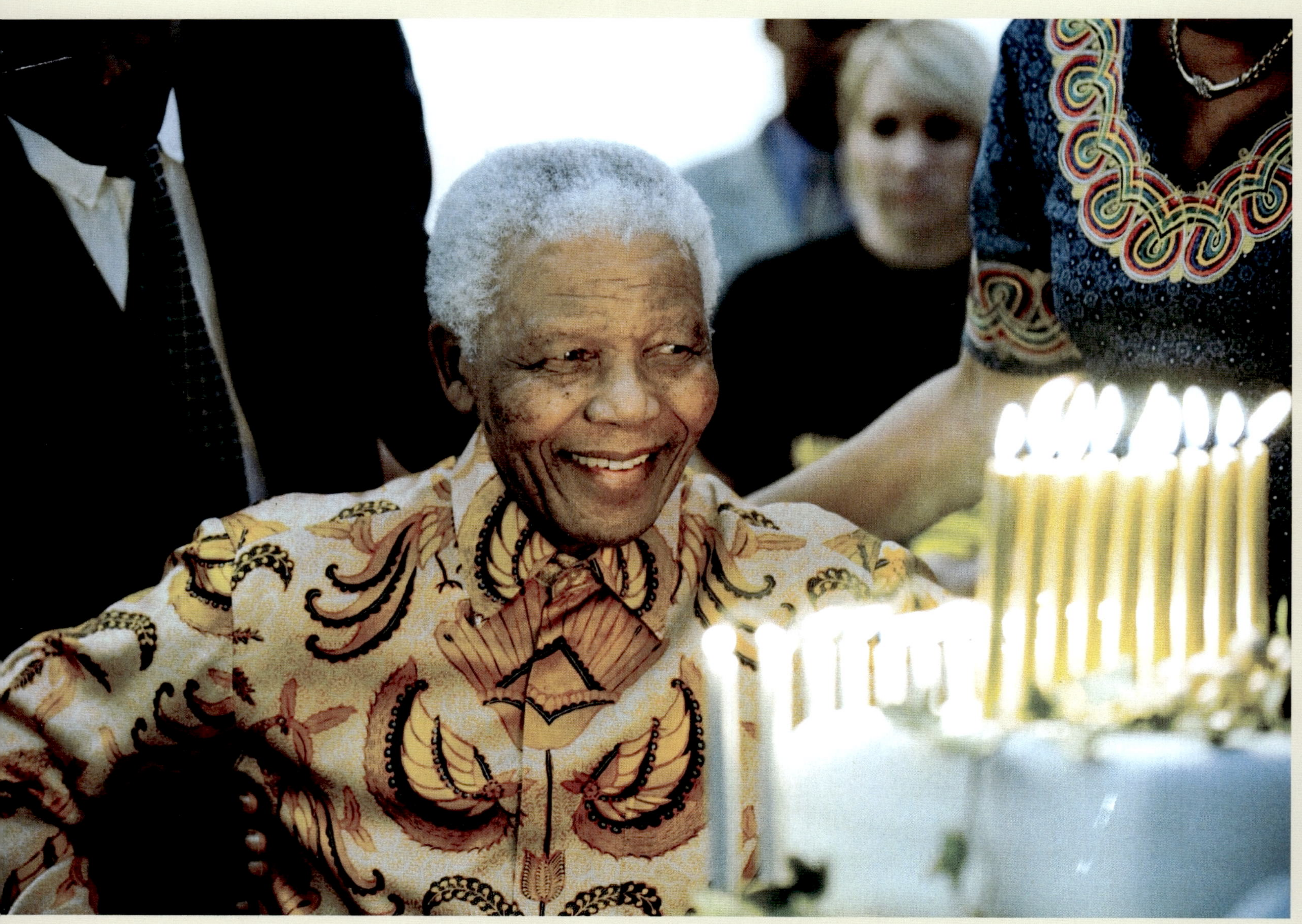

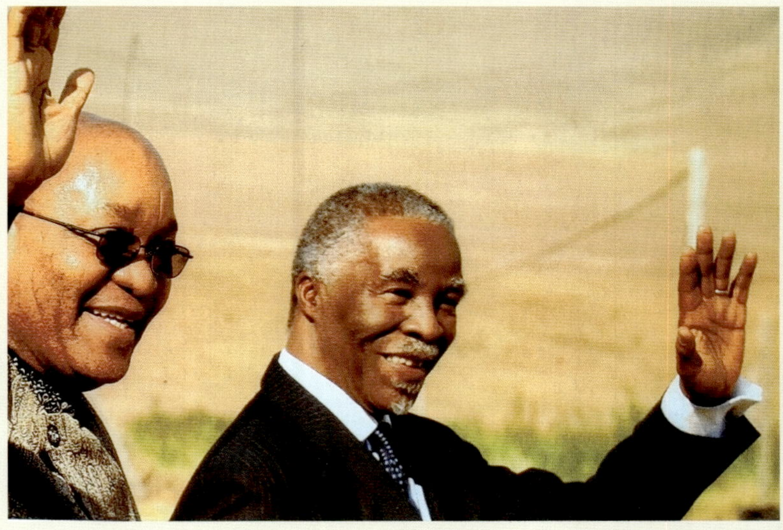

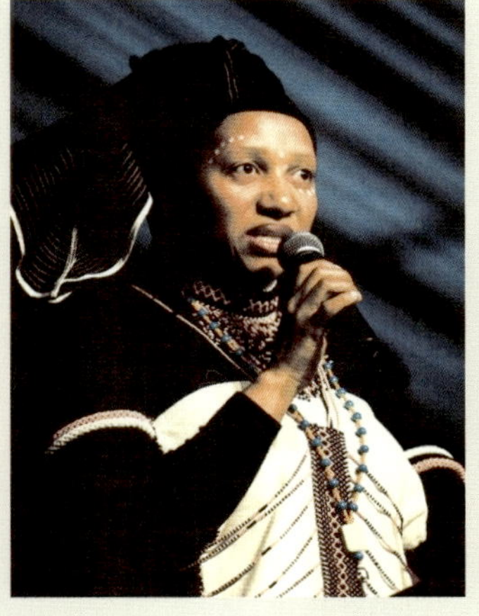

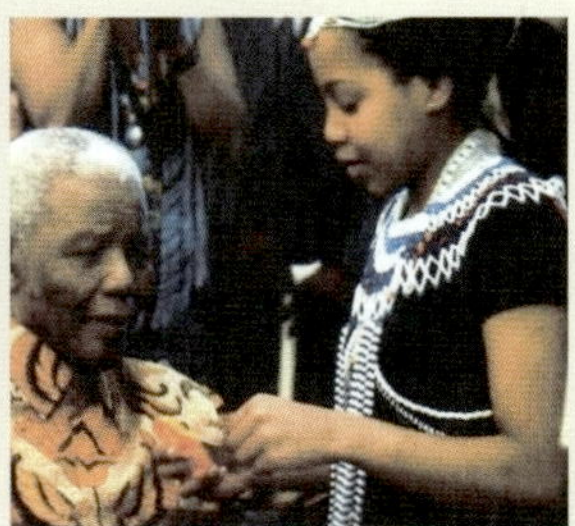

Above: President Jacob Zuma and President Thabo Mbeki.

Above (*center*): Tata's granddaughter, Nandi Mandela, was MC at the ninetieth birthday.

Right: Chief Buthelezi (*right*) and King Goodwill Zwelithini, king of the Zulus, at the ninetieth birthday party.

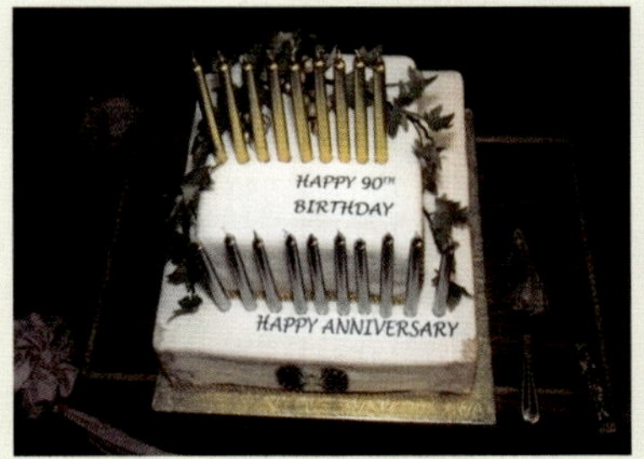

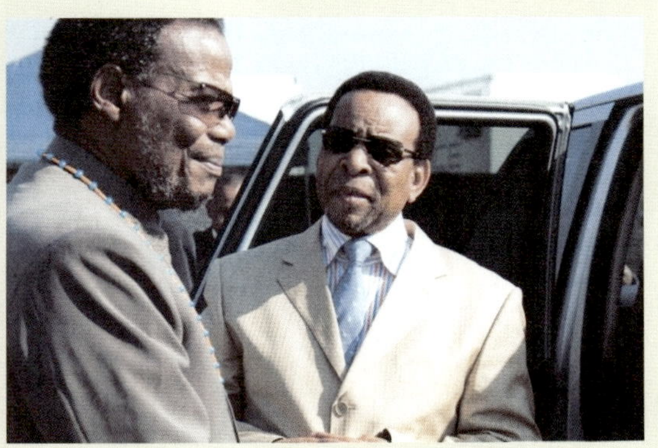

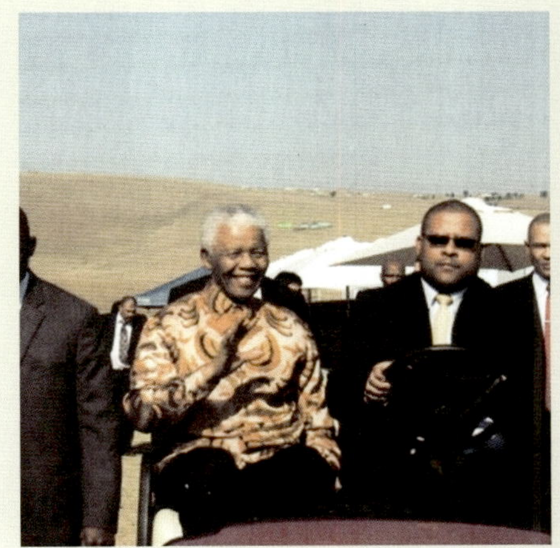

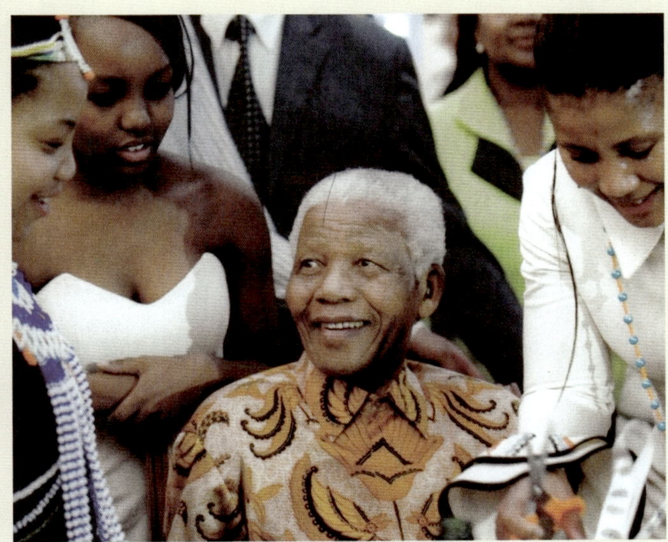

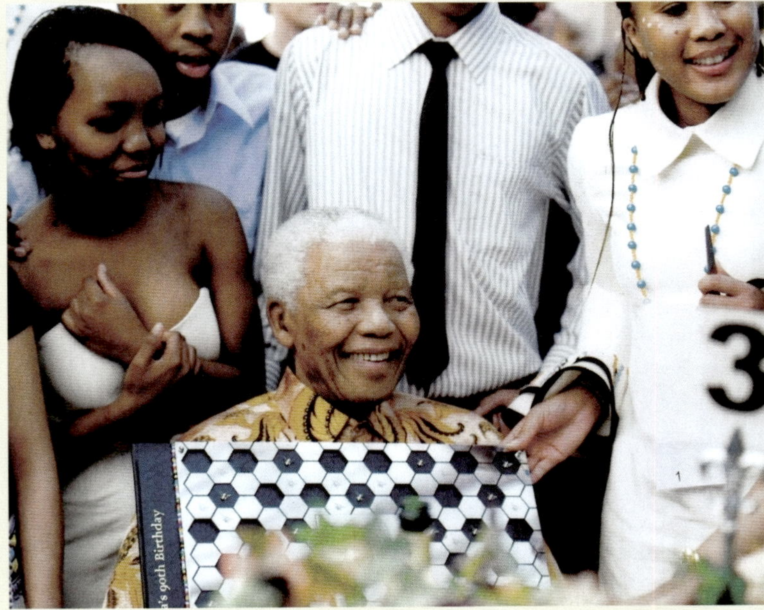

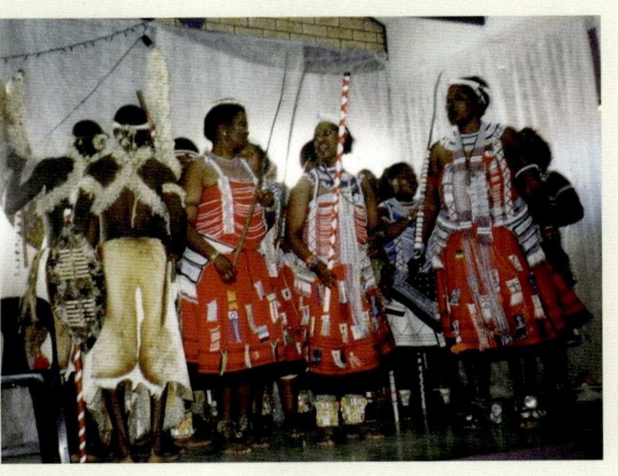

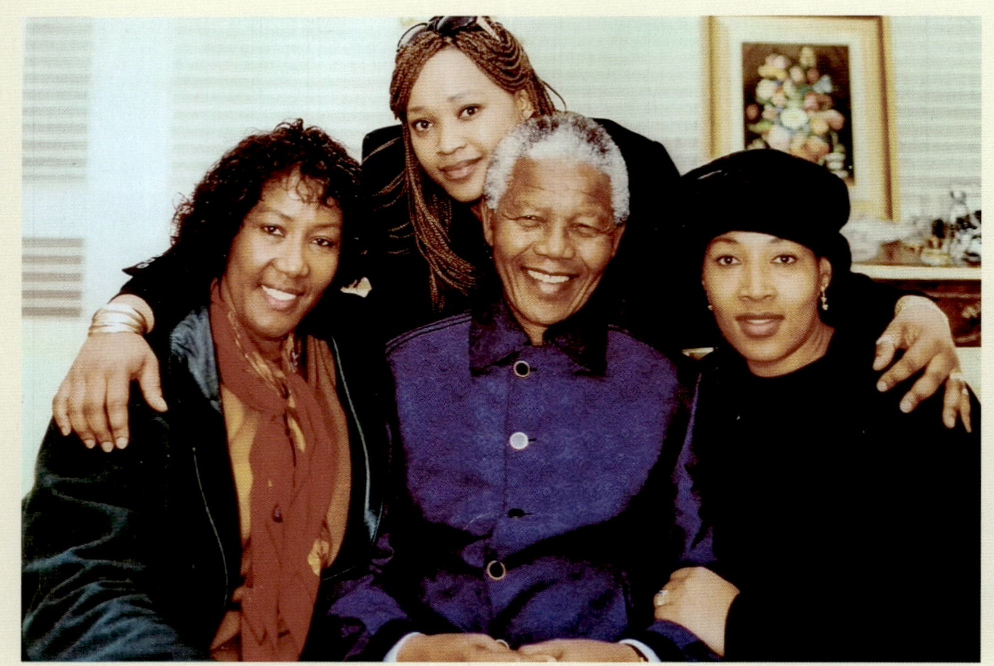

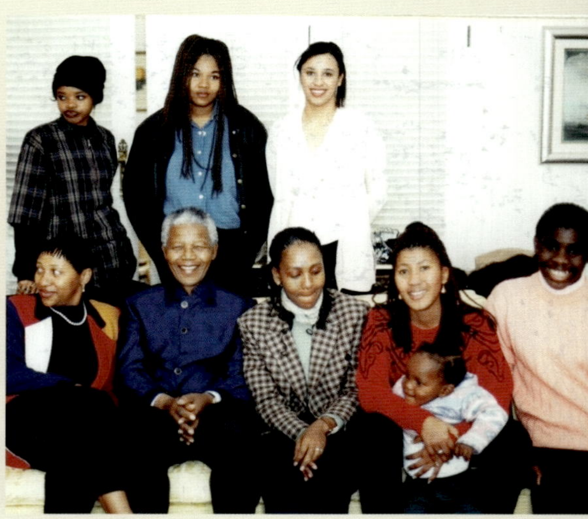

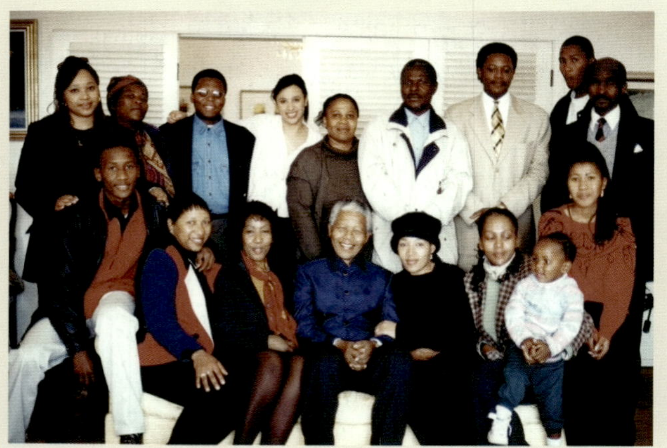

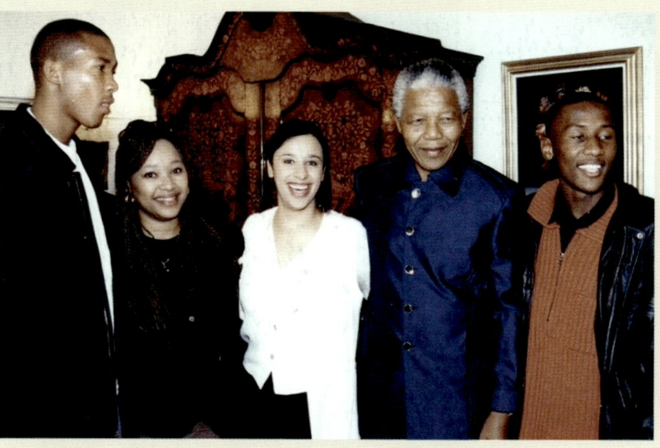

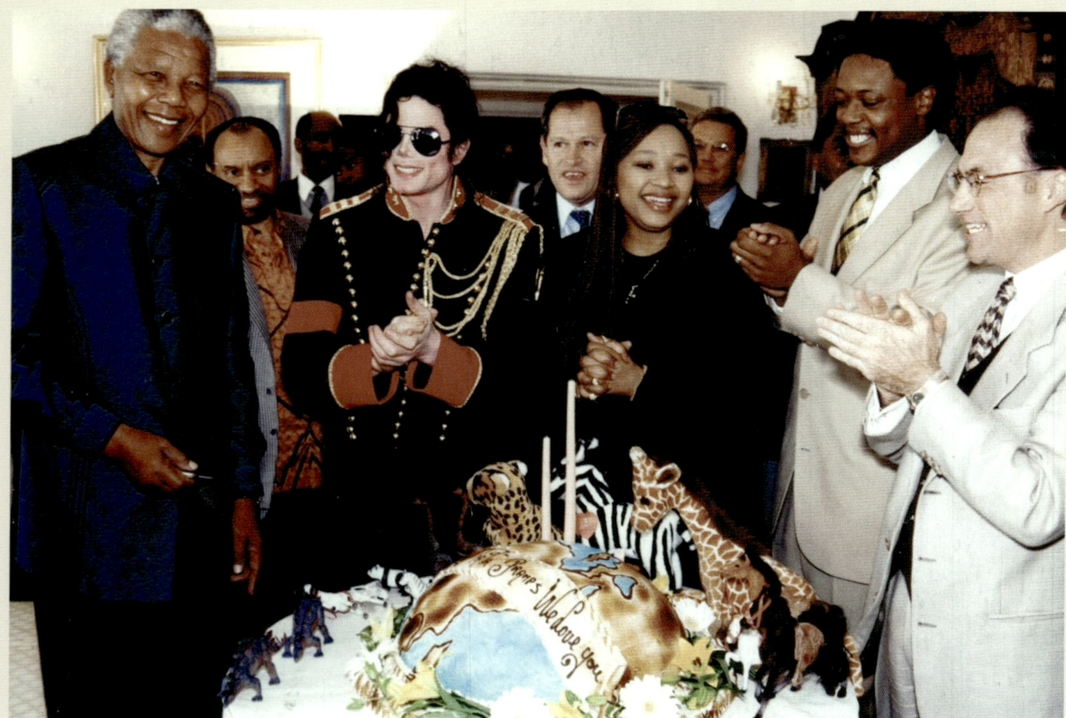

Tata with his children, grandchildren, and Michael Jackson on his birthday in 1996. Michael was in South Africa on a tour and had befriended my sister, Zindziswa.

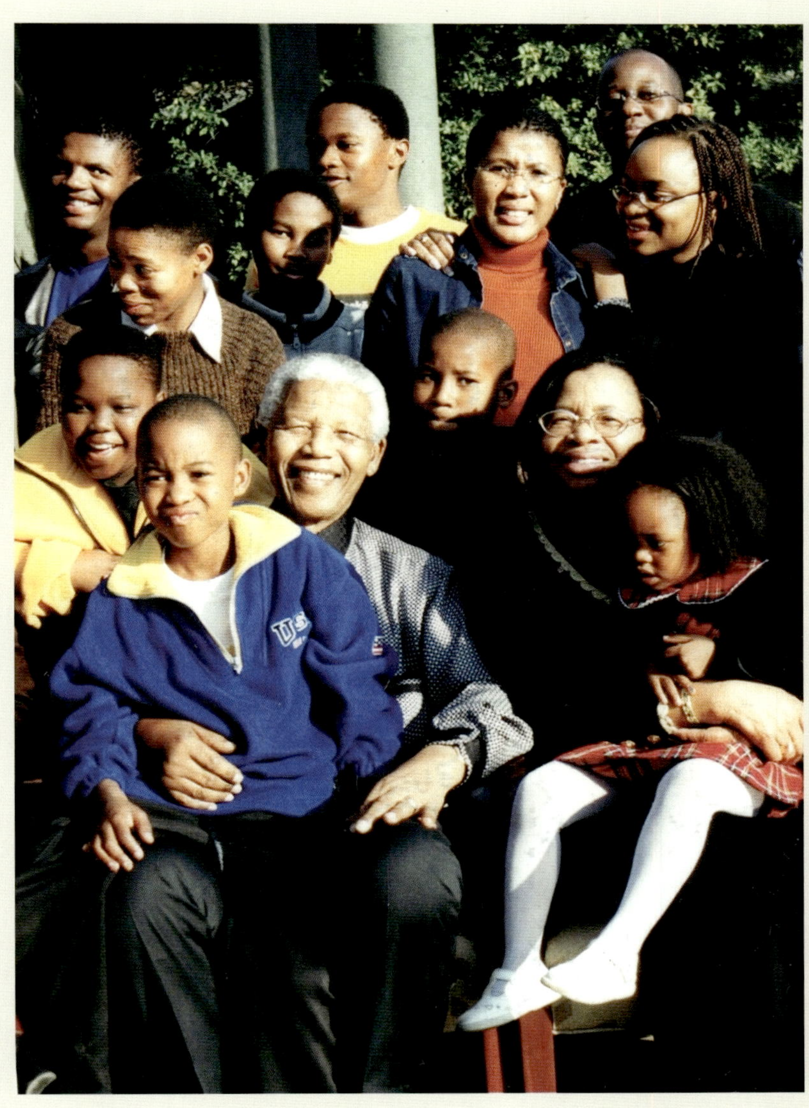

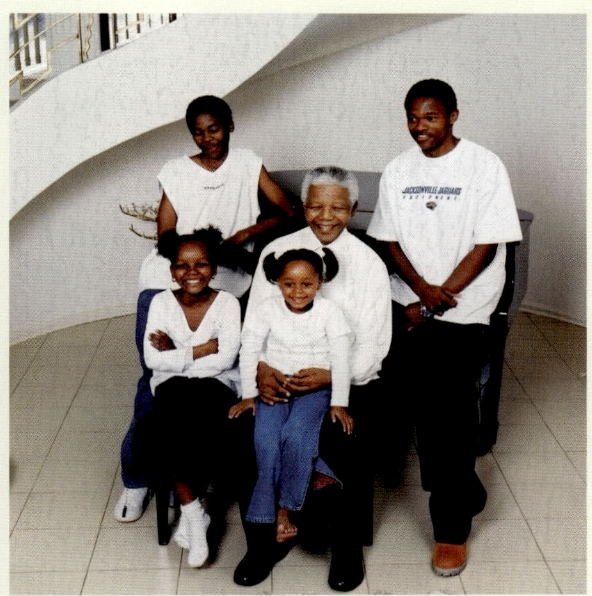

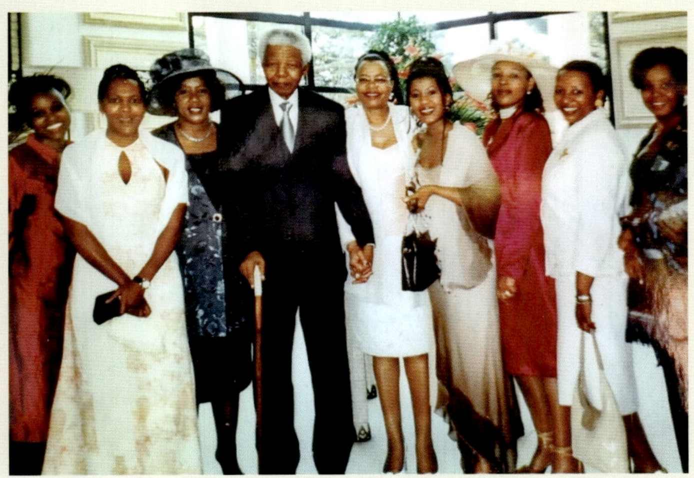

Tata with his children, grandchildren, and Graça at various events.

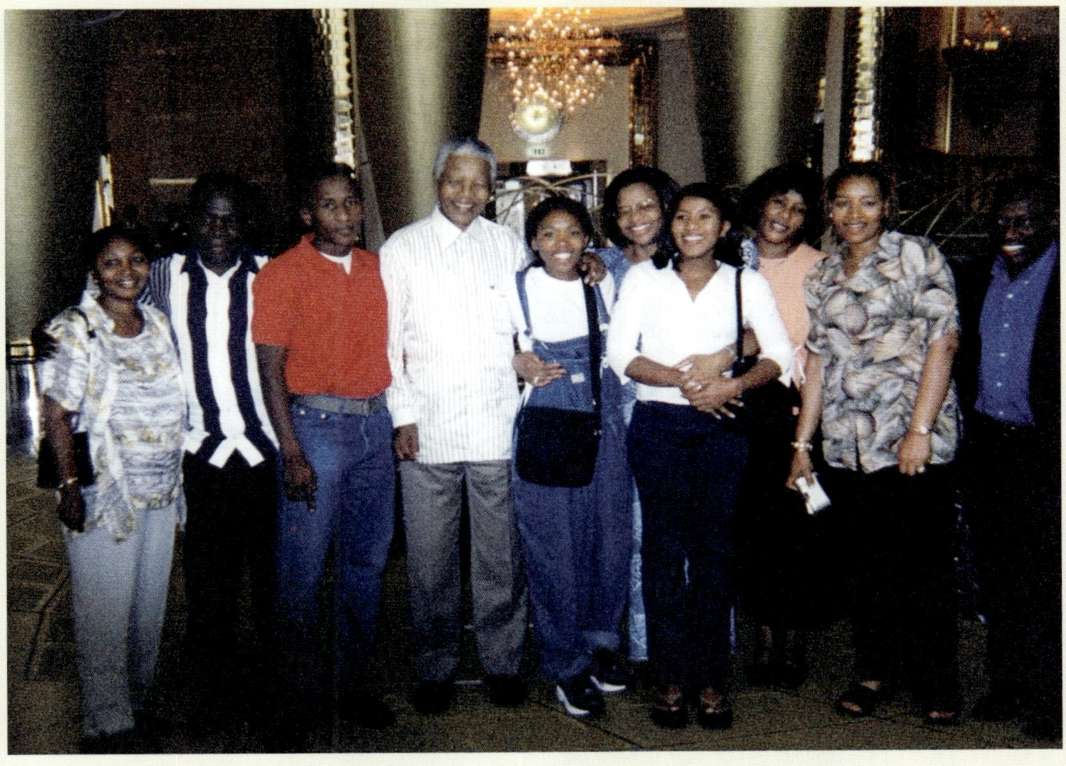

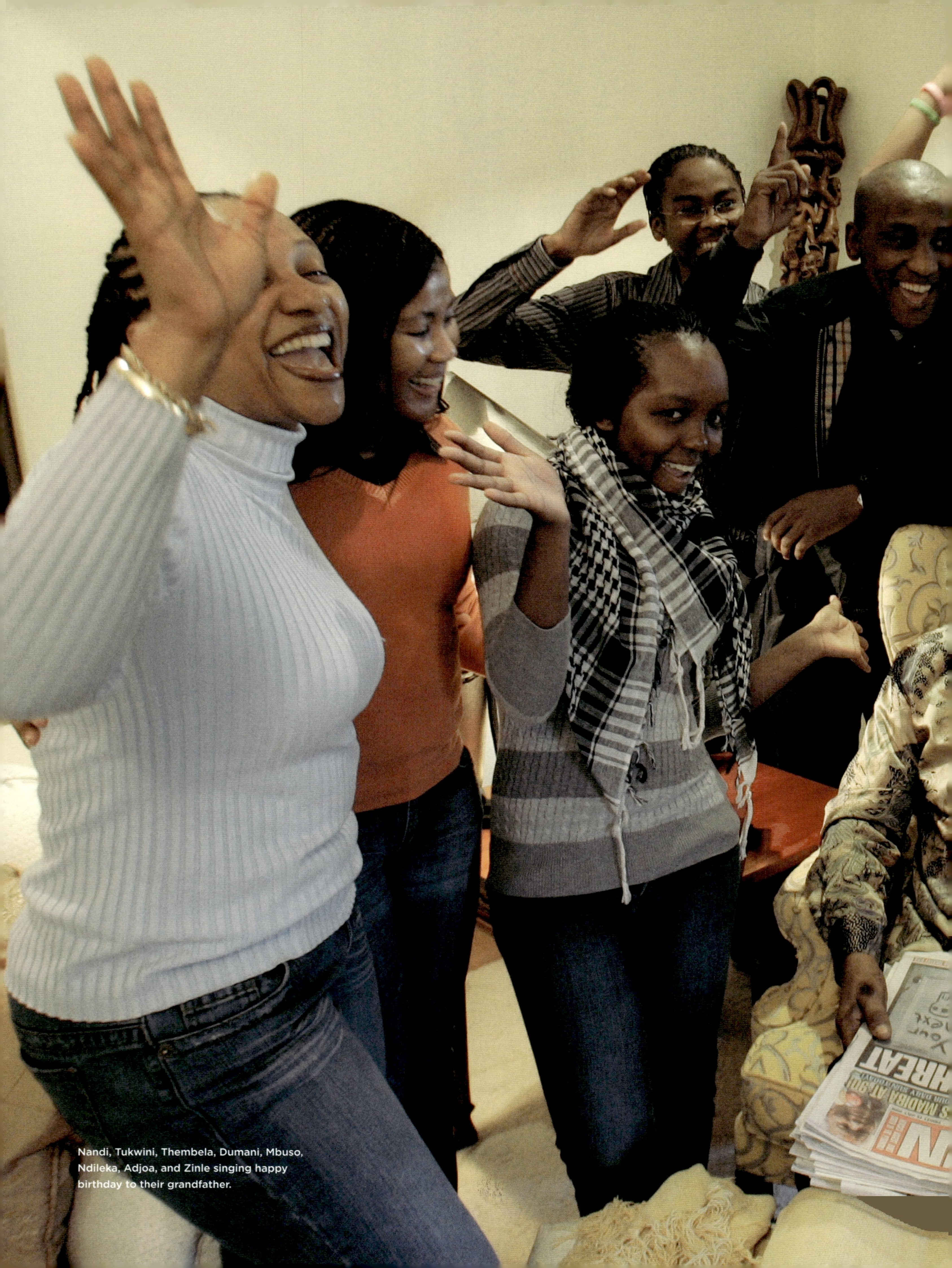

Nandi, Tukwini, Thembela, Dumani, Mbuso, Ndileka, Adjoa, and Zinle singing happy birthday to their grandfather.

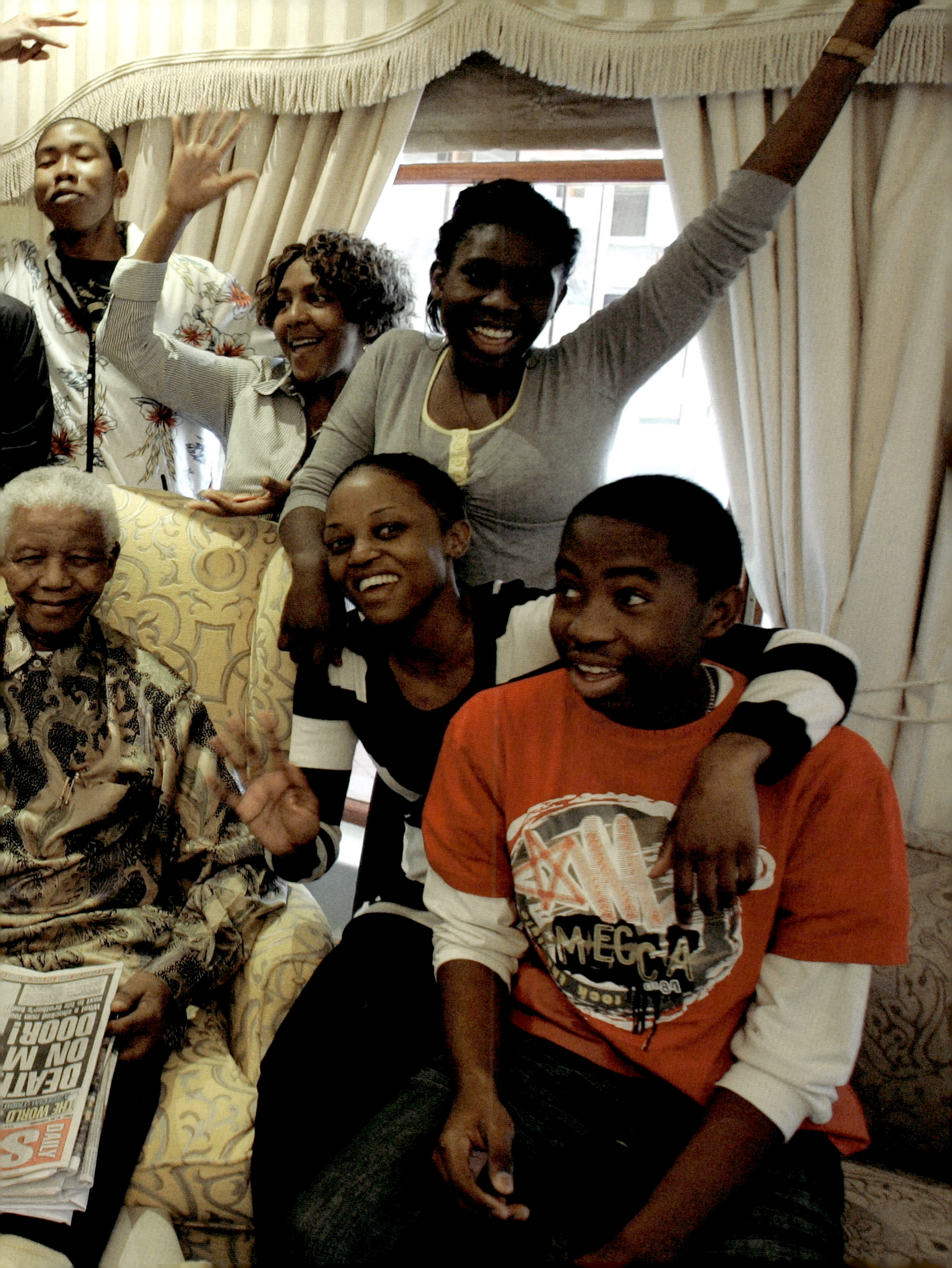
DOOR!
THE WORLD
MECCA

6

1980–1990

A Movement Ignites

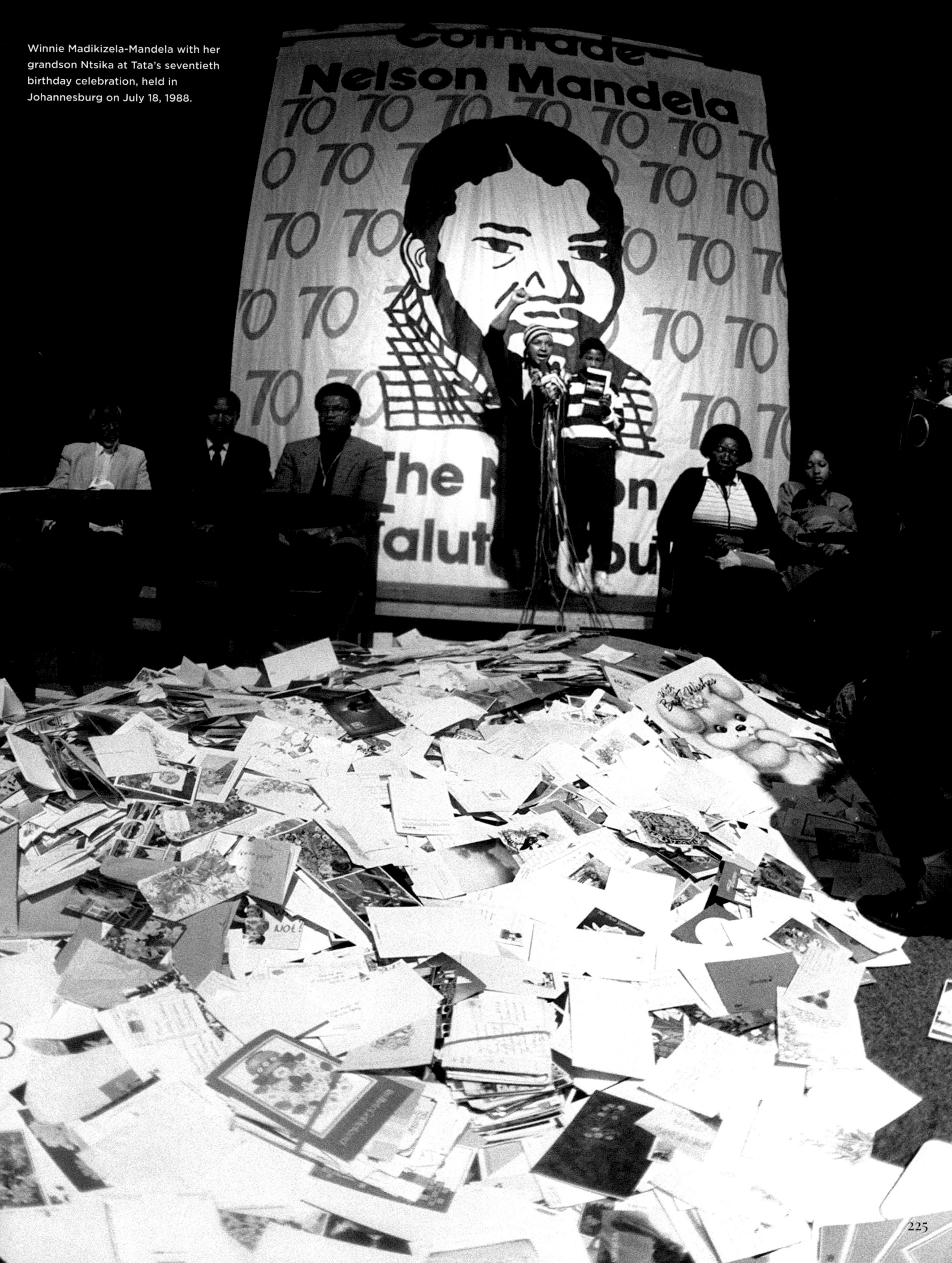

Winnie Madikizela-Mandela with her grandson Ntsika at Tata's seventieth birthday celebration, held in Johannesburg on July 18, 1988.

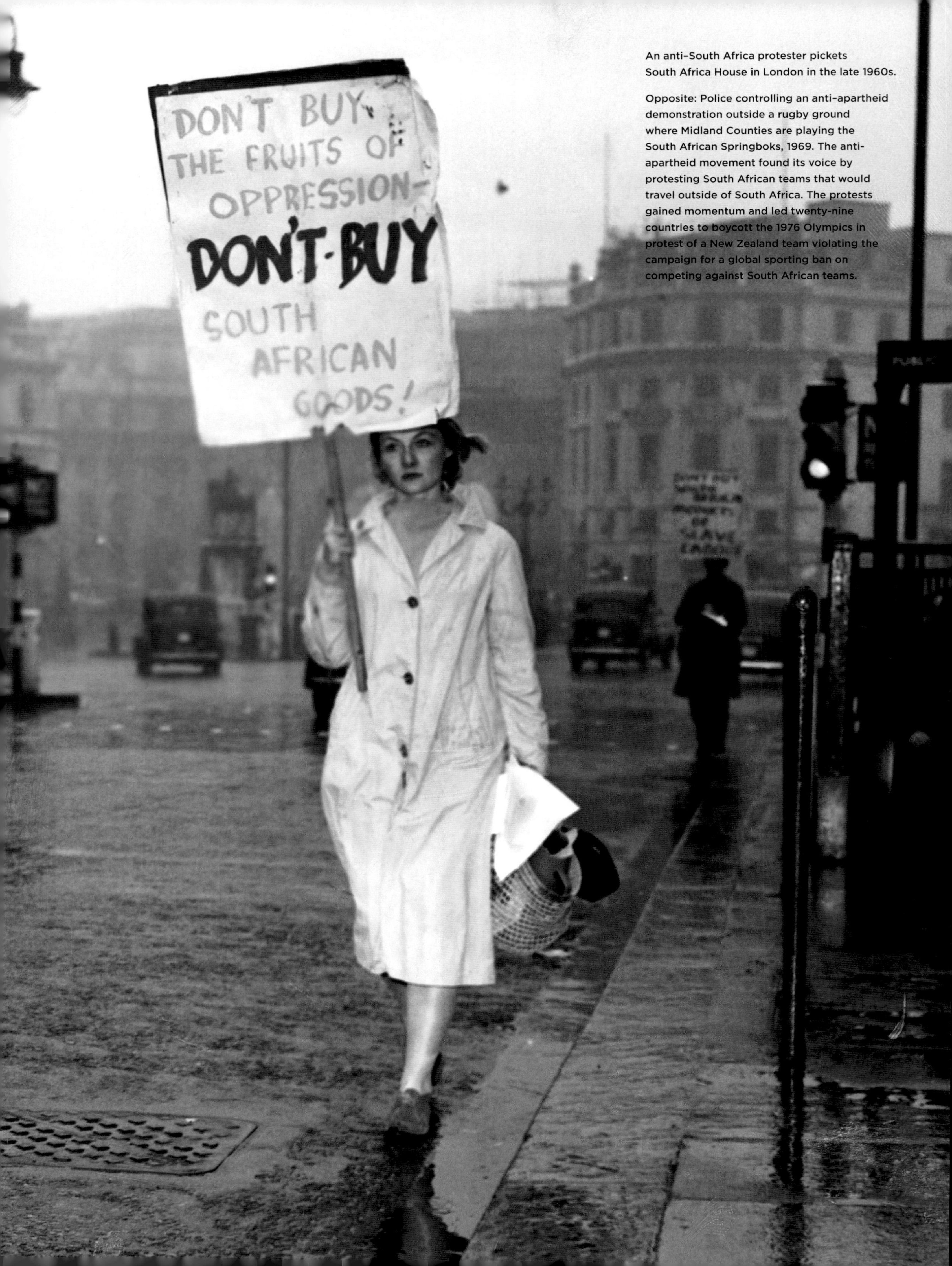

An anti–South Africa protester pickets South Africa House in London in the late 1960s.

Opposite: Police controlling an anti-apartheid demonstration outside a rugby ground where Midland Counties are playing the South African Springboks, 1969. The anti-apartheid movement found its voice by protesting South African teams that would travel outside of South Africa. The protests gained momentum and led twenty-nine countries to boycott the 1976 Olympics in protest of a New Zealand team violating the campaign for a global sporting ban on competing against South African teams.

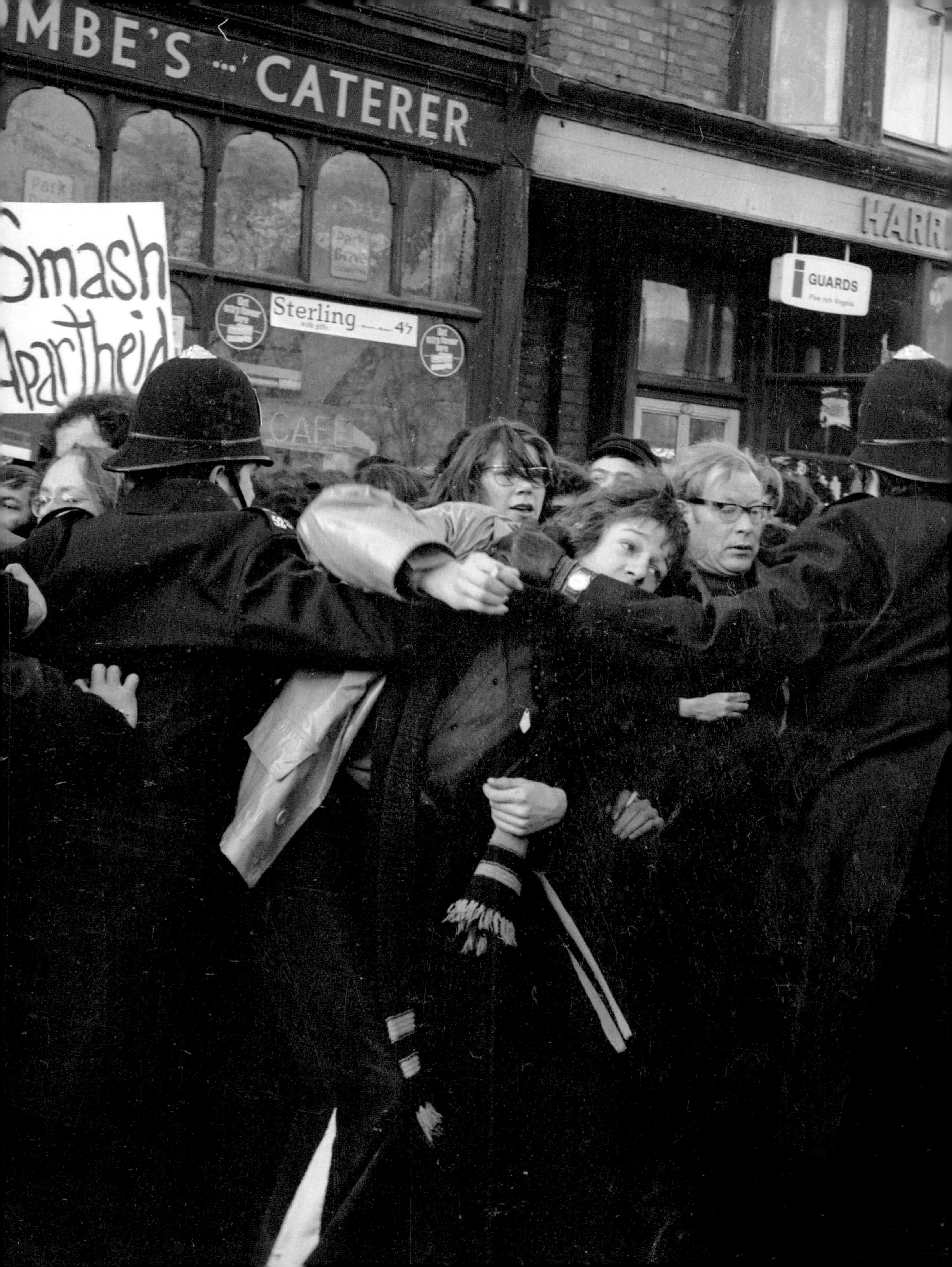

MBE'S ... CATERER
Smash Apartheid
Sterling
4/7
CAFE
HARR
GUARDS

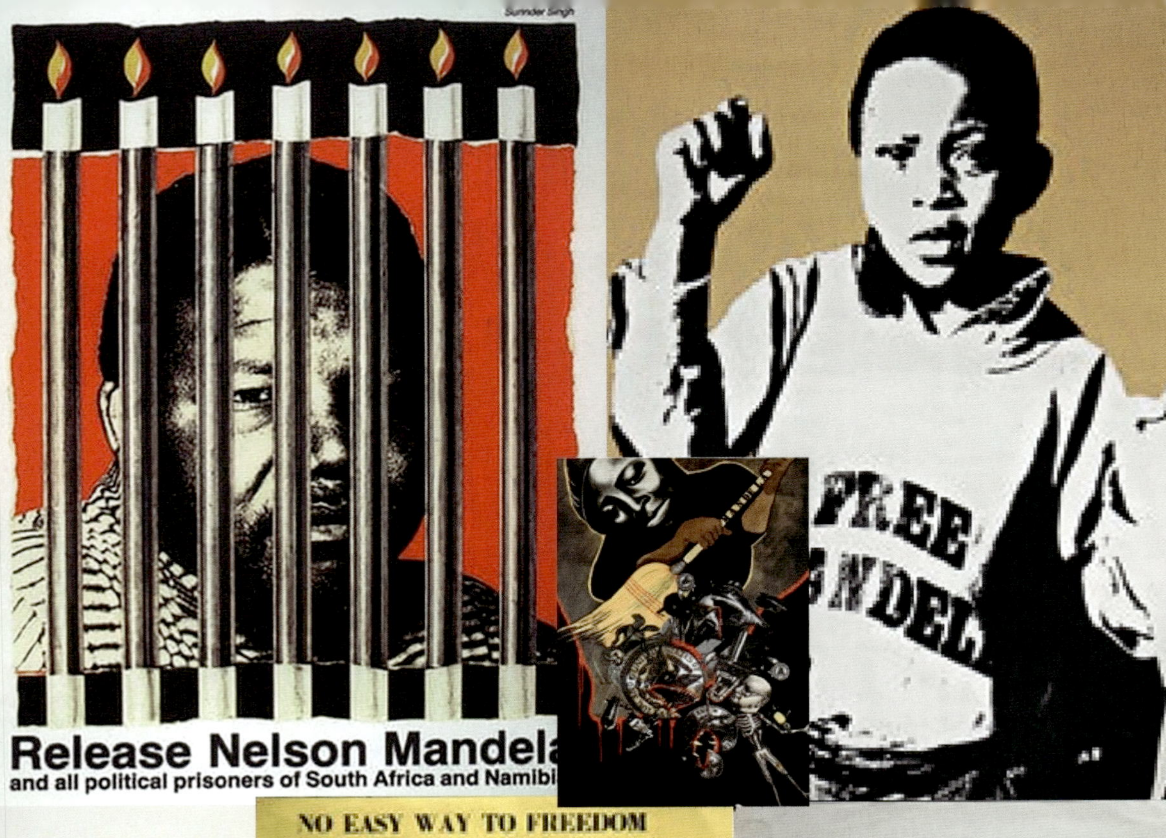
Surinder Singh
Release Nelson Mandela
and all political prisoners of South Africa and Namibi
FREE
NDEL

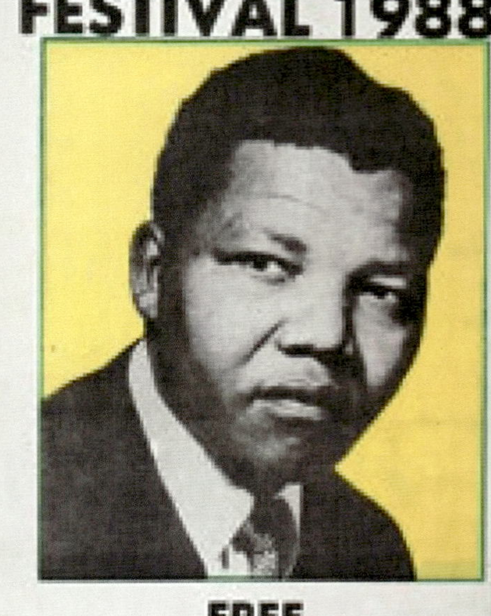
NOTTING HILL
FESTIVAL 1988
FREE
NELSON MANDEL
OF THE
AFRICAN
NATIONAL CONGRESS

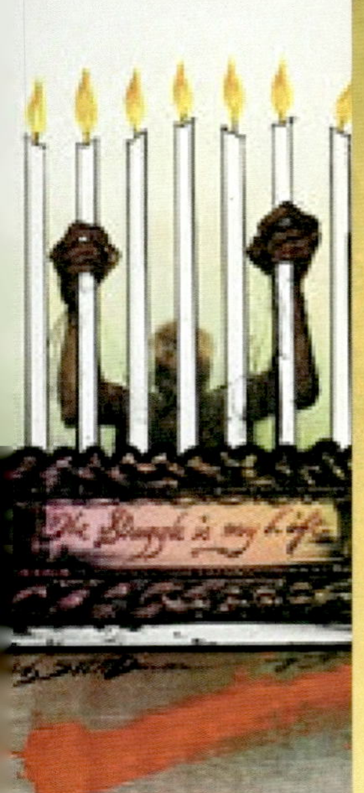

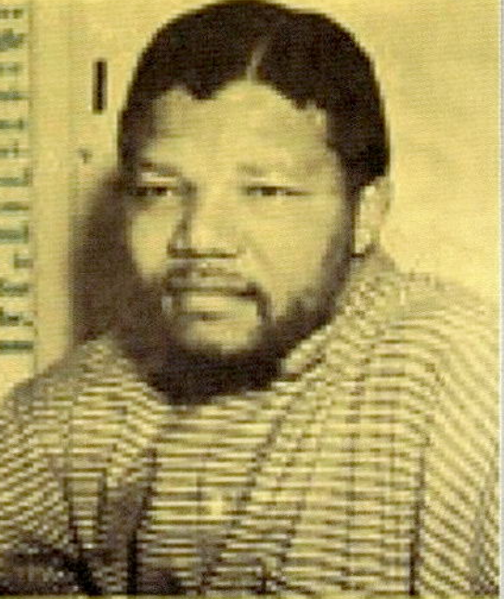
NO EASY WAY TO FREEDOM
NELSON
MANDELA
18th July 1978
60th Birthday
"During my lifetime I have dedicated myself to this struggle of the African people. I have fought against White domination, and I have fought against Black domination. I have cherished the ideal of a democratic and free society in which all persons live together in harmony and with equal opportunities. It is an ideal which I hope to live for and to achieve. But if needs be, it is an ideal for which I am prepared to die."

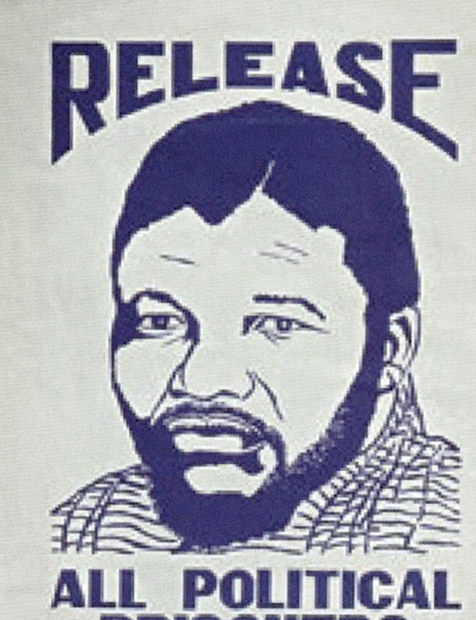
RELEASE
ALL POLITICAL
PRISONERS

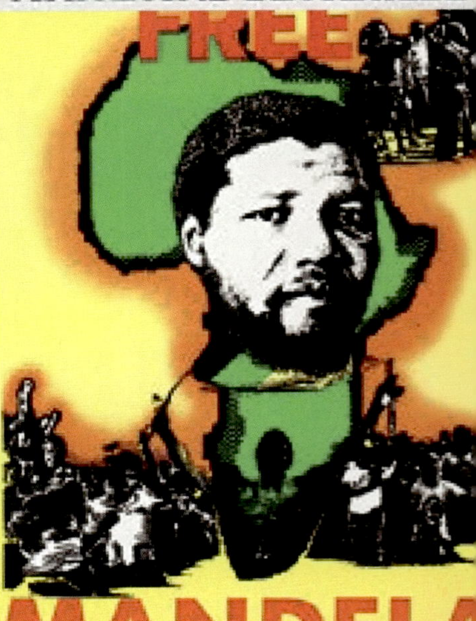
FREE
MANDELA

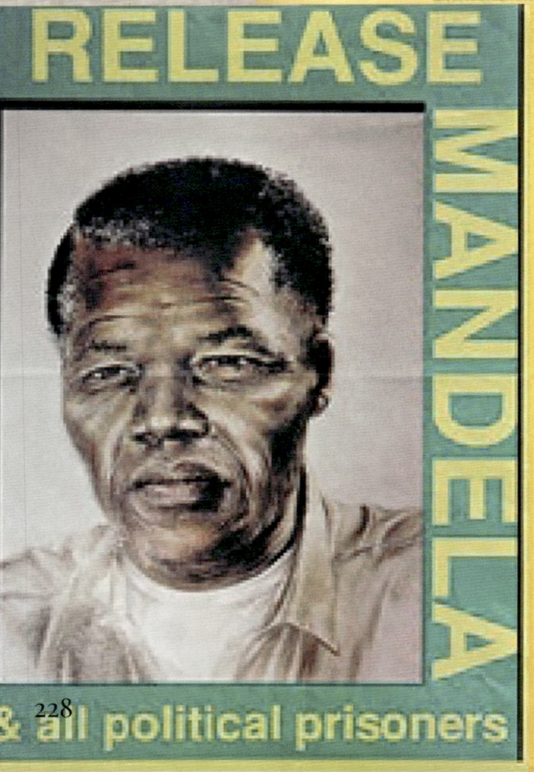
RELEASE
MANDELA
& all political prisoners

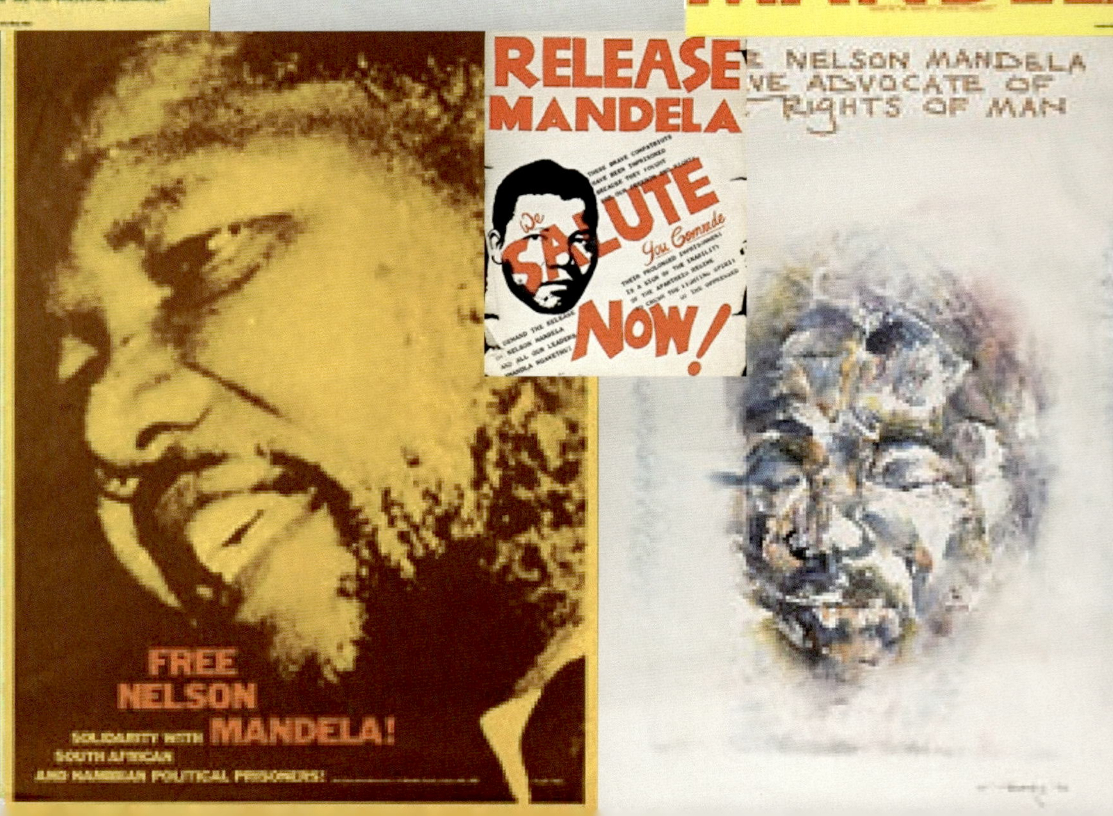
FREE
NELSON
MANDELA!
SOLIDARITY WITH
SOUTH AFRICAN
AND NAMIBIAN POLITICAL PRISONERS!
RELEASE
MANDELA
We
SALUTE
You Comrade
NOW!
E NELSON MANDELA
VE ADVOCATE OF
RIGHTS OF MAN

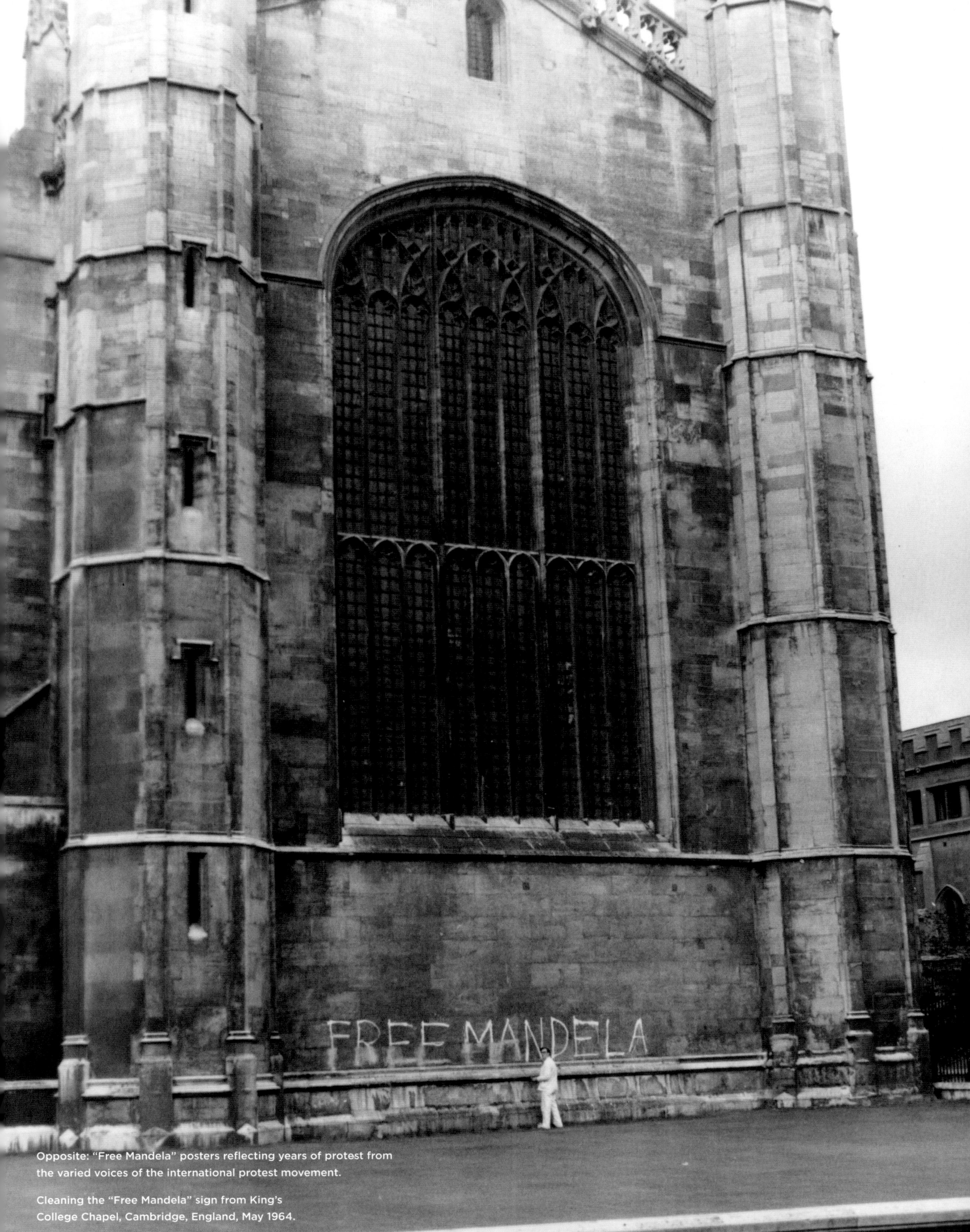

Opposite: "Free Mandela" posters reflecting years of protest from the varied voices of the international protest movement.

Cleaning the "Free Mandela" sign from King's College Chapel, Cambridge, England, May 1964.

Right and below: Anti-apartheid protesters during the Springboks' 1969 match against the North and Midlands rugby team at Linksfield Stadium, Aberdeen.

Bottom: Various posters carried by anti-apartheid marchers on their way through Manchester to the White City Stadium, where the Springboks rugby team was playing North-West Counties in 1969.

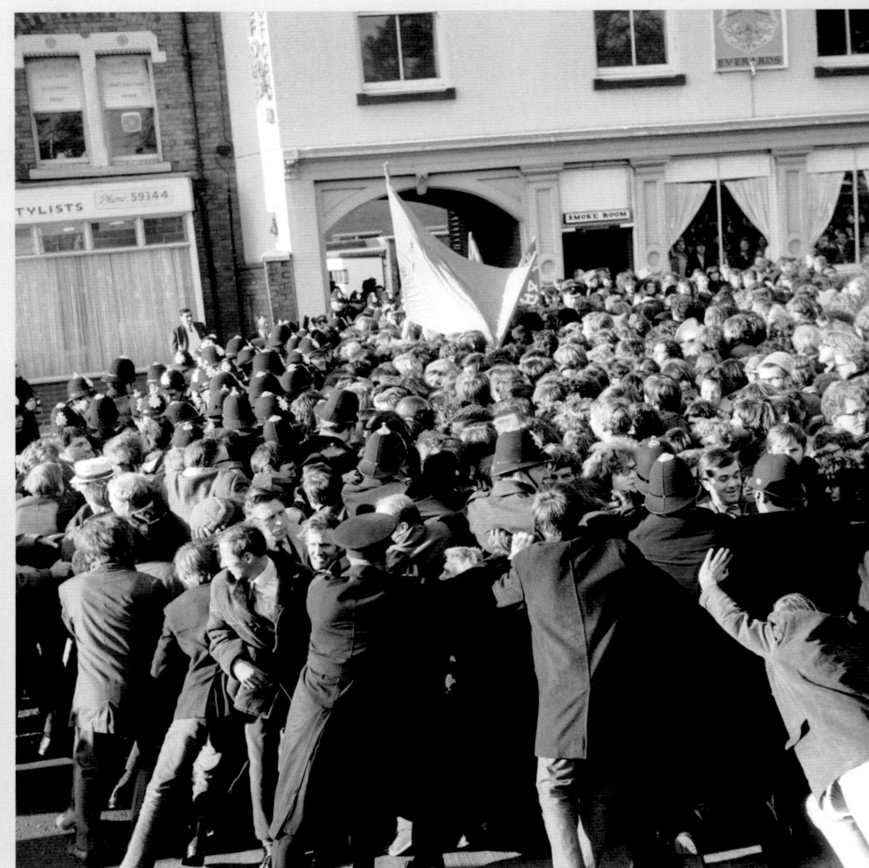

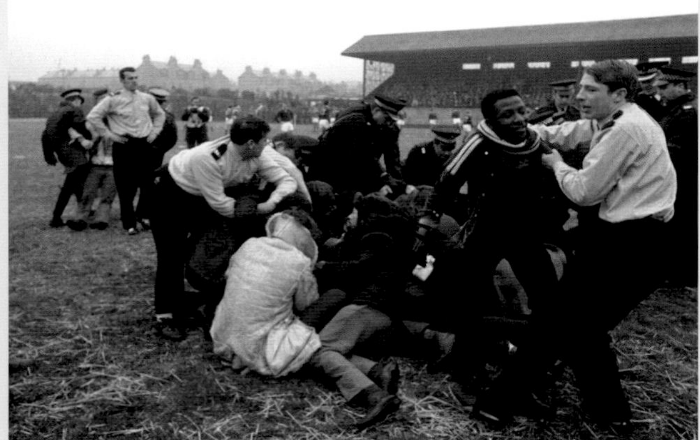

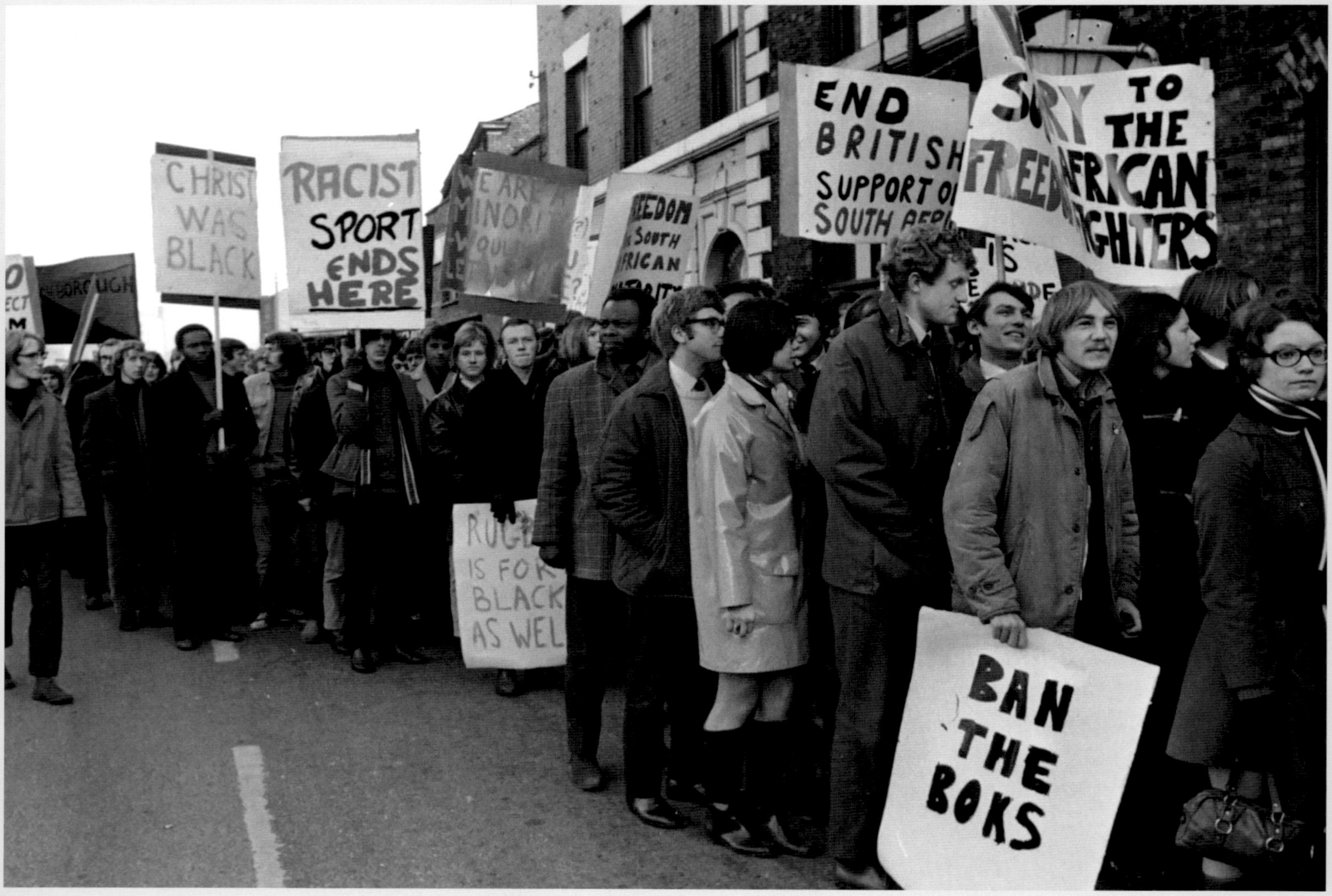

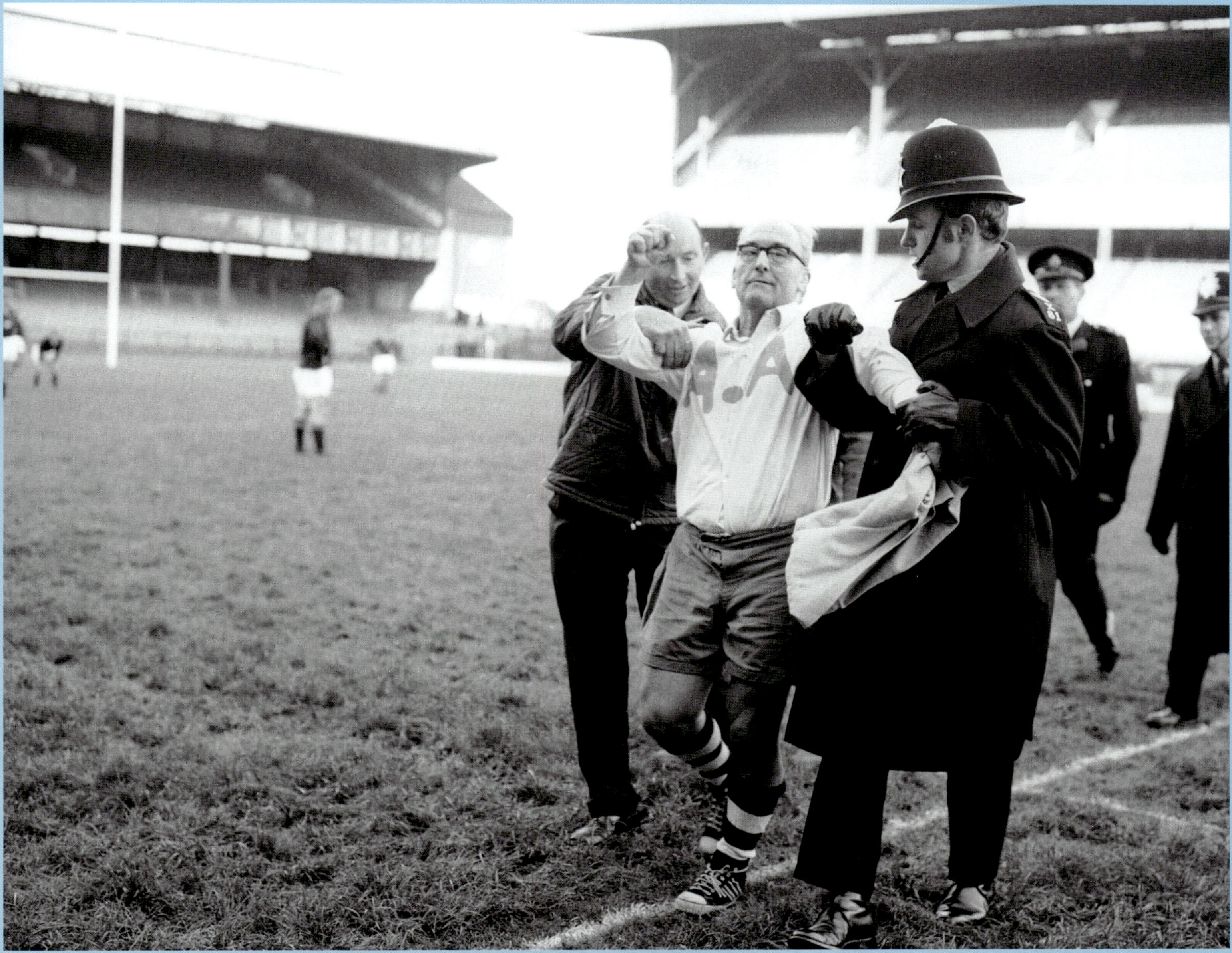

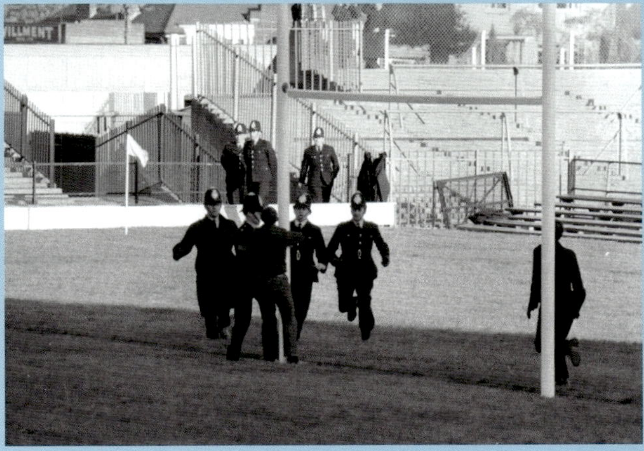

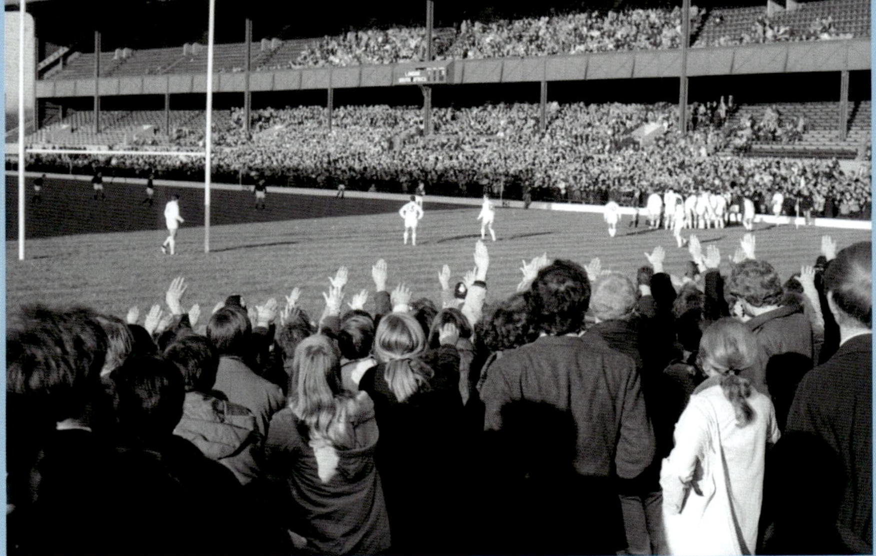

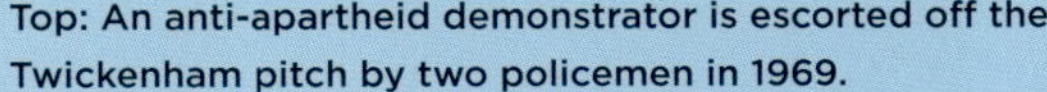

Top: An anti-apartheid demonstrator is escorted off the Twickenham pitch by two policemen in 1969.

Above (*left*): A man about to be tackled by policemen as he tries to climb a goalpost at Twickenham, where the Springboks were meeting Oxford University in the opening match of their 1969 tour.

Above (*right*): That same year, anti-apartheid demonstrators sarcastically whistle and shout "Sieg heil" at the rugby match between London Counties and the Springboks at Twickenham.

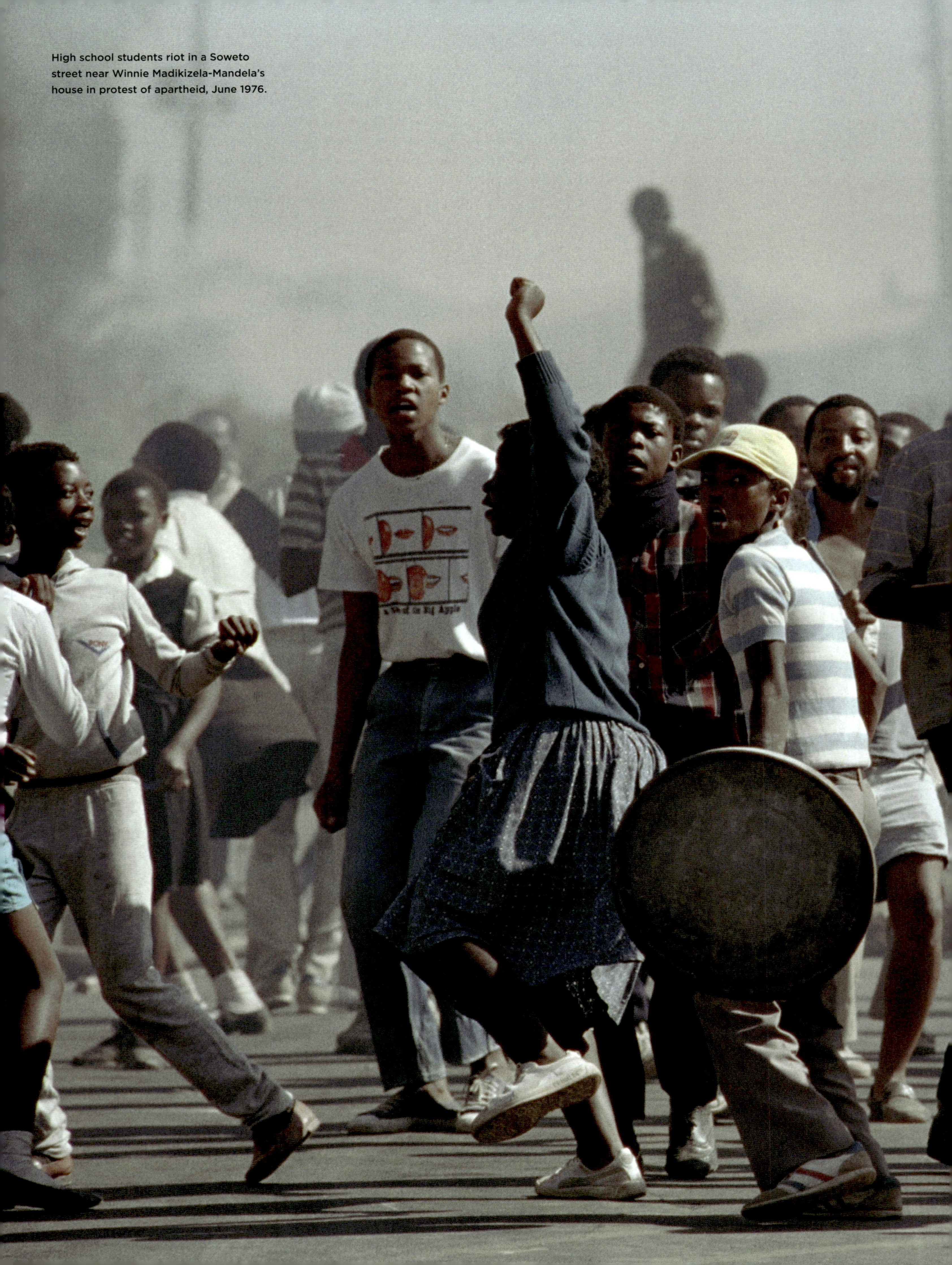

High school students riot in a Soweto street near Winnie Madikizela-Mandela's house in protest of apartheid, June 1976.

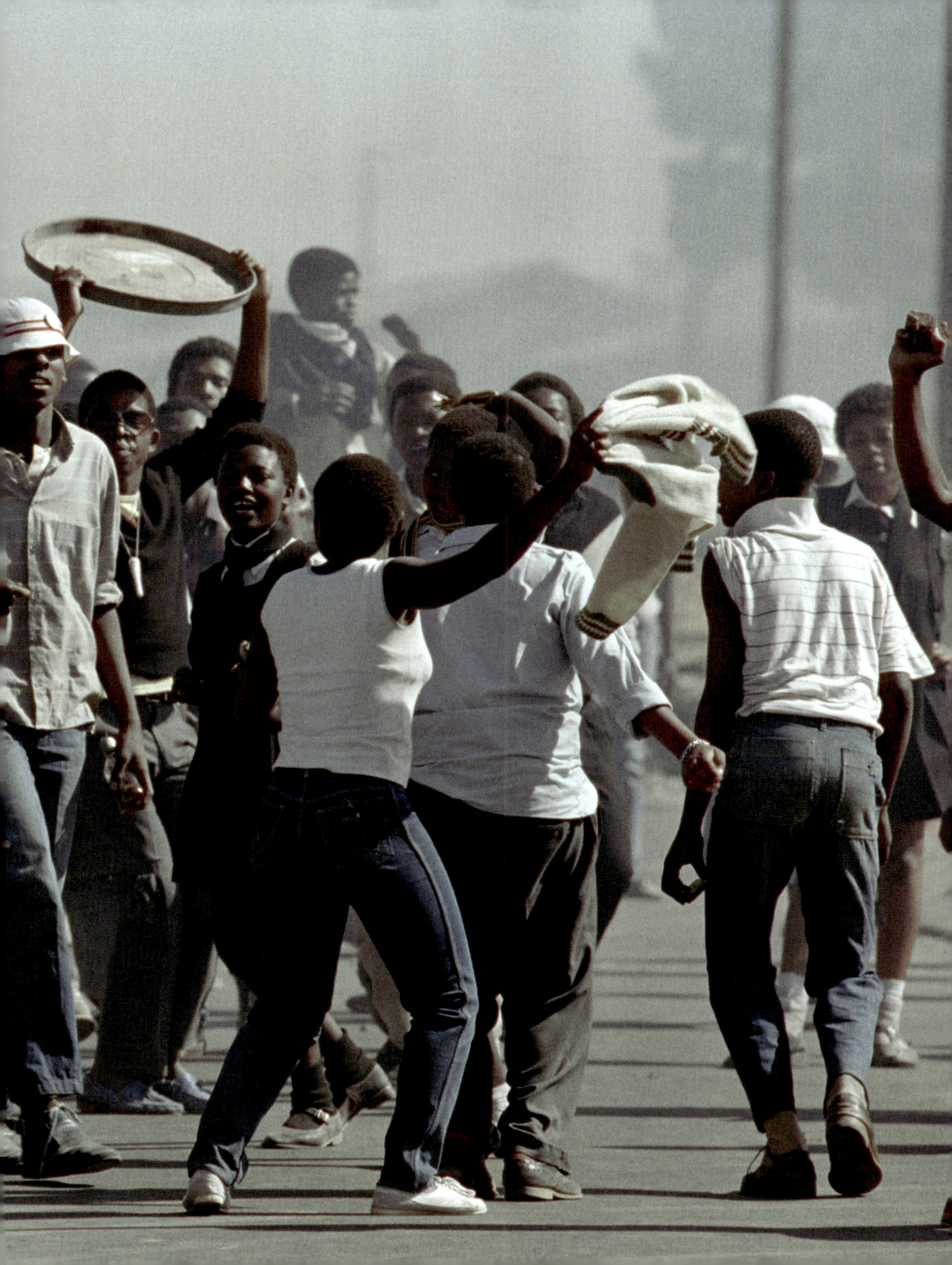

Young Africans singing and holding a Release Mandela banner at the International Year of the Youth (IYY) cultural meeting, 1987. IYY provided unity in actions and the impetus for forming a new national youth organization, culminating in the launch of the South African Youth Congress (SAYCO).

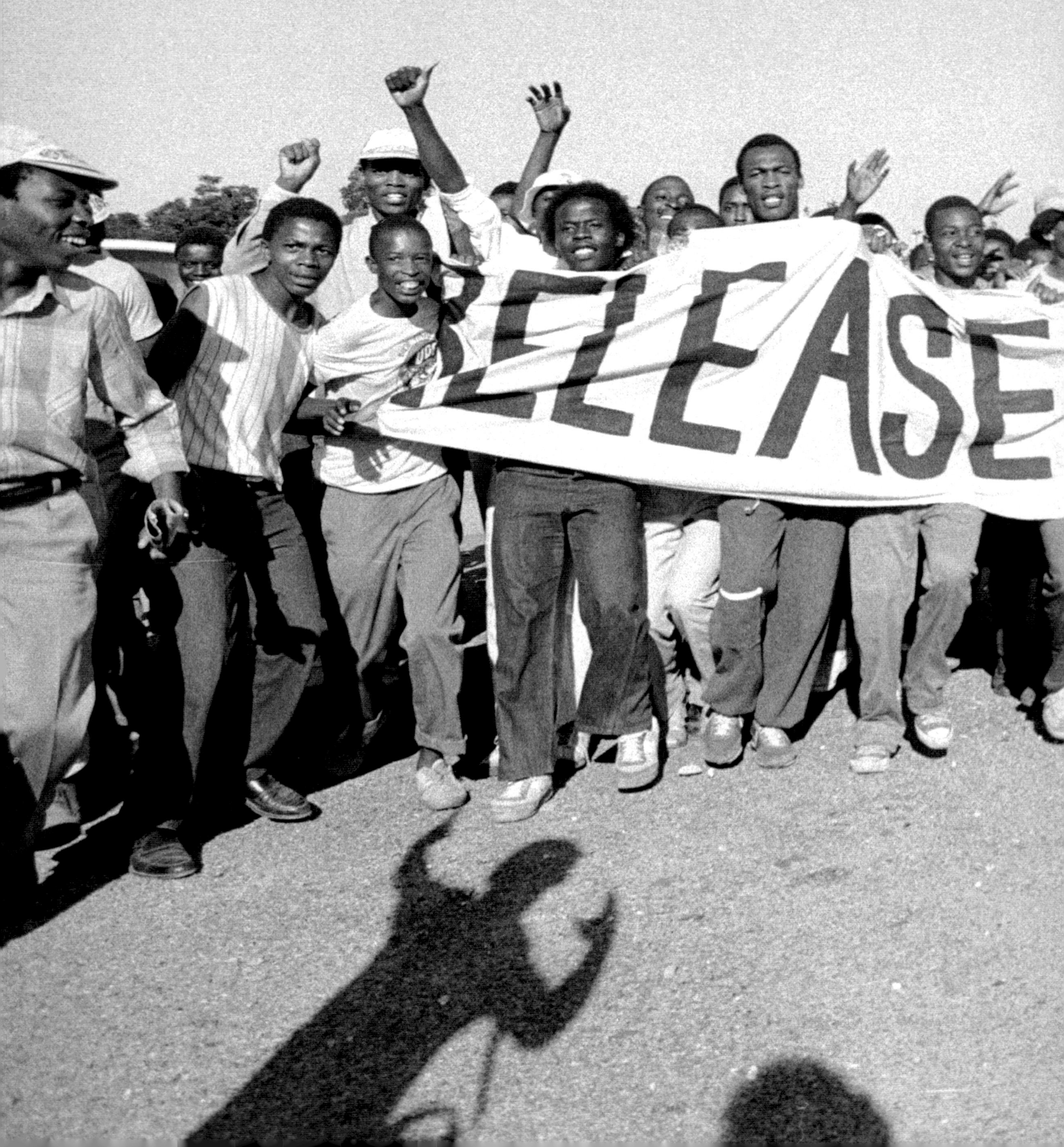

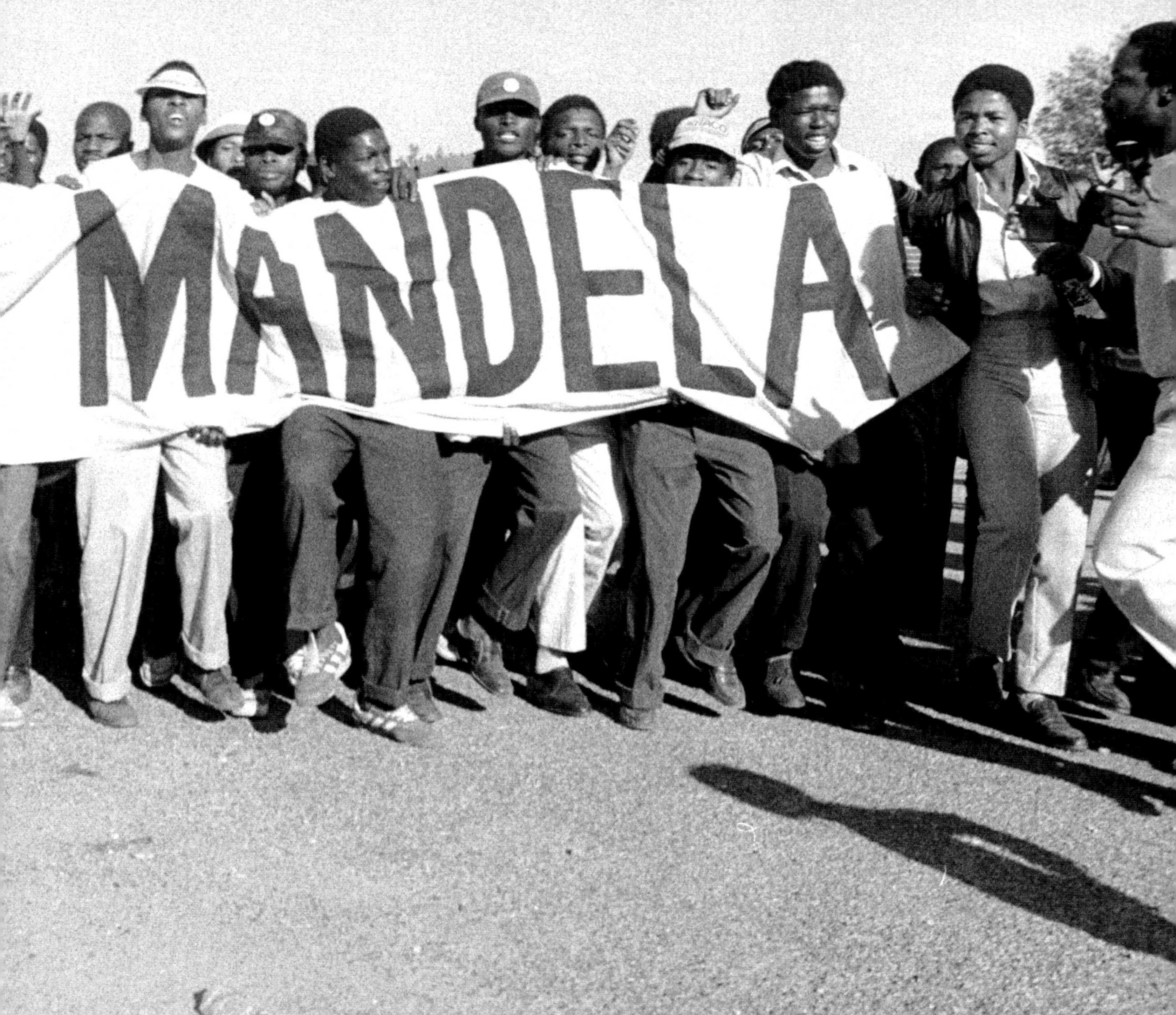
MANDELA

Thousands of protesters march for the release of Tata in Johannesburg, 1987.

Today South Africa is truly a diverse country, where all races are equal before the law, thanks to the efforts of our national heroes from all liberation movements. Yet the freedoms we enjoy today would not have been achieved without the support of many people around the globe who raised their voices through protest demonstrations, music, concerts, art, and the dedication of politicians and the business leaders who supported the anti-apartheid movement.

The Anti-Apartheid Movement was a British organization with exiled ANC members and supporters, mainly in the United Kingdom and later in other countries. This organization was at the center of the international movement opposing the South African apartheid system and supporting those who were persecuted. It was founded on June 26, 1959. The movement attracted widespread support from students, trade unions, labor, liberal, and communist parties. The Sharpeville Massacre, on March 21, 1960, where the police fired on unarmed African protesters, killing 69 and injuring 250, intensified the Anti-Apartheid Movement's actions.

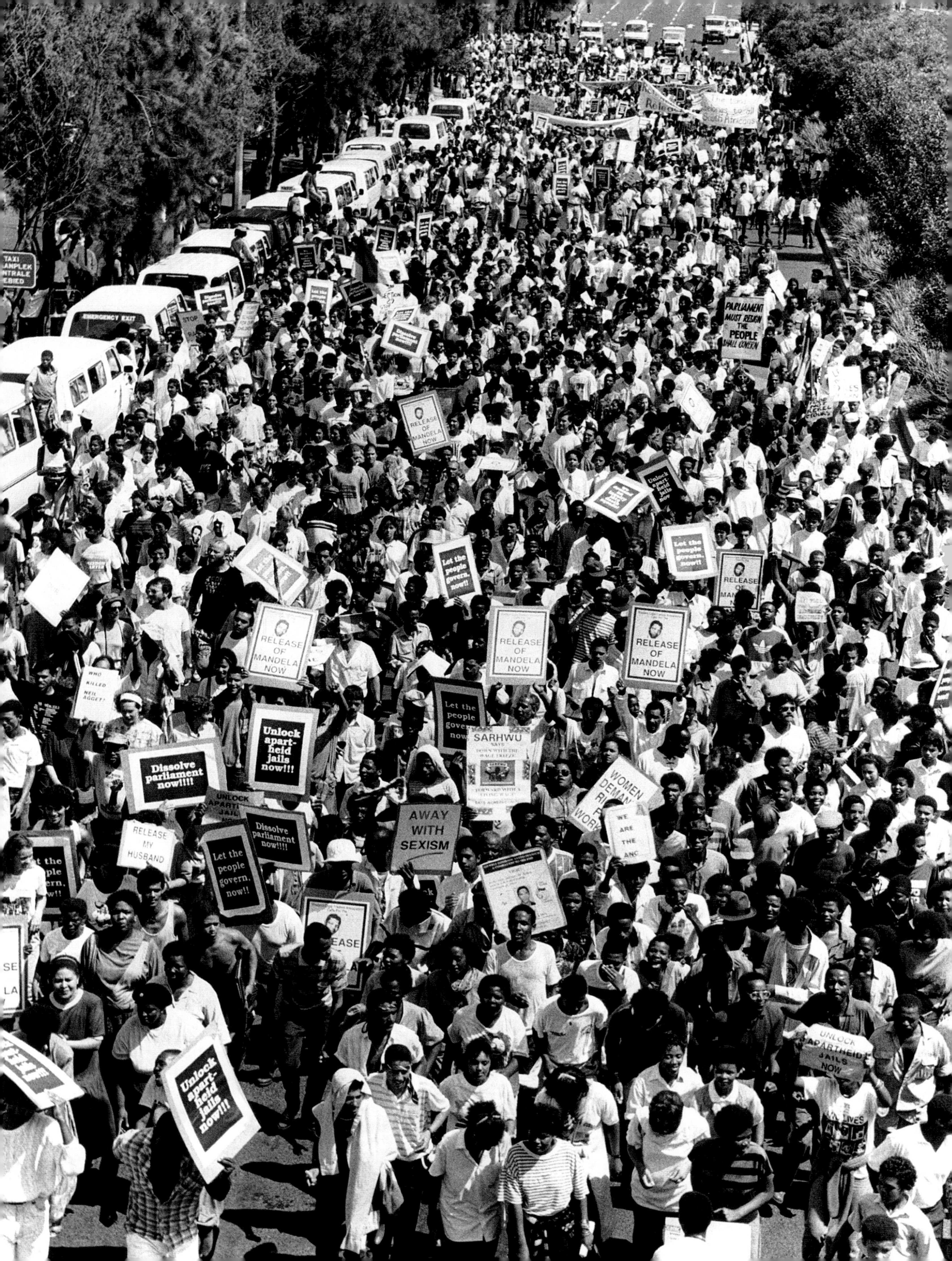

PARLIAMENT MUST RESIGN THE PEOPLE SHALL GOVERN
RELEASE OF MANDELA NOW
Unlock apartheid jails now
Let the people govern, now!!
WHO KILLED NEIL AGGET?
Unlock apart-heid jails now!!!
Dissolve parliament now!!!!
SARHWU SAYS DOWN WITH THE WAGE FREEZE
FORWARD WITH A LIVING WAGE
AWAY WITH SEXISM
RELEASE MY HUSBAND
WE ARE THE ANC
UNLOCK APARTHEID JAILS NOW
EMERGENCY EXIT

Mandela supporters outside Victor Verster Prison in 1989, where Tata spent the last fourteen months of his imprisonment.

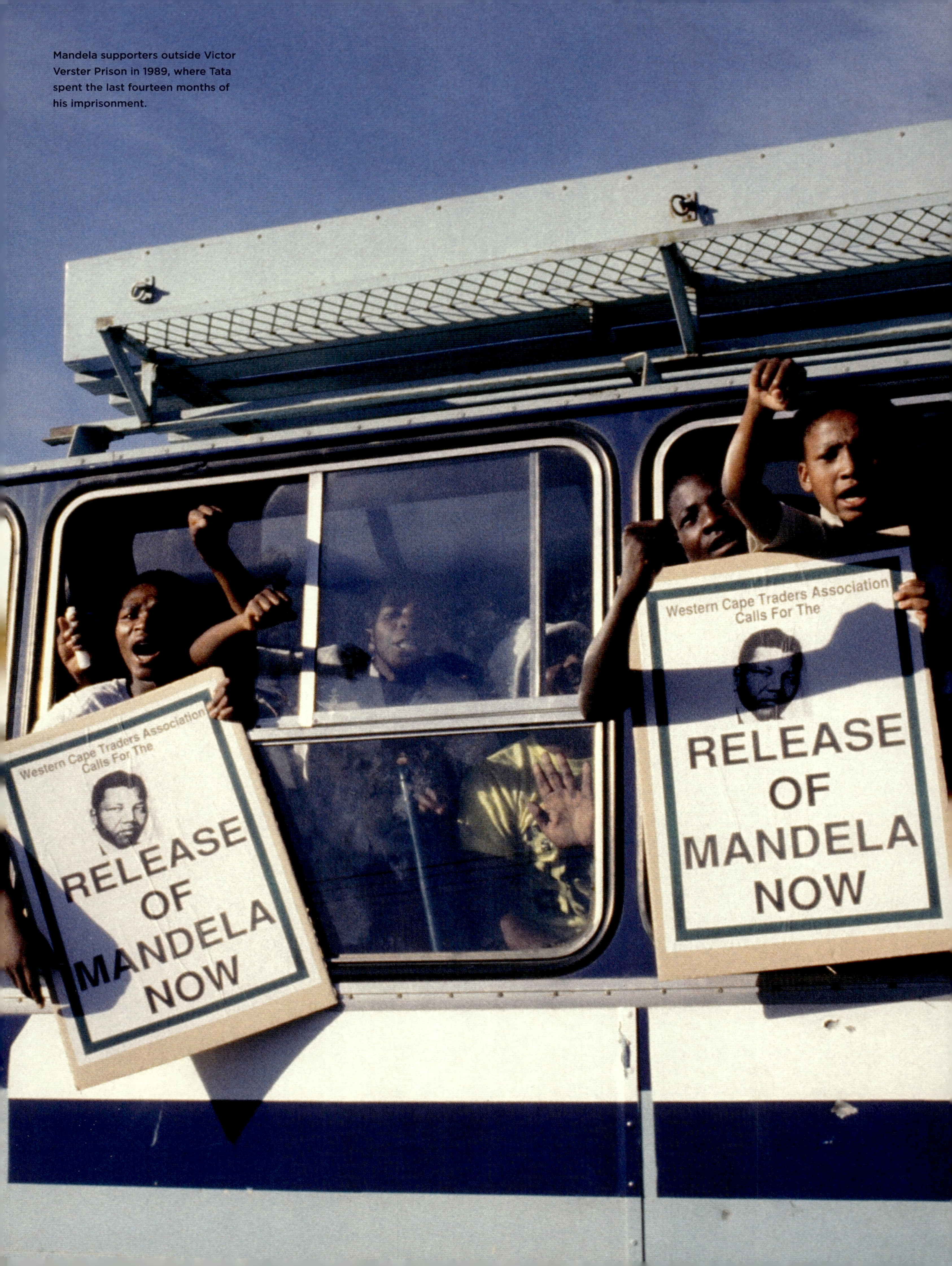

In the 1980s, supporters in London advised the Anti-Apartheid Movement to personalize the liberation struggle. Tata was chosen to be the voice and a name to be used for the movement's campaign.

By then Tata's name had become well-known around the world. So the Free Mandela campaign was not about freeing him alone, it was a movement for the liberation of all political prisoners and the end of apartheid in South Africa. Tata was a symbolic figure for the liberation struggle. The Free Mandela campaign gained prominence when Glasgow's local authority gave Tata the freedom of the city in 1981, while he was still serving a life sentence on Robben Island. Later, eight cites in the UK followed Glasgow's example. A number of events helped to put a spotlight on the atrocities of the apartheid regime. In 1984, The Special, A.K.A. Special Music Group, released the hit single "Free Nelson Mandela" and it reached no. 9 on the UK music charts. In 1986, artists at Clapham Common in London organized a Freedom Festival concert, which was attended by 250,000 people. In 1988, the "Nelson Mandela 70th Birthday Tribute" was held at Wembley Stadium in London and was attended by 100,000 people; it is estimated that 600 million people in more than 60 countries watched the event on television. The international campaign to release Tata from prison became a global campaign and went far beyond the UK. Today, South Africa is a politically free and democratic country though still plagued with a number of socioeconomic challenges. I am personally grateful to the millions of people around the world who participated in the movement to abolish apartheid. A majority were my fellow South Africans—the sung and unsung heroes who were daily experiencing the violence and oppression of the apartheid system. But there were large numbers of supporters across the world—in the UK, Ireland, Holland, Sweden, Cuba, India, Australia, New Zealand, Jamaica, Palestine, African countries, and the US. Some of these people had not been to South Africa nor had they experienced violence or oppression. This global support gave us a lot of inspiration and encouragement and furnished yet further proof that in the struggle for a free democratic South Africa, we could count on the world.

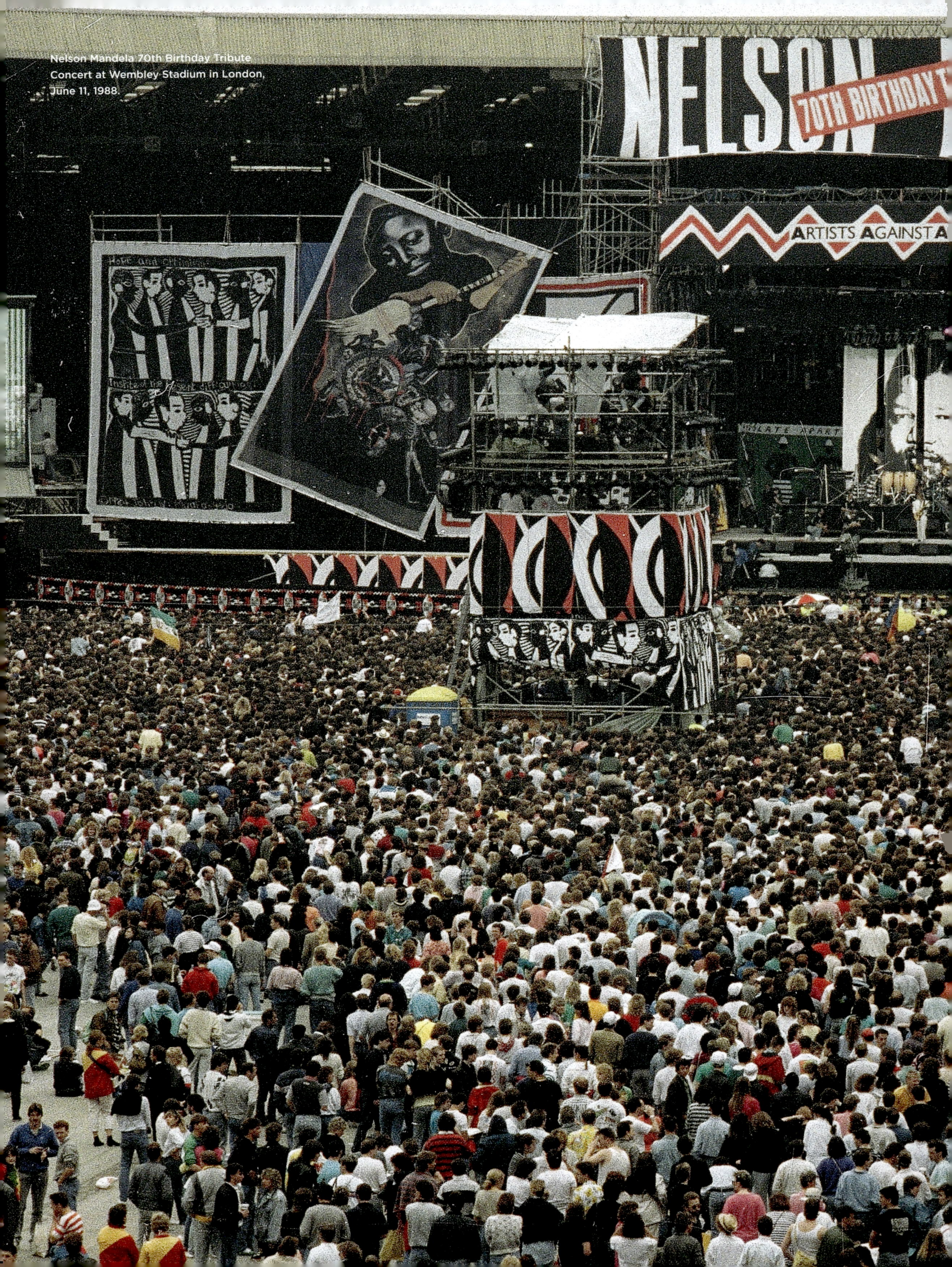

Nelson Mandela 70th Birthday Tribute Concert at Wembley Stadium in London, June 11, 1988.

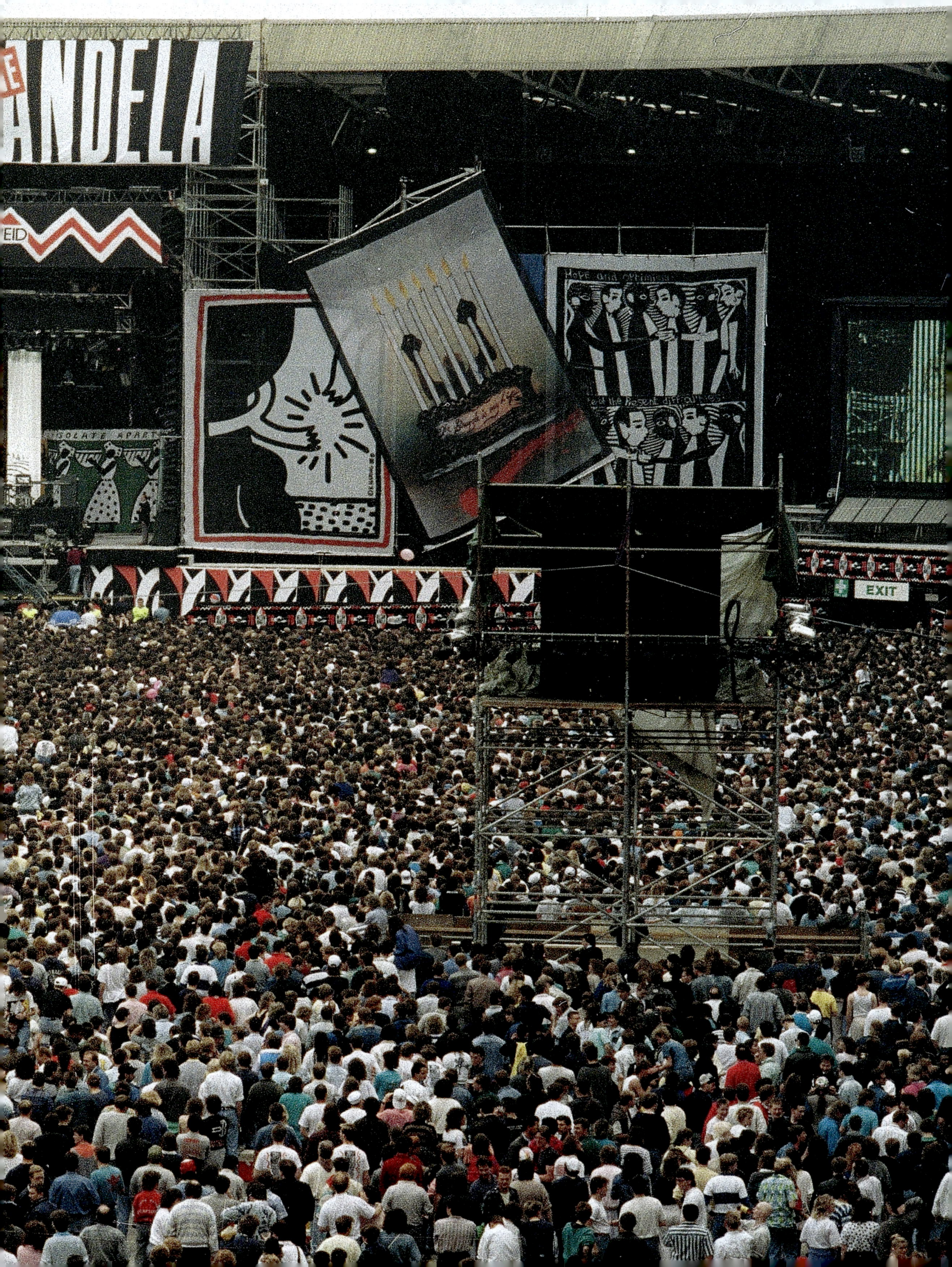
ANDELA
EXIT

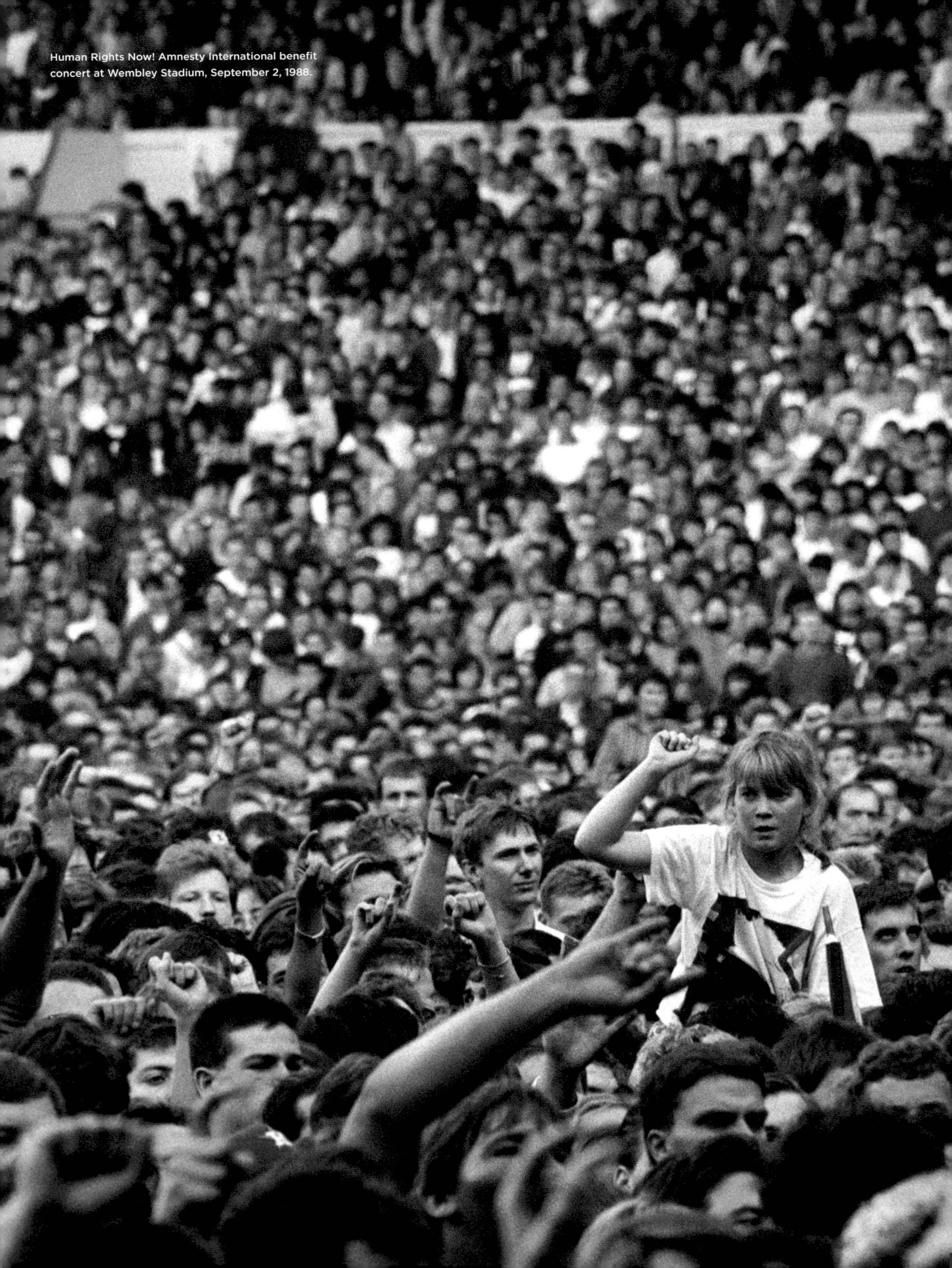

Human Rights Now! Amnesty International benefit concert at Wembley Stadium, September 2, 1988.

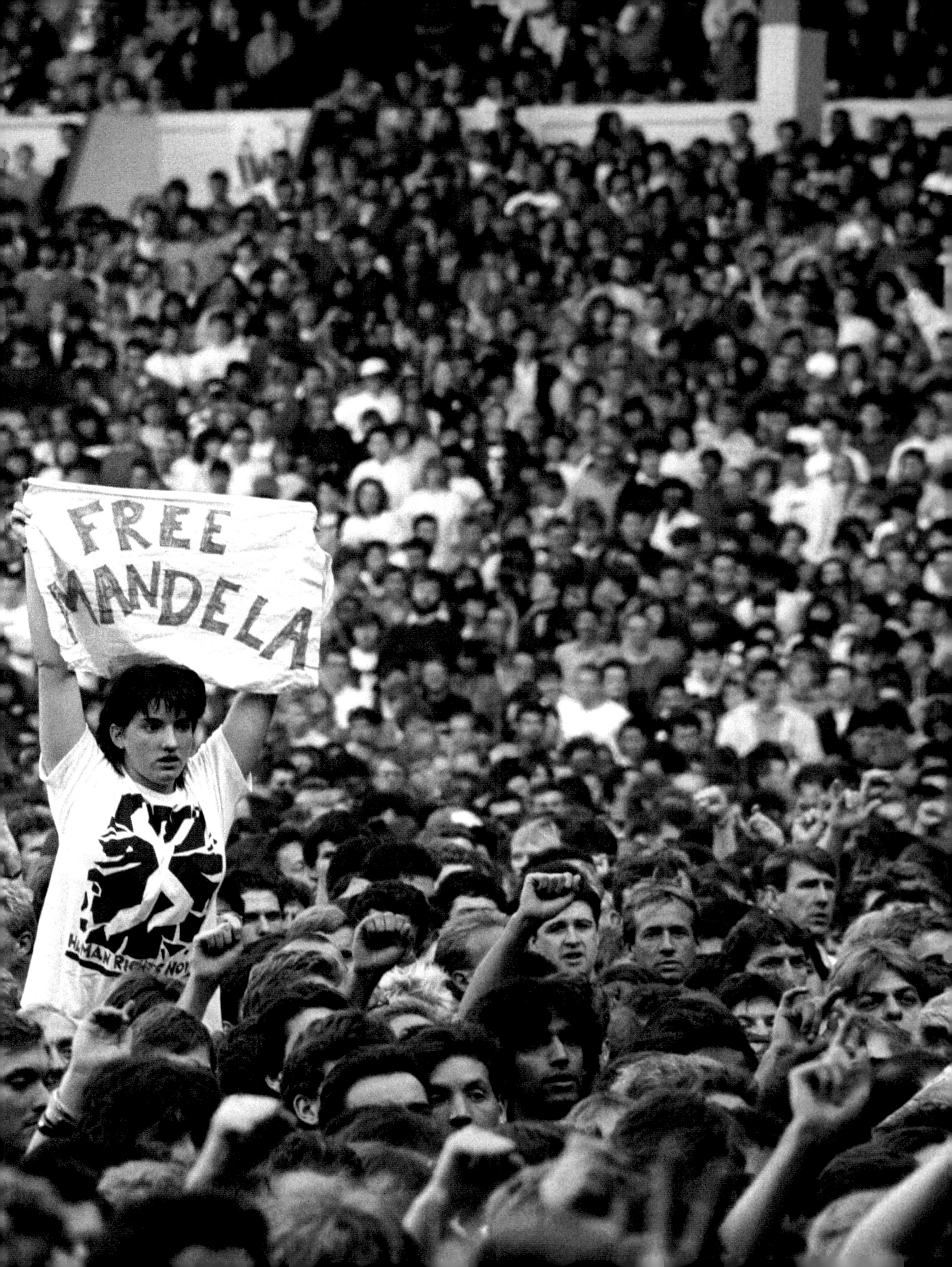
FREE
MANDELA

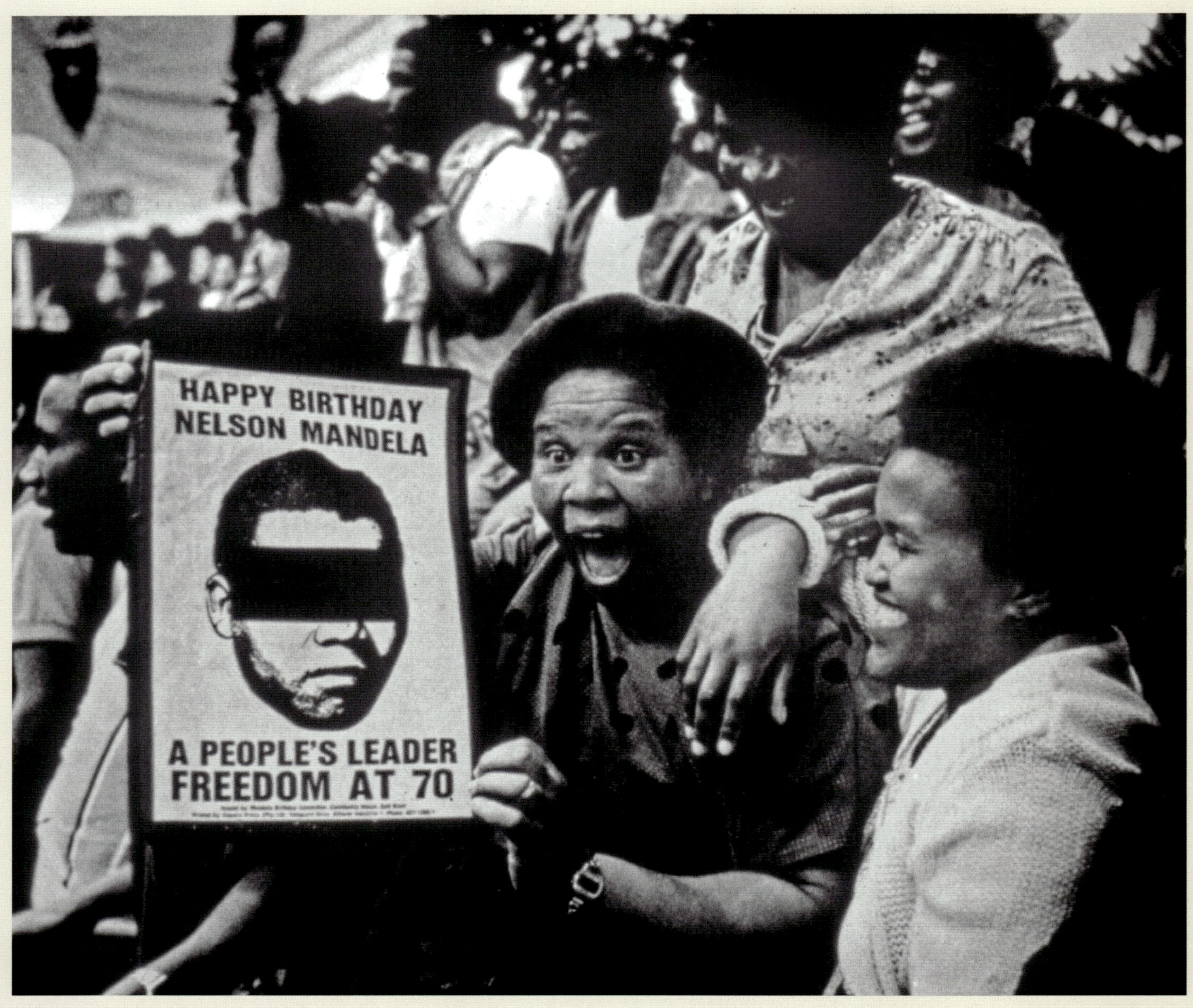

Women participate in an illegal rally at Western Cape University in Cape Town in celebration of Tata's seventieth birthday, 1988.

In South Africa, the government continued, and intensified, its brutal reaction to protests and uprisings. The reaction to external and internal pressure was to increase its violent tactics.

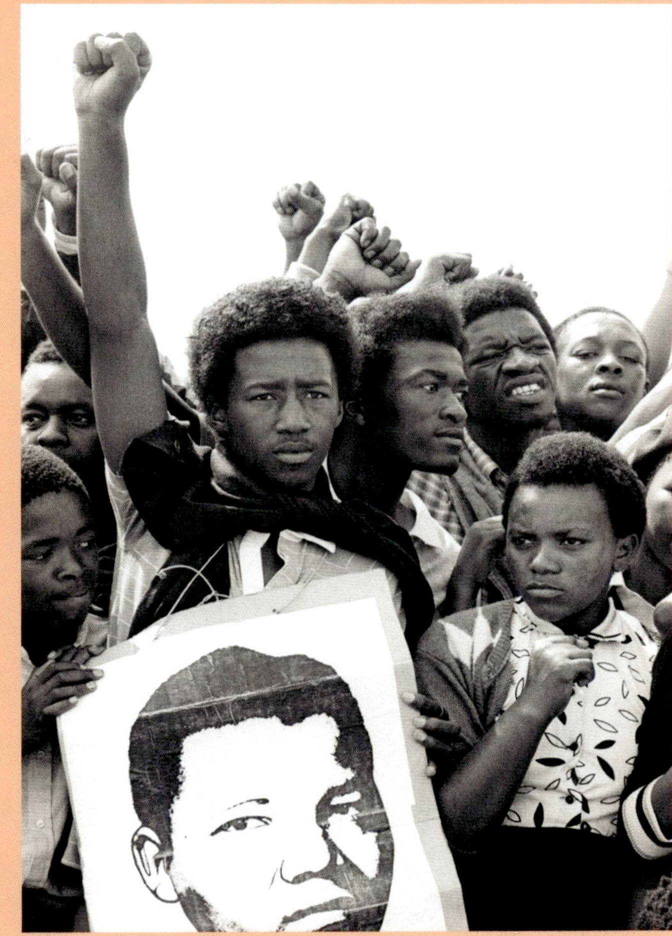

Right: A protester carries a portrait of Tata during the funerals for victims of police repression in South African townships.

Below: Police horsewhip demonstrators in order to break up a march to Tata's prison.

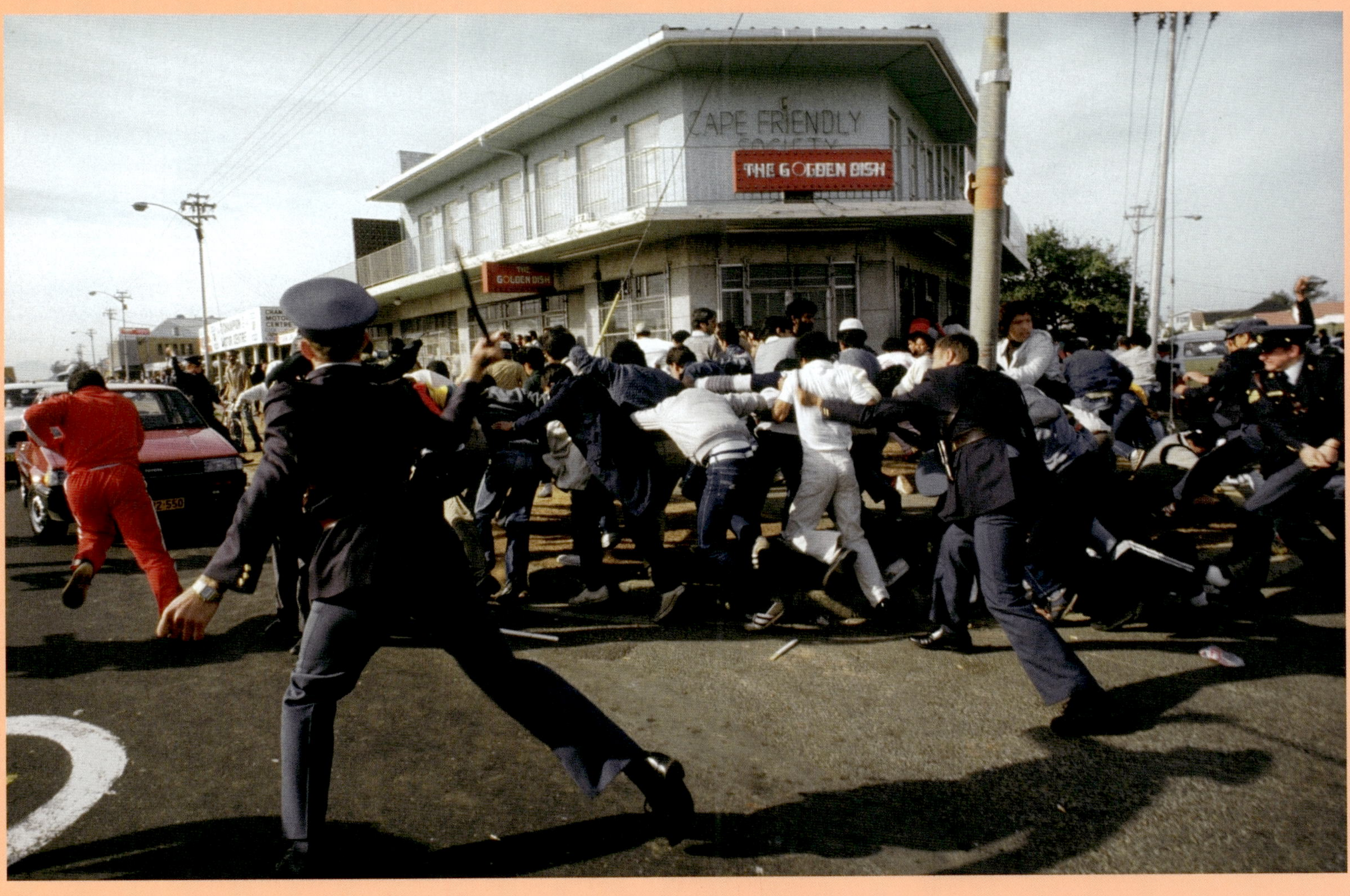

Ultimately, the global movements against apartheid proved that we are all part of a greater whole. Our lives are inextricably bound to one another, and when others are humiliated, diminished, or discriminated against because of their race, gender, class, or geographical location, we all suffer.

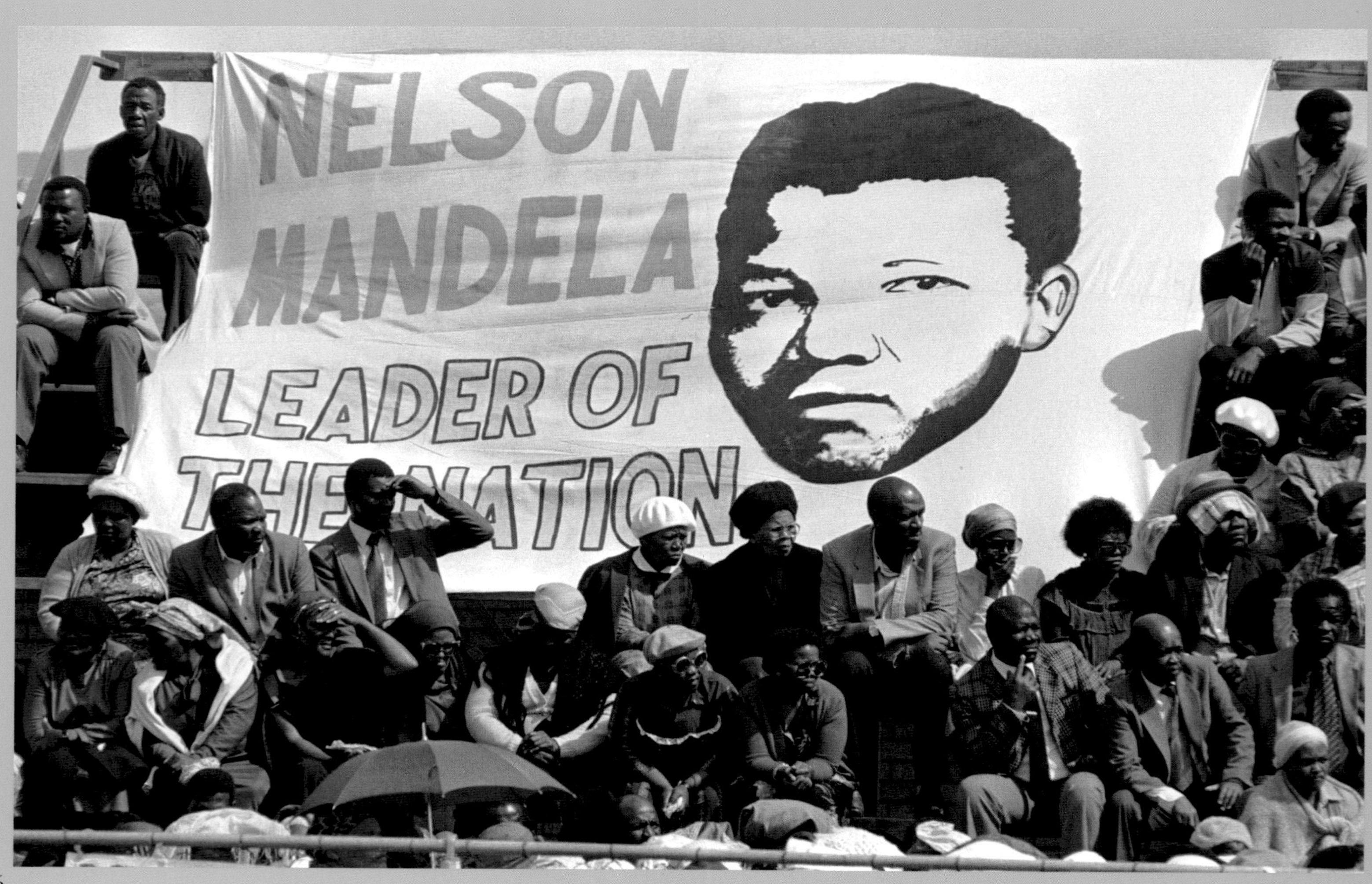

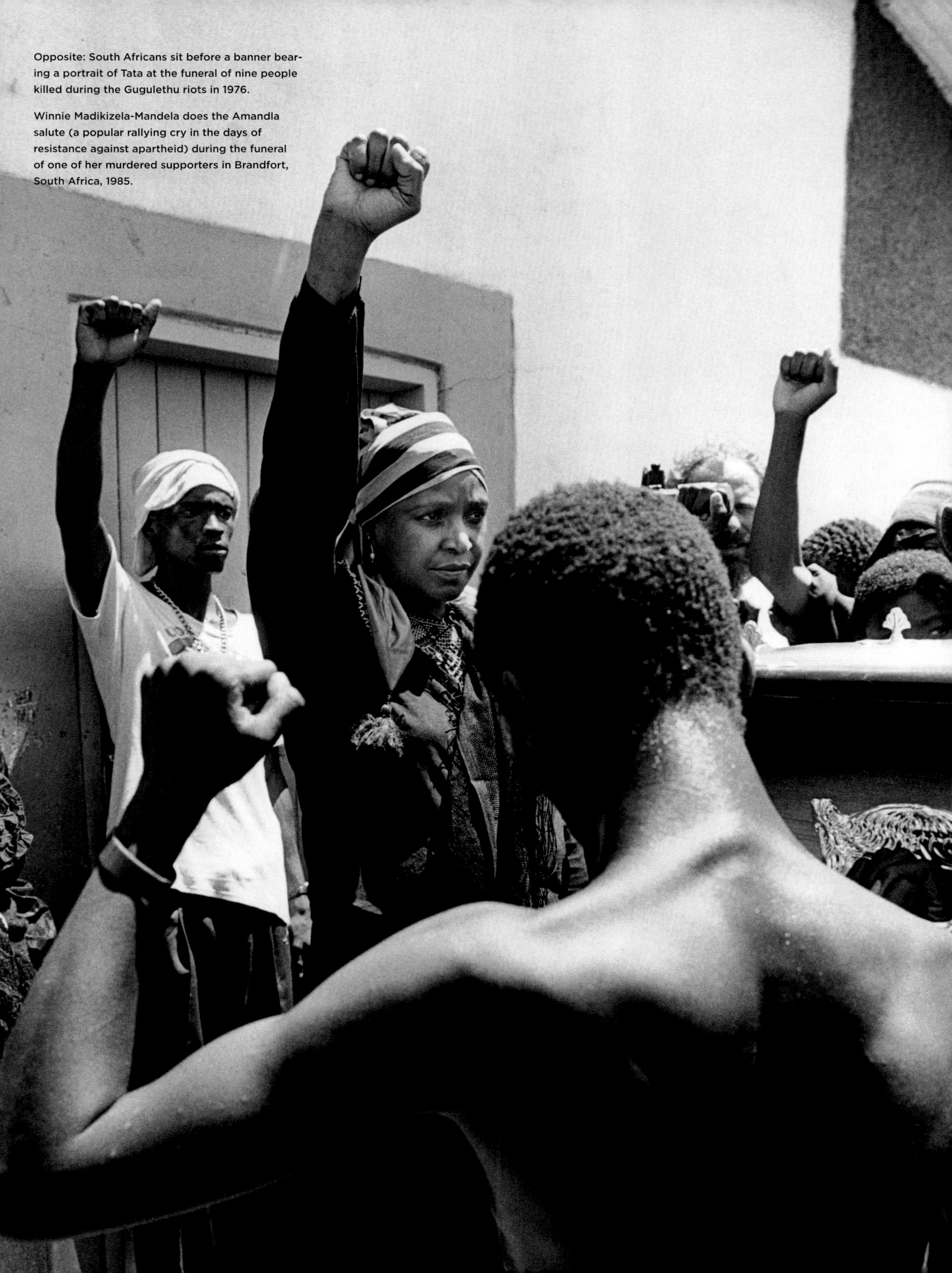

Opposite: South Africans sit before a banner bearing a portrait of Tata at the funeral of nine people killed during the Gugulethu riots in 1976.

Winnie Madikizela-Mandela does the Amandla salute (a popular rallying cry in the days of resistance against apartheid) during the funeral of one of her murdered supporters in Brandfort, South Africa, 1985.

Marchers along 42nd Street in New York display banners and signs protesting the racial policies in South Africa, 1986.

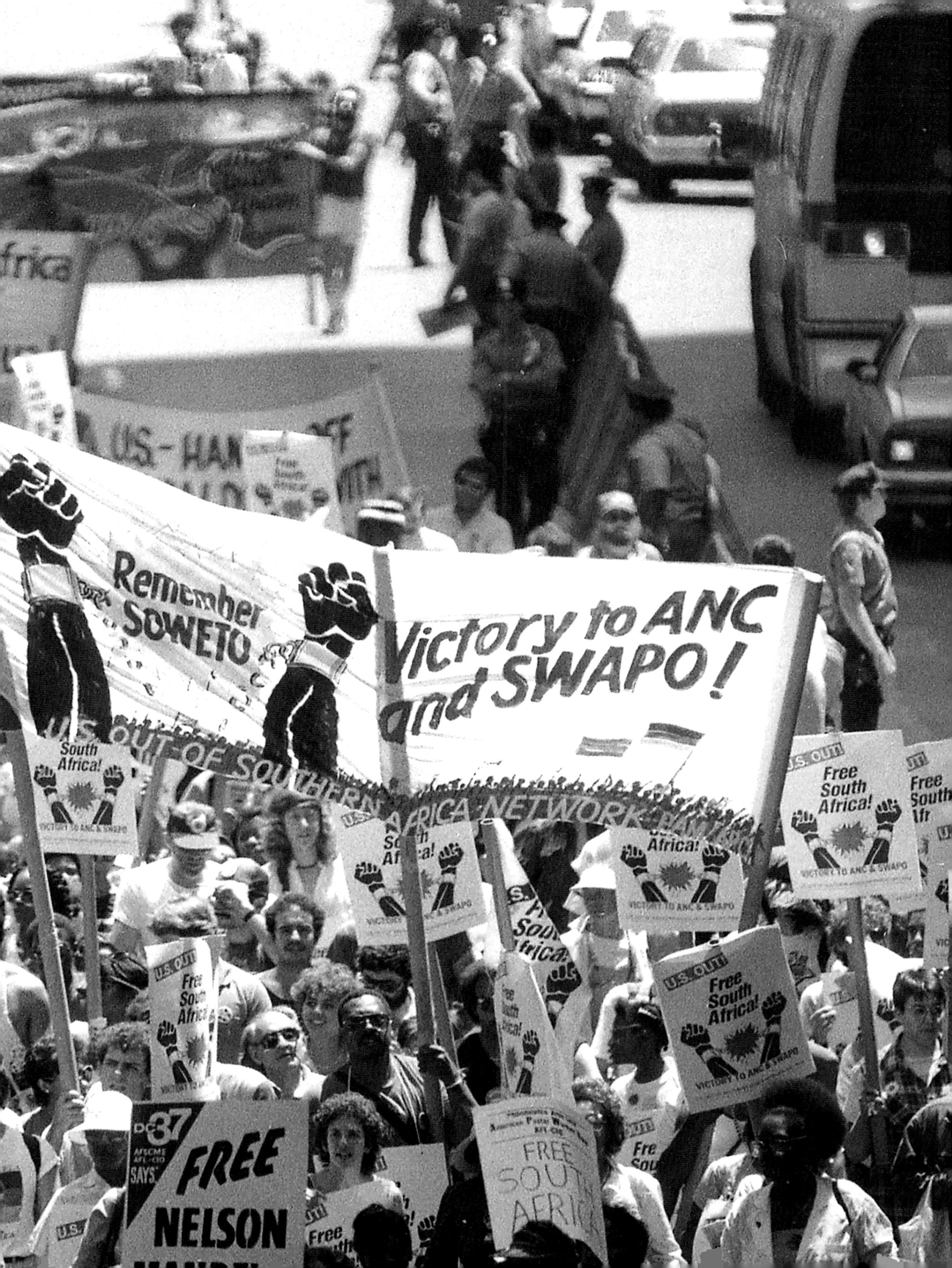

Remember SOWETO
Victory to ANC and SWAPO!
U.S. OUT OF SOUTHERN AFRICA NETWORK
U.S. OUT!
Free South Africa!
VICTORY TO ANC & SWAPO
DC 37 AFSCME AFL-CIO SAYS:
FREE NELSON
FREE SOUTH AFRICA

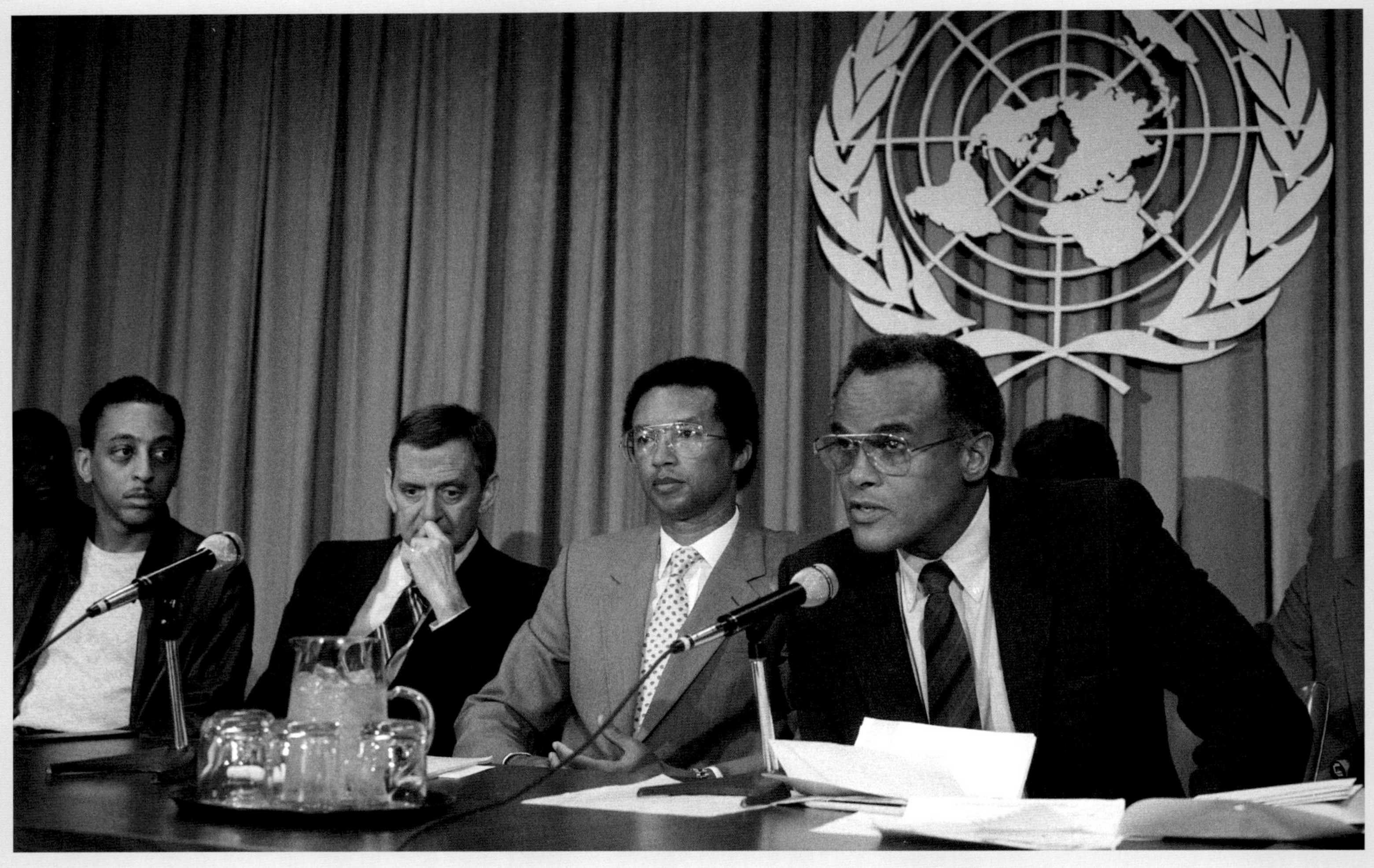

Singer and actor Harry Belafonte speaks at a news conference at the United Nations Headquarters to announce the formation of Artists and Athletes Against Apartheid. At left are actors Gregory Hines and Tony Randall and tennis notable Arthur Ashe, September 1983.

There is much more that unites us than divides us. By supporting each other in defiance of borders, we created bonds that grew stronger than ever, bonds that swayed public sentiment around the world.

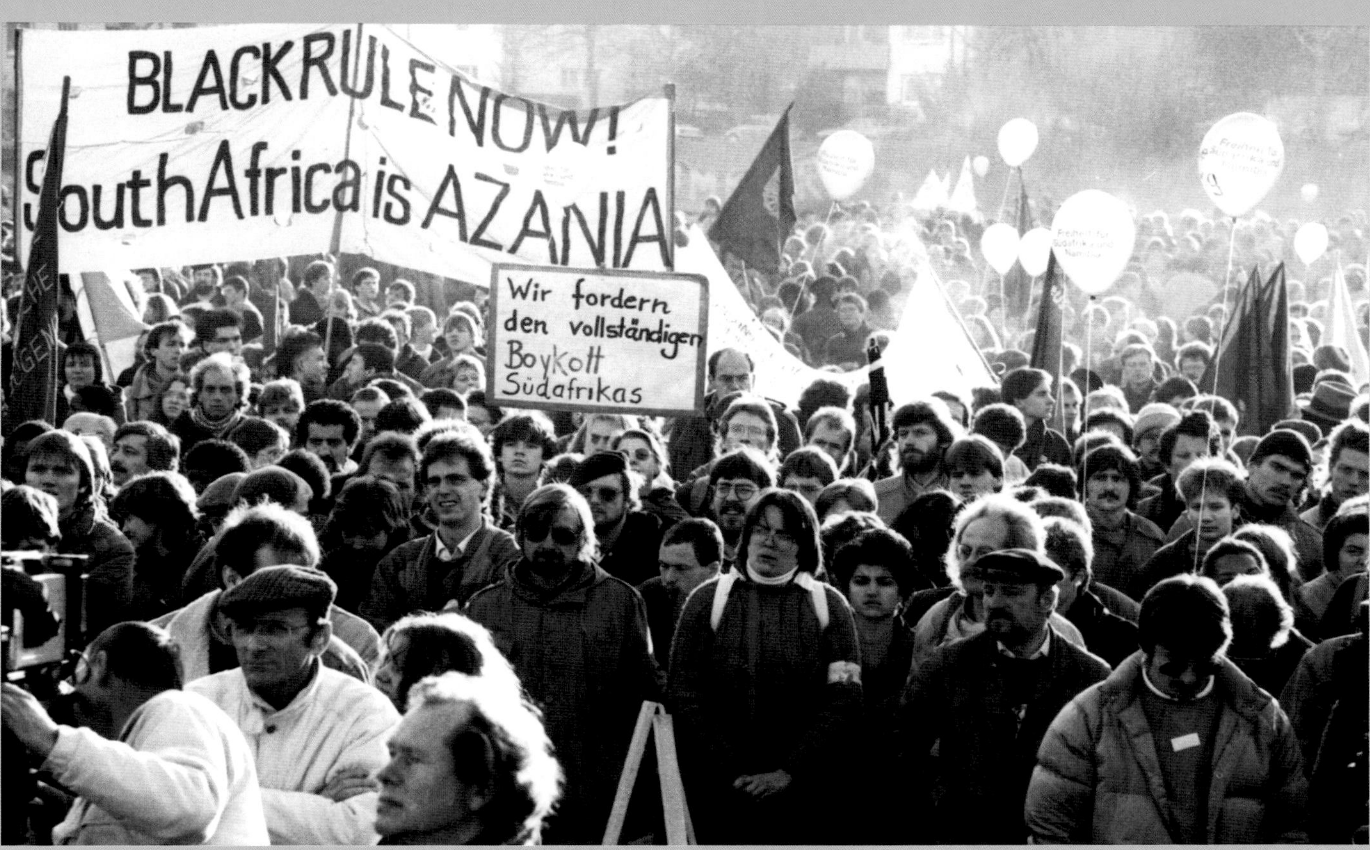

This page: Demonstrations against apartheid in Bonn, Germany, 1986.

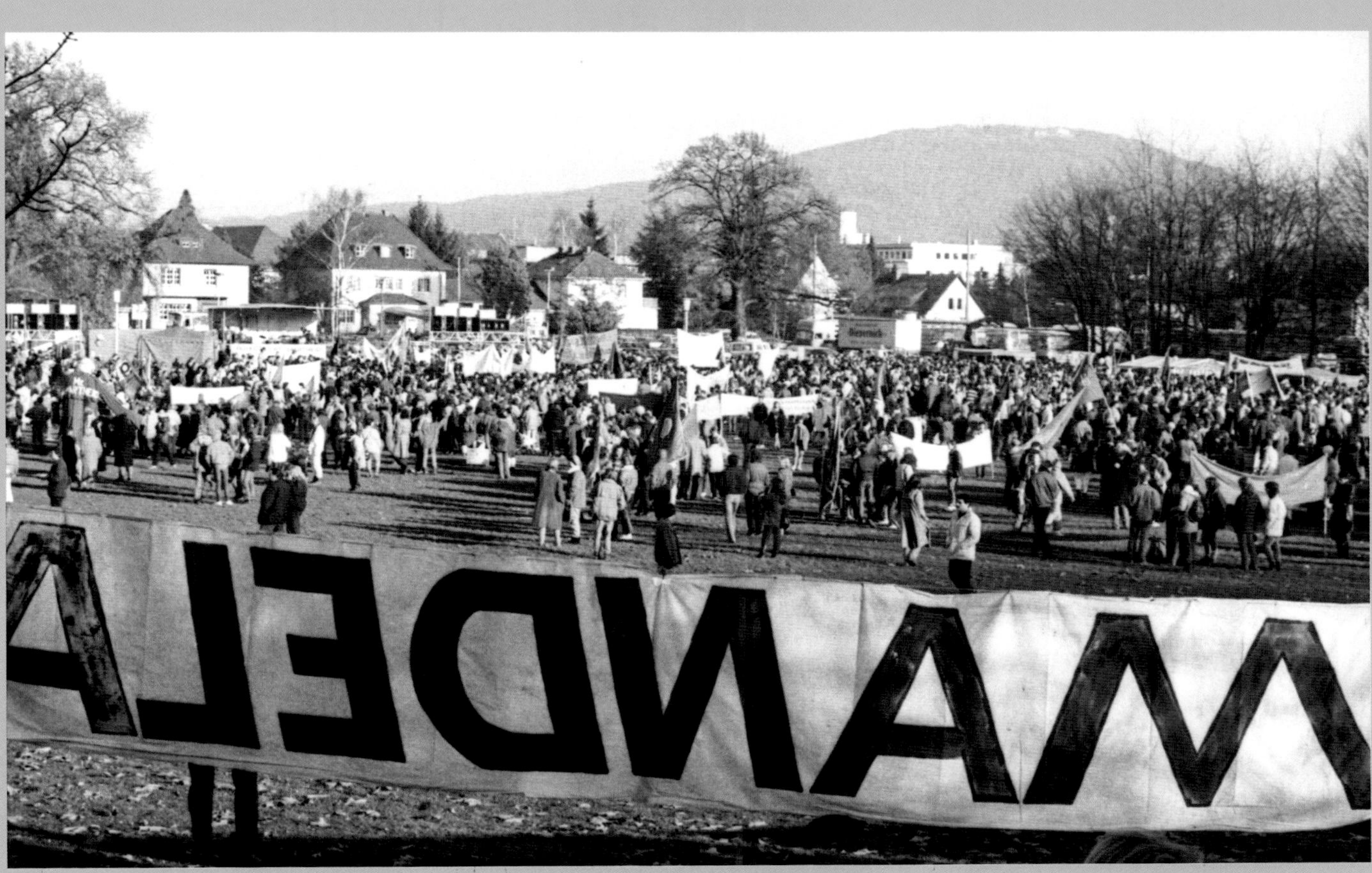

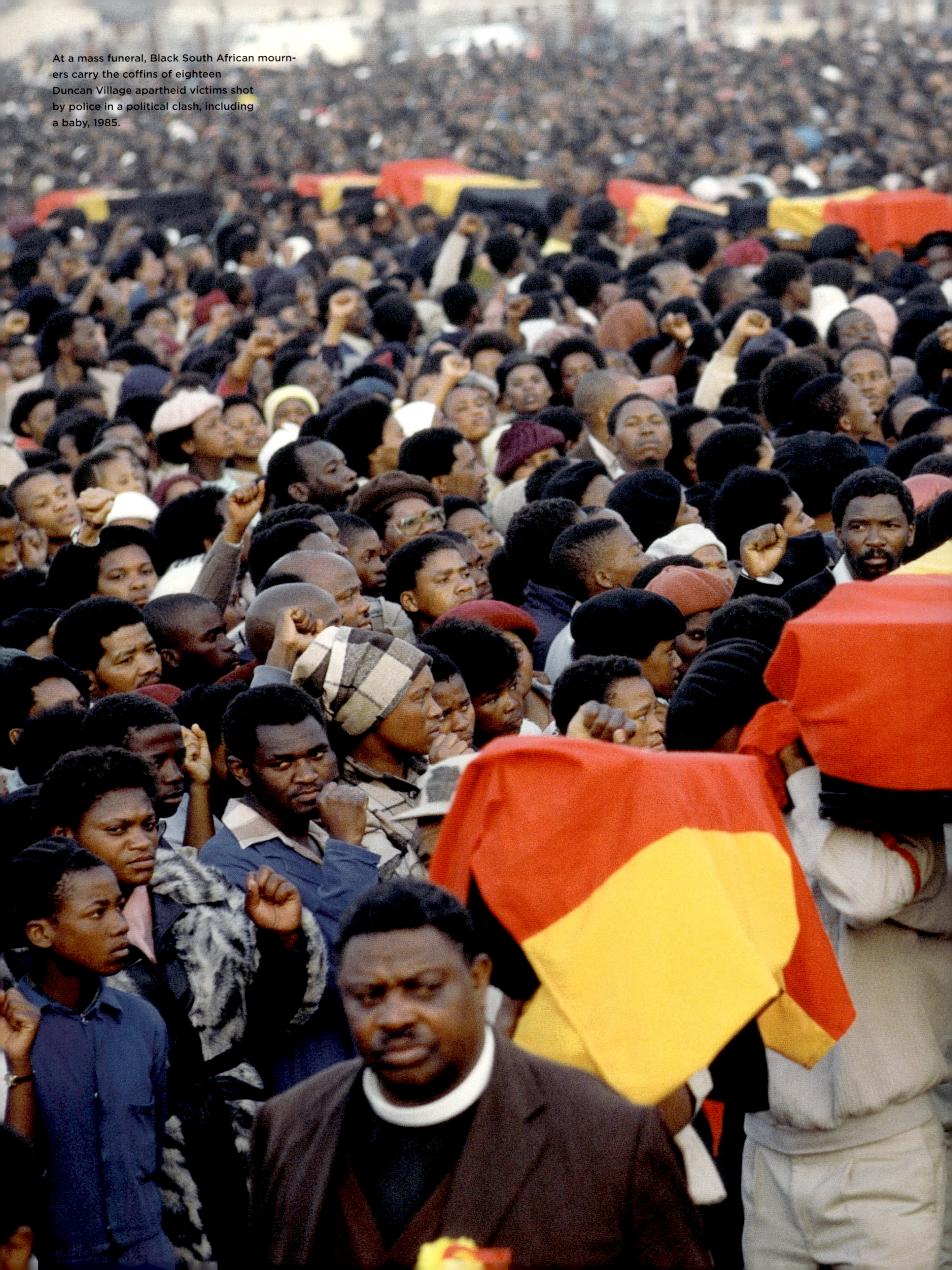

At a mass funeral, Black South African mourners carry the coffins of eighteen Duncan Village apartheid victims shot by police in a political clash, including a baby, 1985.

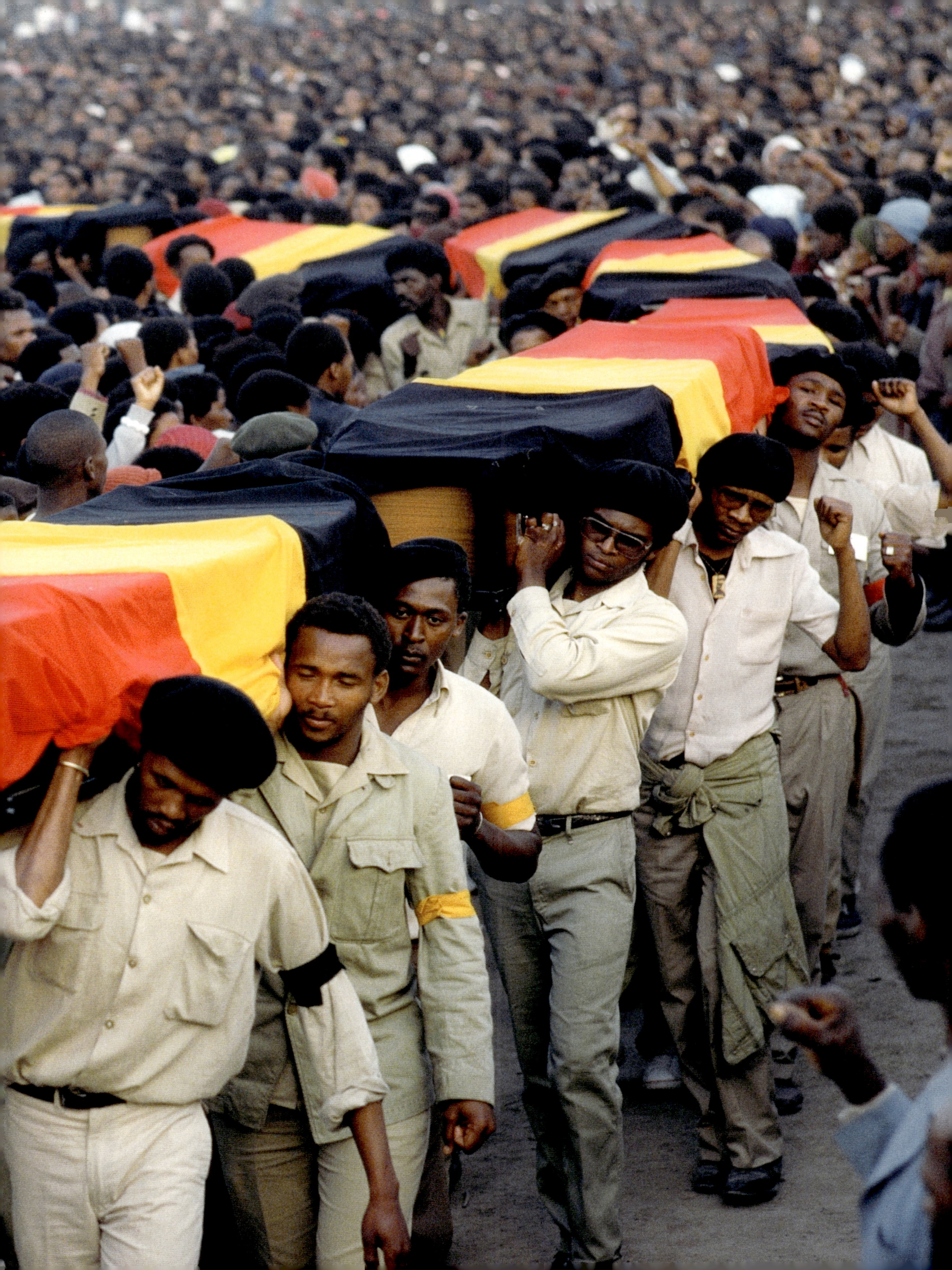

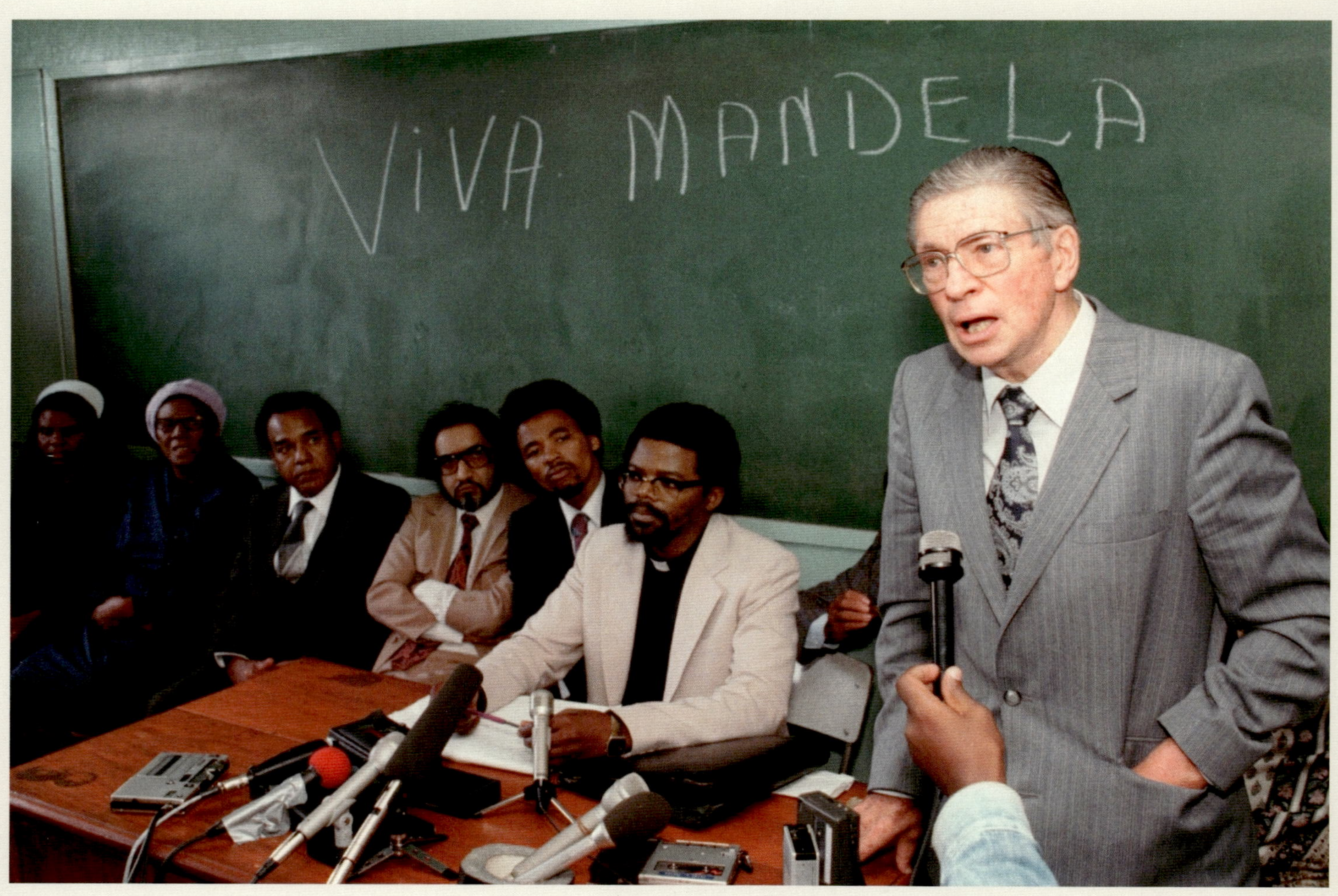

Above: Pro-Mandela press conference in 1986.

Opposite: Anti-apartheid demonstrators standing vigil for a Commonwealth decision in favor of economic sanctions against South Africa, 1986.

Thank you to all those around the globe, both alive and those who have passed on. I will be eternally grateful that I had wonderful moments with Tata as a free man. As Tata said in *Long Walk to Freedom*,

“I was not born with a hunger to be free. I was born free—free in every way that I could know. Free to run in the fields.”

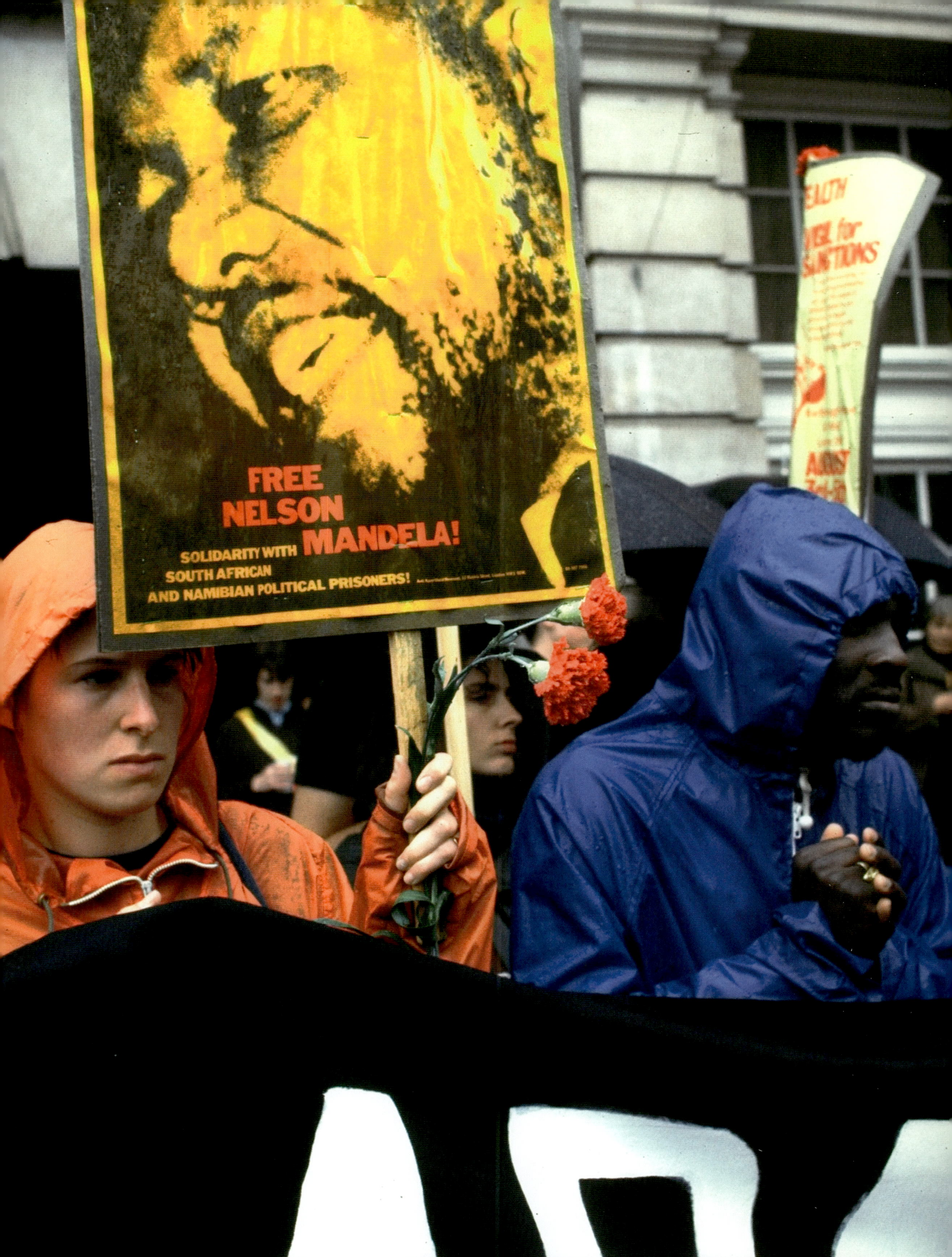
FREE
NELSON
MANDELA!
SOLIDARITY WITH
SOUTH AFRICAN
AND NAMIBIAN POLITICAL PRISONERS!

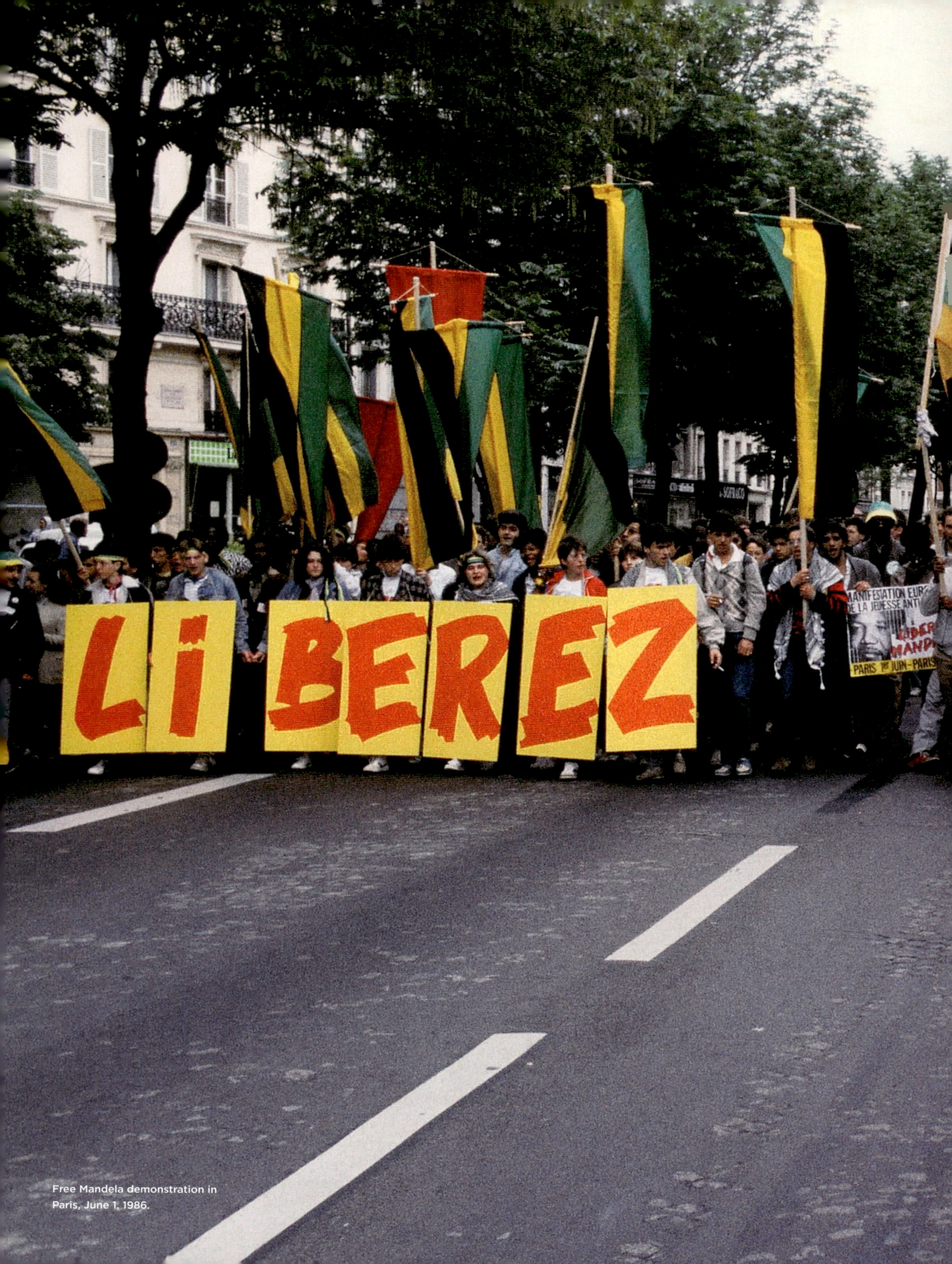

Free Mandela demonstration in Paris, June 1, 1986.

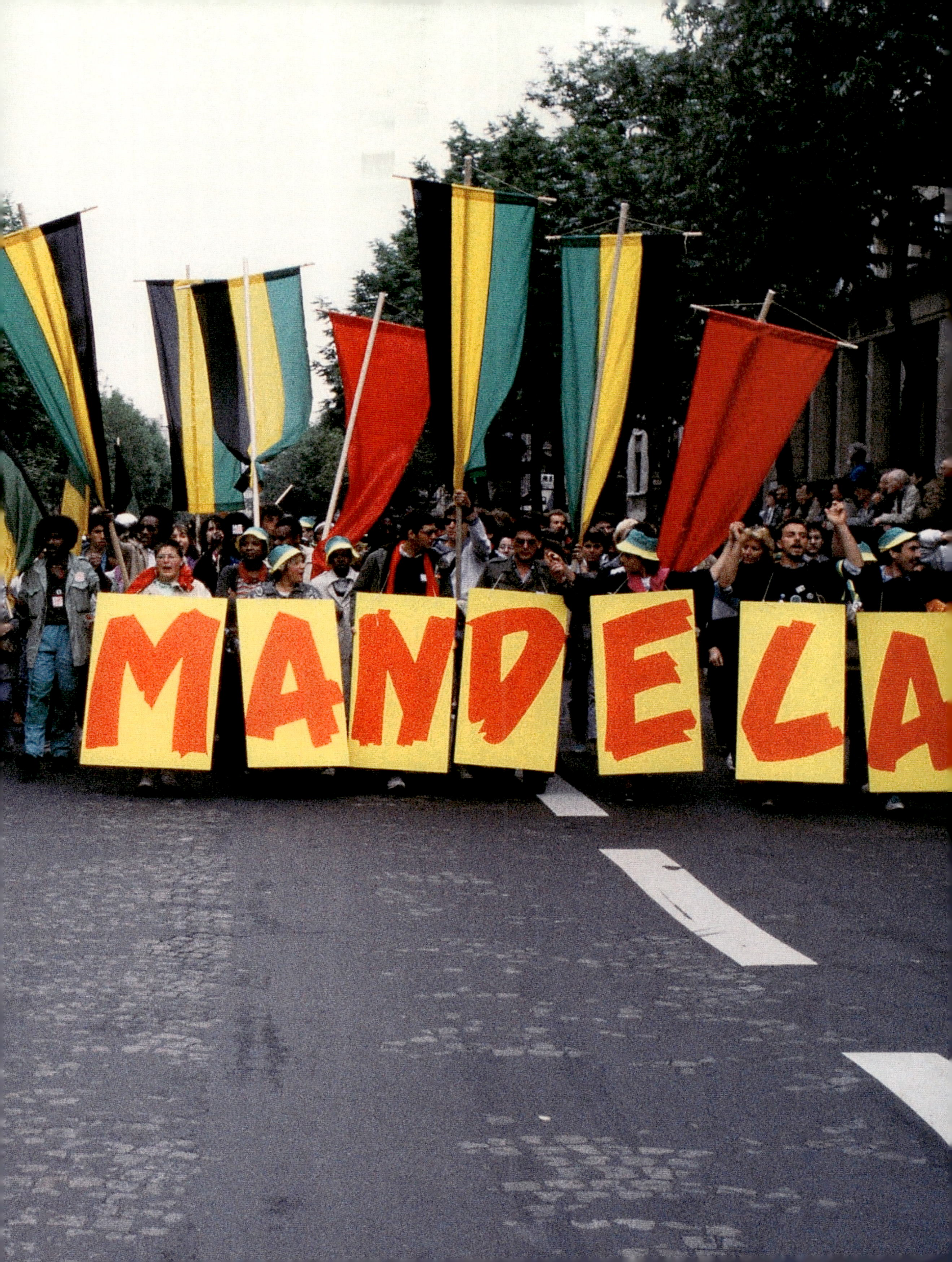
MANDELA

7
1990–2013

Embracing the Nation, Africa, and the World

MANDELA

His stand for justice and humanity
Cost him the rights of liberty.
For twenty-seven anguished years he paid
The price for equality, long delayed.
To end apartheid was his cause,
And to end racially based laws.
The world called for his release,
And for apartheid to decrease.
Finally, the day of hope arrived,
Prince Mandela had survived.
As he walked from his prison cell,
Around the globe, cheers did swell.
His stride was strong and dignified,
The years of suffering were belied.
He disavowed the warriors' sword,
A Nobel Peace Prize was his reward.
His presidency included all races,
He ruled with the utmost graces.
Vocal in the fight against AIDS,
His activism will not be stayed.
Madiba is his Xhosa clan name,
And by all, a leader proclaimed.
A respected statesman of our day,
He continues in his principled way.

Author, Dr. Pinkie Andrews

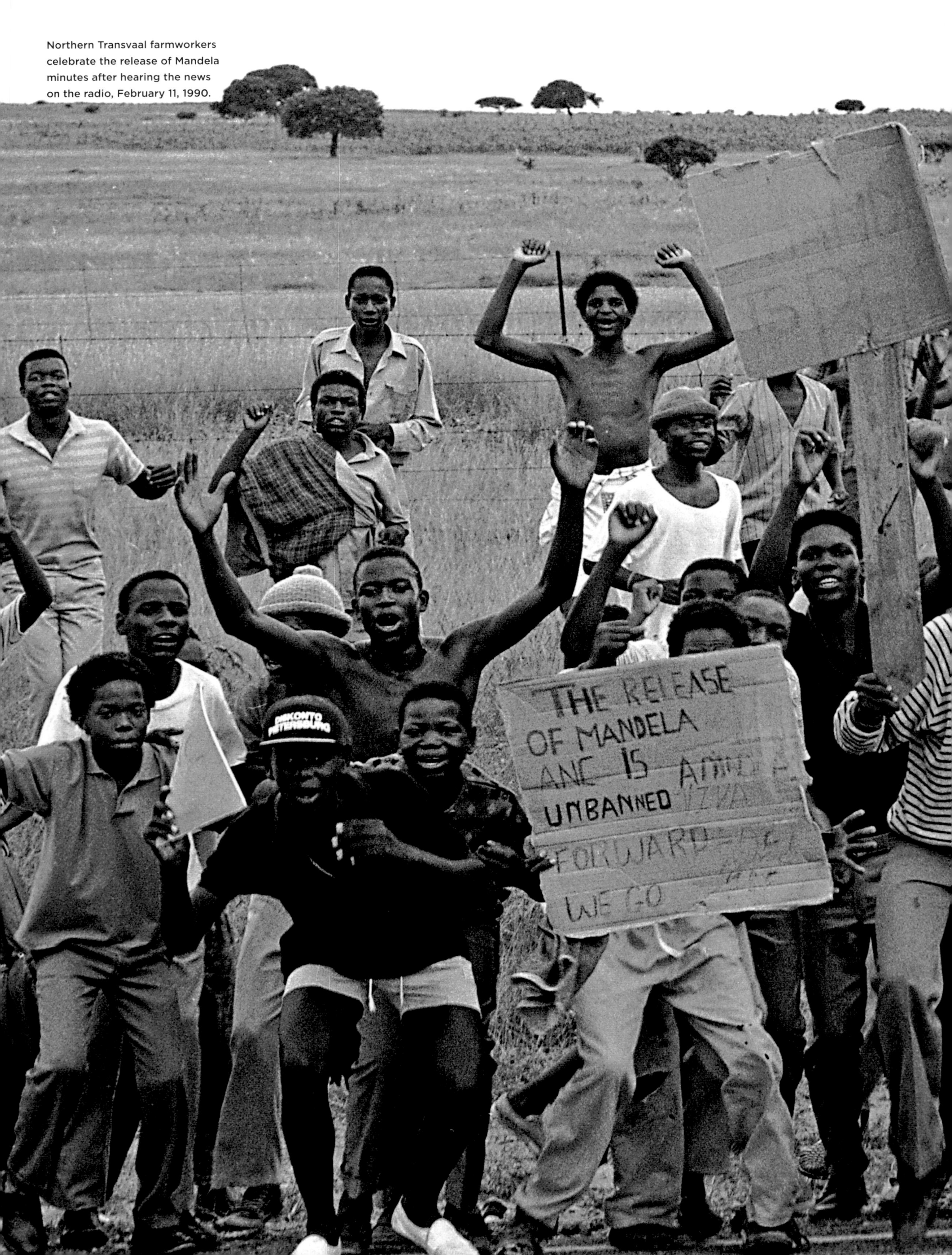

Northern Transvaal farmworkers celebrate the release of Mandela minutes after hearing the news on the radio, February 11, 1990.

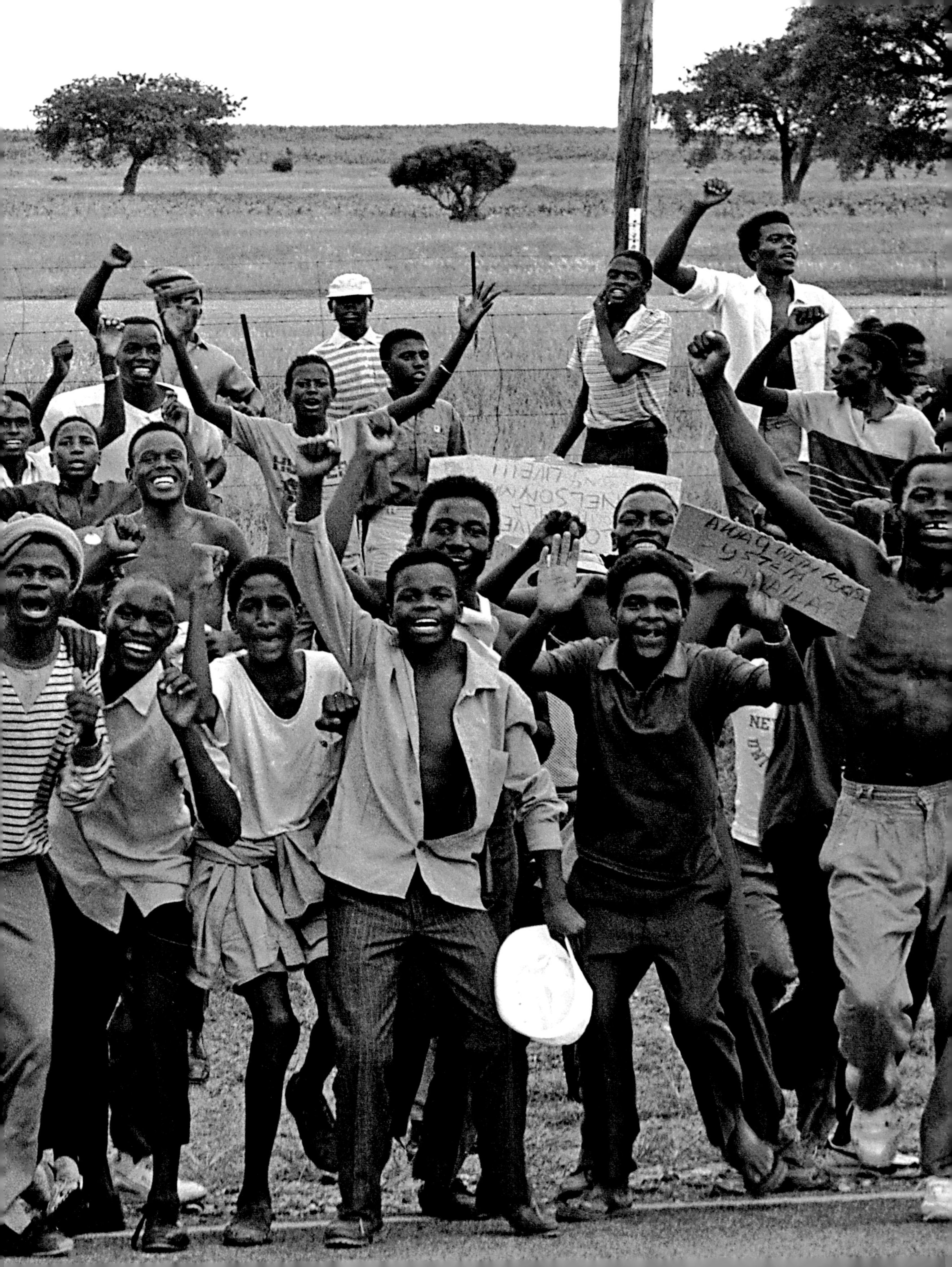

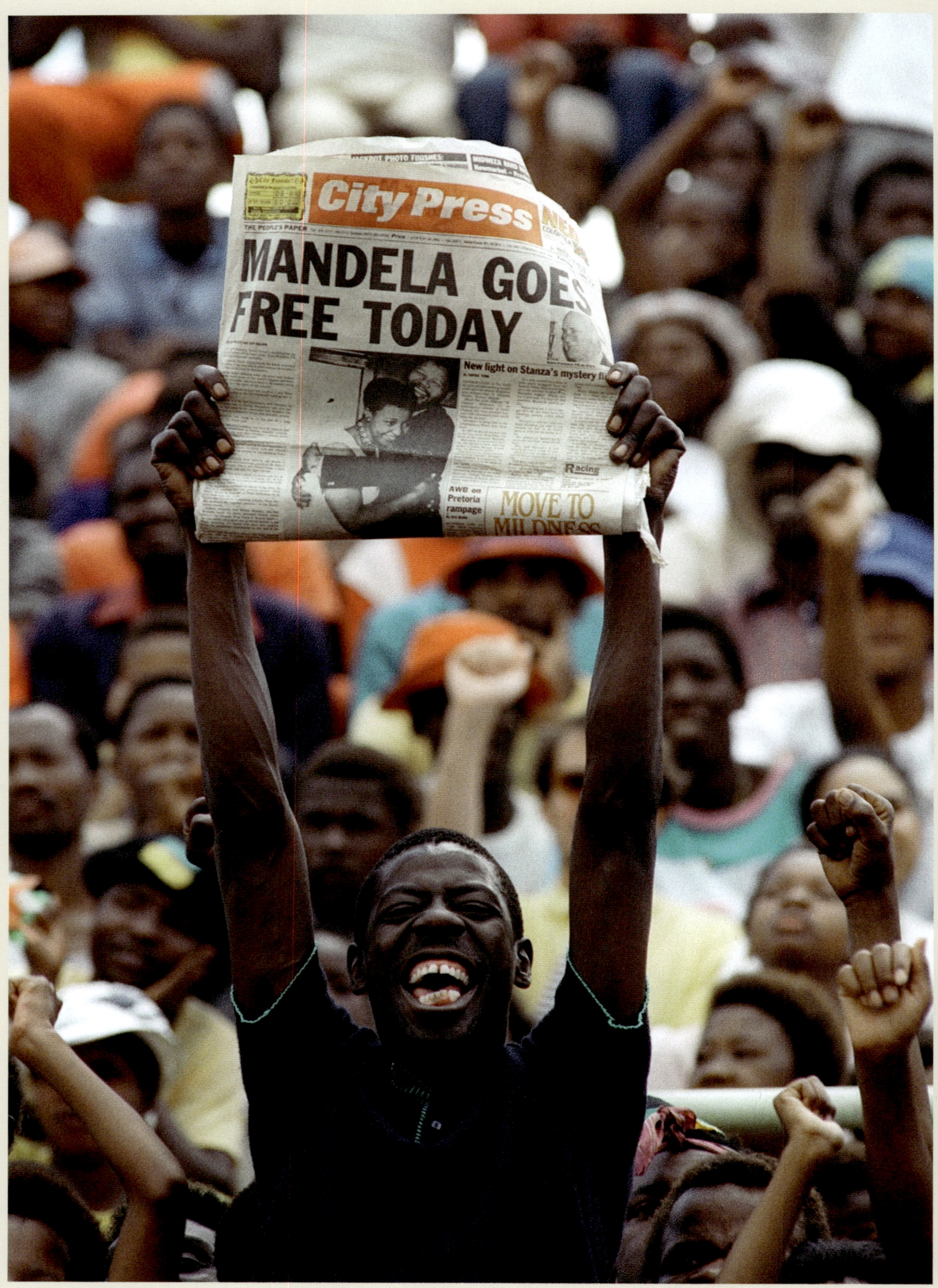

A Sowetan holds up a newspaper announcing Tata's release.

Opposite: Tata raises his fist during a rally in Soweto on February 13, 1990.

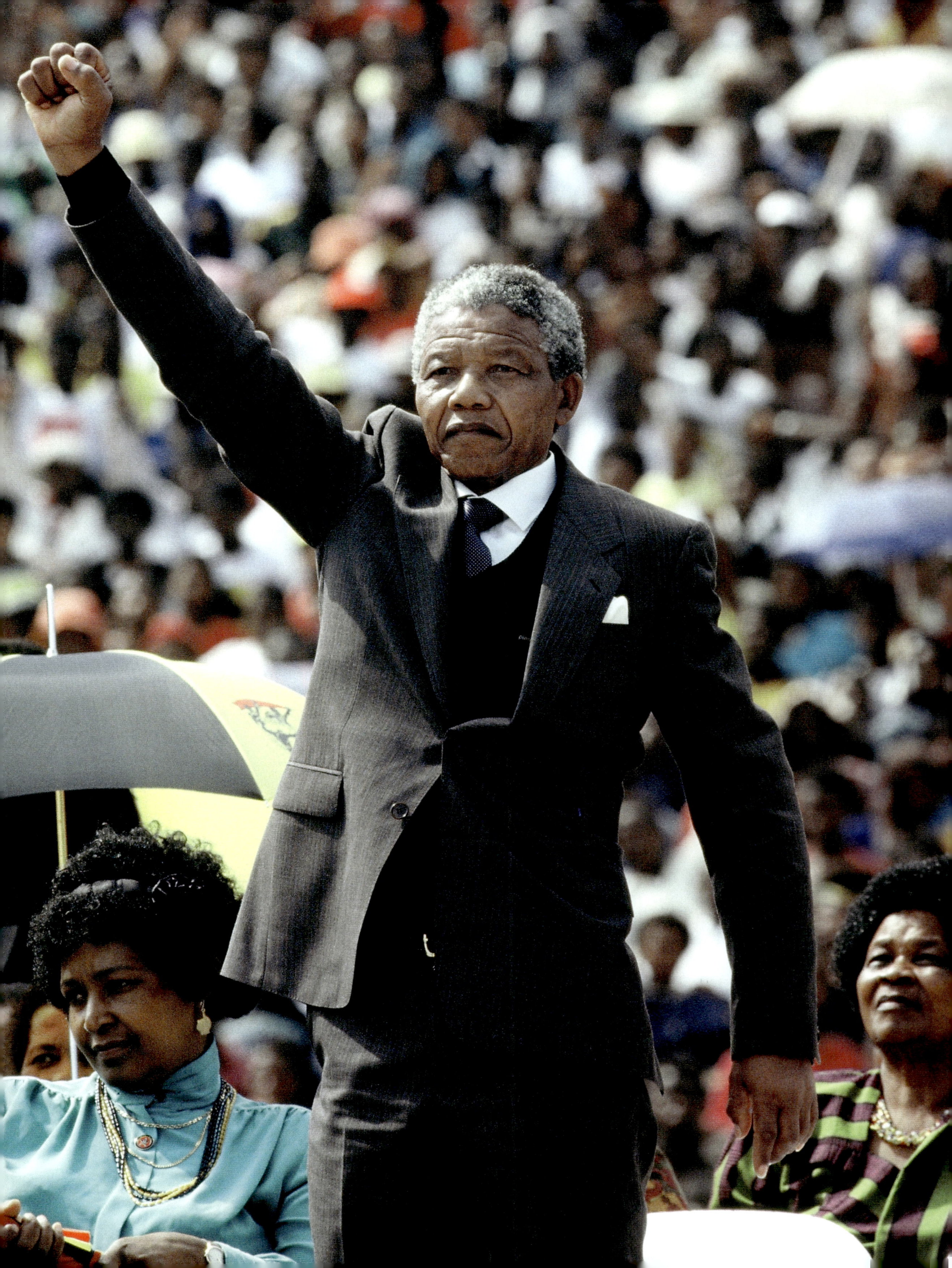

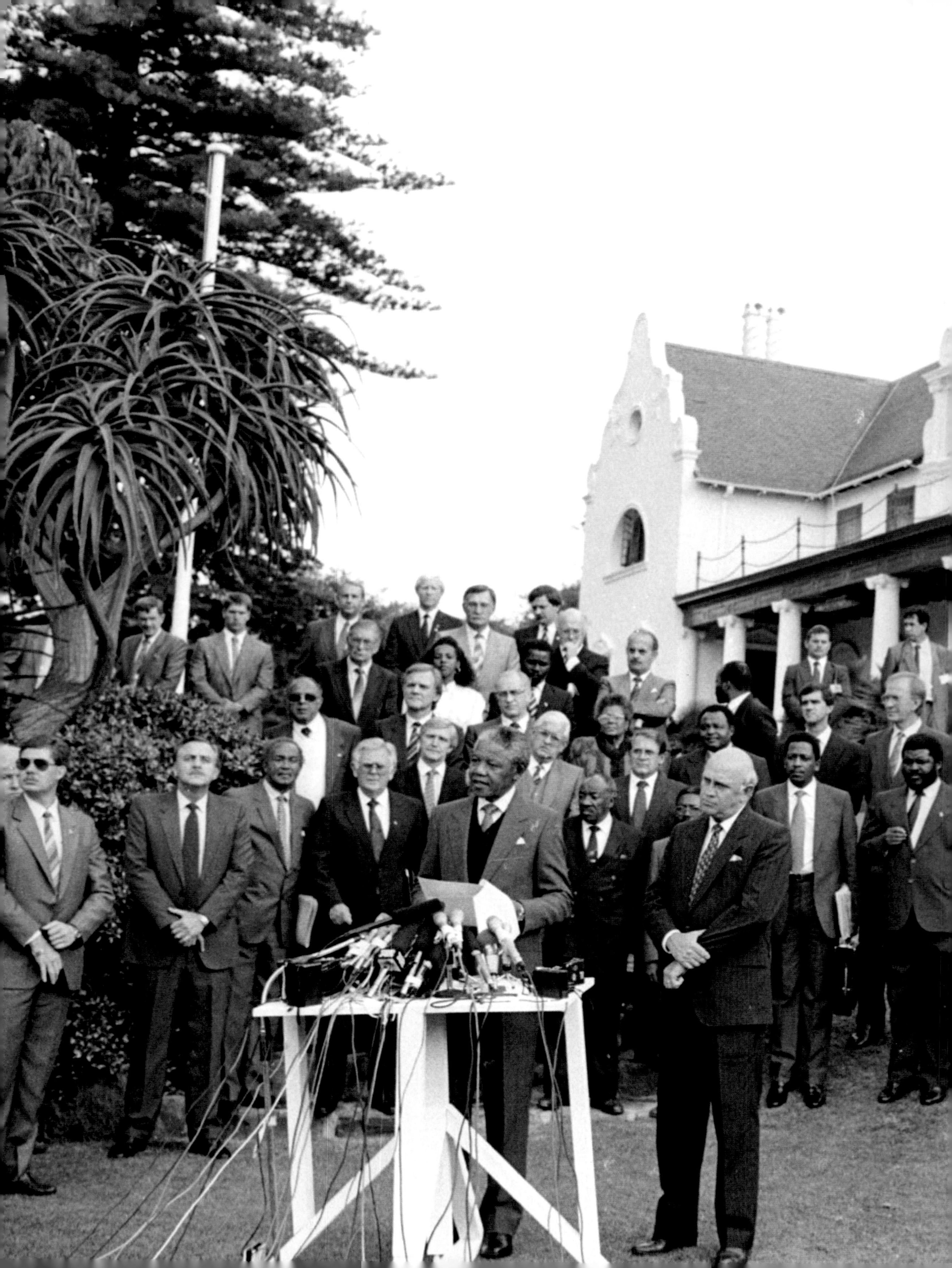

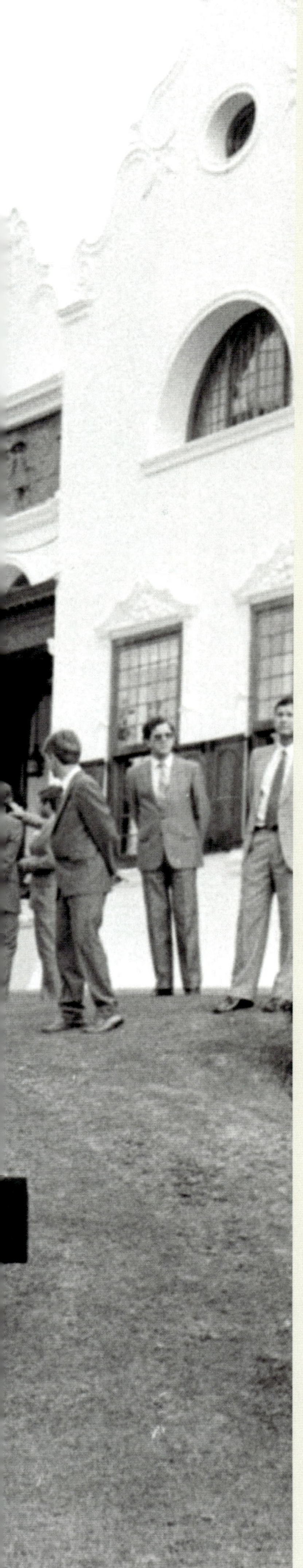

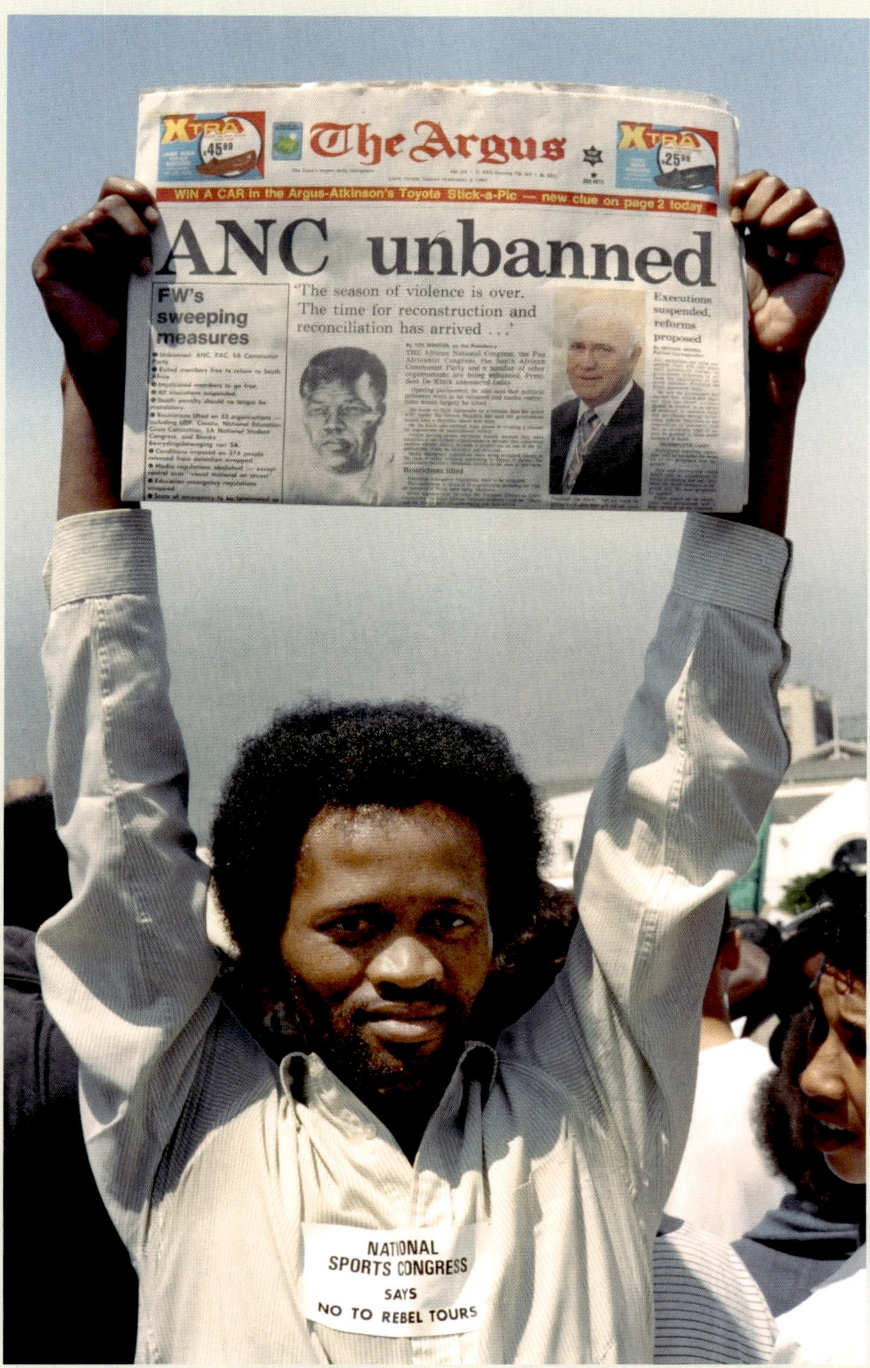

Opposite: Tata and state president of South Africa F. W. de Klerk address the media following breakthrough talks with the government at the Groote Schuur Estate in Cape Town on May 5, 1990.

Above: A young man holds a local newspaper announcing that the ANC is unbanned, on February 2, 1990, in Cape Town, during a demonstration of anti-apartheid marchers demanding the release of all the political prisoners in South Africa, including anti-apartheid leader and ANC member Nelson Mandela.

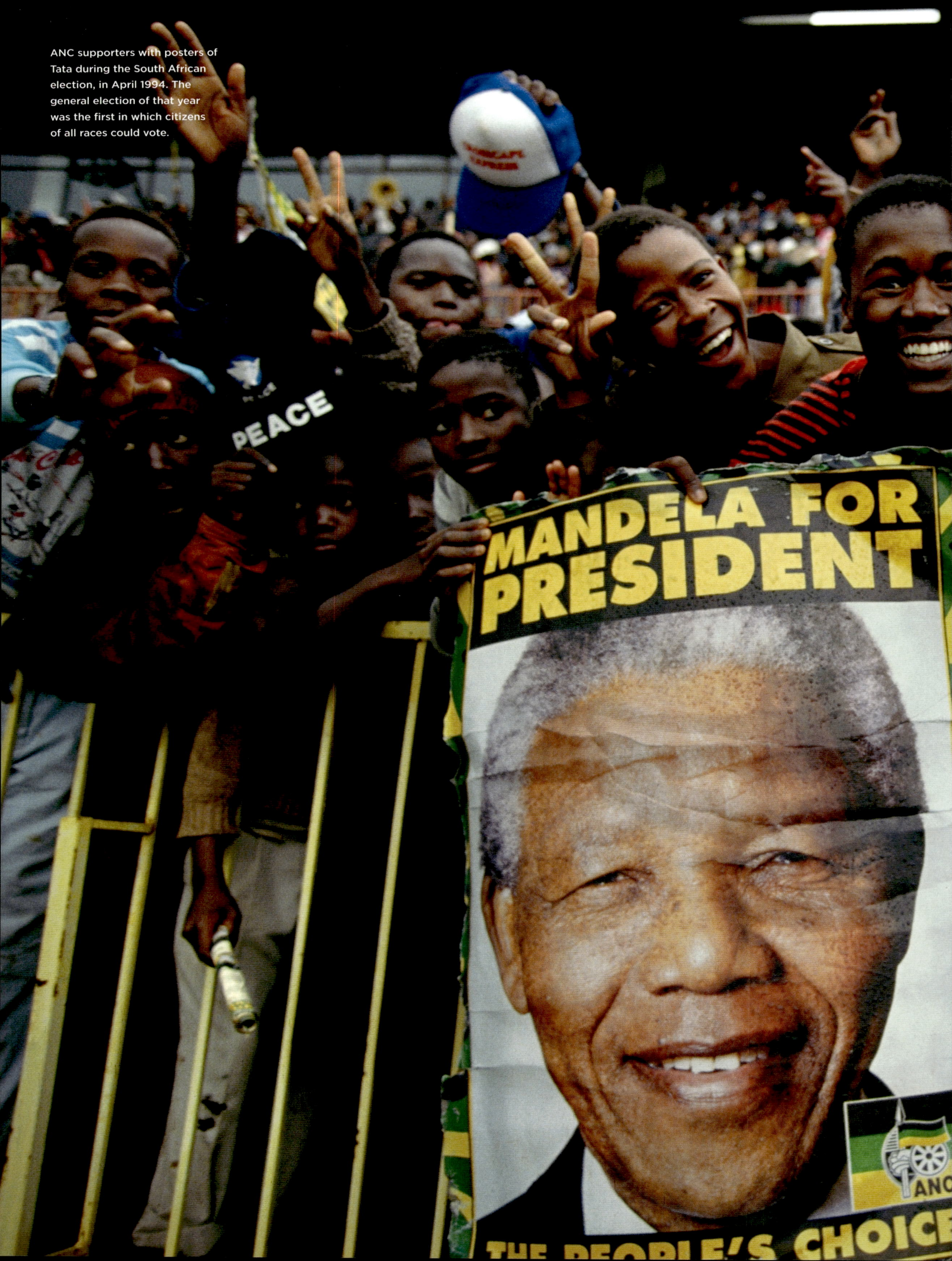

ANC supporters with posters of Tata during the South African election, in April 1994. The general election of that year was the first in which citizens of all races could vote.

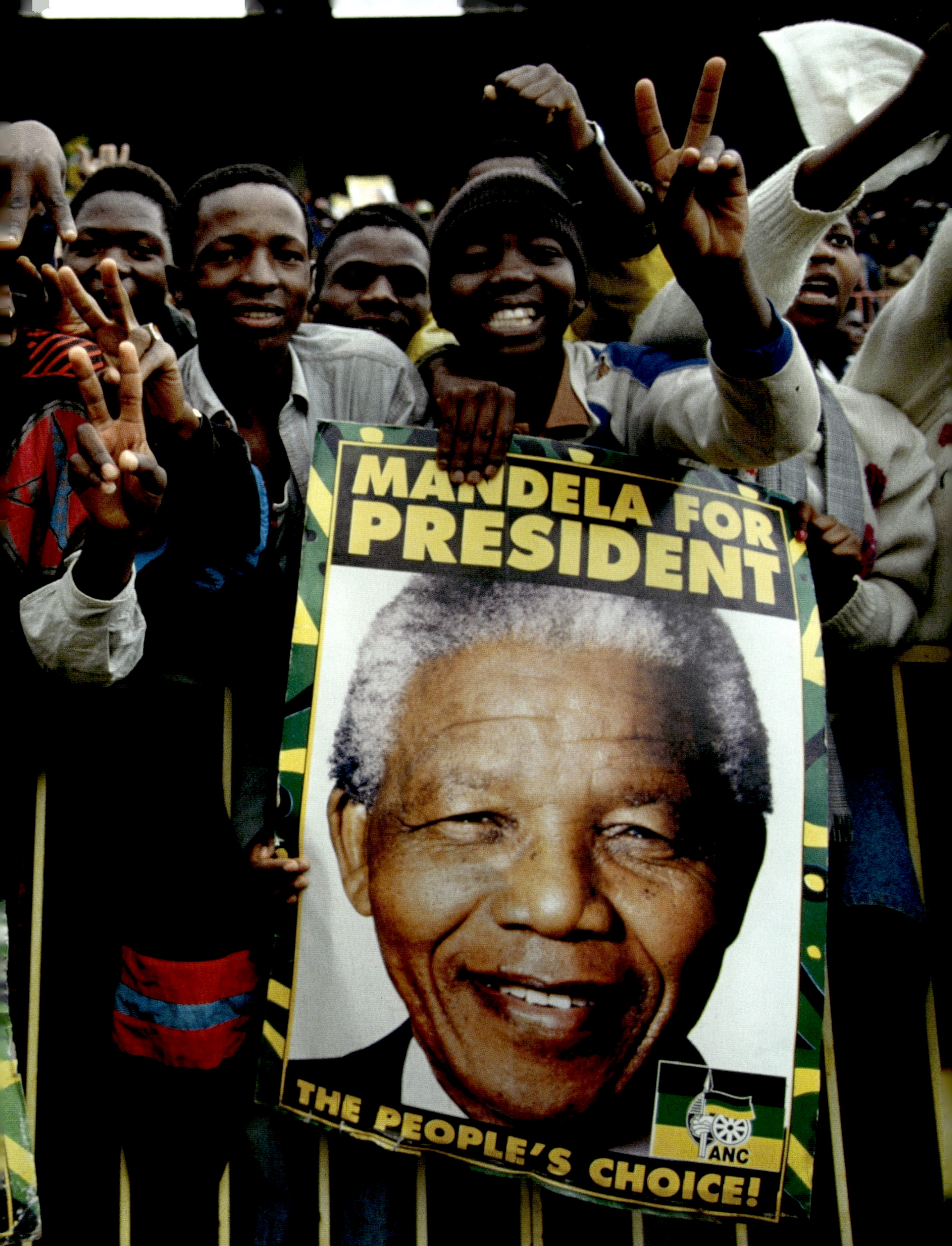
MANDELA FOR PRESIDENT
THE PEOPLE'S CHOICE!
ANC

This page and opposite: Tata campaigning throughout South Africa in 1993 and 1994.

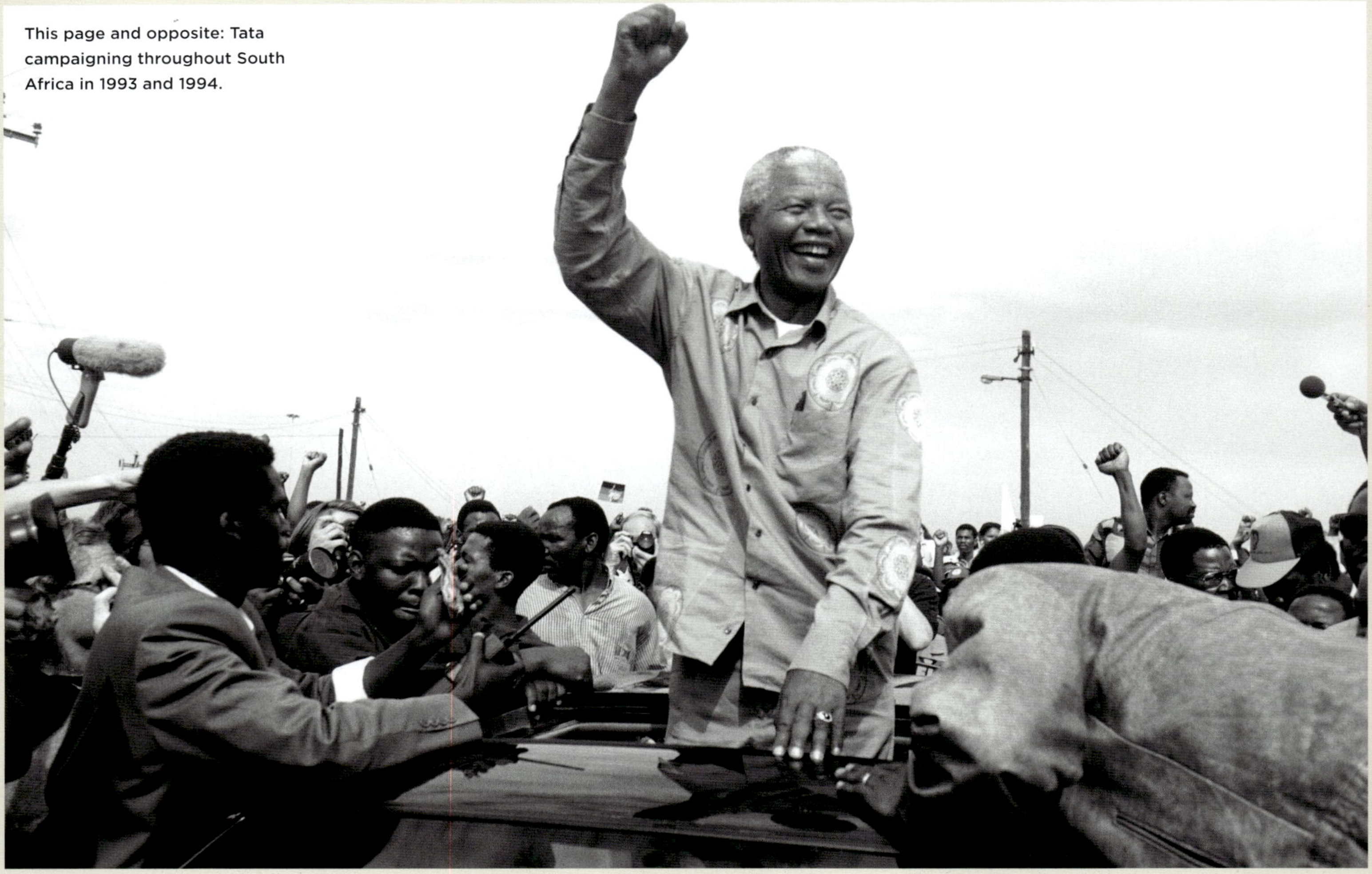

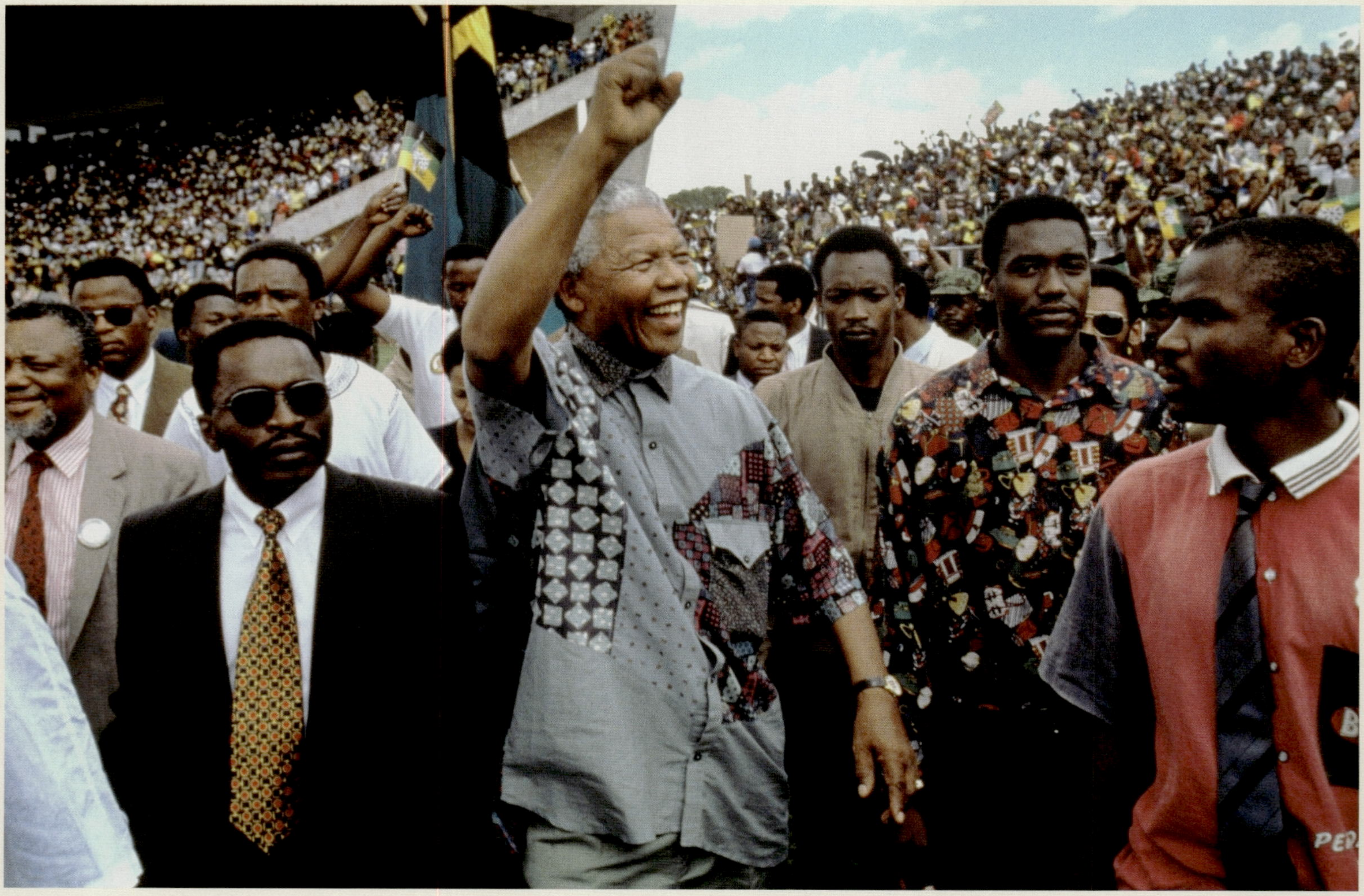

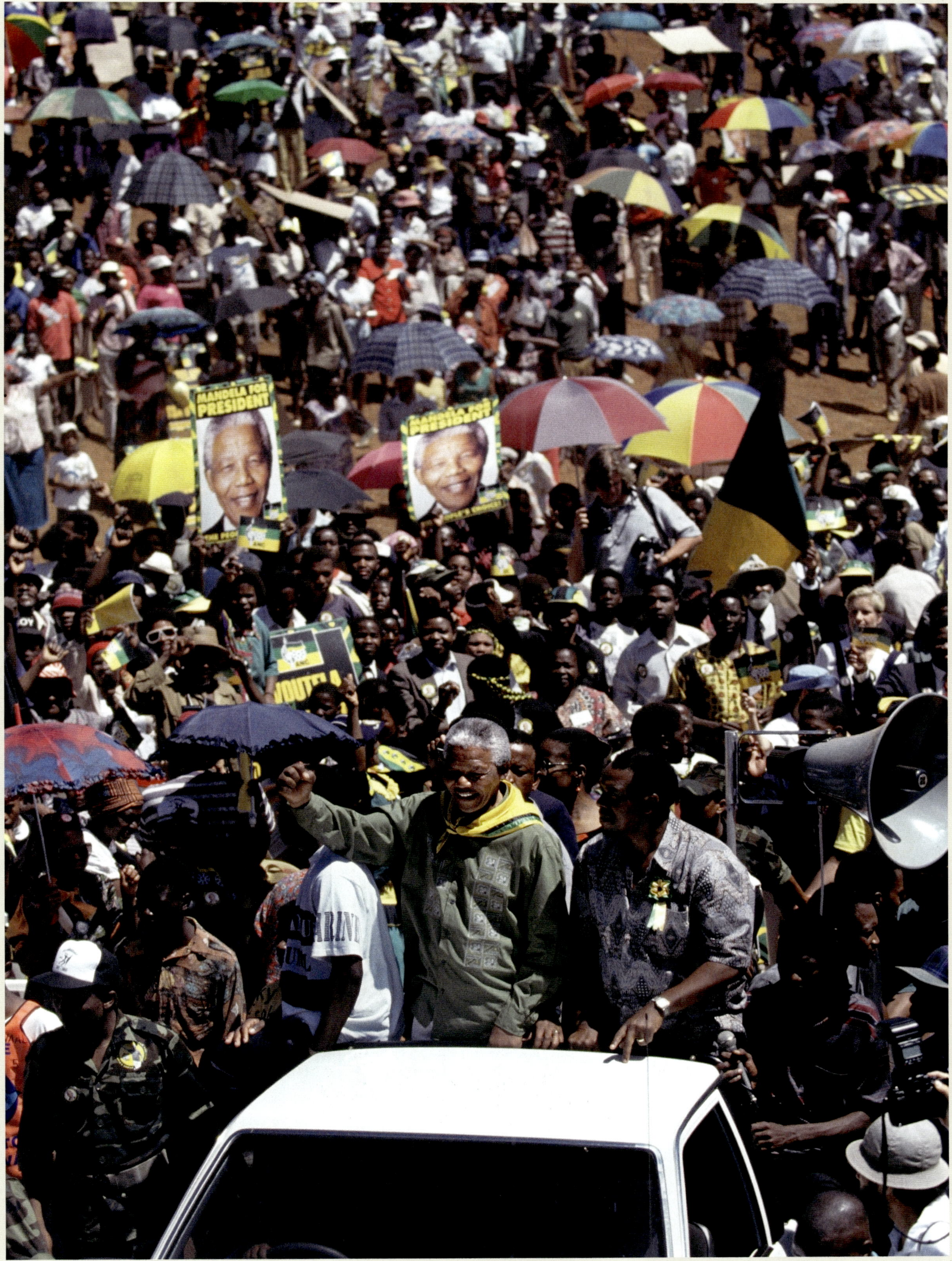
MANDELA FOR
PRESIDENT
MANDELA FOR
PRESIDENT

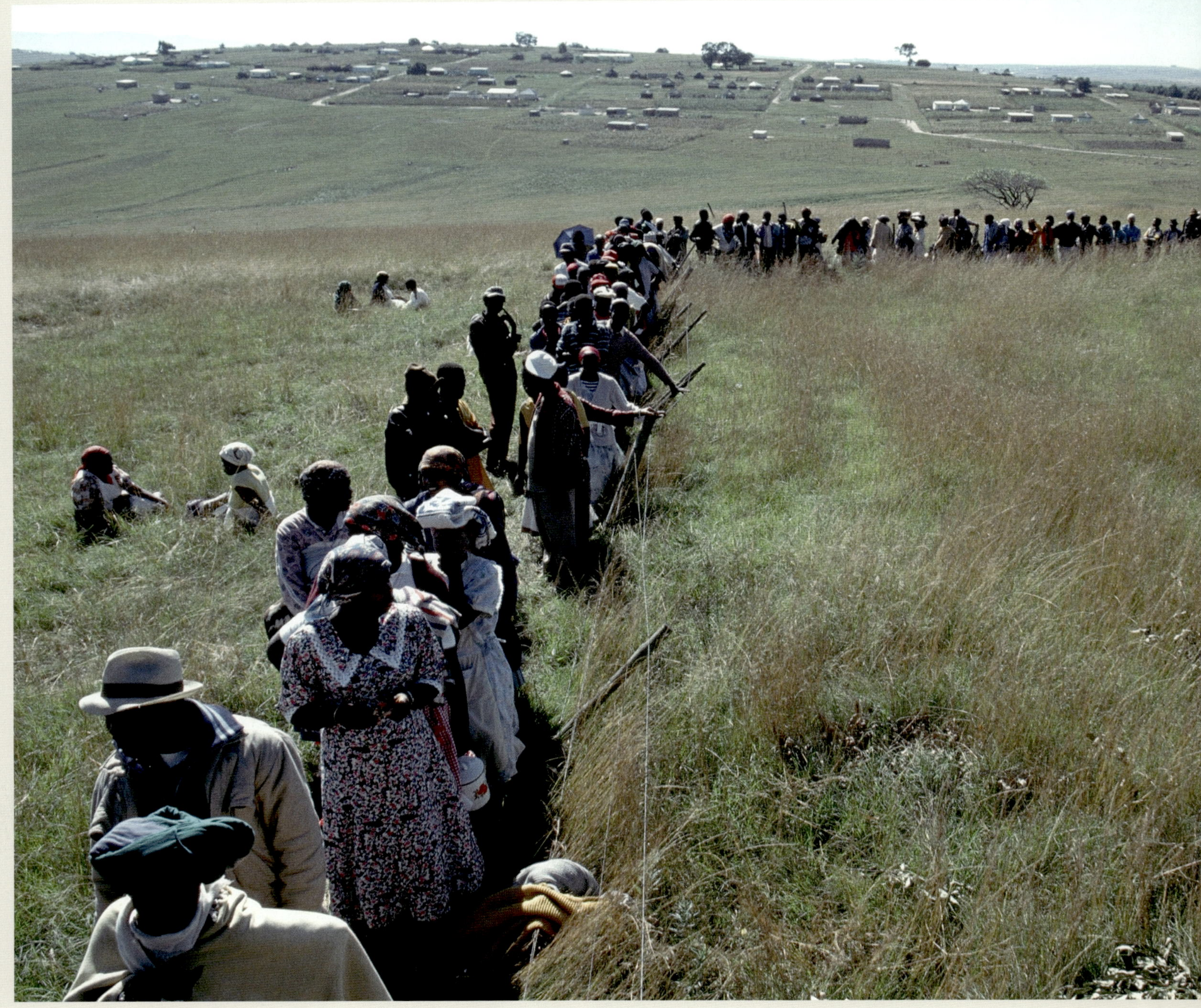

Hundreds of people waiting in line to vote in Tata's home village in 1994.

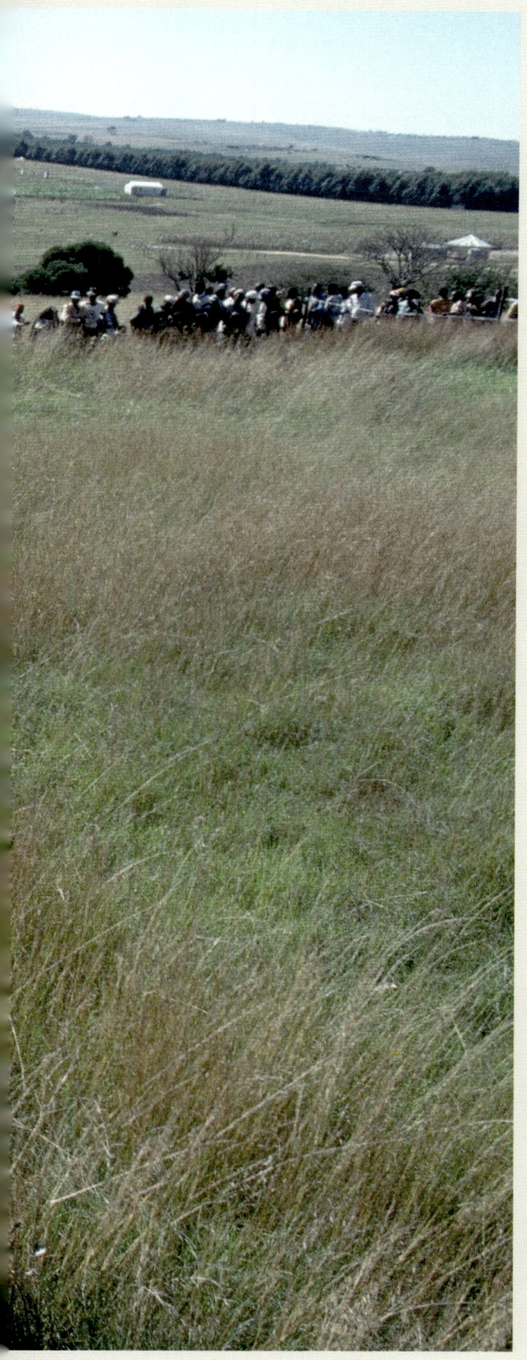

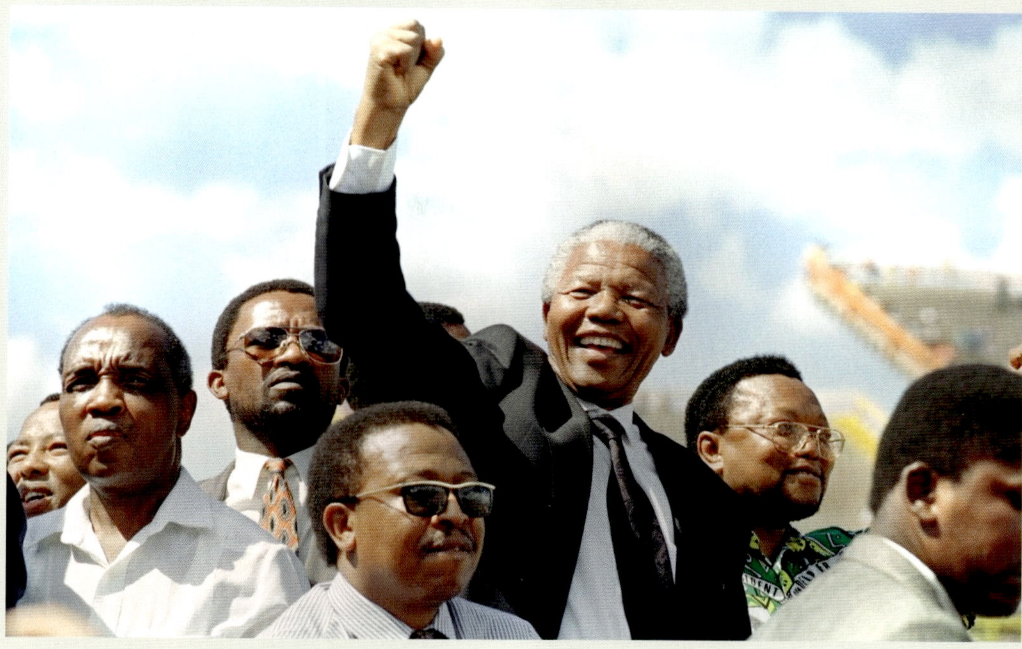

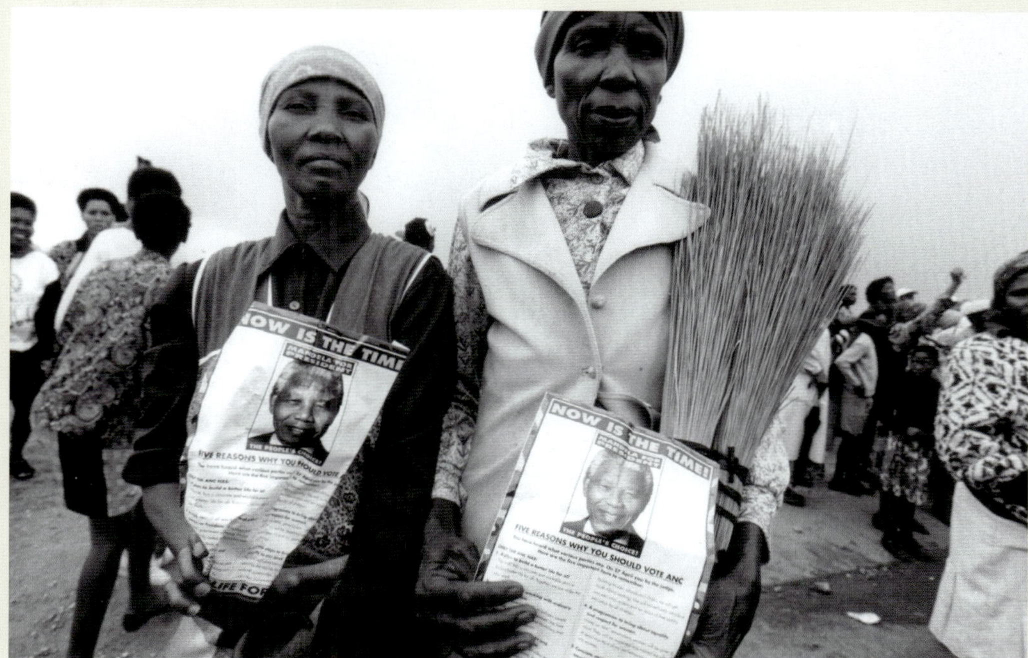

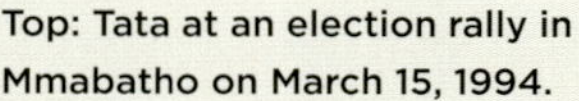

Top: Tata at an election rally in Mmabatho on March 15, 1994.

Middle: Tata's supporters at a rally held in the township of Bophuthatswana.

Right: Voters in an urban township line up to vote for the first time.

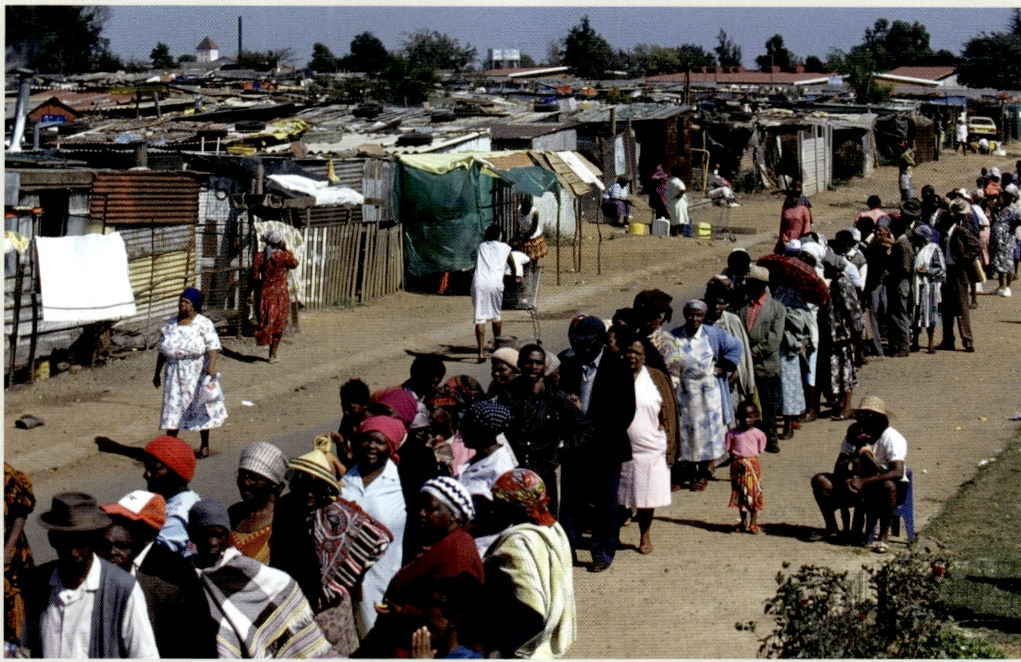

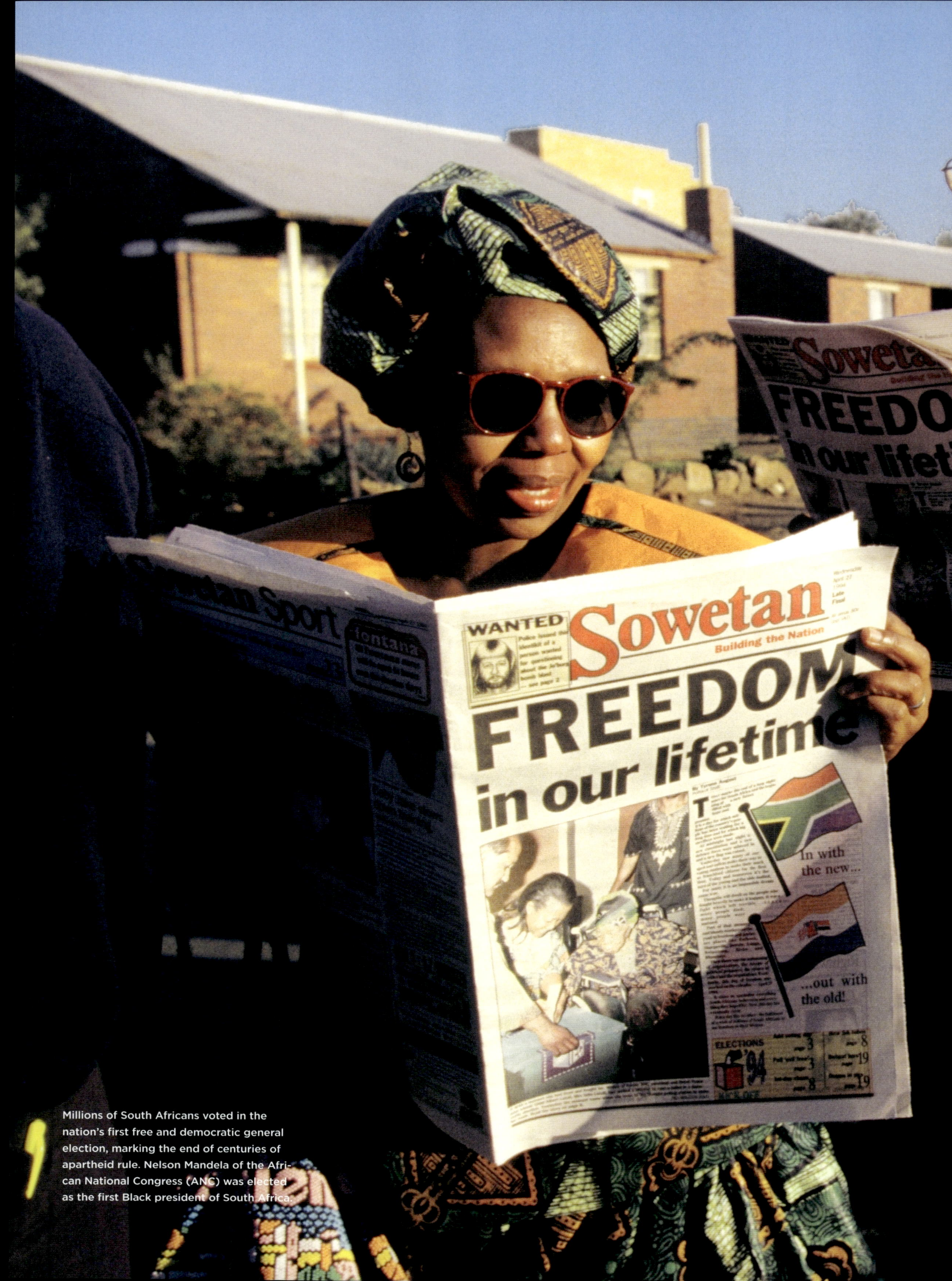

Millions of South Africans voted in the nation's first free and democratic general election, marking the end of centuries of apartheid rule. Nelson Mandela of the African National Congress (ANC) was elected as the first Black president of South Africa.

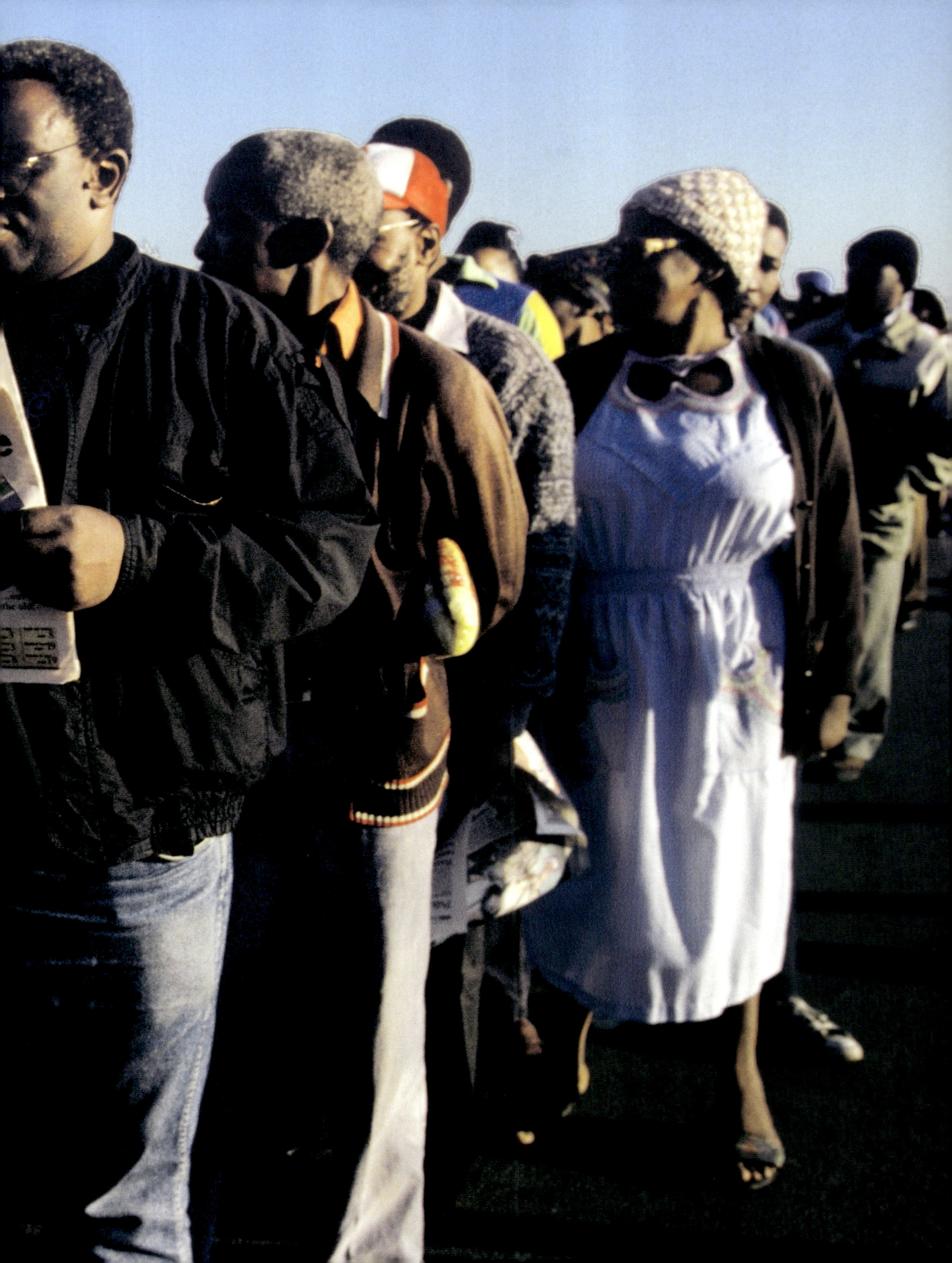

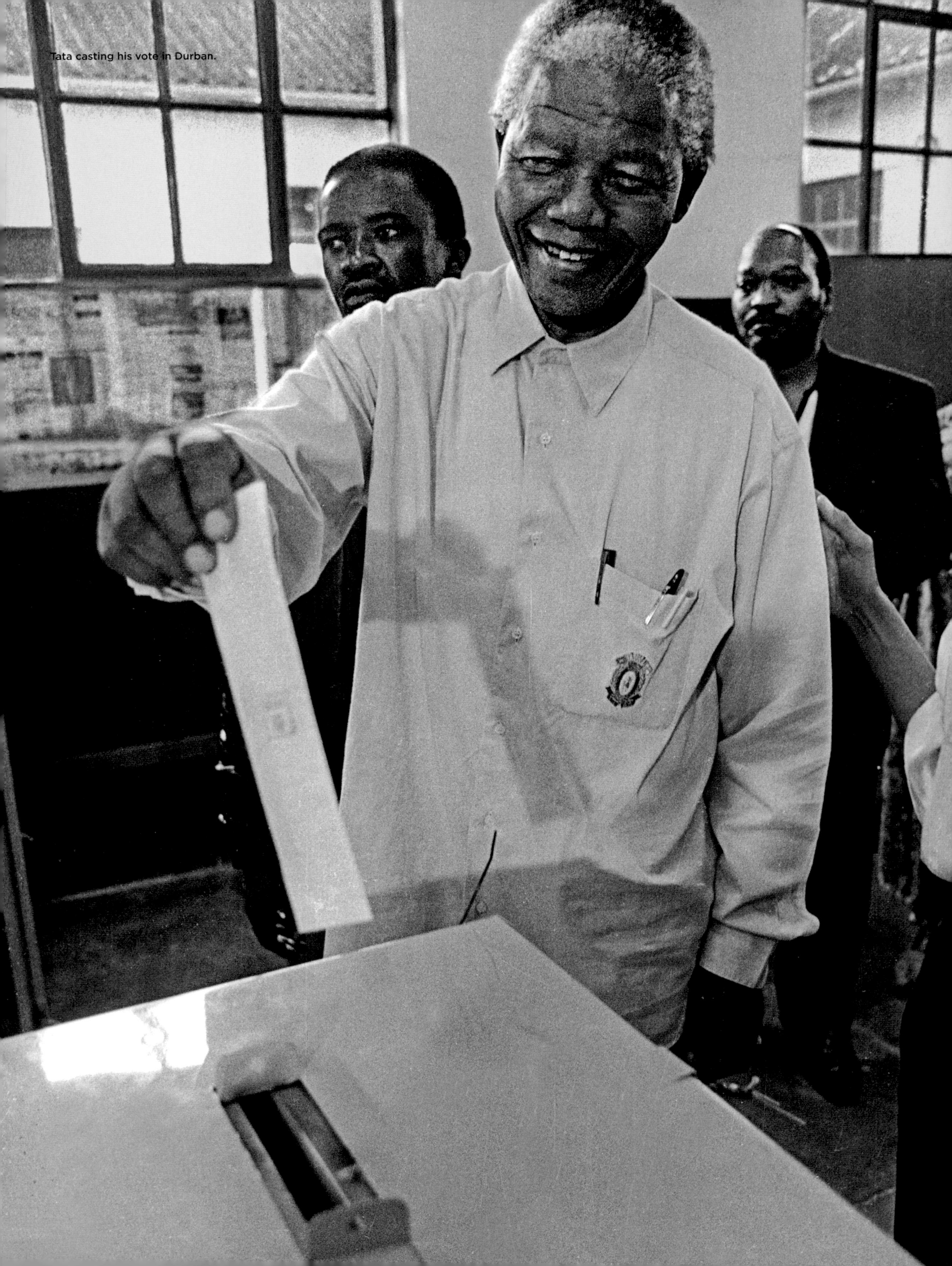

Tata casting his vote in Durban.

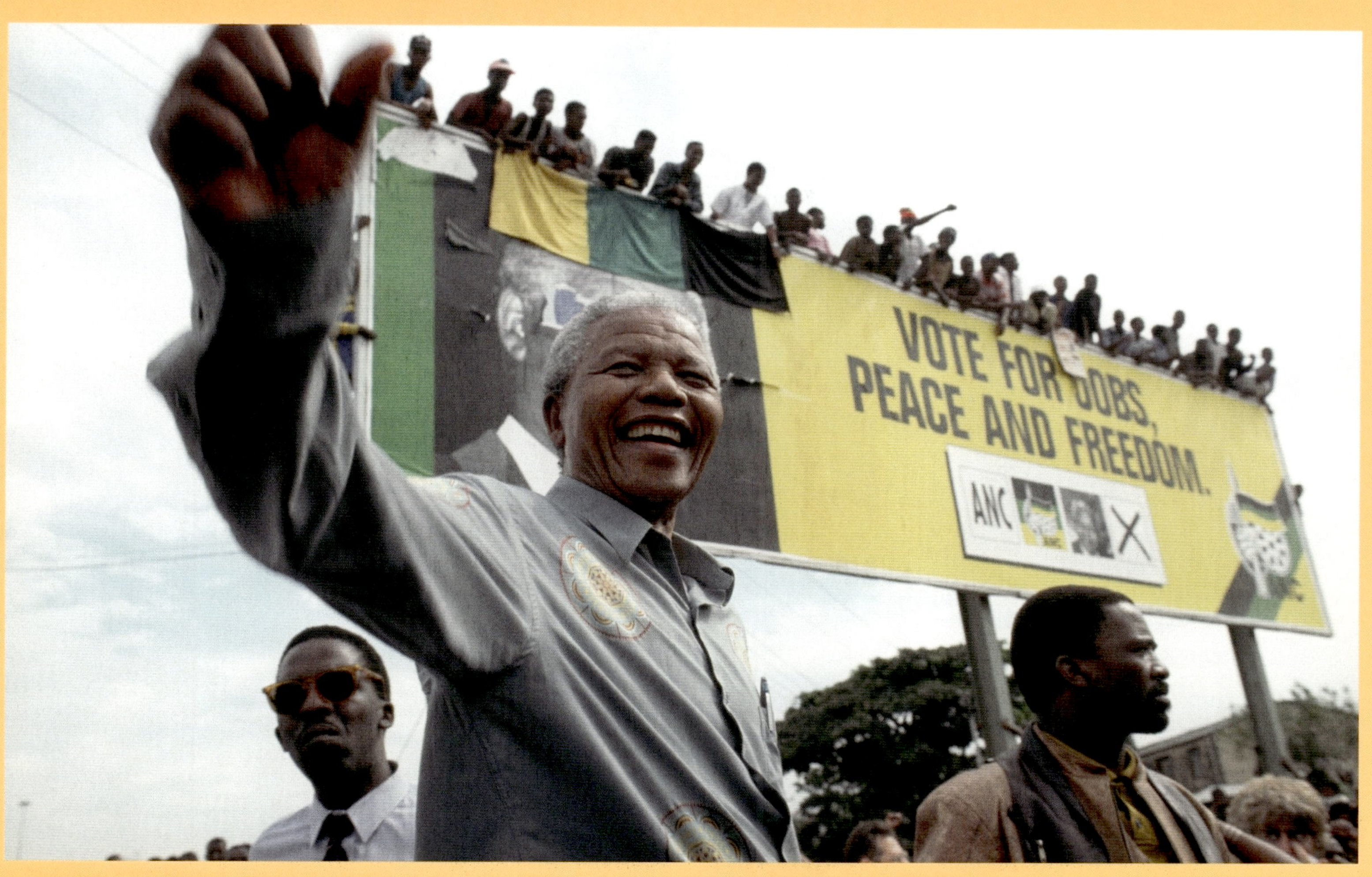

Tata was unanimously elected by parliament as the first president of a democratic South Africa. On May 10, 1994, he was inaugurated as president of the Republic of South Africa. The democratic elections were preceded by a long transition of power from the apartheid regime to an African National Congress–led government, as a result of negotiations among different constituencies, which started when Tata, in consultation with the ANC headquarters in Lusaka, Zambia, was still in prison. The ANC won 62 percent of the national vote. A government of national unity was formed.

BALLOT PAPER

(Make a cross next to the party or organisation of your choice) : Vote for ONE party only

PAN AFRICANIST CONGRESS		PAC		
XIMOKO PROGRESSIVE PARTY		XPP		
AFRICAN NATIONAL CONGRESS		ANC		
AFRIKANER-VOLKSUNIE		AVU		
CONSERVATIVE PARTY		CP		
DEMOCRATIC PARTY		DP		
DIKWANKWETLA PARTY OF SOUTH AFRICA		DPSA		
INKATHA FREEDOM PARTY		IFP		
NATIONAL PARTY		NP		

*This is a sample and not an official ballot paper.
Some of the above political parties / organisations may choose not to enter the elections.
A Project Vote / Veetu Ballot Form

Top: Tata's supporters cheer from atop a billboard during his campaign for president.

Above: A sample ballot from the 1994 election.

From the beginning, Tata was committed to serving only a single five-year term.

On May 10, 1994, my father gave a powerful speech at his inauguration as president of the Republic of South Africa:

Your Majesties
Your Highnesses
Distinguished Guests
Comrades and Friends

Today, all of us do, by our presence here, and by our celebrations in other parts of our country and the world, confer glory and hope to newborn liberty.

Out of the experience of an extraordinary human disaster that lasted too long, must be born a society of which all humanity will be proud. Our daily deeds as ordinary South Africans must produce an actual South African reality that will reinforce humanity's belief in justice, strengthen its confidence in the nobility of the human soul, and sustain all our hopes for a glorious life for all.

All this we owe both to ourselves and to the peoples of the world who are so well represented here today.

To my compatriots, I have no hesitation in saying that each one of us is as intimately attached to the soil of this beautiful country as are the famous jacaranda trees of Pretoria and the mimosa trees of the bushveld.

Each time one of us touches the soil of this land, we feel a sense of personal renewal. The national mood changes as the seasons change. We are moved by a sense of joy and exhilaration when the grass turns green and the flowers bloom.

That spiritual and physical oneness we all share with this common homeland explains the depth of the pain we all carried in our hearts as we saw our country tear itself apart in a terrible conflict, and as we saw it spurned, outlawed, and isolated by the peoples of the world, precisely because it has become the universal base of the pernicious ideology and practice of racism and racial oppression.

We, the people of South Africa, feel fulfilled that humanity has taken us back into its bosom, that we, who were outlaws not so long ago, have today been given the rare privilege to be host to the nations of the world on our own soil.

We thank all our distinguished international guests for having come to take possession with the people of our country of what is, after all, a common victory for justice, for peace, for human dignity.

We trust that you will continue to stand by us as we tackle the challenges of building peace, prosperity, non-sexism, non-racialism, and democracy.

We deeply appreciate the role that the masses of our people and their political mass democratic, religious, women, youth, business, traditional, and other leaders have played to

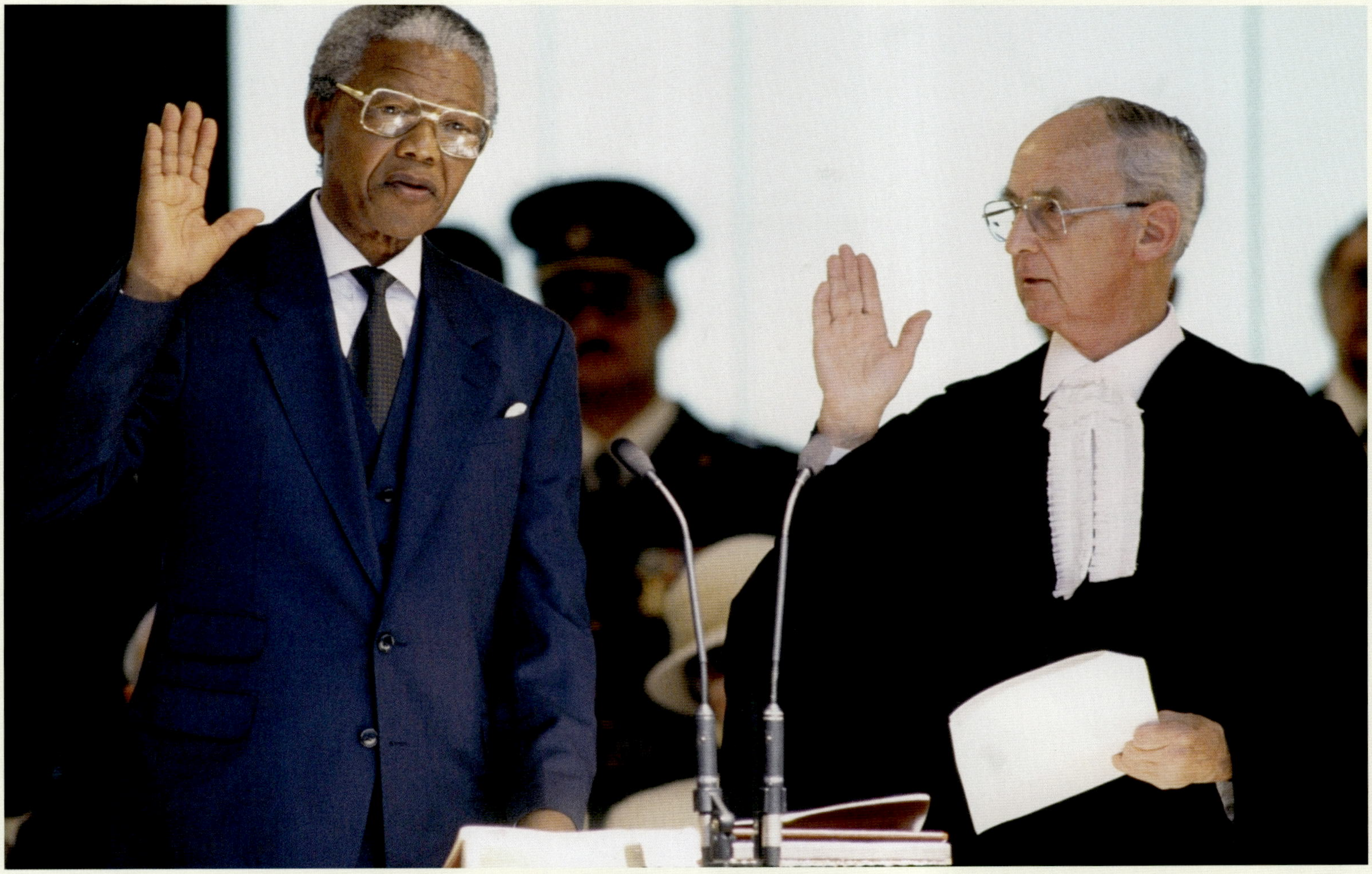

Tata being sworn as president of the Republic of South Africa on May 10, 1994.

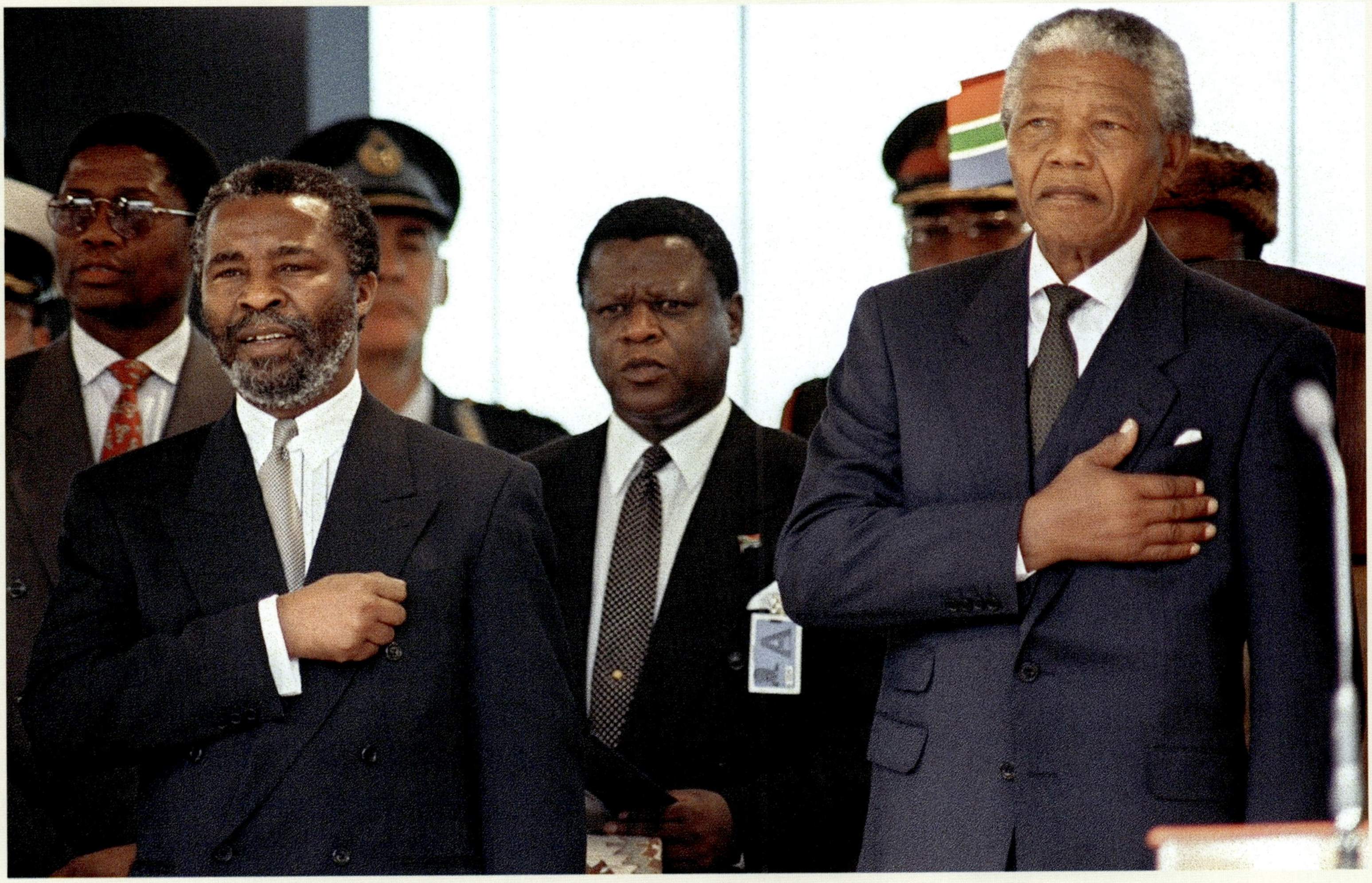

Vice President Thabo Mbeki and Tata during his inauguration at the Union Building in Pretoria.

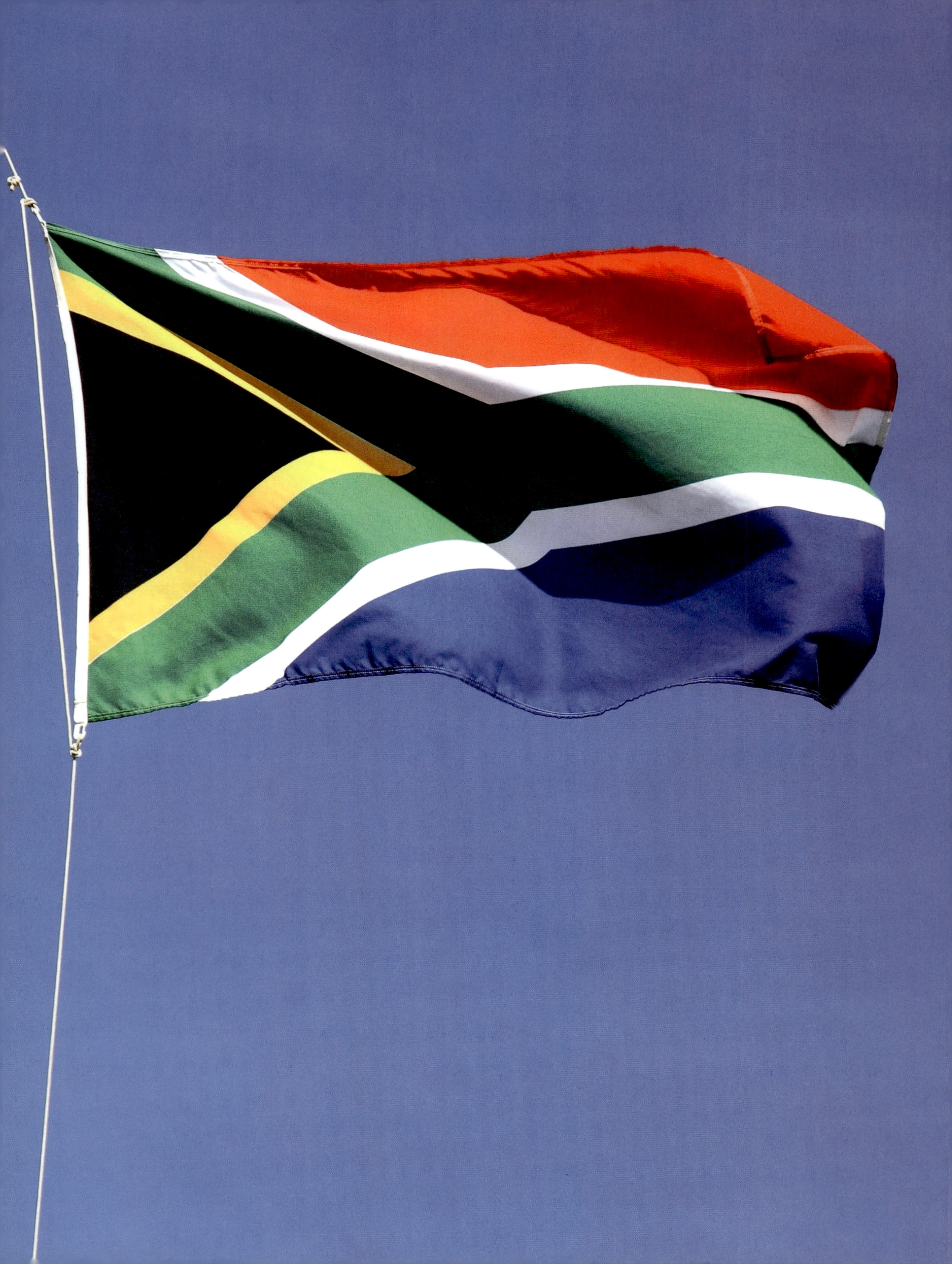

bring about this conclusion. Not least among them is my second deputy president, the Honorable F. W. de Klerk.

We would also like to pay tribute to our security forces, in all their ranks, for the distinguished role they have played in securing our first democratic elections and the transition to democracy, from blood-thirsty forces which still refuse to see the light.

The time for the healing of the wounds has come.

The moment to bridge the chasms that divide us has come.

The time to build is upon us.

We have, at last, achieved our political emancipation. We pledge ourselves to liberate all our people from the continuing bondage of poverty, deprivation, suffering, gender, and other discrimination.

We succeeded to take our last steps to freedom in conditions of relative peace.

We commit ourselves to the construction of a complete, just, and lasting peace.

We have triumphed in the effort to implant hope in the breasts of the millions of our people. We enter into a covenant that we shall build the society in which all South Africans, both black and white, will be able to walk tall, without any fear in their hearts, assured of their inalienable right to human dignity, a rainbow nation at peace with itself and the world.

As a token of its commitment to the renewal of our country, the new interim Government of National Unity will, as a matter of urgency, address the issue of amnesty for various categories of our people who are currently serving terms of imprisonment.

We dedicate this day to all the heroes and heroines in this country and the rest of the world who sacrificed in many ways and surrendered their lives so that we could be free. Their dreams have become reality.

Freedom is their reward.

We are both humbled and elevated by the honor and privilege that you, the people of South Africa, have bestowed on us, as the first president of a united, democratic, non-racial, and non-sexist South Africa, to lead our country out of the valley of darkness.

We understand it still that there is no easy road to freedom.

We know it well that none of us acting alone can achieve success.

We must therefore act together as a united people, for national reconciliation, for nation building, for the birth of a new world.

Let there be justice for all.

Let there be peace for all.

Let there be work, bread, water, and salt for all.

Let each know that for each the body, the mind, and the soul have been freed to fulfill themselves.

Never, never, and never again shall it be that this beautiful land will again experience the oppression of one by another and suffer the indignity of being the skunk of the world.

Let freedom reign.

The sun shall never set on so glorious a human achievement!

God bless Africa! Thank you.

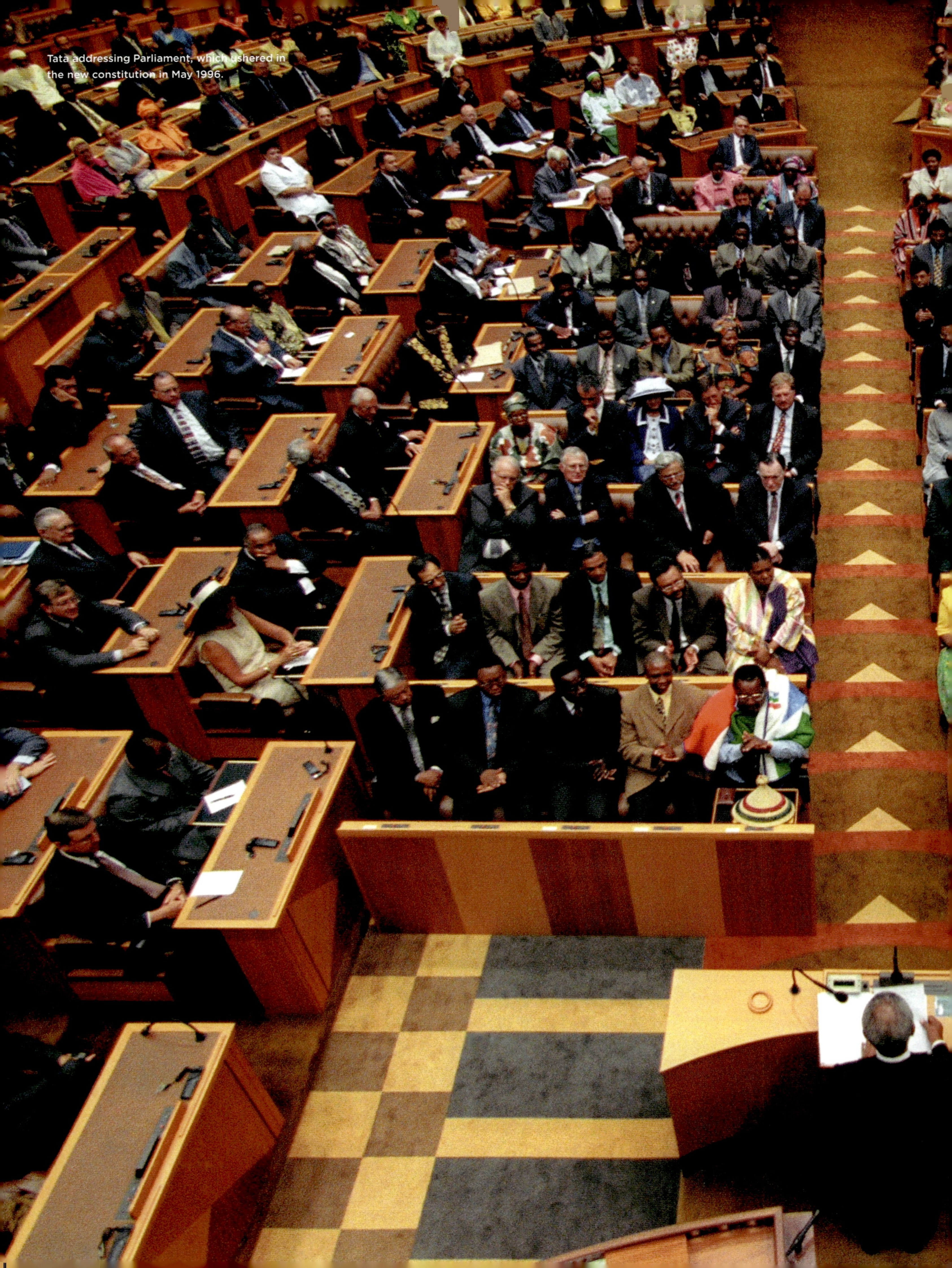

Tata addressing Parliament, which ushered in the new constitution in May 1996.

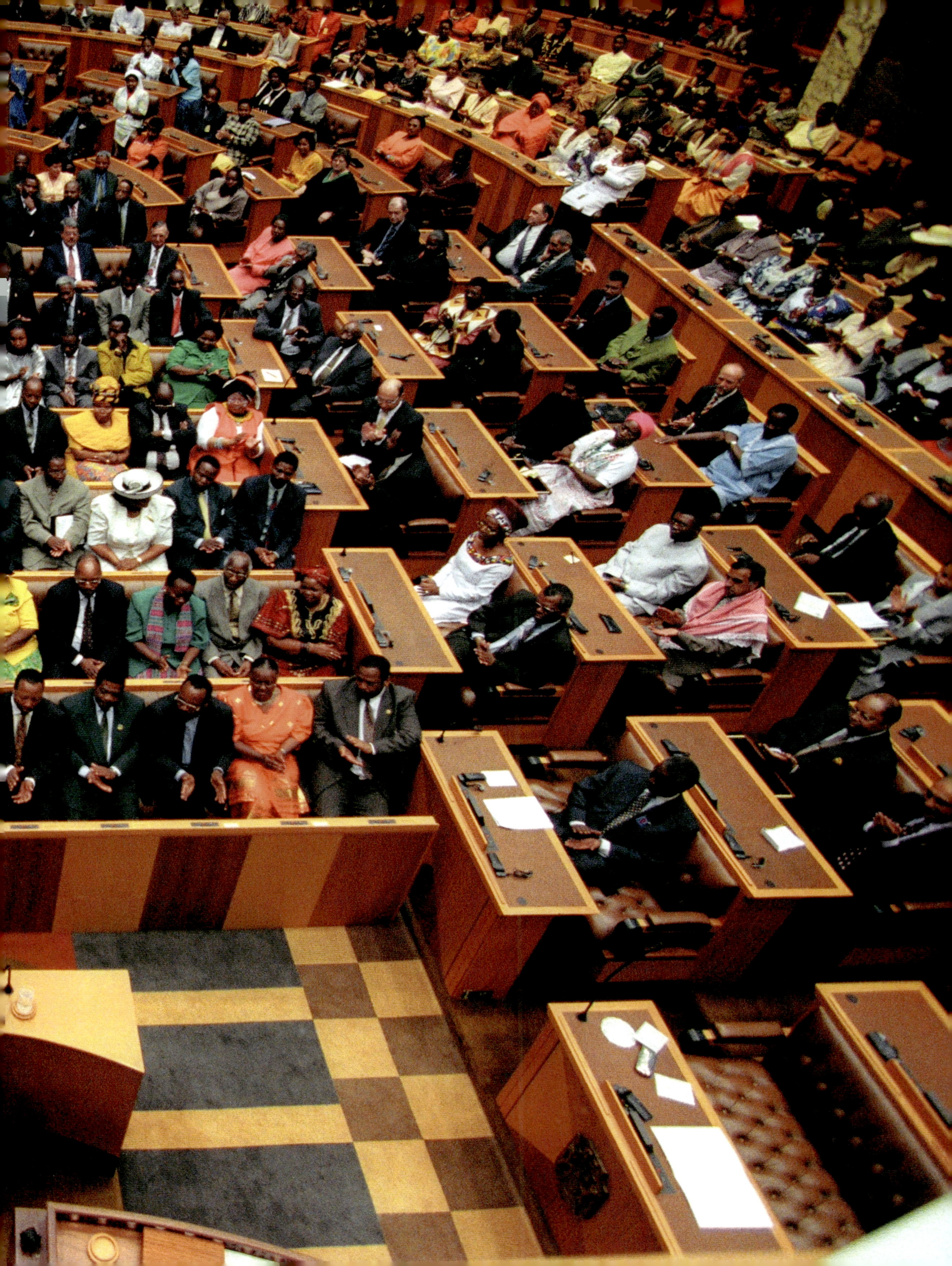

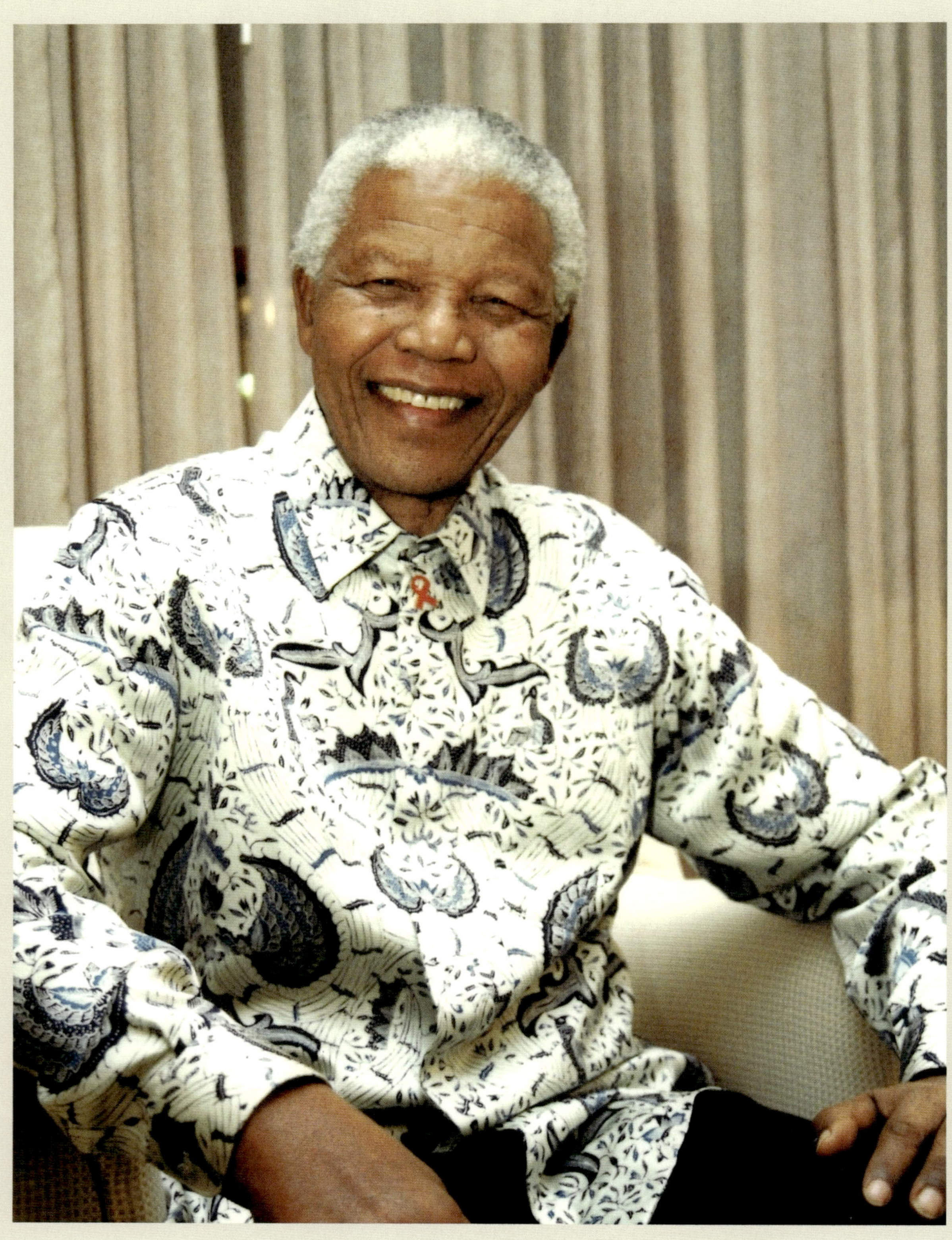

When Tata walked out of prison in 1990, he did not consider himself a free man; for him, there was no freedom for one man without the freedom for all. He fought hard to bequeath us the political freedom all South Africans enjoy today.

"Of course, you cannot know a man completely, his character, his principles, sense of judgment, not till he's shown his colors, ruling the people, making laws. Experience, there's the test."

Creon in *Antigone* by Sophocles

Tata viewed his life as part of the revolutionary generation that was called upon to change history and create a united democratic society. Tata fought for the healing of our nation and abhorred strife among races. Following deep discussions, it was Tata and his comrades' conciliatory tone, moral nobility, calm persuasion, and adept negotiating skills that created unity.

Upon assuming office, Tata announced a number of presidential initiatives, including free health care for mothers and children, as well as food programs in primary schools. His administration practiced disciplined management of public finances in which tight controls on public expenditure eliminated a public debt of 250 billion South African rands, while at the same time redirecting resources from richer communities to poor ones. In 1999, the Mandela government took steps to alleviate poverty by building low-cost homes, extending clean water, expanding the provisions of health care, and spending more money in schools in Black neighborhoods. Despite these measures, unemployment continued to rise.

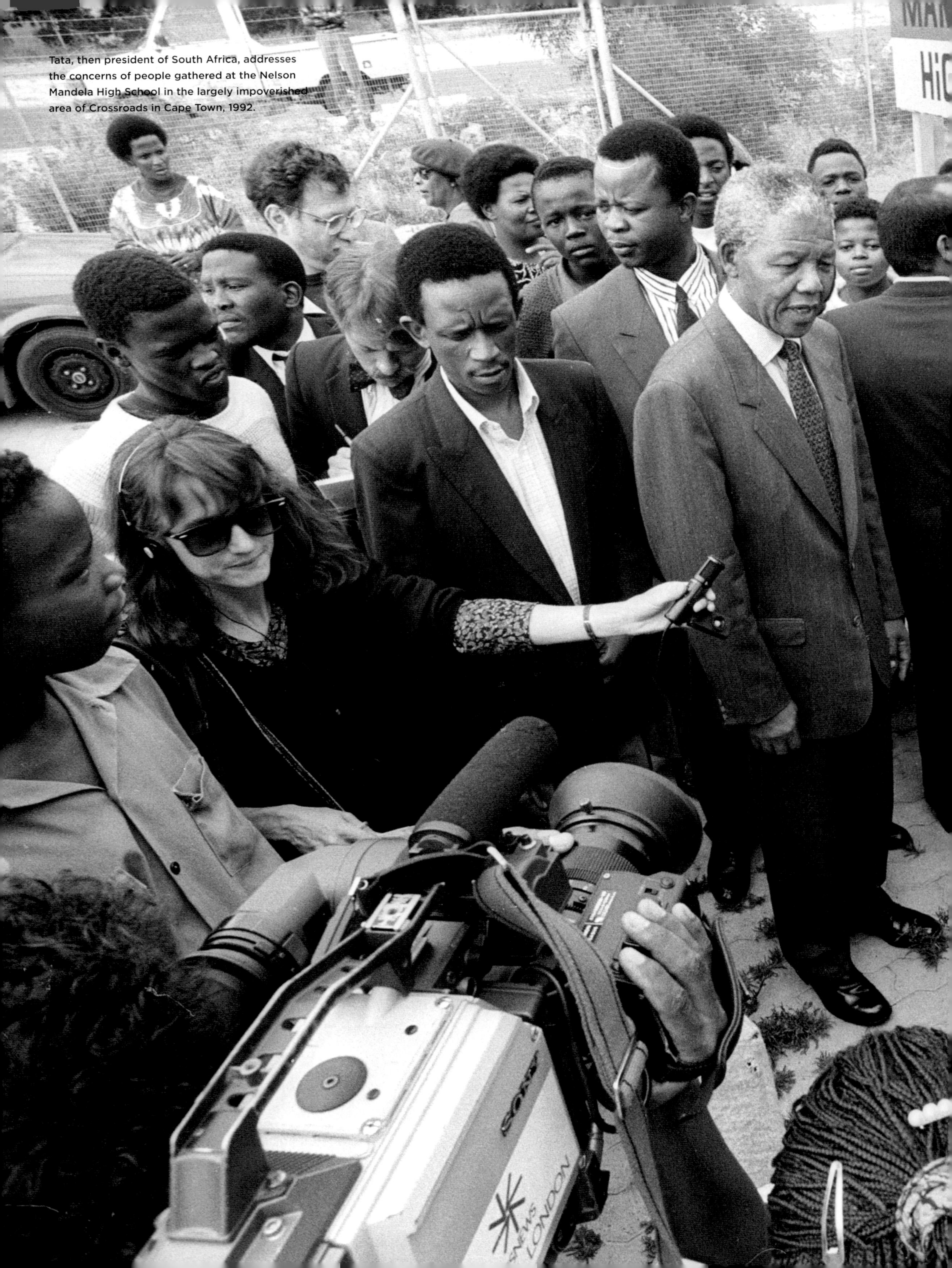

Tata, then president of South Africa, addresses the concerns of people gathered at the Nelson Mandela High School in the largely impoverished area of Crossroads in Cape Town, 1992.

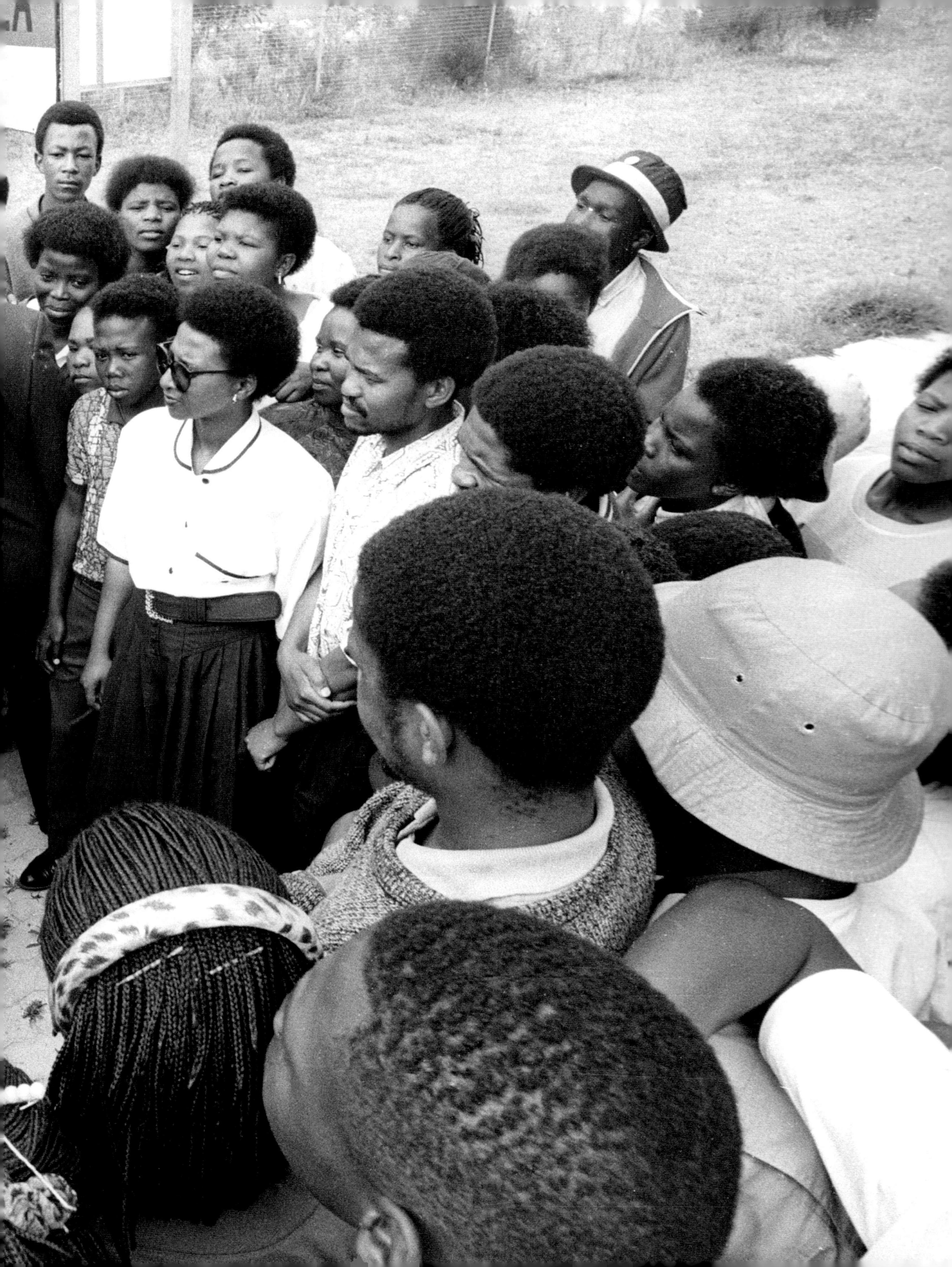

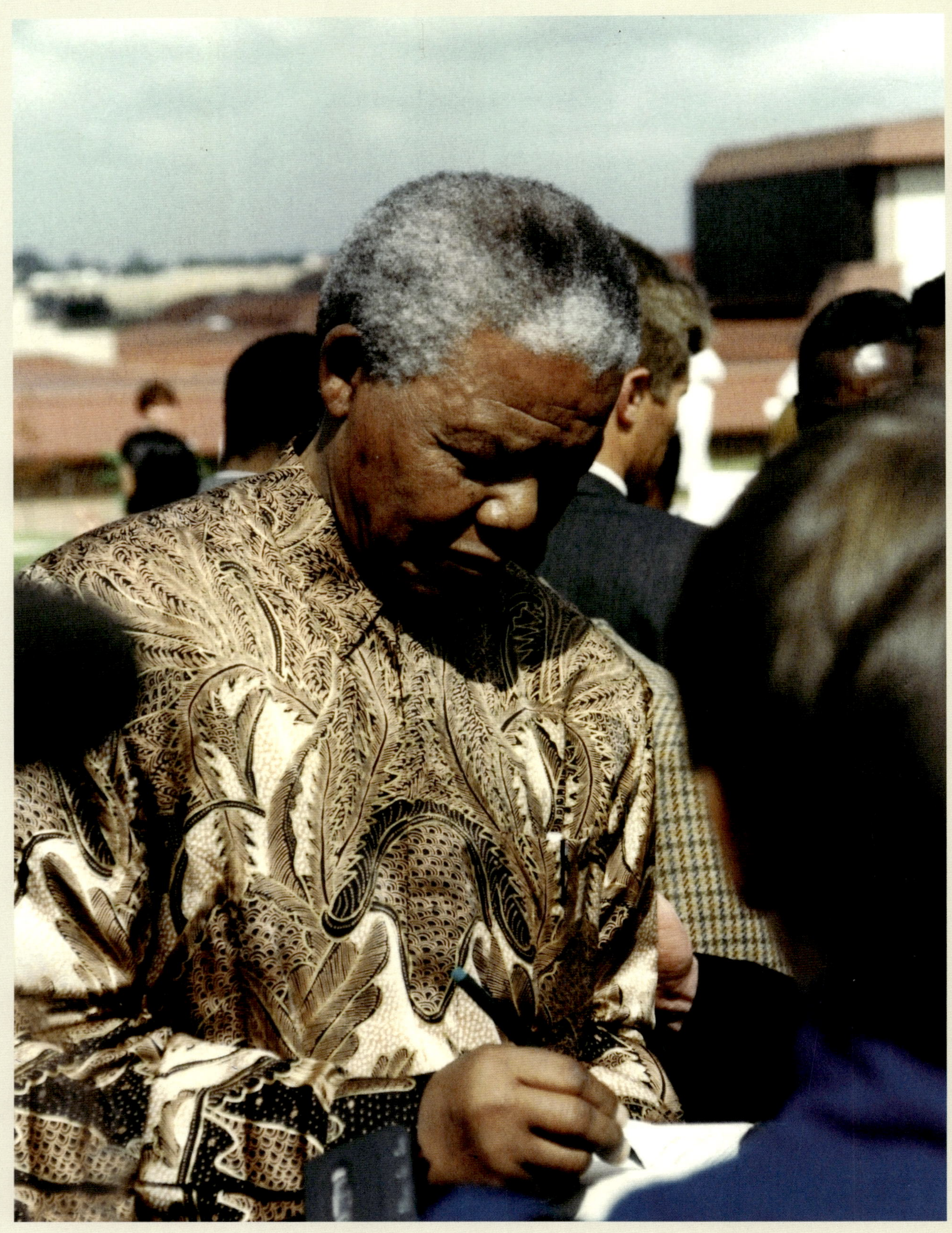

"There can be no keener revelation of a society's soul than the way it treats its children."

From a speech Tata gave at the launch of the Nelson Mandela Children's Fund, May 8, 1995

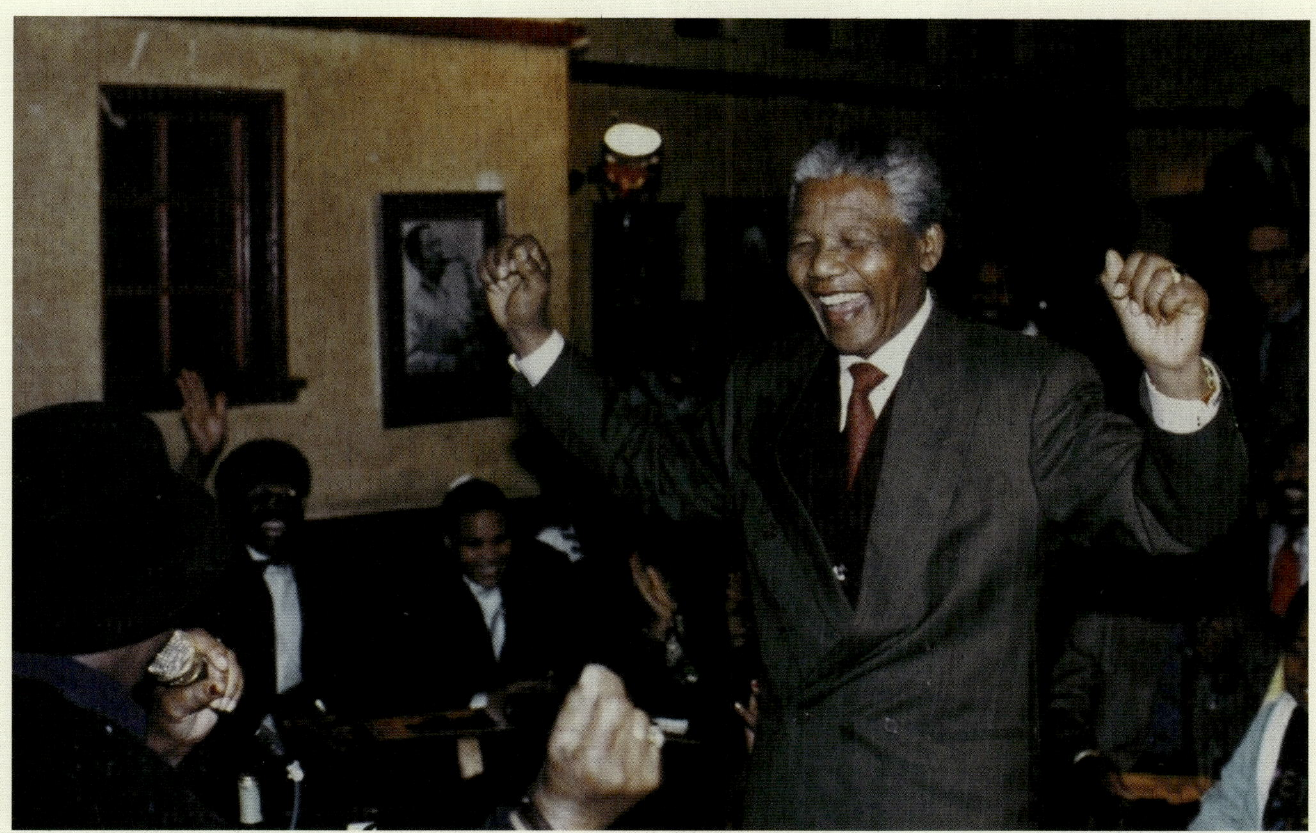

Tata enjoying music on a trip to Portugal prior to his presidency.

Prior to his inauguration, the Mandela government-in-waiting encouraged the right-wing and historically revolutionary Inkatha Freedom Party to participate in the elections and be part of a coalition government. This compromise was a masterstroke; it created stability that allowed a government of national unity to exist. At the beginning of his administration, Tata used his position as president of the republic to appoint ministers from outside his party, both to reassure former and potential adversaries, and to achieve broader diversity in his cabinet. The brutal history of state-sanctioned racism had left scars; few within or without the political sphere felt confident in a peaceful transition from apartheid to a multiracial democracy.

Tata's inclusive social nationalism was an effort to ground the country and inspire optimism by suggesting the possibilities of a reconciliation of political factions and a better balance of racial representation in government. However, the economic policies established by Tata's administration failed to reduce poverty rates for the majority of Black people. Tata and his cabinet had assumed office with no experience in elections, parliamentary practices, or state legislation; they went directly from prison and the bush to the senior offices and administration of a complex, sophisticated, and highly developed country. Such have been the challenges faced by postcolonial leaders in countries across the continent of Africa, with or without my father's commitment to a peaceful ideology.

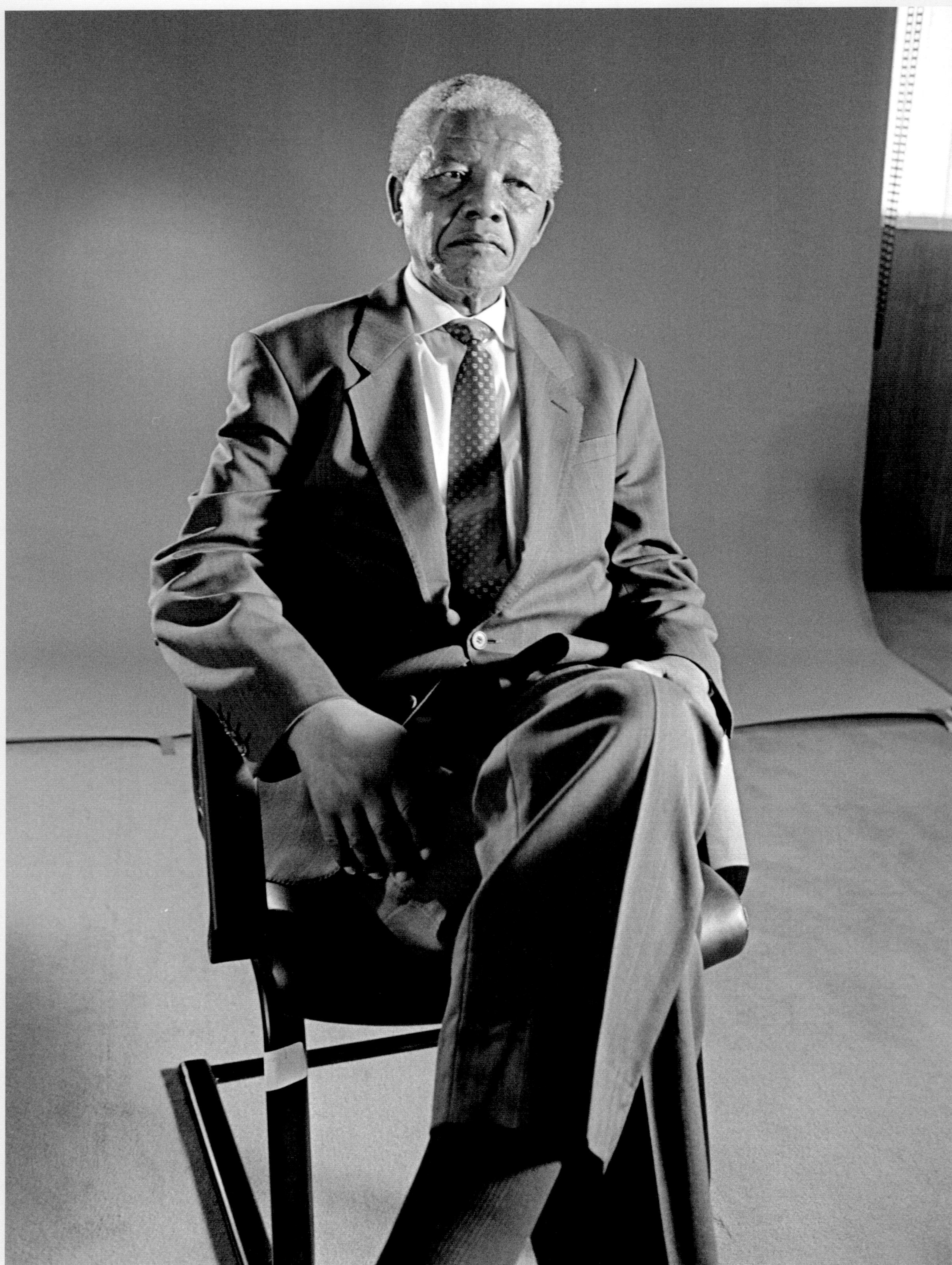

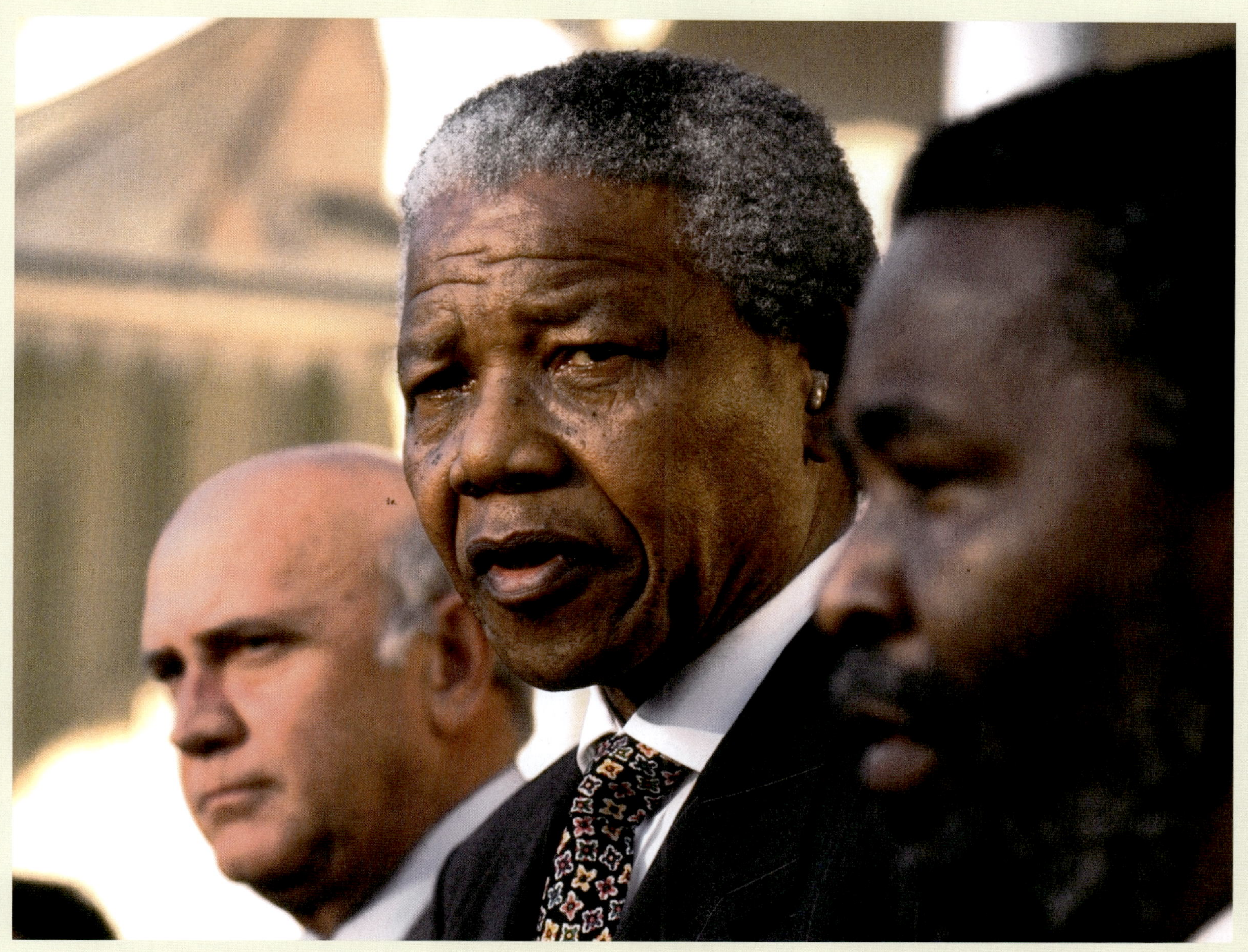

Opposite: Tata sitting for a photographer, circa 1995.

Above: Tata flanked by deputy presidents Thabo Mbeki (*right*) and F. W. de Klerk.

Even today, true freedom remains elusive for millions of unemployed youth and others mired in poverty. Tata recognized the enormous challenges that lay ahead, even in South Africa's hour of victory. In a speech on April 27, 1998, he said:

"Our freedom and our rights will only gain their full meaning as we succeed together in overcoming the divisions and inequalities of our past and improving the lives of, especially, the poor."

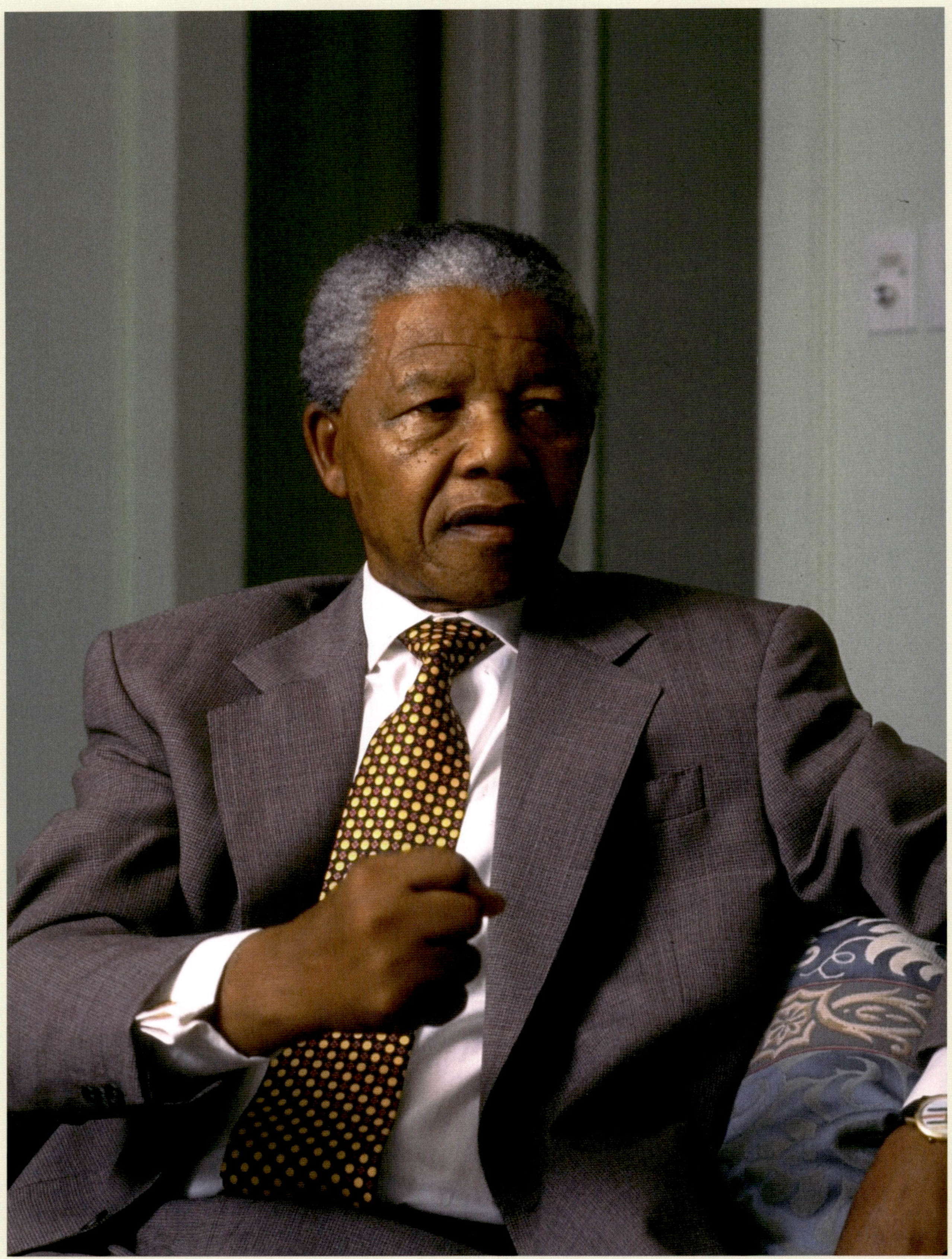

Above: Tata, during an interview with *Time* magazine.

Opposite: Tata meeting with President George H. W. Bush in the White House, June 1990.

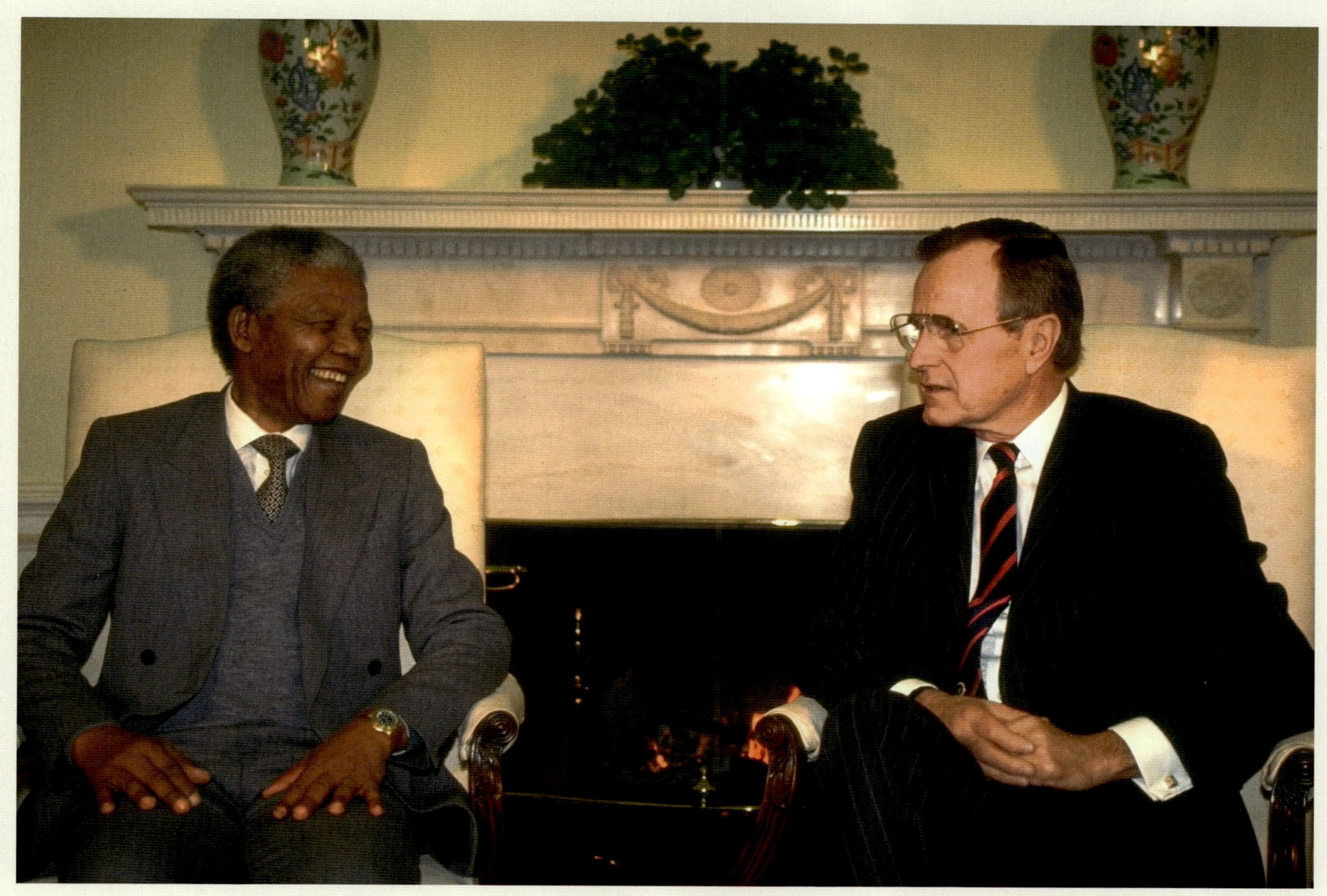

"Though the old lines no longer have the force of the laws, they are still visible in social and economic life—in our residential areas, in our workplaces, between rich and poor. When we celebrate the start that we have made in undoing that legacy, it is in the knowledge there is still much to be done."

Tata in his book, *From Freedom to the Future*

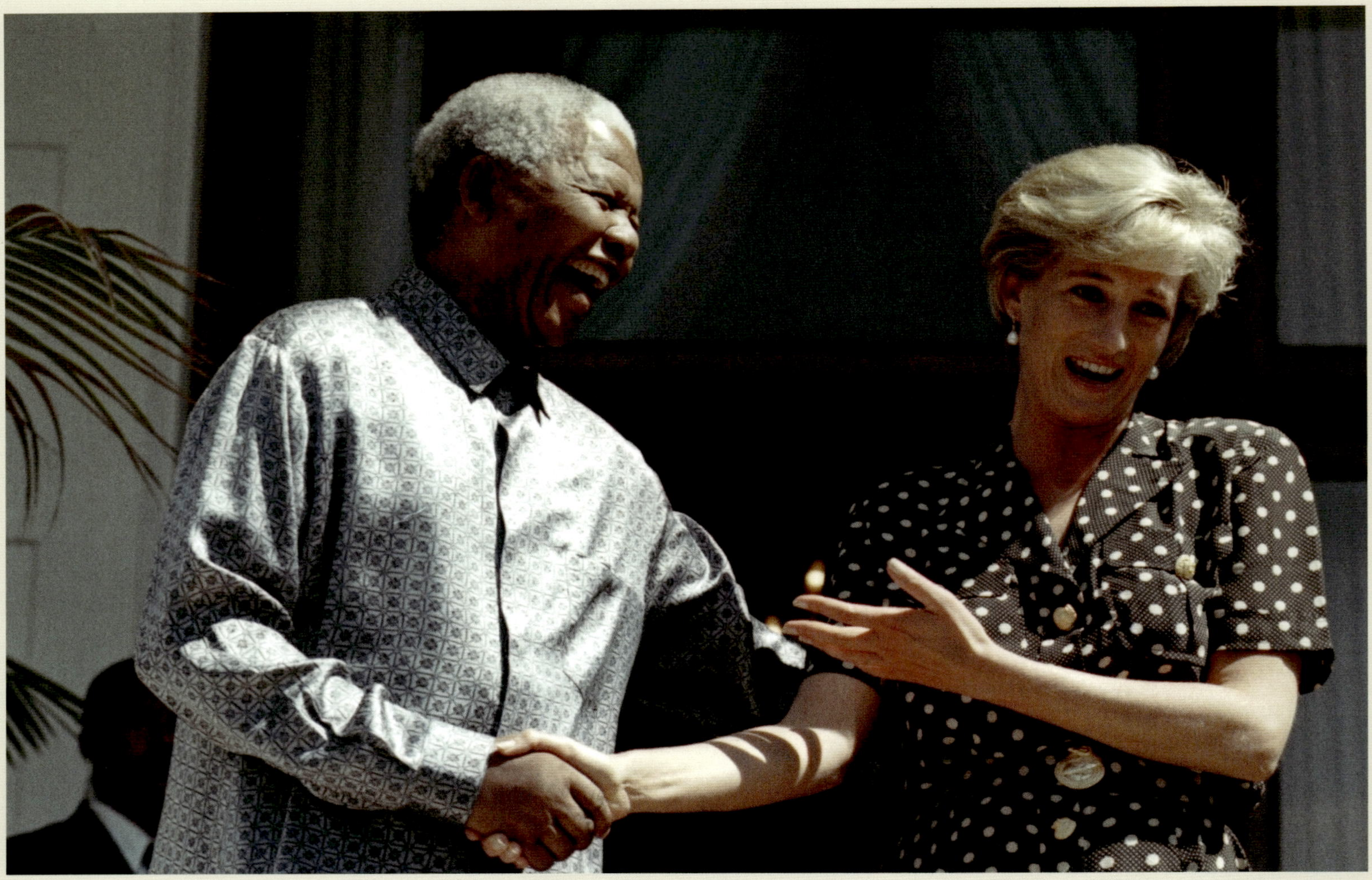

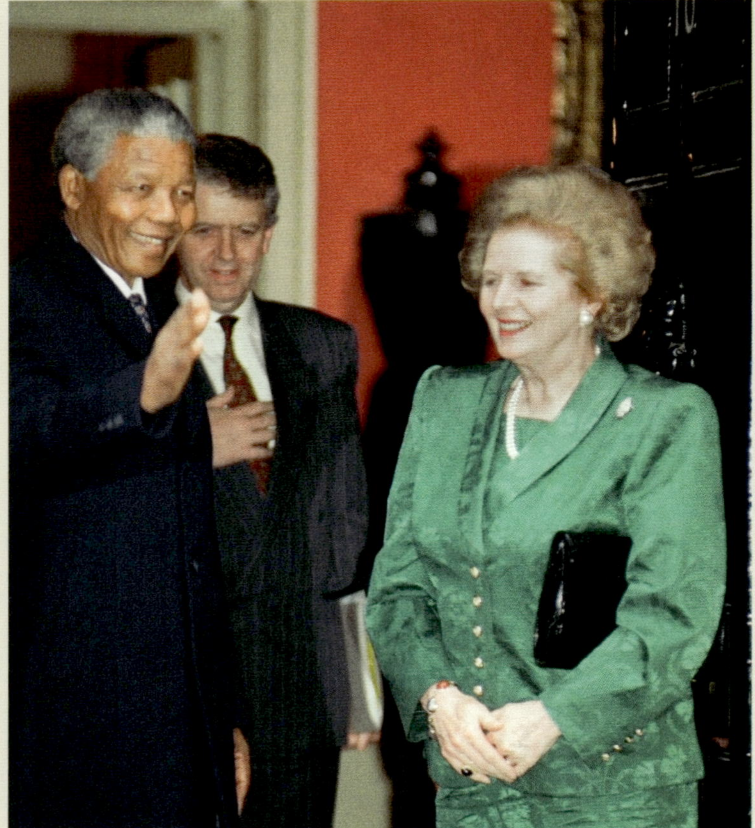

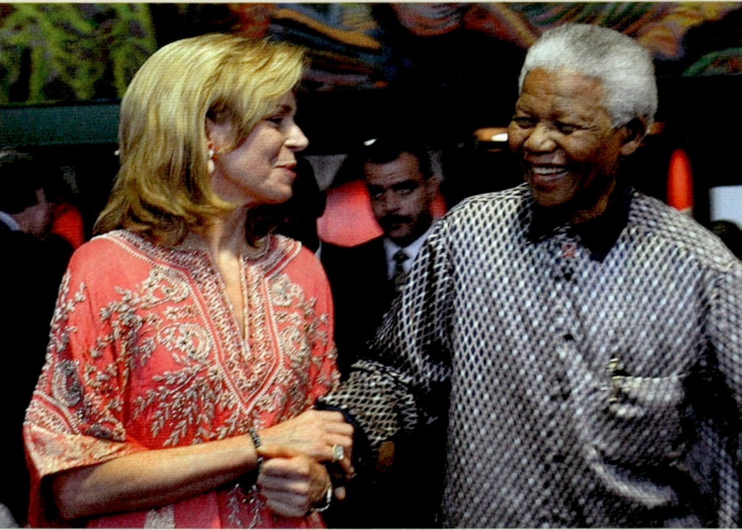

Top: Tata meeting Diana, Princess of Wales, in Cape Town, March 1997.

Left: Tata meeting Prime Minister Margaret Thatcher, July 4, 1990.

Above: Queen Noor of Jordan and Tata at the opening of the fifth World Parks Congress in Durban on September 8, 2003.

Tata was loved and revered across the globe by ordinary people, international political leaders, and celebrities.

He particularly loved and admired Princess Diana. He felt she displayed courage in embracing people with AIDS, especially children, and also for going to Angola to raise awareness about the demining of landmines. Tata truly admired people who would rise above bitterness and revenge and use their capacity to demonstrate generosity of spirit as Diana did during her short life.

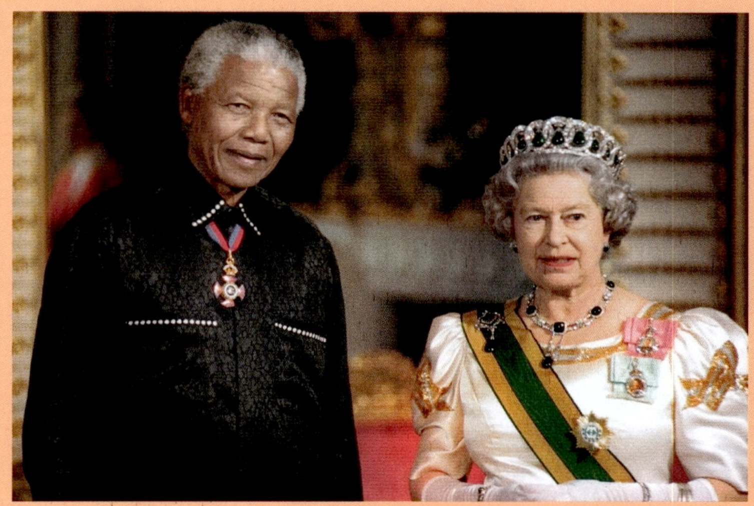

Tata and Queen Elizabeth II enjoyed a warm friendship, referring to each other by their first names.

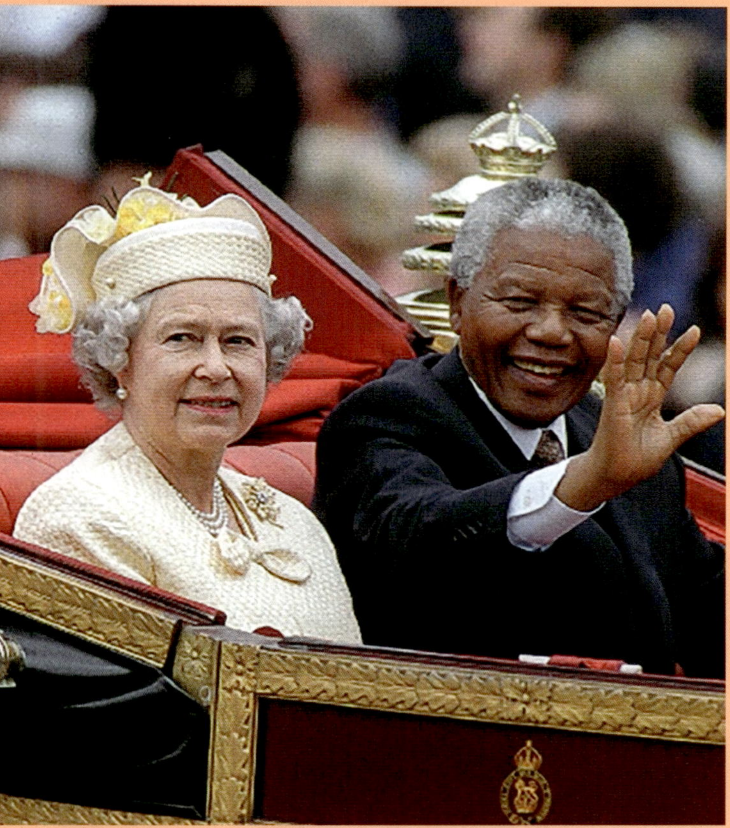

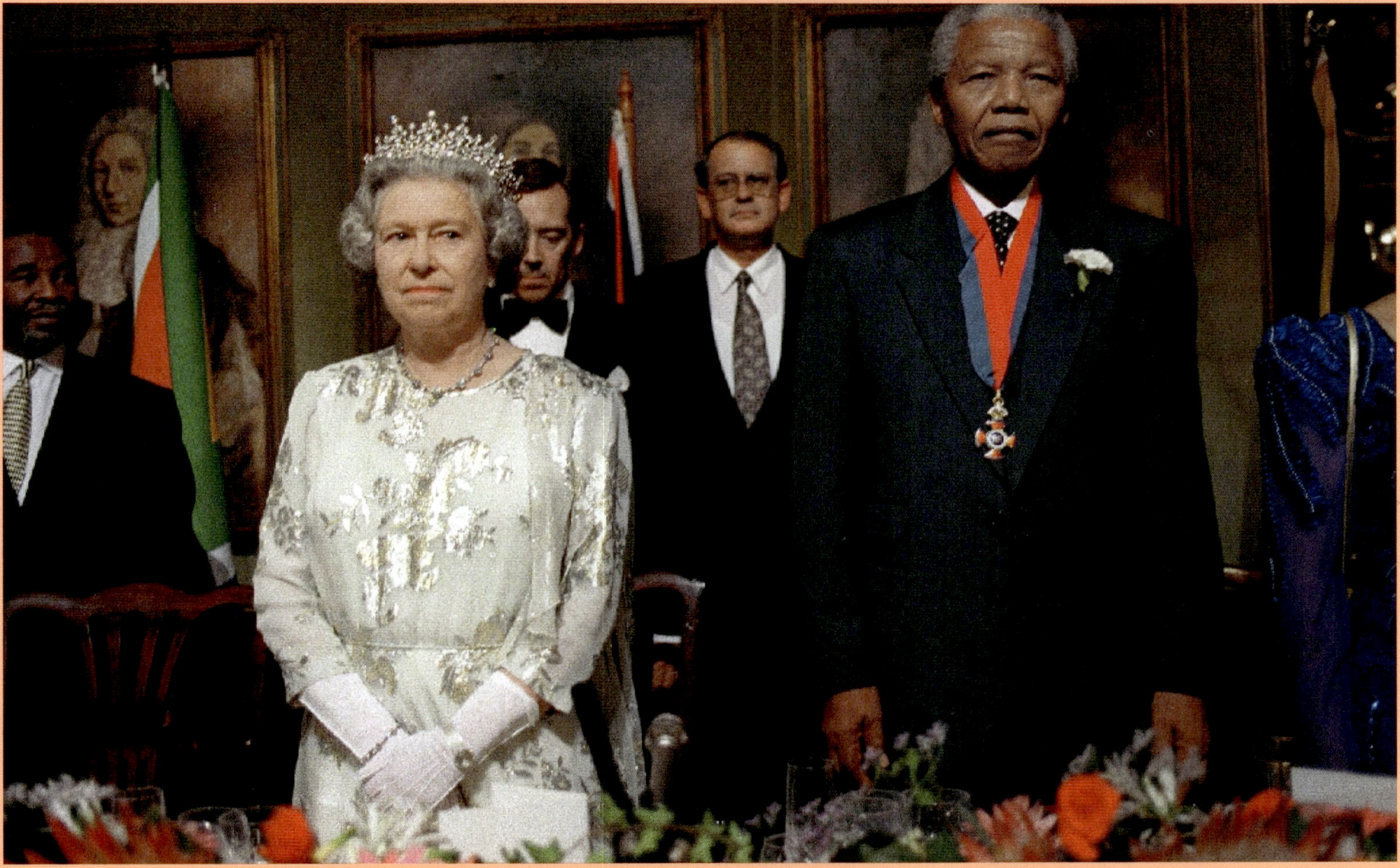

Tata welcomed many international leaders. Those who were friends of the ANC and those who deemed the ANC as a terrorist movement. His depth of moral character formed from childhood and through the toughest of circumstances made him naturally treat all individuals as ordinary human beings who are capable of being the best versions of themselves. As president Fidel Castro stated in a speech to the South African parliament in 1988:

"Nelson Mandela will go down in history because he was able to draw from his soul all the poison accumulated by such unjust punishment."

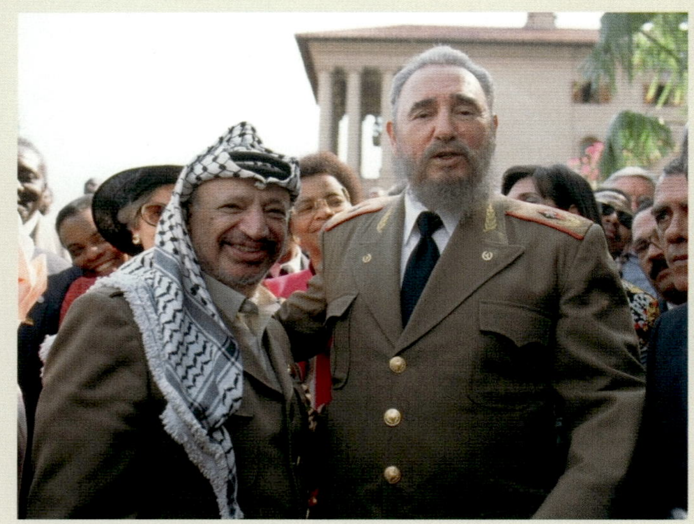

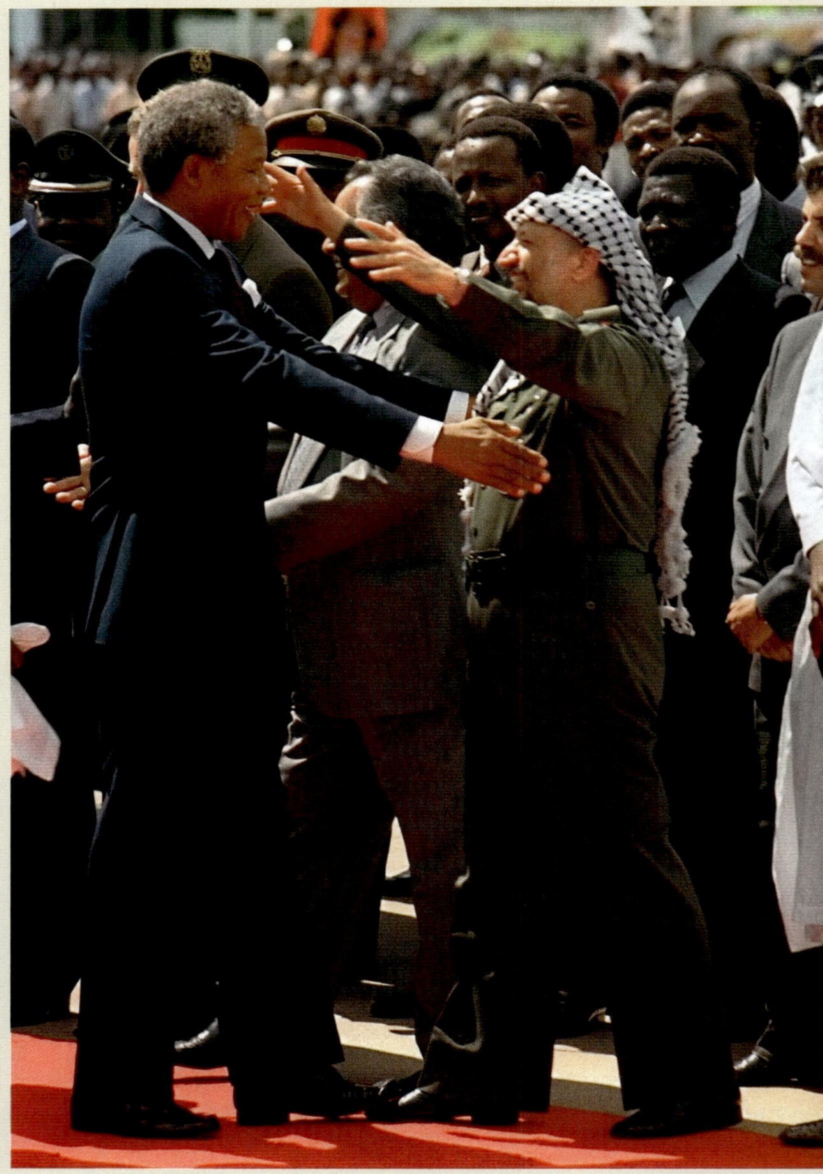

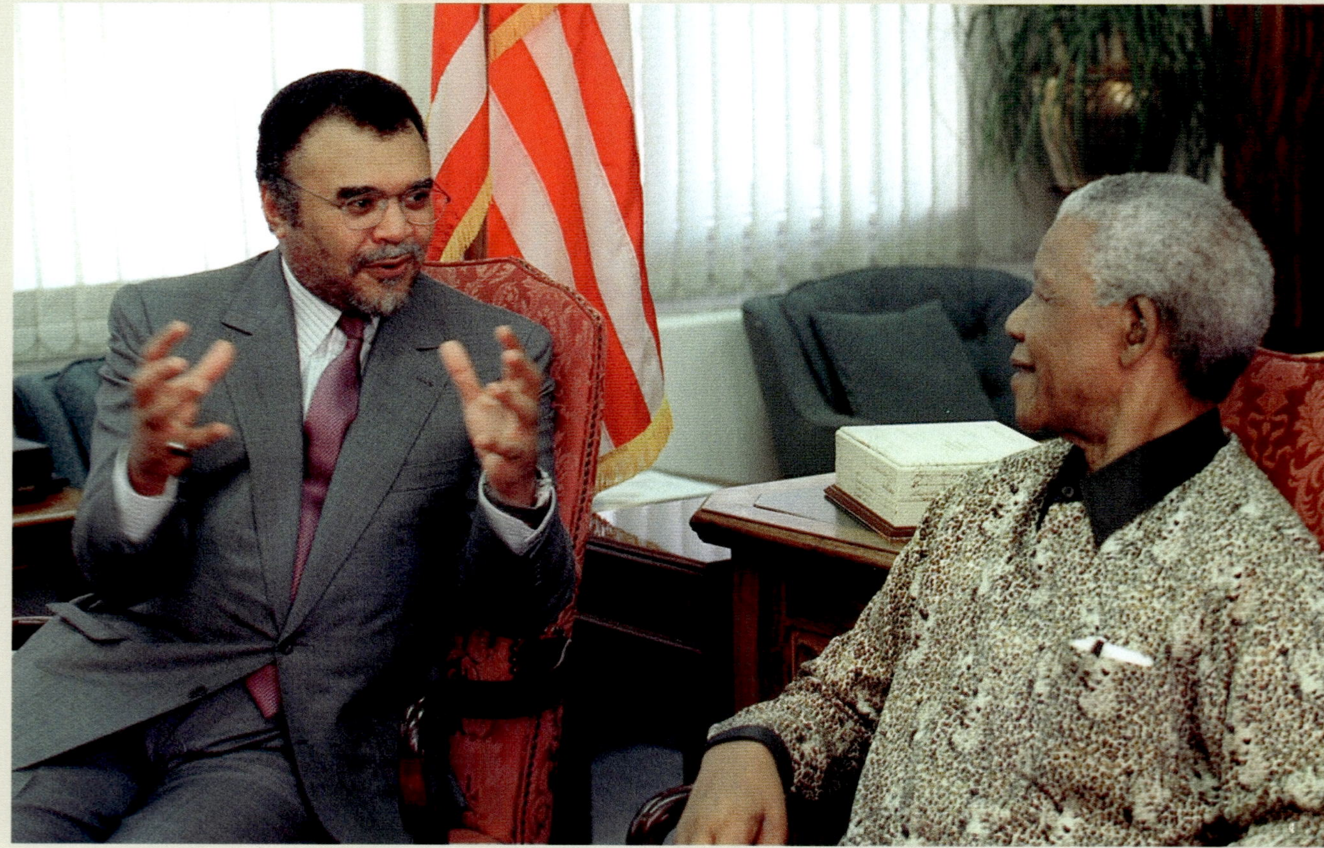

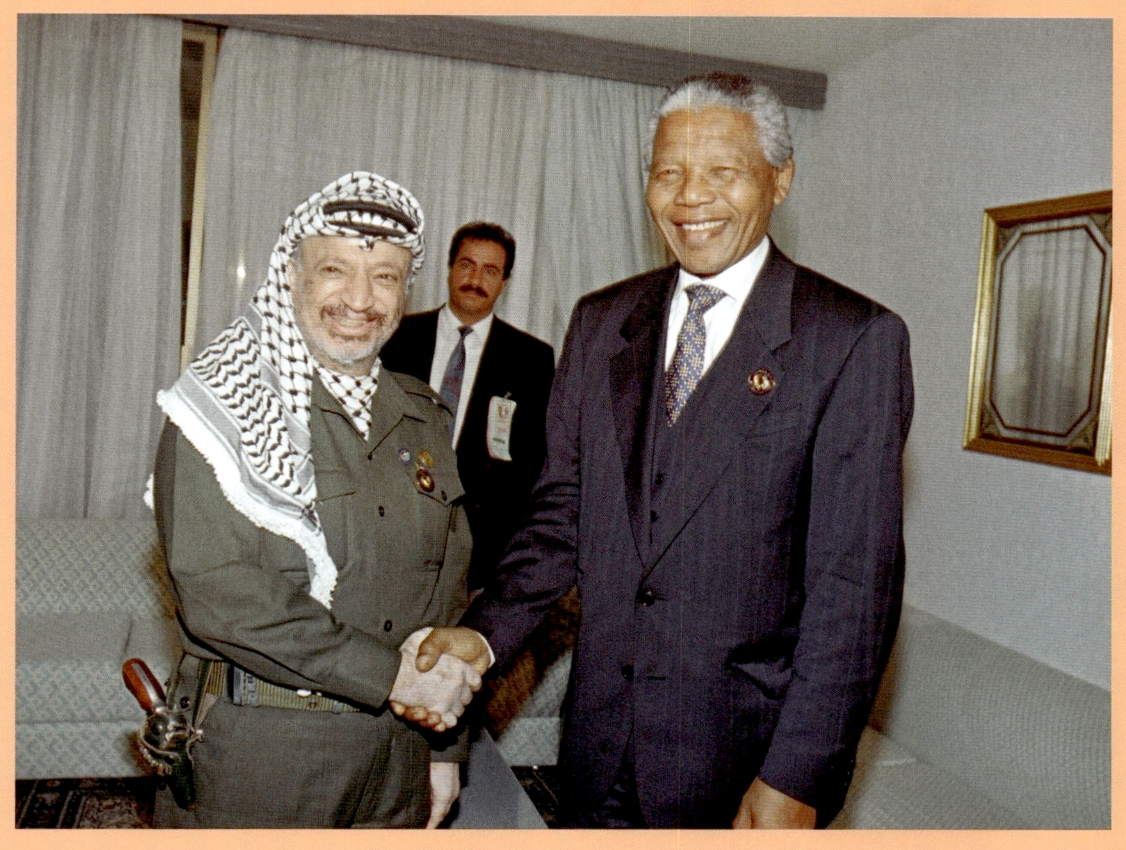

Opposite (*top*): Tata greets Palestine Liberation Organization (PLO) chairman Yasser Arafat on his arrival in Lusaka, Zambia, February 1990. This was Tata's first trip to a foreign country after his release from prison.

Opposite (*center*): Yasser Arafat and Cuban President Fidel Castro at Tata's presidential inauguration ceremony.

Opposite (*bottom*): Tata meeting with Saudi Arabia's Prince Bandar on October, 22, 1999, at the South African Embassy in Washington, DC.

Left: Yasser Arafat greeting Tata on June 13, 1994, at the Organisation of African Unity summit (OAU) in Tunis, Tunisia.

Bottom: Tata and Fidel Castro at the opening of the 12th Non-Aligned Movement summit in Durban on September 2, 1998.

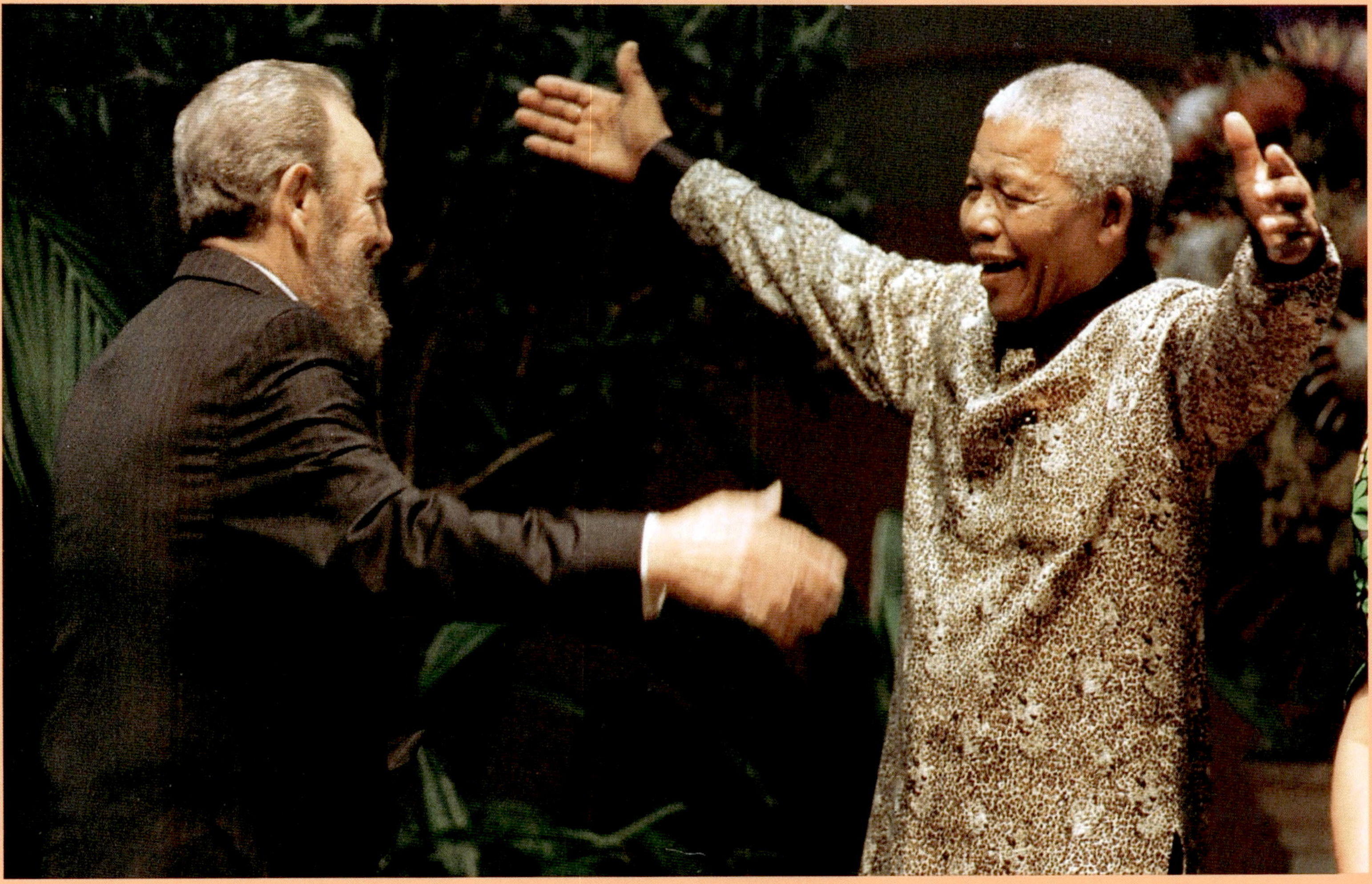

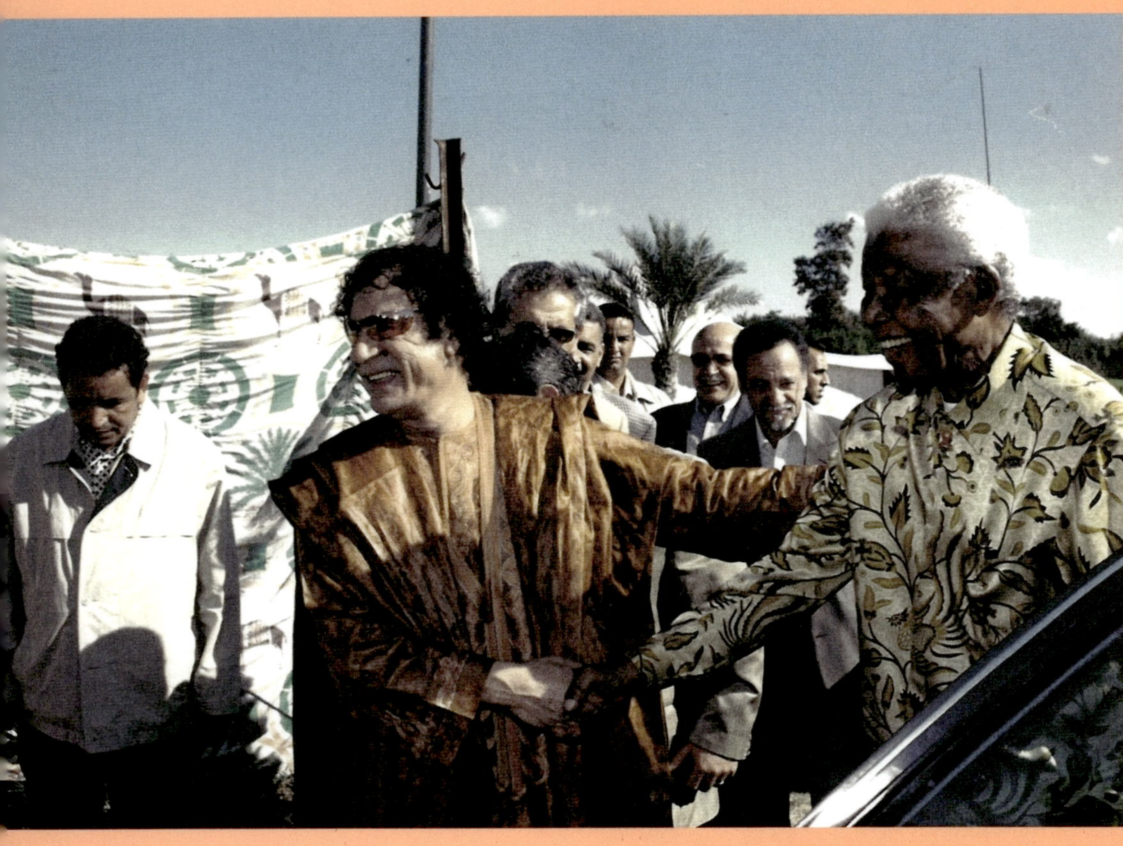

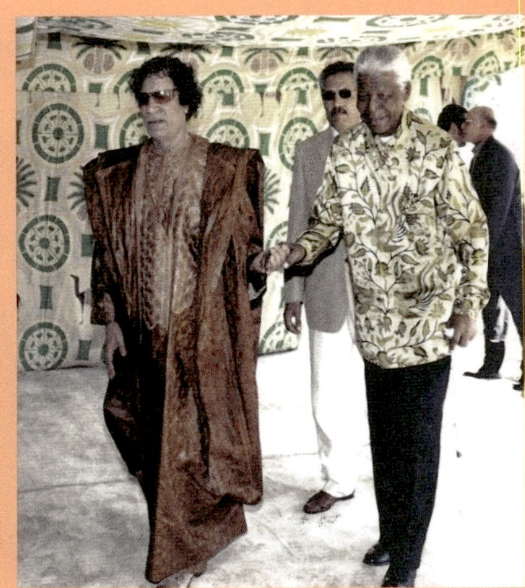

Opposite: Tata in Libya with Muammar Gaddafi while president.

This page: Tata remained friendly with Gaddafi into his retirement years.

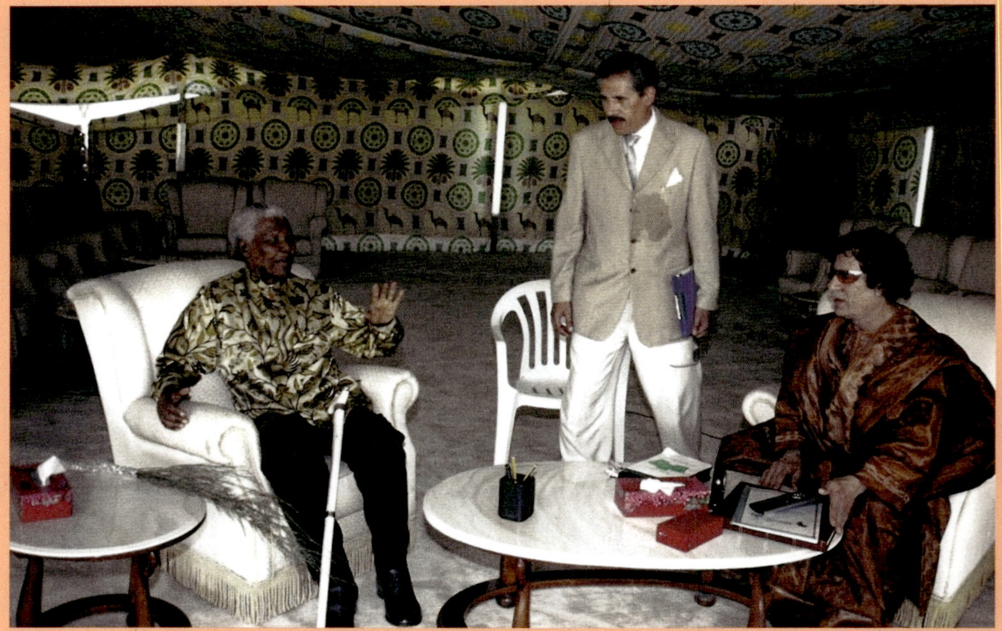

"One of the mistakes which political analysts make is to think their enemies should be our enemies. Our attitude towards any country is determined by the attitude of that country to our struggle. Yasser Arafat, Colonel Gaddafi [and] Fidel Castro support our struggle to the hilt."

Tata from a town-hall-style interview on *Nightline* with Ted Koppel when asked why he aligns himself with leaders who are not models of human rights, June 1990.

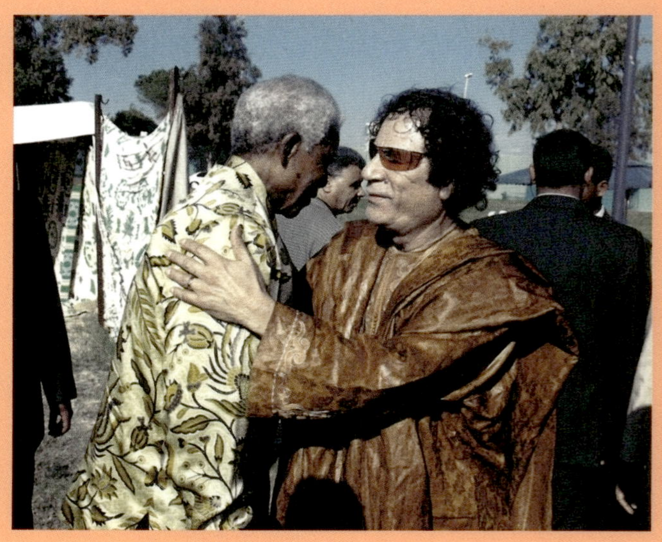

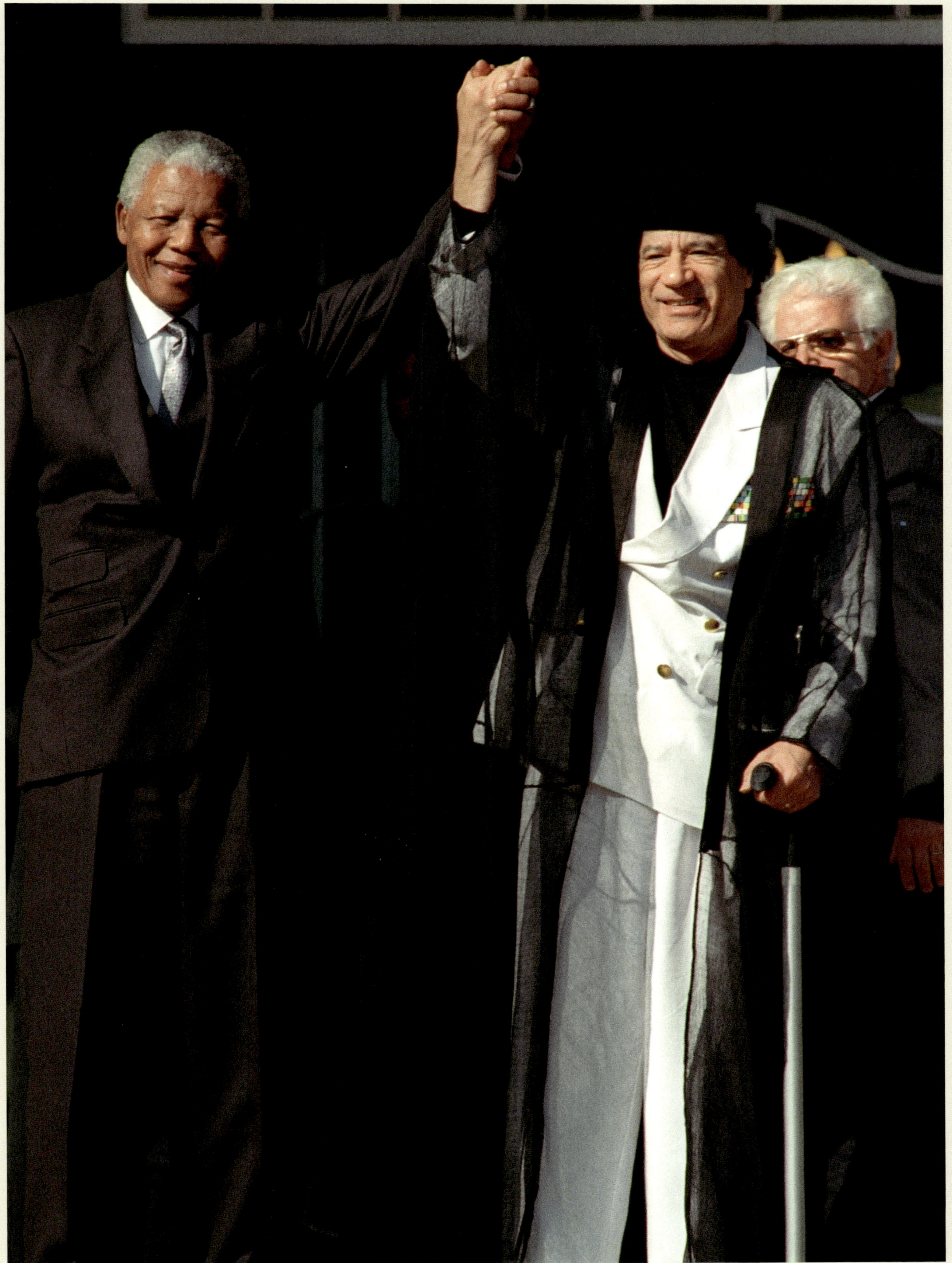

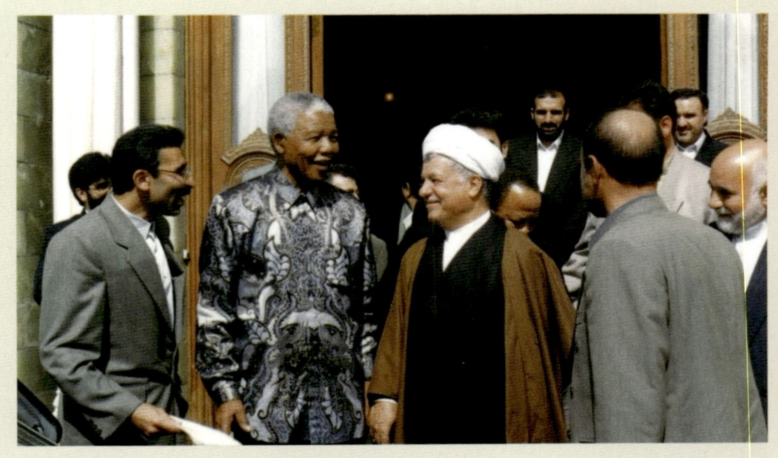

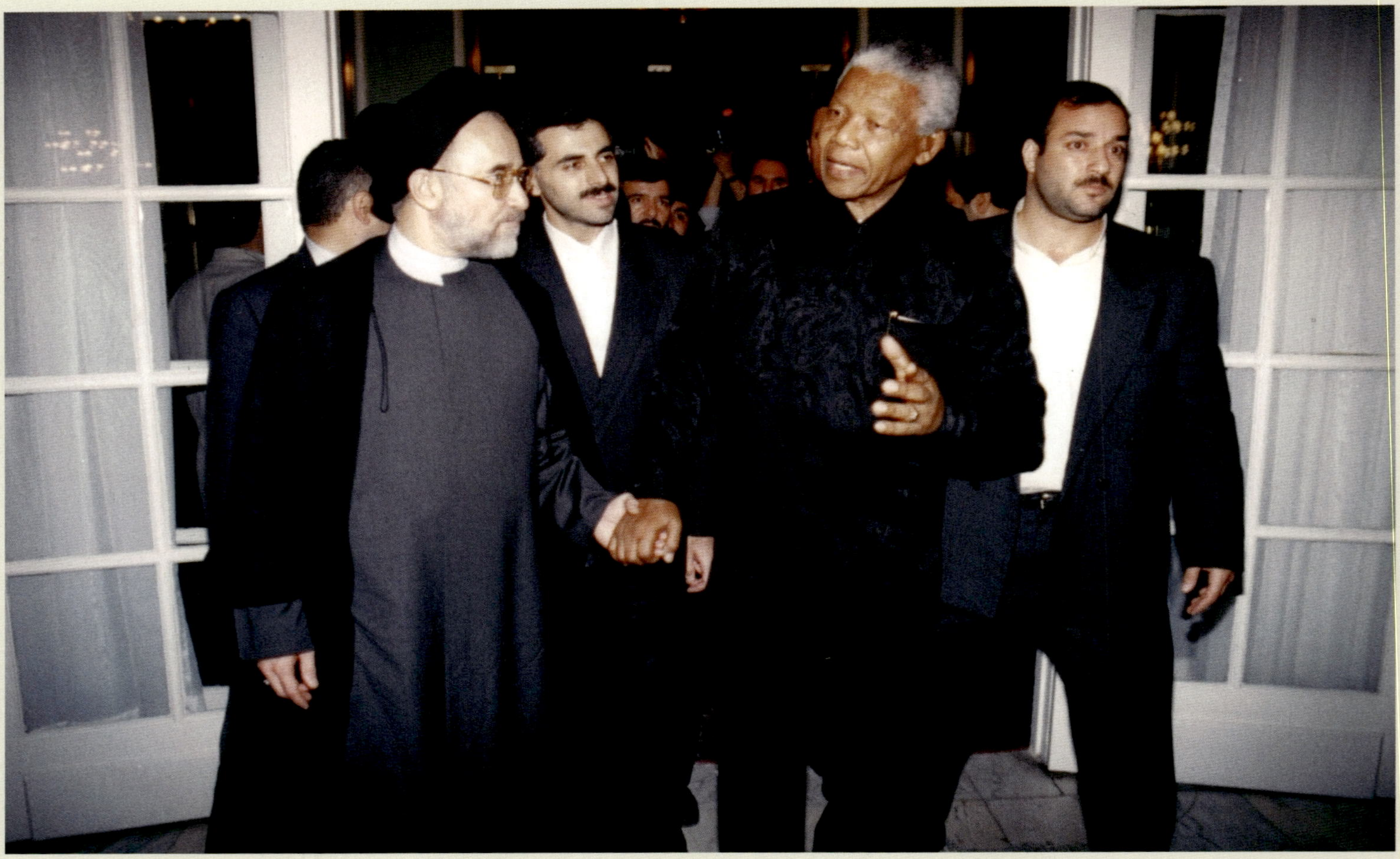

This page: Tata meeting with Iran's supreme leader Ayatollah Ali Khamenei in Tehran on October 17, 1999. Iran had always been a strong political and financial backer of the African National Congress.

Opposite: Tata speaking after his release in 1990.

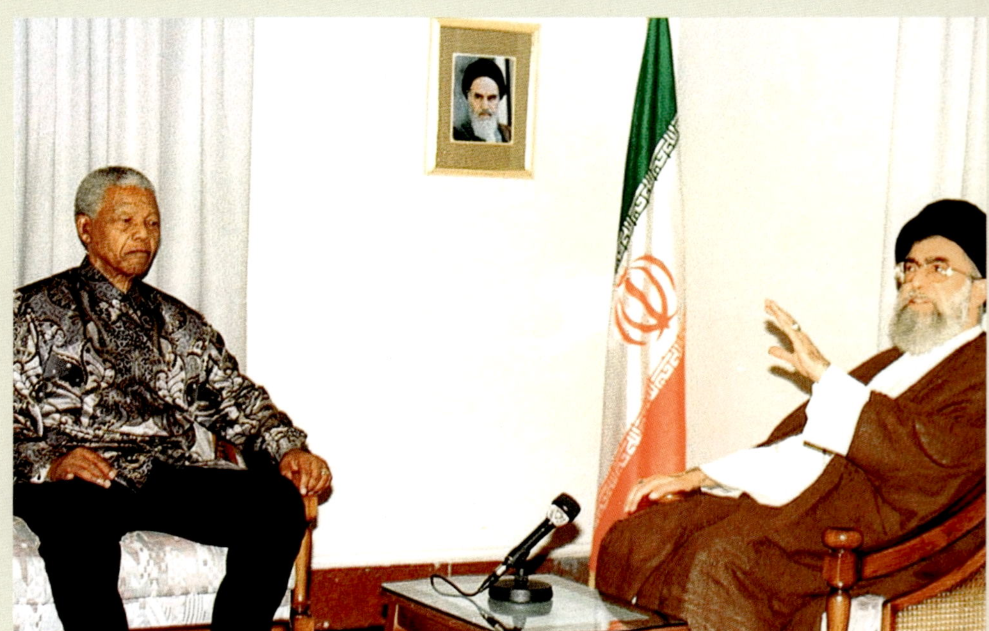

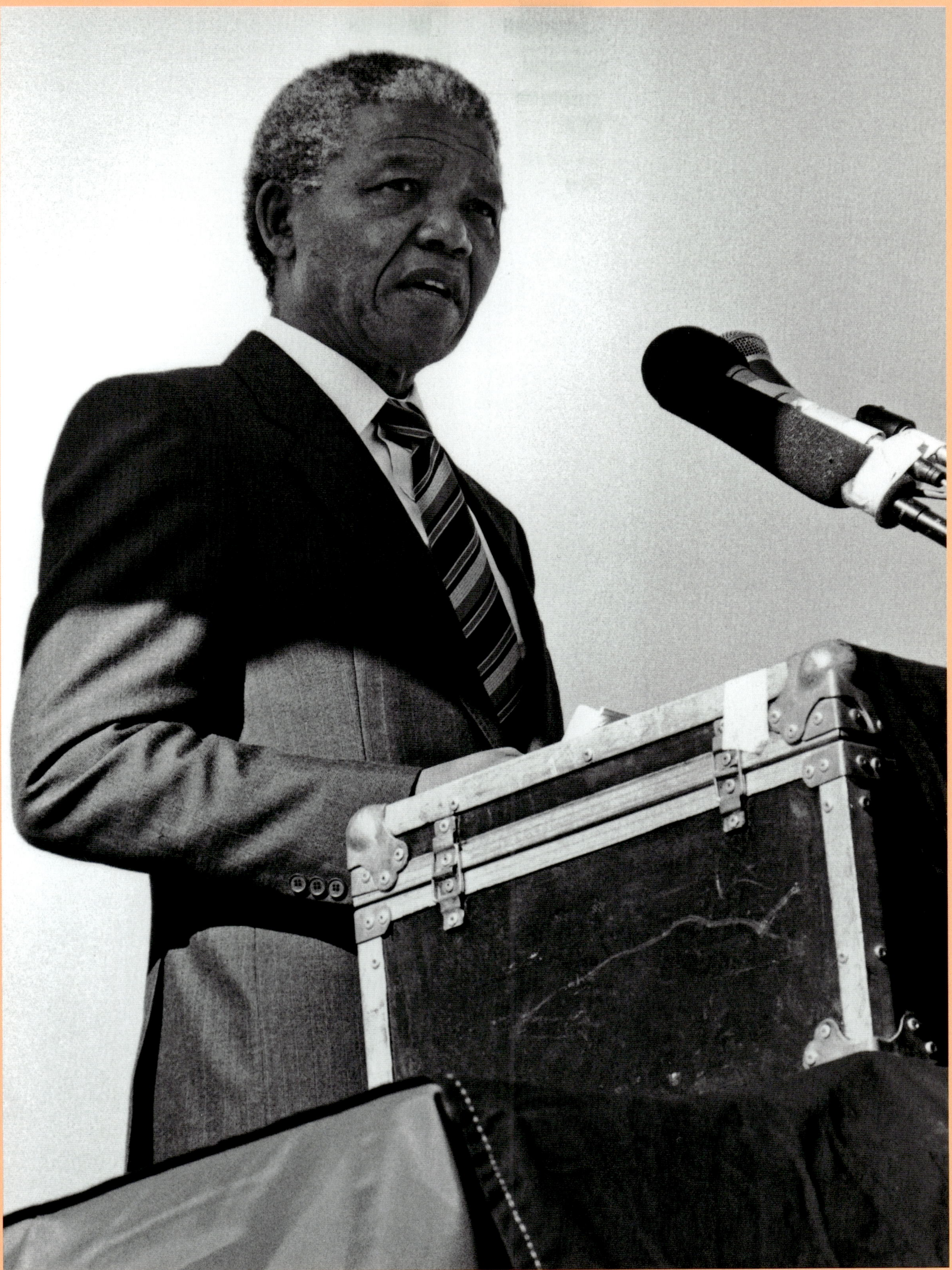

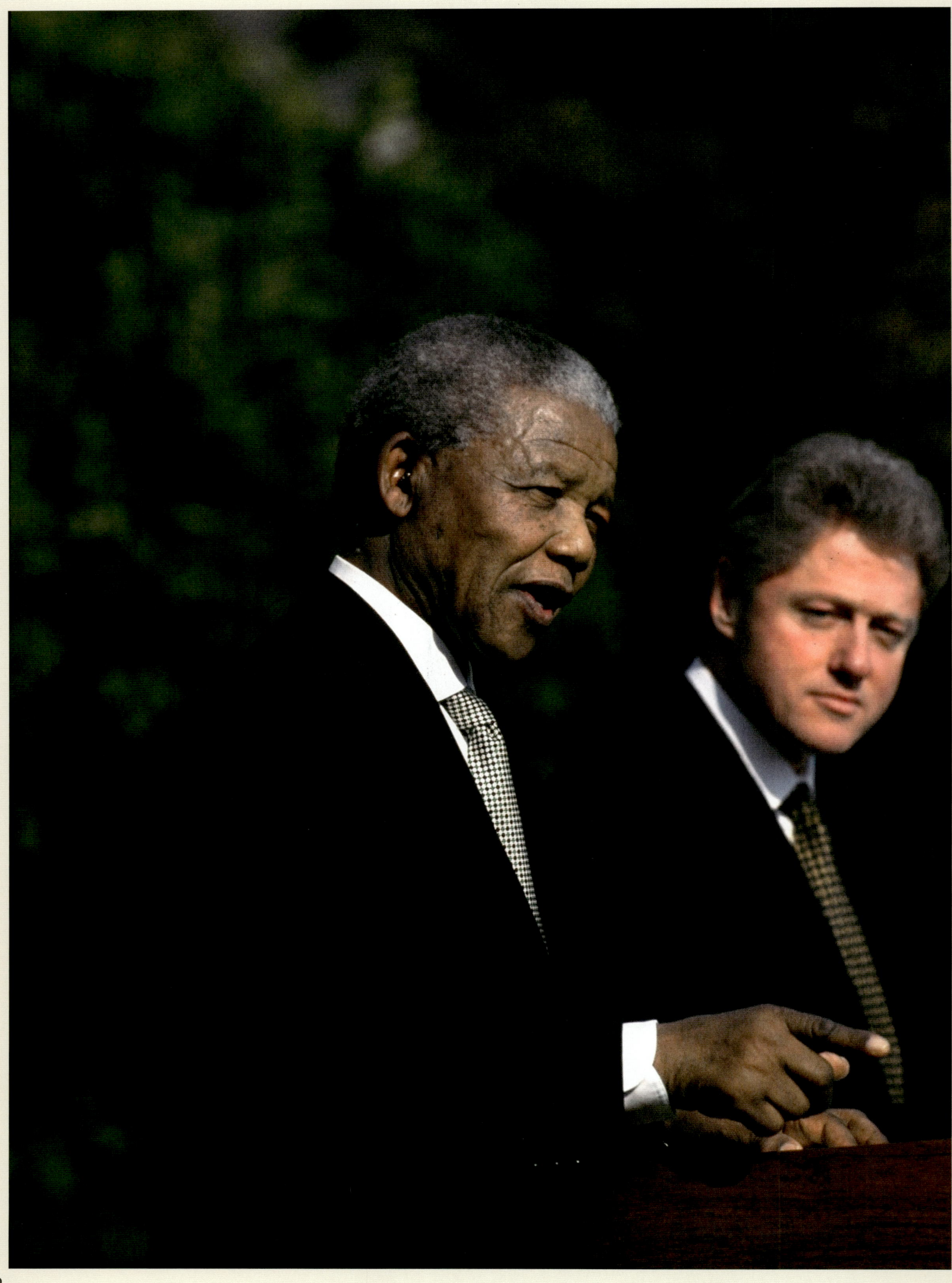

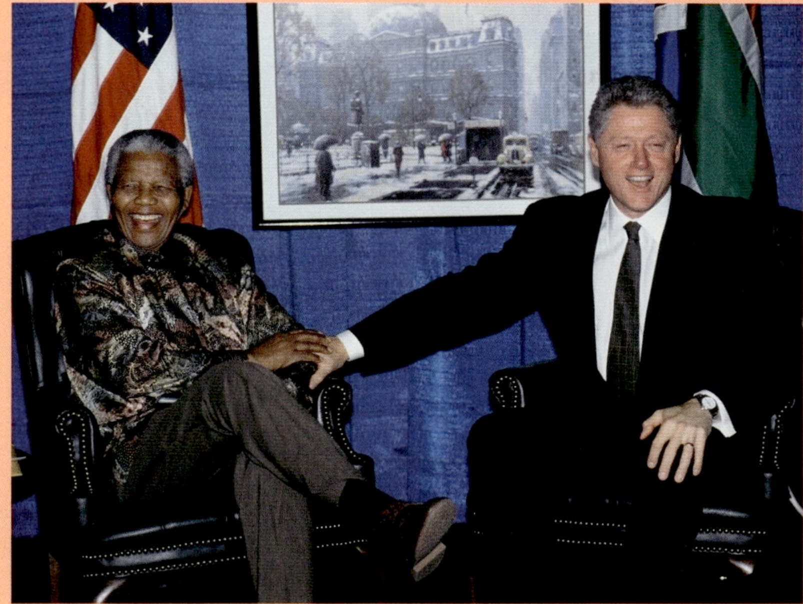

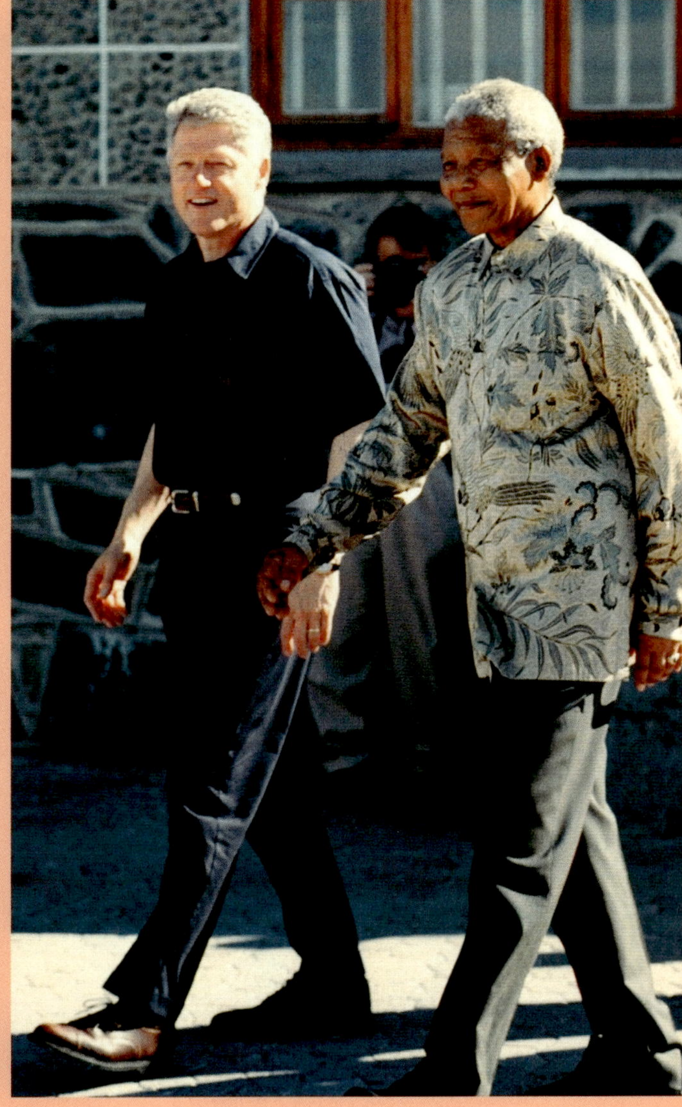

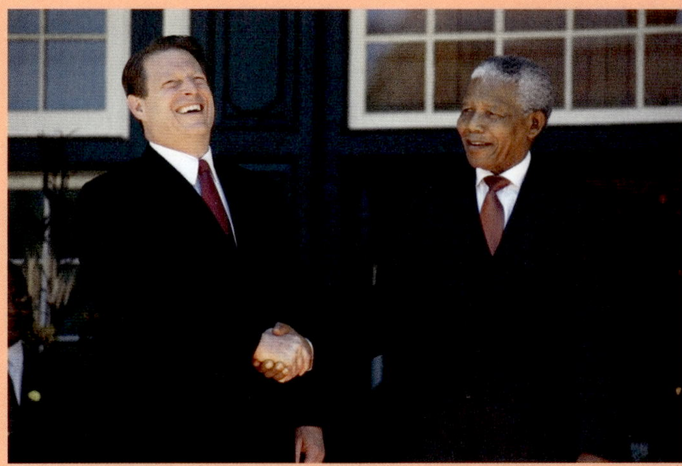

Opposite: Tata holding a joint news conference with President Bill Clinton on the White House's South Lawn.

This page: Tata with President Bill Clinton, Vice President Al Gore, and future Secretary of State Hillary Clinton.

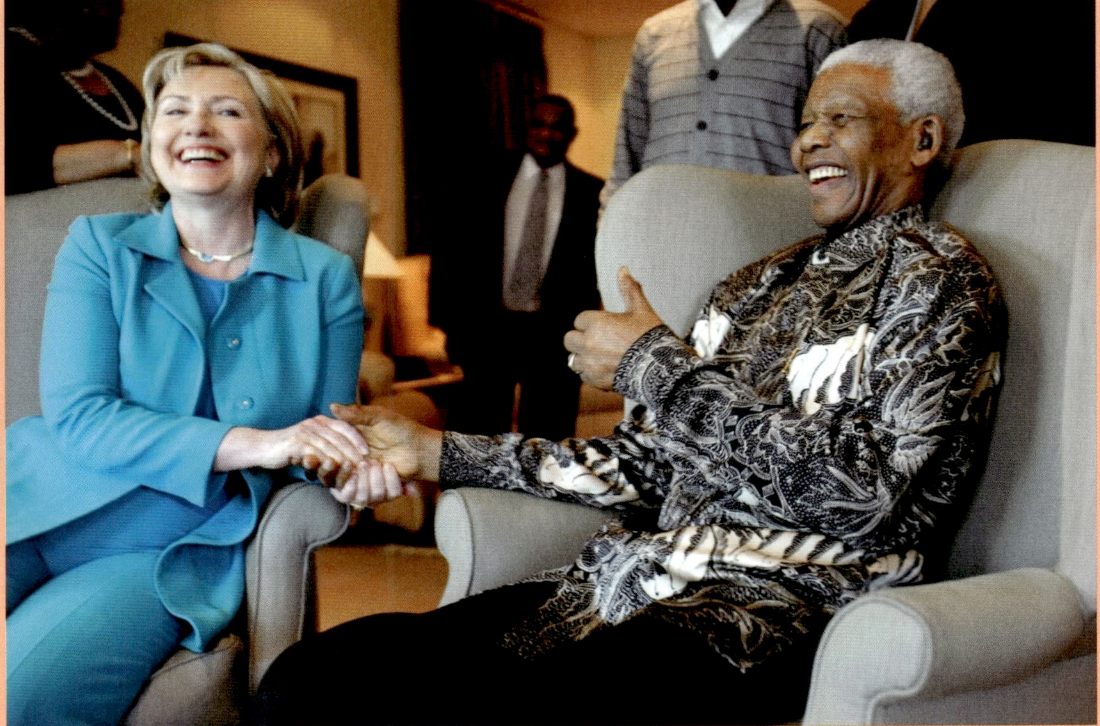

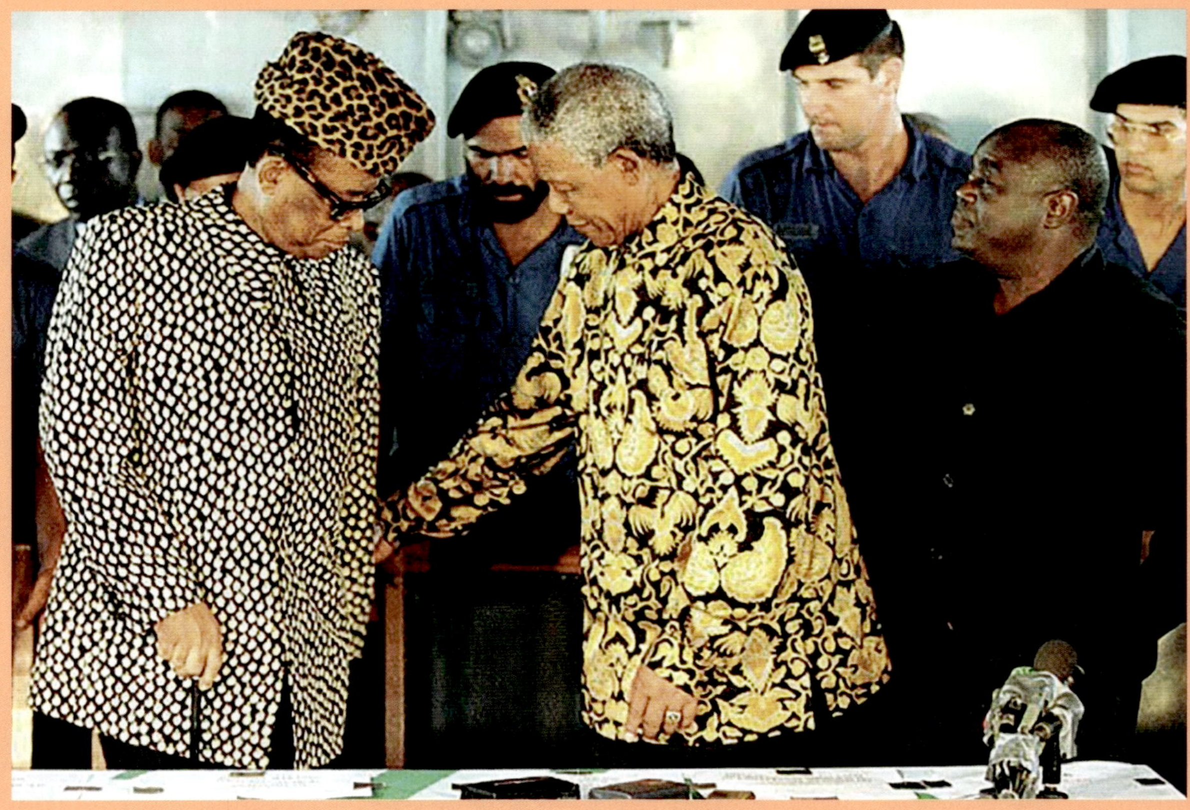

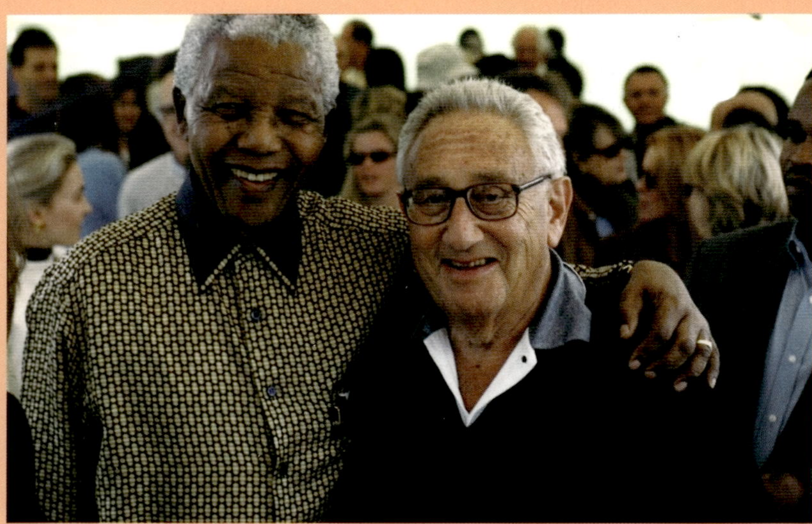

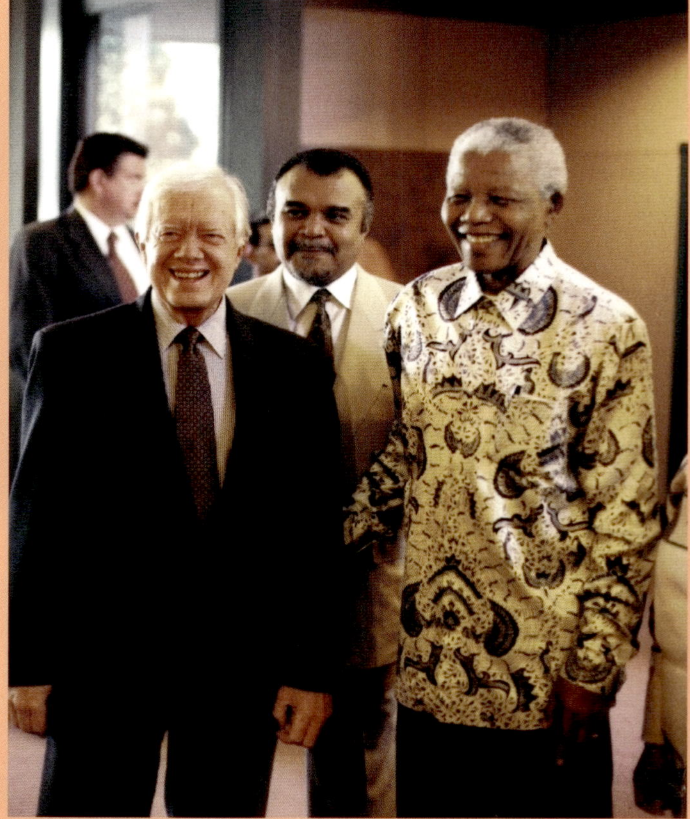

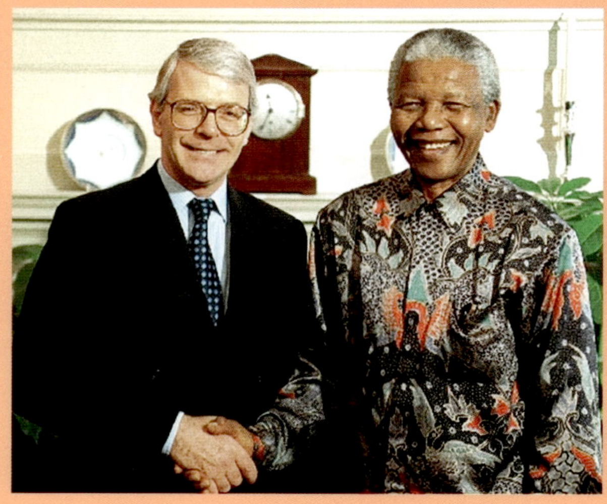

Top: Tata with President Mobutu Sese Seko of Zaire (now the Democratic Republic of the Congo).

Above (*left*): Tata with former US Secretary of State Henry Kissinger.

Above (*right*): Tata with President Jimmy Carter and Prince Bandar.

Left: Tata with Prime Minister John Major.

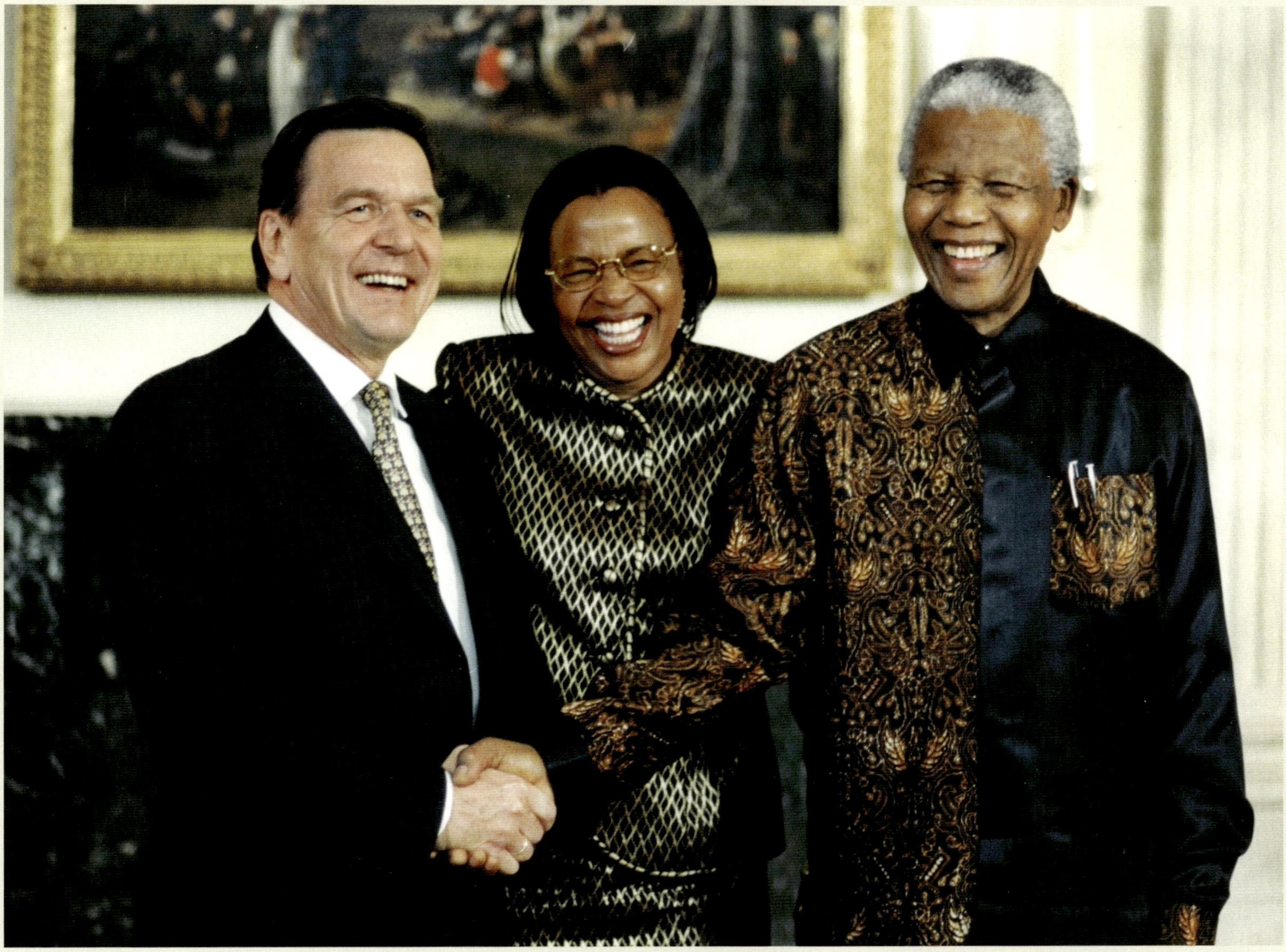

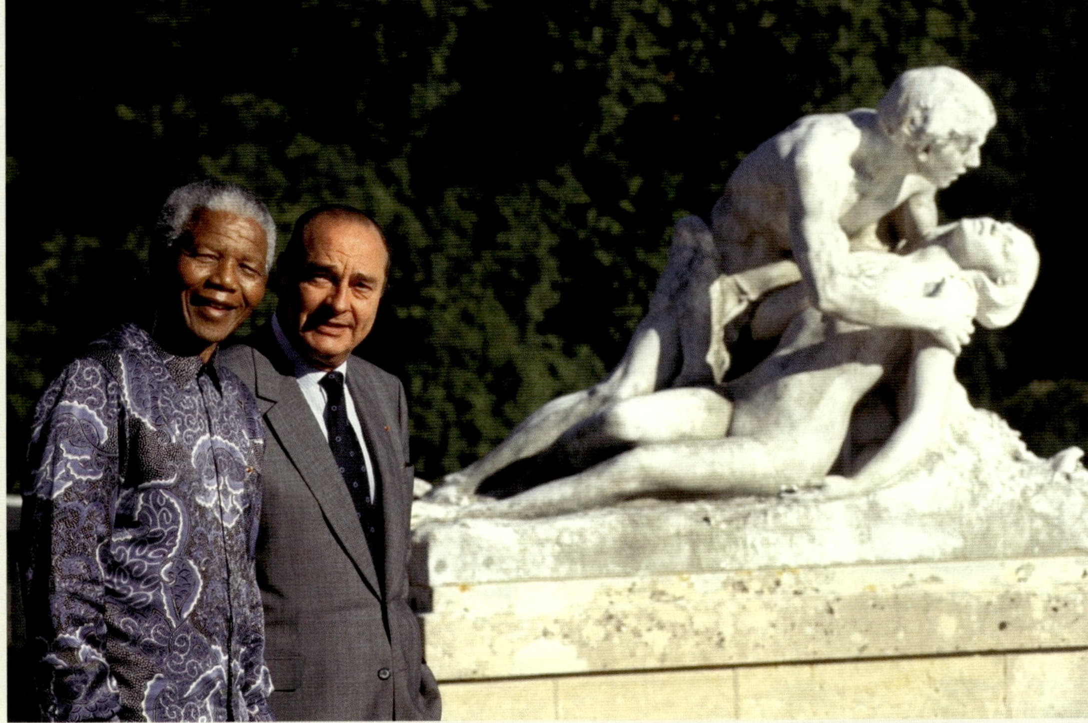

Above: Tata and Graça Machel in Baden-Baden in Germany with Chancellor Gerhard Schröder, 1999.

Left: Tata with President Jacques Chirac during a visit to France, July 1, 1996.

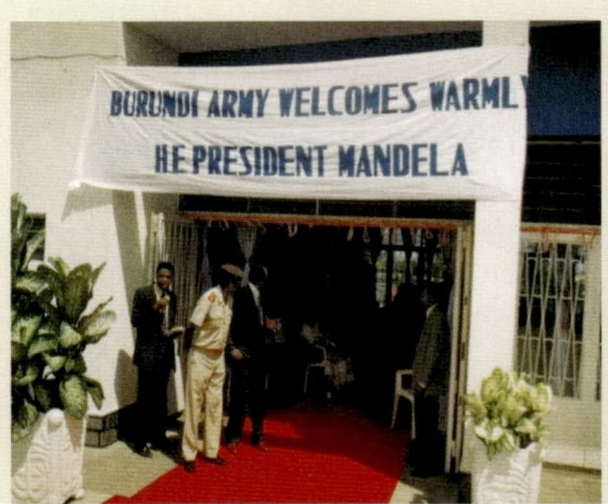

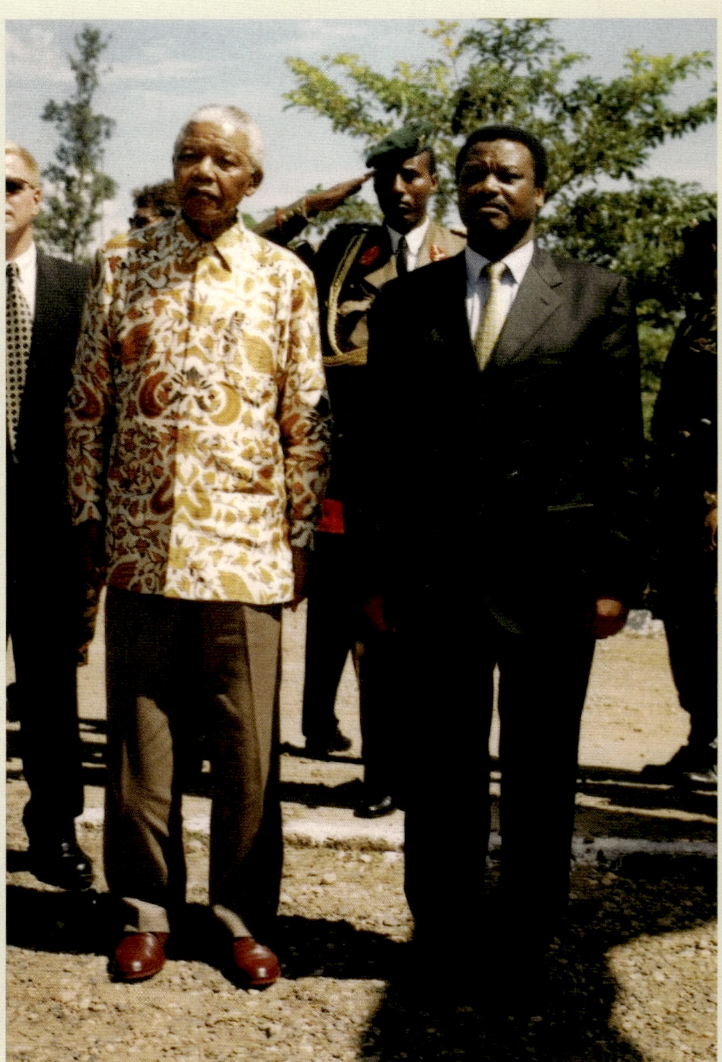

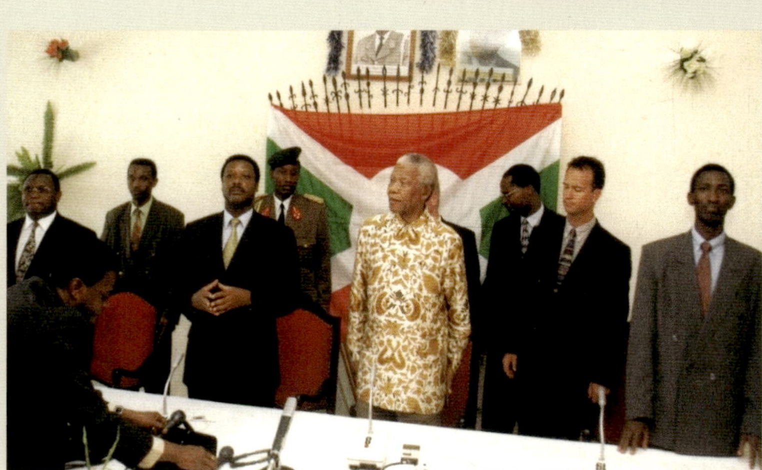

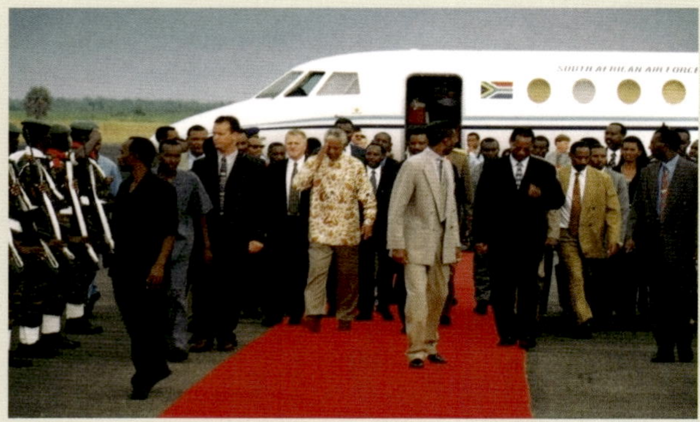

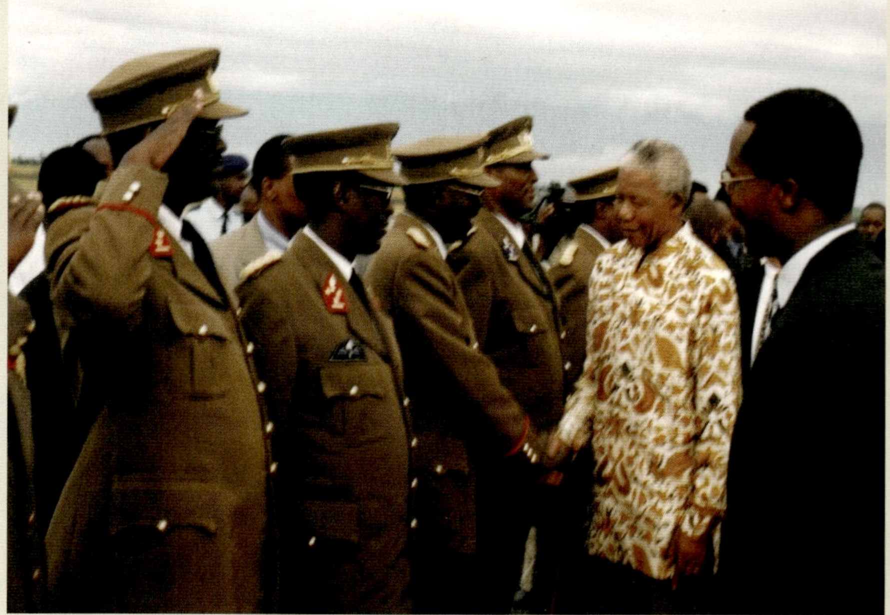

Tata was appointed as a mediator in the Burundi Peace Negotiations in December 1999. In his formal title as Facilitator, he called for the inclusion of all sides in the peace talks. He strongly felt that no individual, political party, or women's group should be excluded. Tata's inclusion of women's issues in the process was considered a turning point in the peace talks, which included the issues of human rights abuses against women and women's land rights.

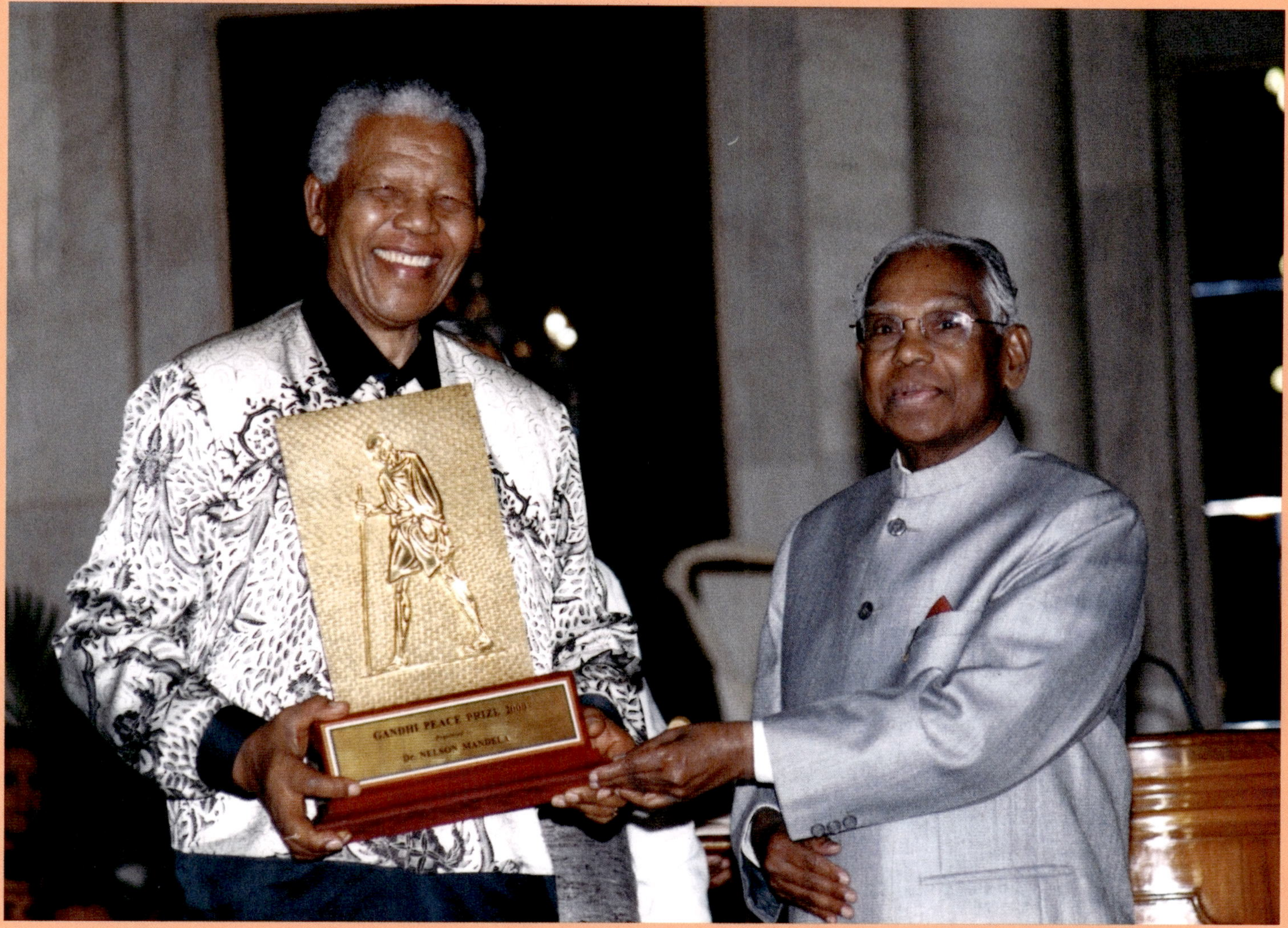

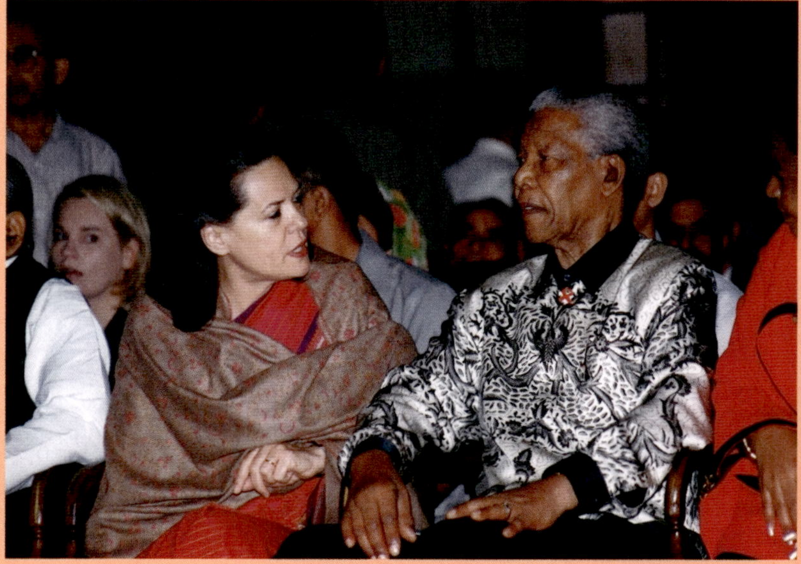

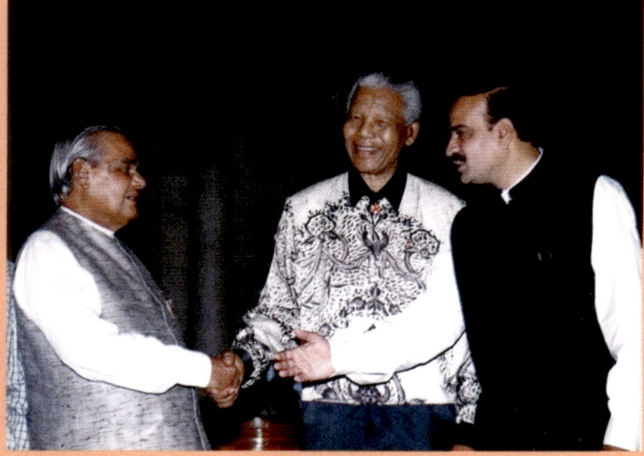

Tata receiving the International Gandhi Peace Prize in New Delhi, India, on March 16, 2010.

Tata believed in the unifying power of sport to bring people togther.

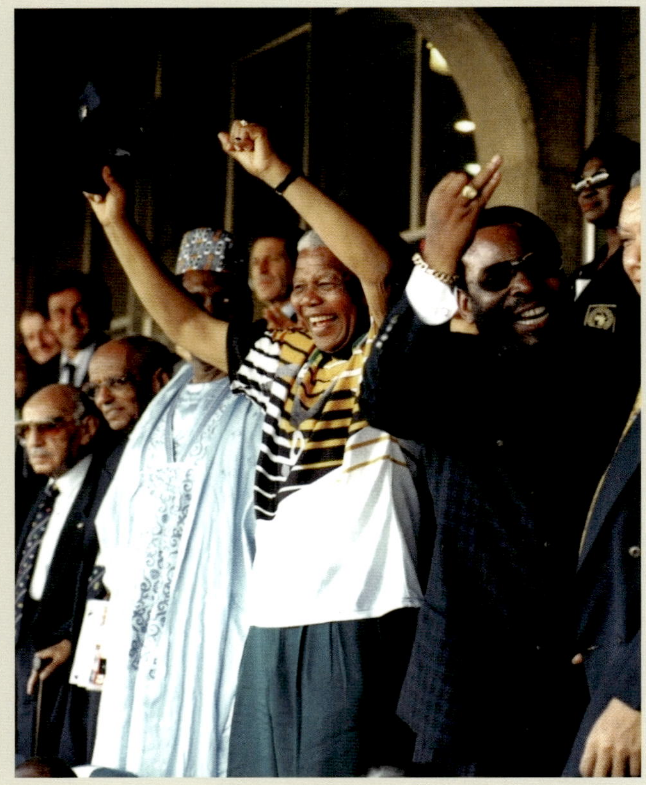

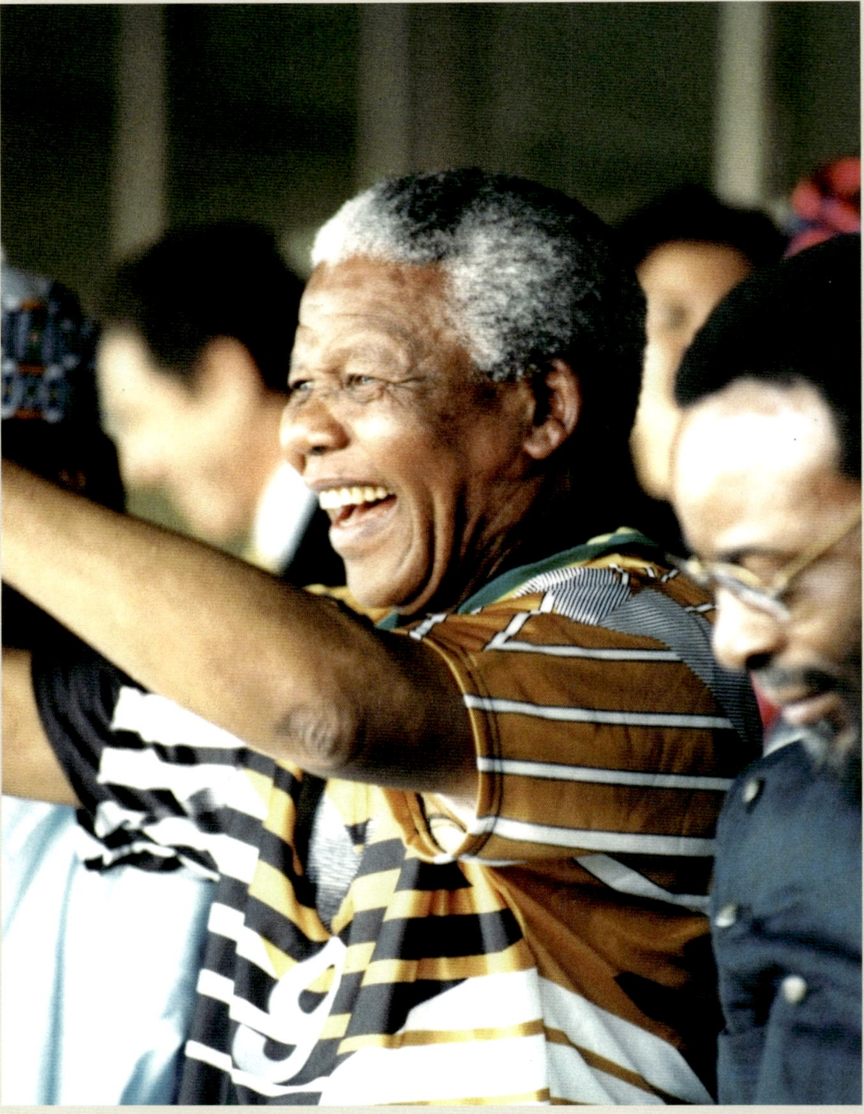

This page and following pages: A lifelong sports fan, Tata at the African Nations Cup final, February 3, 1996. South Africa won the match against Tunisia 2-0.

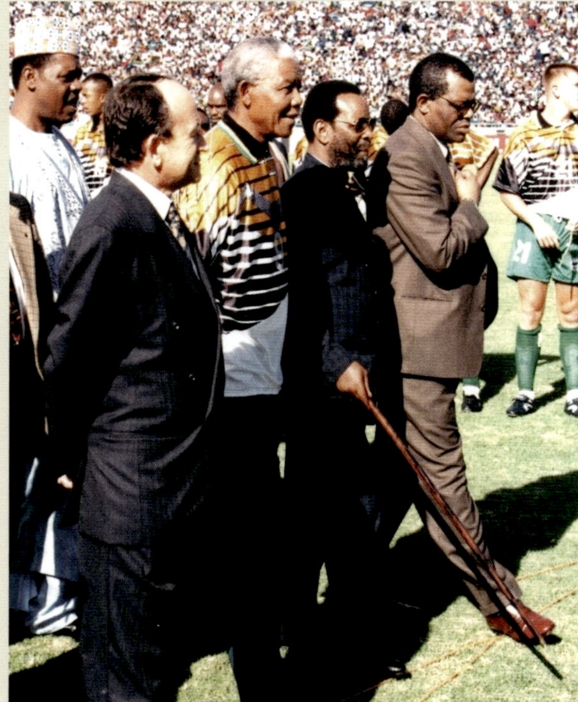

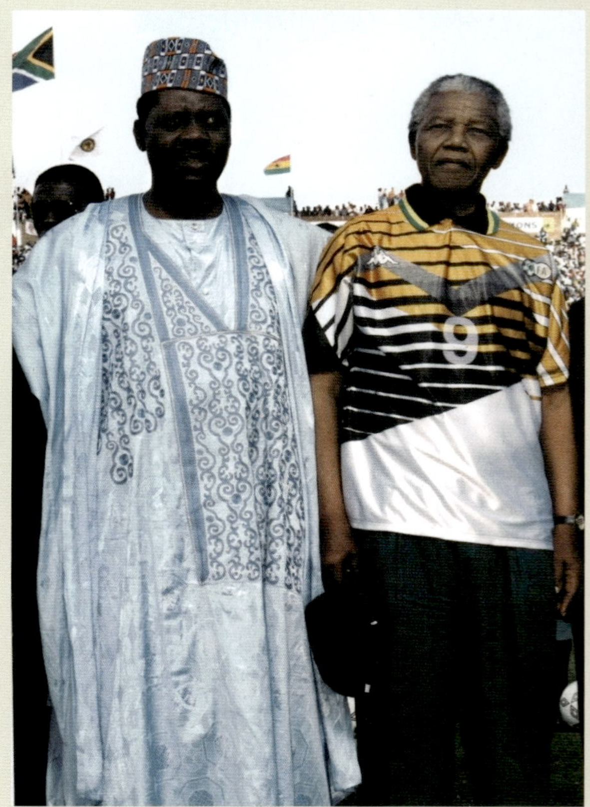

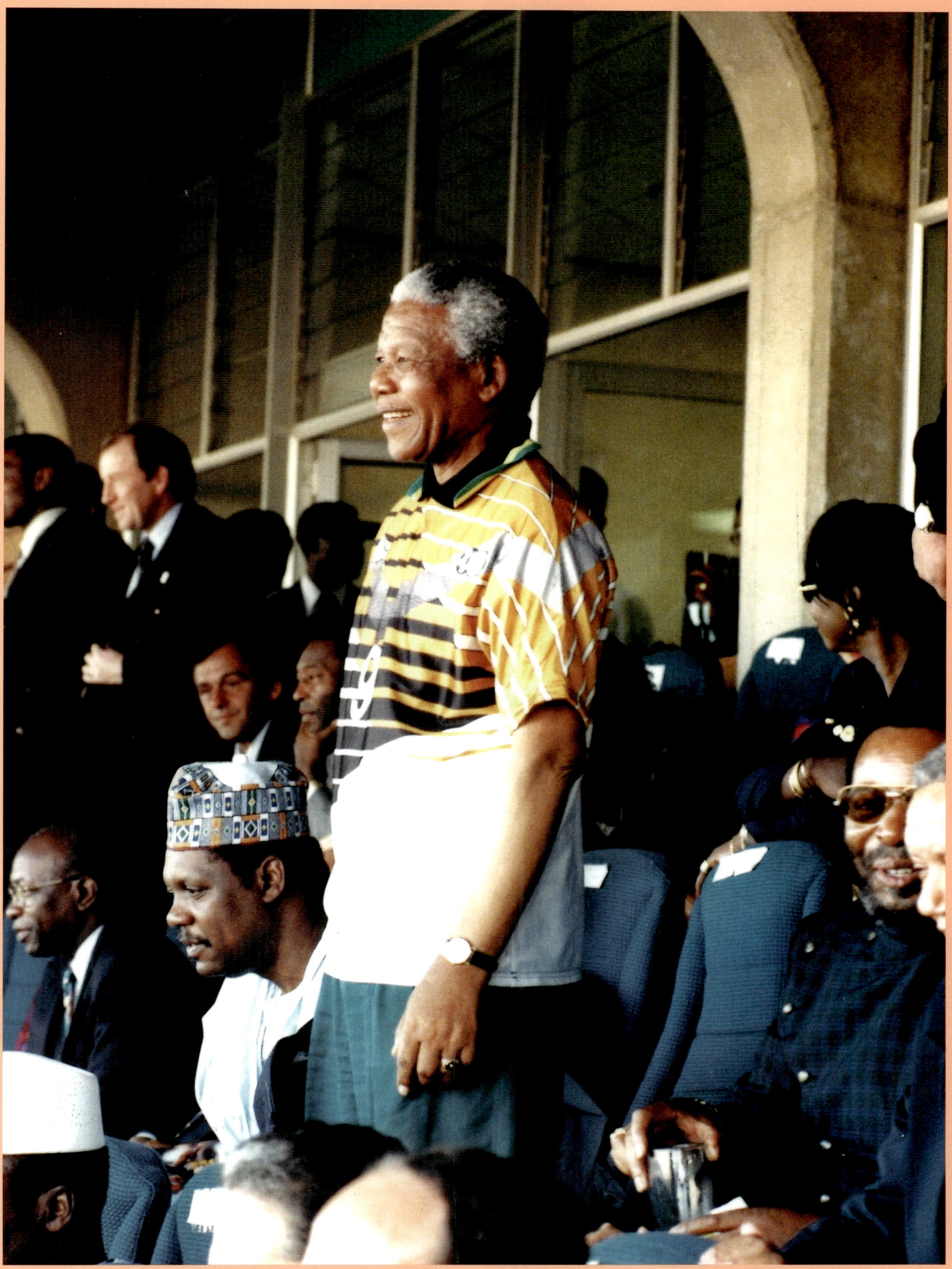

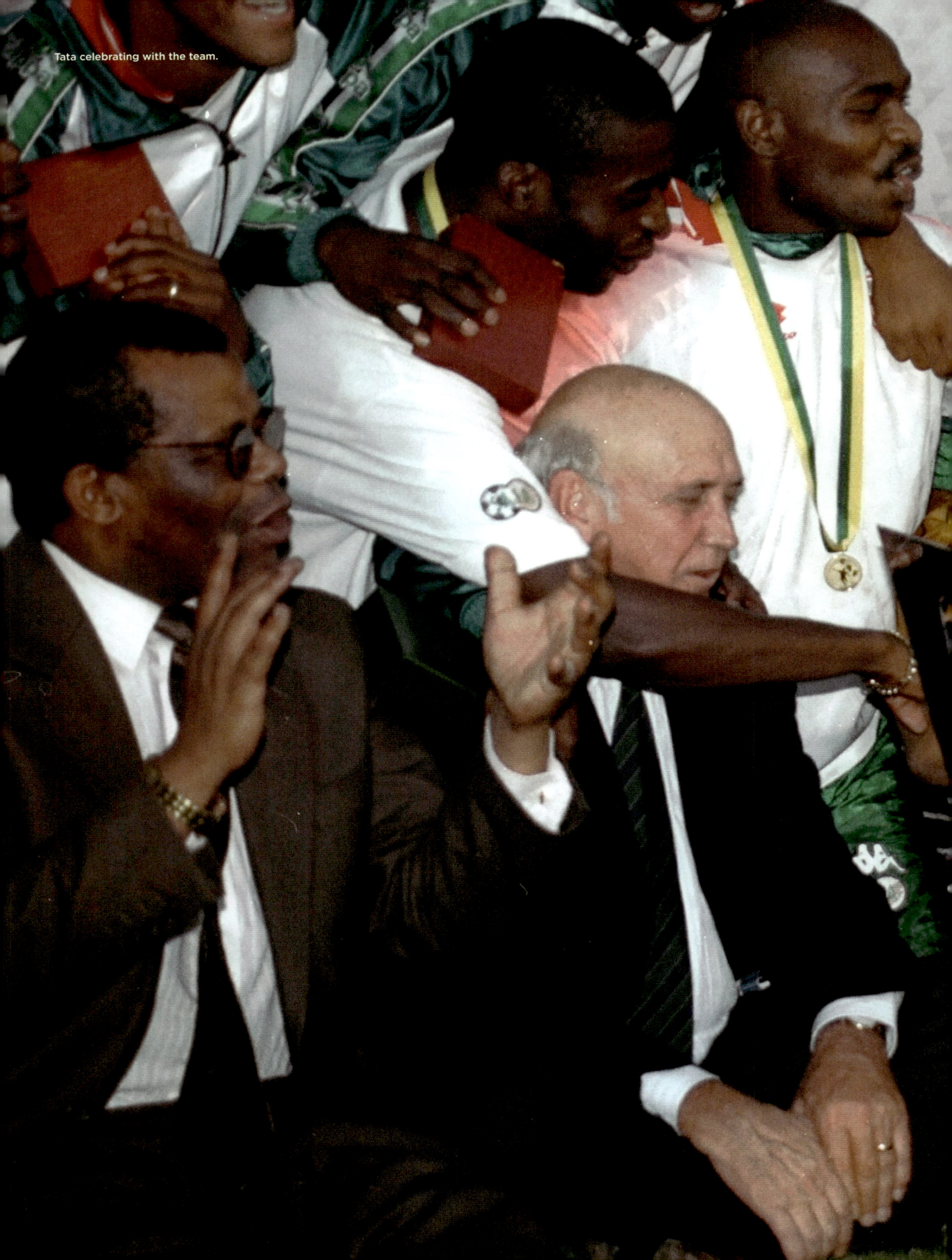
Tata celebrating with the team.

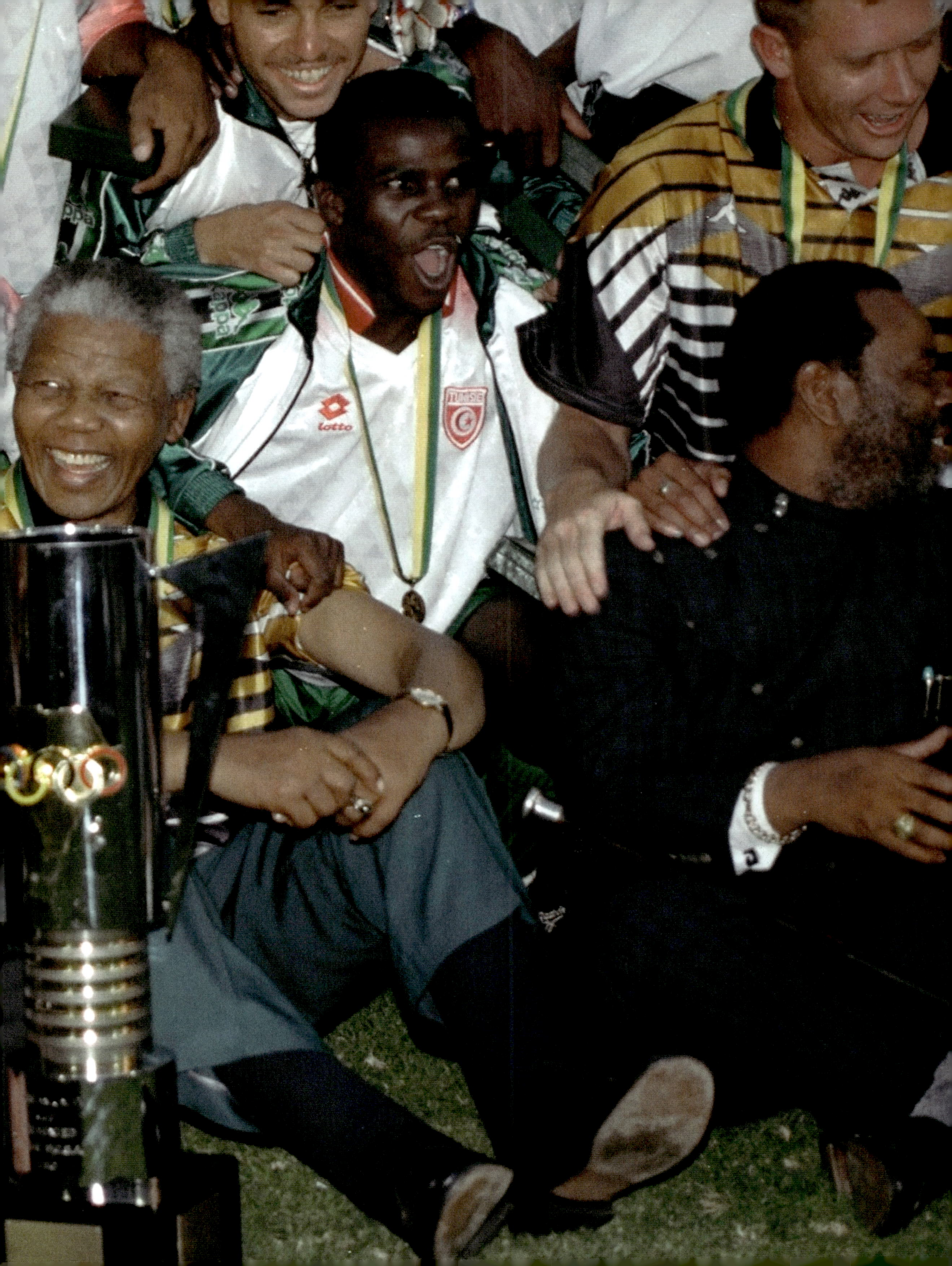
lotto

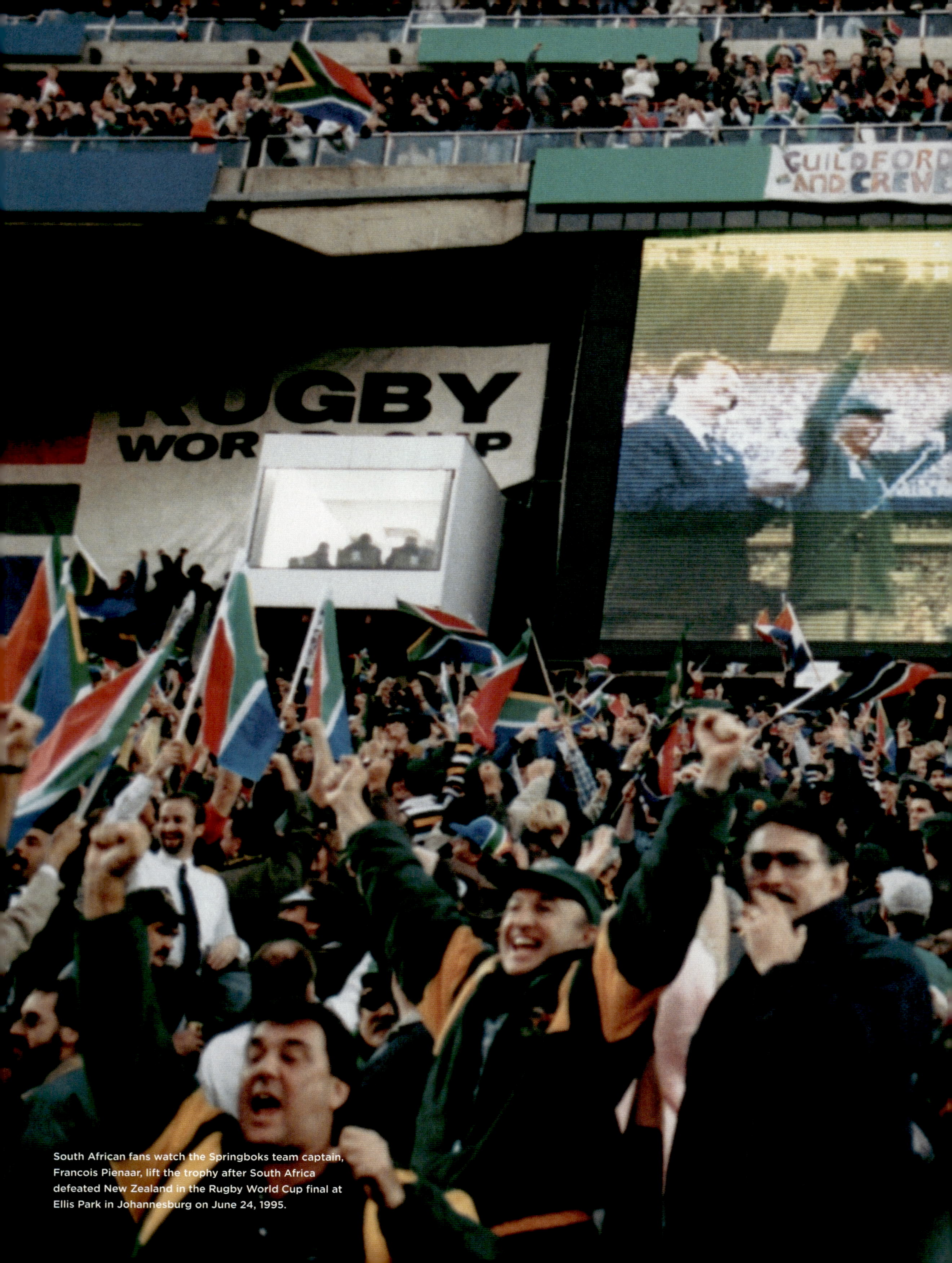

South African fans watch the Springboks team captain, Francois Pienaar, lift the trophy after South Africa defeated New Zealand in the Rugby World Cup final at Ellis Park in Johannesburg on June 24, 1995.

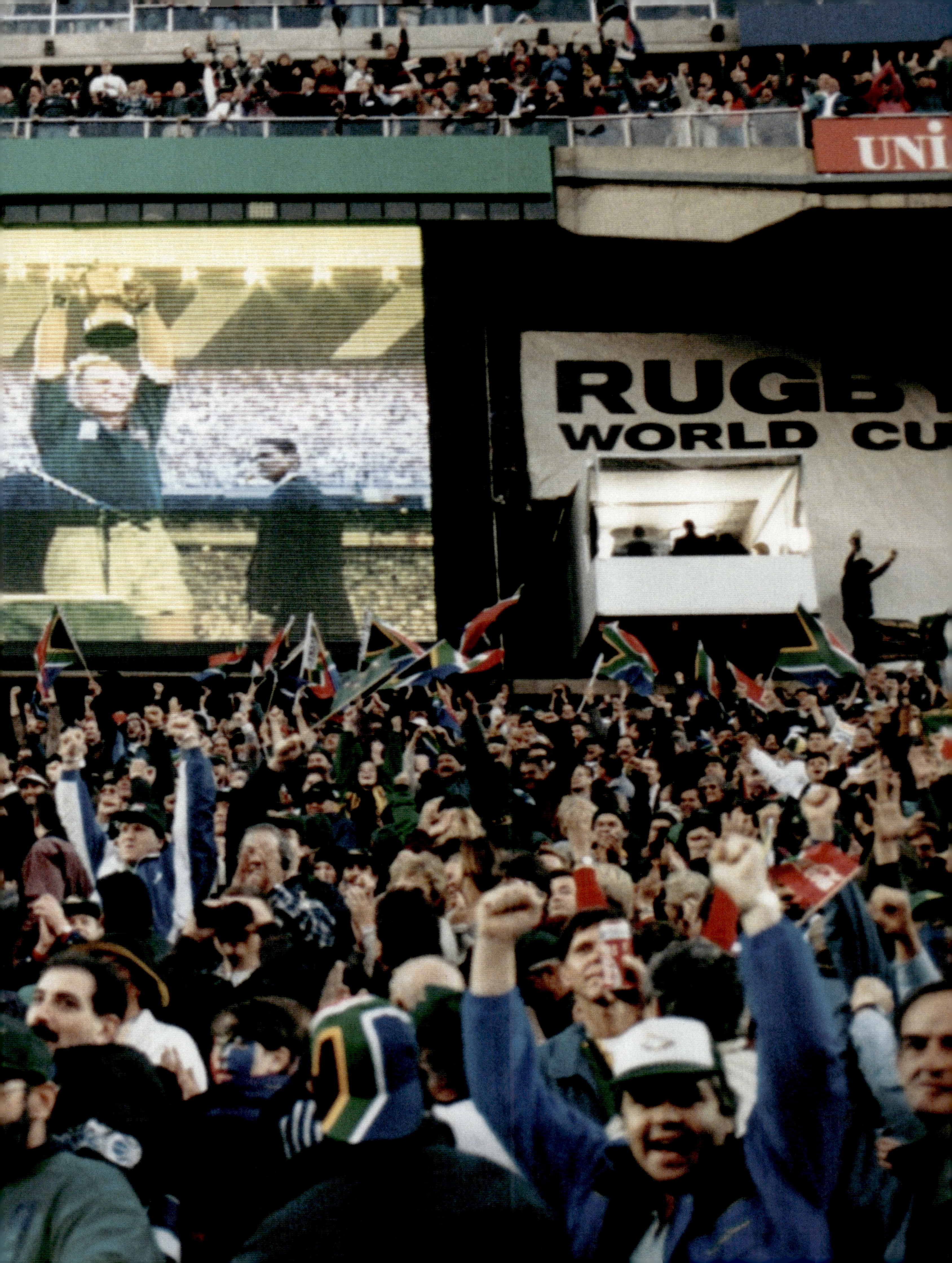
UNI
RUGB
WORLD CU

Opposite: Tata presenting Francois Pienaar with the William Webb Ellis Trophy.

This page: Tata was invited to this game and saw this as a strategic opportunity to unite Blacks and whites, the oppressed and the oppressors, to use sport to bridge the racial divide in South Africa.

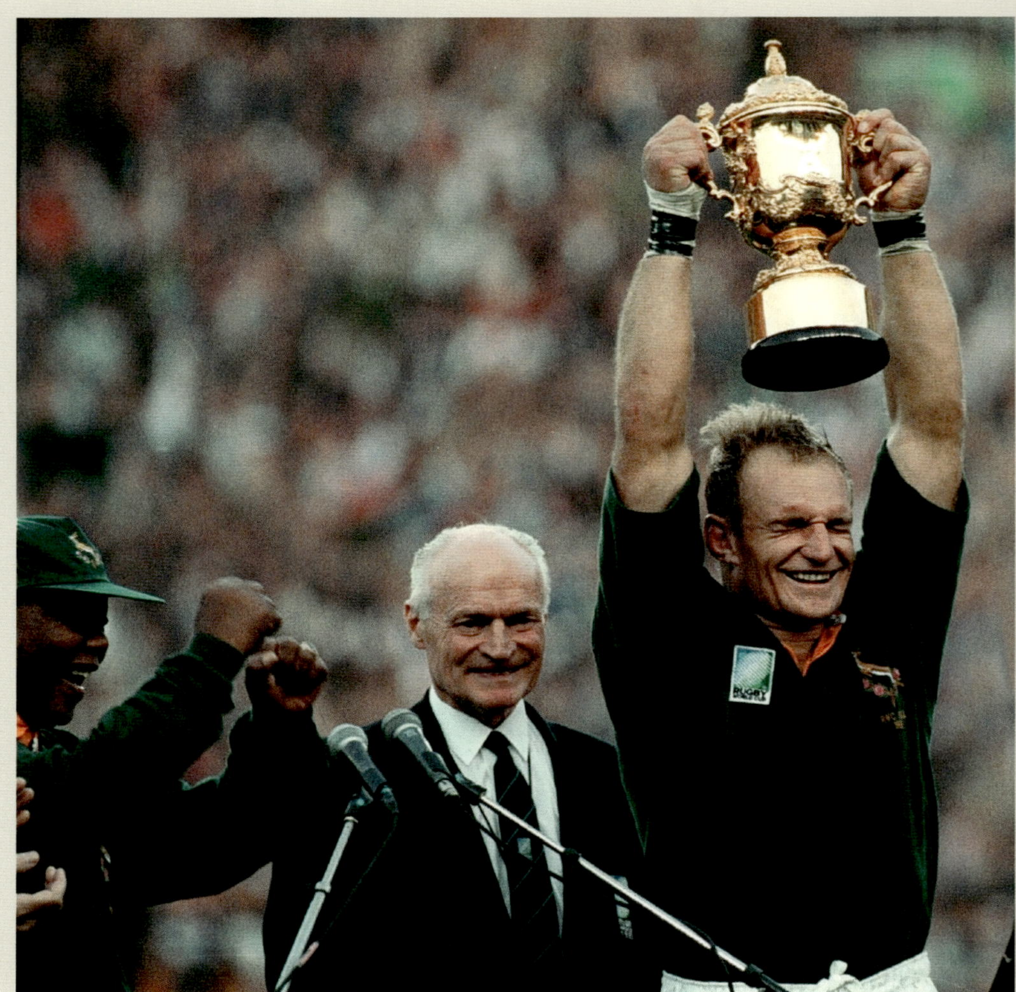

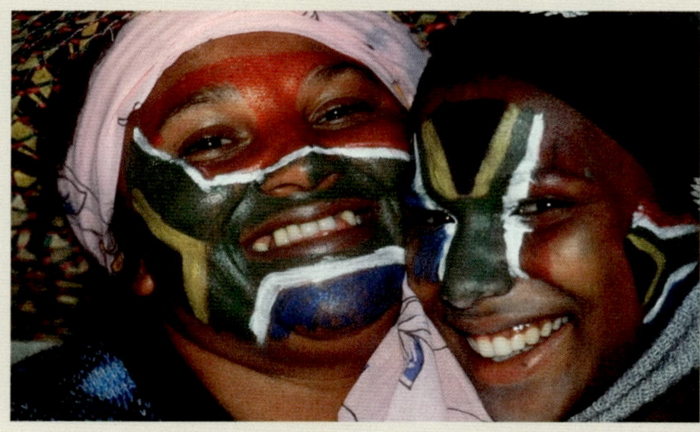

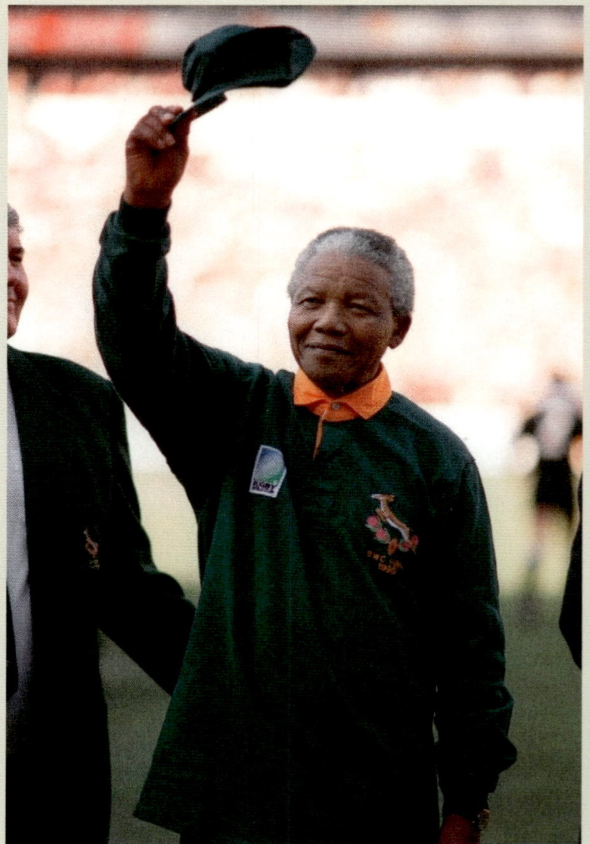

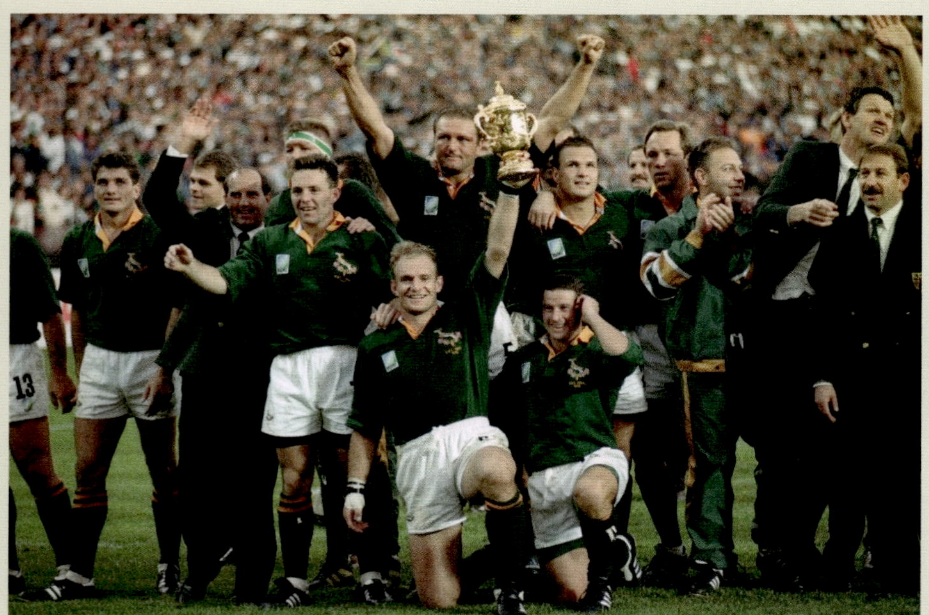

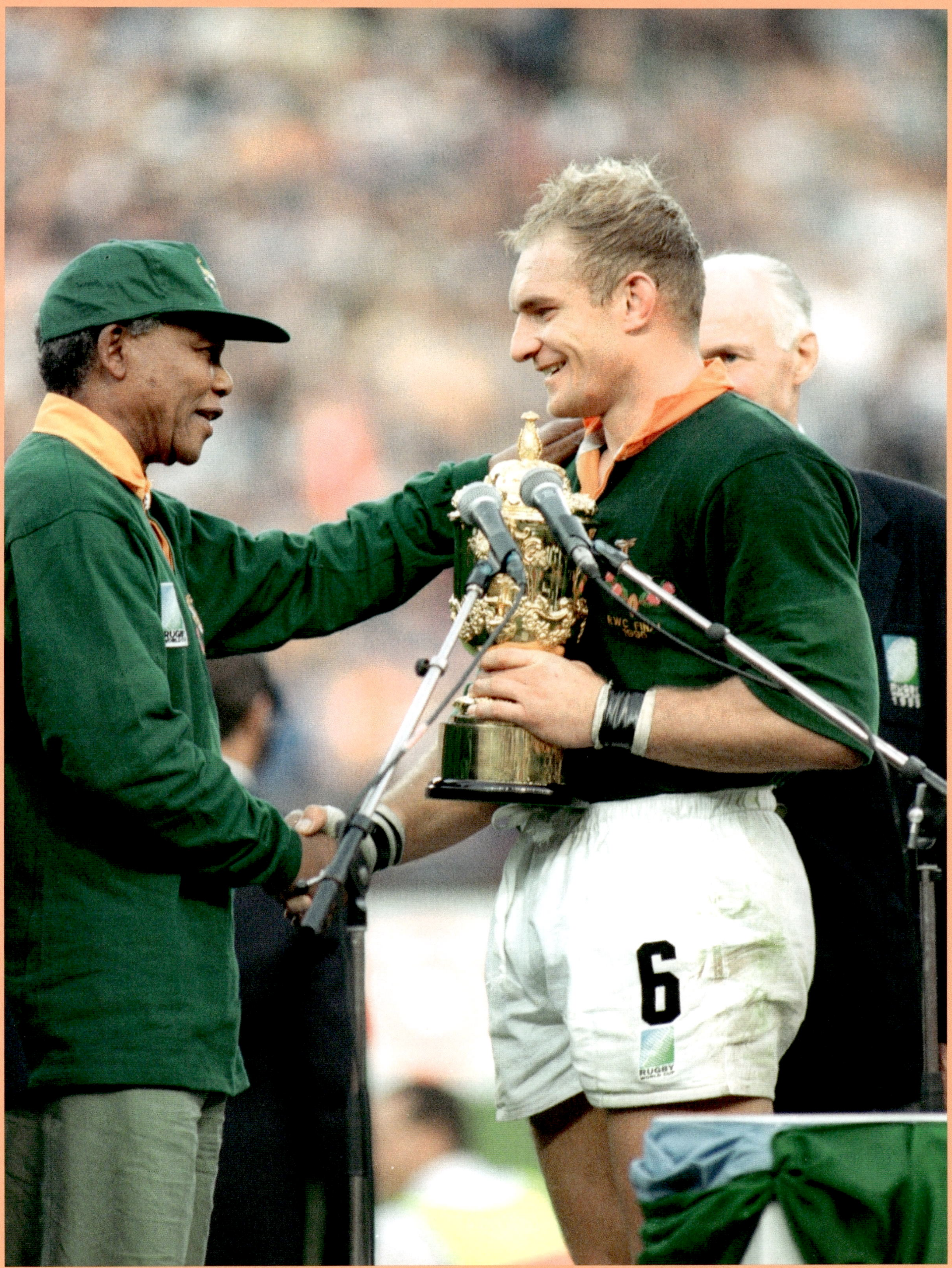
6
RUGBY

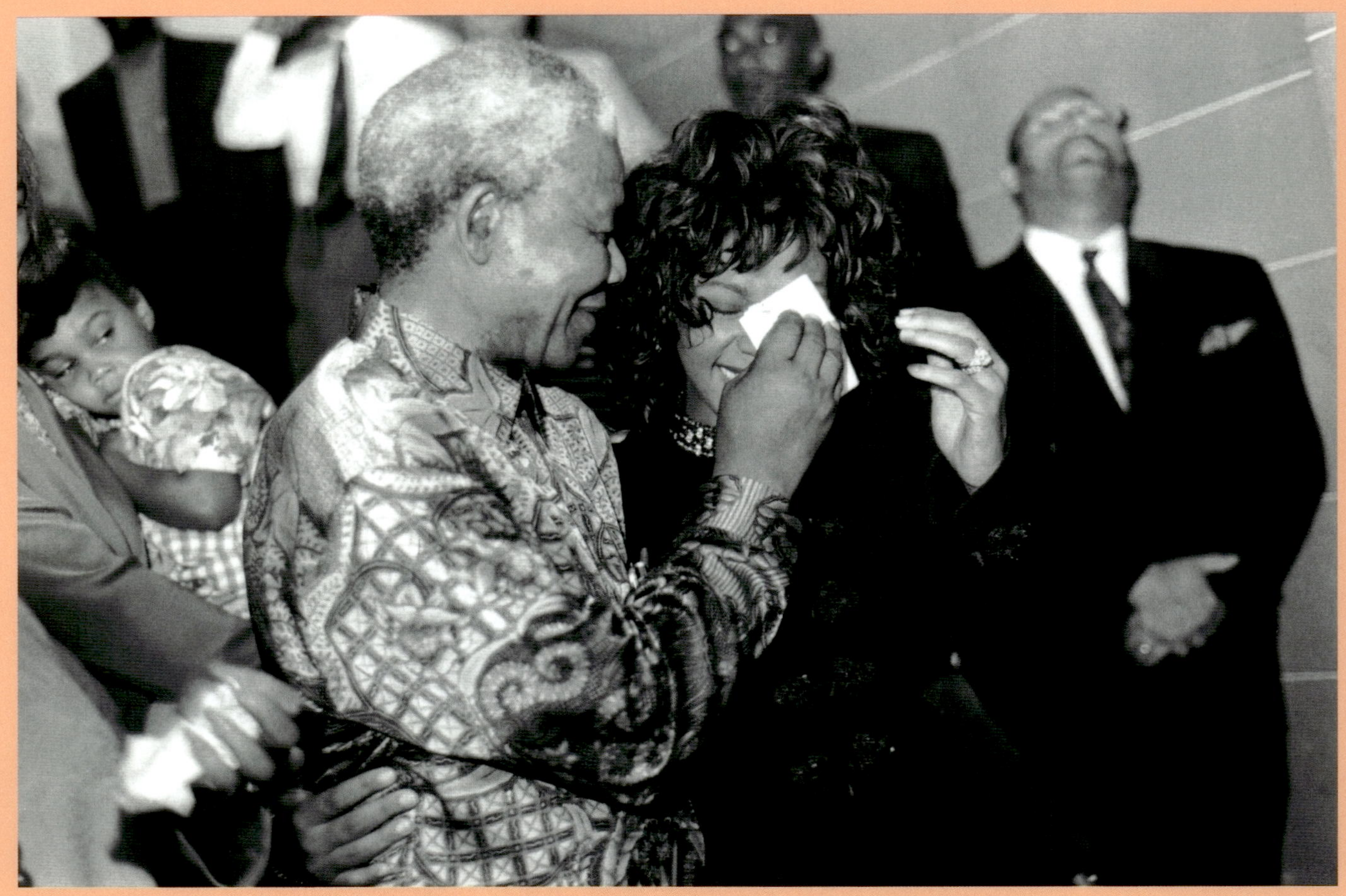

Above: Tata with Whitney Houston.

Right: Tata with Beyoncé.

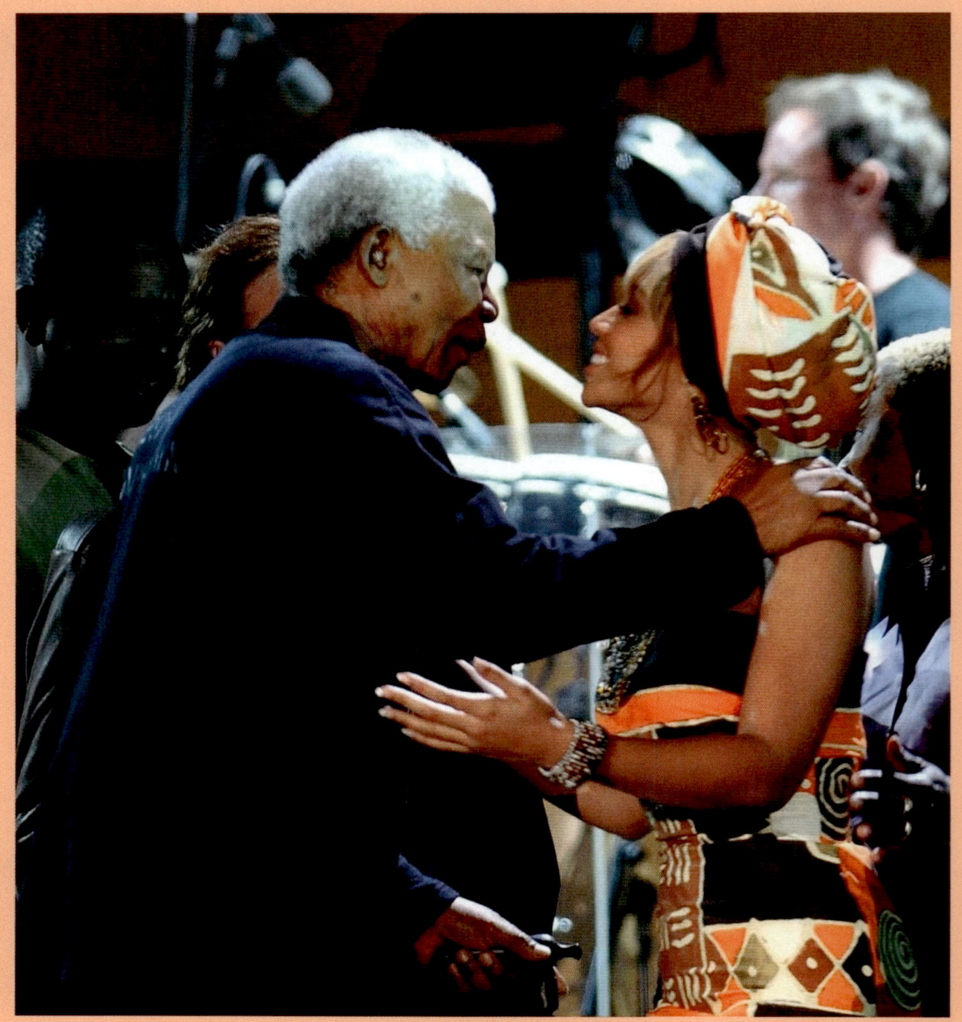

Tata did not consider himself a celebrity and genuinely loved people whether they were famous or not. Yet many celebrities kept South Africa's cause alive throughout the world during the anti-apartheid movement's dark days, and Tata was always happy to welcome and thank them for their continued support.

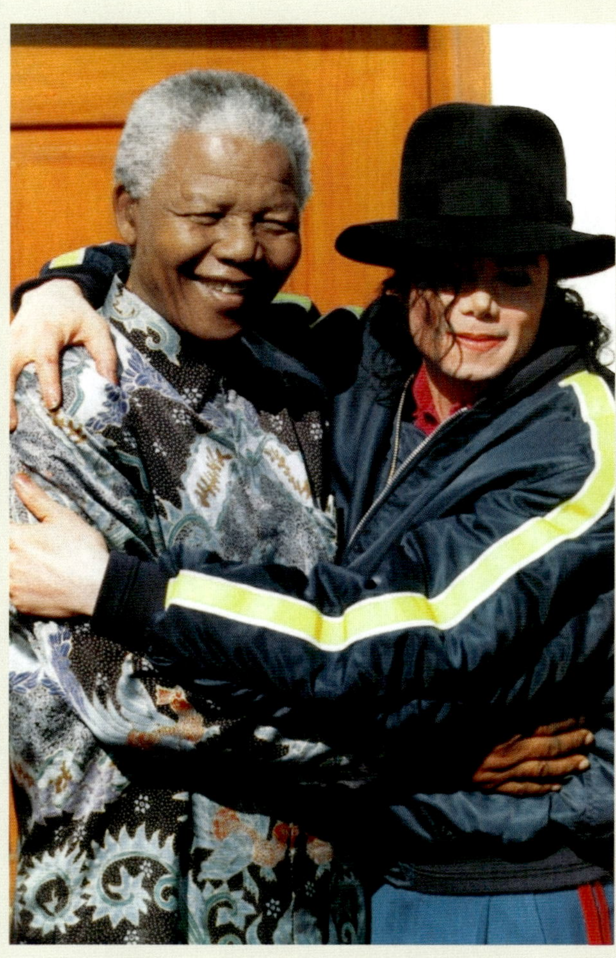

Left: Tata with Michael Jackson.

Below: Tata and Bono.

Bottom (*left to right*): Dave Stewart, Roger Taylor, Brian May, Peter Gabriel, and Annie Lennox, the artists who created and supported the Mandela Freedom Concert at Wembley in 1988.

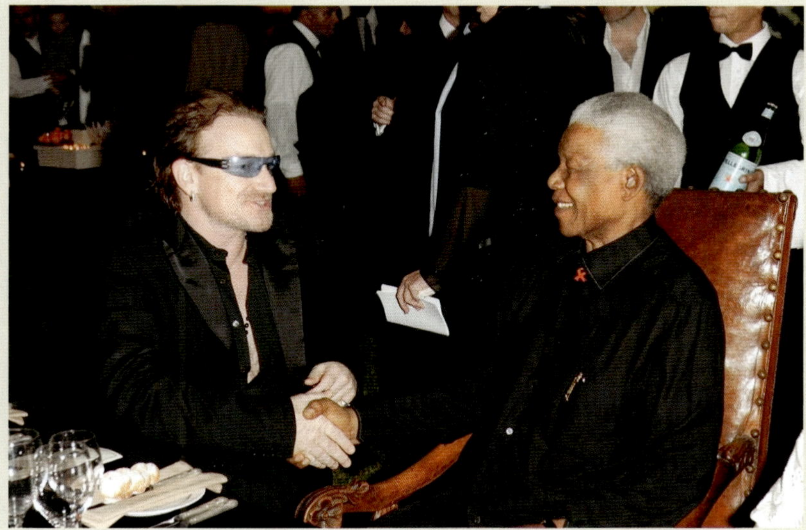

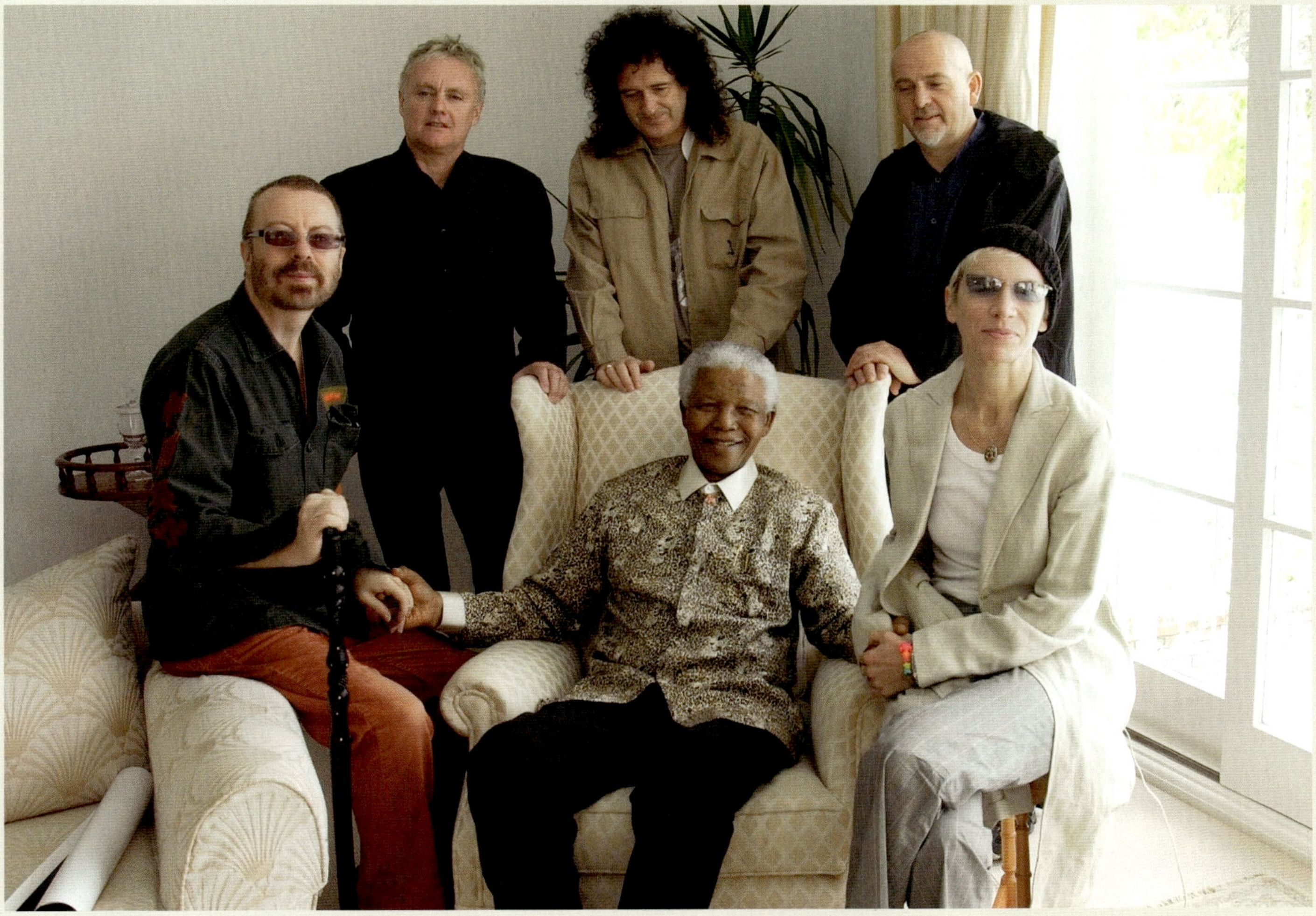

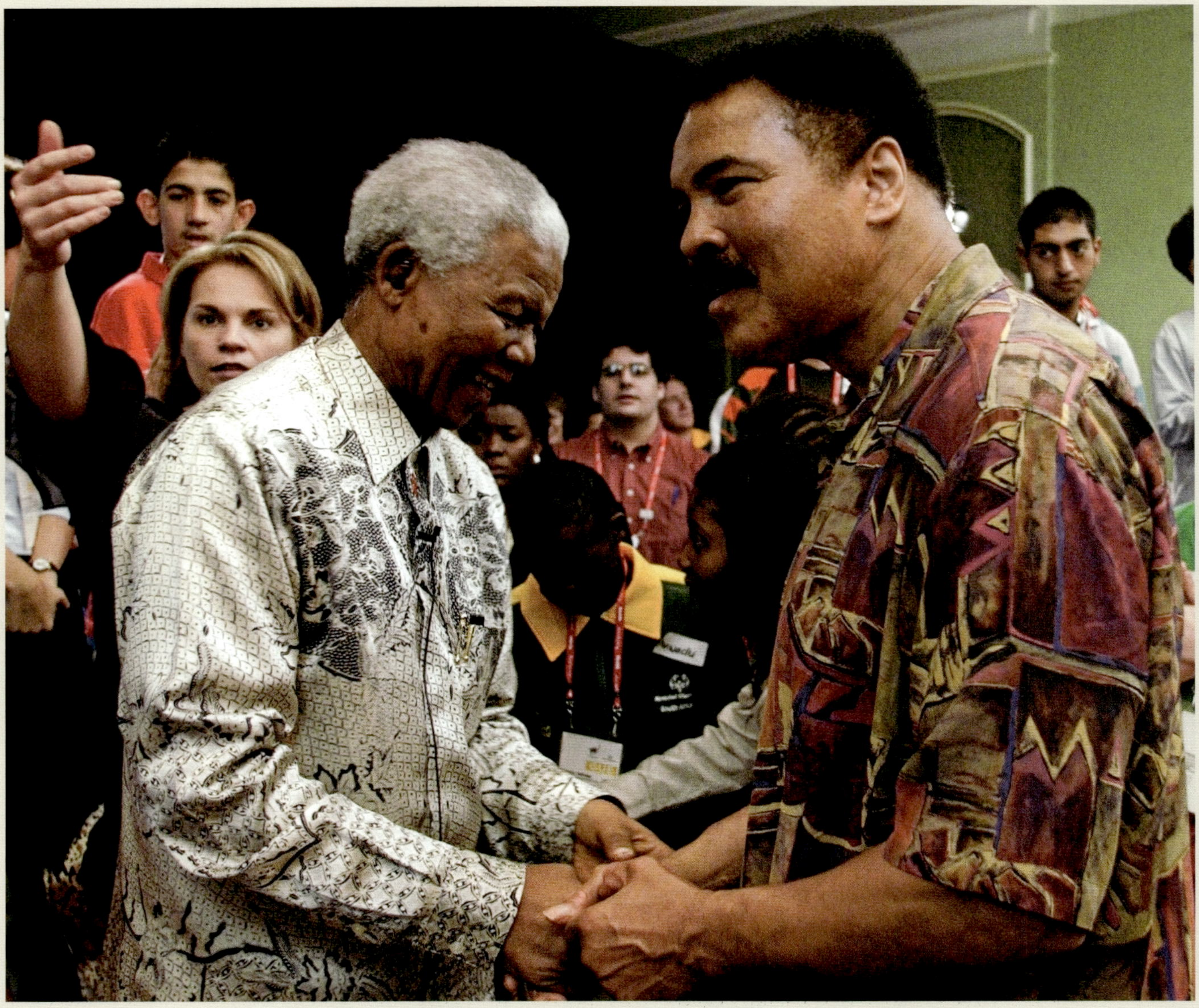

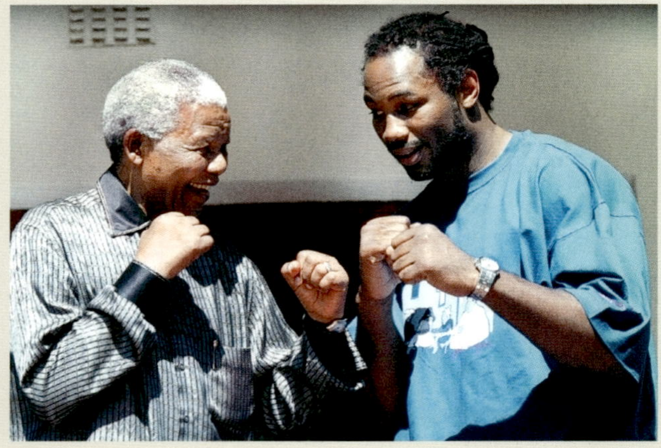

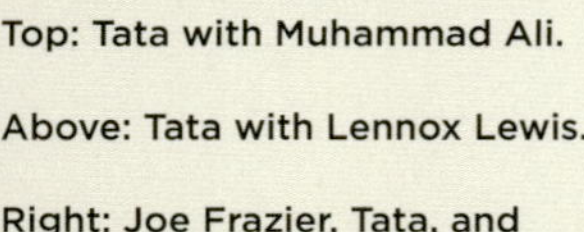

Top: Tata with Muhammad Ali.

Above: Tata with Lennox Lewis.

Right: Joe Frazier, Tata, and Butch Lewis.

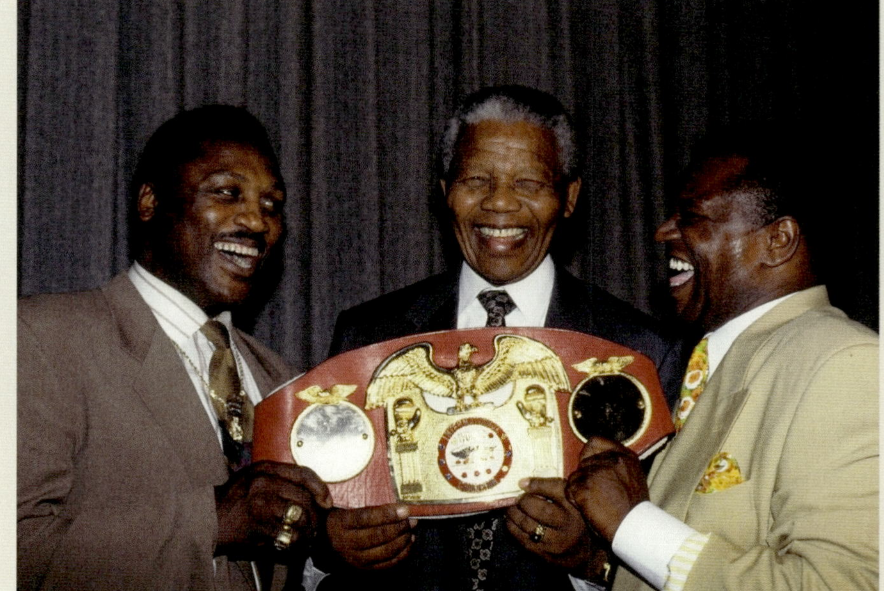

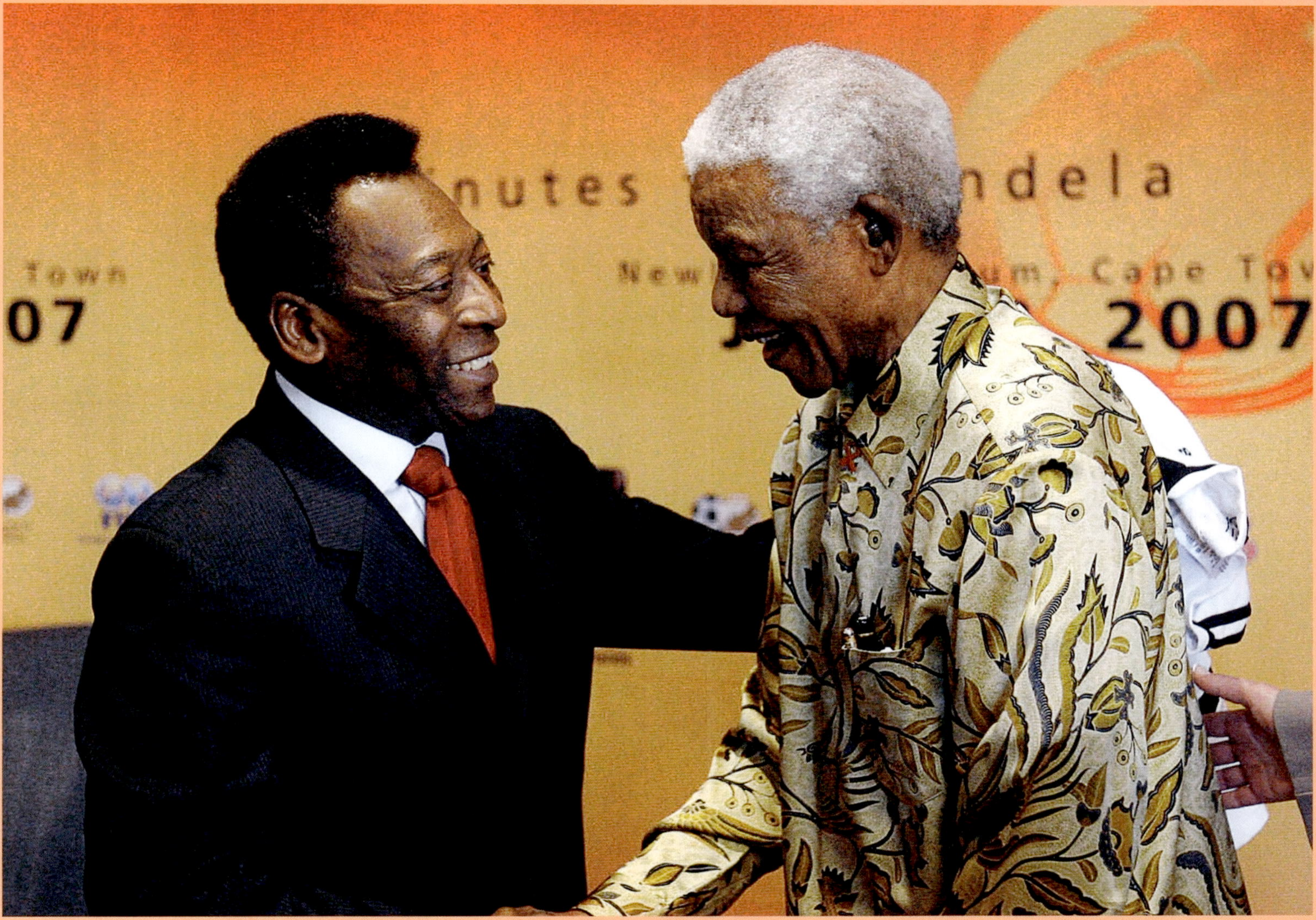

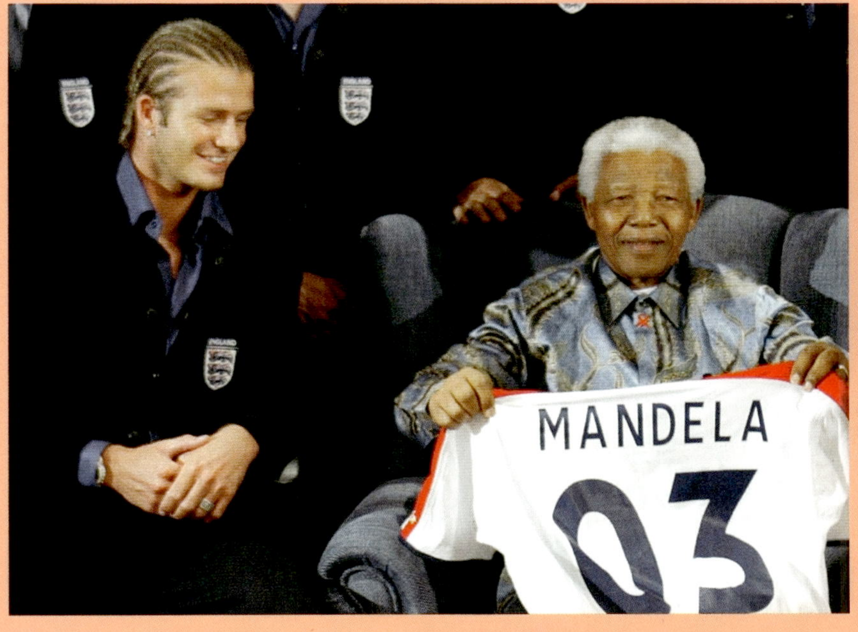

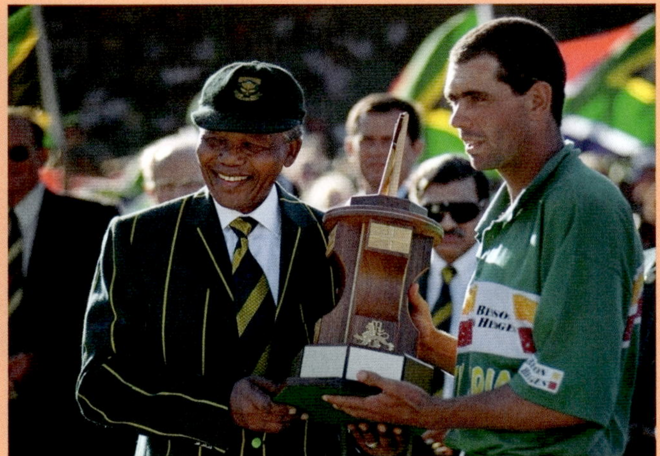

Top: Tata with Pelé.

Left: Tata with David Beckham.

Above: Tata with cricketer Hansie Cronje.

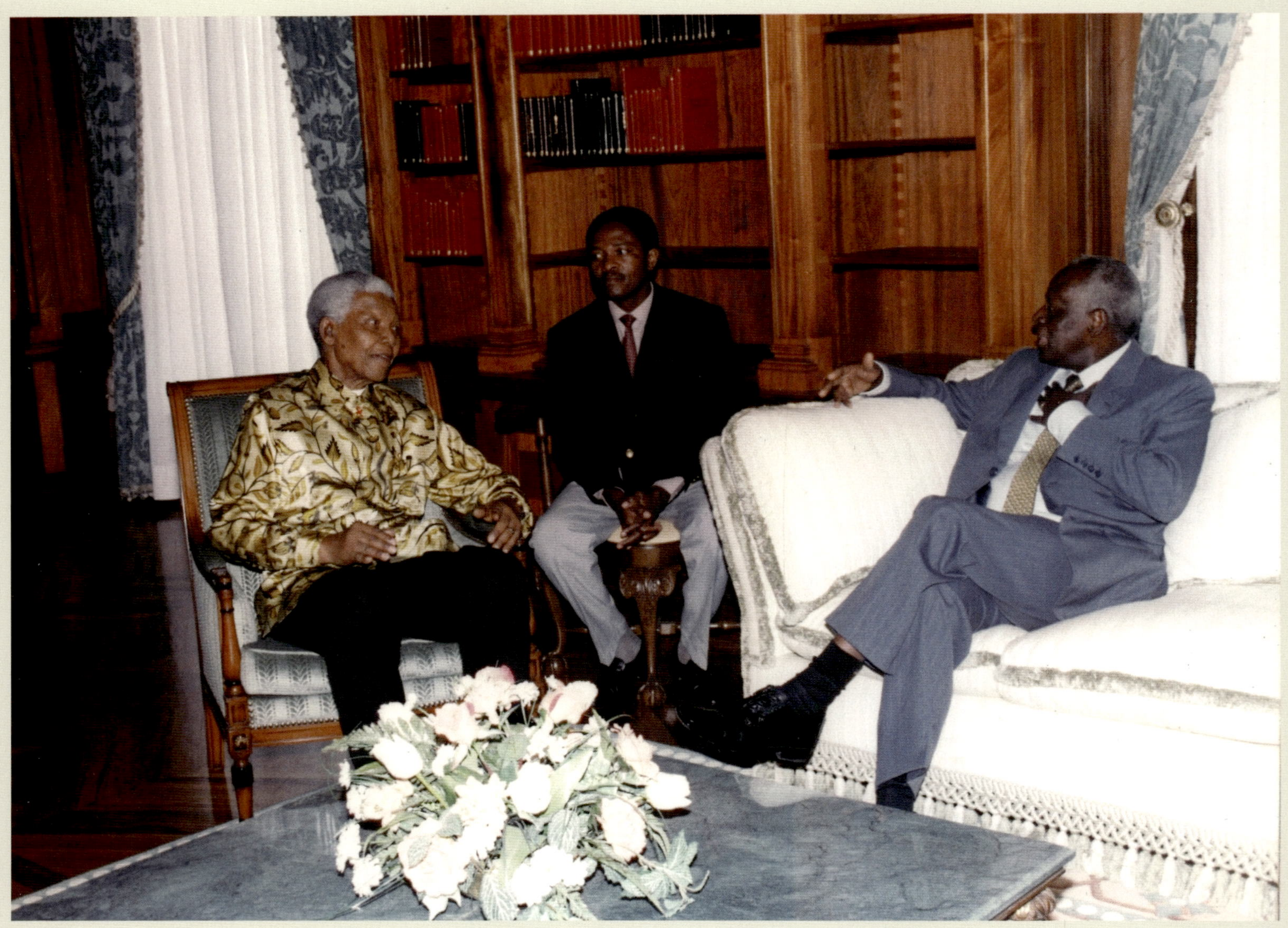

Above: Tata with President José Eduardo dos Santos of Angola.

Opposite: Tata with the president of Tunisia, Zine El Abidine Ben Ali.

"True Freedom requires hard work by all of us, employers and workers, teachers and students, government and communities. On the part of all of us, wherever we stand in society, it requires us to work together to resolve the disparities of the past."

Tata in his book, *From Freedom to the Future*

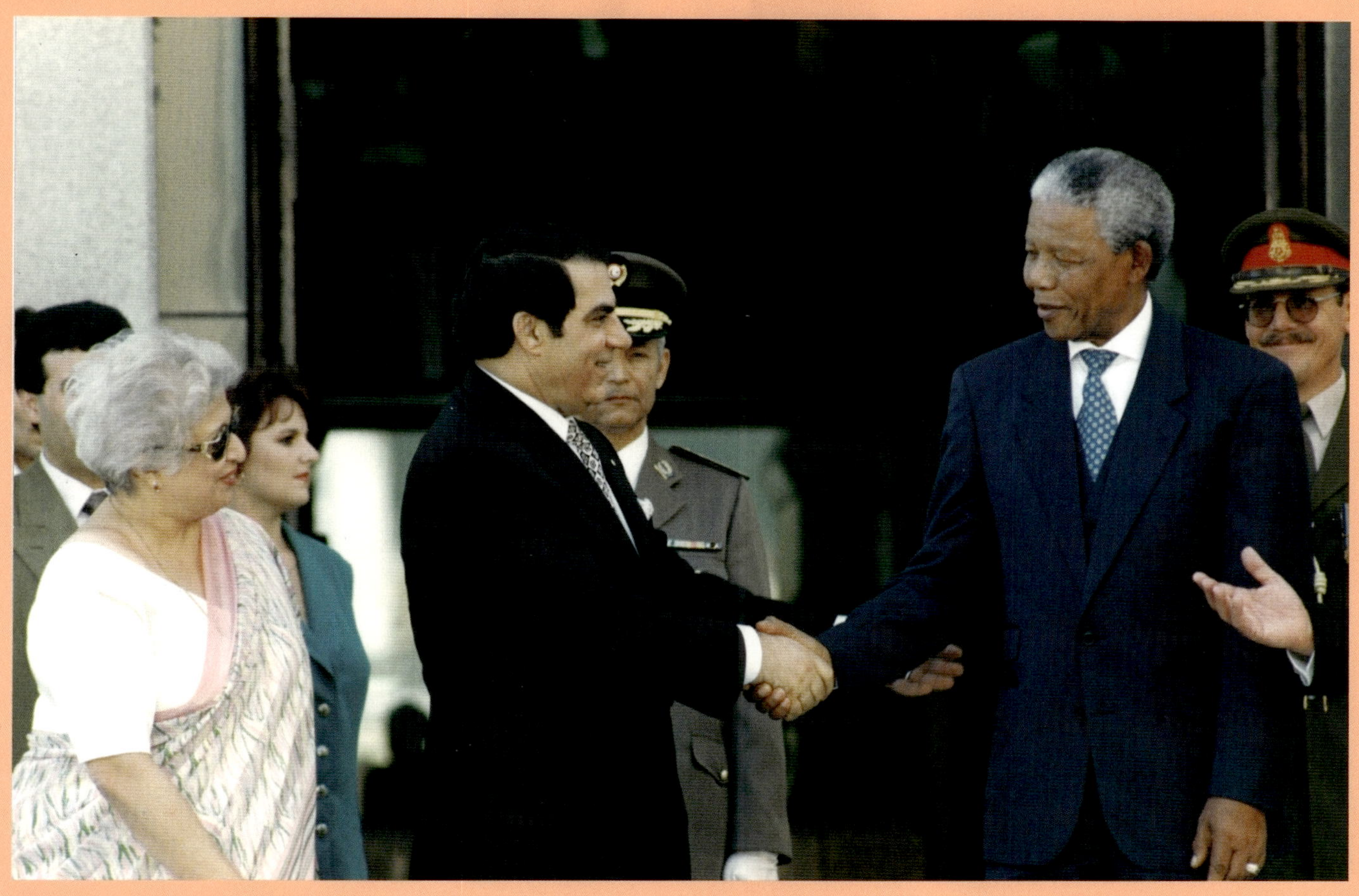

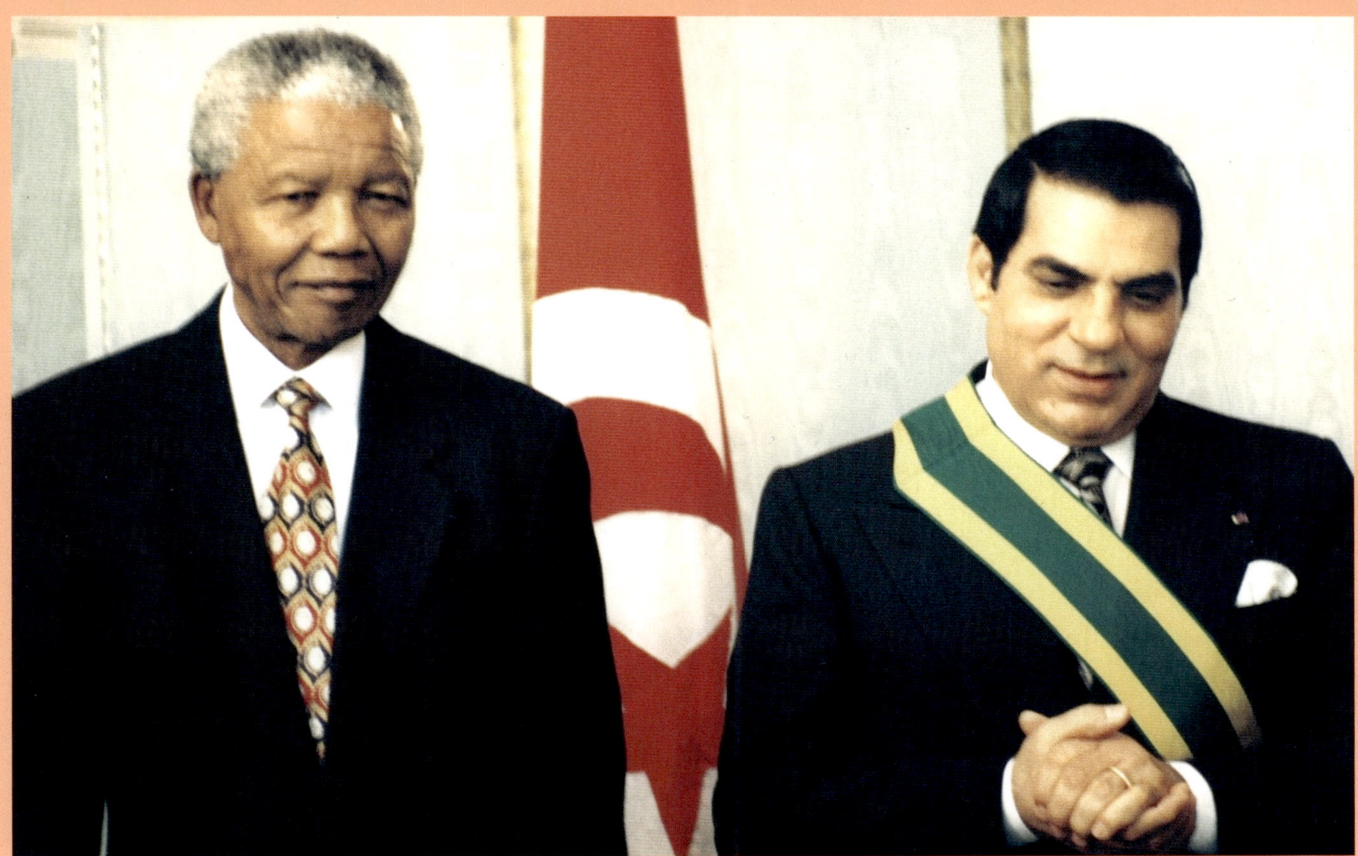

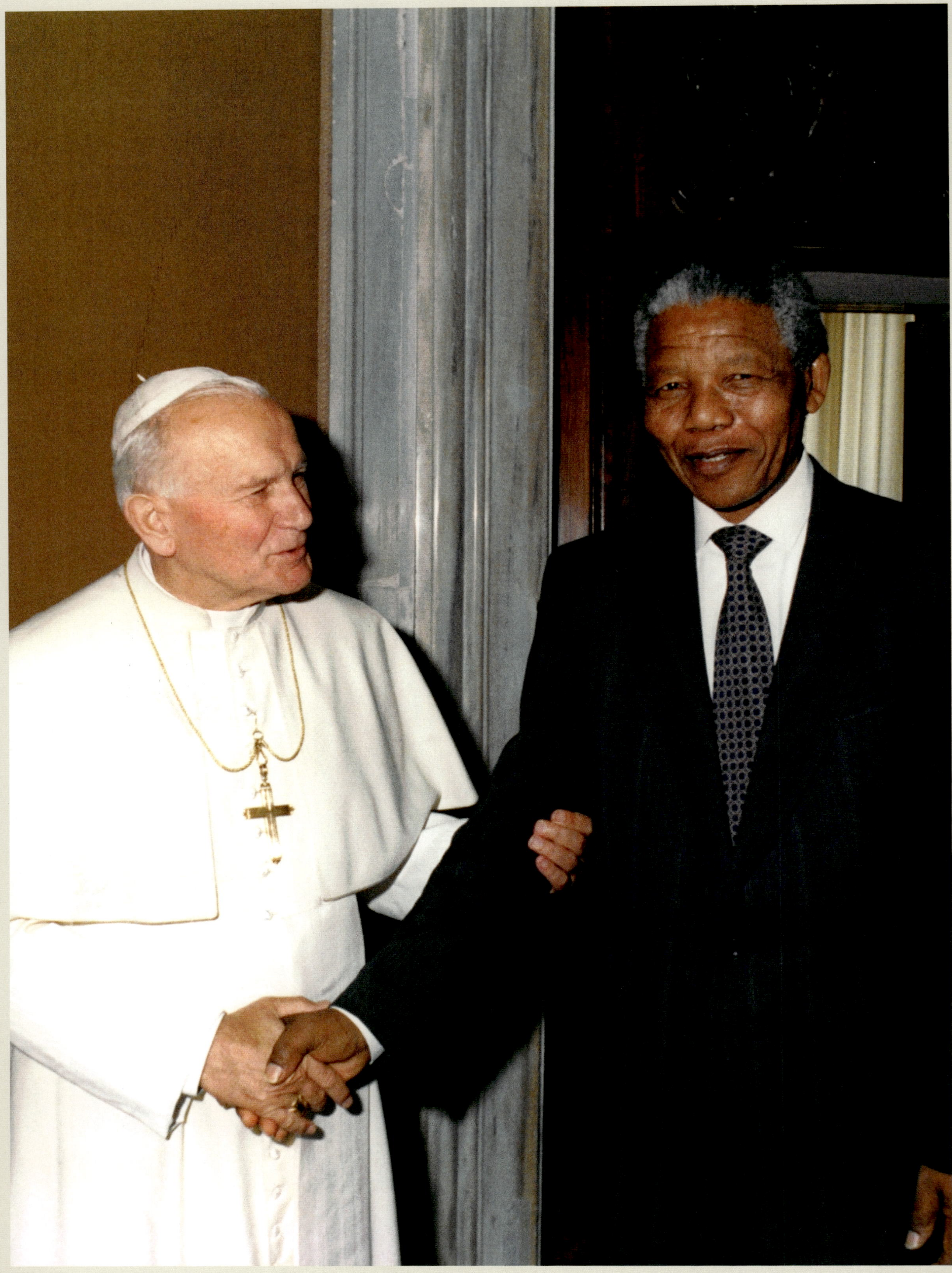

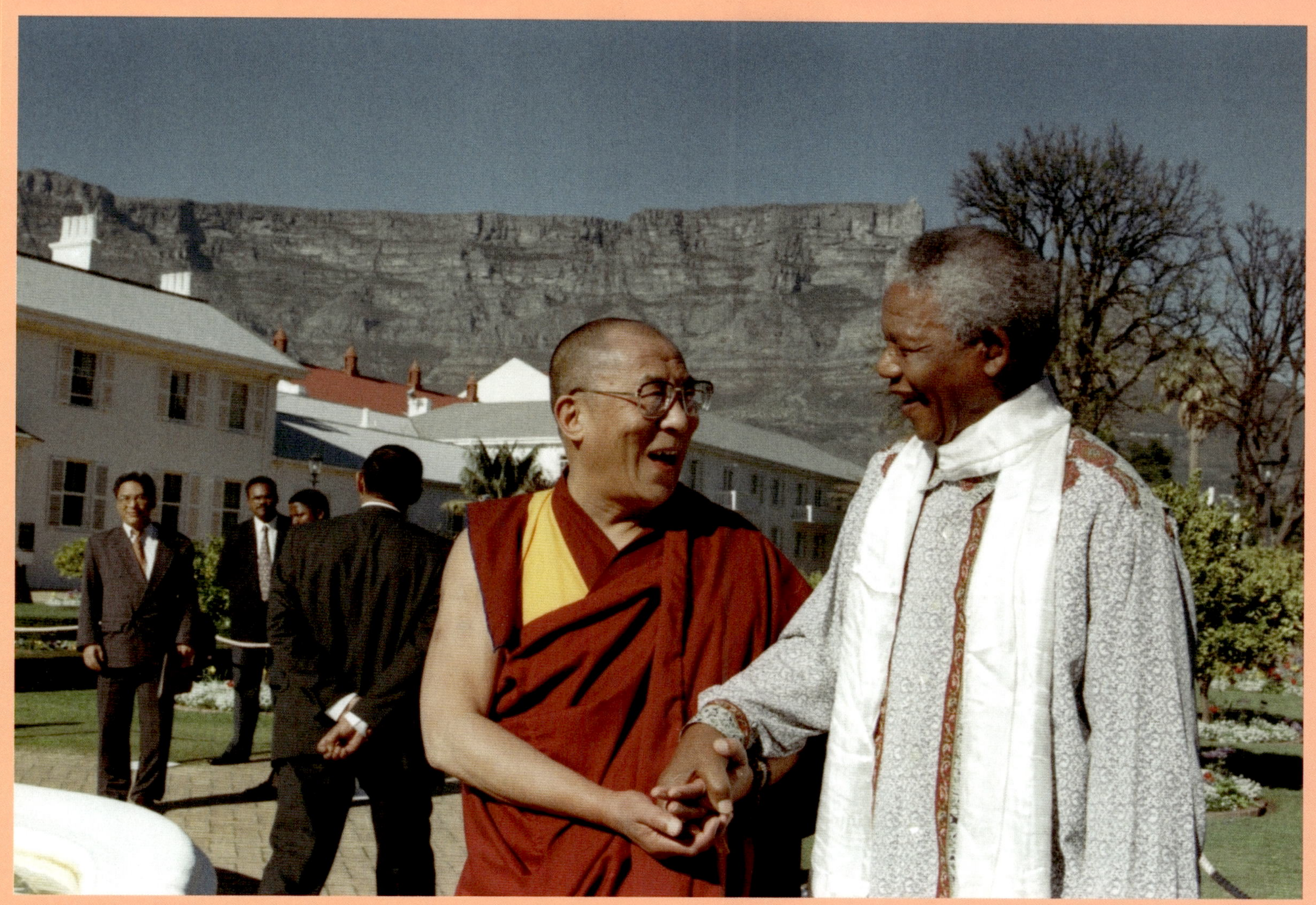

Opposite: Tata with Pope John Paul II in Rome on October 15, 1990.

Above: Tata with the Dalai Lama in Cape Town, August 1996.

"There is a word in South Africa—ubuntu—that describes his greatest gift, his recognition that we are all bound together in ways that can be invisible to the eye; that there is a oneness to humanity; that we achieve ourselves by sharing ourselves with others, and caring for those around us."

Barack Obama at the 2018 annual Mandela Lecture in Johannesburg

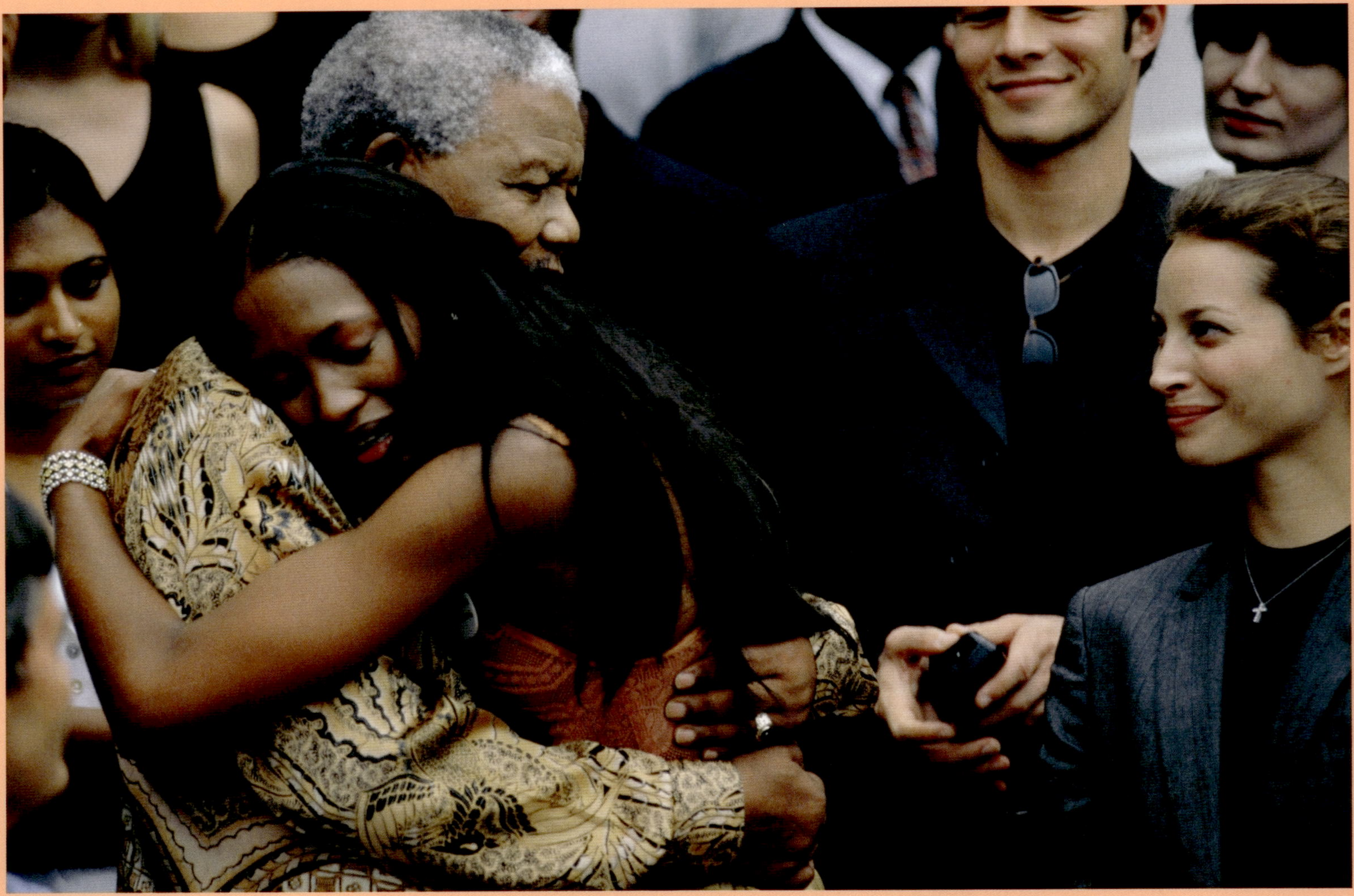

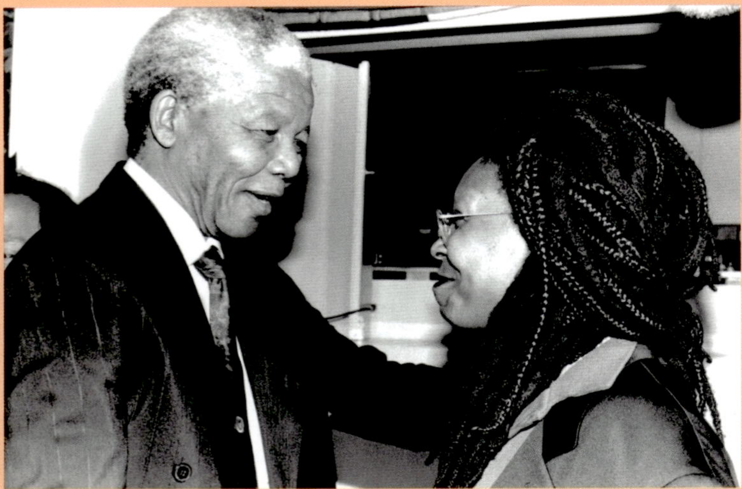

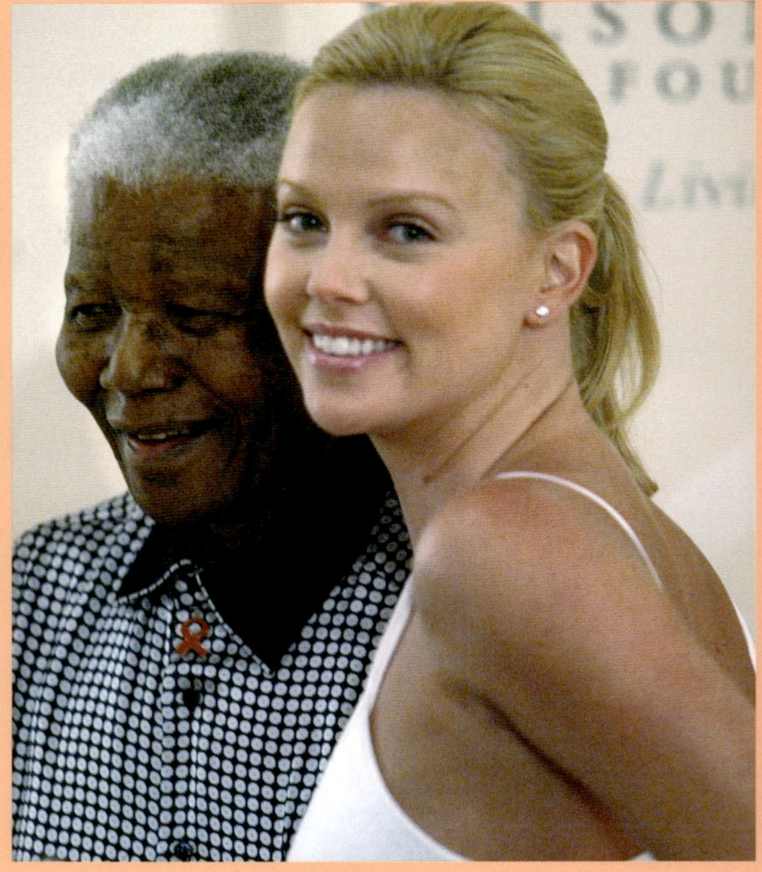

Top: Tata with Naomi Campbell and Christy Turlington while they were in South Africa to support the Mandela Children's Fund.

Above: Tata with Whoopi Goldberg.

Right: Tata with fellow South African Charlize Theron.

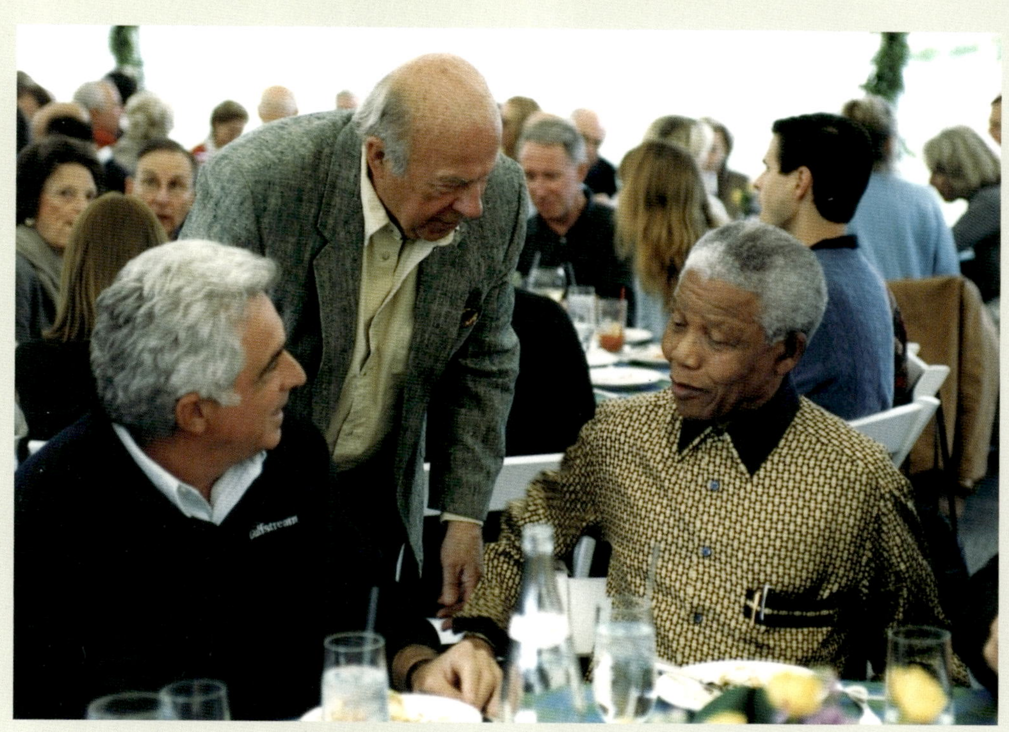

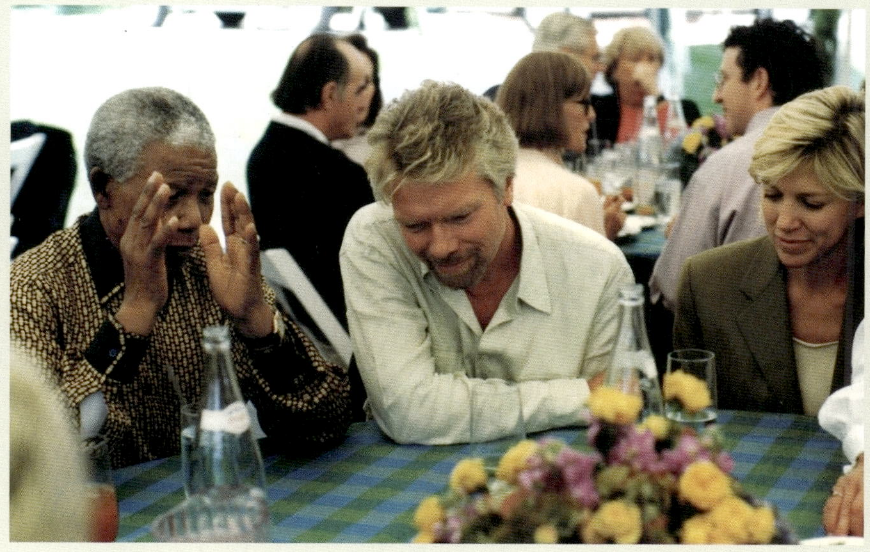

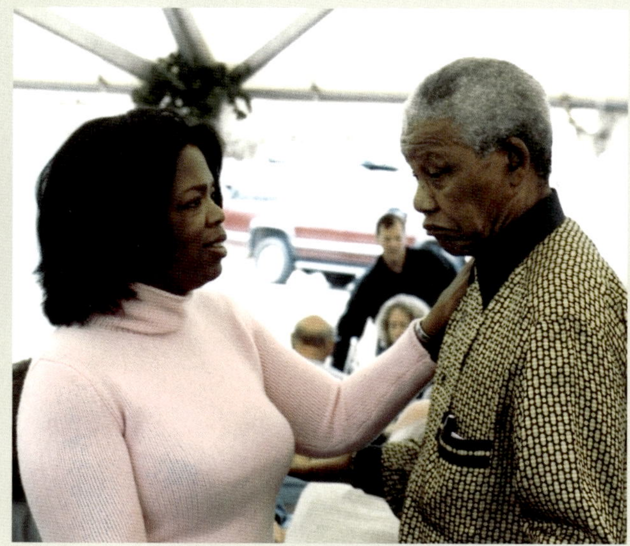

Luncheon in Los Angeles in honor of Tata.

Top: Tata with Ted Forstmann and George Schultz.

Middle (*left*): With Richard Branson.

Middle (*right*): With Oprah.

Right: With Kevin Costner, Martha Stewart, and others.

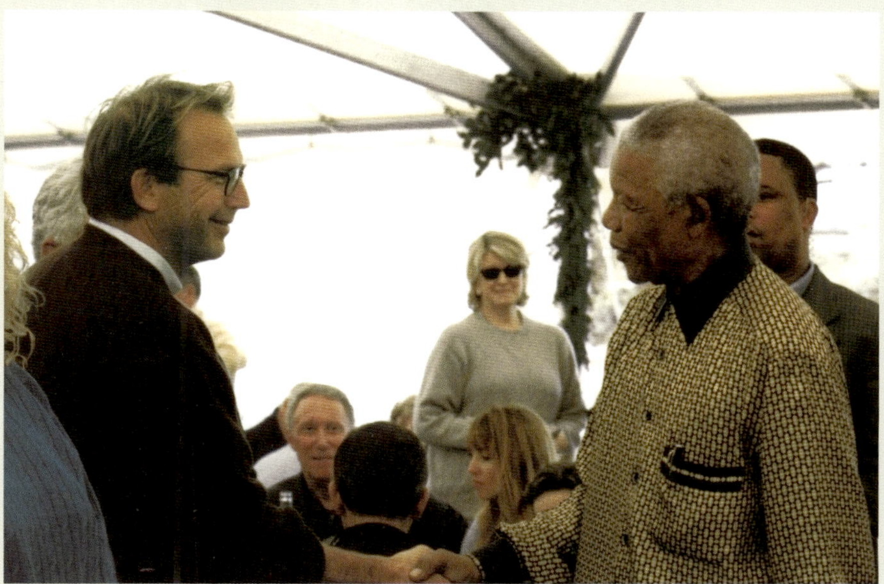

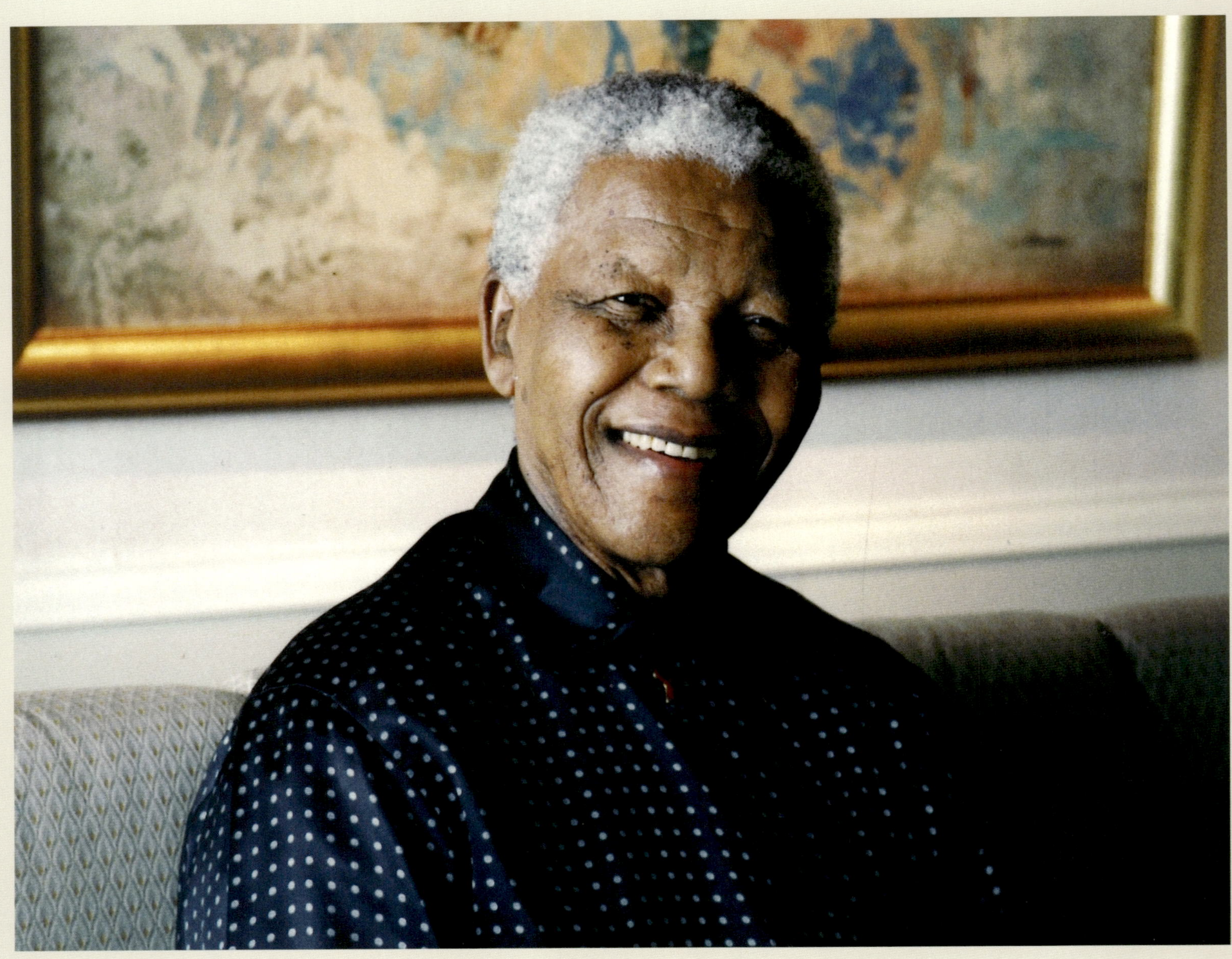

"As we overcame the obstacles that lay before us then, we will meet those of today. The foundation for a better life has been laid, and the building has begun. Today, let us renew our pledge to work together, to make South Africa into a land of our dreams."

Such were the parting words Tata made as he passed the baton from his generation to the next. And as a realist, he also understood that there was still much work to be done.

Tata in his last parliamentary speech as he was stepping down as president

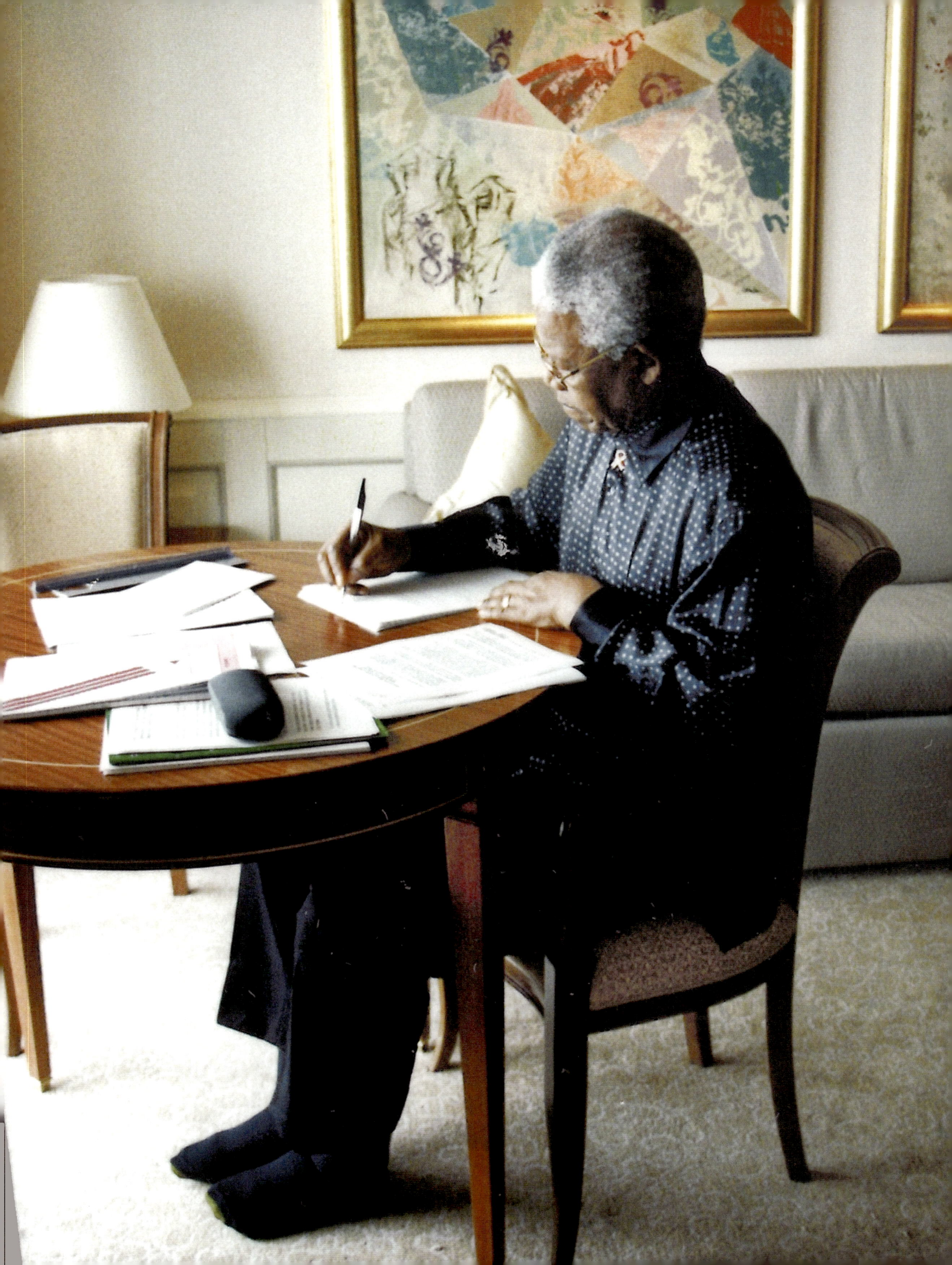

8

The Legacy

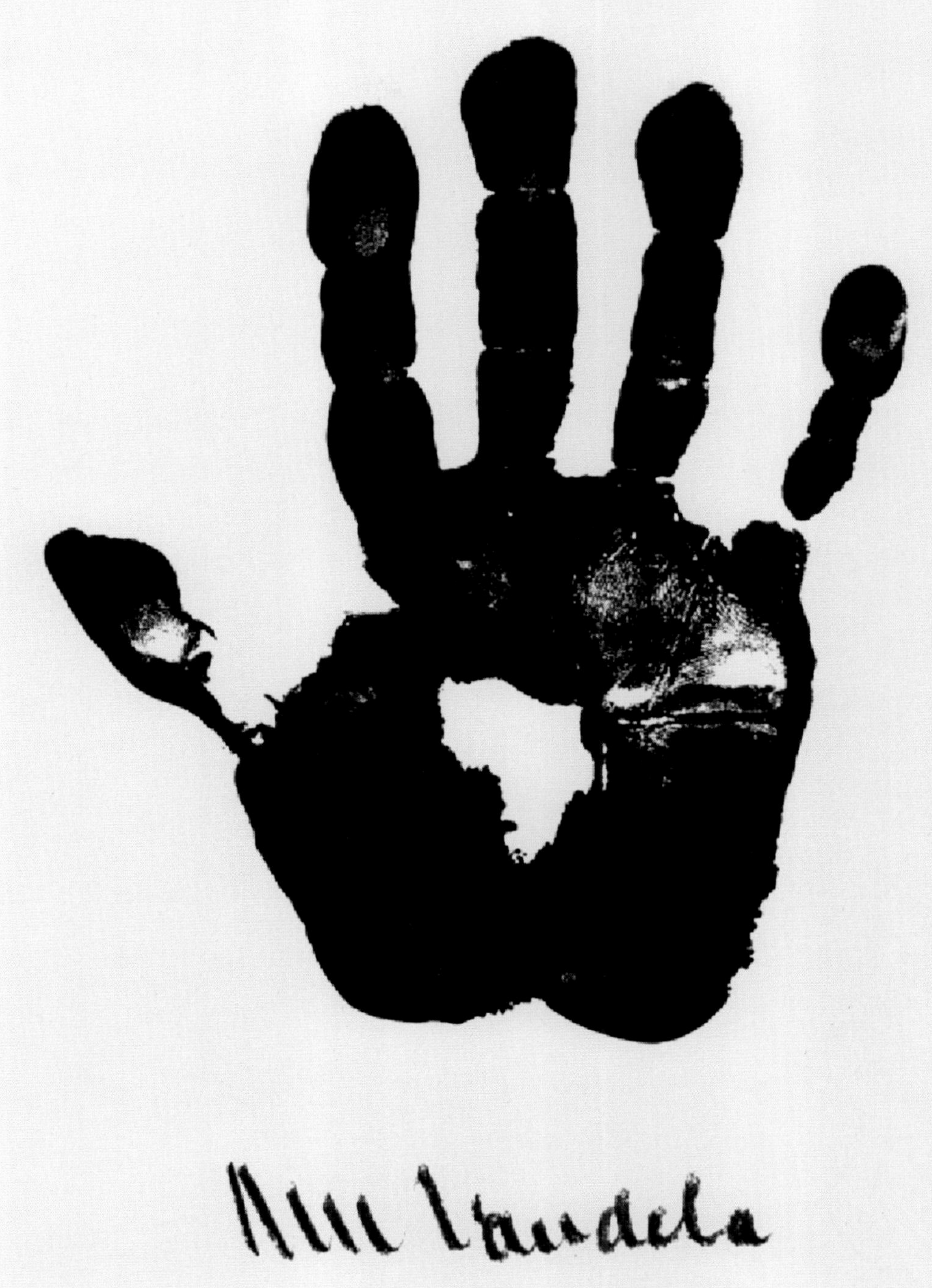

Tata lived so that others might live and that the happiness of others might reign. He died so that liberty might not perish and freedom and justice might reign.

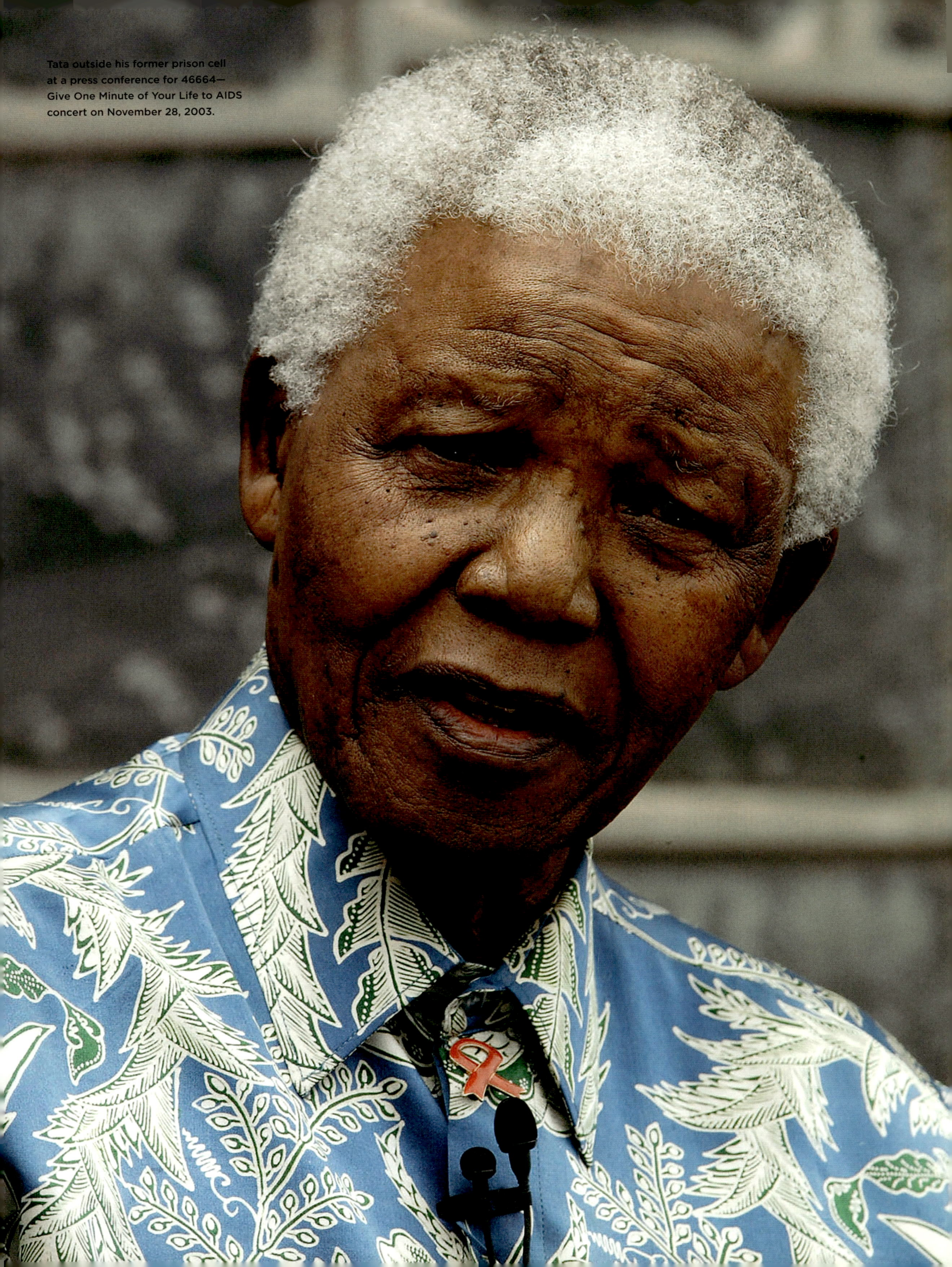

Tata outside his former prison cell at a press conference for 46664—Give One Minute of Your Life to AIDS concert on November 28, 2003.

"[Mandela's] inspiration lives on in the heart of every African patriot. He is the symbol of the self-sacrificing leadership our struggle has thrown up and our people need. He is unrelenting, yet capable of flexibility and delicate judgment. He is an outstanding individual, but he knows that he derives his strength from the great masses of people, who make up the freedom struggle in our country.

Oliver Tambo, London, 1965

Few leaders in the history of the world have attracted such worldwide veneration as is bestowed on Tata. Despite several articles published after his death that were critical of his life after retiring as president, the widespread adoration of this beloved son of Africa has not waned. As journalist Adrian Hadland has put it, "[Mandela's] reputation remains as impressive as it is unsullied."

Tata is widely seen as a personification of the core values that informed his life and for which he spent most of his life fighting. His character, courage, humility, and compassion have granted him, even in death, an unprecedented moral authority. He is, in the words of Anthony Sampson, "a universal hero."

As journalist Fred Khumalo wrote, he is remembered "as the first president of a free South Africa, a man who saved that country from a full-scale racial civil war; a man who, for generations to come, will remain an iconic presence in the firmament of influential personalities the world over."

However, as a daughter, I can see that Tata had his weaknesses. He was not perfect, nor was he, during his lifetime, beyond criticism. Like all of us, he had feet of clay. As a man, Tata was passionate and sensitive; he did not take kindly to being questioned by younger people.

He was very stubborn in some things—it was his way. He would forget that the world he grew up in and the world that his own children grew up in were completely different.

He was, however, a charismatic and magnetic man. Tata did not explicitly say, "These are the values that I stand for, and these are the values that you as my people should aspire to." He was instead an embodiment of these values. We were able to discern them through the way he conducted his life.

Wherever he went and in whatever he did, he respected and defended the dignity of everybody, regardless of their social or economic status. Tata remained, and remains, a man of the people, revered around the globe.

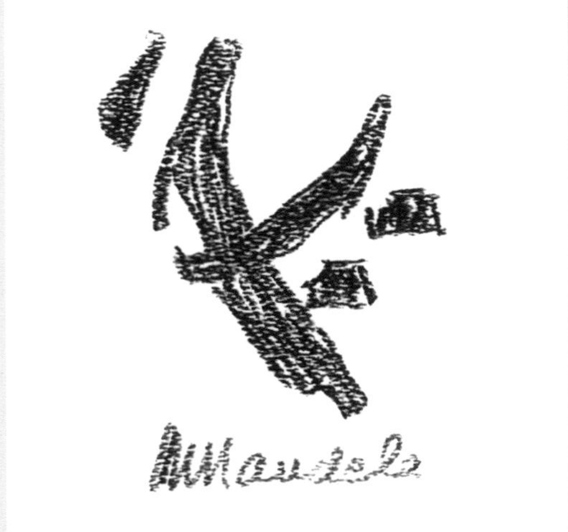

Tata's sketches were often his way of symbolizing profound ideas.

Courage

"I learned that courage was not the absence of fear, but the triumph over it. The brave man is not he who does not feel afraid but he who conquers that fear."

Tata in *Long Walk to Freedom*

It took courage to fight the cruel, brutal system of apartheid, to be prepared to die for the belief in justice. When Tata decided during his long years of imprisonment to negotiate with the government, he knew that such a decision would lead to criticism by his colleagues. Yet as Walter Sisulu said, "I regard that as one of the most courageous moments when a man is alone in the face of that situation, particularly in politics where you have a lot of criticism from everyone."

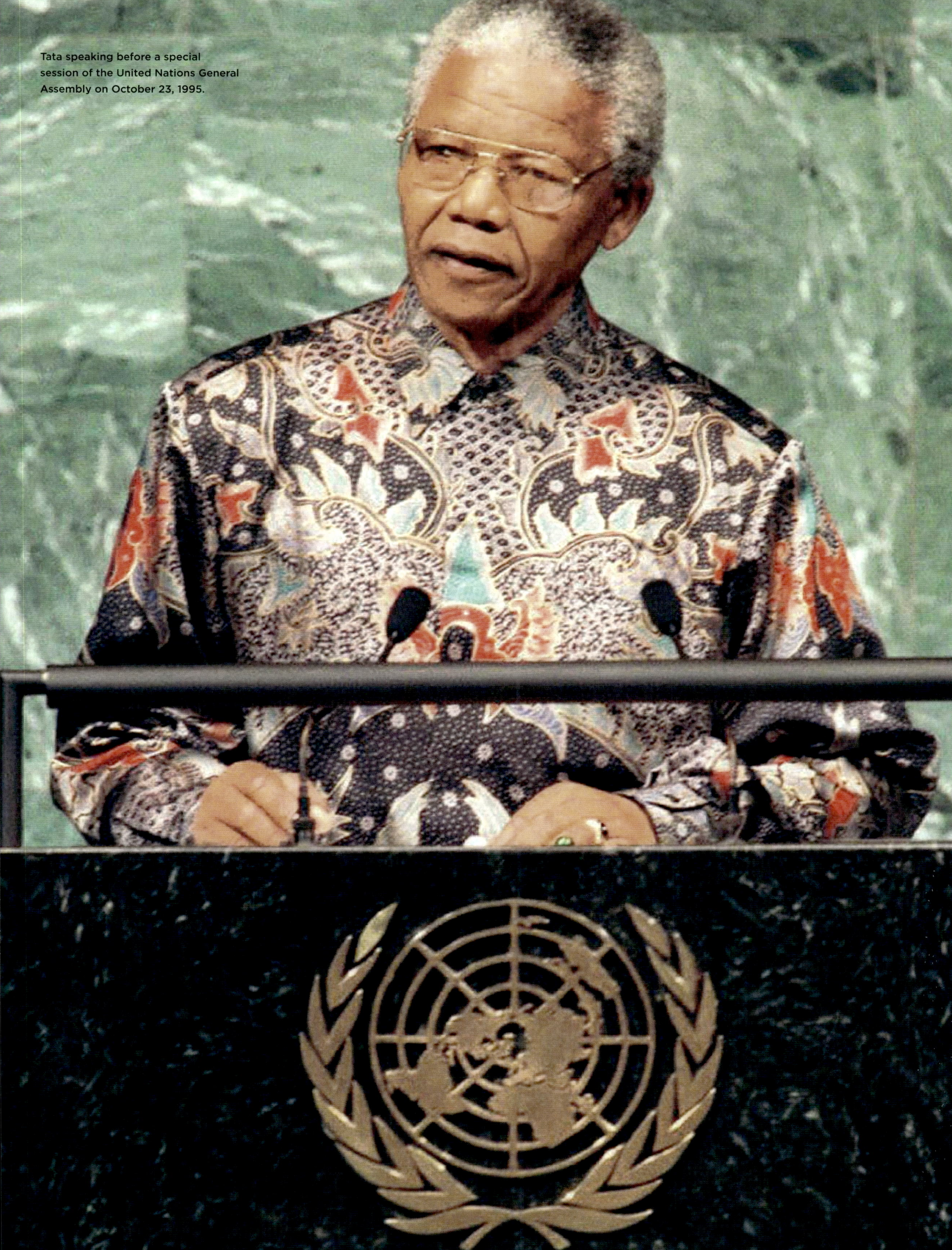

Tata speaking before a special session of the United Nations General Assembly on October 23, 1995.

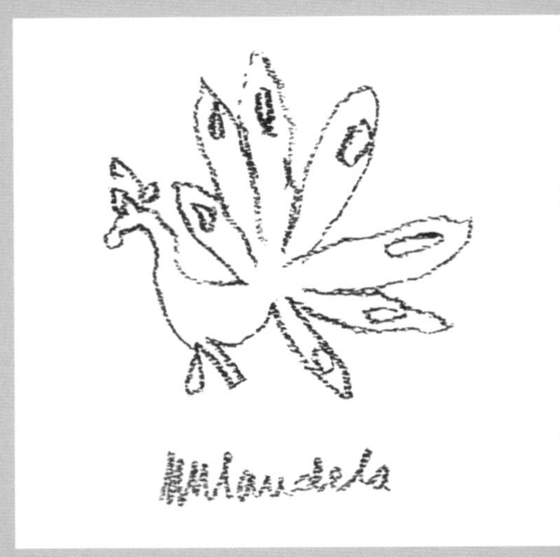

Integrity

"The first thing is to be honest with yourself. You can never have an impact on society if you have not changed yourself." Tata

As a member of the population who were, and who remain, the victims of oppression and poverty, Tata was loyal to his cause, fighting against both white domination and Black domination. He proved his honesty and integrity by aligning his life's mission with the statement he read at the Rivonia Trial, the trial that led to his imprisonment, and fighting for a truly nonracial South African society.

He never compromised with the perpetrators of racial oppression, and he expected each of us as individuals—both victims and perpetrators—to take responsibility for our actions and not remain robots programmed by fate. "Everyone can rise above their circumstances and achieve success if they are dedicated to and passionate about what they do," he said.

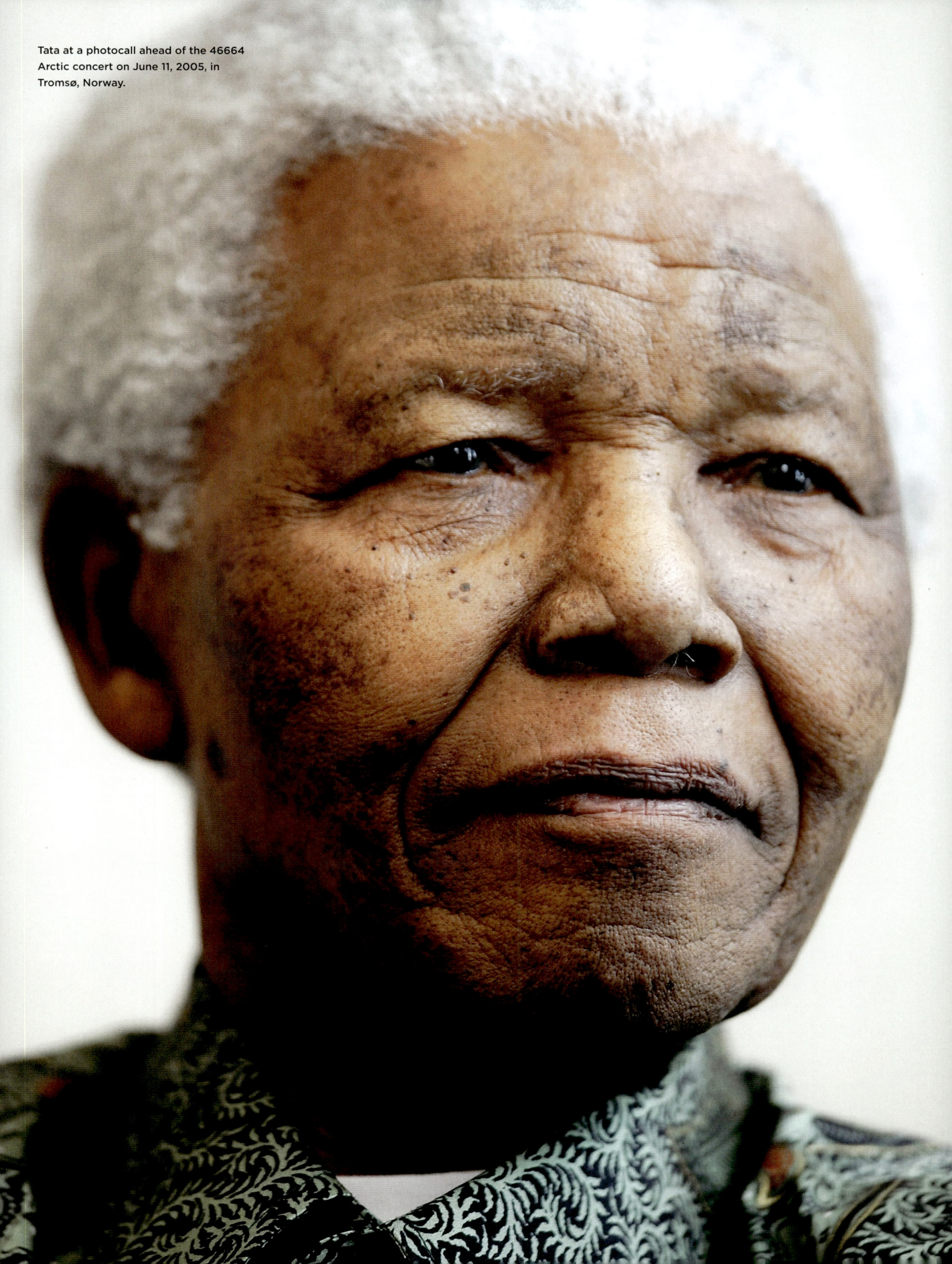

Tata at a photocall ahead of the 46664 Arctic concert on June 11, 2005, in Tromsø, Norway.

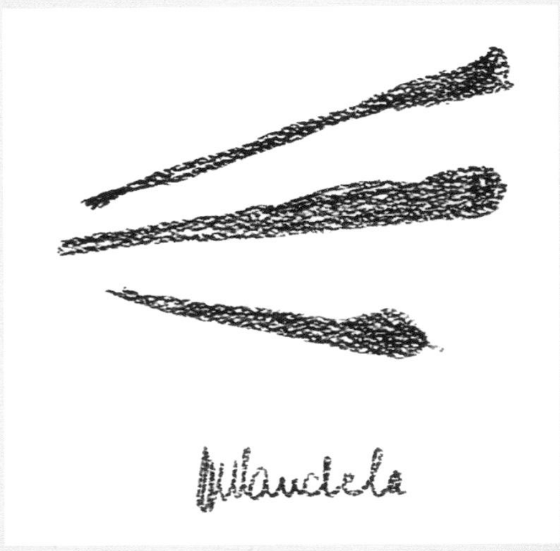

Perseverance

"There are few misfortunes in the world that you cannot turn into a personal triumph if you have the iron will and the necessary skill."

Tata

When Tata joined the African National Congress in 1944, he knew that the struggle for freedom would be long and difficult. He and his comrades understood that they were dealing with a brutal, oppressive regime and the journey required not just courageous men and women, but ones who were willing to persevere until the end. They learned that the struggle for freedom was all-consuming and it meant sacrificing one's personal and family life. He knew early on that he could be imprisoned or sent to the gallows, but he was determined to push on. In Tata's own words, in *Long Walk to Freedom*: "After climbing a great hill, one only finds that there are many more hills to climb."

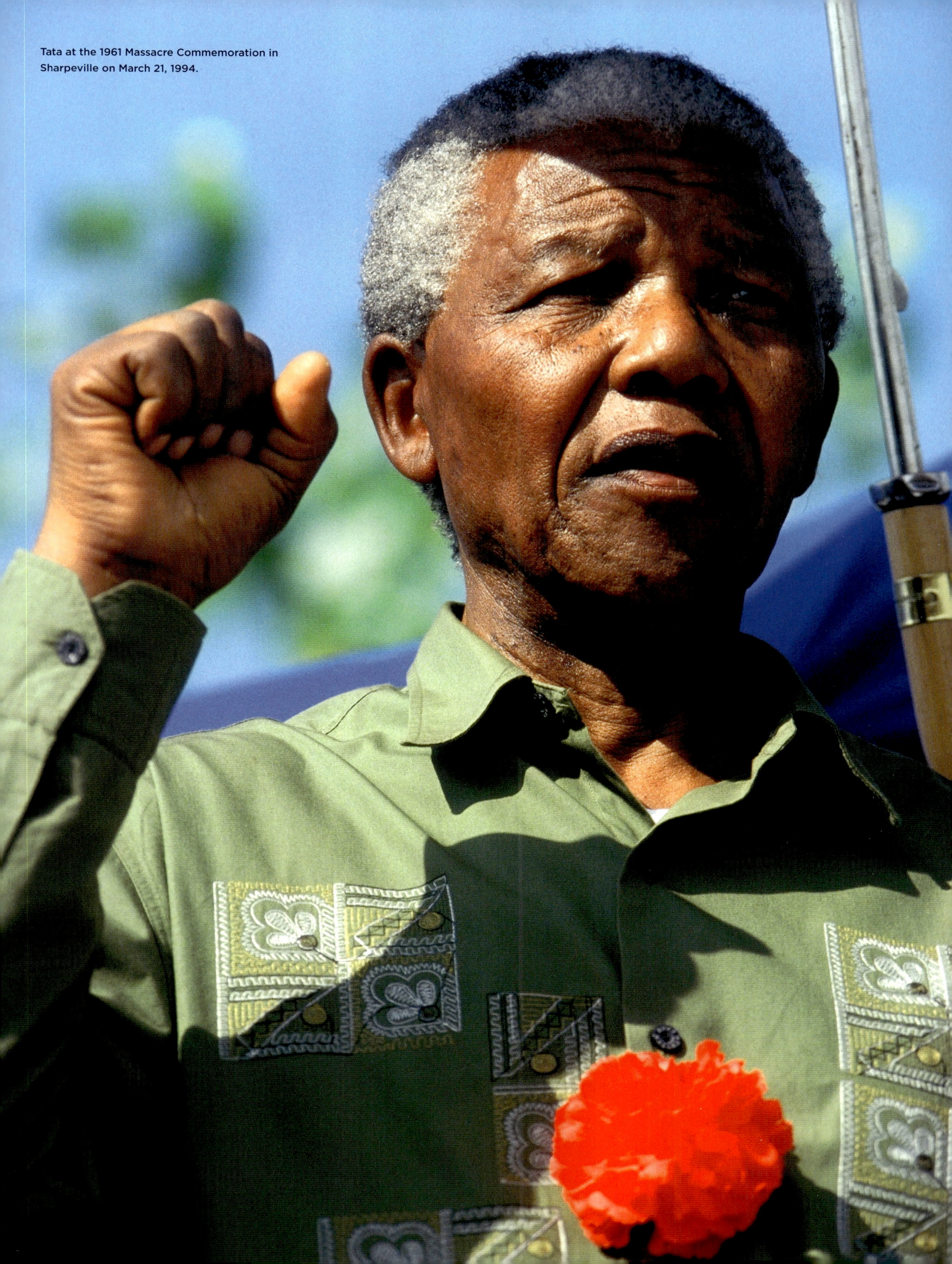
Tata at the 1961 Massacre Commemoration in Sharpeville on March 21, 1994.

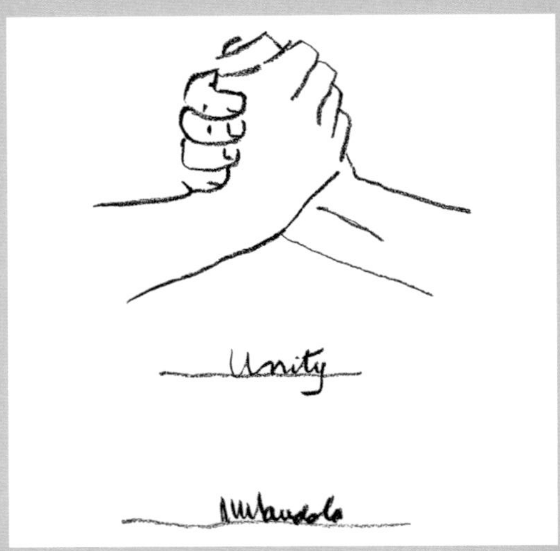

Forgiveness

"I always knew that deep down in every human heart, there is mercy and generosity." Tata

"Madiba was . . . a symbol of tolerance and through patient acceptance of 'the other' showed us how we can cohabitate despite daunting challenges."

Dr. Frannie A. Léautier, Tanzanian academic and activist

"Mandela proved in his being and teachings that science is right: there are no races, genetically speaking. There is only one race and that is the human race. He showed us that our differences are miniscule and skin-deep; that all maligned feelings of superior or inferior self-worth, ethnicity, racism, tribalism, cultural arrogance, gender violence, religious intolerance are all man-made and can be remedied by us." **Jay Naidoo, South African activist**

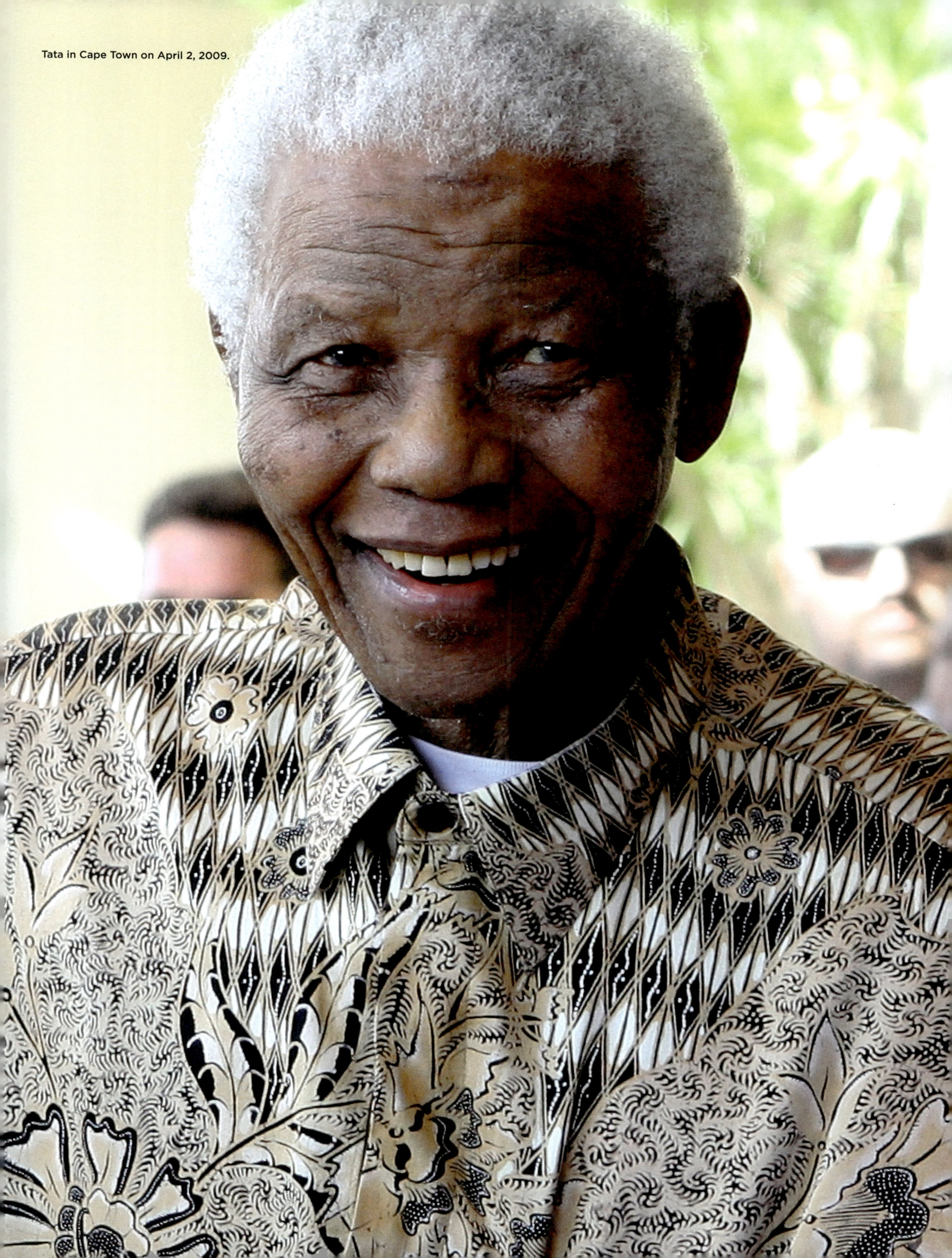

Tata in Cape Town on April 2, 2009.

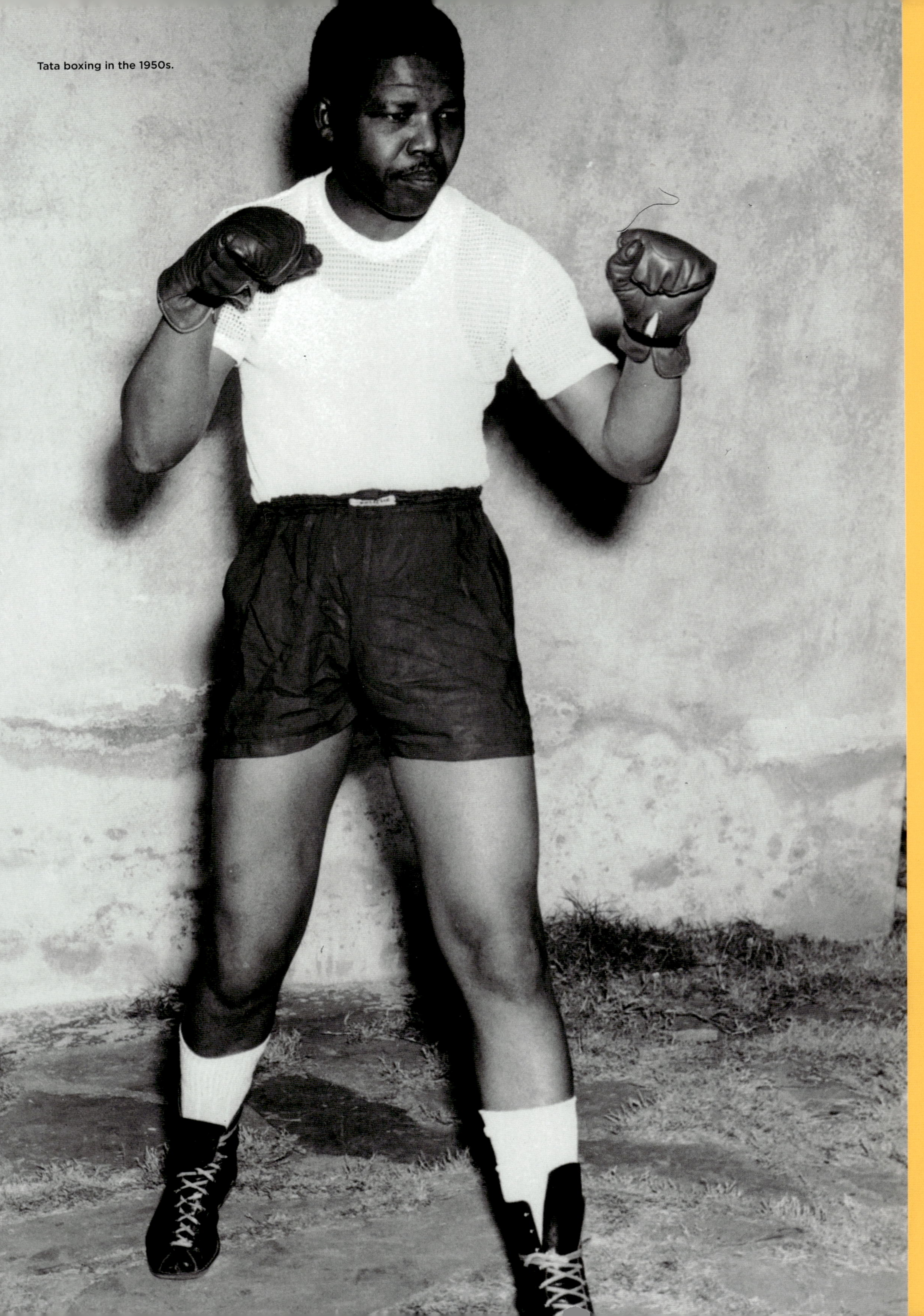

Tata boxing in the 1950s.

His Legacy in Sports

"Mandela understood sports' power to deliver a message, level societal playing fields, and explode myths of racial identity/inferiority. One of his most prickly challenges was creating a new South Africa where everyone felt they belonged. He knew the value of sports as a source of pride, an important escape hatch, a ladder out of isolation and deprivation."

Johnette Howard, sportswriter

Tata was a big fan of boxing. When he was at the University of Fort Hare, he enjoyed both boxing and long-distance running. He continued training as a boxer, just to keep fit, at the weight-lifting club at the Donaldson Orlando Community Centre in Soweto almost every evening. He would take my brother Thembi with him after he turned ten years old.

Tata's interest was focused more on the mechanics of boxing as a physical pursuit than on the violence of it as a sport. He enjoyed the discipline of training and even seemed to find catharsis in the exertion of it. He spoke often of boxing as a source of both physical and mental release for him—an exercise in movement and meditation, strength and strategy.

“Now I can see my grave, now I can die.”

Tata in May 2004, after securing South Africa’s successful bid to host the 2010 World Cup

“Nelson Mandela was an angel who walked the earth.”

Francois “Faf” du Plessis, South African cricketer after Tata’s passing

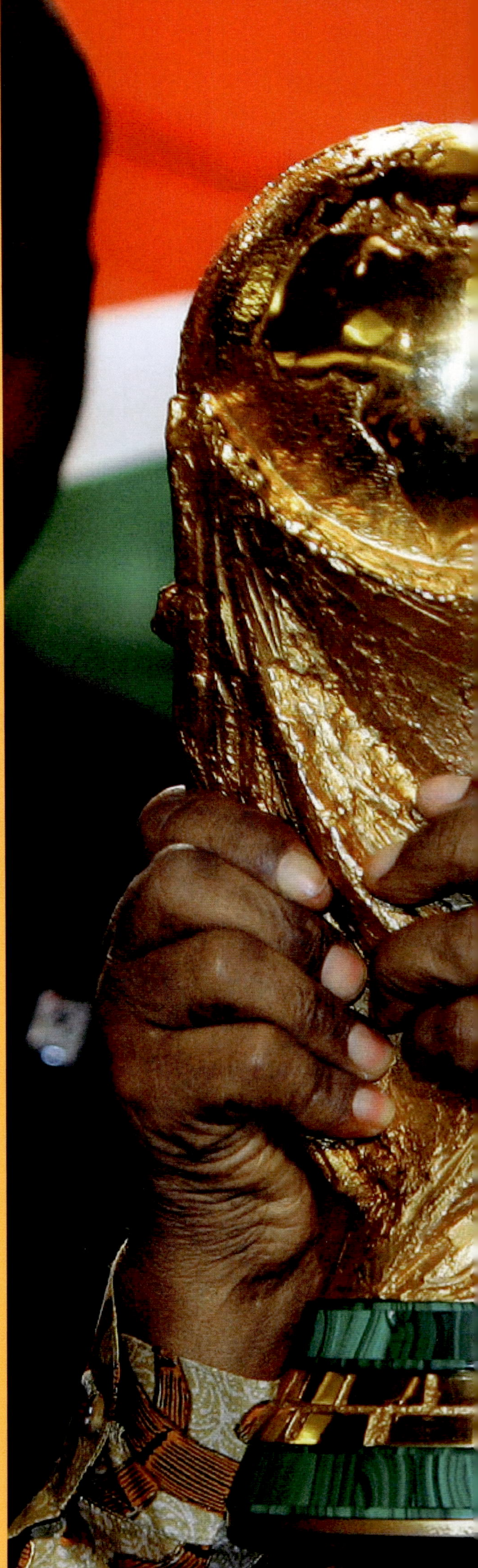

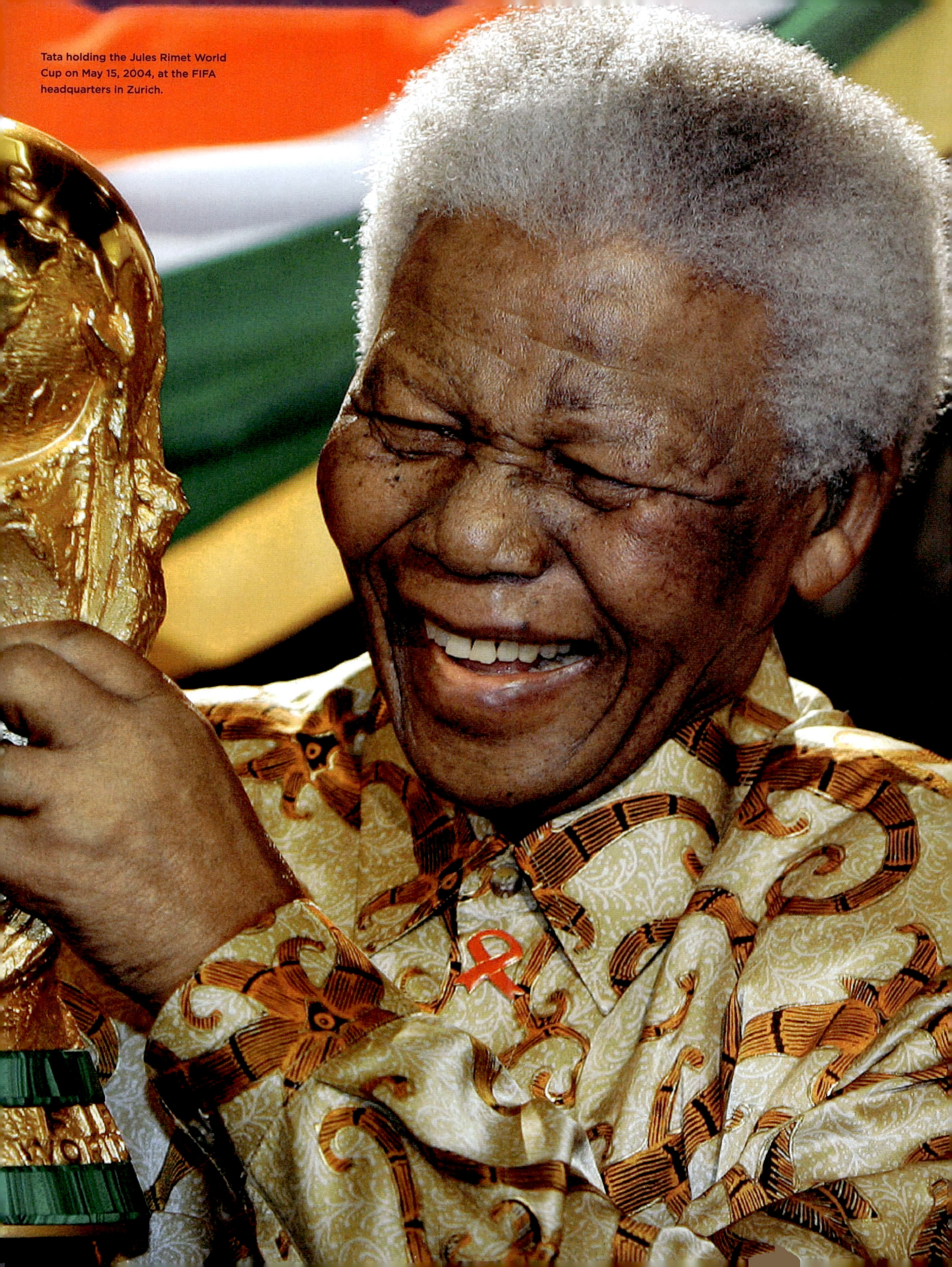
Tata holding the Jules Rimet World Cup on May 15, 2004, at the FIFA headquarters in Zurich.

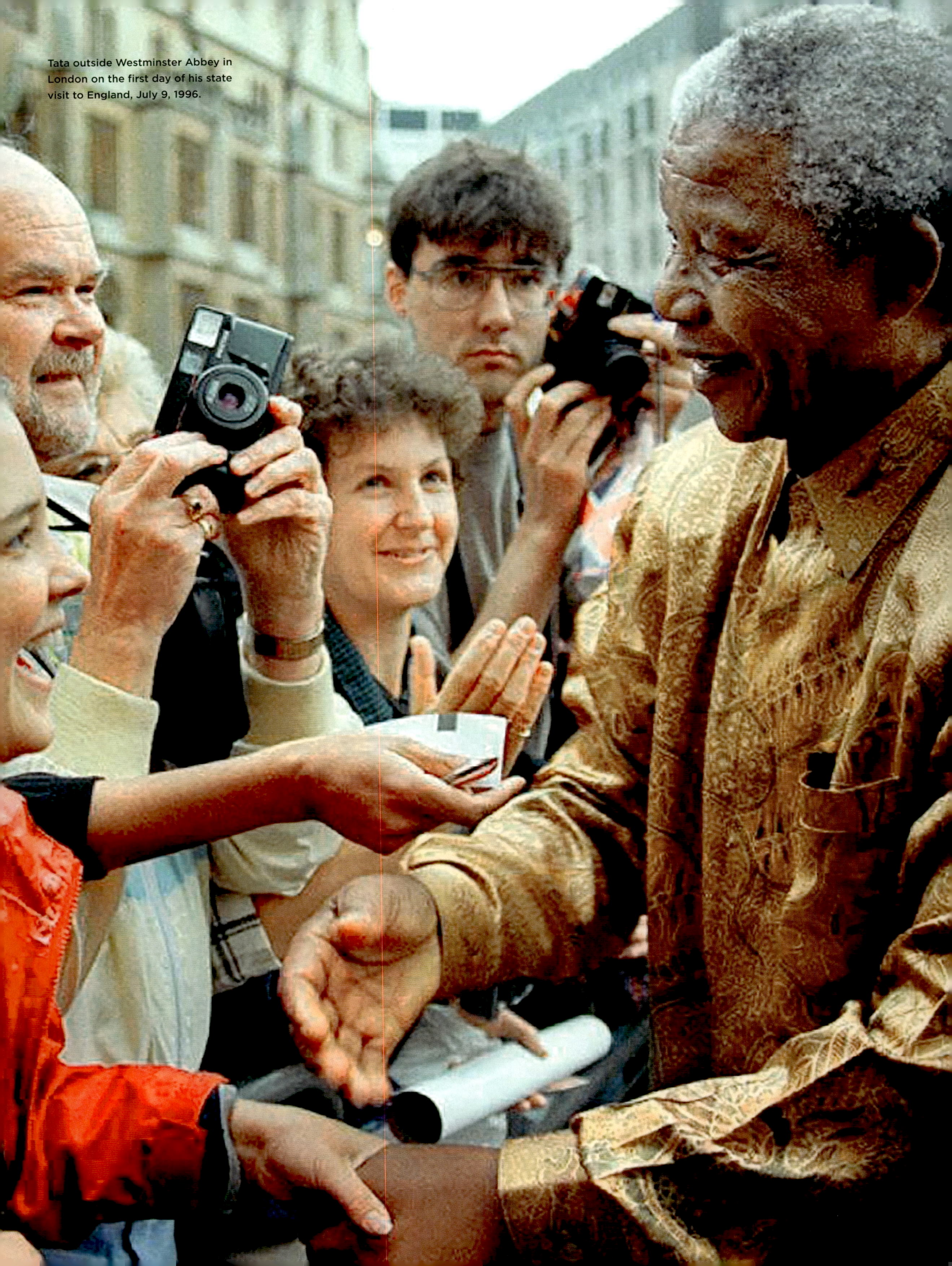

Tata outside Westminster Abbey in London on the first day of his state visit to England, July 9, 1996.

In Praise of President Mandela

Our family pays tribute to you, as one of the greatest men of all time. You symbolize the ultimate of the potential in every human being. You teach in the conduct of your life, and in the leadership of our great country that possibly can be probability, and that every achievement is attainable, if the potential in all of us is accessed.

I speak on behalf of my family when I praise you for your generosity of spirit, your magnanimity of soul, and the impeccable diplomacy with which you have transformed this country into one based on democracy, equality, and freedom.

I speak on behalf of myself when I praise you for clarifying my perception of priority, for instilling in me at the brink of my adult life a sense of social justice and the role that I can play in developing our society.

You have placed in the South African nation's hands the tools with which to rebuild respect and mutual love, based not on retribution and acrimony, but on the basic tenets of the divine word: LOVE.

Nicole Forman, an admirer of Tata whom I think captured a popular sentiment. Tata always mentioned that he was open to hear from everyone, not just the famous or those in a position of power

A Tribute From Your Progeny: Ah! Madiba

Remember the laughs,
remember the smiles,
remember the times we had for a while,
remember the good,
remember the bad,
remember the love that we once had,
remember with a smile,
remember with a tear,
remember the times you held me in fear,
remember the kisses,
remember the hugs.
Whatever you do, don't forget us.

A poem that captured my feelings for Tata, by poet Erin Stack

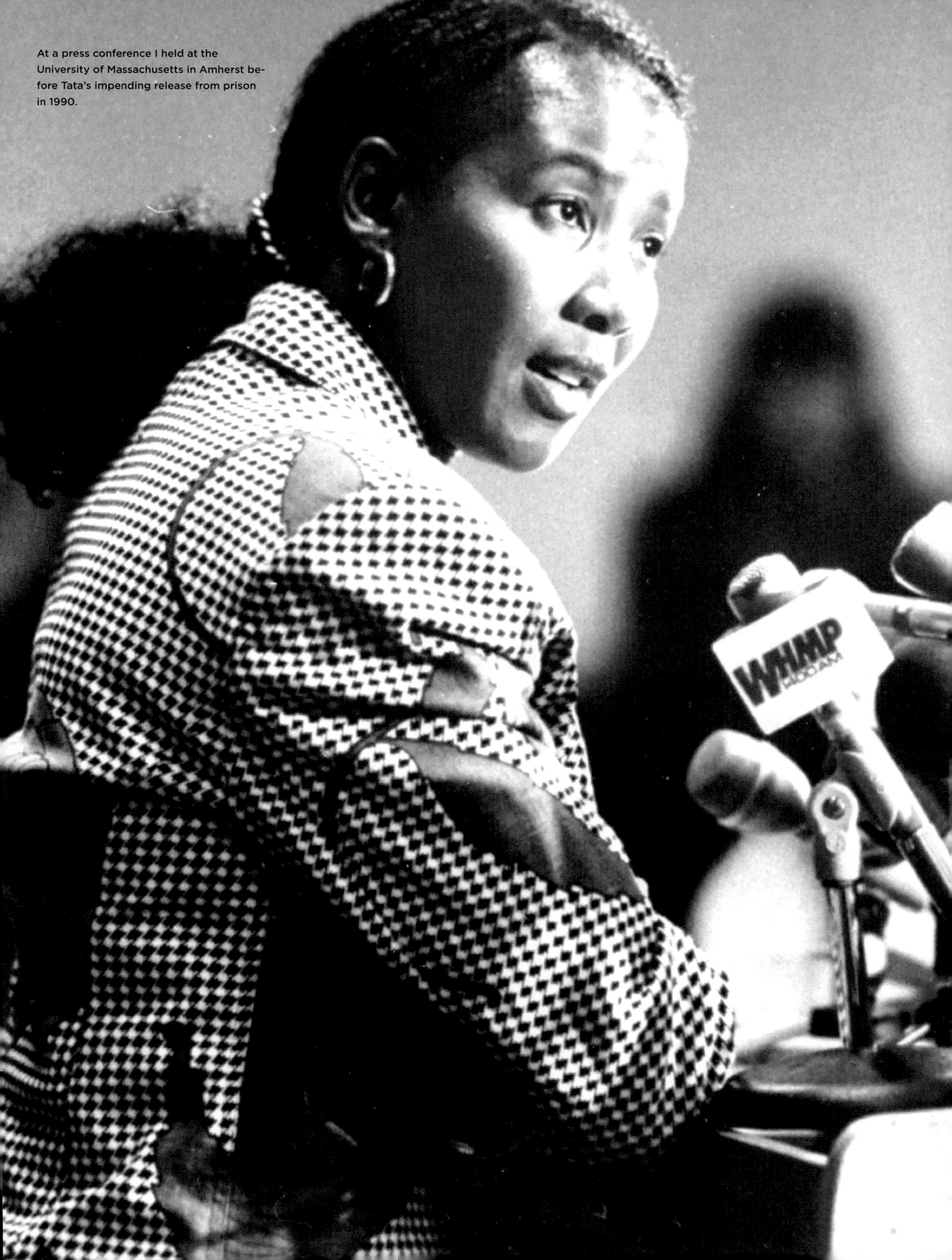

At a press conference I held at the University of Massachusetts in Amherst before Tata's impending release from prison in 1990.

World Leaders Pay Tribute to Madiba

On August 29, 2007, a nine-foot bronze statue of Tata was unveiled in London's Parliament Square. It stands facing the House of Commons, along with other statues of such leaders as Winston Churchill, Benjamin Disraeli, and Abraham Lincoln.

Long before his release from Robben Island, there was a great deal of interest in Tata and his comrades. People from all over the globe protested, held concerts, prayers, and vigils in support of his and his comrades' release from life imprisonment. After he became the first president of a free democratic South Africa, he was honored with the Nobel Peace Prize in 1993, in official decrees, and spontaneously by communities—fans, artists, scholars, and children—in every country he visited. Today we live in a world of upheaval, where honorable and thoughtful leadership is in short supply. Tata, however, is revered as a person of character, wisdom, commitment, and self-sacrifice, who effected true and lasting change.

As the Voice of America reported, "Tens of thousands of South Africans gathered Tuesday in a soccer stadium near Soweto to bid farewell to anti-apartheid icon Nelson Mandela, a man loved around the world for his long, difficult fight to end apartheid and bring equality to South Africa. The memorial service in Johannesburg also brought together dignitaries and celebrities from around the world."

"A giant of history."

Barack Obama

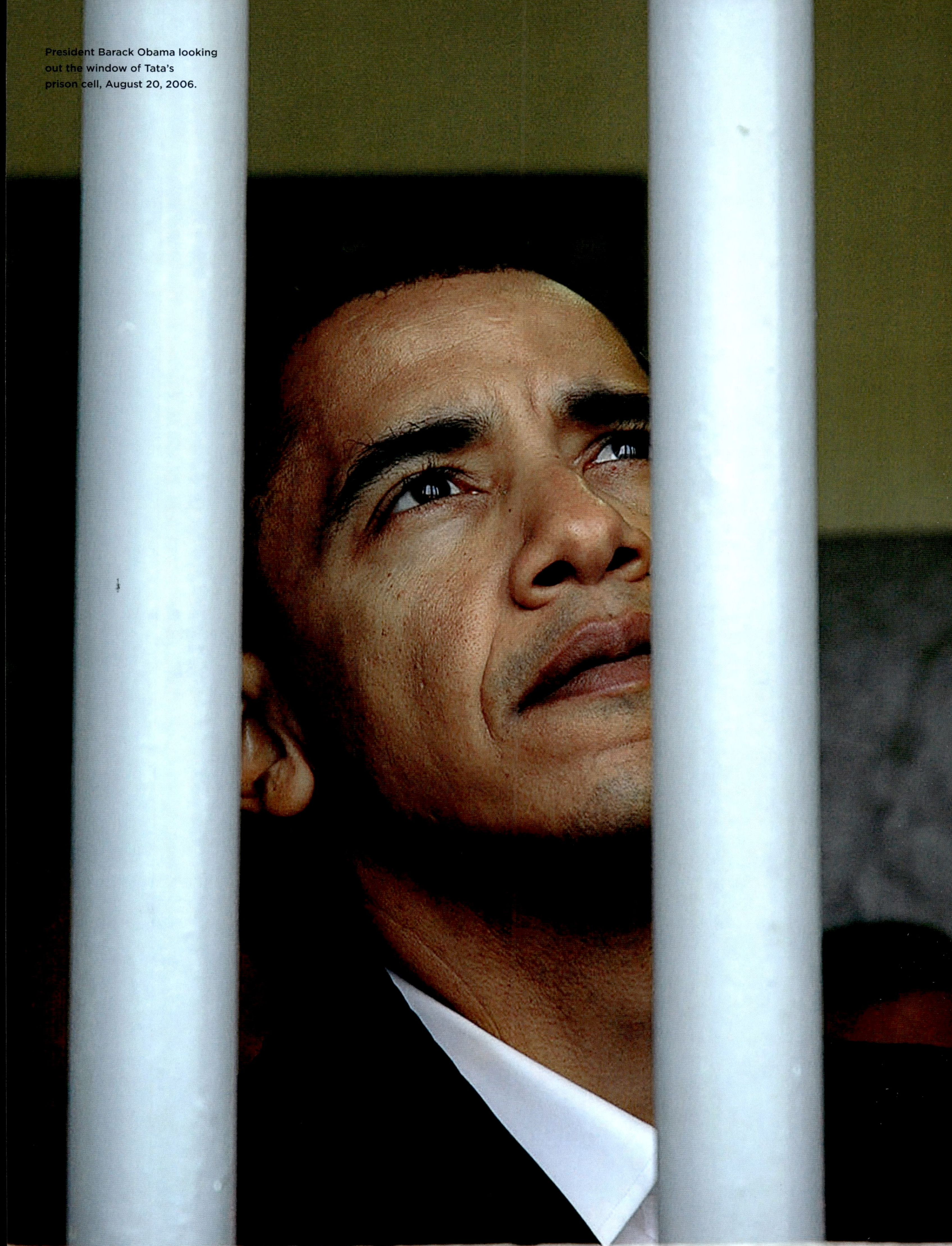

President Barack Obama looking out the window of Tata's prison cell, August 20, 2006.

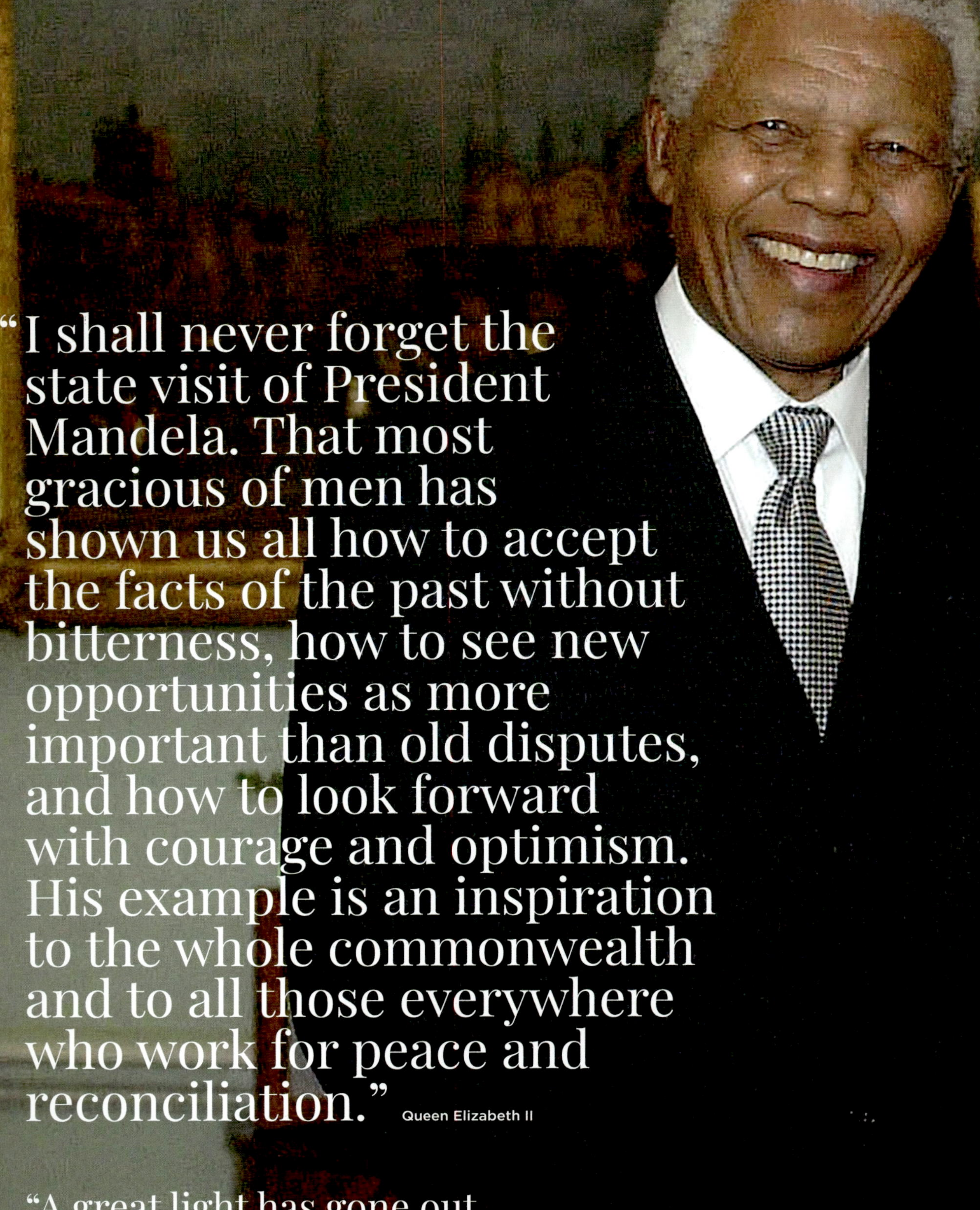

"I shall never forget the state visit of President Mandela. That most gracious of men has shown us all how to accept the facts of the past without bitterness, how to see new opportunities as more important than old disputes, and how to look forward with courage and optimism. His example is an inspiration to the whole commonwealth and to all those everywhere who work for peace and reconciliation." Queen Elizabeth II

"A great light has gone out. Since the day he stood up against the odious apartheid system, I admired him as a fighter for freedom, inflexible, stately in the face of trials." President Jacques Chirac of France

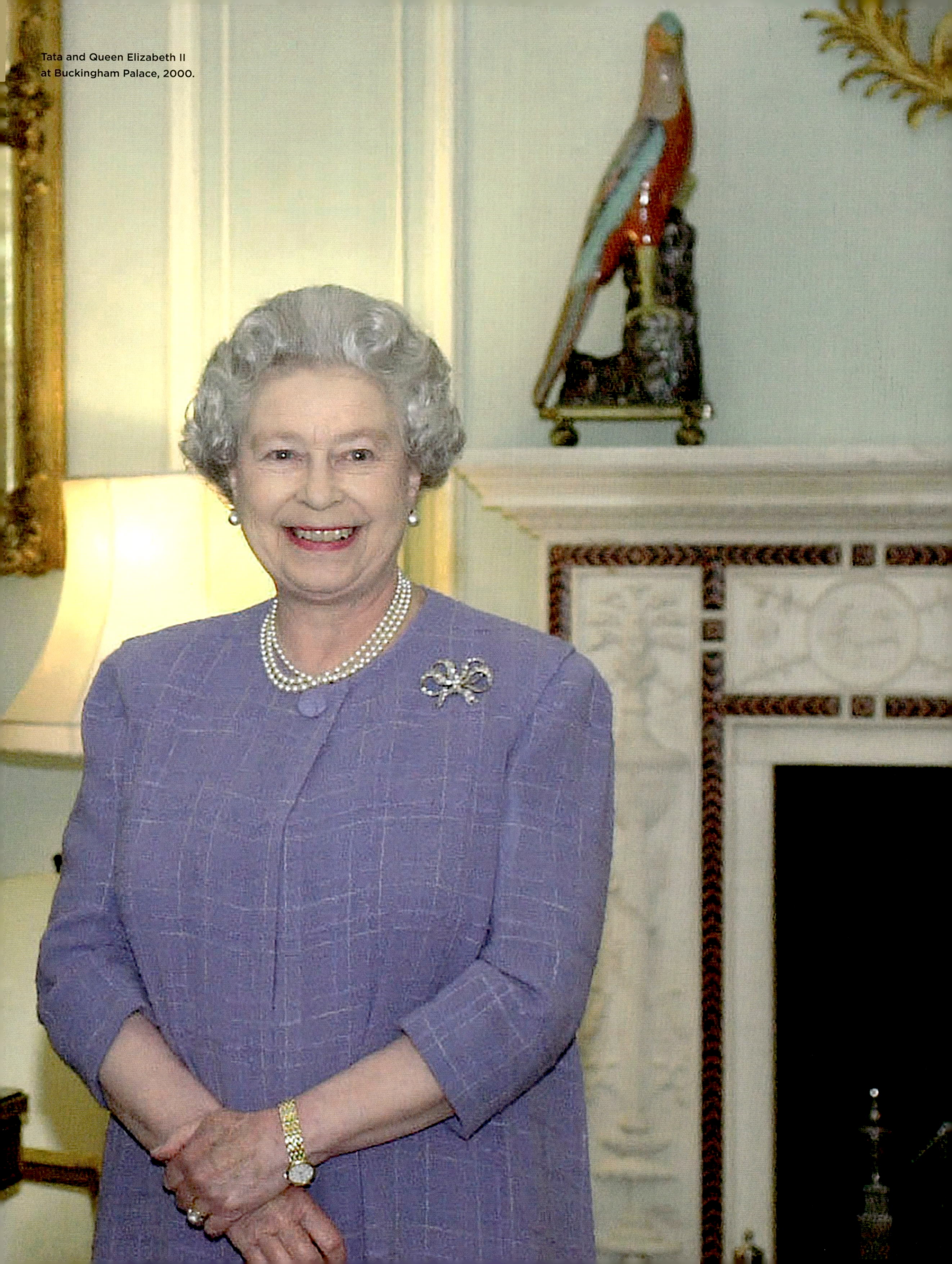

Tata and Queen Elizabeth II
at Buckingham Palace, 2000.

"I was honored to be the first American president to welcome Mr. Mandela to the White House. It remains a genuine highlight from those four years I was privileged to hold that high office. . . . I viewed Nelson Mandela as one of the great moral leaders during that hopeful and transformative era of global change . . . Following his twenty-seven years of wrongful imprisonment, it would have been understandable if Mr. Mandela had harbored and expressed more animosity—more bitterness—toward his political adversaries. That he didn't is one of the more remarkable examples of grace and dignity I have ever witnessed."

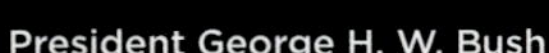

President George H. W. Bush

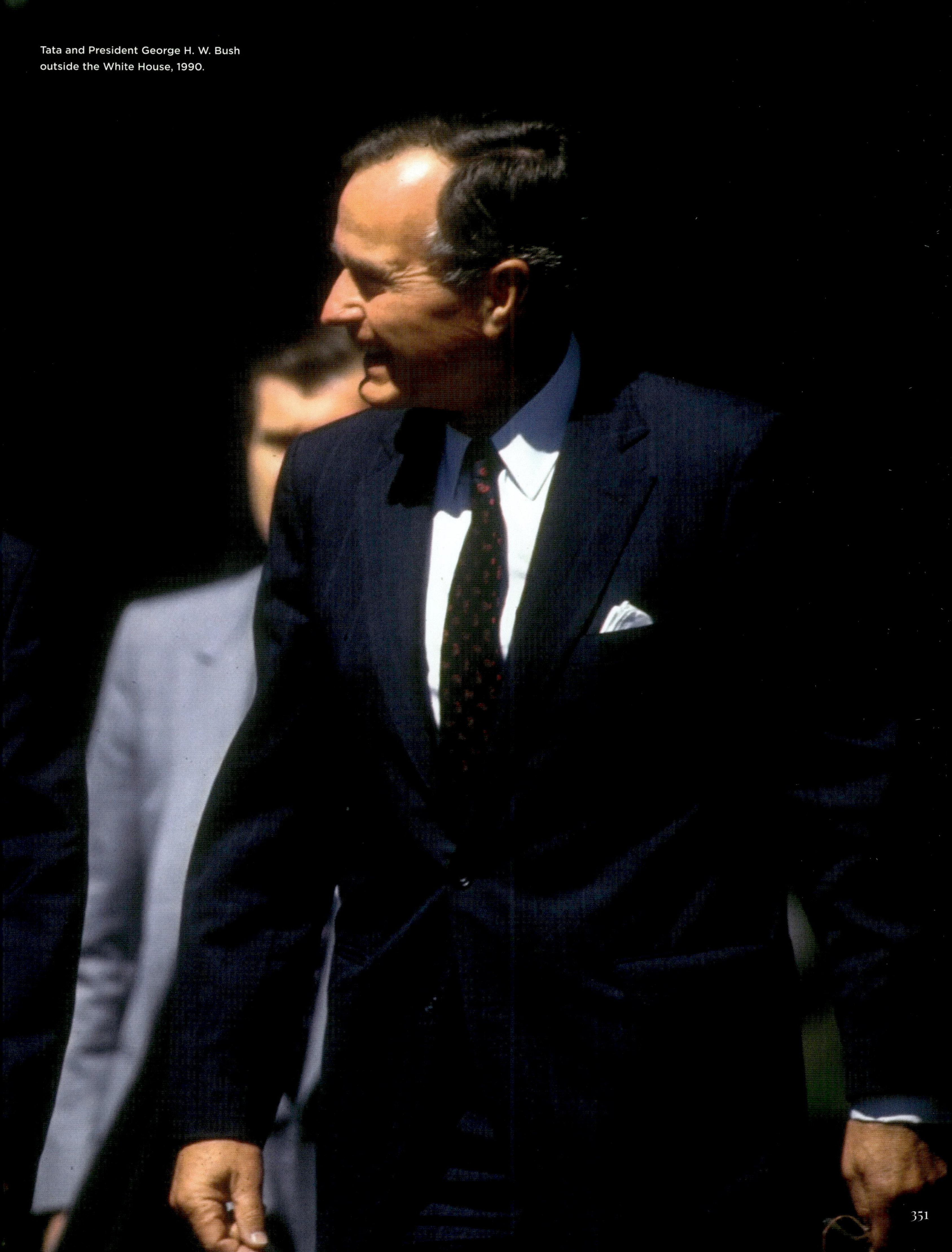

Tata and President George H. W. Bush outside the White House, 1990.

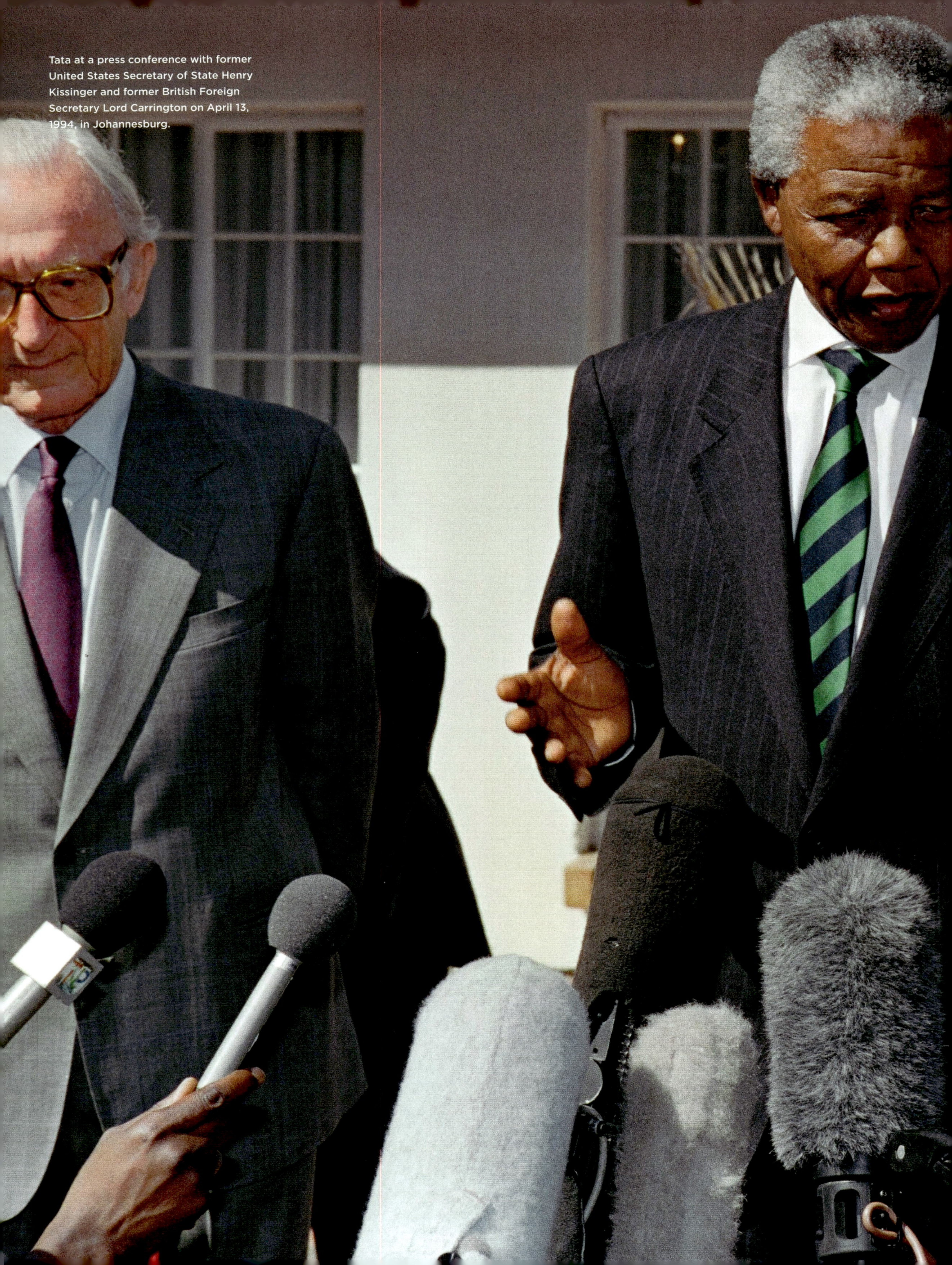

Tata at a press conference with former United States Secretary of State Henry Kissinger and former British Foreign Secretary Lord Carrington on April 13, 1994, in Johannesburg.

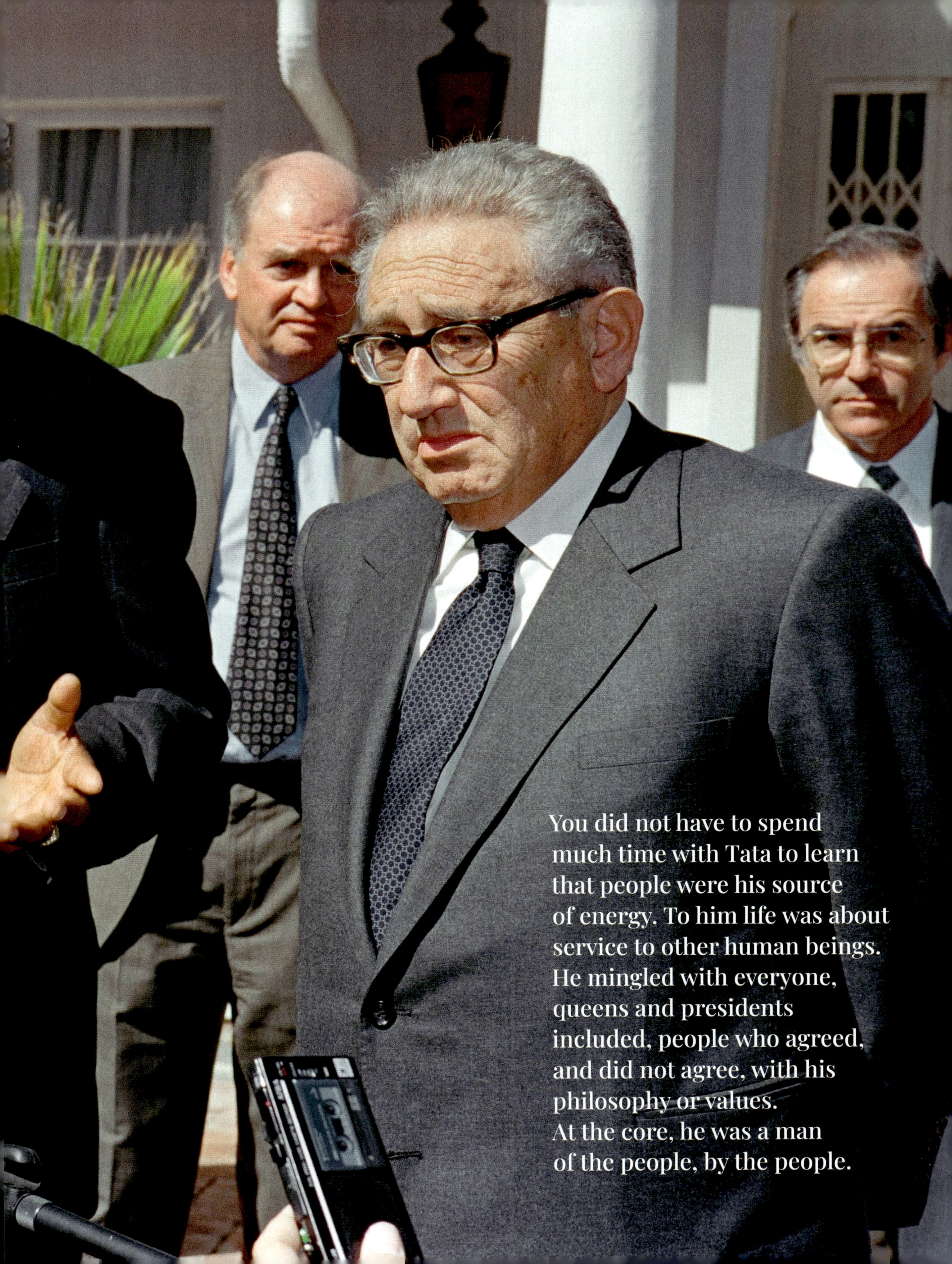

You did not have to spend much time with Tata to learn that people were his source of energy. To him life was about service to other human beings. He mingled with everyone, queens and presidents included, people who agreed, and did not agree, with his philosophy or values. At the core, he was a man of the people, by the people.

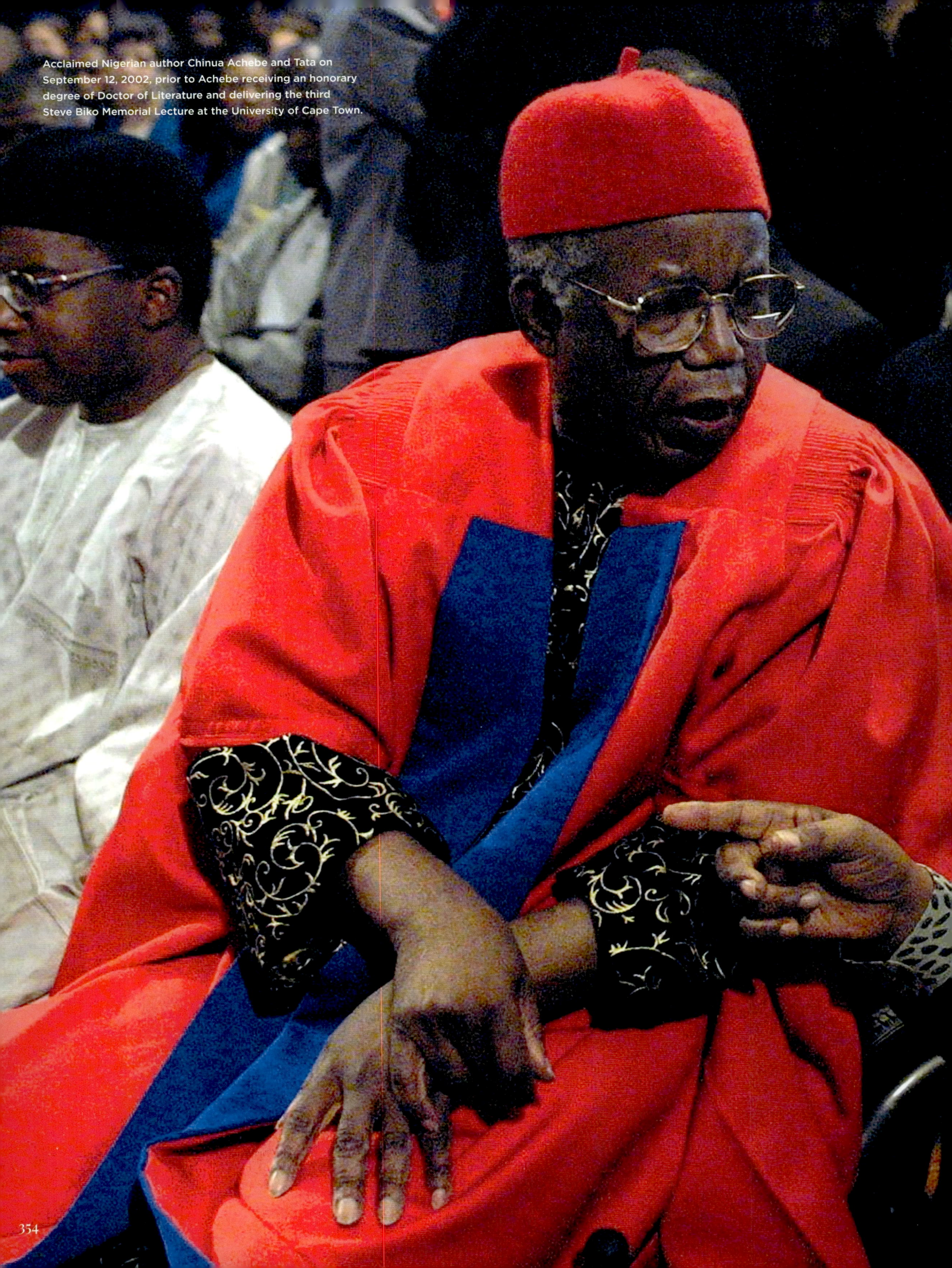

Acclaimed Nigerian author Chinua Achebe and Tata on September 12, 2002, prior to Achebe receiving an honorary degree of Doctor of Literature and delivering the third Steve Biko Memorial Lecture at the University of Cape Town.

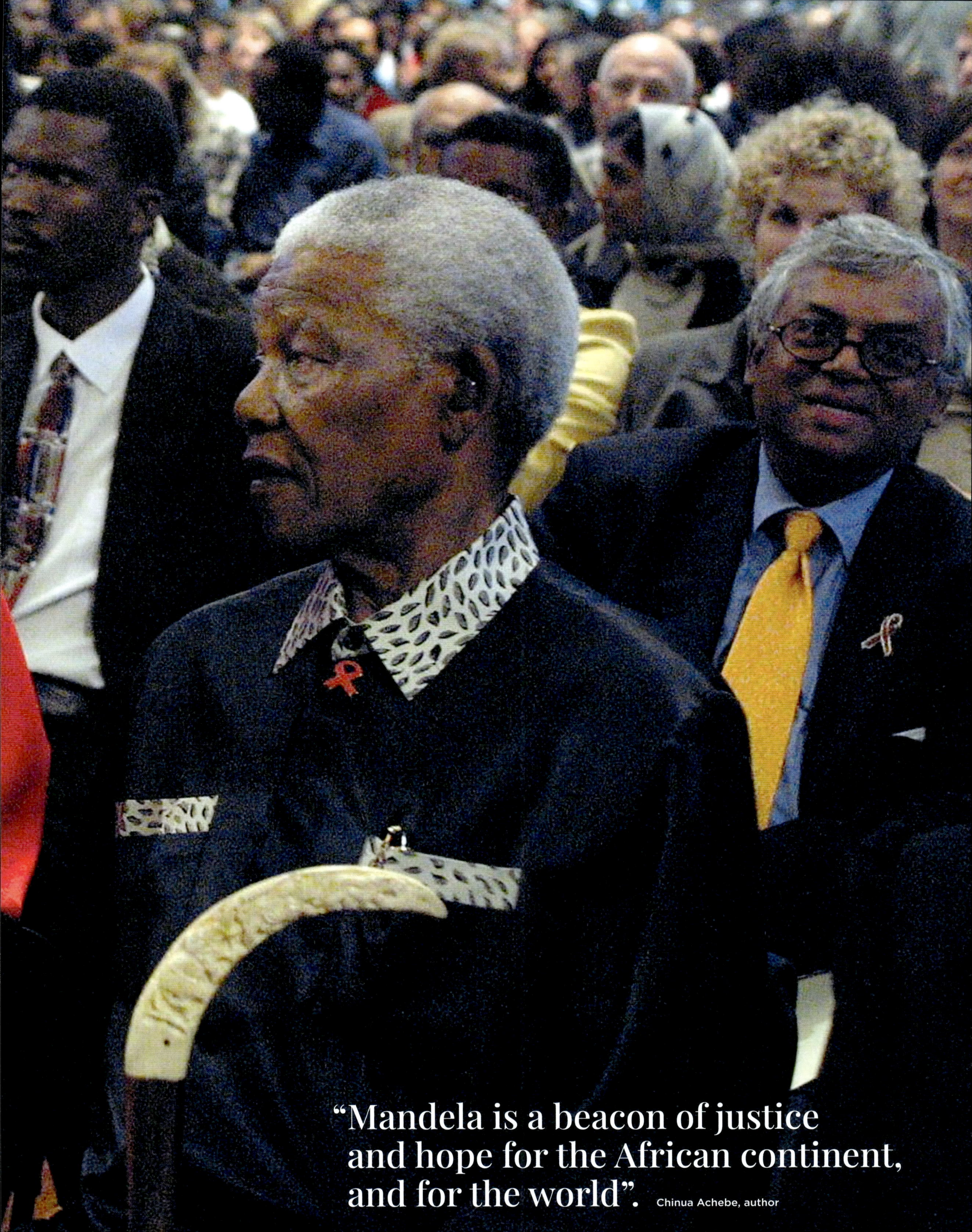

“Mandela is a beacon of justice and hope for the African continent, and for the world”. Chinua Achebe, author

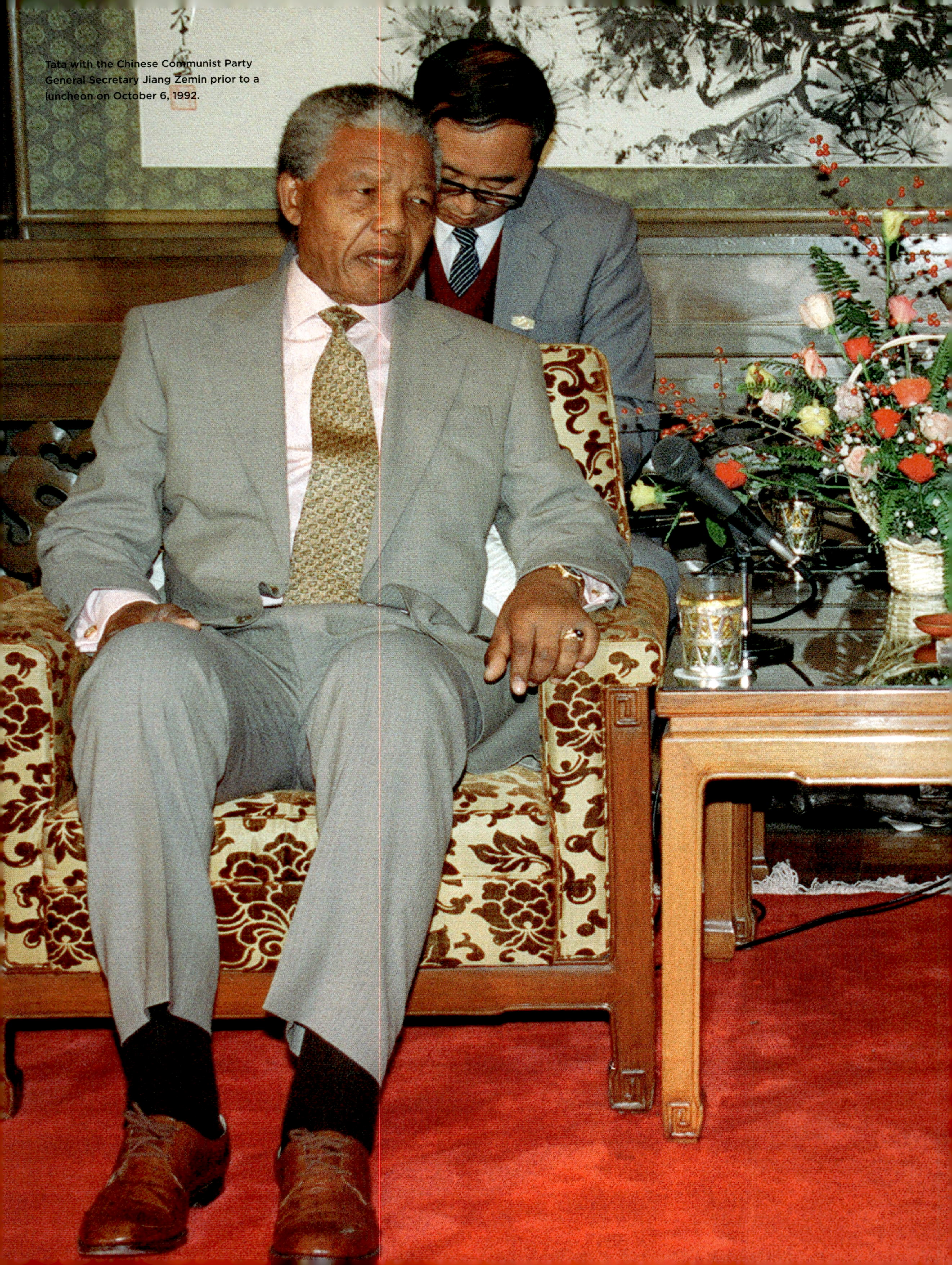

Tata with the Chinese Communist Party General Secretary Jiang Zemin prior to a luncheon on October 6, 1992.

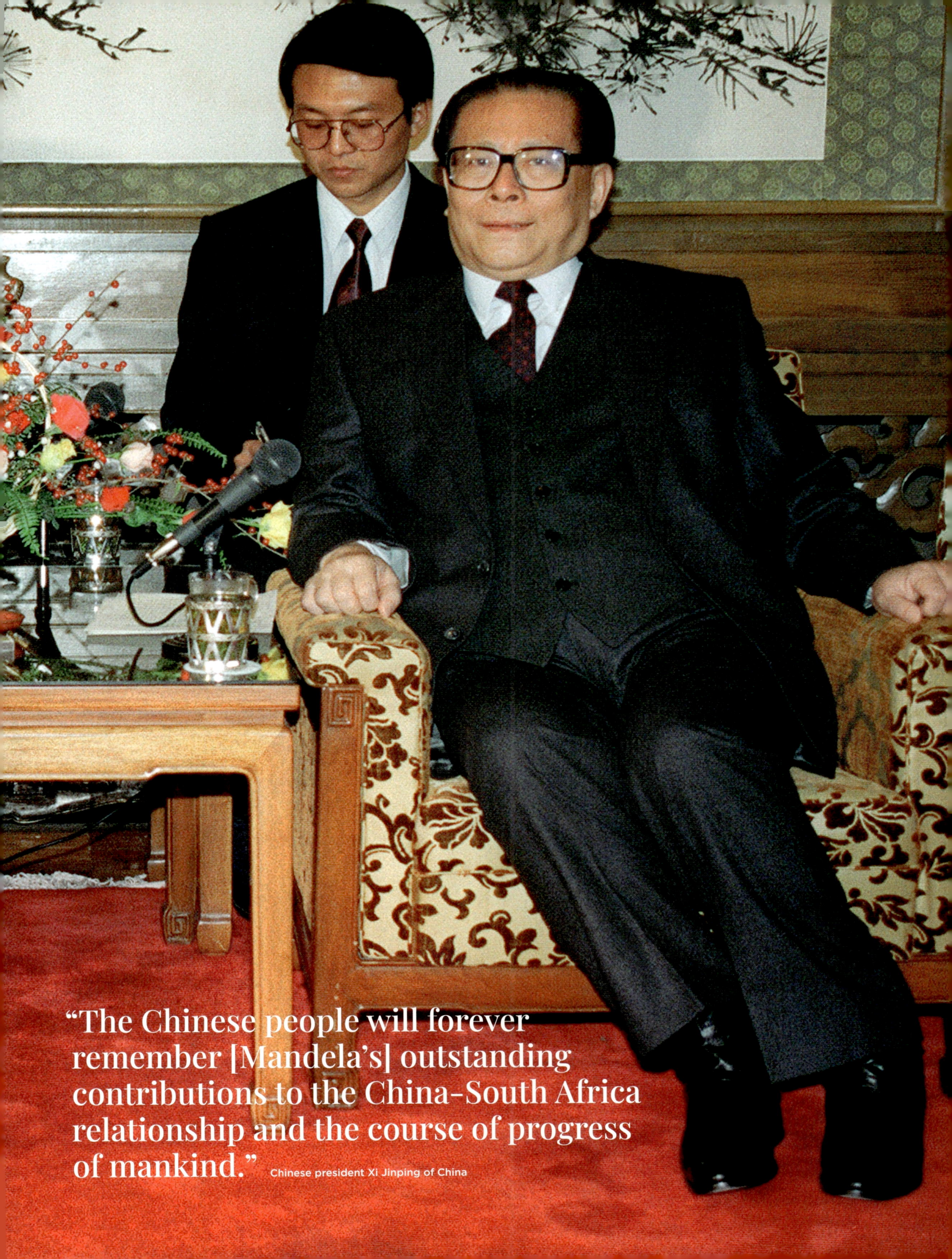

"The Chinese people will forever remember [Mandela's] outstanding contributions to the China-South Africa relationship and the course of progress of mankind." Chinese president Xi Jinping of China

"South Africa has lost a hero. They've lost a father, friend, and mentor. Nelson Mandela was more than one of the greatest leaders of our time. He was one of our greatest teachers. He taught by example. He sacrificed so much and was willing to give up everything for freedom and equality, for democracy and justice. His compassion stands out most."

United Nations Secretary-General Ban Ki-moon

"Mandela was a great human being . . . He made us all understand that nobody should be penalized for the color of his skin, for the circumstances into which he is born. He also made us understand that we can change the world—we can change the world by changing attitudes, by changing perceptions. For this reason I would like to pay him tribute as a great human being who raised the standard of humanity."

Aung San Suu Kyi, Nobel Peace Prize laureate

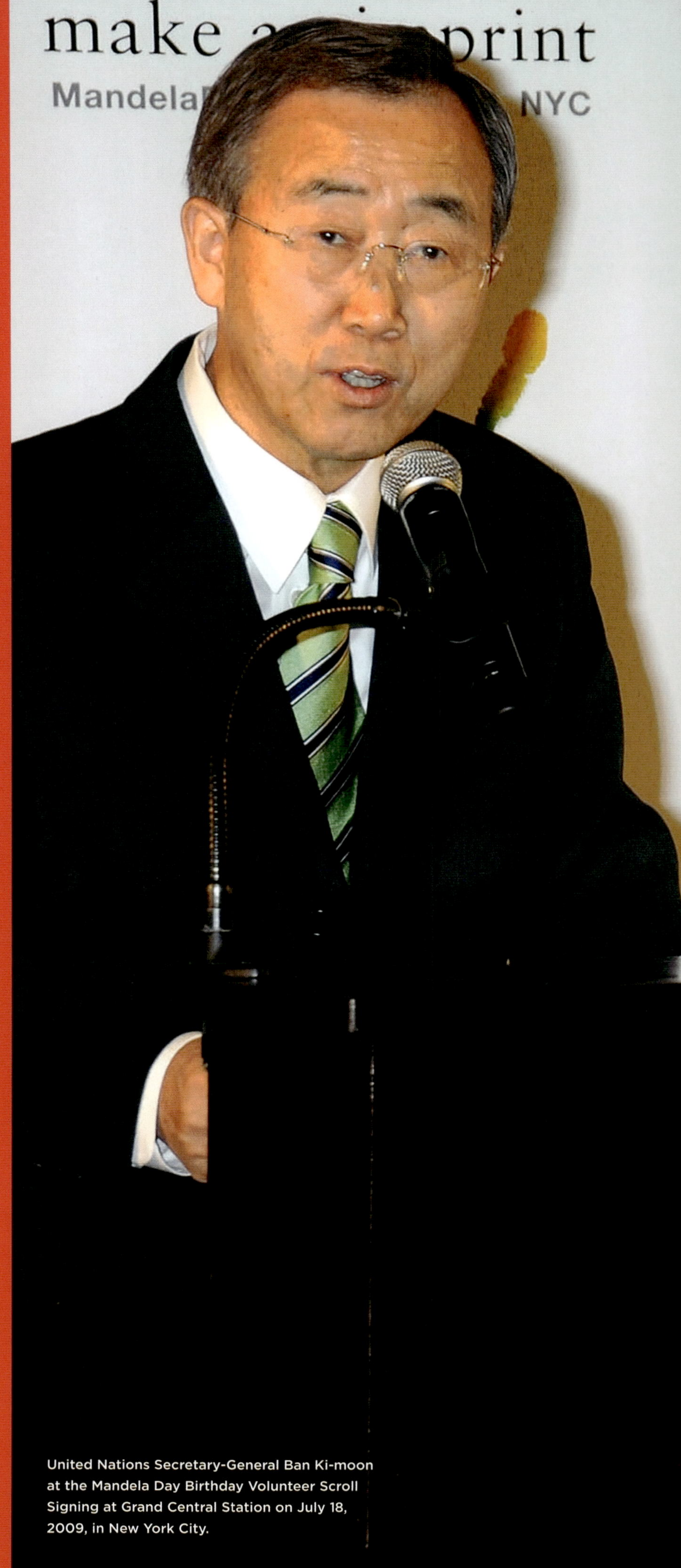

United Nations Secretary-General Ban Ki-moon at the Mandela Day Birthday Volunteer Scroll Signing at Grand Central Station on July 18, 2009, in New York City.

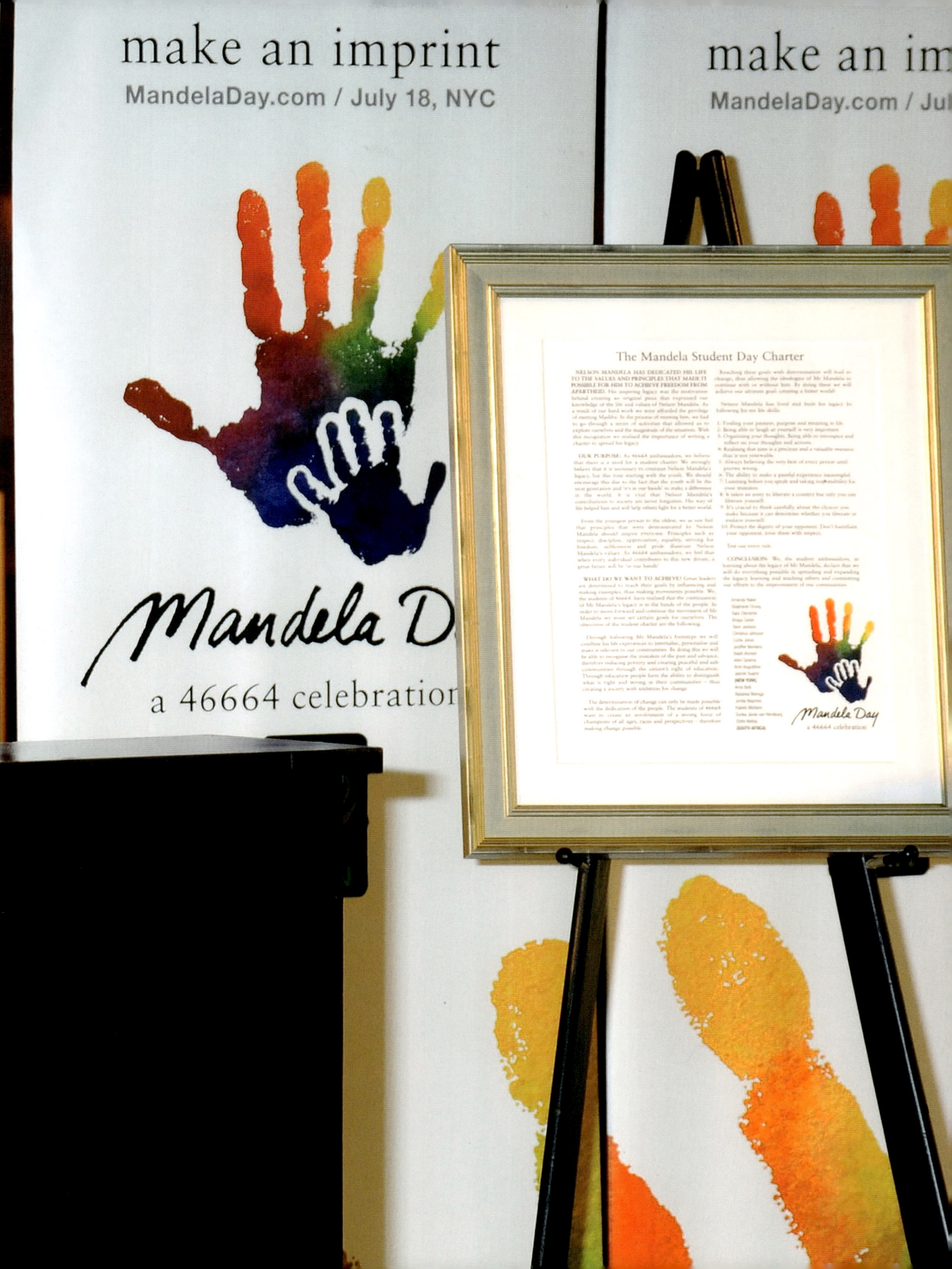
make an imprint
MandelaDay.com / July 18, NYC
The Mandela Student Day Charter
Mandela Day
a 46664 celebration

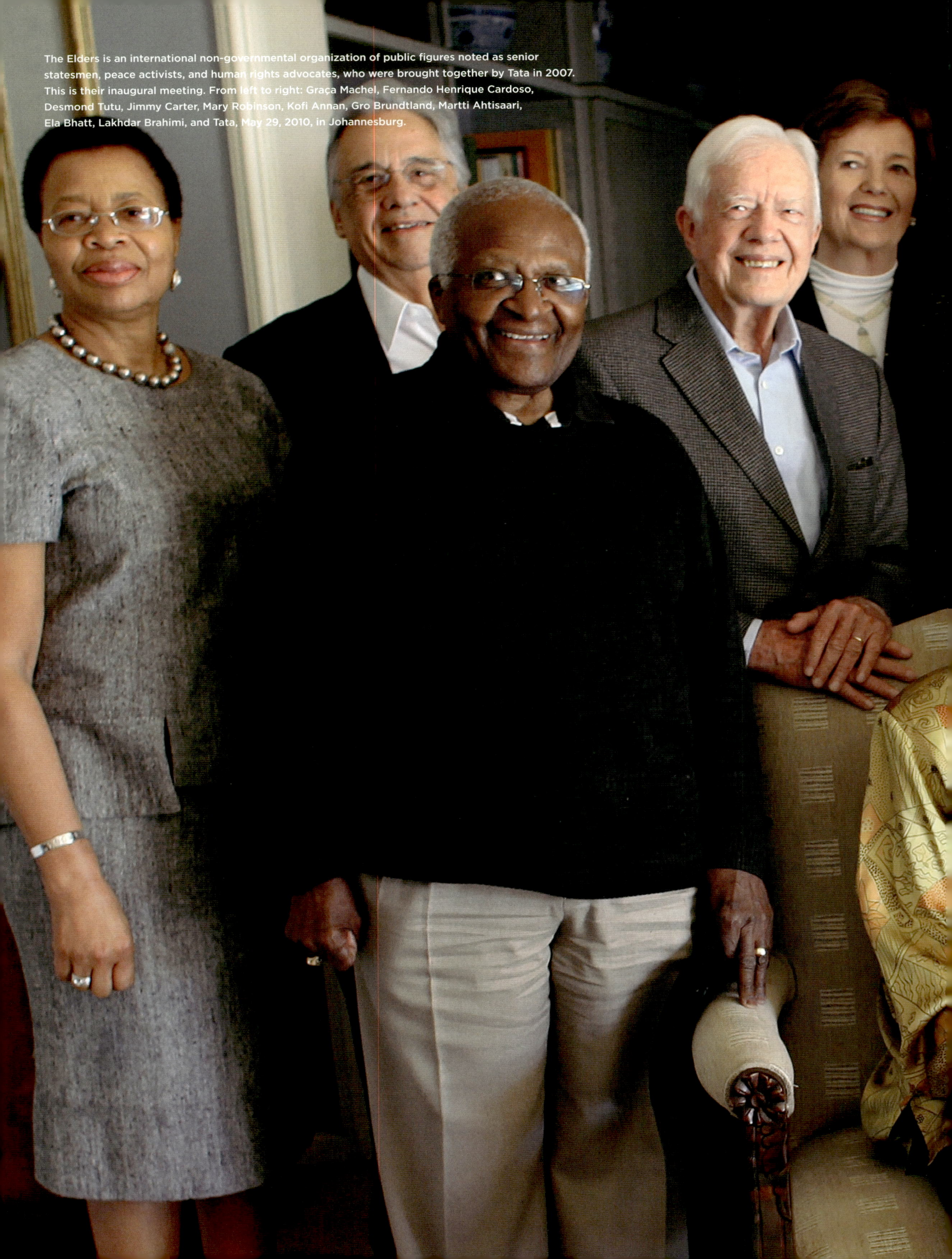

The Elders is an international non-governmental organization of public figures noted as senior statesmen, peace activists, and human rights advocates, who were brought together by Tata in 2007. This is their inaugural meeting. From left to right: Graça Machel, Fernando Henrique Cardoso, Desmond Tutu, Jimmy Carter, Mary Robinson, Kofi Annan, Gro Brundtland, Martti Ahtisaari, Ela Bhatt, Lakhdar Brahimi, and Tata, May 29, 2010, in Johannesburg.

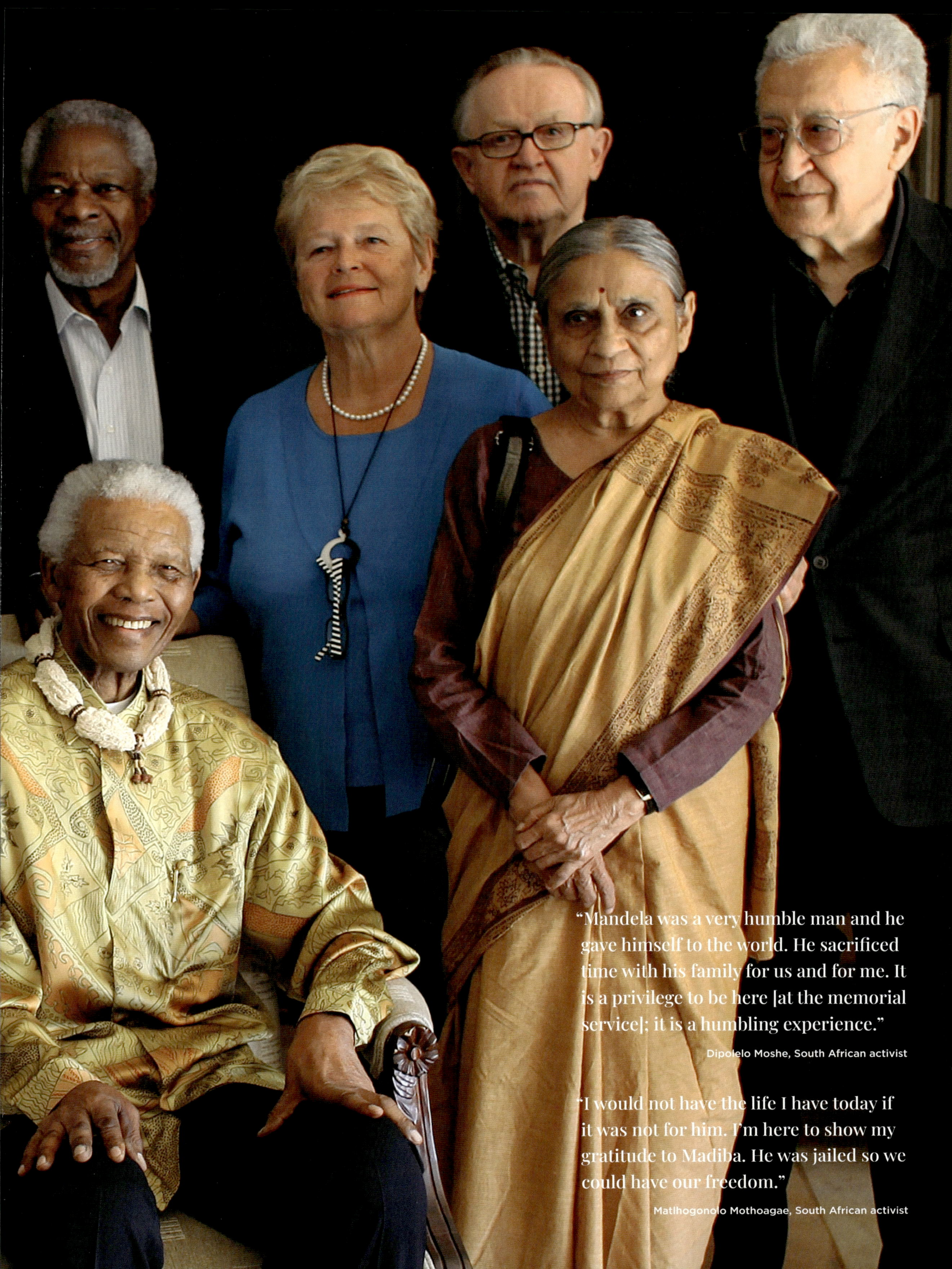

"Mandela was a very humble man and he gave himself to the world. He sacrificed time with his family for us and for me. It is a privilege to be here [at the memorial service]; it is a humbling experience."

Dipolelo Moshe, South African activist

"I would not have the life I have today if it was not for him. I'm here to show my gratitude to Madiba. He was jailed so we could have our freedom."

Matlhogonolo Mothoagae, South African activist

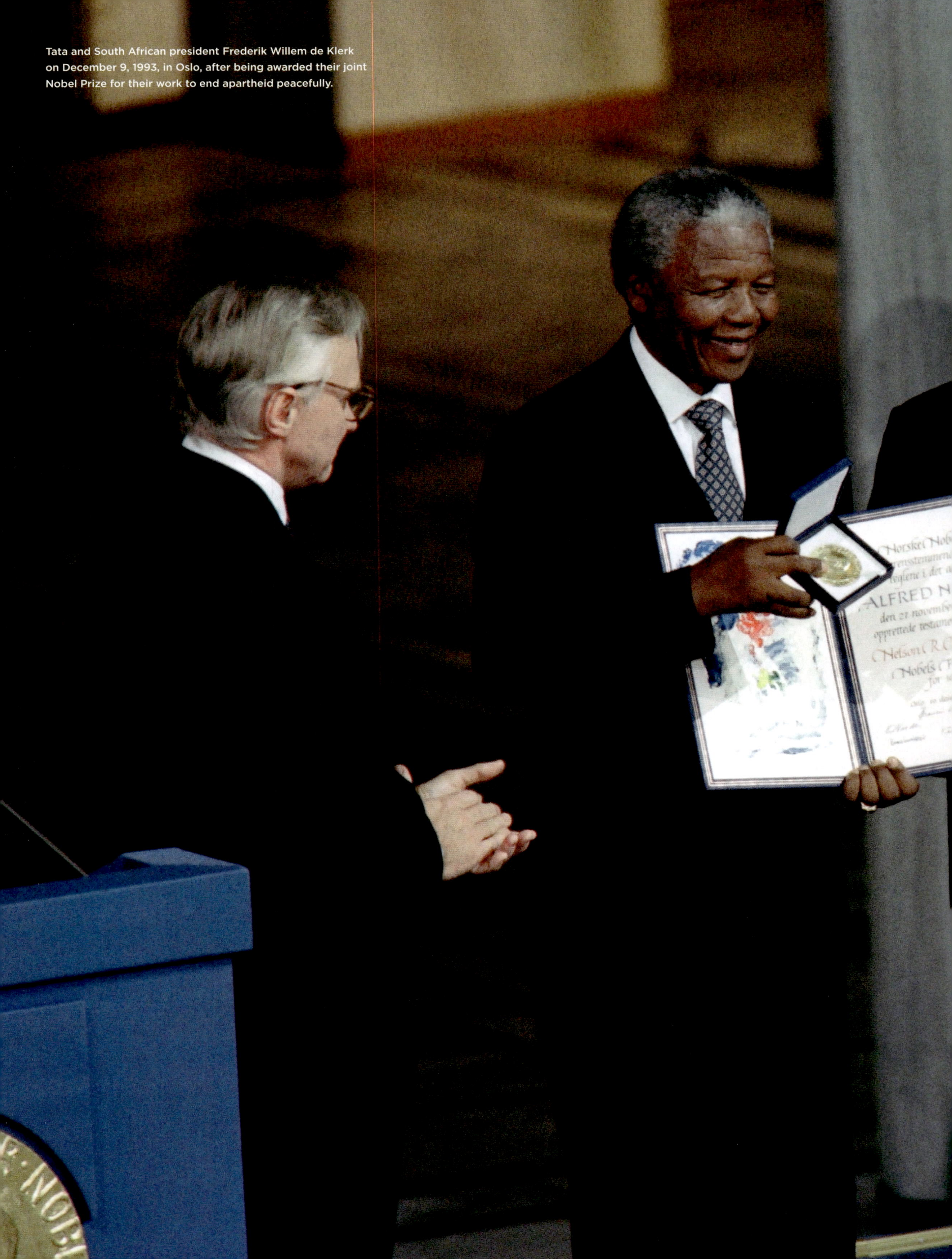

Tata and South African president Frederik Willem de Klerk on December 9, 1993, in Oslo, after being awarded their joint Nobel Prize for their work to end apartheid peacefully.

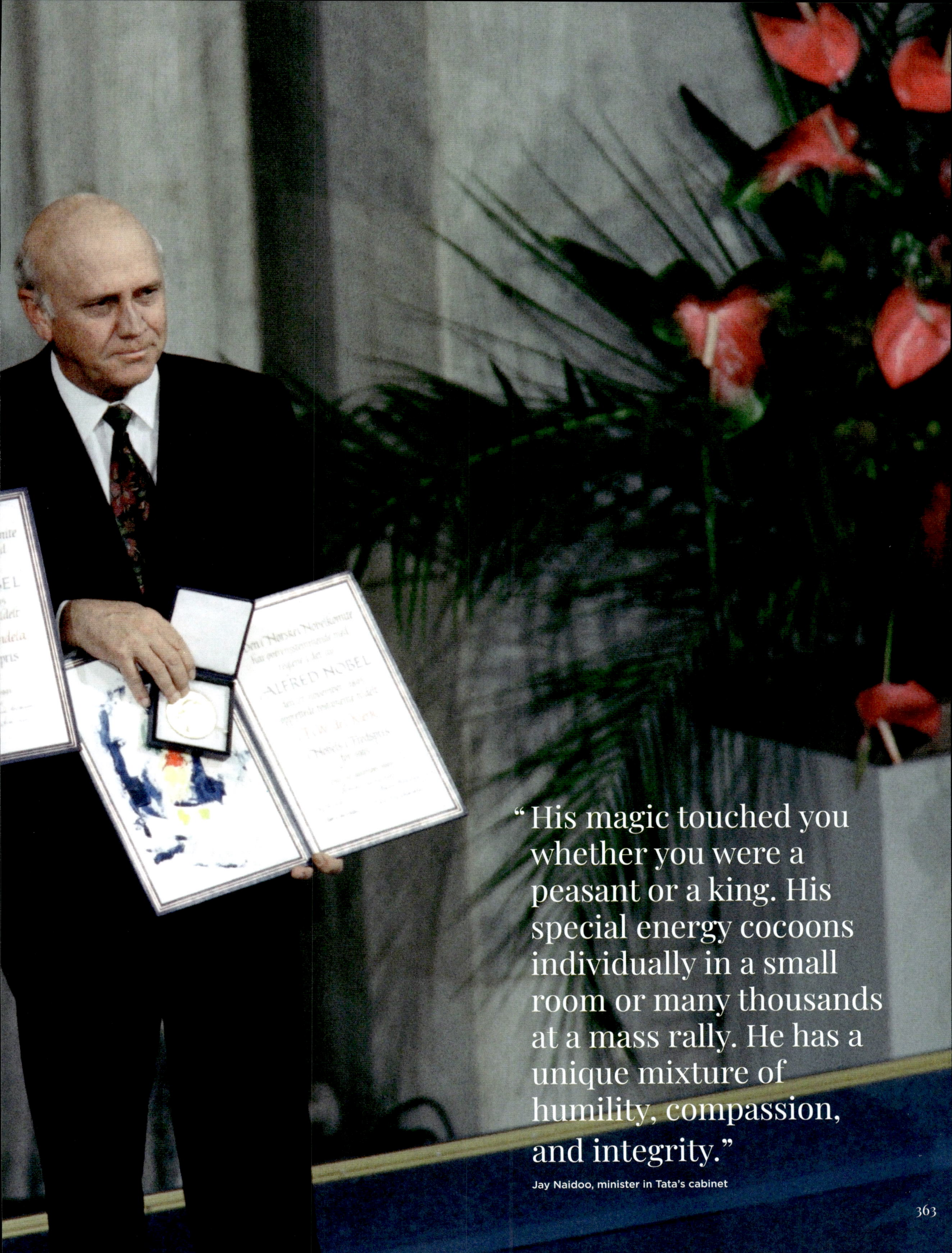

“His magic touched you whether you were a peasant or a king. His special energy cocoons individually in a small room or many thousands at a mass rally. He has a unique mixture of humility, compassion, and integrity.”

Jay Naidoo, minister in Tata’s cabinet

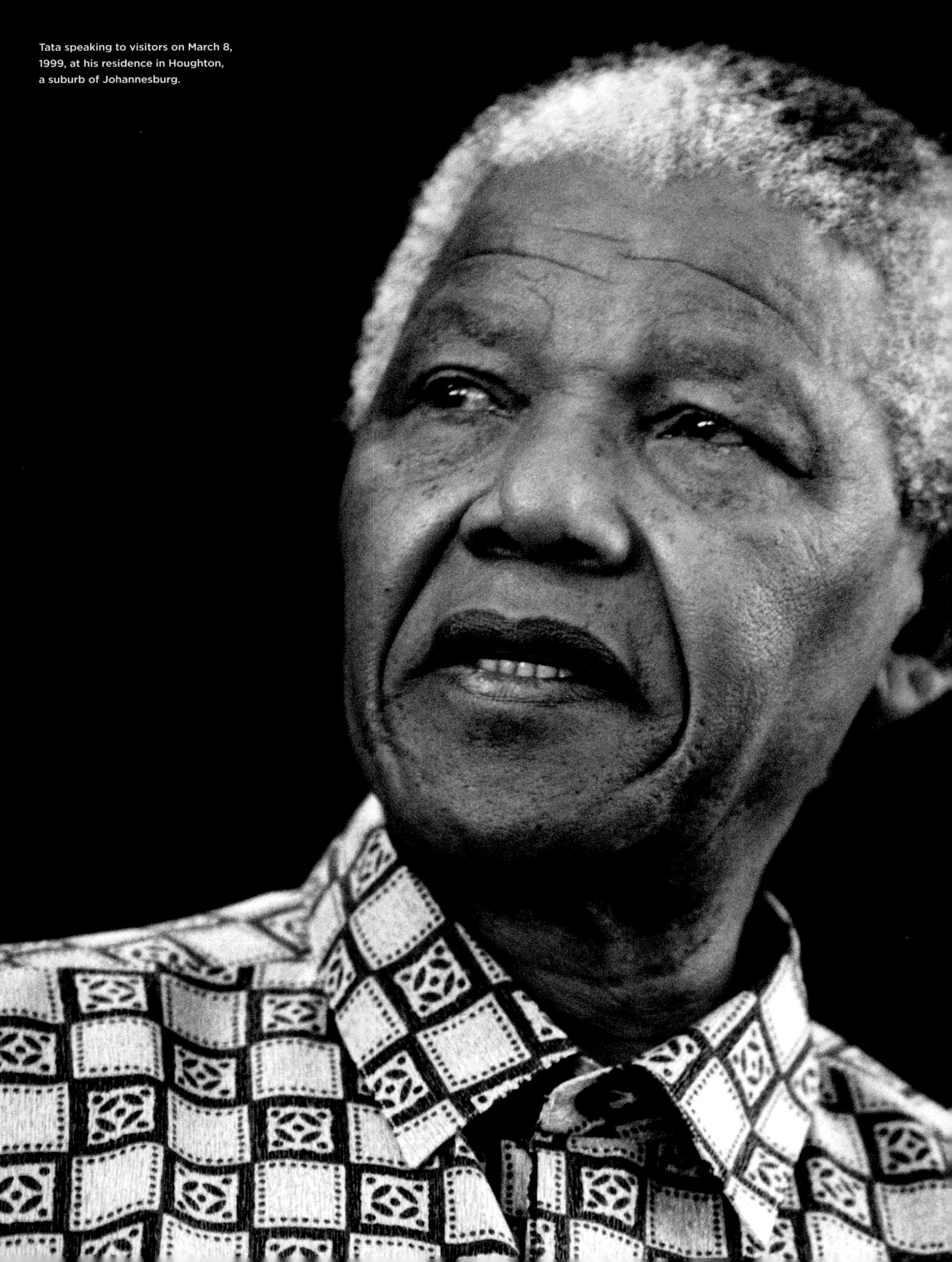

Tata speaking to visitors on March 8, 1999, at his residence in Houghton, a suburb of Johannesburg.

"My greatest moment was at a show in Frankfurt in 1997 for a joint Africa-Germany NGO summit. I ended my performance with 'Asimbonanga.' As we began the final chorus, the crowd roared and I was puzzled because it was a strange moment for them to acknowledge the song. Then, out of the corner of my eye, I saw Nelson Mandela. He had walked on stage and was doing this special Madiba dance move to the music."

Johnny Clegg, South African musician

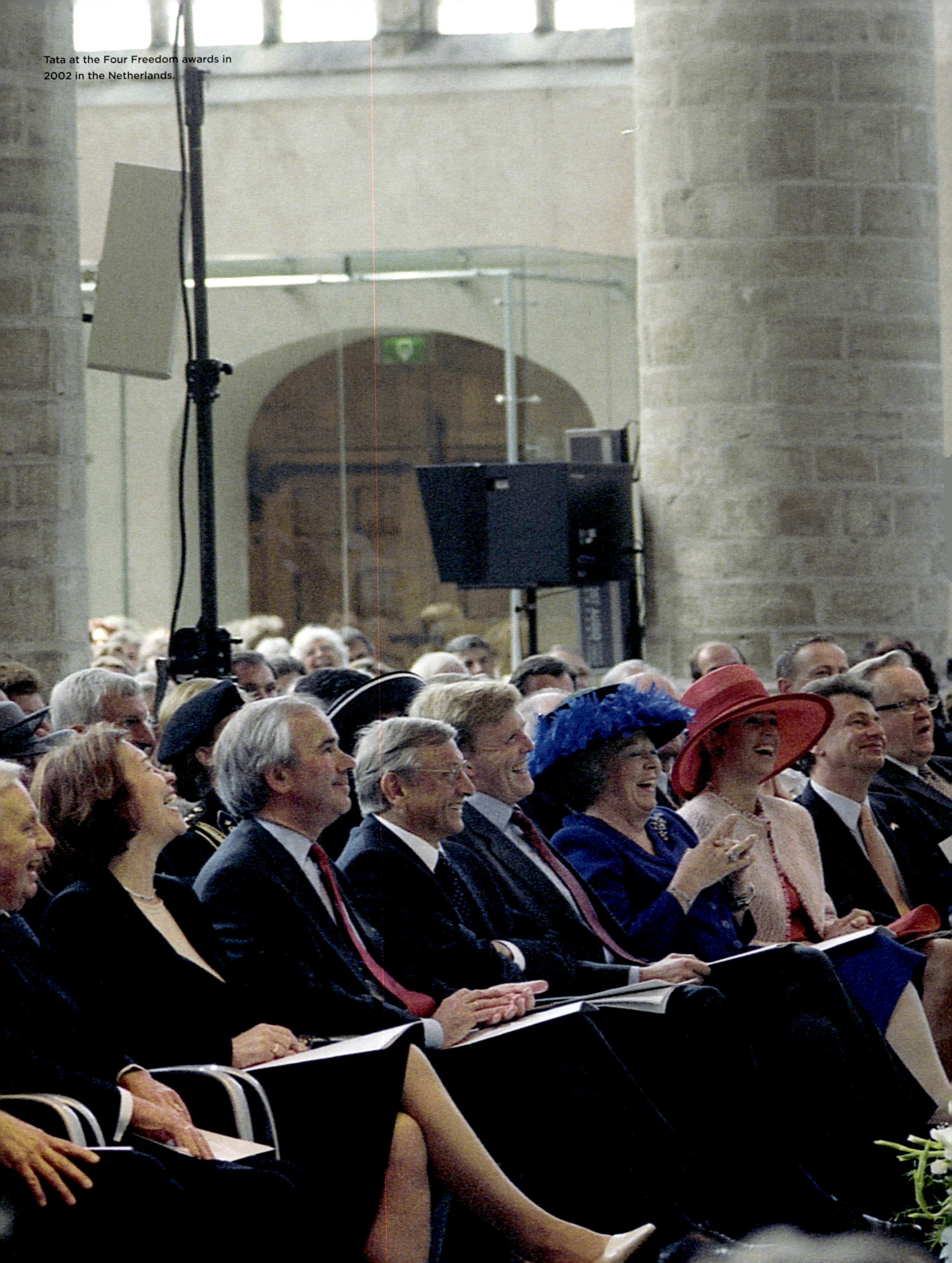

Tata at the Four Freedom awards in 2002 in the Netherlands.

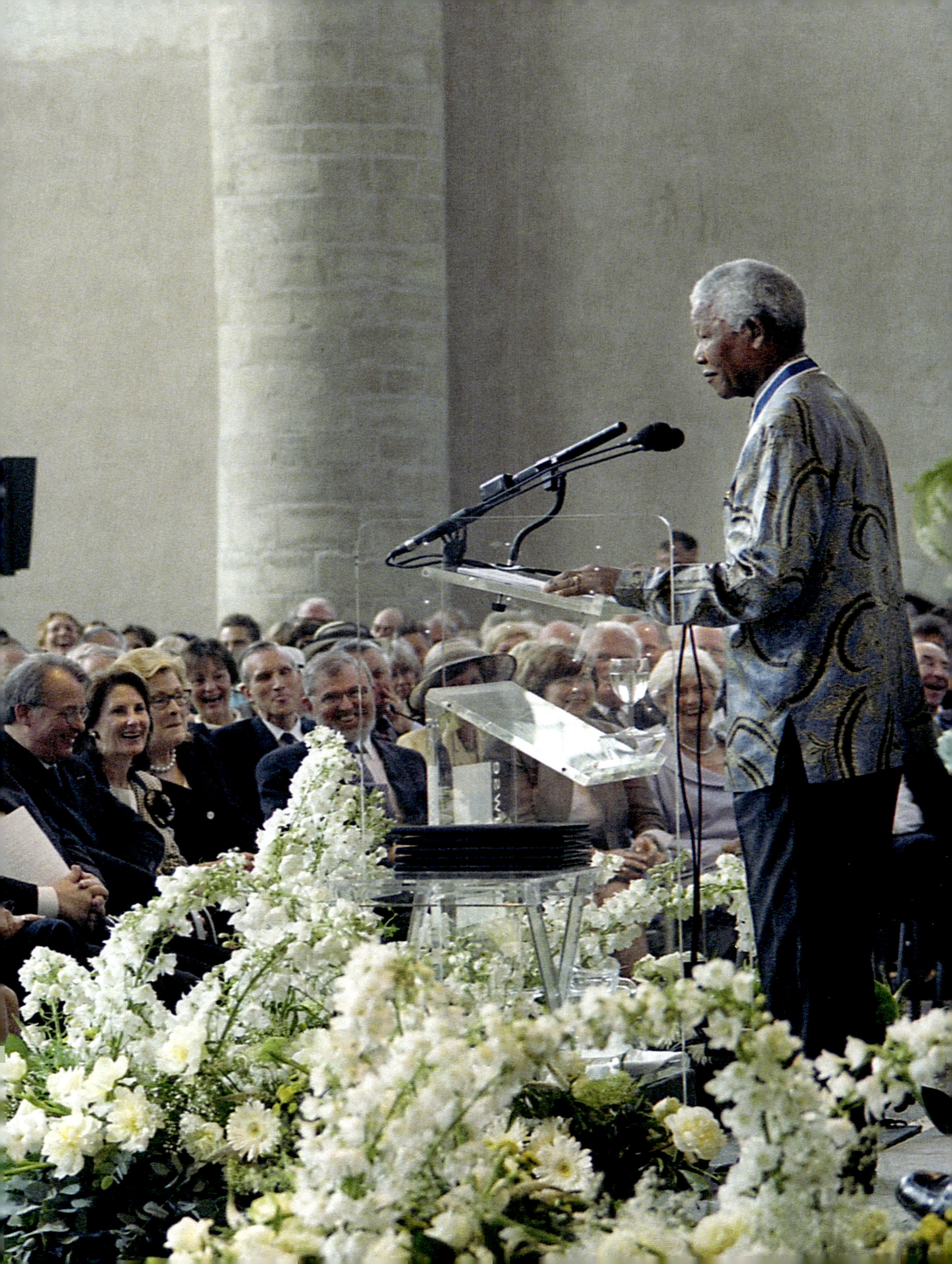

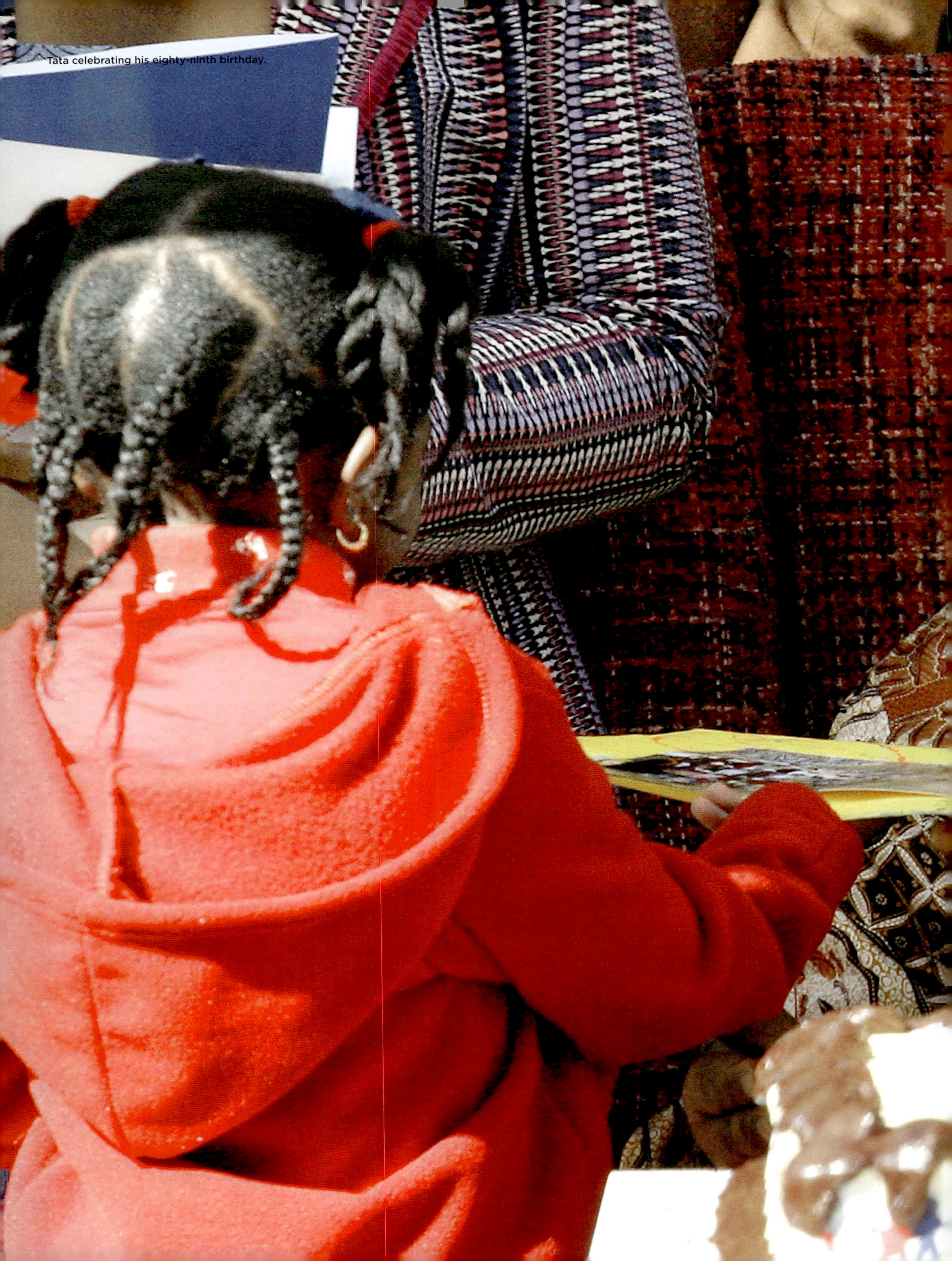

Tata celebrating his eighty-ninth birthday.

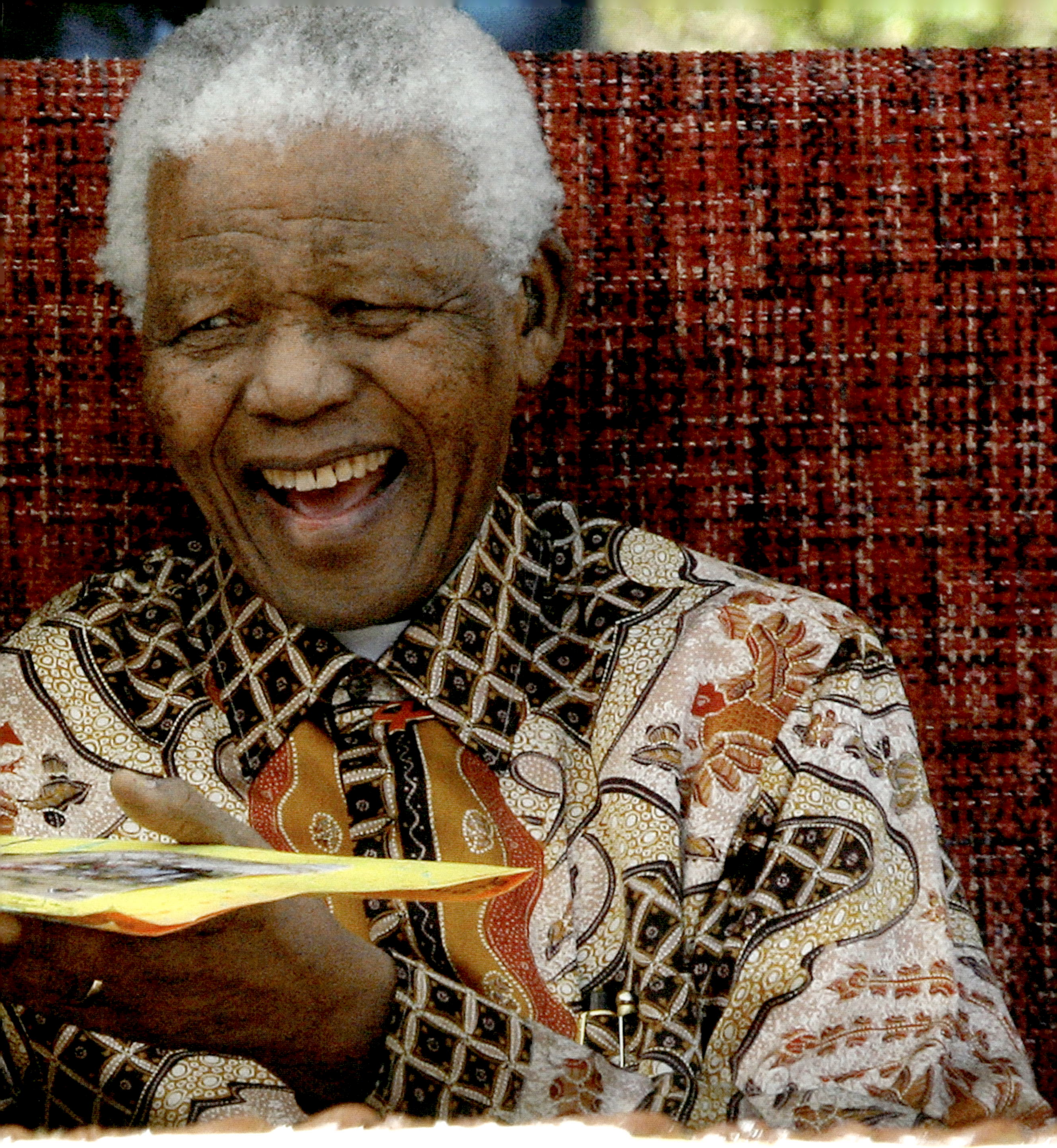

"In this world of such abundance, surely we can find the means to assure that no child will go hungry, no pregnant woman will be too weak to survive childbirth, and that every one of the nearly six million children who die next year because of malnutrition will be saved."

Tata, in Johannesburg, May 6, 2000

Tata saluting the South African military health service band that came to play a specially composed march and birthday song on his eighty-fifth birthday.

"It is no easy thing to rest while millions still bear the burden of poverty and insecurity. But my days will be filled with contentment to the extent that hands are joined across social divides and national boundaries, between continents and over oceans, to give effect to that common humanity in whose name we have together made the long walk to where we are today."

Tata in Johannesburg, March 19, 1998

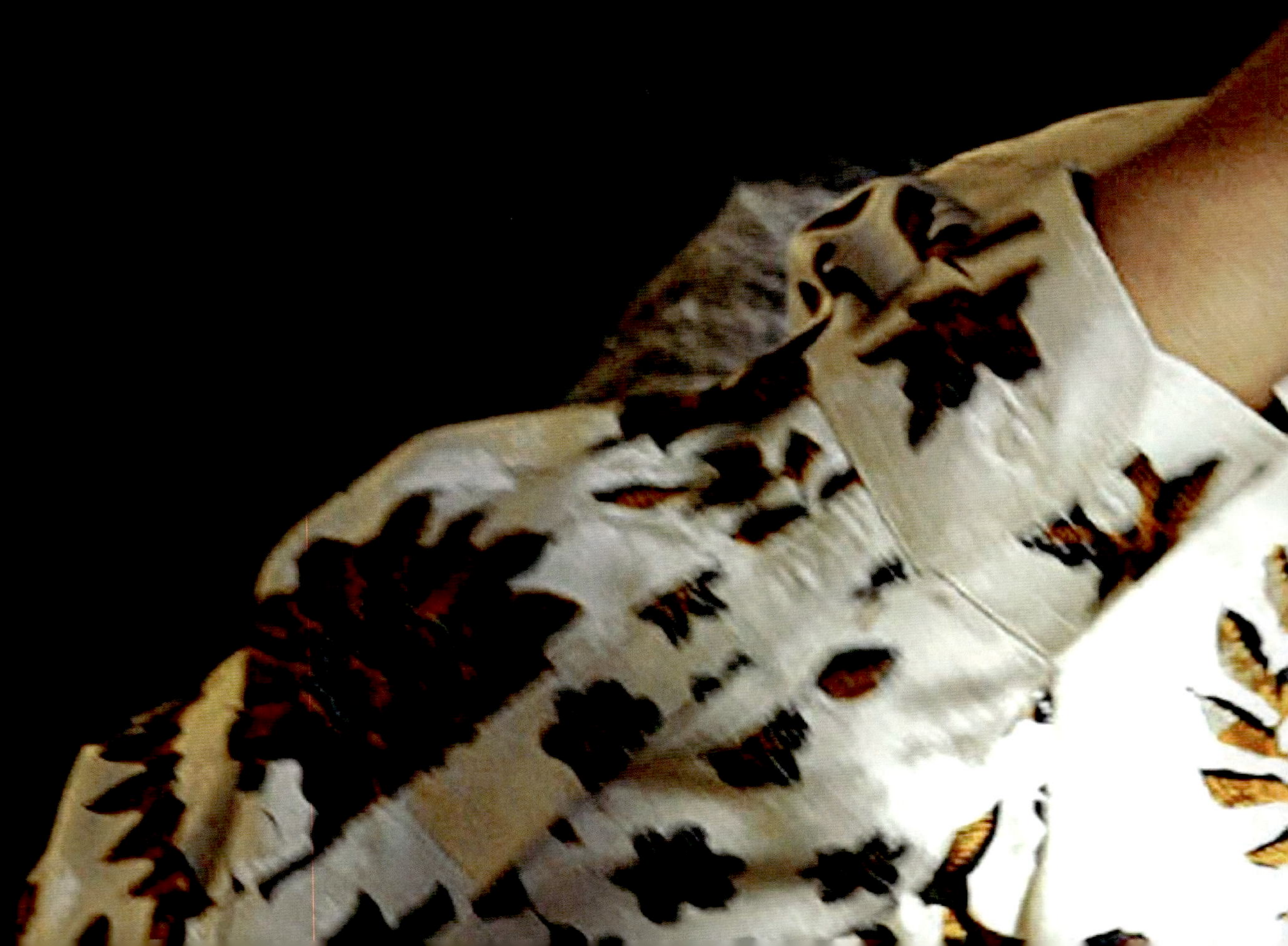

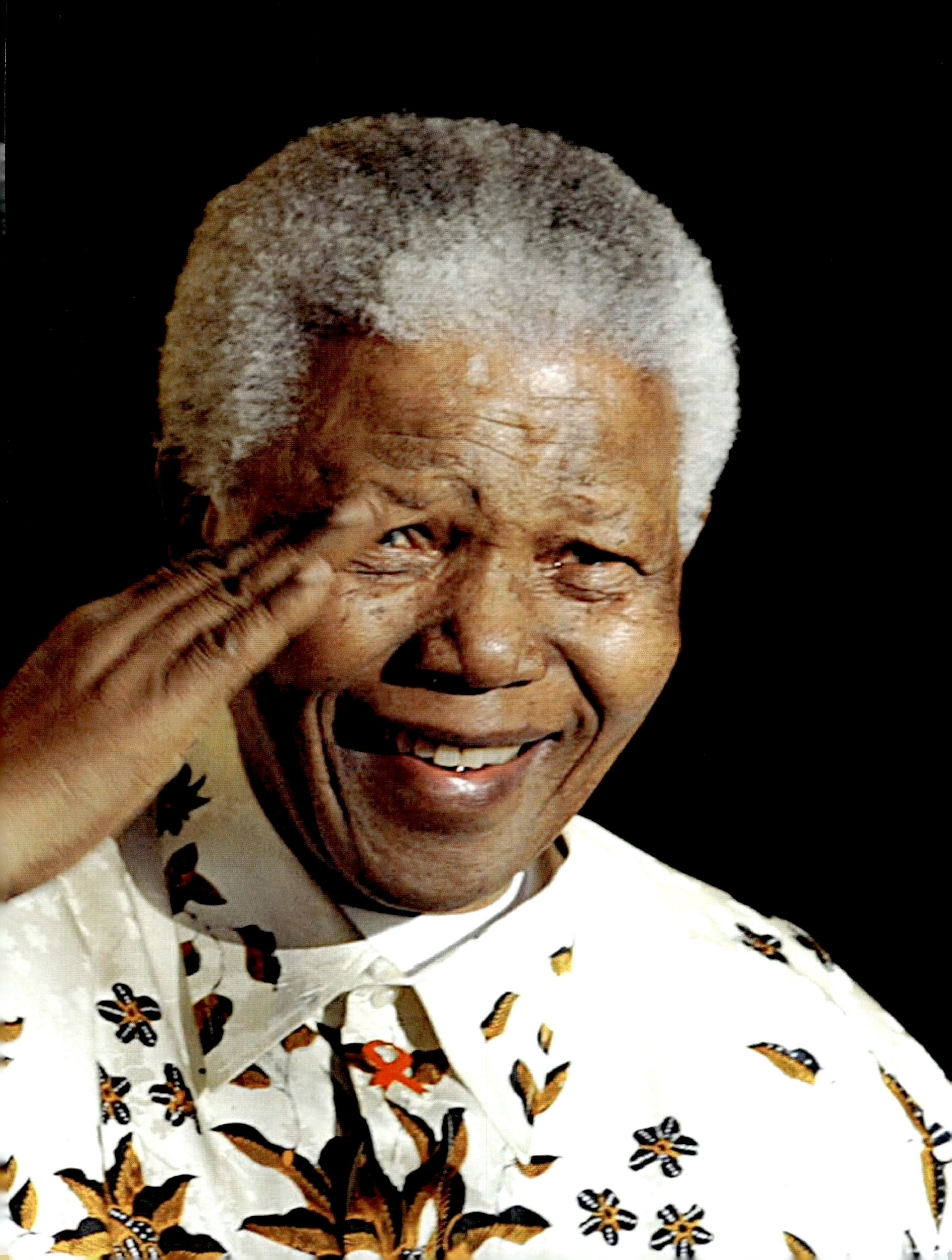

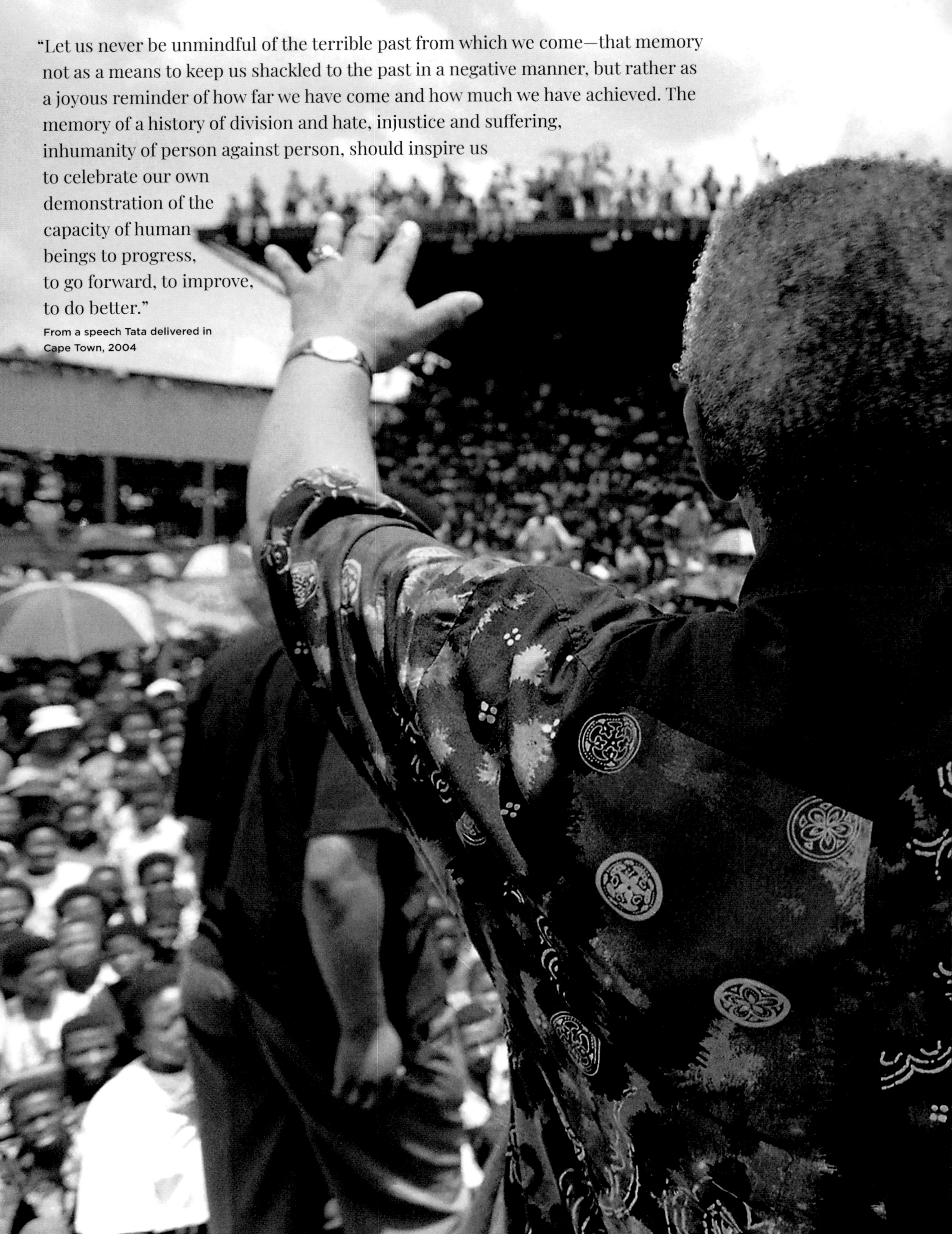

"Let us never be unmindful of the terrible past from which we come—that memory not as a means to keep us shackled to the past in a negative manner, but rather as a joyous reminder of how far we have come and how much we have achieved. The memory of a history of division and hate, injustice and suffering, inhumanity of person against person, should inspire us to celebrate our own demonstration of the capacity of human beings to progress, to go forward, to improve, to do better."

From a speech Tata delivered in Cape Town, 2004

Tata salutes large crowds on January 31, 1994, in Ikageng Stadium, a township just outside the western Transvaal city Potchefstroom, during his two-day campaign swing for the April 27 all-race general elections.

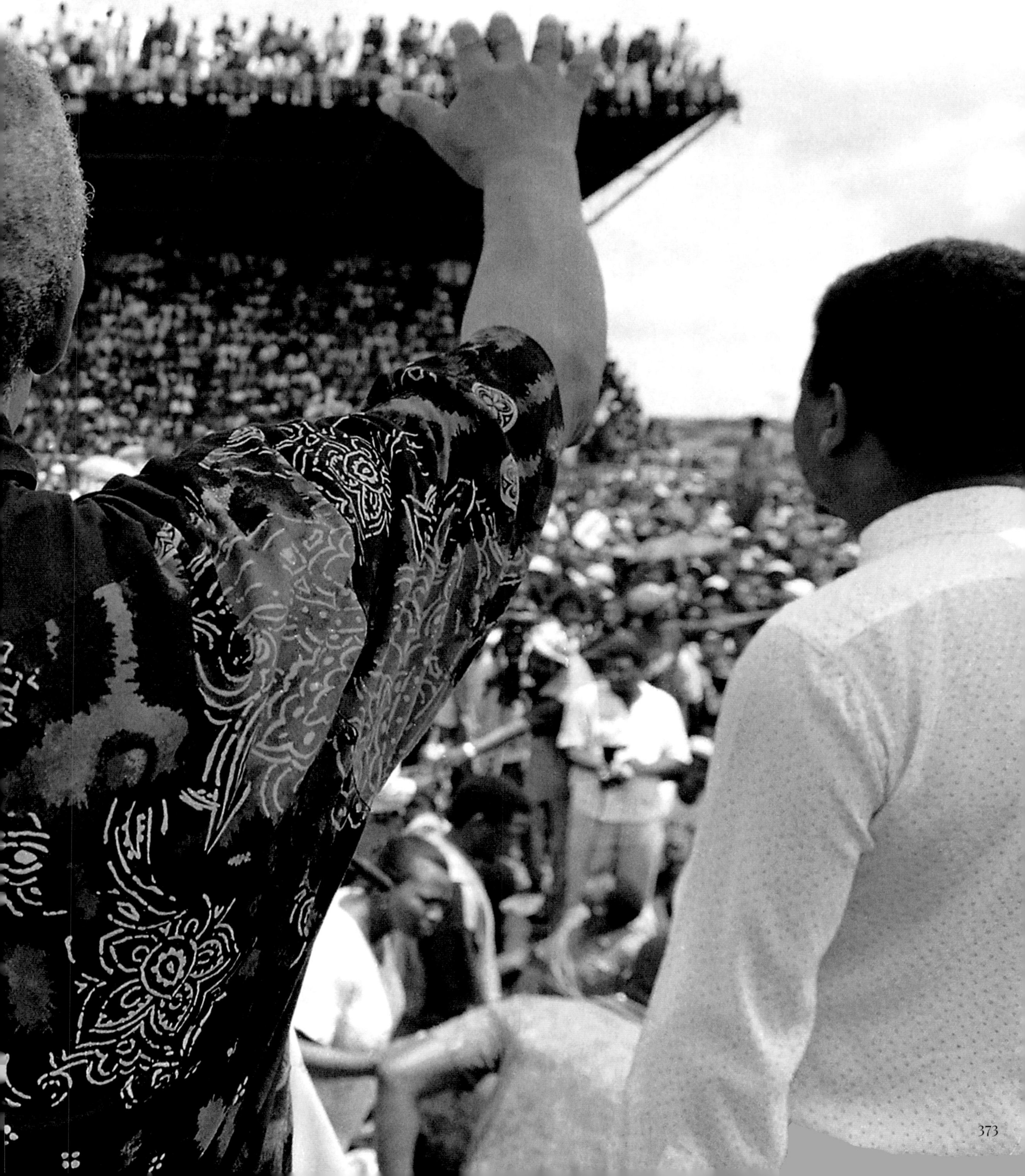

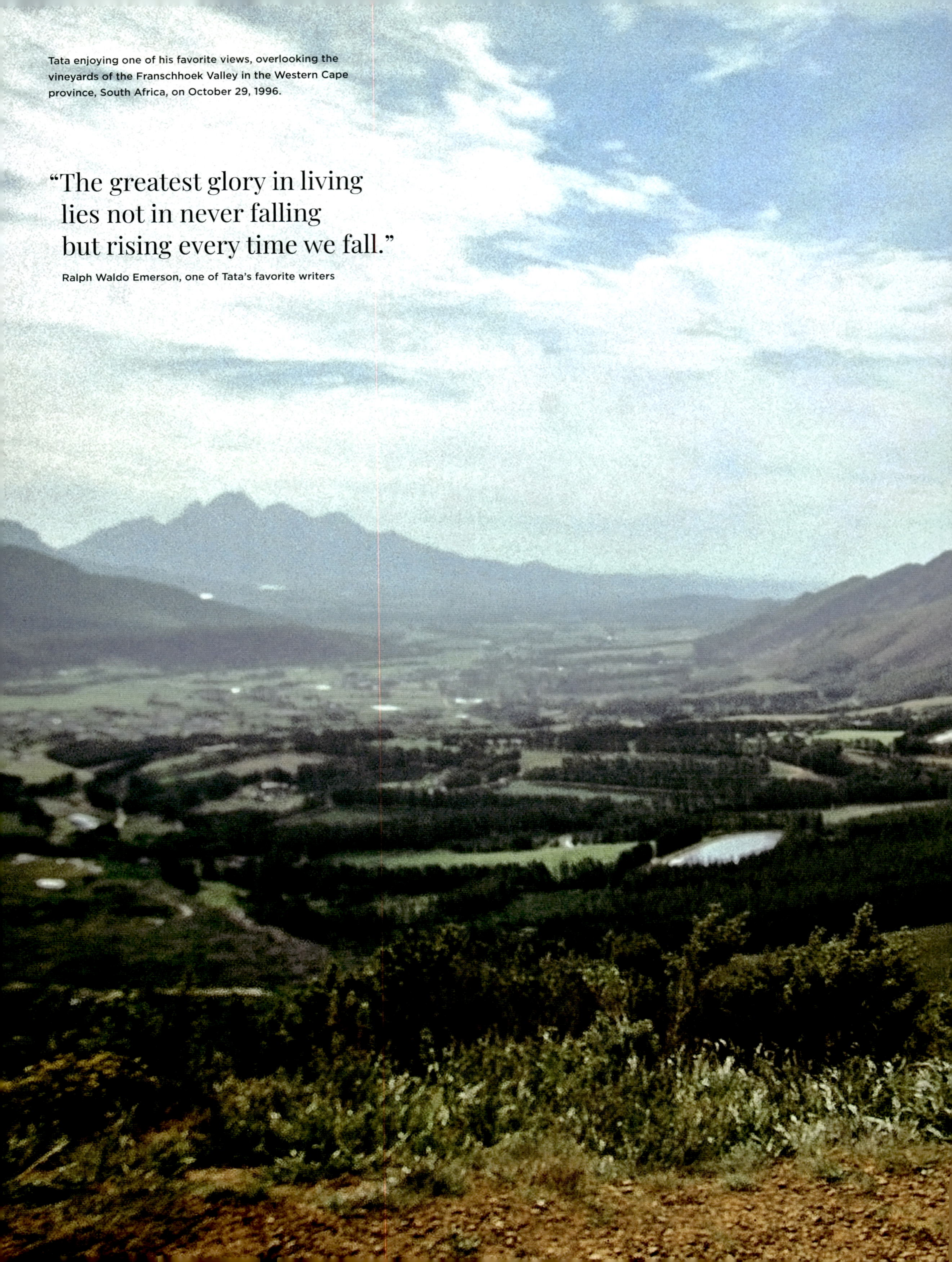

Tata enjoying one of his favorite views, overlooking the vineyards of the Franschhoek Valley in the Western Cape province, South Africa, on October 29, 1996.

"The greatest glory in living lies not in never falling but rising every time we fall."

Ralph Waldo Emerson, one of Tata's favorite writers

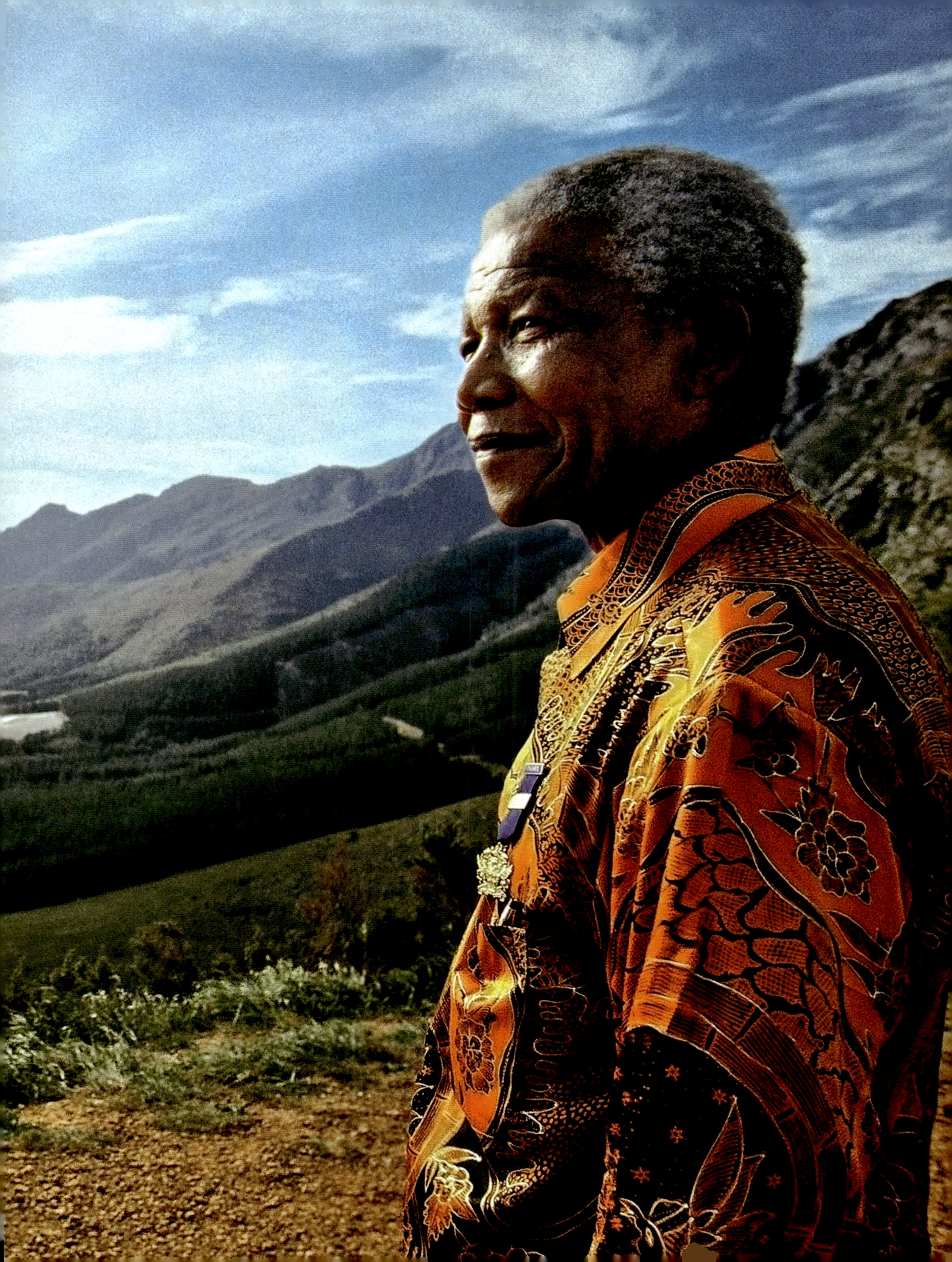

Afterword

Tukwini Mandela

When my grandfather passed on, I was relieved.

Some people will recoil in horror at this and ask how I could say such a thing. I can say it with some serious conviction because I know what my grandfather went through when he became ill.

In my culture, when a loved one passes on, they become an ancestor, their name and spirit echo through the ages. More importantly, their spirit echoes in us, their descendants, as we are part of them, and they are part of us. They remind us that we are torchbearers to our names and legacies, to be passed down from one generation to the next. A torchbearer is not to take the responsibility that has been bestowed on them lightly. It is heavy or light, depending on the attitude of the bearer. Does the bearer feel pride, responsibility, honor or does the bearer feel obligated to carry out his duties. For those who feel the lightness of carrying the torch—they are aware of their ancestor's spirit that runs through them. They can call on that spirit for help, guidance, and illumination when things become dark. I feel light carrying my family's torch because I know that my ancestors are with me, willing me to carry my grandfather's legacy with pride and willing my mother to tell the true story of Nelson Mandela and not some whitewashed version, which I always find incessantly annoying. On the 5th of December 2013, Madiba took his last breath and became my family's ancestor. I remember that day so clearly, as his children and grandchildren all stood around him as he transitioned to the spiritual realm. To say that his transition was a spiritual experience is not an apt way of describing it. It felt as if my grandfather was transferring some of that beautiful light of his to us, and that it was now up to us to carry the beautiful legacy that he and his ancestors had created. When I watched the news footage from the previous night, as they were transporting him to the hospital, the lights from the convoy and other cars on the road shone so brightly; there was a magical quality to it. It is as if the angels were accompanying him home. My grandfather was such a force of nature, he seemed to make anything happen by the sheer force of his will, so I never imagined a time when he would not be with us, even when he was gravely ill. But once angels' work is done on this earth, they all must go home.

A few years before, my grandfather started telling us openly that he was dying, at which point we would ignore him and change the subject. My grandfather had no compunction about confronting his own death. He did not seem afraid at all, he knew it was near, that his ancestors were calling, and he was determined to prepare us for it by broaching the subject as often as he could. I don't know of any of my family members who talked about my grandfather's death at all; it would mean that we had to acknowledge that he was becoming frail, starting to forget certain things. . . . Then, Madiba became ill and the circus began in earnest. What to do, what to do? Everyone was just bumbling back and forth not wanting to confront and deal with what was really in front of them. Some tried very hard to take advantage of his frailty, the unwelcome local and international press descended into our lives,

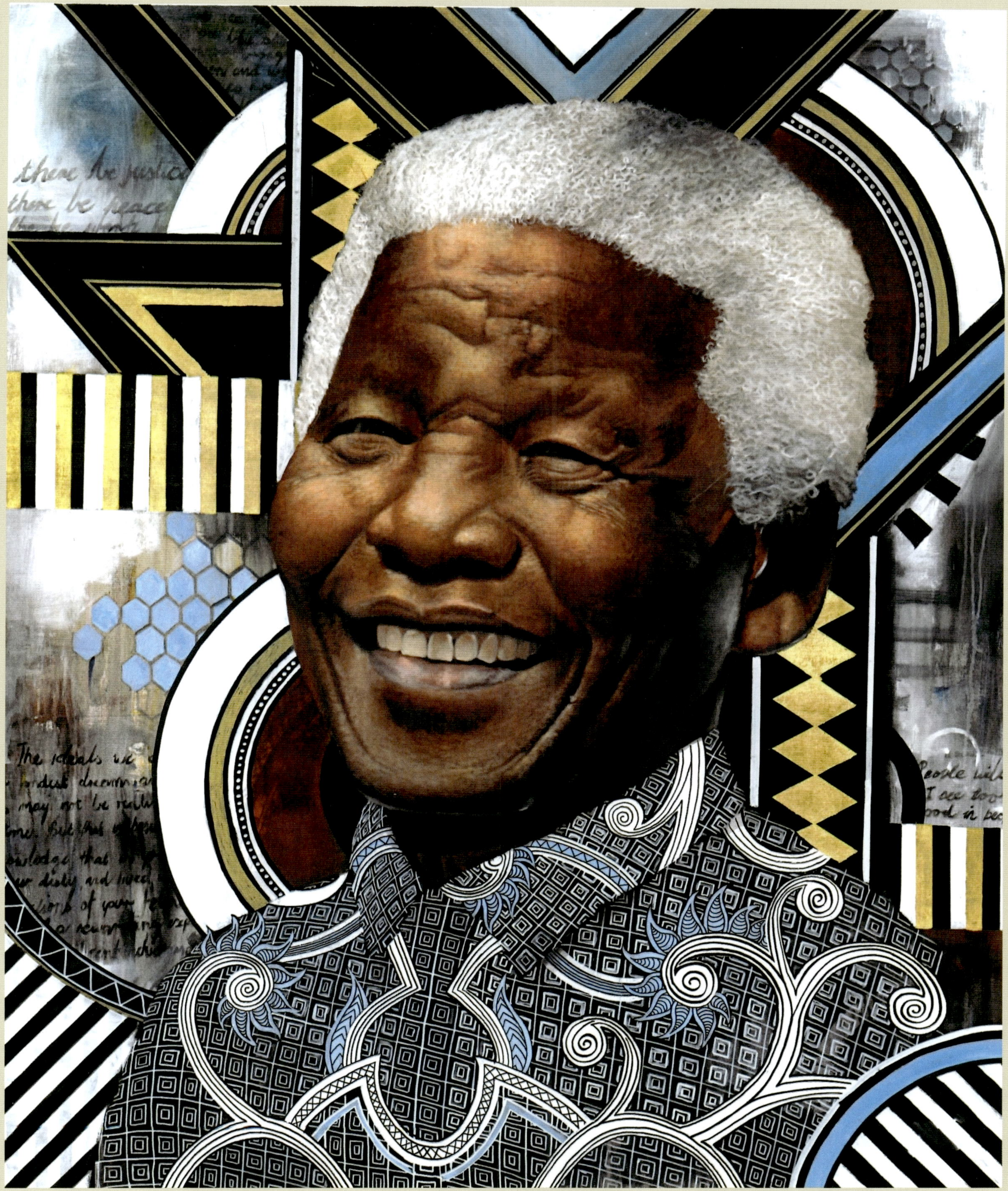

Painting by Loyiso Mkize.

(Continued)

taking incessant pictures, and wanted daily updates. It was truly maddening. That's when my mother decided to put a stop to the nonsense and protect her father from the wolves outside and within. She was the only one strong enough to do it. She approached the state so he could have twenty-four hour care, she and some of the grandchildren made it a point to spend as much time with him as possible, so he did not feel alone, even if it meant just sitting there quietly with him and holding his hand or reading a book, while he read his newspapers.

Then my mother did the "unthinkable" and broached the subject of Madiba's funeral plans with the state. Some members of government were not prepared for this discussion and did not want to be prepared. Then the South African media had a field day: "How could his own daughter start talking about her father's funeral?" Another outlet declared, "It is taboo to talk about someone's burial in African culture." This elicited the proverbial eye roll and sucking of teeth from some family members, including myself, who were sick of all the posturing and self-appointed family spokespeople and so-called friends who "knew what Madiba wanted." My mother would not be deterred, and she dragged the South African government kicking and screaming into a seven-year planning marathon that ended up being a beautiful and well-planned send-off of Madiba, South Africa's first democratically elected president. It must be noted that President Jacob Zuma and some of the government officials gave my family their full support and backing and were not interested in the disingenuous accusations being leveled at my mother.

After my grandfather's passing, I had some time to reflect on why people seemed to think that my grandfather was this magical creature that just fell from the sky with no sense of place. Why did some feel that the Mandela name belonged to a benign "we" as opposed to his beneficiaries—his progeny? Why did they feel that they had the right to exploit this name for their benefit only, but when Madiba's progeny used the name (a name they own and have every right to) for their own benefit, this was seen as unacceptable and profiteering? It became crystal clear to me, my mother, and my siblings that the battle lines for who controlled our own name had already been drawn and if we allowed people who were nonentities to my family and my legacy to control our name, and in the long run, our destiny, our legacy would be defiled and destroyed by profiteers and thieves. I use these strong terms on purpose, to illustrate the danger in this situation and in this story. Families lose their legacies and their names because they don't have the strength of character to control their own names and stories. Moreover, did people actually know the real Nelson Mandela, who and what formed him as a human being, a freedom fighter, and ultimately a worldwide statesman? Of course, my grandfather embodied all of these titles with a great sense of ease, as if they were meant to be part of him; but the Nelson Mandela that people think they knew was not formed by some unknown force. He himself said that he was shaped by the values of his ancestral roots, that his political awakening took place a decade before he moved to Johannesburg and joined the ANC. I remember reading the first one hundred pages of *Long Walk to Freedom*—what I learned in those pages gave me pause. There in those pages came alive the people who shaped Nelson Mandela, the man and statesman: his father Gadla Henry Mandela, a "prime minister" (because no such title existed at the time) of Thembuland, an adviser to kings, and a custodian of Xhosa history. A progressive who did not believe in maintaining the status quo for the benefit of the elite or the privileged few. Madiba described his father as a man with a stubborn sense of fairness, a man who possessed a proud rebelliousness that he saw in himself. The King Regent Chief Jongintaba, who looked after my grandfather after his father's passing and taught him about leadership. Madiba was destined to be a counselor to kings after his father, and the king regent was determined to honor the man who put him on the throne, Nelson Mandela's father. The king regent often said to him: "It is not for you to spend your life mining the white man's gold, never knowing how to write your name."

I was equally struck by some of Madiba's quotes from *Long Walk to Freedom*:

> My later notion of leadership was profoundly influenced by observing the regent and his court. I watched and learned from the tribal meetings that were regularly held at the Great Place palace. Everyone who wanted to speak did so. It was democracy in its purest form. There may have been a hierarchy of importance among the speakers, but everyone was heard: chief and subject, warrior and medicine man, shopkeeper and farmer, landowner, and labourer. The foundation for self-government was that all men were free to voice their opinions and were equal in their value as citizens.
>
> At first, I was astonished by the vehemence—and candor—with which people criticized the regent. He was not above criticism—in fact he was often the principal target of it. But no matter how serious the charge, the regent simply listened, not defending himself, showing no emotion at all. The meetings would continue until consensus was reached. They ended in unanimity or not at all. Unanimity, however, might be an agreement to disagree, to wait for a more propitious time to propose a solution. Democracy meant all men were to be heard and a decision was taken together as a people. Majority rule was a foreign notion. A minority was not to be crushed by a majority.

I, as his grandchild, then realized that my grandfather was making it abundantly clear that his journey to political awareness was most definitely shaped by the cultural roots of his ancestors. My grandfather was shaped by his past as much as he was shaped by a future that he had no idea would see him imprisoned, lose his family, and eventually become the first democratically elected president of South Africa and worldwide statesman.

My grandfather had a very strong sense of place, and he considered himself a torchbearer of his name and admired his father who was a force to be reckoned with himself. This book tells the story of Nelson Mandela from the beginning—a flawed human being who accomplished great feats despite all of the challenges before him, including death. I'm very proud of this book, and I hope it will give the young generation some insight into what sacrifices all of those who came before us made so that we can enjoy the freedoms we currently have. It's a challenge to us that we must never take these hard-won freedoms for granted; because in the blink of an eye, they can disappear. I'm sending a clarion call to all torchbearers: even in the twenty-first century, the struggle still continues and we can never be tired.

Maki Mandela
Acknowledgments

In Honor Of An Extraordinary Life is an illustrated book of Tata's life featuring his winding journey as a son, brother, husband, father, freedom fighter, statesman, and a great son of the Thembu. Tata passed away on December 5, 2013, to join the world of the ancestors. As a daughter I mourned the times when Tata was alive but not present, and that mourning intensified at his passing away, not out of sorrow but because of failing nerves that this great son had left too soon. Winter set in just for a brief moment and soon gave way to spring, as I reminded myself that the nobility of his soul has merged with other souls that have gone before him. I am also cognizant that Tata would want me to build on the legacy he left me. That is why, through this book, I honor his life, because I embody all that is good in him. By remembering Tata through this book, I can step into my true power and realize my highest potential.

I would like to thank the DMA team, Sam Sohaili, Marc Beckman, and Nancy Chanin, who came up with the idea of the book. I am especially grateful to Sam, who worked tirelessly to make sure that the book was turned from an idea into reality and clearly captured the vision I had for this book. My appreciation to Monica Davis, who translated my handwritten notes into a typed manuscript.

I appreciate all the work my daughter, Tukwini, did for this project; being a steadfast assistant to me, collecting all the pictures, and scanning the chapters, and sending them to Sam. Thank you very much. You are a wonderful daughter and my pillar of strength. To my sons, thank you for your support and encouragement.

My special thanks goes to the Rizzoli team, Charles Miers, Anthony Petrillose, and Gisela Aguilar, who patiently guided this work and have been active collaborators on this project from the beginning to the end.

I am truly grateful to all those who helped to resurrect the memory of Tata and helped me bring his life into the present time, with an illustrated book. Celebrating those who have gone before me, especially Tata, is truly an honor for me.

House of Mandela

We are the proud progeny of the Royal House of Mandela; an African family dedicated to the preservation of our history, culture, and family. Our history, culture, and values are closely linked with the life and times of Africa, her people, resilience, compassion, and courage.

The Mandela name is one of heritage, strong values, and royalty. The Mandelas are the descendants of a royal bloodline that dates back to the 18th century when Thembu Land was part of the royal kingdom of the Eastern Cape. Our legacy traces back to King Ngubengcuka, the king of the Thembus; and to a small village in the Eastern Cape, where the great Chief Mphakanyiswa of Mvezo and father to Nelson Rolihlahla Mandela ruled. Our history is steeped in tradition, family values, and a strong sense of community. We are proud of our heritage and believe that only when we understand and appreciate where we come from is it possible to achieve a state of enlightenment and progress in our journey through life.

As Africans, we believe that community is an extension of our family and we strive to uphold our values in the way we interact with everyone around us. Openness, honesty, empathy, and patience are the cornerstones of how we form bonds with our immediate and extended families. We strongly believe in a sense of humility, integrity, and a common notion that our problems can be solved more effectively when we open our hearts, our minds, and come together.

Bee Totem

The Bee is the Mandela family's totem symbol and represents the House of Mandela. It is the literal translation of the family patriarch's name, Rolihlahla, colloquially meaning, "One who is brave enough to challenge the status quo."

First published in the United States of America
in 2023 by **Rizzoli International Publications, Inc.**
300 Park Avenue South
New York, NY 10010
www.rizzoliusa.com

Creative Director: **Sam Sohaili**, DMA United
Art Directors: **Eduardo Vallejo**,
Saari Kirschner, **Dorothy Wann**

Publisher: **Charles Miers**
Associate Publisher: **Anthony Petrillose**
Editor: **Gisela Aguilar**
Production Manager: **Maria Pia Gramaglia**
Managing Editor: **Lynn Scrabis**
Design Coordinator: **Olivia Russin**

Printed in Italy

2023 2024 2025 2026 2027 / 10 9 8 7 6 5 4 3 2 1

ISBN: 978-0-8478-7200-8
Library of Congress Control Number: 2022932324

Visit us online:
Facebook.com/RizzoliNewYork
Twitter: **@Rizzoli_Books**
Instagram.com/RizzoliBooks
Pinterest.com/RizzoliBooks
Youtube.com/user/RizzoliNY
Issuu.com/Rizzoli

Photo Credits

© AFP/Getty Images page 40 (top right), 87 (bottom left), 102 (bottom right), 103 (bottom right), 144-145, 265, 298 (bottom), 301 (bottom), 302 (top), 317 (top), 356-357

© Alain BUU/Getty Images page 303 (bottom)

© Alexander Joe/Getty Images page 292 (bottom right), 370-371

© Alf Kumalo/Africa Media Online page 180 (bottom), 188

© Alice Mertens and Joan Broster page 14-15, 17, 19, 24-25, 30-31, 34-35, 39

© Al Pereira/Getty Images page 316 (bottom right)

© AM Duggan-Cronin, McGregor Museum page 43

© Andrew Lichtenstein/Getty Images page 271 (middle)

© Anna Zieminski/Getty Images page 354-355

© API/Getty Images page 85, 90, 91 (bottom), 92-93, 109, 127, 130 (bottom), 320

© Apic/Getty Images page 73 (top), 338

© Archive Photos/Getty Images page 62

© Associated Press page 134 (bottom), 136-137, 142-143, 222-223, 372-373

© API/Getty Images page 85, 90, 91 (bottom), 92-93, 109, 127, 130 (bottom), 320

© Bernard Bisson/Getty Images page 243, 244

© Bettmann/Getty Images page 66, 67 (middle), 68-69, 72 (bottom), 74-75, 102 (bottom left), 120 (bottom right), 248

© Brent Stirton/Getty Images page 44-45

© Brooks Kraft/Getty Images page 268 (bottom), 269, 271 (bottom), 272-273

© Bruno Hadjih/Anzenberger/Redux page 32-33

© Chris Jackson/Getty Images page 337

© Cloete Breytenbach/Daily Express London page 152, 153 (bottom)

© Contraband Collection/Alamy Stock Photo page 228 (bottom left)

Courtesy Makaziwe Mandela page 36, 37, 38, 98, 122, 161, 162, 163, 164, 165, 166, 167, 168, 169, 170, 171, 172, 173, 175, 177, 179, 180 (top), 182 (top right), 184, 186, 187, 190, 191, 192, 193, 194 (bottom left and right), 196 (top and bottom left), 197, 198, 199, 202, 204, 205, 206, 207, 208, 209, 210, 211, 212, 213, 214, 215, 216, 217, 218, 219, 220, 221, 282, 286, 296, 298 (top and middle), 302 (middle left), 303 (top), 304, 305, 306, 307, 318, 319, 323, 324, 325, 327, 330, 332, 334, 377, 384

Courtesy Nelson Mandela Foundation page 46-47, 49 (top left), 61, 91 (top), 118, 149

© Dave Benett/Getty Images page 314 (bottom), 358-359

© David Cooper/Getty Images page 194 (top)

© David Rogers/Getty Images page 312 (middle right), 313

© David Thomson/Getty Images page 342

© David Turnley/Getty Images page 230-231, 254

© DEA/N. Cirani/Getty Images page 40 (top left)

© Denver Post/Getty Images page 196 (bottom right)

© Diane Walker/Getty Images page 300

© Dirck Halstead/Getty Images page 291, 350-351

© Dr. Peter Magubane page 287

© Drum Social Histories/BAHA/Africa Media Online page 77, 107, 112-113, 114-115, 116

© Ejor/Getty Images page 70-71

© Evans/Getty Images page 56-57

© Fethi Belaid/Getty Images page 295 (top)

© Francois Lochon/Getty Images page 256-257

© Franck Fife/Getty Images page 340-341

© Gallo Images/Getty Images page 78, 79 (top), 200 (top), 235

© Georges De Keerle/Getty Images page 79 (middle), 263

© Georges Merillon/Getty Images page 335

© Gerard Julien/Getty Images page 362-363

© Getty Images page 250, 315 (top right and bottom), 317 (bottom left), 328, 333, 360-361

© Gideon Mendel/Getty Images page 245

© Gille de Vlieg / Africa Media Online page 232-233

© GL Archive/Alamy Stock Photo page 49 (top right)

© Graeme Williams/Panos Pictures page 228 (bottom middle right)

© Greg Marinovich/Africa Media Online page 260-261

© Guy Tillim/Africa Media Online page 53 (left)

© Guy Tillim/Getty Images page 21

© Hulton Deutsch/Getty Images page 28, 87 (top), 120 (bottom left), 226

© Hulton/Getty Images page 110-111, 227, 242

© Ira Wyman/Getty Images page 301 (top right)

© Jeff J. Mitchell/Getty Images page 50-51

© Joe Eldridge/Alamy Stock Photo page 182 (bottom)

© John Stillwell/Getty Images page 302 (bottom)

© Julian Parker/Getty Images page 293 (top right)

© Jurgen Schadeberg/Getty Images page 73 (bottom), 82, 83, 88, 89, 95, 103 (bottom left), 104-105, 106, 117, 121 (bottom), 156, 288

© Ken Goff/Getty Images page 348-349

© Keystone-France/Getty Images page 67 (bottom), 87 (middle left), 99, 108, 130 (top)

© Koto Bolofo/CXA page 147, 148, 154, 155, 157

© Leon Neal/Getty Images page 275 (bottom)

© Lily Franey/Getty Images page 299

© Louise Gubb/Getty Images page 18, 58, 150-151, 174, 252-253, 277 (top), 301 (middle left), 322 (top), 374-375

© Marion Kaplan/Alamy Stock Photo page 128-129

© Mark Thompson/Getty Images page 308-309

© Mary Benson Estate/Getty Images page 84, 119 (left)

© Matthew Ashton/EMPICS/Getty Images page 317 (bottom right)

© Matthew Willman/Getty Images page 26

© Media24/Gallo Images/Getty Images page 312 (top), 314 (top), 315 (top left), 316 (bottom left), 322 (middle and bottom), 368-369

© Mike Hewitt/Getty Images page 312 (middle left)

© Mirrorpix/Getty Images page 238-239, 292 (bottom left)

© Morne Pretorius page 23

© National Library of Scotland page 49 (bottom)

© Nelson Mandela Foundation/Matthew Willman page 159

© New York Daily News/Getty Images page 246-247

© Odd Andersen/Getty Images page 295 (bottom)

© PA Images/Getty Images page 228, 229, 240-241, 293 (top left)

© Paul Popper/Popperfoto/Getty Images page 100

© Per-Anders Pettersson/Getty Images page 268 (top), 364-365

© Peter Dunne/Getty Images page 251

© Peter Turnley/Getty Images page 270, 275 (top), 294 (top right)

© Philip Littleton/Getty Images page 294 (top right)

© Pictorial Press Ltd/Alamy Stock Photo page 153 (top)

© Popperfoto/Getty Images page 67 (top), 72 (top), 96, 103 (top)

© Radu Sigheti/Reuters Pictures page 158

© Rajesh Jantilal/Getty Images page 53 (right)

© Ray McManus/Getty Images page 316 (top)

© Reuters/Alamy Stock Photo page 134 (top), 139, 140, 278

© Richard Lautens/Getty Images page 41

© Rodger Bosch/Getty Images page 347

© Rolls Press/Popperfoto/Getty Images page 87 (middle right)

© Sahm Doherty/Getty Images page 254

© Shaun Botterill/Getty Images page 310-311, 312 (bottom)

© South Photography/Gallo Images. Getty Images page 274

© Spaarnestad Photo/Bridgeman Images page 200 (bottom left and right), 201

© Steve Liss/Getty Images page 345

© STF/Getty Images page 119 (right)

© Terrence Spencer/Popperfoto/Getty Images page 42, 102 (top), 121 (top)
© The Roosevelt Foundation and Wilma Wijers page 366-367

© Three Lions/Getty Images page 101

© Tim Graham/Getty Images page 293 (bottom)

© Timothy Clary/Getty Images page 331

© Tom Stoddart Archive/Getty Images page 266-267

© Trevor Samson/Getty Images page 262

© TSJ Merlyn Licensing BV/Gallo Images/Getty Images page 236, 264, 280-281, 284-285, 292 (top), 297, 302 (middle right), 321

© Ullstein Bild/Getty Images page 40 (bottom), 64-65, 249

© Universal History Archive/Getty Images page 52, 120 (top), 123

© UWC, Robben Island, Mayibuye Archives page 124, 125

© UWC, Robben Island, Mayibuye Archives/Eli Weinberg page 182 (top left)

© vkilikov/Shutterstock page 54-55

© Wally McNamee/Getty Images page 301 (top left)

© Walter Dhladhla/Getty Images page 79 (bottom), 225, 271 (top), 277 (bottom), 352-353

© William Campbell/Getty Images page 289, 290

© William Philpott/Getty Images page 294 (bottom)

© Wits University Archives page 80-81

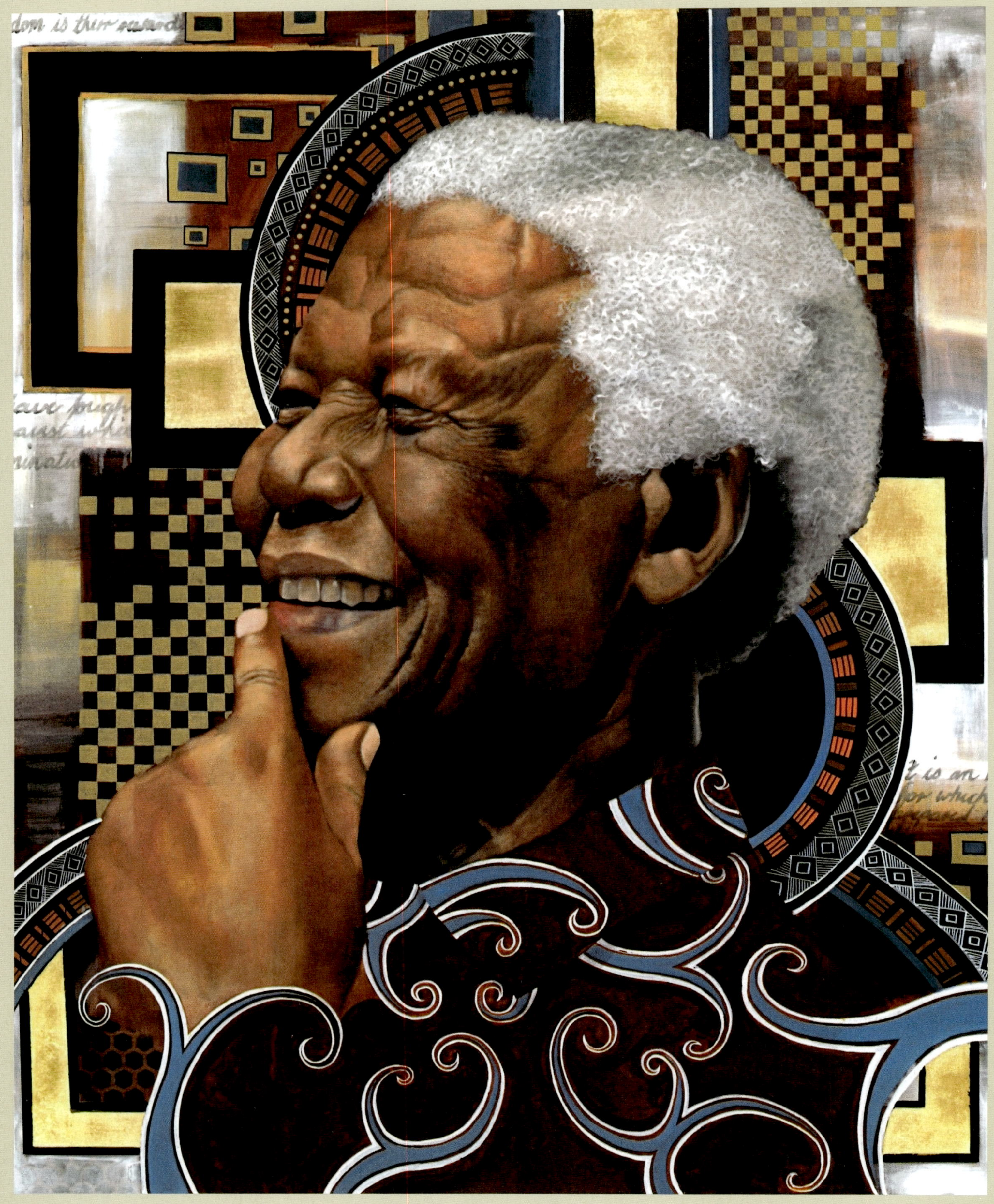

Painting by Loyiso Mkize.

Tata, you have joined the spirit world of the ancestors and we will always honor your memory. Maki

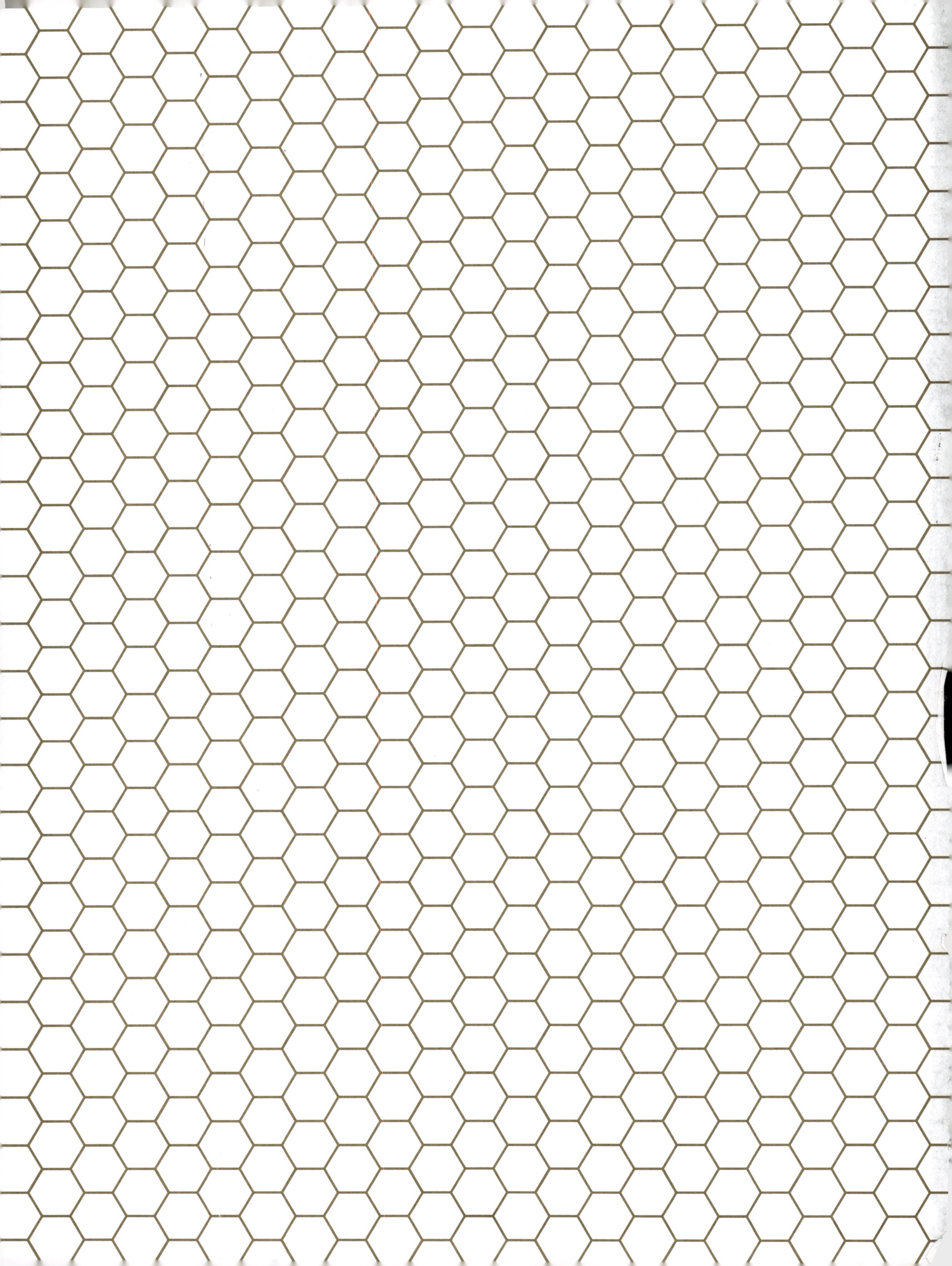